marketing

Fifth Edition

Dhruv Grewal, PhD
Babson College

Michael Levy, PhD
Babson College

marketing,
fifth edition

SENIOR VICE PRESIDENT, PRODUCTS & MARKETS: **KURT L. STRAND**
VICE PRESIDENT, GENERAL MANAGER, PRODUCTS & MARKETS: **MICHAEL RYAN**
VICE PRESIDENT, CONTENT DESIGN & DELIVERY: **KIMBERLY MERIWETHER DAVID**
MANAGING DIRECTOR: **SUSAN GOUIJNSTOOK**
BRAND MANAGER: **KIM LEISTNER**
DIRECTOR, PRODUCT DEVELOPMENT: **MEGHAN CAMPBELL**
LEAD PRODUCT DEVELOPER: **KELLY DELSO**
PRODUCT DEVELOPER: **LAI MOY**
MARKETING MANAGER: **ELIZABETH SCHONAGEN**
DIRECTOR, CONTENT DESIGN & DELIVERY: **TERRI SCHIESL**
PROGRAM MANAGER: **MARY CONZACHI**
CONTENT PROJECT MANAGERS: **CHRISTINE VAUGHAN; DANIELLE CLEMENT**
BUYER: **LAURA M. FULLER**
DESIGN: **MATT DIAMOND**
CONTENT LICENSING SPECIALISTS: **MICHELLE D. WHITAKER; DEANNA DAUSENER**
ILLUSTRATIONS: **LIZ DEFRAIN**
STUDENT IMAGE: **STUART JENNER/GETTY IMAGES**
COMPOSITOR: **APTARA®, INC.**
TYPEFACE: **10/12 STIX MATHJAX MAIN**
PRINTER: **R. R. DONNELLEY**

M: MARKETING, FIFTH EDITION

Published by McGraw-Hill Education, 2 Penn Plaza, New York, NY 10121. Copyright © 2017 by McGraw-Hill Education. All rights reserved. Printed in the United States of America. Previous edition © 2015, 2013, 2011 and 2009. No part of this publication may be reproduced or distributed in any form or by any means, or stored in a database or retrieval system, without the prior written consent of McGraw-Hill Education, including, but not limited to, in any network or other electronic storage or transmission, or broadcast for distance learning.

Some ancillaries, including electronic and print components, may not be available to customers outside the United States.

This book is printed on acid-free paper.

3 4 5 6 7 8 9 LMN 21 20 19 18 17

ISBN   978-1-259-44629-0

MHID   1-259-44629-8

All credits appearing on page or at the end of the book are considered to be an extension of the copyright page.

Library of Congress Control Number: 2015953831

The Internet addresses listed in the text were accurate at the time of publication. The inclusion of a website does not indicate an endorsement by the authors or McGraw-Hill Education, and McGraw-Hill Education does not guarantee the accuracy of the information presented at these sites.

mheducation.com/highered

brief contents

section one
ASSESSING THE MARKETPLACE
chapter 1 Overview of Marketing 3
chapter 2 Developing Marketing Strategies and a Marketing Plan 21
chapter 3 Social and Mobile Marketing 47
chapter 4 Marketing Ethics 67
chapter 5 Analyzing the Marketing Environment 83

section two
UNDERSTANDING THE MARKETPLACE
chapter 6 Consumer Behavior 101
chapter 7 Business-to-Business Marketing 127
chapter 8 Global Marketing 145

section three
TARGETING THE MARKETPLACE
chapter 9 Segmentation, Targeting, and Positioning 169
chapter 10 Marketing Research 193

section four
VALUE CREATION
chapter 11 Product, Branding, and Packaging Decisions 217
chapter 12 Developing New Products 237
chapter 13 Services: The Intangible Product 263

section five
VALUE CAPTURE
chapter 14 Pricing Concepts for Establishing Value 283

section six
VALUE DELIVERY: DESIGNING THE CHANNEL AND SUPPLY CHAIN
chapter 15 Supply Chain and Channel Management 307
chapter 16 Retailing and Omnichannel Marketing 327

section seven
VALUE COMMUNICATION
chapter 17 Integrated Marketing Communications 349
chapter 18 Advertising, Public Relations, and Sales Promotions 371
chapter 19 Personal Selling and Sales Management 397

Endnotes 417
Name Index 441
Company Index 446
Subject Index 451

contents

section one
ASSESSING THE MARKETPLACE

CHAPTER 1   OVERVIEW OF MARKETING   3

WHAT IS MARKETING?   5

Marketing Is about Satisfying Customer Needs and Wants   6

Marketing Entails an Exchange   7

Marketing Requires Product, Price, Place, and Promotion Decisions   7

Marketing Can Be Performed by Both Individuals and Organizations   10

SOCIAL AND MOBILE MARKETING 1.1:
Snacks, Team, Players, and Promotions   11

Marketing Affects Various Stakeholders   12

Marketing Helps Create Value   12

ADDING VALUE 1.1: Smartphone? Try Smart Glasses, Smart Monitors, Smart . . .   14

How Do Marketing Firms Become More Value Driven?   15

Marketing Analytics   15

MARKETING ANALYTICS 1.1: Location, Location, Analytics: Starbucks' Use of Data to Place New Stores   16

ETHICAL AND SOCIETAL DILEMMA 1.1:
Beckoning Consumers with iBeacon   18

CHAPTER 2   DEVELOPING MARKETING STRATEGIES AND A MARKETING PLAN   21

WHAT IS A MARKETING STRATEGY?   23

Customer Excellence   24

Operational Excellence   25

Product Excellence   26

Locational Excellence   26

Multiple Sources of Advantage   26

THE MARKETING PLAN   26

Step 1: Define the Business Mission   28

Step 2: Conduct a Situation Analysis   28

Step 3: Identify and Evaluate Opportunities Using STP (Segmentation, Targeting, and Positioning)   30

SOCIAL AND MOBILE MARKETING 2.1:
Truly Mobile Pizza   33

Step 4: Implement Marketing Mix and Allocate Resources   33

ADDING VALUE 2.1: Online Retail Meets Bricks and Mortar: Tesco's HomePlus Virtual Stores   35

Step 5: Evaluate Performance Using Marketing Metrics   36

ETHICAL AND SOCIETAL DILEMMA 2.1:
How a Faulty Gearbox Changed Volkswagen's Entire Approach to China   38

MARKETING ANALYTICS 2.1: The First Name in Predictive Analytics: Google   39

Strategic Planning Is Not Sequential   42

GROWTH STRATEGIES   42

Market Penetration   42

Market Development   43

Product Development   44

Diversification   44

CHAPTER 3   SOCIAL AND MOBILE MARKETING   47

THE 4E FRAMEWORK FOR SOCIAL MEDIA   48

Excite the Customer   49

SOCIAL AND MOBILE MARKETING 3.1:
Late-Night Laughs to Order   50

Educate the Customer   50

ADDING VALUE 3.1: Educating Customers Using HubSpot   51

Experience the Product or Service   52

Engage the Customer   52

CATEGORIES OF SOCIAL MEDIA 53
Social Network Sites 53

ADDING VALUE 3.2: Effective Friending 54
Media-Sharing Sites 55
Thought-Sharing Sites 56

GOING MOBILE AND SOCIAL 57
App Pricing Models 59

HOW DO FIRMS ENGAGE THEIR CUSTOMERS USING
SOCIAL MEDIA? 60
Listen 60
Analyze 62
Do 62

MARKETING ANALYTICS 3.1: Finding a Perfect
Match: How eHarmony Leverages Users' Data to Identify
Dates—and Their Consumption Patterns 63

CHAPTER 4   MARKETING ETHICS   67

MARKETING ANALYTICS 4.1: How Kellogg's Uses
Analytics to Address GMO Concerns 69

THE SCOPE OF MARKETING ETHICS 70
Influence of Personal Ethics 70
Ethics and Corporate Social Responsibility 71
A Framework for Ethical Decision Making 72

ADDING VALUE 4.1: The Barefoot
Entrepreneur 73

INTEGRATING ETHICS INTO MARKETING STRATEGY 75
Planning Phase 76
Implementation Phase 76

SOCIAL AND MOBILE MARKETING 4.1: Who
Tweeted Me to Buy a Ford Fiesta? 77
Control Phase 77

CORPORATE SOCIAL RESPONSIBILITY 78

ADDING VALUE 4.2: Walmart Wants to Be the
Corporate "Good Guy" 80
Sustainability 81

**CHAPTER 5   ANALYZING THE MARKETING
ENVIRONMENT   83**

A MARKETING ENVIRONMENT ANALYSIS
FRAMEWORK 84

THE IMMEDIATE ENVIRONMENT 85
Company Capabilities 85
Competitors 85
Corporate Partners 86

MACROENVIRONMENTAL FACTORS 86
Culture 86
Demographics 88

SOCIAL AND MOBILE MARKETING 5.1:
Understanding Connections, Both with and by
Young Consumers 88

ADDING VALUE 5.1: Where Gender Matters—and
Where It Doesn't 91
Social Trends 92

ADDING VALUE 5.2: Transforming Grocery Stores
into Health Providers 93

ETHICAL AND SOCIETAL DILEMMA 5.1: Green
Cereal? 94
Technological Advances 95
Economic Situation 95

MARKETING ANALYTICS 5.1: When the
Best Is Good Enough: Netflix's Stellar Predictive
Analytics 96
Political/Regulatory Environment 97

SOCIAL AND MOBILE MARKETING 5.2:
The News from This Year's CES 97
Responding to the Environment 99

section two
UNDERSTANDING THE MARKETPLACE

CHAPTER 6   CONSUMER BEHAVIOR   101

THE CONSUMER DECISION PROCESS 103
Need Recognition 103
Search for Information 105

MARKETING ANALYTICS 6.1: Tax Time Tactics
by H&R Block 105

SOCIAL AND MOBILE MARKETING 6.1:
The Future of Health Is Mobile 107
Evaluation of Alternatives 108

ETHICAL AND SOCIETAL DILEMMA 6.1:
Wearing the "Healthy" Label: Natural and
Organic Foods   110

Purchase and Consumption   111
Postpurchase   111

FACTORS INFLUENCING THE CONSUMER DECISION
PROCESS   113

Psychological Factors   114

ETHICAL AND SOCIETAL DILEMMA 6.2: Can
Marketing Be Life Threatening? Allegations of
Unethical Practices by Pharmaceutical Firms   117

Social Factors   118
Situational Factors   120

ADDING VALUE 6.1: Doing Everything Right—H-E-B
Supermarkets   121

SOCIAL AND MOBILE MARKETING 6.2:
Ensuring Mobile Dominance through In-Store
Promotions   123

INVOLVEMENT AND CONSUMER BUYING DECISIONS   123

Extended Problem Solving   124
Limited Problem Solving   124

**CHAPTER 7   BUSINESS–TO–BUSINESS
MARKETING   127**

B2B MARKETS   129

Manufacturers and Service Providers   129
Resellers   130
Institutions   130

MARKETING ANALYTICS 7.1: Clouding over
Computing Power   131

Government   131

SOCIAL AND MOBILE MARKETING 7.1:
iPads Go to Work   132

THE BUSINESS-TO-BUSINESS BUYING PROCESS   132

Stage 1: Need Recognition   133
Stage 2: Product Specification   133
Stage 3: RFP Process   133
Stage 4: Proposal Analysis, Vendor Negotiation,
and Selection   134

Stage 5: Order Specification   134
Stage 6: Vendor Performance Assessment Using
Metrics   134

THE BUYING CENTER   135

Organizational Culture   136

ETHICAL AND SOCIETAL DILEMMA 7.1: Is It
Business or Bribery?   137

Building B2B Relationships   138

SOCIAL AND MOBILE MARKETING 7.2:
Making the Most of LinkedIn   139

THE BUYING SITUATION   140

ADDING VALUE 7.1: Getting Out the Message with
Inbound Marketing   141

CHAPTER 8   GLOBAL MARKETING   145

ASSESSING GLOBAL MARKETS   147

Economic Analysis Using Metrics   147
Analyzing Infrastructure and Technological
Capabilities   150
Analyzing Governmental Actions   151

ETHICAL AND SOCIETAL DILEMMA 8.1:
How Chinese Regulations Change Car-Buying
Practices   151

Analyzing Sociocultural Factors   153
The Appeal of the BRIC Countries   155

SOCIAL AND MOBILE MARKETING 8.1:
The Growth of Social Networking—Brazil's Free
Market versus China's Restrictions   158

CHOOSING A GLOBAL ENTRY STRATEGY   159

Exporting   159
Franchising   160
Strategic Alliance   160
Joint Venture   160
Direct Investment   161

ADDING VALUE 8.1: Tata Starbucks and the
Indian Coffee Culture   161

CHOOSING A GLOBAL MARKETING STRATEGY   162

Target Market: Segmentation, Targeting, and
Positioning   162

ADDING VALUE 8.2: Ponying Up the Latest
Ford Mustang   163

section three
TARGETING THE MARKETPLACE

**CHAPTER 9   SEGMENTATION, TARGETING,
AND POSITIONING   169**

THE SEGMENTATION, TARGETING, AND POSITIONING
PROCESS   170

Step 1: Establish the Overall Strategy or Objectives 170
Step 2: Use Segmentation Methods 171

SOCIAL AND MOBILE MARKETING 9.1: Is Facebook Over? 173

MARKETING ANALYTICS 9.1: A Complete Ecosystem for Coffee Drinkers: The Starbucks Mobile Plan 178

ETHICAL AND SOCIETAL DILEMMA 9.1: Congressional Hearings and the Ethical Considerations for Modern Loyalty Programs 180

Step 3: Evaluate Segment Attractiveness 180

ADDING VALUE 9.1: Are Baby Boomers Too Old for TV? Some Networks Seem to Think So 182

Step 4: Select a Target Market 182
Step 5: Identify and Develop Positioning Strategy 186
Positioning Methods 188
Positioning Using Perceptual Mapping 189

CHAPTER 10 MARKETING RESEARCH 193

THE MARKETING RESEARCH PROCESS 195
Marketing Research Process Step 1: Defining the Objectives and Research Needs 196
Marketing Research Process Step 2: Designing the Research 196

ADDING VALUE 10.1: A Key Motivation for Waking Teens Early on Weekends Disappears—McDonald's Hints at Breakfast All Day 197

Marketing Research Process Step 3: Collecting the Data 198
Marketing Research Process Step 4: Analyzing the Data and Developing Insights 198
Marketing Research Process Step 5: Developing and Implementing an Action Plan 199

SECONDARY DATA 200
Inexpensive External Secondary Data 201
Syndicated External Secondary Data 201

SOCIAL AND MOBILE MARKETING 10.1: Nielsen Seeks to Track Viewership, regardless of the Media People Use to Watch 202

Internal Secondary Data 203

MARKETING ANALYTICS 10.1: Google Analytics Promises Movie Studios the Ability to Predict Performance, Weeks Prior to Opening 205

PRIMARY DATA COLLECTION TECHNIQUES 206
Social Media 207
In-Depth Interviews 208
Focus Group Interviews 209
Survey Research 209
Panel- and Scanner-Based Research 211
Experimental Research 211
Advantages and Disadvantages of Primary and Secondary Research 212

THE ETHICS OF USING CUSTOMER INFORMATION 213

ETHICAL AND SOCIETAL DILEMMA 10.1: Oh, Say, Can You See? The Implications of Mannequins That Capture Shoppers' Demographic Data 213

section four
VALUE CREATION

CHAPTER 11 PRODUCT, BRANDING, AND PACKAGING DECISIONS 217

COMPLEXITY AND TYPES OF PRODUCTS 218
Complexity of Products 218
Types of Products 219

PRODUCT MIX AND PRODUCT LINE DECISIONS 220

MARKETING ANALYTICS 11.1: How Macy's Defines Its Assortment through Analytics 221

SOCIAL AND MOBILE MARKETING 11.1: Axe Brand's Anarchy Fragrance and Graphic Novel 223

BRANDING 224
Value of Branding for the Customer 224
Brand Equity for the Owner 226

ETHICAL AND SOCIETAL DILEMMA 11.1: (Not) Marketing Sugary Drinks to Kids 227

BRANDING STRATEGIES 229
Brand Ownership 229
Naming Brands and Product Lines 230
Brand and Line Extensions 230
Co-Branding 231
Brand Licensing 231
Brand Repositioning 232

PACKAGING 232

ADDING VALUE 11.1: The Global Appeal and Rebranding Efforts of American Airlines 233

ETHICAL AND SOCIETAL DILEMMA 11.2: Calories 0, Vitamins 0: How Much Information Can Water Labels Provide? 234

Product Labeling 235

CHAPTER 12 DEVELOPING NEW PRODUCTS 237

WHY DO FIRMS CREATE NEW PRODUCTS? 239
Changing Customer Needs 239
Market Saturation 240

ADDING VALUE 12.1: Carmakers Look for an Edge, above and below the Hood 241

Managing Risk through Diversity 242
Fashion Cycles 242
Improving Business Relationships 242

DIFFUSION OF INNOVATION 243
Innovators 245
Early Adopters 245
Early Majority 245
Late Majority 246
Laggards 246
Using the Diffusion of Innovation Theory 246

HOW FIRMS DEVELOP NEW PRODUCTS 248
Idea Generation 248

MARKETING ANALYTICS 12.1: Data That Help the Brand and the Customer: GM's Big Data Use 249

SOCIAL AND MOBILE MARKETING 12.1: When Microsoft Plays Catch-Up 251

Concept Testing 252
Product Development 253

ETHICAL AND SOCIETAL DILEMMA 12.1: Should Firms Test on Animals? 254

Market Testing 255
Product Launch 255
Evaluation of Results 256

THE PRODUCT LIFE CYCLE 256
Introduction Stage 257
Growth Stage 257
Maturity Stage 258
Decline Stage 259
The Shape of the Product Life Cycle Curve 260
Strategies Based on Product Life Cycle: Some Caveats 260

CHAPTER 13 SERVICES: THE INTANGIBLE PRODUCT 263

SERVICES MARKETING DIFFERS FROM PRODUCT MARKETING 265
Intangible 266
Inseparable Production and Consumption 266
Heterogeneous 266

ADDING VALUE 13.1: Carbonite's Secure Online Backup 267
Perishable 268

PROVIDING GREAT SERVICE: THE GAPS MODEL 268
The Knowledge Gap: Understanding Customer Expectations 270

ADDING VALUE 13.2: The Broadmoor Manages Service Quality for a Five-Star Rating 271

MARKETING ANALYTICS 13.1: Using Analytics to Reduce Wait Time at Kroger 272

The Standards Gap: Setting Service Standards 274
The Delivery Gap: Delivering Service Quality 275
The Communications Gap: Communicating the Service Promise 276

SOCIAL AND MOBILE MARKETING 13.1: Linking American Express Members to Purchases 277

ETHICAL AND SOCIETAL DILEMMA 13.1: Fake Reviews 278
Service Quality and Customer Satisfaction and Loyalty 279

SERVICE RECOVERY 279
Listening to the Customers and Involving Them in the Service Recovery 280
Finding a Fair Solution 280
Resolving Problems Quickly 281

section five
VALUE CAPTURE

CHAPTER 14 PRICING CONCEPTS FOR ESTABLISHING VALUE 283

THE FIVE Cs OF PRICING 285
Company Objectives 285

ADDING VALUE 14.1: Using Price to Position the Apple Watch 288
Customers 289

MARKETING ANALYTICS 14.1: Airlines Offer Prices Based on Customers' Willingness to Pay   293

    Costs   294
    Break-Even Analysis and Decision Making   295
    Competition   297
    Channel Members   299

PRICING STRATEGIES   299
    Everyday Low Pricing (EDLP)   299
    High/Low Pricing   299
    New Product Pricing Strategies   300

ETHICAL AND SOCIETAL DILEMMA 14.1: Is It Really 45 Percent Off?   301

LEGAL AND ETHICAL ASPECTS OF PRICING   303
    Deceptive or Illegal Price Advertising   303
    Predatory Pricing   304
    Price Discrimination   304
    Price Fixing   304

section six
VALUE DELIVERY: DESIGNING THE CHANNEL AND SUPPLY CHAIN

CHAPTER 15   SUPPLY CHAIN AND CHANNEL MANAGEMENT   307

THE IMPORTANCE OF MARKETING CHANNEL/SUPPLY CHAIN MANAGEMENT   309

ADDING VALUE 15.1: The Beans May Be Slow Cooked, but the Delivery Is Quick   309

    Marketing Channels Add Value   310
    Marketing Channel Management Affects Other Aspects of Marketing   311

DESIGNING MARKETING CHANNELS   311
    Direct Marketing Channel   312
    Indirect Marketing Channel   312

MANAGING THE MARKETING CHANNEL AND SUPPLY CHAIN   312
    Managing the Marketing Channel and Supply Chain through Vertical Marketing Systems   314
    Managing Marketing Channels and Supply Chains through Strategic Relationships   316

ETHICAL AND SOCIETAL DILEMMA 15.1: Do Customers Care More about the Newest iPhone or about Working Conditions in China?   318

MAKING INFORMATION FLOW THROUGH MARKETING CHANNELS   319
    Data Warehouse   320

MAKING MERCHANDISE FLOW THROUGH MARKETING CHANNELS   321
    Distribution Centers versus Direct Store Delivery   321

    The Distribution (or Fulfillment) Center   322
    Inventory Management through Just-in-Time Inventory Systems   324

CHAPTER 16   RETAILING AND OMNICHANNEL MARKETING   327

CHOOSING RETAILING PARTNERS   329
    Channel Structure   330
    Customer Expectations   330
    Channel Member Characteristics   331
    Distribution Intensity   331

IDENTIFY TYPES OF RETAILERS   332
    Food Retailers   332
    Supermarkets   333

ADDING VALUE 16.1: Meet the Captain and Visit the Island   334

    General Merchandise Retailers   335
    Service Retailers   338

DEVELOPING A RETAIL STRATEGY USING THE FOUR PS   338
    Product   338

ADDING VALUE 16.2: The Home Depot—Providing Customers Better Access to Products   339

    Price   340
    Promotion   340
    Place   342

BENEFITS OF STORES FOR CONSUMERS   343

MARKETING ANALYTICS 16.1: In-Store and Online Analytics at IKEA   343

BENEFITS OF THE INTERNET AND OMNICHANNEL RETAILING   344
    Deeper and Broader Selection   344
    Personalization   344
    Expanded Market Presence   345

EFFECTIVE OMNICHANNEL RETAILING   345
   Integrated CRM   345
   Brand Image   346
   Pricing   346
   Supply Chain   346

section seven
VALUE COMMUNICATION

CHAPTER 17   INTEGRATED MARKETING COMMUNICATIONS   349

COMMUNICATING WITH CONSUMERS   351
   The Communication Process   351
   How Consumers Perceive Communication   353
   The AIDA Model   354

SOCIAL AND MOBILE MARKETING 17.1:
Making the Old New by Turning a Classic Campaign into a Mobile Event   355

ELEMENTS OF AN INTEGRATED MARKETING COMMUNICATIONS STRATEGY   357
   Advertising   357
   Public Relations   358

ETHICAL AND SOCIETAL DILEMMA 17.1:   Too Skinny   358
   Sales Promotions   359
   Personal Selling   359
   Direct Marketing   359
   Online Marketing   360

ETHICAL AND SOCIETAL DILEMMA 17.2:   The Consumer Privacy Bill of Rights   360

   PLANNING FOR AND MEASURING IMC SUCCESS   362
   Goals   362
   Setting and Allocating the IMC Budget   362

ADDING VALUE 17.1:
Changing Priceline by Killing Captain Kirk—and Then Bringing Him Back   363

   Measuring Success Using Marketing Metrics   364
   Planning, Implementing, and Evaluating IMC Programs—an Illustration of Google Advertising   366

MARKETING ANALYTICS 17.1:
Puma's Use of Google Analytics   366

CHAPTER 18   ADVERTISING, PUBLIC RELATIONS, AND SALES PROMOTIONS   371

STEP 1: IDENTIFY TARGET AUDIENCE   373
STEP 2: SET ADVERTISING OBJECTIVES   374
   Informative Advertising   375
   Persuasive Advertising   375
   Reminder Advertising   375
   Focus of Advertisements   376

ETHICAL AND SOCIETAL DILEMMA 18.1:
Getting to the Truth   378

STEP 3: DETERMINE THE ADVERTISING BUDGET   378
STEP 4: CONVEY THE MESSAGE   379
   The Message   379
   The Appeal   379

STEP 5: EVALUATE AND SELECT MEDIA   381
   Mass and Niche Media   382
   Choosing the Right Medium   382
   Determining the Advertising Schedule   382

STEP 6: CREATE ADVERTISEMENTS   383

SOCIAL AND MOBILE MARKETING 18.1:
Simplicity as a Strength and as a Weakness: Twitter's Advertising Formats and Future Plans   383

ETHICAL AND SOCIETAL DILEMMA 18.2:
When Makeup Companies Really Do Make Up Models' Faces   385

STEP 7: ASSESS IMPACT USING MARKETING METRICS   386
REGULATORY AND ETHICAL ISSUES IN ADVERTISING   387
PUBLIC RELATIONS   388
SALES PROMOTION   390
   Types of Sales Promotion   390

MARKETING ANALYTICS 18.1: How CVS Uses Loyalty Data to Define Coupons 391

Using Sales Promotion Tools 394

CHAPTER 19 PERSONAL SELLING AND SALES MANAGEMENT 397

THE SCOPE AND NATURE OF PERSONAL SELLING 398

Personal Selling as a Career 399
The Value Added by Personal Selling 399

SOCIAL AND MOBILE MARKETING 19.1: Personal Selling Goes Virtual 400

THE PERSONAL SELLING PROCESS 402

Step 1: Generate and Qualify Leads 402

ADDING VALUE 19.1: College Athletics Turn to the Pros for Sales Help 403

Step 2: Preapproach and the Use of CRM Systems 404

ADDING VALUE 19.2: Selling in the Cloud: The Growth and Success of Salesforce.com 405

Step 3: Sales Presentation and Overcoming Reservations 406
Step 4: Closing the Sale 407
Step 5: Follow-Up 407

MANAGING THE SALES FORCE 408

Sales Force Structure 408
Recruiting and Selecting Salespeople 409
Sales Training 410
Motivating and Compensating Salespeople 411

ETHICAL AND LEGAL ISSUES IN PERSONAL SELLING 413

The Sales Manager and the Sales Force 413
The Sales Force and Corporate Policy 413

ETHICAL AND SOCIETAL DILEMMA 19.1: When Realtors Become Reality Stars 414

The Salesperson and the Customer 414

Endnotes 417
Name Index 441
Company Index 446
Subject Index 451

marketing

Fifth Edition

Chapter one

overview of marketing

S howing a remarkable flair for understatement, the chief executive officer (CEO) of Starbucks, Howard Schultz, recently admitted, "We have a lot going on."[1] Let's think about all the things Starbucks is doing at the moment, in its attempt to market itself as an appealing product and service provider for all its customers, both current and potential.

Its ubiquitous stores—from the long-standing locations in U.S. cities and towns to international expansion into a vast range of new nations—are easy to locate and visit. A recent count showed that the chain maintains more than 20,000 stores, spanning 66 countries.[2] By making sure its stores, with their familiar siren logo, are easy to find, Starbucks guarantees that most people can readily find a place to get their coffee fix.

Starbucks vigorously competes with the likes of McDonald's, Dunkin' Donuts, and independent coffeehouses. Not too long ago, McDonald's was not a true competitor in the coffee market because all it sold was plain coffee. But when it started promoting its McCafés, Starbucks was quick to

LEARNING OBJECTIVES

After reading this chapter, you should be able to:

LO 1-1   Define the role of marketing in organizations.

LO 1-2   Describe how marketers create value for a product or service.

respond, to make sure it stayed in the lead. Starbucks' "coffee war" with Dunkin' Donuts is famous in the areas in which they compete head-to-head.[3] Independent coffeehouses and smaller regional chains, seen by many as being more hip and less commercial, also continually nip at Starbucks' heels.

Starbucks continues to innovate and expand with a variety of products, making them available in various locations beyond its own stores. Unsatisfied with dominating just the coffee market, it added Tazo teas to its product line early in its history; more recently it

continued on p. 4

© Bill Hogan/Chicago Tribune/MCT via Getty Images

continued from p. 3

purchased the Teavana chain of tea stores.[4] In addition, it purchased the Evolution Fresh line of fresh juices and sells bags of its own brand of ground coffee K-Cups, whole beans, as well as coffee-flavored ice cream in not only its own stores but also in grocery stores. But the expansion is not limited to beverages. For example, Starbucks' latest collaboration with Danone, the yogurt company, is developing a new line of dairy products called Evolution Fresh to sell in various outlets.[5]

There are plenty of jokes about how Starbucks manages to charge upwards of $5 for a jolt of caffeine, but a quick glance at its marketing methods and strategies helps explain why it can do so. The products it sells are appealing to customers and fulfill their needs: they taste good, are available readily and conveniently, and offer the benefit of helping them wake up to start their day (or stay awake for a long night of studying). Thus the exchange of money for coffee—or tea or juice or yogurt or a nice pastry—they regard as a

continued from p. 4

good value, despite the relatively high cost. The lines outside the doors of many Starbucks locations at 8:00 a.m. demonstrate this perceived value.

Starbucks also connects with fans through social marketing channels, including its popular My Starbucks Idea site. The site is an innovative approach designed to develop new products. Customers share ideas about everything "Starbucks," from store designs to new drink recipes. They can also join one of the many discussions in the customer forums. Additionally, the site connects customers to its Twitter and Facebook sites, and also links people to its mobile phone applications (apps) that they can use to pay for drinks or other products in Starbucks stores.

It's a lot to be going on, indeed. But by adopting the principles and methods of marketing that this textbook covers, Starbucks has created a market that it continues to dominate, bringing benefits to the company and its shareholders, as well as to consumers. ■

LO 1-1 | Define the role of marketing in organizations.

WHAT IS MARKETING?

Unlike other subjects you may have studied, marketing already is very familiar to you. You start your day by agreeing to do the dishes in exchange for a freshly made cup of coffee. Then you fill up your car with gas. You attend a class that you have chosen and paid for. After class, you pick up lunch (and maybe a frozen dessert) at the cafeteria, which you eat while reading a book on your iPad. Then you leave campus to have your hair cut and take in a movie. On your bus ride back to school, you pass the time by buying a few songs from Apple's iTunes. In each case, you have acted as the buyer and made a decision about whether you should part with your time and/or money to receive a particular product or service. If, after you return home, you decide to sell some clothes on eBay that you don't wear much anymore, you have become a seller. In each of these transactions, you were engaged in marketing.

The American Marketing Association states that "**marketing** is the activity, set of institutions, and processes for creating, *capturing,* communicating, delivering, and exchanging offerings that have value for customers, clients, partners, and society at large."[6] What does this definition really mean? Good

marketing is not a random activity; it requires thoughtful planning with an emphasis on the ethical implications of any of those decisions on society in general. Firms develop a **marketing plan** (Chapter 2) that specifies the marketing activities for a specific period of time. The marketing plan also is broken down into various components—how the product or service will be conceived or designed, how much it should cost, where and how it will be promoted, and how it will get to the consumer. In any exchange, the parties to the transaction should be satisfied. In our previous example, you should be satisfied or even delighted with the song you downloaded, and Apple should be satisfied with the amount of money it received from you. Thus, the core aspects of marketing are found in Exhibit 1.1. Let's see how these core aspects look in practice.

marketing An organizational function and a set of processes for creating, *capturing*, communicating, and delivering value to customers and for managing customer relationships in ways that benefit the organization and its stakeholders.

marketing plan A written document composed of an analysis of the current marketing situation, opportunities and threats for the firm, marketing objectives and strategy specified in terms of the four Ps, action programs, and projected or pro forma income (and other financial) statements.

▼ **EXHIBIT 1.1** Core Aspects of Marketing

- Marketing helps create value.
- Marketing is about satisfying customer needs and wants.
- Marketing entails an exchange.
- Marketing requires product, price, place, and promotion decisions.
- Marketing can be performed by both individuals and organizations.
- Marketing affects various stakeholders.

Marketing

Marketing Is about Satisfying Customer Needs and Wants

Understanding the marketplace, and especially consumer needs and wants, is fundamental to marketing success. In the broadest terms, the marketplace refers to the world of trade. More narrowly, however, the marketplace can be segmented or divided into groups of people who are pertinent to an organization for particular reasons. For example, the marketplace for soft drinks may include most people in the world, but as Pepsi and Coke battle each other worldwide, they divide the global population into a host of categories: men versus women, calorie-conscious or not, people who prefer carbonated versus noncarbonated drinks, and multiple categories of flavor preferences, among others.[7] If you manufacture a beverage with zero calories, you want to know for which marketplace segments your product is most relevant, then make sure you build a marketing strategy that targets those groups. Certain diet- and health-conscious customers may prefer Diet Coke or Diet Pepsi; others may opt for bottled water products like Dasani or Aquafina.

Although marketers would prefer to sell their products and services to everyone, it is not practical to do so. Because marketing costs money, good marketers carefully seek out potential customers who have both an interest in the product and an ability to buy it. For example, most people need some form of transportation, and many people probably would like to own the new hybrid from Lexus. Starting at more than $120,000, the Lexus LS 600h L is one of the most sophisticated hybrid cars on the market. But Lexus is not actually interested in everyone who wants an LS 600h L, because not everyone can afford to spend that much on a car. Instead, Lexus defines its viable target market as those consumers who want and can afford such a product.[8] Although not all companies focus on such a specific, and wealthy, target, all marketers are interested in finding the buyers who are most likely to be interested in their offerings.

> Although marketers would prefer to sell their products and services to everyone, it is not practical to do so."

Coke and Pepsi have divided the world into two camps: Coke-lovers and Pepsi-lovers. Which are you?
© Carlo Allegri/Reuters/Corbis

What type of customer would buy a $120,000 hybrid car?
© Ian Langsdon/EPA/Newscom

You can exchange your money on the iTunes Store for the latest Katy Perry album.
© Christie Goodwin/Entertainment/Getty Image

song you heard, multiple songs, or the entire new album. You begin with the song you heard, which you continue to love after hearing it several times. Therefore, you go back to iTunes and take advantage of its offer to complete the album by downloading the rest of the songs to your iTunes library. Your billing information is already in the company's system, so you do not have to enter your credit card number or other information. Furthermore, iTunes creates a record of your purchase, which it uses, together with your other purchase trends, to create personalized recommendations of other albums or songs that you might like. Thus, Apple uses the valuable information you provide to facilitate future exchanges and solidify its relationship with you.

Marketing Entails an Exchange

Marketing is about an **exchange**—the trade of things of value between the buyer and the seller so that each is better off as a result. As depicted in Exhibit 1.2, sellers provide products or services, then communicate and facilitate the delivery of their offering to consumers. Buyers complete the exchange by giving money and information to the seller. Suppose you learn about a new Katy Perry album by hearing one of her songs on SiriusXM Satellite Radio. The same day, a friend tweets on her Twitter account that she loves the new album, and you visit the Katy Perry Facebook fan page, which is full of recommendations. From there, you click into the iTunes Store, where you can purchase the

Marketing Requires Product, Price, Place, and Promotion Decisions

Marketing traditionally has been divided into a set of four interrelated decisions and consequent actions known as the **marketing mix**, or **four Ps**: product, price, place, and promotion (as defined in Exhibit 1.3).[9] The four Ps are the controllable set of decisions or activities that the firm uses to respond to the wants of its target markets. But what does each of these activities in the marketing mix entail?

Product: Creating Value Although marketing is a multifaceted function, its fundamental purpose is to create value by developing a variety of offerings, including goods, services, and ideas, to satisfy customer needs.[10] Take, for example, a cup of coffee. At one time, people in the United

▼ **EXHIBIT 1.2** Exchange: The Underpinning of Seller–Buyer Relationships

Communications and delivery

Goods/services producers (sellers)

Money and information

Customers/ consumers (buyers)

goods Items that can be physically touched.

States made a pot of coffee at home or picked up a cup on the run from a McDonald's or Dunkin' Donuts. Because Starbucks and competitive firms realize customers have needs beyond just buying a cup of joe, they are offering their customers a variety of options. This variety includes lattes, cappuccinos, macchiatos, Frappuccinos, hot chocolates, smoothies, teas, bottled juices, Refreshers, and regular brewed coffee, providing customers with interesting choices for which they are willing to pay a premium. The experience of watching the coffee being made by a barista in a setting that often resembles a quaint café in Florence, Italy, adds to the perceived value of the product, and to the price!

Goods are items that you can physically touch. Nike shoes, Pepsi-Cola, a Frappuccino, Kraft cheese, Tide, an iPad, and countless other products are examples of goods. As we describe at the start of Chapter 2, Nike primarily makes shoes but also adds value to its products by, for example, offering custom designs under its Nike ID brand that increase their fashionable appeal and enlisting popular celebrities such as Rafael Nadal to add their names to the designs.

▼ **EXHIBIT 1.3** The Marketing Mix

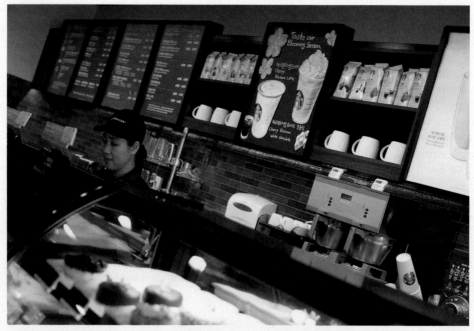

Marketers have transformed coffee from a simple morning drink into an entire experience that adds value for the customer.
© SeongJoon Cho/Bloomberg via Getty Images

" ALTHOUGH MARKETING IS A MULTIFACETED FUNCTION, ITS FUNDAMENTAL PURPOSE IS TO CREATE VALUE BY DEVELOPING A VARIETY OF OFFERINGS. "

Unlike goods, **services** are intangible customer benefits that are produced by people or machines and cannot be separated from the producer. When people buy tickets—whether for airline travel, a sporting event, or the theater—they are paying not for the physical ticket stub but of course for the experience they gain. For people who like to drink their coffee in a cozy, warm setting, Starbucks offers an experience that feels like home but encourages social interaction. Hotels, insurance agencies, and spas similarly provide services. Getting money from your bank, whether through an ATM or from a teller, is another example of using a service. In this case, cash machines usually add value to the banking experience because they are conveniently located, fast, and easy to use.

Many offerings in the market combine goods and services.[11] When you go to an optical center, you get your eyes examined

Price: Capturing Value

Everything has a price, although it doesn't always have to be monetary. Price, therefore, is everything the buyer gives up—money, time, and/or energy—in exchange for the product.[12] Marketers must determine the price of a product carefully on the basis of the potential buyer's belief about its value. For example, United Airlines can take you from New York to Denver. The price you pay for that service depends on how far in advance you book the ticket, the time of year, and whether you want to fly coach or business class. If you value the convenience of buying your ticket at the last minute for

> "When people buy tickets—whether for airline travel, a sporting event, or the theater—they are paying not for the physical ticket stub but of course for the experience they gain."

(a service) and purchase new contact lenses (a good). If you attend a Bruno Mars concert, you can be enthralled by the world-class performance. To remember the event, you might want to pick up a shirt or a souvenir from the concert. With these tangible goods, you can relive and remember the enjoyment of the experience over and over again.

Ideas include thoughts, opinions, and philosophies; intellectual concepts such as these also can be marketed. Groups promoting bicycle safety go to schools, give talks, and sponsor bike helmet poster contests for the members of their primary market—children. Then their secondary target market segment, parents and siblings, gets involved through their interactions with the young contest participants. The exchange of value occurs when the children listen to the sponsors' presentation and wear their helmets while bicycling, which means they have adopted, or become "purchasers," of the safety idea that the group marketed.

a ski trip between Christmas and New Year's Day and you want to fly business class, you can expect to pay four or five times as much as you would for the cheapest available ticket. That is, you have traded off a lower price for convenience. For marketers, the key to determining prices is figuring out how much customers are willing to pay so that they are satisfied with the purchase and the seller achieves a reasonable profit.

Place: Delivering the Value Proposition

The third P, place, represents all the activities necessary to get the product to the right customer when that customer wants it. For Starbucks, that means expanding its storefronts

Rafael Nadal plays tennis in Nike shoes.
© Matthias Hangst/Getty Images Sport/Getty Images.

When you attend a Bruno Mars concert you are paying for a service.
© Rich Polk/Getty Images Entertainment/Getty Images for Clear Channel

business-to-consumer (B2C) marketing The process in which businesses sell to consumers.

business-to-business (B2B) marketing The process of buying and selling goods or services to be used in the production of other goods and services, for consumption by the buying organization, or for resale by wholesalers and retailers.

consumer-to-consumer (C2C) marketing The process in which consumers sell to other consumers.

constantly and proactively, so that it is easy for caffeine junkies to find their fix. Creative locations, such as kiosks at the baggage claim in airports or small booths in grocery stores, represent the chain's effort to improve its offering on this dimension of the marketing mix.

Place more commonly deals specifically with retailing and marketing channel management, also known as *supply chain management. Supply chain management* is the set of approaches and techniques that firms employ to efficiently and effectively integrate their suppliers, manufacturers, warehouses, stores, and other firms involved in the transaction (e.g., transportation companies) into a seamless value chain in which merchandise is produced and distributed in the right quantities, to the right locations, and at the right time, while minimizing systemwide costs and satisfying the service levels required by the customers. Many marketing students initially overlook the importance of marketing channel management, because a lot of these activities are behind the scenes. But without a strong and efficient marketing channel system, merchandise isn't available when customers want it. Then customers are disappointed, and sales and profits suffer.

Promotion: Communicating the Value Proposition

Even the best products and services will go unsold if marketers cannot communicate their value to customers. Promotion is communication by a marketer that informs, persuades, and reminds potential buyers about a product or service to influence their opinions and elicit a response. Promotion generally can enhance a product's or service's value. When the publisher of the well-known Babar books wanted to celebrate the 80th anniversary of the series, it initiated a $100,000 campaign. Working in collaboration with toy and bookstores, the campaign did not just suggest people buy the books and read about an elephant king. Instead, it embraced a sense of nostalgia and evoked a simpler time, in which grandparents might read pleasant stories to their grandchildren.[13]

Such collaborative promotions can be especially effective tactics for marketers, particularly if they can team up with a popular sport, as Social and Mobile Marketing 1.1 details.

Marketing Can Be Performed by Both Individuals and Organizations

Imagine how complicated the world would be if you had to buy everything you consumed directly from producers or manufacturers. You would have to go from farm to farm buying your food and then from manufacturer to manufacturer to purchase the table, plates, and utensils you needed to eat that food. Fortunately, marketing intermediaries, such as retailers, accumulate merchandise from producers in large amounts and then sell it to you in smaller amounts. The process by which businesses sell to consumers is known as **business-to-consumer (B2C) marketing**, whereas the process of selling merchandise or services from one business to another is called **business-to-business (B2B) marketing**. With the advent of various Internet auction sites (e.g., eBay) and social media, consumers have started marketing their products and services to other consumers. This third category, in which consumers sell to other consumers, is **consumer-to-consumer (C2C) marketing**. These marketing transactions are illustrated in Exhibit 1.4.

Individuals can also undertake activities to market themselves. When you apply for a job, for instance, the research you do about the firm, the résumé and cover letter you submit with

> " Imagine how complicated the world would be if you had to buy everything you consumed directly from producers or manufacturers. "

▼ **EXHIBIT 1.4** Marketing Can Be Performed by Both Individuals and Organizations

Manufacturer (makes monitors)		Retailer (sells PCs & monitors)		Consumer A		Consumer B
	B2B		B2C		C2C	

Social & Mobile Marketing
Snacks, Teams, Players, and Promotions[i]

Sponsorships of sports teams are nothing new. Firms have been naming stadiums, providing gear, and calling themselves the "official product of" popular sporting events and teams for years. But such promotions can take on new life and new facets when they bring the power of social media marketing to bear on their campaigns.

Take the example of Mondelēz International and its latest deal in conjunction with various soccer teams and players. The company maintains such well-known brands as Chips Ahoy! and Oreo cookies, Wheat Thins and Ritz crackers, Cadbury candies, and Sour Patch Kids Stride gum. Thus its product assortment is quite strongly geared toward children and families.

Recent trends suggest that more children today play soccer (17.1 percent of them play at least once a year) than other sports such as baseball (13.4 percent), football (4.5 percent), or hockey (1.1 percent). Mondelēz was quick to make the connection and entered into a sponsorship agreement that made it the official snack brand of the U.S. men's and women's national soccer teams. Furthermore, it signed individual sponsorship deals with some stars of the sport, such as Alex Morgan, Omar Gonzalez, and Clint Dempsey.

Despite this popularity among children and their infamous soccer moms, soccer still struggles in television ratings compared with other sports. Accordingly, the promotional campaigns associated with the sponsorship have very little to do with television. Instead, the focus is on in-store and social media efforts.

In conjunction with its sponsorship of U.S. soccer, Mondelēz has entered into a partnership with Twitter to increase its advertising spending at the site. In return, Twitter will share its real-time marketing expertise, offer customized marketing research findings, and host various training programs for the packaged-goods company.

This effort represents a continuation of Mondelēz's already strong social media presence. For example, Oreo has nearly 35 million followers on Facebook. It also won praise for its quick thinking during the power outage at Super Bowl XLVII, when it immediately tweeted, "You can still dunk in the dark." By linking a snack that appeals to children with a sport they love, Mondelēz vastly increases the chances that moms will bring the tasty cookies for a postgame celebration with the little league team.

Mondelēz is the official snack brand for the U.S. men's and women's national soccer teams. To appeal to its young target market, it uses social media instead of television. Pictured here, wearing a Sour Patch Kids T-shirt, is U.S. soccer star Alex Morgan giving a "high five."
© Stephen Brashear/AP Photo for Mondelez International

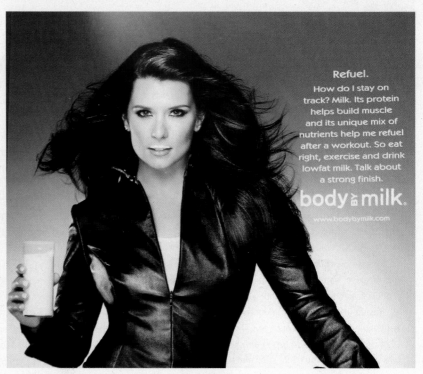

The "Milk Life" and "Body by Milk" marketing campaigns create a high level of awareness for the milk industry.
Left: Courtesy of Lowe Campbell Ewald and MilkPEP; Right: © Jonathan Ferrey/Getty Images

your application, and the way you dress for an interview and conduct yourself during it are all forms of marketing activities. Accountants, lawyers, financial planners, physicians, and other professional service providers also constantly market their services one way or another.

Marketing Affects Various Stakeholders

Most people think of marketing as a way to facilitate the sale of products or services to customers or clients. But marketing can also affect several other stakeholders (e.g., supply chain partners, society at large). Partners in the supply chain include wholesalers, retailers, or other intermediaries such as transportation or warehousing companies. All of these entities are involved in marketing to one another. Manufacturers sell merchandise to retailers, but the retailers often have to convince manufacturers to sell to them. After many years of not being able to purchase products from Ralph Lauren because it sells below the manufacturers' suggested retail price (MSRP), TJX Companies, Inc., operators of Marshall's and TJMaxx, among others, is now Ralph Lauren's largest customer.[14]

Marketing also can aim to benefit an entire industry or society at large. The dairy industry targets its "Milk Life" and "Body by Milk" campaigns at different target segments, including parents, their children, and athletes. Through this campaign, the allied milk producers have created high levels of awareness about the benefits of drinking milk, including the high levels of protein, potassium, and calcium it provides. The focus is largely

on how drinking milk for breakfast fits in with a healthy lifestyle that helps people maintain their focus, weight, and muscle mass. Even the industry's charitable campaigns resonate with this notion: The Milk Drive, run in conjunction with Feeding America, seeks to ensure that local food banks are sufficiently stocked with this nutritious, frequently requested item. Such campaigns benefit the entire dairy industry and promote the health benefits of drinking milk to society at large.

Marketing Helps Create Value

Marketing didn't get to its current prominence among individuals, corporations, and society at large overnight.[15] To understand how marketing has evolved into its present-day, integral business function of creating value, let's look for a moment at some of the milestones in marketing's short history (see Exhibit 1.5).

Production-Oriented Era Around the turn of the 20th century, most firms were production oriented and believed that a good product would sell itself. Henry Ford, the founder of Ford Motor Company, once famously remarked, "Customers can have any color they want so long as it's black." Manufacturers were concerned with product innovation, not with satisfying the needs of individual consumers, and retail stores typically were considered places to hold the merchandise until a consumer wanted it.

Sales-Oriented Era Between 1920 and 1950, production and distribution techniques became more sophisticated and the Great Depression and World War II conditioned customers to consume less or manufacture items themselves, so they

▼ **EXHIBIT 1.5** Marketing Evolution: Production, Sales, Marketing, and Value

Photos (left to right): © Ryan McVay/Getty Images RF; © CMCD/Getty Images RF; © Ted Dayton Photography/Beateworks/ Corbis RF; © Ryan McVay/Getty Images RF; © McGraw-Hill Education/Mark Dierker, photographer

planted victory gardens instead of buying produce. As a result, manufacturers had the capacity to produce more than customers really wanted or were able to buy. Firms found an answer to their overproduction in becoming sales oriented: they depended on heavy doses of personal selling and advertising.

discovering and providing what consumers wanted and needed; to compete successfully, they would have to give their customers greater value than their competitors did. (The importance of value is appropriately incorporated into the AMA definition of marketing discussed earlier.)

> ## Most successful firms today are market oriented.

Market-Oriented Era

After World War II, soldiers returned home, got new jobs, and started families. At the same time, manufacturers turned from focusing on the war effort toward making consumer products. Suburban communities, featuring cars in every garage, sprouted up around the country, and the new suburban fixture, the shopping center, began to replace cities' central business districts as the hub of retail activity and a place to just hang out. Some products, once in limited supply because of World War II, became plentiful. And the United States entered a buyers' market—the customer became king! When consumers again had choices, they were able to make purchasing decisions on the basis of factors such as quality, convenience, and price. Manufacturers and retailers thus began to focus on what consumers wanted and needed before they designed, made, or attempted to sell their products and services. It was during this period that firms discovered marketing.

Value-Based Marketing Era

Most successful firms today are market oriented.[16] That means they generally have transcended a production or selling orientation and attempt to discover and satisfy their customers' needs and wants. Before the turn of the 21st century, better marketing firms recognized that there was more to good marketing than simply

Value reflects the relationship of benefits to costs, or what you *get* for what you *give*.[17] In a marketing context, customers seek a fair return in goods and/or services for their hard-earned

Gucci provides value to its target customers.
© Tomohiro Ohsumi/Bloomberg/Getty Images

value Reflects the relationship of benefits to costs, or what the consumer *gets* for what he or she *gives*.

money and scarce time. They want products or services that meet their specific needs or wants *and* that are offered at a price that they believe is a good value. A good value, however, doesn't necessarily mean the product or service is inexpensive. If it did, luxury goods manufacturers like Porsche or Gucci would go out of business. There are customers willing to pay asking prices for all types of goods at all price levels because to those individuals, what they get for what they give is a good value.

A creative way to provide value to customers is to engage in **value cocreation**.[18] In this case, customers can act as collaborators to create the product or service. When clients work with their investment advisers, they cocreate their investment portfolios; when Nike allows customers to custom design their sneakers, they are cocreating. Adding Value 1.1 examines how companies are adding value to smartphones by developing smart accessories.

In the next section, we explore the notion of value-based marketing further. Specifically, we look at various options for attracting customers by providing them with better value than the competition does. Then we discuss how firms compete on the basis of value. Finally, we examine how firms transform the value concept into their value-driven activities.

Adding Value   1.1

Smartphone? Try Smart Glasses, Smart Monitors, Smart...[ii]

It may be hard to imagine, but just a few short years ago the idea of being able to talk to someone while away from home was a massive added value. Then the value added became being able check e-mail on a phone. Such offerings seem incredibly basic today. Obviously, the "smart" market is a dynamic and rapidly changing one in which the definition of what constitutes value also changes constantly.

Some of the most modern smart gadgets seek to make it easier for people to engage in their day-to-day activities. An app by Mercedes-Benz allows car owners to unlock their doors or open the trunk with their phones. Alternatively, an external device, Hone, attaches to key chains and allows smartphone users to activate a visual and audio signal so that they can find their car keys wherever they left them (e.g., in the freezer, tucked in a drawer).

For exercise fans, the Nike Fit band calculates steps taken, calories burned, and time spent exercising, then syncs the information gathered from the wristband with a mobile app that combines all the information in one place. The UP band, by Jawbone, tracks all this information, as well as sleep times and food intake. Thus it can tell users how long they took to fall asleep and how many hours of deep sleep they actually got. Then it promises to summarize this information in "Insights," which suggest recommendations based on individual trends. If a person sleeps poorly after snacking late in the day, UP will recommend no more eating after 8:00 p.m., for example. For even more adventurous exercisers, the Crash Sensor, a device made to mount onto a bicycle helmet, alerts emergency contacts if a crash occurs and provides coordinates so that emergency crews can find a hiker lost in the wilderness.

Other smart tools are a little more forward thinking, moving us into a future world in which connecting to anyone, anywhere doesn't even require our thumbs. Perhaps the most widely talked about version is Google Glass, the technology that puts the web in the corner of users' vision and allows them to connect, using only eye movement. This revolutionary innovation

Smartphones and related connected devices/apps, such as Google Glass, are revolutionizing the marketplace.
© Rex Features via AP Photo

appears likely to change virtually everything (pun intended). However, its rollout has been slow thus far and the company has sought to avoid moving smartphone apps to Glass. So Google has created guidelines for developing "Glassware": keep the information concise, keep alerts relevant, make tasks easy, and make information provision timely.

Nearly as ubiquitous as the chatter about the device are the concerns about it. Critics have questioned how Google Glass might alter social interactions, cause accidents by people focused on the web rather than where they are walking, and even rewire our cognitive capacities. The promise of Google Glass is so intriguing, though, that consumers are lining up to pay around $1,500 for the potential to mess with their brain matter.

LO 1-2 Describe how marketers create value for a product or service.

How Do Marketing Firms Become More Value Driven?

Firms become value driven by focusing on four activities. First, they share information about their customers and competitors across their own organization and with other firms that help them get the product or service to the marketplace, such as manufacturers and transportation companies. Second, they strive to balance their customers' benefits and costs. Third, they concentrate on building relationships with customers. Fourth, they need to take advantage of new technologies and connect with their customers using social and mobile media.

Marketing Analytics

Modern marketers rely on sophisticated data analytics to define and refine their approaches to their customers and their markets. Companies such as Starbucks, CVS, Kroger, Netflix, and Amazon collect massive amounts of data about how, when, why, where, and what people buy, then analyze those data to inform their choices. In Marketing Analytics 1.1, we detail just one use of these data by the coffee giant—namely, to decide where to put its stores.

Balancing Benefits with Costs

Value-oriented marketers constantly measure the benefits that customers perceive against the cost of their offerings. They use available customer data to find opportunities to satisfy their customers' needs better, keep down costs, and develop long-term loyalties. For example, IKEA does not have highly paid salespeople to sell its furniture, but its simple designs mean customers can easily choose a product and assemble it themselves.

> "To build relationships, firms focus on the lifetime profitability of the relationship, not how much money is made during each transaction."

Building Relationships with Customers

During the past couple of decades, marketers have begun to develop a **relational orientation** as they have realized that they need to think about their customers in terms of relationships rather than transactions.[19] To build relationships, firms focus on the lifetime profitability of the relationship, not how much money is made during each transaction. Thus, Apple makes its innovations compatible with existing products to encourage consumers to maintain a long-term relationship with the company across all their electronic needs.

This relationship approach uses a process known as **customer relationship management (CRM)**, a business

relational orientation A method of building a relationship with customers based on the philosophy that buyers and sellers should develop a long-term relationship.

customer relationship management (CRM) A business philosophy and set of strategies, programs, and systems that focus on identifying and building loyalty among the firm's most valued customers.

Kroger collects massive amounts of data about how, when, why, where, and what people buy, then analyze those data to better serve its customers.
© Daniel Acker/Bloomberg via Getty Images

To balance benefits with costs, IKEA does not offer significant sales assistance, but does showcase products in a simulated home environment to facilitate decision making. To keep costs low, many products are sold unassembled.
© Alex Segre/Alamy.

Marketing Analytics

Location, Location, Analytics: Starbucks' Use of Data to Place New Stores[iii]

By now, nearly everyone on the planet recognizes the green mermaid logo that proudly sits atop every Starbucks sign, poster, and cup. The ubiquitous coffee giant maintains more than 22,000 locations in over 66 countries. But its growth has not been without a few stumbles and bumps in the road. For example, in the last decade, hundreds of newly opened stores had to be closed because of their poor performance. In analyzing how the company got to that point, Starbucks' manager of global market planning Patrick O'Hagan explained that many of the stores never should have opened. However, the staff in charge of these location choices had been inundated with so much data, they were unable to use them to make profitable decisions. Thus, the Starbucks story reveals a great deal about the importance of data analytics.

Starbucks began using Esri's Geographic Information Systems (GIS) technology as far back as the 1990s. But it has perfected its applications of the GIS-provided predictive analytics only recently. Currently, it is using the information gleaned from the technology to plan 1,500 new locations. With the system's ArcGIS Online tool, Starbucks obtains a graphical summary of the GIS data in map form. These data include both location information and demographic details, which the software analyzes according to pertinent criteria. The applications allow Starbucks' staff to pinpoint ideal locations that are likely to attract substantial traffic and thus boost chainwide sales, such that "ArcGIS allows us to create replicable consumer applications that are exactly what they need." Because the GIS technology is accessible

Starbucks uses Geographic Information Systems (GIS) technology to pinpoint ideal locations and determine which kinds of stores to open in those locations.
© Bhandol/Alamy

through both desktops and mobile devices, location experts in the field also can combine the high-tech insights with their real-world observations.

Not only does the GIS technology help Starbucks determine the ideal locations for new stores, but it also can enable the company to decide which kinds of stores to open. For example, many of the 1,500 planned new stores will feature drive-through windows; others will be smaller stores, strategically placed to provide the greatest customer convenience. The new approach already has been proving effective, according to results that show that the most recent newly opened stores, particularly those in the Americas, consistently are producing great returns and exceeding hurdle rates.

Apple makes its new products compatible with existing ones to maintain a long-term relationship with its customers.
© Spencer Platt/Getty Images News/Getty Images

philosophy and set of strategies, programs, and systems that focus on identifying and building loyalty among the firm's most valued customers.[20] Firms that employ CRM systematically collect information about their customers' needs and then use that information to target their best customers with the products, services, and special promotions that appear most important to them.

Connecting with Customers Using Social and Mobile Media
Marketers are steadily embracing new technologies, such as social and mobile media, to allow them to connect better with their customers and thereby serve their needs more effectively. Businesses take social and mobile media seriously, including these advanced tools in the development of their marketing strategies. In turn, 93 percent of marketers assert that they use social media tools for their businesses.[21] That's largely because approximately 4.2 billion people link to some social media sites through their mobile devices.[22]

Yet even with this astounding penetration, only 10 percent of the world's population uses Facebook—which means 90 percent

> "Customers who book hotels using travel agencies become loyal to the agency that gives them the lowest prices, rather than to any particular hotel brand."

still has not signed up. The United States and United Kingdom may be approaching saturation, but there is still huge growth potential for social networks. Before users can sign up for Facebook, though, they need access to high-speed Internet.[23] Other countries continue to experience higher Facebook growth rates as they gain greater Internet access, and as Facebook becomes available in more languages (around 70 currently). The global average Internet penetration rate hovers below 40 percent, with massive populations in Africa and Asia still limited in their access.[24]

Beyond social media sites, online travel agencies such as Expedia, Travelocity, Orbitz, Priceline, and Kayak have become the first place that users go to book travel arrangements. According to the U.S. Travel Association, in addition to asking friends and relying on their own experience, 10 percent of travelers turned to destination websites, 9 percent relied on websites run by specific providers, another 5 percent used social networking, and 4 percent of them depended on their mobile devices to plan their trips.[25] Customers who book hotels using travel agencies become loyal to the agency that gives them the lowest prices, rather than to any particular hotel brand. So hotels are using social media and mobile applications to lure customers back to their specific brands by engaging in conversations with them on Facebook and allowing fans of the page to book their hotel reservations through Facebook. Some hotel chains have mobile applications that allow customers to make changes to their reservations, shift check-in and check-out

times, and add amenities or services to their stays. The hotels know a lot about their customers because they collect information about their previous visits, including the type of room they stayed in, their preferences (from pillows to drinks consumed from the minibar), and the type of room service they prefer.

Several restaurant chains are exploiting location-based social media applications, such as HappyCow Vegin'Out, Yelp, Foodspotting, inBloom, and Alfred.[26] By using location-based apps on mobile phones, customers can find restaurants that cater to their specific dietary requirements (such as HappyCow, which identifies nearby vegetarian restaurants) or find well-rated (by Yelp users) restaurants nearby. The result is that users are driving the way brands and stores are interacting with social media. Location-based services are thus appealing, though they also may create some concerns, as Ethical and Societal Dilemma 1.1 describes.

Buffalo Wild Wings suggests that its diners check in to its locations using their phones. The target customers for this chain are young and tech savvy, and with its in-house games and sports broadcasts, Buffalo Wild Wings is uniquely situated to encourage customers to connect and bring their friends along. It offers contests and encourages frequent visits to win. Customers can earn free chicken wings or soft drinks within

Marketers connect with customers by using social and mobile media.
Courtesy of Intelity

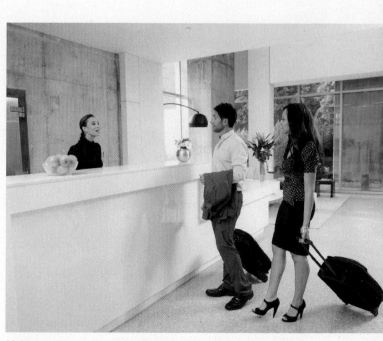
Make travel arrangements online either through Facebook or your mobile app and check-in is a breeze.
© Erik Isakson/Getty Images RF

ethical&societal dilemma

Beckoning Consumers with the iBeacon[iv]

When iPad and iPhone owners updated their systems to iOS 7, they also transformed their devices into a new type of communication channel, whether they realized it or not. Specifically, the latest operating system update installed iBeacon software onto their mobile devices.

The iBeacon software works as a location service, such that transmitters can send messages to any user with an iPhone or iPad that has been updated to iOS 7. Apple soon announced that it already had installed transmitters into all of its U.S. stores. When Apple fans visit the stores, the iBeacon location service will push notifications to them based on their specific location. A shopper who pauses by the updated MacBook Air might receive a message on her phone about its battery life or compatibility with her phone. Another consumer who breezes past the phones could receive a reminder that he is eligible for an upgrade.

This application is notable; it indicates that Apple has jumped ahead of its competitors in devising and implementing hypertargeted, micro-location-based marketing. For its retail stores, the software reveals not just whether a potential customer is in the same town or near the parking lot, but also whether a shopper is literally standing near the accessory display.

This rollout in the Apple stores appears to be just the tip of the iceberg. Recent model iPhones and iPads can not only receive messages using the iBeacon software but also be easily configured to serve as a transmitter of iBeacon messages. This means that virtually every retailer that invests in an iPad can use the software similar to the way Apple uses it: pushing notifications to shoppers who are already in the store, locating them precisely, and learning exactly how they move through the store. One estimate suggests that there are approximately 200 million potential iBeacon transmitters already in circulation—even before the functionality has gained widespread acclaim.

For Apple, the competitive advantage appears nearly insurmountable because when users updated to iOS 7, they also opted in to the iBeacon application, agreeing to accept the micro-location-based push notifications. Other stores will need to get consumers to agree to receive similar messages. For big retailers such as Walmart, it might not be hard; they can simply include the software in their regular apps that consumers already may have downloaded.

Furthermore, Apple has essentially blazed the trail for this latest innovation for retail. Combining its dominance in the tablet market, popularity in the mobile phone market, and first-mover advantages in the location service market, it appears that the iBeacon is set to become the standard.

But even if Apple has thought ahead about how to make sure users adopt the iBeacon, it might not have considered all the implications for users' privacy. Are companies responsible for making sure their customers know their identity and location are being revealed to marketers all the time? Or are customers the ones responsible for opting out of such location-based services?

This Estimote Beacon enables Apple users to opt in to receive micro-location-based messages in physical locations, helping them find products, deals, and more information about their surroundings.
Courtesy of Estimote, Inc.

their first three visits. Other contests encourage patrons to upload photos of the crowd's reaction to a big play. Moreover, customers can develop their own challenges from their bar stools. Approximately 10,000 people participated in 33,000 challenges, and 5,000 rewards were given out in the first week of Buffalo Wild Wings' contests by using location-based applications.[27] ∎

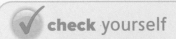

check yourself

1. Does providing a good value mean selling at a low price?
2. How are marketers connecting with customers through social and mobile media?

Increase your engagement and learning with Connect Marketing.

These Connect activities, available only through your Connect course, have been designed to make the following concepts more meaningful and applicable:

▶ Introduction to Marketing: Dunkin' Donuts Video Case

▶ Creating Value in the Marketplace: Zipcar Case Analysis

▶ The Marketing Mix—Travel Goods and Service: Click and Drag Activity

▶ Delivering Value: Pinkberry versus Red Mango Video Case

▶ Value Creation through The Marketing Mix: iSeeit! Video

 SMARTBOOK™   **iSeeit!**

two

developing marketing strategies and a **marketing plan**

N ike is dedicated to providing both top athletes and their casual counterparts all the tools they need to compete at their highest levels. It constantly seeks to improve its own performance through innovation and in-depth analyses of its competitors.

Created by runners in Oregon, Nike began in the early 1970s as an American company, focused mainly on the American market.[1] Its first running shoes featured a then-innovative design with a waffle-patterned sole. The customers were mainly elite runners, determined to find the lightest shoe they could. But Nike running shoes were gaining popularity among casual athletes.

By 1984 the company had gone public, and it had found Michael Jordan. Thus the entire market—and the very concept of sponsorship—changed forever. The Air Jordan line of basketball shoes turned Nike into a massive success, with broad appeal to sports fans of virtually all ages and profiles. Nike continues to affiliate with high-profile, elite basketball players, including dozens of NBA All-Stars such as Kyrie Irving, Carmelo Anthony, and LeBron James.[2]

continued on p. 22

LEARNING OBJECTIVES

After reading this chapter, you should be able to:

LO 2-1 Define a marketing strategy.

LO 2-2 Describe the elements of a marketing plan.

LO 2-3 Analyze a marketing situation using SWOT analyses.

LO 2-4 Describe how a firm chooses which consumer group(s) to pursue with its marketing efforts.

LO 2-5 Outline the implementation of the marketing mix as a means to increase customer value.

LO 2-6 Summarize portfolio analysis and its use to evaluate marketing performance.

LO 2-7 Describe how firms grow their business.

© Jin Lee/Bloomberg via Getty Images

navigation*continued from p. 21*

Waffle-soled shoes and athletic partnerships sparked the notion of innovative ideas as the keys to victory. The company continues to introduce new and exciting concepts at a rapid pace rarely matched by other firms. For example, Nike's partnership with Apple allows runners with the Nike+ Sensor inserted in their shoes to program their iPhones or iPods to play a collection of songs that matches their distance or time goals.[3] The sensor also keeps track of their speed and distance, and Nike saves the data and provides platforms for social interactions among runners in the same area.

Going a step further down the tech road, Nike also has introduced the FuelBand, a flexible wrist monitor that keeps track of how much a person moves during the day. The simple interface turns red if movement is insufficient and green when the goal is in reach. Nike also provides a means for users to share the Nike-Fuel points they have earned throughout the day online. With these moves, "Nike has transformed itself into a digital force," a role that improves its competitiveness across its various product lines.[4]

The Nike FuelBand allows athletes to track their workouts seamlessly.
© Bebeto Matthews/AP Photo

Alongside its digitally oriented strategy, Nike demonstrates its innovation in another modern realm: creative sustainability. By paying attention to its broader environment, Nike recognized that it needed to be more environmentally conscious, for three main reasons. First, when resources become scarcer, competition for them increases, which means higher costs. Second, rising energy costs means Nike's production costs would rise even further. Third, if it could divorce its own growth from reliance on such scarce resources, Nike realized that it would not be limited in its expansion.[5] For example, it has changed the production process for its clothing lines to make it more environmentally efficient. With its new Color Dry system, Nike not only eliminates water completely from the dyeing process but also reduces the chemicals needed and minimizes the amount of dye that gets wasted. Nike estimates that it reduces energy consumption by 63 percent.[6]

These strategies clearly have been working. Nike's annual revenues and profits have increased by approximately 60 percent in the past decade.[7] Furthermore, its market share continues to increase, outpacing both the average growth of the market and its competitors' rates of growth.[8]

22 SECTION 1 | Assessing the Marketplace

continued from p. 22

In this chapter, we start by discussing a *marketing strategy,* which outlines the specific actions a firm intends to implement to appeal to potential customers. Then we discuss how to do a *marketing plan,* which provides a blueprint for implementing the marketing strategy. The chapter concludes with a discussion of strategies firms use to grow. ■

| LO 2-1 | Define a marketing strategy. |

WHAT IS A MARKETING STRATEGY?

A **marketing strategy** identifies (1) a firm's target market(s), (2) a related marketing mix (its four Ps), and (3) the bases on which the firm plans to build a sustainable competitive advantage. A **sustainable competitive advantage** is an advantage over the competition that is not easily copied and can be maintained over a long period of time. A competitive advantage acts like a wall that the firm has built around its position in a market. This wall makes it hard for outside competitors to contact customers inside—otherwise known as the marketer's target market. Of course, if the marketer has built a wall around an attractive market, competitors will attempt to break down the wall. Over time, advantages will erode because of these competitive forces, but by building high, thick walls, marketers can sustain their advantage, minimize competitive pressure, and boost profits for a longer time. Thus, establishing a sustainable competitive advantage is key to long-term financial performance.

For Nike, its thickest wall is the result of its solid foundation of innovation, which has produced a strong brand and a loyal customer base. Customers know the Nike swoosh well and consider the brand as a first option when they need running, basketball, or even just casual athletic shoes. This appeal reflects Nike's careful targeting and marketing mix implementation. In terms of the four Ps, Nike is constantly trying to come up with new versions of its relatively basic products, namely, shoes and related apparel. To sell these varied products, it relies on multiple channels: online, in dedicated Nike stores and superstores, and through independent retailers such as Foot Locker. Its pricing spans a broad range, from lower-end, simpler options for casual shoes to the most expensive, technically sophisticated, highly reputed lines associated with big-name athletes. And these popular athletes are central to its promotion efforts. Nike remains dominant in most athletic fields, and it feels confident about expanding further.

marketing strategy A firm's target market, marketing mix, and method of obtaining a sustainable competitive advantage.

sustainable competitive advantage Something the firm can persistently do better than its competitors.

> " A competitive advantage acts like a wall that the firm has built around its position in a market. This wall makes it hard for outside competitors to contact customers inside. "

Foot Locker is one of many independent retailers that carry Nike shoes.
© Patrick T. Fallon/Bloomberg via Getty Images

There are four macro, or overarching, strategies that focus on aspects of the marketing mix to create and deliver value and to develop sustainable competitive advantages, as we depict in Exhibit 2.1:[9]

- **Customer excellence:** Focuses on retaining loyal customers and excellent customer service.

- **Operational excellence:** Achieved through efficient operations and excellent supply chain and human resource management.

- **Product excellence:** Having products with high perceived value and effective branding and positioning.

- **Locational excellence:** Having a good physical location and Internet presence.

▼ **EXHIBIT 2.1** Macro Strategies for Developing Customer Value

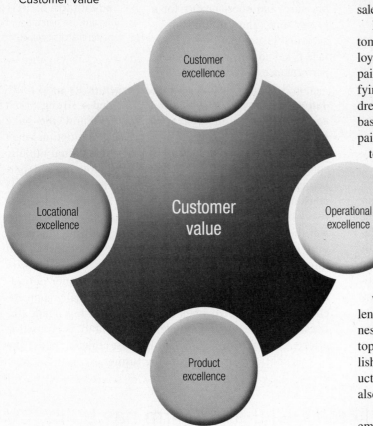

Customer Excellence

Customer excellence is achieved when a firm develops value-based strategies for retaining loyal customers and provides outstanding customer service.

Retaining Loyal Customers Sometimes the methods a firm uses to maintain a sustainable competitive advantage help attract and maintain loyal customers. For instance, having a strong brand, unique merchandise, and superior customer service all help solidify a loyal customer base. In addition, having loyal customers is, in and of itself, an important method of sustaining an advantage over competitors.

Loyalty is more than simply preferring to purchase from one firm instead of another.[10] It means that customers are reluctant to patronize competitive firms. Loyal customers buy Nike apparel for all their sporting and casual endeavors, even if adidas goes on sale or opens a new store right around the corner from their house.

More and more firms realize the value of achieving customer excellence through focusing their strategy on retaining loyal customers. Nike doesn't think in terms of selling a single pair of fashionable shoes for $100; instead, it focuses on satisfying the customer who buys track shoes for herself, Cole Haan dress shoes for her spouse, soccer shoes for her daughter, and basketball shoes for her son. Conservatively, she might buy five pairs of shoes every year for 20 years. She is not a $100 customer; combining all purchases for her family over the years, she is at least a $10,000 shoe customer—and that doesn't even count the shorts, shirts, and socks she adds to her purchases. Viewing customers with a lifetime value perspective, rather than on a transaction-by-transaction basis, is key to modern customer retention programs.[11]

One way to build customer loyalty is to provide your target market something unique. For example, when *Self* magazine recognized that its target markets of millennial female readers were interested in fashion as well as fitness, it sought to become a provider of content related to both topics.[12] In addition to expanding the editorial content published in the magazine, *Self* has applied its brand to other products, such as yoga mats and a dramatic romance movie, that also appeal to its target market.

Another method of achieving customer loyalty creates an emotional attachment through loyalty programs. These loyalty programs, which constitute part of an overall customer relationship management (CRM) program, prevail in many industries, from airlines to hotels to movie theaters to retail stores. With such programs, firms can identify members through the loyalty card or membership information the consumer provides when he or she makes a purchase. Using that purchase information, analysts determine which types of merchandise certain groups of customers are buying and thereby tailor their offering to better meet the needs of their loyal customers. For instance, by analyzing their databases, banks develop profiles of customers who have defected in the past and use that information to identify customers who may defect in the

> "Using that purchase information, analysts determine which types of merchandise certain groups of customers are buying and thereby tailor their offering to better meet the needs of their loyal customers."

Disney's employees and cast members provide the highest level of customer service.
© Tao Images/agefotostock

operational excellence Involves a firm's focus on efficient operations and excellent supply chain management.

future. Once it identifies these customers, the firm can implement special retention programs to keep them.

Providing Outstanding Customer Service

Marketers also may build sustainable competitive advantage by offering excellent customer service,[13] though consistency in this area can prove difficult. Customer service is provided by employees, and invariably, humans are less consistent than machines. Firms that offer good customer service must instill its importance in their employees over a long period of time so that it becomes part of the organizational culture.

Disney offers excellent examples of both of these types of customer excellence. First, Disney's My Magic system enables visitors to swipe their Magic Band wristbands to make purchases, open their hotel room door, get dinner reservations, or check in for rides, throughout the park and its grounds. The system also enables Disney to collect a remarkable amount of information about what each guest is doing, at virtually every moment of his or her visit to its theme parks.[14]

Second, its customer service is virtually unparalleled. Visitors to Disney parks are greeted by "assertively friendly" staff who have been extensively trained to find ways to provide better service. The training includes information about how to recognize the signs that a visitor is lost, so the Disney employee can offer help locating a destination. It also highlights the need to communicate frequently and collaboratively about every aspect of the park, so a custodian at one end of the Magic Kingdom likely knows what time a restaurant on the other side

opens.[15] Although it may take considerable time and effort to build such a reputation for customer service, once a marketer has earned a good service reputation, it can sustain this advantage for a long time because a competitor is hard pressed to develop a comparable reputation.

Operational Excellence

Firms achieve **operational excellence**, the second way to achieve a sustainable competitive advantage, through their efficient operations, excellent supply chain management, and strong relationships with their suppliers.

All marketers strive for efficient operations to get their customers the merchandise they want, when they want it, in the required quantities, and at a lower delivered cost than that of their competitors. By so doing, they ensure good value to their customers, earn profitability for themselves, and satisfy their customers' needs.

Firms achieve efficiencies by developing sophisticated distribution and information systems as well as strong relationships with vendors. Like customer relationships, vendor relations must be developed over the long term and generally cannot be easily offset by a competitor.[16]

You are likely aware of, and perhaps have taken advantage of, Amazon's Prime shipping program, offering free two-day shipping on all orders for $99 a year. Perhaps you have paid for overnight delivery with Amazon, or if you live in one of the eleven cities in the United States that offer it, you may have paid for same-day shipping. With attractive shipping options like these, how are other online retailers able to compete? One innovative solution is being offered by eBay. Understanding that many customers want products quickly, the eBay Now service offers a personal buyer that will not only purchase the product you want locally, but deliver the product in "about an hour"! Operational excellence is required for eBay to execute this program effectively. Not only does it need to have the technology to coordinate the personal buyers, but it needs to have an effective human resources hiring program that selects and trains employees capable of going the extra mile to please its customers.[17]

> *BLOOMBERG BUSINESSWEEK'S* TOP GLOBAL BRANDS—SUCH AS COCA-COLA, IBM, MICROSOFT, GOOGLE, GE, MCDONALD'S, INTEL, APPLE, DISNEY, AND SAMSUNG—ARE ALL LEADERS IN THEIR RESPECTIVE INDUSTRIES, AT LEAST IN PART BECAUSE THEY HAVE STRONG BRANDS AND A CLEAR POSITION IN THE MARKETPLACE.

product excellence Involves a focus on achieving high-quality products; effective branding and positioning is key.

locational excellence A method of achieving excellence by having a strong physical location and/or Internet presence.

marketing plan A written document composed of an analysis of the current marketing situation, opportunities and threats for the firm, marketing objectives and strategy specified in terms of the four Ps, action programs, and projected or pro forma income (and other financial) statements.

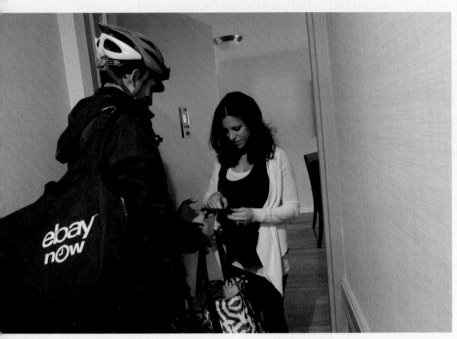

Is two days too long to wait for delivery? With eBay's Now service you can get your product the same day.
© Tina Feinberg/Redux

Product Excellence

Product excellence, the third way to achieve a sustainable competitive advantage, occurs by providing products with high perceived value and effective branding and positioning. Some firms have difficulty developing a competitive advantage through their merchandise and service offerings, especially if competitors can deliver similar products or services easily. However, others have been able to maintain their sustainable competitive advantage by investing in their brand itself; positioning their product or service using a clear, distinctive brand image; and constantly reinforcing that image through their merchandise, service, and promotion. For instance, *Bloomberg Businessweek*'s top global brands—such as Coca-Cola, IBM, Microsoft, Google, GE, McDonald's, Intel, Apple, Disney, and Samsung—are all leaders in their respective industries, at least in part because they have strong brands and a clear position in the marketplace.[18]

Locational Excellence

Locational excellence is particularly important for retailers and service providers. Many say "The three most important things in retailing are location, location, location." For example, most people will not walk or drive very far when looking to buy a cup of coffee. A competitive advantage based on location is sustainable because it is not easily duplicated. McDonald's has developed a strong competitive advantage with its location selection. The high density of stores it has established in some markets makes it very difficult for a competitor to enter that market and find good locations. After all, if McDonald's has a store on the corner of a busy intersection, no other competitor can take that location, and will instead have to settle for a less-worthy spot.

Multiple Sources of Advantage

In most cases, a single strategy, such as low prices or excellent service, is not sufficient to build a sustainable competitive advantage. Firms require multiple approaches to build a "wall" around their position that stands as high as possible.

Southwest Airlines consistently has positioned itself as a carrier that provides good service at a good value—customers get to their destinations on time for a reasonable price without having to pay extra for checked luggage. At the same time, its customers know not to have extraordinary expectations, unlike those they might develop when they purchase a ticket from Singapore Airlines. They don't expect food service or seat assignments. But they do expect—and even more important, get—on-time flights that are reasonably priced. By developing its unique capabilities in several areas, Southwest has built a very high wall around its position as the value player in the airline industry, which has resulted in a huge cadre of loyal customers.

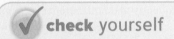

✓ check yourself

1. What are the various components of a marketing strategy?
2. List the four macro strategies that can help a firm develop a sustainable competitive advantage.

LO 2-2 Describe the elements of a marketing plan.

THE MARKETING PLAN

Effective marketing doesn't just happen. Firms like Nike carefully plan their marketing strategies to react to changes in the environment, the competition, and their customers by creating a marketing plan. A **marketing plan** is a written document composed of an analysis of the current marketing situation, opportunities and threats for the firm, marketing objectives and

planning phase The part of the strategic marketing planning process when marketing executives, in conjunction with other top managers (1) define the mission or vision of the business and (2) evaluate the situation by assessing how various players, both in and outside the organization, affect the firm's potential for success.

implementation phase The part of the strategic marketing planning process when marketing managers (1) identify and evaluate different opportunities by engaging in segmentation, targeting, and positioning (see also *segmentation, targeting, and positioning*) and (2) implement the marketing mix using the four Ps.

control phase The part of the strategic marketing planning process when managers evaluate the performance of the marketing strategy and take any necessary corrective actions.

strategy specified in terms of the four Ps, action programs, and projected or pro forma income (and other financial) statements.[19] The three major phases of the marketing plan are planning, implementation, and control.[20]

Although most people do not have a written plan that outlines what they are planning to accomplish in the next year, and how they expect to do it, firms do need such a document. It is important that everyone involved in implementing the plan knows what the overall objectives for the firm are and how they are going to be met. Other stakeholders, such as investors and potential investors, also want to know what the firm plans to do. A written marketing plan provides a reference point for evaluating whether or not the firm has met its objectives.

A marketing plan entails five steps, depicted in Exhibit 2.2. In Step 1 of the **planning phase**, marketing executives, in conjunction with other top managers, define the mission and/or vision of the business. For the second step, they evaluate the situation by assessing how various players, both in and outside the organization, affect the firm's potential for success. In the **implementation phase**, marketing managers identify and evaluate different opportunities by engaging in a process known as segmentation, targeting, and positioning (STP) (Step 3). They then are responsible for implementing the marketing mix using the four Ps (Step 4). Finally, the **control phase** entails evaluating the performance of the marketing strategy using marketing metrics and taking any necessary corrective actions (Step 5).

As indicated in Exhibit 2.2, it is not always necessary to go through the entire process for every evaluation (Step 5). For instance, a firm could evaluate its performance in Step 5, then go directly to Step 2 to conduct a situation audit without redefining its overall mission.

We first discuss each step involved in developing a marketing plan. Then we consider ways of analyzing a marketing situation, as well as identifying and evaluating marketing opportunities. We also

▼ **EXHIBIT 2.2** The Marketing Plan

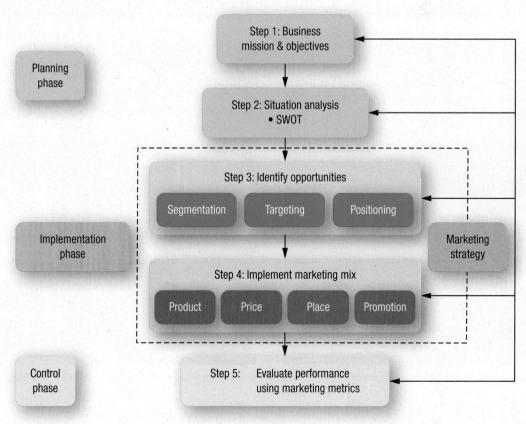

examine some specific strategies marketers use to grow a business. Finally, we consider how the implementation of the marketing mix increases customer value.

Step 1: Define the Business Mission

The **mission statement**, a broad description of a firm's objectives and the scope of activities it plans to undertake,[21] attempts to answer two main questions: What type of business are we? What do we need to do to accomplish our goals and objectives? These fundamental business questions must be answered at the highest corporate levels before marketing executives can get involved. Most firms want to maximize stockholders' wealth by increasing the value of the firms' stock and paying dividends.[22] Let's look at Nike and adidas as examples:

- **Nike's Mission Statement:** "To bring inspiration and innovation to every athlete* in the world," and then with its asterisk, defines an athlete by quoting one of its founders: "If you have a body, you are an athlete."[23]

- **adidas' Mission Statement:** "The adidas group strives to be the global leader in the sporting goods industry with brands built on a passion for sport and a sporting lifestyle."[24]

> *What type of business are we? What do we need to do to accomplish our goals and objectives?*

For both of these firms, marketing is primarily responsible for enhancing the value of the company's offering for its customers and other constituents, whether in pursuit of a profit or not. Another key goal or objective often embedded in a mission statement relates to how the firm is building its sustainable competitive advantage.

However, owners of small, privately held firms frequently have other objectives, such as achieving a specific level of income and avoiding risks. Nonprofit organizations Movember and the "Pink Ribbon" campaign instead have nonmonetary objectives:

- **Movember's Vision Statement:** "To have an everlasting impact on the face of men's health."[25]

- **Pink Ribbon International's Mission Statement:** "To create a global community to support breast cancer patients, survivors and their families all over the world . . . by facilitating forums and blogs where thoughts, experience and information can be shared."[26]

LO 2-3 Analyze a marketing situation using SWOT analyses.

Step 2: Conduct a Situation Analysis

After developing its mission, a firm would perform a **situation analysis** using a **SWOT analysis** that assesses both the internal environment with regard to its **S**trengths and **W**eaknesses and the external environment in terms of its **O**pportunities and **T**hreats. In addition, it should assess the opportunities and uncertainties of the marketplace due to changes in **C**ultural, **D**emographic, **S**ocial, **T**echnological, **E**conomic, and **P**olitical forces (CDSTEP). These factors are

Both Nike's and adidas' ads reflect their mission statements. Nike's ads (left) consistently inspire athletes to excel; adidas' ads (right) emphasize passion for sports.
Left: © Matthew Chattle/Alamy; Right: © Stephen Shaver/Bloomberg via Getty Images

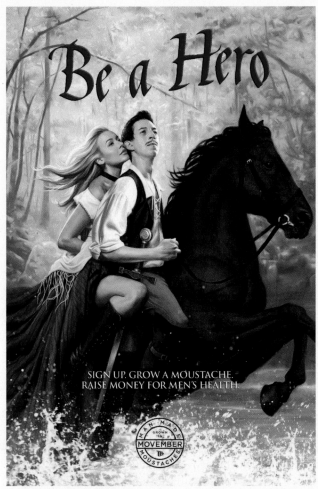

The objective of a nonprofit organization Movember is to have an everlasting impact on the face of men's health.
Photographer: Matt Barnes, Studio/Production Company: Westside Studio, Advertising Agency: BBDO Toronto, Art Director/Copywriter: Jeff Cheung

Pink Ribbon is a nonprofit organization that supports breast cancer patients, survivors, and their families.
© David Westing/Getty Images

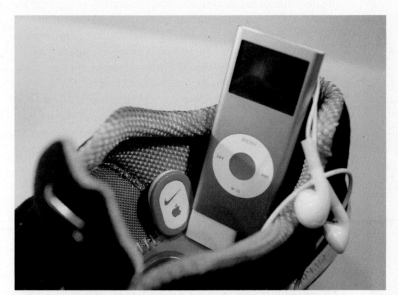

Nike's strengths include its innovative product tradition. It was the first to introduce the Nike+ iPod, a sensor that when inserted into shoes gives the runner instant feedback on factors such as running time, distance, pace, and calories burned.
© Bongarts/Getty Images Publicity/Getty Images for Nike

discussed in more detail in Chapter 5. With this information, firms can anticipate and interpret change, so they can allocate appropriate resources.

Consider how Nike might conduct a SWOT analysis, as outlined in Exhibit 2.3. We focus on Nike here, but we also recognize that its marketing managers might find it helpful to perform parallel analyses for competitors, such as adidas. Because a company's strengths (Exhibit 2.3, upper left) refer to the positive internal attributes of the firm, in this example we might include Nike's great brand recognition and the visibility of the celebrities who wear its products. Furthermore, its introductions of the Nike+ iPod, FuelBand, and Flyknit were the first of their kind, continuing the innovative tradition that has marked Nike since it first came up with waffle-soled running shoes. Its name recognition makes consumers more likely to try out these innovations when they appear on the market—especially when they see their favorite athlete wearing similar apparel on the court or in the field.

Yet every firm has its weaknesses, and Nike is no exception. Weaknesses (Exhibit 2.3, upper right) are negative attributes of the firm. Nike relies heavily—perhaps even too heavily—on its

		Environment		Evaluation	
		Positive		**Negative**	
Nike	**Internal**	**Strengths**		**Weakness**	
		Strong brand		Overreliance on footwear	
		Strong celebrity endorsers		Scandals involving celebrity endorsers	
		Innovative products			
	External	**Opportunity**		**Threats**	
		Emerging countries		Cheaper imports	
		Other fashion segments		Imitation products	
				Retail becoming price competitive	
adidas	**Internal**	**Strengths**		**Weakness**	
		Strong brand		Management of numerous brands	
		Portfolio of brands			
		Strong global presence			
	External	**Opportunity**		**Threats**	
		Emerging countries		Cheaper imports	
				Imitation products	
				Recessionary forces	

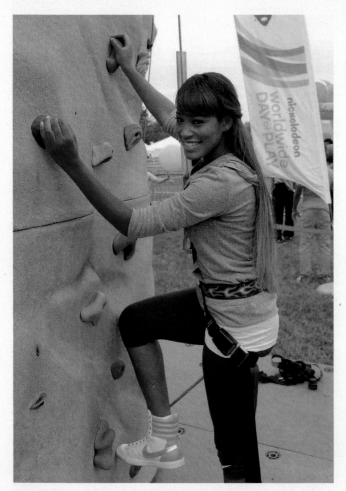

Keke Palmer is wearing her Nikes at a Nickelodeon event.
© Larry Busacca/Getty Images Entertainment/Getty Images for Nickelodeon

athletic shoe lines, especially for running and basketball. It also aligns itself closely with the athletes that serve as its brand ambassadors, highlighting them as "heroes." But on multiple occasions these athletes have become embroiled in scandals that are embarrassing and potentially damaging to the brand. Furthermore, in response to the popular emergence of other shoe options, such as "toning" and "barefoot" models, Nike has largely suggested they are fads that will not last, stressing instead its traditional athletic shoe models and innovating new forms.[27]

Opportunities (Exhibit 2.3, lower left) pertain to positive aspects of the external environment. Among Nike's opportunities, it appears determined to pursue dominance in other, sometimes niche, sports markets. Although not the official sponsor of the 2014 Sochi Winter Olympics, Nike took advantage of the opportunity to build a strong connection with the games. It launched a "Play Russian" campaign in Russia that featured Russian Olympic hopefuls (Adelina Sotnikova and Alexander Ovechkin, among others) and implied the country's harsh winters were the perfect conditioning for winter athletes.[28]

Another notable opportunity for Nike is growth in global markets. It sells products in 170 countries worldwide through independent distributors, Nike stores, the website, and licenses.[29] It aims to expand further, and it has devoted significant resources to improving its prominence among European football players and fans.[30]

Finally, threats (Exhibit 2.3, lower right) represent the negative aspects of the company's external environment. For example, its widespread market dominance makes Nike the primary target for all its competitors,[31] from adidas to New Balance to Li Ning, China's largest shoemaker. All of these firms want to take market share from Nike, which means it must constantly be a little bit on the defensive. Furthermore, as Nike itself acknowledges: "Our products face intense competition. . . . Failure to maintain our reputation and brand image could negatively impact our business. . . . If we are unable to anticipate consumer preferences and develop new products, we may not be able to maintain or increase our net revenues and profits."[32]

LO 2-4	Describe how a firm chooses which consumer group(s) to pursue with its marketing efforts.

Step 3: Identify and Evaluate Opportunities Using STP (Segmentation, Targeting, and Positioning)

After completing the situation audit, the next step is to identify and evaluate opportunities for increasing sales and profits using

segmentation, targeting, and positioning (STP). With STP, the firm first divides the marketplace into subgroups or segments, determines which of those segments it should pursue or target, and finally decides how it should position its products and services to best meet the needs of those chosen targets (more details on the STP process can be found in Chapter 9).

Segmentation

Many types of customers appear in any market, and most firms cannot satisfy everyone's needs. For instance, among Internet users some do research online, some shop, some look for entertainment, and many do all three. Each of these groups might be a **market segment** consisting of consumers who respond similarly to a firm's marketing efforts. The process of dividing the market into groups of customers with different needs, wants, or characteristics—who therefore

segmentation, targeting, and positioning (STP)
Firms use these processes to identify and evaluate opportunities for increasing sales and profits.

market segment A group of consumers who respond similarly to a firm's marketing efforts.

market segmentation
The process of dividing the market into groups of customers with different needs, wants, or characteristics—who therefore might appreciate products or services geared especially for them.

might appreciate products or services geared especially for them—is called **market segmentation**.

Let's look at Hertz, the car rental company. The example in Exhibit 2.4 reveals some of the segments that Hertz targets.

> ❝ MANY TYPES OF CUSTOMERS APPEAR IN ANY MARKET, AND MOST FIRMS CANNOT SATISFY EVERYONE'S NEEDS. ❞

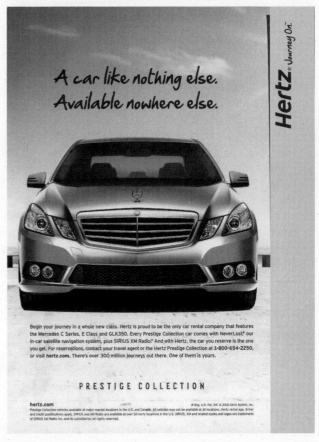

Hertz targets several markets. Its Adrenaline Collection (left) appeals to single people and couples wanting to have fun; while its Prestige Collection (right) appeals to its business customers and families who prefer a luxurious ride.

Left and right: Courtesy The Hertz Corporation.

target marketing or targeting The process of evaluating the attractiveness of various segments and then deciding which to pursue as a market.

market positioning Involves the process of defining the marketing mix variables so that target customers have a clear, distinctive, desirable understanding of what the product does or represents in comparison with competing products.

With the Adrenaline Collection, Hertz offers up the Chevrolet Camaro or Corvette, seeking to appeal to thrill seekers and gear heads on vacation. Its Prestige Collection features various Cadillac and Infiniti models, targeting business customers and families who prefer a luxurious ride. With its Green Collection of cars such as the Toyota Prius and Ford Fusion, and even some electric vehicle options in selected locations, Hertz appeals to environmentally conscious customers. It also offers commercial vans for service customers with its Commercial Van/Truck Collection.[33] Thus, Hertz uses a variety of demographics—gender, age, income, interests—to identify customers who might want the Prestige, Green, and Adrenaline Collections, but it also applies psychological or behavioral factors, such as a need to move possessions across town, to identify likely consumers of its commercial vans.

Targeting

After a firm has identified the various market segments it might pursue, it evaluates each segment's attractiveness and decides which to pursue using a process known as **target marketing** or **targeting**. For example, Hertz realizes that its primary appeal for the SUV/Minivan/4x4 collection centers on young families, so the bulk of its marketing efforts for this business is directed toward that group.

Soft drink manufacturers also divide their massive markets into submarkets or segments. Coca-Cola, for instance, makes several different types of Coke, including regular, Coke II, and Cherry Coke. Among its diet colas, it targets Coke Zero to men and Diet Coke to women because men prefer not to be associated with diets. It also markets Sprite to those who don't like dark colas, Fruitopia and

> Firms typically are most successful when they focus on opportunities that build on their strengths relative to those of their competition.

Minute Maid for more health-conscious consumers, and Dasani bottled water for purists.

Positioning

Finally, when the firm decides which segments to pursue, it must determine how it wants to be positioned within those segments. **Market positioning** involves the process of defining the marketing mix variables so that target customers have a clear, distinctive, desirable understanding of what the product does or represents in comparison with competing products. Hertz positions itself as a quality car (and truck) rental company that is the first choice for each of its target segments. In its marketing communications it stresses that customers will get peace of mind when they rent from Hertz, the market leader in the car rental business, and be able to enjoy their journey (e.g., leisure consumers) and reduce travel time (e.g., business consumers).[34]

To segment the coffee-drinker market, Starbucks uses a variety of methods, including geography (e.g., college campuses versus shopping/business districts) and benefits (e.g., drinkers of caffeinated versus decaffeinated products). After determining which of those segments represent effective targets, Starbucks positions itself as a firm that develops a variety of products that match the wants and needs of the different market segments—espresso drinks, coffees, teas, bottled drinks, pastries, and cooler foods.

After identifying its target segments, a firm must evaluate each of its strategic opportunities. A method of examining which segments to pursue is described in the Growth Strategies section later in the chapter. Firms typically are most successful when they focus on opportunities that build on their strengths relative to those of their competition. In Step 4 of the marketing plan, the firm implements its marketing mix and allocates resources to different products and services.

For example, Pizza Hut decided to jump on changing consumer desires for rapid access to its offering by constantly expanding its mobile applications, but it also found its positioning as a convenient option appealing to more markets than it even expected, as Social and Mobile Marketing 2.1 reveals.

▼ **EXHIBIT 2.4** Hertz Market Segmentation Illustration

	Segment 1	Segment 2	Segment 3	Segment 4	Segment 5
Segments	Single thrill seekers and gear heads on vacation	Business customers and families who prefer a luxurious ride	Environmentally conscious customers	Families	Commercial customers
	Adrenaline Collection	Prestige Collection	Green Collection	SUV/Minivan/4x4	Commercial Van/Truck
Cars Offered	Corvette ZHZ	Infiniti QX56	Toyota Prius	Toyota Rav 4	
	Chevrolet Camaro	Cadillac Escalade	Ford Fusion	Ford Explorer	Ford Cargo Van

Social & Mobile Marketing

Truly Mobile Pizza[i]

The pizza delivery business has always been mobile in one sense, but Pizza Hut is making sure that it spreads into mobile commerce as well. This first-mover introduced its mobile website in 2007, an iPhone application in 2009, and apps for the iPad, Android, and Windows Mobile 7 in 2010. By 2013, it had partnered with Microsoft to become the first restaurant to offer orders through Xbox 360 consoles.

The decision to go mobile was based on a few insights that Pizza Hut gleaned from its market research. In particular, if it did not offer mobile access quickly, its competitors might be the first to do so in the competitive pizza delivery market. The Pizza Hut app lets customers order food through a user-friendly experience, but it also makes sure to identify the closest store locations for delivery or pickup service to further emphasize convenience.

Without much information to identify the consumers who would use the app, Pizza Hut anticipated more orders from college-age men, who do not like to cook and want their food on demand, but also are not willing to stop a video game to take the time to order food through more traditional channels. The assumption seemed reasonable—but it also was dead wrong. Further market research, based on the introduction of the app, has shown that there are just as many pizza connoisseurs 55 years and older with iPhones as there are 13- to 24-year-olds ordering the pies.

Pizza Hut's mobile app makes ordering pizza a piece of cake.
Courtesy Pizza Hut.

| LO 2-5 | Outline the implementation of the marketing mix as a means to increase customer value. |

Step 4: Implement Marketing Mix and Allocate Resources

When the firm has identified and evaluated different growth opportunities by performing an STP analysis, the real action begins. It has decided what to do, how to do it, and how many resources should be allocated to it. In the fourth step of the planning process, marketers implement the actual marketing mix—product, price, promotion, and place—for each product and service on the basis of what they believe their target markets will value. At the same time, marketers make important decisions about how they will allocate their scarce resources to their various products and services.

Product and Value Creation Products These products include services and constitute the first of the four Ps. Because the key to the success of any marketing program is the creation of value, firms attempt to develop products and services that customers perceive as valuable enough to buy. Dyson fans and fan heaters draw in and redirect surrounding air

Dyson creates value with its innovative products (left). It can therefore charge significantly more than the price of conventional fans (right).
Left: Courtesy Dyson, Inc.; Right: © Stockbyte/PunchStock RF

without potentially dangerous or fast-spinning blades or visible heating elements. Although more expensive than conventional fans and space heaters, these sculpturally beautiful appliances are perceived by consumers to be a valuable alternative to products that haven't significantly changed since the early 1900s.

Price and Value Capture
Recall that the second element of the marketing mix is price. As part of the exchange process, a firm provides a product or a service, or some combination thereof, and in return, it gets money. Value-based marketing requires that firms charge a price that customers perceive as giving them a good value for the product they receive. Clearly, it is important for a firm to have a clear focus in terms of what products to sell, where to buy them, and what methods to use in selling them. But pricing is the only activity that actually brings in money and therefore influences revenues. If a price is set too high, it will not generate much volume. If a price

is set too low, it may result in lower-than-optimal margins and profits. Therefore, price should be based on the value that the customer perceives. Dyson fans can retail for $150 or more while conventional fans retail for around $25. Customers can decide what they want from their fan and choose the one at the price they prefer.

Place and Value Delivery
For the third P, place, the firm must be able, after it has created value through a product and/or service, to make the product or service readily accessible when and where the customer wants it. Dyson therefore featured its new fans prominently on its website but also made sure to place them on Amazon and in Bed Bath and Beyond stores. In these locations, consumers previously found other Dyson products, and they likely would look for fans there too. Adding Value 2.1 takes a look at a unique new place to shop for groceries: subway stations!

> " IF A PRICE IS SET TOO HIGH, IT WILL NOT GENERATE MUCH VOLUME. IF A PRICE IS SET TOO LOW, IT MAY RESULT IN LOWER-THAN-OPTIMAL MARGINS AND PROFITS. "

Adding Value   2.1

Online Retail Meets Bricks and Mortar: Tesco's HomePlus Virtual Stores[ii]

South Korea is known for its tech innovations, introduced by highly creative companies and embraced by a forward-thinking consumer public. But the top app in this tech-savvy nation isn't associated with some space-age fantasy. Instead, it pertains to a seemingly perpetual, distinctly old-fashioned task: grocery shopping.

The international retailer Tesco chose Korea as the site to open its HomePlus virtual stores back in 2011. In subway stations, virtual stores began appearing on LCD screens. Shoppers on their way to or from work could scan the barcodes or QR codes for the items they wanted to purchase with their smartphones. The virtual stores are laid out in a grid, similar to a brick-and-mortar store, which helped shoppers feel familiar with the radically new approach. Furthermore, the app allows them to schedule home delivery, such that fresh produce, food for their pets, replenished cleaning supplies, and maybe even dinner for themselves can be waiting on their doorstep when they get home.

The remarkable success of this app has prompted Tesco to expand the placement of HomePlus stores to bus depots and other commuter routes. Within about six months of the introduction, nearly 1 million consumers had downloaded and used the HomePlus app.

Despite the success and popularity of HomePlus, Tesco continues to keep its physical stores open, with no plans to eliminate them. Two main features demand this dual approach. First, Korea is somewhat unique in terms of its significant embrace and acceptance of virtual tools and high-tech options. In many other countries, including Tesco's UK home market, and in rural areas where access to public spaces like bus stops is just as challenging as getting to the local store, acceptance may be less widespread. Even in Korea, consumers tend to use HomePlus for dry goods but still like to be able to touch and feel vegetables and fruit before buying them.

Second, for many people, shopping is an enjoyable pastime that gets them out of their houses or offices for a brief time. Noting this persistent preference, Tesco is seeking to integrate virtual offerings more effectively into some of its stores. For example, it is considering plans to add interactive tablets in its in-store cafés. Customers could take a break, have a cup of tea, and type in a few ingredients that sound appealing to them. The tablets then might produce recipes that match the ingredients, along with a map showing the customers where to find each needed item.

The HomePlus Virtual Stores have created a whole new way of providing the third P, place, and value delivery.
© Paul Brown/Rex Features via AP Photo.

integrated marketing communications (IMC) Represents the promotion dimension of the four Ps; encompasses a variety of communication disciplines—general advertising, personal selling, sales promotion, public relations, direct marketing, and electronic media—in combination to provide clarity, consistency, and maximum communicative impact.

metric A measuring system that quantifies a trend, dynamic, or characteristic.

Promotion and Value Communication Integrated marketing communications (IMC) represents the fourth P, promotion. It encompasses a variety of communication disciplines—advertising, personal selling, sales promotion, public relations, direct marketing, and online marketing including social media—in combination to provide clarity, consistency, and maximum communicative impact.[35] Using the various disciplines of its IMC program, marketers communicate a *value proposition,* which is the unique value that a product or service provides to its customers and how it is better than and different from those of competitors.

One of Dyson's promotions for its new fans related to both the second and third Ps, price and place. That is, it made a select number of fans available on Groupon at a heavily discounted price, to encourage people to try the innovations.

Step 5: Evaluate Performance Using Marketing Metrics

The final step in the planning process includes evaluating the results of the strategy and implementation program using marketing metrics. A **metric** is a measuring system that quantifies a trend, dynamic, or characteristic. Metrics are used to explain why things happened and also project the future. They make it possible to compare results across regions, strategic business units (SBUs), product lines, and time periods. The firm can determine why it achieved or did not achieve its performance goals with the help of these metrics. Understanding the causes of the performance, regardless of whether that performance exceeded, met, or fell below the firm's goals, enables firms to make appropriate adjustments.

Typically, managers begin by reviewing the implementation programs, and their analysis may indicate that the strategy (or even the mission statement) needs to be reconsidered. Problems can arise both when firms successfully implement poor strategies and when they poorly implement good strategies.

Who Is Accountable for Performance? At each level of an organization, the business unit and its manager should be held accountable only for the revenues, expenses, and profits that they can control. Thus, expenses that affect several levels of the organization (such as the labor and capital expenses associated with operating a corporate headquarters) shouldn't be arbitrarily assigned to lower levels. In the case of a store, for example, it may be appropriate to evaluate performance objectives based on sales, sales associate productivity, and energy costs. If the corporate office lowers prices to get rid of merchandise and therefore profits suffer, then it's not fair to assess a store

Dyson invoked two of the 4Ps, price and place, by making a select number of fans available on Groupon at a heavily discounted price.
© digitallife/Alamy

" Understanding the causes of the performance, regardless of whether that performance exceeded, met, or fell below the firm's goals, enables firms to make appropriate adjustments. "

Promotional discounts are one way General Mills is trying to save the cereal industry.
© Joe Raedle/Staff/Getty Images

Ethical and Societal Dilemma 2.1 describes how Volkswagen dealt effectively with a product safety concern in China, adjusting to customers' expectations and leveraging the data it received.

Performance Objectives, Marketing Analytics, and Metrics

Many factors contribute to a firm's overall performance, which makes it hard to find a single metric to evaluate performance.[37] One approach is to compare a firm's performance over time or to competing firms, using common financial metrics such as sales and profits. Another method of assessing performance is to view the firm's products or services as a portfolio. Depending on the firm's relative performance, the profits from some products or services are used to fuel growth for others.

With its extensive data, Google claims that it can use a combination of metrics to predict the performance of a major motion picture, up to a month prior to the date it opens in theaters. Using search volume for the movie title in combination with several other metrics, such as the season and whether the movie is a sequel, Google promises a 94 percent accurate prediction of box office performance. Other proprietary metrics include the volume of clicks on search ads. If, for example, one movie prompted 20,000 more paid clicks than another film, it will bring in approximately $7.5 million more in revenues during its opening weekend. Beyond the implications for opening weekend, Google asserts that weekday searches in the weeks leading up to the release offer better predictors of continued revenues. That is, if a film fan searches for a movie title on a Tuesday, she or he is more likely to hold off on seeing the movie, rather than rushing out during opening weekend.[38] Google's extensive analytics abilities support its competitive tactics in other markets too, as Marketing Analytics 2.1 describes.

Financial Performance Metrics

Some commonly used metrics to assess performance include revenues, or sales, and profits. For instance, sales are a global measure of a firm's activity level. However, a manager could easily increase sales by lowering prices, but the profit realized on that merchandise (gross margin) would suffer as a result. An attempt to maximize one metric may therefore lower another. Thus, managers must understand how their actions affect multiple performance metrics. It's usually unwise to use only one metric because it rarely tells the whole story.

In addition to assessing the absolute level of sales and profits, a firm may wish to measure the relative level of sales and profits. For example, a relative metric of sales or profits is its increase or decrease over the prior year. In addition, a firm may

manager's performance based on the resulting decline in store profit.

Performance evaluations are used to pinpoint problem areas. Reasons performance may be above or below planned levels must be examined. If a manager's performance is below planned levels, was it because the sales force didn't do an adequate job, because the economy took a downward turn, because competition successfully implemented a new strategy, or because the managers involved in setting the objectives aren't very good at making estimates? The manager should be held accountable only in the case of the inadequate sales force job or setting inappropriate forecasts.

When it appears that actual performance is going to be below the plan because of circumstances beyond the manager's control, the firm can still take action to minimize the harm. For example, the cereal industry has been beset by a wealth of setbacks due to trends in the wider consumer environment. People seek to cut carbohydrates out of their diets, but cereal is mostly carbs. Many consumers are recognizing their allergies to gluten, but many cereals include wheat as a main ingredient. In response, the largest cereal maker General Mills (GM) has called on its competitors to step up their marketing efforts to save the industry. Leading the way, it increased its advertising budget by 7 percent and initiated promotional discounts on some of its most popular cereal brands, including Cheerios.[36]

In remarkable cases such as this, marketing managers must ask themselves several relevant questions: How quickly were plans adjusted? How rapidly and appropriately were pricing and promotional policies modified? In short, did I react to salvage an adverse situation, or did my reactions worsen the situation?

> " Sales are a global measure of a firm's activity level. However, a manager could easily increase sales by lowering prices, but the profit realized on that merchandise (gross margin) would suffer as a result. "

ethical&societal dilemma

How a Faulty Gearbox Changed Volkswagen's Entire Approach to China[iii]

When China's central television agency CCTV revealed in an exposé that Volkswagen cars being sold in the country contained faulty gearboxes, the company faced a massive public relations crisis. Volkswagen is the market leader in China, and the allegations threatened to derail its double-digit annual growth in the vastly appealing emerging market. Instead, its response provides a template for other multinational firms operating in China, as well as a lesson that the company itself continues to take to heart in all its customer communications.

To start, when confronted unexpectedly with the news report, Volkswagen Group China's newly named vice president of PR & Communications responded promptly and sincerely with an apology. Although the fault with the gearboxes had little potential to be dangerous to drivers, the flaw represented an inconvenience that troubled these consumers, so Volkswagen was quick and honest in apologizing for letting down its customers. Such a move was particularly effective in China, where consumers consider corporate attitudes of primary importance.

Following the apology, Volkswagen issued an immediate recall and replaced all faulty gearboxes for free. It also provided complementary software upgrades when necessary. In the meantime, other executives continued to apologize, demonstrating that the company was taking full responsibility for any failure.

Learning from her ongoing interviews with journalists about the failure and recall, the vice president of PR & Communications also told the executive board in Germany that it needed to revise its approach to the Chinese market, to avoid being perceived as too arrogant. Because the company already had the top market position, customers viewed press releases touting its sales achievements as bragging. Seeking to establish a more humble image, communications by Volkswagen China Group shifted to emphasize more human elements, such as its continued campaign to increase the uses of child safety seats. In addition, all marketing communications for China are now written initially in Chinese and, if necessary, translated into English, rather than the other way around, which had been the standard.

Some of these elements are global; a product safety issue demands an apology and a recall, no matter where it takes place. But Volkswagen's experience also recommends some specific traits of marketing communications in China, including humility, personification, and deep sincerity.

Volkswagen turned lemons into lemonade in China when it immediately apologized for selling cars with faulty gearboxes, recalled and fixed the cars, and repositioned its communications to be more humble and caring about its customers.
© AP Photo

Marketing Analytics

The First Name in Predictive Analytics: Google[iv]

In the world of analytics, Google has made a significant name for itself because, from the moment it was established, Google has put predictive analytics at the heart of the company. As the most widely used search engine, Google needs to be able to predict which websites and pages a person is seeking, based on just a few keywords. Google is so successful at this method that few users even bother going to the second page of the results list in a Google search. Google now offers Google Analytics for companies to help improve their online presence by providing insights into customers' web searching behavior. In addition, Google now uses its analytics for more than just its search engine. They were critical to the development of Android software, Apple's biggest competitor in the smartphone domain. Now with the help of its sophisticated analytics, Google is taking on Apple in another domain as well: cars.

In Google's 2015 Android boot camp, the company officially introduced its Android Auto dashboard interface, which will face off against Apple's CarPlay. Data analytics have played a big role in the development of these systems. Study after study has shown how dangerous using one's phone while driving is. Data even show that driving while using a smartphone is equitable to driving while under the influence of alcohol. These startling results have spurred top phone system manufacturers' interest in creating dashboard platforms. When Google debuted Android Auto, it was clear that extensive analytics went into the development of every feature.

For example, Google developed a driver distraction lab to learn what tasks people do frequently when driving. These data informed which

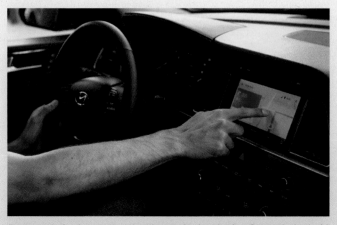

Data analytics have played a big role in developing Google's Android Auto dashboard interface to help keep drivers safe while using electronic dashboard functions.
© Elijah Nouvelage/Reuters/Corbis

functions would be included and how they would work in the Android Auto system. According to Google's studies, no action should take longer than two seconds, so every function of Android Auto must be "glanceable." In addition, the interface does not include any "back" or "recent" buttons. Not only are social media apps blocked, but texting is accessible only through voice commands. With these improvements in the connection between phones and cars, data analytics are helping make the world both more convenient and safer.

---

compare its growth in sales or profits relative to other benchmark companies (e.g., Coke may compare itself to Pepsi).

The metrics used to evaluate a firm vary depending on (1) the level of the organization at which the decision is made and (2) the resources the manager controls. For example, while the top executives of a firm have control over all of the firm's resources and resulting expenses, a regional sales manager has control over only the sales and expenses generated by his or her salespeople.

Let's look at Nike's sales revenue and profits (after taxes) and compare them with those of adidas (Exhibit 2.5).

> **LO 2-6** Summarize portfolio analysis and its use to evaluate marketing performance.

Portfolio Analysis In portfolio analysis, management evaluates the firm's various products and businesses—its "portfolio"—and allocates resources according to which products are expected to be the most profitable for the firm in

▼ **FIGURE 2.5** Performance Metrics: Nike vs. adidas

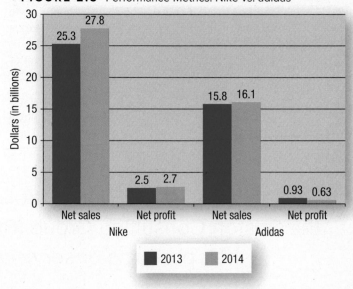

Nike — Net sales: 25.3 (2013), 27.8 (2014); Net profit: 2.5 (2013), 2.7 (2014)
Adidas — Net sales: 15.8 (2013), 16.1 (2014); Net profit: 0.93 (2013), 0.63 (2014)
Dollars (in billions)
■ 2013 ■ 2014

the future. Portfolio analysis is typically performed at the **strategic business unit (SBU)** or **product line** level of the firm, though managers also can use it to analyze brands or even individual items. An SBU is a division of the firm itself that can be managed and operated somewhat independently from other divisions and may have a different mission or objectives. For example, Goodyear is one of the largest tire firms in the world, selling its products on six continents in over 180 countries and with sales of approximately $21 billion. Its four SBUs are organized by geography: North American; Europe, Middle East, African; Latin American; and Asia Pacific.[39]

A product line, in contrast, is a group of products that consumers may use together or perceive as similar in some way. One line of product for Goodyear could be car, van, sport-utility vehicle (SUV), and light truck while another line could be high-performance tires or aviation tires.

One of the most popular portfolio analysis methods, developed by the Boston Consulting Group (BCG), requires that firms classify all their products or services into a two-by-two matrix, as depicted in Exhibit 2.6.[40] The circles represent brands, and their sizes are in direct proportion to the brands' annual sales. The horizontal axis represents the relative market share.

In general, **market share** is the percentage of a market accounted for by a specific entity,[41] and is used to establish the product's strength in a particular market. It is usually discussed in units, revenue, or sales. A special type of market share metric, **relative market share**, is used in this application because it provides managers with a product's relative strength, compared with that of the largest firm in the industry.[42] The vertical axis is the **market growth rate**, or the annual rate of growth of the specific market in which the product competes. Market growth rate thus measures how attractive a particular market is. Each quadrant has been named on the basis of the amount of resources it generates for and requires from the firm.

Stars Stars (upper left quadrant) occur in high-growth markets and are high market share products. That is, stars often require a heavy resource investment in such things as promotions and new

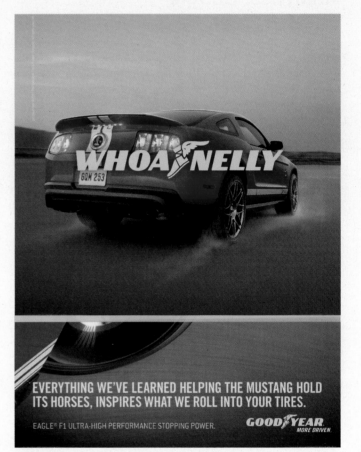

Goodyear, one of the largest tire firms in the world, organizes its strategic business units by geography. This ad for high-performance tires, one of Goodyear's many product lines, was designed for its North American SBU.

Courtesy ©2008 The Goodyear Tire & Rubber Company. All rights reserved. Agency: McCann Erickson/New York, NY. Creative Director: Craig Markus; Art Director: Tim Dillingham; Copywriter: Mark Ronquillo; Photographer: ©2007 Graham Westmoreland/Friend and Johnson.

production facilities to fuel their rapid growth. As their market growth slows, stars will migrate from heavy users of resources to heavy generators of resources and become cash cows.

> " One of the most popular portfolio analysis methods, developed by the Boston Consulting Group (BCG), requires that firms classify all their products or services into a two-by-two matrix. "

increase their market share. Managers must decide whether to infuse question marks with resources generated by the cash cows, so that they can become stars, or withdraw resources and eventually phase out the products. Brand A, for instance, is currently a question mark, but by infusing it with resources, the firm hopes to turn it into a star.

Dogs Dogs (lower right quadrant) are in low-growth markets and have relatively low market shares. Although they may generate enough resources to sustain themselves, dogs are not destined for "stardom" and should be phased out unless they are needed to complement or boost the sales of another product or for competitive purposes. In the case depicted in Exhibit 2.6, the company has decided to stop making Brand B.

Now let's look at Apple and some of its products.[43] The four that we will focus our attention on are:

- iPhone
- iPod
- iMac Desktop
- iPad

Cash Cows Cash cows (lower left quadrant) are in low-growth markets but are high market share products. Because these products have already received heavy investments to develop their high market share, they have excess resources that can be spun off to those products that need it. For example, the firm may decide to use the excess resources generated by Brand C to fund products in the question mark quadrant.

Question Marks Question marks (upper right quadrant) appear in high-growth markets but have relatively low market shares; thus, they are often the most managerially intensive products in that they require significant resources to maintain and potentially

Let's consider each of these products and place them into the BCG matrix based on the data. The iPhone has clearly been the star, with growth rates nearing 90 percent in some years.

The iPod tells a different story. With a staggering absolute market share consistently above 75 percent, its relative market share is 100 percent, and with more than 300 million iPods sold in a little over 10 years, it definitely has been an important product for Apple. Unfortunately, the MP3 market is contracting and sales of iPods have slowed to their lowest level. Combine the lack of growth with a large relative market share and it is likely that the iPod is a cash cow for Apple.[44]

In which Boston Consulting Group quadrant do these products fit?
Left: © McGraw-Hill Education/Mark Dierker, photographer; Right: © Stanca Sanda/Alamy

Although popular with graphic designers, the growth rate of the Mac Desktop has slowed enough that it has even declined in some recent quarters. Given that it also has a small relative market share in the desktop market, the iMac can be tentatively classified as a dog. But Apple should probably not get rid of the iMac because it risks alienating its loyal customers.

Then we have the iPad, with an incredible sales growth rate from 2010 to 2011 of 333 percent, and sales of approximately 55 million units as of early 2012. But its market share and growth rate have since slowed. Where on the BCG matrix would you classify the iPad? Does its continued excellent market enter it into the star category? Or is the erosion of its growth enough to make it a question mark?

The big question for Apple is, will Apple Watch become a star?
© PG Pictures/Alamy RF.

Although quite useful for conceptualizing the relative performance of products or services and using this information to allocate resources, the BCG approach, and others like it, is often difficult to implement in practice. In particular, it is difficult to measure both relative market share and industry growth. Furthermore, other measures easily could serve as substitutes to represent a product's competitive position and the market's relative attractiveness. Another issue for marketers is the potential self-fulfilling prophecy of placing a product or service into a quadrant. Whether it is classified as a star or a question mark has profound implications on how it is treated and supported within the firm. Question marks require more marketing and production support.

Strategic Planning Is Not Sequential

The planning process in Exhibit 2.2 suggests that managers follow a set sequence when they make strategic decisions. Namely, after they've defined the business mission, they perform the situation analysis, identify strategic opportunities, evaluate alternatives, set objectives, allocate resources, develop the implementation plan, and, finally, evaluate their performance and make adjustments. But actual planning processes can move back and forth among these steps. For example, a situation analysis may uncover a logical alternative, even though this alternative might not be included in the mission statement, which would mean that the mission statement would need to be revised. The development of the implementation plan also might reveal that insufficient resources have been allocated to a particular product for it to achieve its objective. In that case, the firm would need to either change the objective or increase the resources; alternatively, the marketer might consider not investing in the product at all.

Now that we have gone through the steps of the marketing plan, let's look at some growth strategies that have been responsible for making many marketing firms successful.

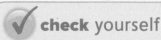

check yourself

1. What are the five steps in creating a marketing plan?
2. What tool helps a marketer conduct a situation analysis?
3. What is STP?
4. What do the four quadrants of the portfolio analysis represent?

LO 2-7 | Describe how firms grow their business.

GROWTH STRATEGIES

Firms consider pursuing various market segments as part of their overall growth strategies, which may include the four major strategies in Exhibit 2.7.[45] The rows distinguish those opportunities a firm possesses in its current markets from those it has in new markets, whereas the columns distinguish between the firm's current marketing offering and that of a new opportunity. Let's consider each of them in detail.

Market Penetration

A **market penetration strategy** employs the existing marketing mix and focuses the firm's efforts on existing customers. Such a growth strategy might be achieved by attracting new consumers to the firm's current target market or encouraging current customers to patronize the firm more often or buy more merchandise on each visit. A market penetration strategy generally requires greater marketing efforts, such as increased advertising and additional sales and promotions, or intensified distribution efforts in geographic areas in which the product or service already is sold.

▼ **FIGURE 2.7** Markets/Products and Services Strategies

To penetrate its target market, TV network MTV found that it needed new ways to engage its viewers. The young audience to which MTV traditionally appeals consists of text-messaging, video-gaming multitaskers who no longer accept plain video programming on their televisions. Its research determined that interactions with the audience through alternative channels increase ratings for its shows. Therefore, in addition to producing and airing reality shows such as *America's Best Dance Crew* and *Jersey Shore*, MTV has partnered with video game producer Yoostar to offer "Yoostar on MTV" for Xbox 360. The game provides a massive library of constantly updated shows, music videos, and recordings of live events. Fans of these shows can insert themselves into scenes they've already seen their more famous teen peers undergo.[46] On MTV's website, dedicated forums, blogs, and activities for each show also encourage viewers to connect with characters in their shows. Not only can viewers talk about the characters as if they were friends, but they can also buy the products they wear and download the music played during the show.[47]

> "A market penetration strategy generally requires greater marketing efforts, such as increased advertising and additional sales and promotions, or intensified distribution efforts."

Market Development

A **market development strategy** employs the existing marketing offering to reach new market segments, whether domestic or international. Domestically, MTV pursues a market development strategy by targeting older customers who were MTV viewers in their youth, but are now attracted to Music Television shows that are reminiscent of their teenage years. On the other hand, international expansion generally is riskier than domestic expansion because firms must deal with differences in government regulations, cultural traditions, supply chains, and language. However, many U.S. firms, including MTV, enjoy a competitive

To increase market penetration with its young target audience, MTV produces reality shows like America's Best Dance Crew.
© Frank Micelotta/Invsion/AP Photo

advantage in global markets—such as Mexico, Latin America, Europe, China, and Japan—because, especially among young people, U.S. culture is widely emulated for consumer products.

For example, because of rising prosperity worldwide and rapidly increasing access to cable television that offers U.S. programming, fashion trends from the United States have spread to young people in emerging countries. The global MTV generation prefers soft drinks to tea, athletic shoes to sandals, french fries to rice, and credit cards to cash. To achieve such growth, MTV leveraged its existing media content but also delivers culturally relevant content using local DJs and show formats.

Product Development

The third growth strategy option, a **product development strategy**, offers a new product or service to a firm's current target market. Consider MTV's dynamic lineup: The network constantly develops new pilots and show concepts to increase the amount of time viewers can spend watching MTV. Along with its new TV series, MTV develops new online products to engage consumers through more than 25 niche blogs, as well as a website that it uses to dominate a greater share of viewers' minds and time. The sites further encourage viewers to get involved in real-world issues (not *The Real World* issues) through mobile technologies. By visiting the sites, MTV promises that consumers can share mobile content, educate themselves, and take action on important issues.[48]

Diversification

A **diversification strategy**, the last of the growth strategies from Exhibit 2.7, introduces a new product or service to a market segment that currently is not served. Diversification opportunities may be either related or unrelated. In a **related diversification** opportunity, the current target market and/or marketing mix shares something in common with the new opportunity.[49] In other words, the firm might be able to purchase from existing vendors, use the same distribution and/or management information system, or advertise in the same newspapers to target markets that are similar to their current consumers. MTV has pursued a related diversification by introducing TV series that focus on more positive social messages. In series such as *I Used to Be Fat* and *Made*, recognizable and seemingly familiar teens still appeal to viewers and provide a healthy dose of drama. However, the plotlines of these shows focus on how people overcome adversity or struggle with everyday challenges to attain some level of happiness.[50]

MTV's Real World Las Vegas *cast members: Heather Marter, Dustin Zito, Naomi Defensor, and* Real World Cancun *cast member Jasmine Reynaud.*
© Craig Barritt/Getty Images Entertainment/Getty Images

> " THE GLOBAL MTV GENERATION PREFERS SOFT DRINKS TO TEA, ATHLETIC SHOES TO SANDALS, FRENCH FRIES TO RICE, AND CREDIT CARDS TO CASH. "

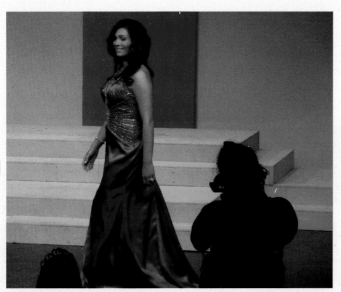

In contrast, in an **unrelated diversification**, the new business lacks any common elements with the present business. Unrelated diversifications do not capitalize on either core strengths associated with markets or with products. Thus, they would be viewed as very risky. For instance, if Nike ventured into the child day care service industry, it would be an unrelated diversification because it is so different from its core business and therefore very risky. ■

unrelated diversification A growth strategy whereby a new business lacks any common elements with the present business.

 check yourself

1. What are the four growth strategies?
2. What type of strategy is growing the business from existing customers?
3. Which strategy is the riskiest?

Shows such as Made *are one of MTV's attempts to diversify its offerings.*
© Eric Litke/The Sheboygan Press/AP Photo

> "Unrelated diversifications do not capitalize on either core strengths associated with markets or with products."

 Increase your engagement and learning with Connect Marketing.

These Connect activities, available only through your Connect course, have been designed to make the following concepts more meaningful and applicable:

▶ The Strategic Planning Process: Disney Timeline Creation Activity

▶ SWOT Analysis—Domino's Pizza: Click and Drag Activity

▶ Implementing the Marketing Mix: Staples Video Case

▶ Marketing Strategy: Spirit Video Case

▶ The Marketing Plan: iSeeit! Video

Chapter three

social and mobile marketing

S ocial media have revolutionized how companies communicate with, listen to, and learn from customers. Their influence is far-reaching, whether firms are selling online or in stores, providing services or products, or dealing primarily with consumers or business customers. Modern listening and analysis tools allow firms to identify salient, pertinent trends and customer input through social media.

Gatorade offers a stellar example of a carefully designed plan for connecting effectively with customers, controlling social media buzz, and responding to trends as they arise. Although Gatorade's basic marketing strategy continues to include famous athletic spokespersons, it constantly seeks new ways to use these superb athletes to help ensure consumers' connections with the brand.

Residing in the marketing department at Gatorade's Chicago headquarters is its Social Media Mission Control Center, which hosts massive monitors that track social media referring to Gatorade and its competitors. One monitor stays on blog trends;

LEARNING OBJECTIVES

After reading this chapter, you should be able to:

LO 3-1 Describe the 4E framework of social media marketing.

LO 3-2 Understand the types of social media.

LO 3-3 Understand various motivations for using mobile applications and how they are priced.

LO 3-4 Recognize and understand the three components of a social media strategy.

another summarizes the topics and sentiments expressed in tweets, all in real time.[1]

According to Gatorade (and its owner, PepsiCo), Mission Control actually has six main missions: (1) monitor online discussions, (2) monitor the sports landscape, (3) engage in proactive social media

continued on p. 48

social media Media content used for social interactions such as YouTube, Facebook, and Twitter.

continued from p. 47

outreach, (4) track media performance, (5) track brand attitudes, and (6) track sports trends and buzz. Through the insights it gathers from consumers, Gatorade can influence not only its marketing communications but also its products and brand.[2]

One day not too long ago, social media chatter indicated consumers' highly favorable responses to a just-released commercial featuring a new song by rapper David Banner. Gatorade worked immediately with Banner to develop the snippet into a full-length song, which it distributed within a day through its Facebook and Twitter sites. Mission Control also is responsible for connecting fans with athletes associated with Gatorade. During the Super Bowl, it hosted discussions through the Ustream social media site.[3]

In addition to this innovative and unique Mission Control Center, Gatorade takes care of "old-school" social media too. Its Facebook page contains little explicit advertising for the brand. Instead, it posts provocative questions in an attempt to get fans to engage in conversations with the brand and one another. Its Twitter feed consists mainly of inspirational sayings and quotes. On YouTube, Gatorade offers easy access to some of its most famous commercials from over the years—ads that have taken on an iconic cult following, including old favorites describing how to "Be Like Mike" and more recent versions that challenge "Is It In You?"[4]

When consumers search for Gatorade on popular search engines, they also see page after page of company-sponsored results, rather than outside comments.[5] As this outcome reveals, Gatorade has done the preliminary work, through search engine optimization and brand building, to control most of what people see online. Although no company can prevent negative comments online (such as common complaints about Gatorade's taste),

Anthony Shop & Social Driver, copyright 2013

Gatorade has managed to ensure that those negative comments are hidden under a wave of positive, company-approved messages. Consumers must look harder to find the criticisms. ∎

LO 3-1 | Describe the 4E framework of social media marketing.

THE 4E FRAMEWORK FOR SOCIAL MEDIA

As we will see throughout the book and as we saw in the chapter opener, social media are becoming integral components of any integrated marketing communications strategy. The term **social media** refers to content distributed through online and mobile technologies to facilitate interpersonal interactions. These media use various firms that offer services or tools to help consumers and firms build connections. Through these connections, marketers and customers share information of all forms—from their thoughts about products or images, to uploaded pictures, music, and videos.

The changes and advances in social, mobile, and online technologies have created a perfect storm, forcing firms to change how they communicate with their customers.

> **THE CHANGES AND ADVANCES IN SOCIAL, MOBILE, AND ONLINE TECHNOLOGIES HAVE CREATED A PERFECT STORM, FORCING FIRMS TO CHANGE HOW THEY COMMUNICATE WITH THEIR CUSTOMERS.**

▼ EXHIBIT 3.1 The 4E Framework for Social Media

The Minnesota Timberwolves excited Facebook fans by offering a chance to win tickets by posting pictures of a dunk to its Pinterest page.
© Genevieve Ross/AP Photo

Traditional ways to market their products using brick-and-mortar stores, traditional mass media (e.g., print, television, radio), and other sales promotional vehicles (e.g., mail, telemarketing) are no longer sufficient for many firms. The presence of social, mobile, and online marketing is steadily expanding relative to these more traditional forms of integrated marketing communications (IMC).

The changing role of traditional media, sales promotions, and retail, coupled with the new social, mobile, and online media, has led to a different way of thinking about the objectives of marketing communications using the 4E framework (see Exhibit 3.1):

- **E**xcite customers with relevant offers.

- **E**ducate them about the offering.

- Help them **e**xperience products, whether directly or indirectly.

- Give them an opportunity to **e**ngage with their social network.

Social and Mobile Marketing 3.1 recounts how Jimmy Fallon got viewers more excited and engaged with his late-night talk show by leveraging the power of social media.

Excite the Customer

Marketers use many kinds of social media–related offers to excite customers, including mobile applications and games to get the customers excited about an idea, product, brand, or company. Firms actively use social networks such as Facebook, Pinterest, and Google+ to communicate deals that are likely to excite consumers, such as when the Minnesota Timberwolves encouraged Facebook fans to post a great shot of a dunk onto their Pinterest page for a chance to win tickets to a game.[6]

To excite customers, an offer must be relevant to its targeted customer. Relevancy can be achieved by providing personalized offers, which are determined through insights and information obtained from customer relationship management and/or loyalty programs. To obtain these insights and information, the firm might use online analytic tools such as Google analytics.

In some cases location-based software and applications help bring the offer to the customers when they are in the

> **The changes and advances in social, mobile, and online technologies have created a perfect storm, forcing firms to change how they communicate with their customers.**

Social media appear to have brought us full circle. In the early days of television, nearly all the advertisements were live. Then taping became the main method. But as recent technologies have made it easy for viewers to speed past or completely skip the advertising messages, some marketers are revisiting the idea of live advertising. This isn't the same old notion though. By recombining an idea from broadcast media with new functionalities enabled by social media, marketers seek to ensure that viewers are not only interested in the new content but even might determine it.

A Lexus-sponsored program, "It's Your Move After Dark," ran on *Late Night with Jimmy Fallon* over the course of four weeks. During the first commercial break on each Thursday's show, a Lexus advertisement prominently displayed a hashtag. By linking to it, viewers could submit their ideas for commercials. Then in a later advertising break during the same show, an improvisational comedy troupe acted out the chosen ideas. The acting troupes—Fun Young Guys, Magnet Theater Touring Company, MB's Dream, and Stone Cold Fox—were all from New York and well known for their comedy. In actuality, their performances took place under the Brooklyn Bridge, adding to the vibrancy and reality of the setting.

To appeal to the widest audience of Fallon fans possible, separate advertisements were chosen and enacted for the East and West Coast broadcasts. The submissions came through a wide variety of media channels, including Facebook, Twitter, and Tumblr. Such ready access, real-time interactivity, and

In an innovative campaign, Jimmy Fallon viewers could submit ideas for Lexus commercials via Twitter and see an improvised version later in the night on the show.
© Theo Wargo/Getty Images

potential influence—together with the promise of funny, totally new advertising content and perhaps even a live, on-air goof—promised that Fallon's youthful, edgy audience wanted to tune in to the commercials, as much as they did to the show.

The advertisements are not the only way Fallon has relied on social media to connect with his audience of course. He has nearly 10 million Twitter followers, and on a regular basis he challenges them to post the funniest, silliest, or craziest responses to topics he provides, such as "#howigotfired," "#whydonttheymakethat," and "#awkwarddate." The best contributions are highlighted on Fallon's Twitter feed but also might make it onto the network broadcast, as he reads out his favorite bits. That is, the consumers of his content also provide some of that content.

On the flip side, content from the traditional television channel constantly makes it onto social media sites. Excerpts from Fallon's shows are some of the most popular YouTube videos, including a skit in which President Barack Obama "slow jams" the news, a sing-along with Carly Rae Jepson and the Roots of "Call Me Maybe" using found materials as instruments, and of course, any skits featuring his pal Justin Timberlake.

Fallon has continued these antics and tactics on the *The Tonight Show*. As long as he keeps his viewers excited and willing to contribute and engage with him, his social media dominance appears likely to persist, regardless of what time he appears on people's televisions.

Check out in seconds.
Get your shopping done faster by scanning products you use all the time for easy reorder.

Shop your way.
Check local inventory at a store near you or choose from our ever-growing online assortment.

Get great savings.
Easily redeem your Staples Rewards® while you shop and check out your Weekly Ad deals.

Staples excites its customers by giving them instant rewards through their mobile phone, while they are in the store.
Courtesy of Staples, Inc.

process of making a purchase decision. For instance, Staples may provide a loyal customer a relevant coupon based on previous purchases through his or her mobile phone, while the customer is in the store—a very relevant and hopefully exciting experience.

Exhibit 3.2 highlights some illustrative and successful social media campaigns because they are exciting and relevant to their audiences.

Educate the Customer

An imperative of well-designed social media marketing offers is that they have a clear call to action to draw customers through their computers, tablets, and mobile devices into online websites or traditional retail stores. When potential customers arrive at the websites or stores, the marketer

Water is Life's "Hashtag Killer" campaign posted videos on YouTube of Haitians reading and responding to tweets to excite individuals to donate to their cause.
Courtesy WATERisLIFE

has a golden opportunity to educate them about its value proposition and communicate the offered benefits. Some of this information may be new, but in some cases, education is all about reminding people about what they already know. Therefore, by engaging in appropriate education, marketers are expanding the overlap of the benefits that they provide with the benefits that customers require. In this sense, the second E of the 4E framework constitutes a method to develop a sustainable competitive advantage. Several social media tools are critical in helping marketers educate their potential customers, such as blogs and blogging tools (e.g., WordPress and Twitter), HubSpot (all-in-one marketing software), YouTube, and Google+, as well as some lesser known options such as Roost or Schedulicity. Adding Value 3.1 highlights how HubSpot can be used to educate customers better.

▼ **EXHIBIT 3.2** Illustrative Social Media Campaigns

Campaign	Description
Justin Bieber's "Girlfriend"	To launch his new perfume, Girlfriend, Justin Bieber launched a $20 million social media campaign focusing on Twitter and Tumblr. He invited fans to help create a 60-second television commercial for the fragrance and post their entries on Tumblr. With over 22 million followers on Twitter and more than 44 million likes on Facebook, this was a great strategy for Bieber to access his young, hip fanbase.
Water is Life "Hashtag Killer"	To drive awareness about serious problems in the developing world, nonprofit Water is Life launched a "Hashtag Killer" campaign in which it took on the insensitive #firstworldproblems hashtag and Twitter meme. It began by creating a video on YouTube in which Haitians read tweets that had been tagged as "#firstworldproblems" such as a child sitting on a mound of dirt saying, "I hate when my leather seats aren't heated." Amazingly, Haitians engaged with the campaign themselves and offered consolation to people with tweets such as: "I'm sorry your leather seats weren't heated. . . . I hope your day gets better!" The campaign was a remarkable success—individuals donated over one million days of clean water.
"One Small Tweet"	After Neil Armstrong's death at age 82, the John F. Kennedy Library and Museum in New York launched a Twitter campaign, "One Small Tweet." The organization set up a website that re-created Armstrong's journey to the moon. For each tweet that included the hashtag "#onesmalltweet" the re-creation moved 100 miles closer to the moon.
"Nike Barbershop"	The "Nike Barbershop" campaign started with a commercial in which Mario Balotelli, striker for soccer club Milan, tells a barber he wants to be remembered. The commercial proceeds with a montage of hairstyles, and ends with Mario sporting a mohawk. But this is just the beginning—viewers could then download the Nike Barbershop app, make pictures of themselves with 10 different iconic soccer hairstyles, and share them with friends. The top posts were flown to one of the real Nike Barbershop physical locations in Buenos Aires, Madrid, Mexico City, Milan, or Paris to get the haircut for real. Finally, Nike created a popup Nike Barbershop in Warsaw for Europe's major soccer tournament.

Adding Value 3.1

Educating Customers Using HubSpot[ii]

Hy-Line Cruises is a ferry company with vessels for travel to and from Cape Cod and Islands, deep-sea fishing trips, and sightseeing. While it had a strong Internet presence through its website, Facebook, and Twitter, it didn't know if its efforts were leading to increased sales. Using HubSpot's SEO (search engine optimization) and blogging tools, Hy-Line began to match its blogging content to the keywords and phrases its potential customers were using. Not only did the new blogging content contain information about ferry services, but it also made recommendations about where to eat and what to do once on the Cape and islands. It also developed a free downloadable Insider's Guide for each destination, and kept track of and—through e-mail— thanked each potential customer. Compared to the previous year

before it started using HubSpot's services, Hy-Line generated 5 times more cruise offers to Nantucket, and 17 times more Fall Daytrip Specials to Martha's Vineyard.

Hy-Line Cruises uses HubSpot to enhance its social media presence.
© Oleg Albinsky/iStock/360/Getty Images RF

Experience the Product or Service

Although most of the top videos on YouTube are funny, silly, or otherwise entertaining, the site's most useful contributions may be the vivid information it provides about a firm's goods and services—how they work, how to use them, and where they can be obtained. YouTube and similar sites can come relatively close to simulating real experiences. Such benefits are very common for products that have long been sold online—so much so that we might forget that it used to be difficult to assess these products before buying them. But today, consumers can download a chapter of a new book to their tablet before buying it. They can try out a software option for a month before buying it. They often can listen to a few seconds or even an entire song before purchasing from iTunes. The diffusion of such products has expanded to feature a wealth of new channels and media options.

For other offerings, such as services, social media again offer experience-based information that was not previously available unless consumers bought and tried the product or service. Need help choosing a new nail polish color or lipstick, or applying a new makeup trend? Check blogs such as *Temptalia* (http://www.temptalia.com), which offers both advice and tutorials. Relied too long on clip-on ties? Head over to *Tie-a-Tie* (http://www.tie-a-tie.net/) to find pictures, videos, and step-by-step instructions on how to manage a Windsor, Pratt, or bowtie knot, as well as advice on what to wear to an interview.

Home Depot has long been a source for do-it-yourselfers (DIYers). But if eager customers forget what the salesclerk said about installing a newly purchased water heater, they can check the retailer's website (http://www6.homedepot.com/how-to/

> "With engagement comes action, the potential for a relationship, and possibly even loyalty and commitment."

index.html) to get detailed, in-depth instructions. They also will find a section that enables them to chat with other users who might have run into similar problems in their own installation projects.

Nikon's Digital Learning Center (see http://www.flickr.com/groups/nikondigitallearningcenter/; http://www.flickr.com/Nikon) provides Flickr members with "tutorials, practical photography tips and advice from Nikon photo professionals to assist them in taking the photos they've always dreamed of capturing."[7] Beyond just providing static photography tips that could be found in a book, Nikon created a two-way dialogue with customers, inviting professional photographers to provide instruction and host question-and-answer sessions, and encouraging users to post their own photos. The more than 64,000 members of the learning center thus learn from others' experiences, even as they create their own.

Engage the Customer

In a sense, the first three Es set the stage for the last one: engaging the customer. With engagement comes action, the potential for a relationship, and possibly even loyalty and commitment. Through social media tools such as blogging and microblogging, customers actively engage with firms and their own social networks. Such engagement can be negative or positive. Positively engaged consumers tend to be more profitable consumers, purchasing 20 to 40 percent more than less engaged customers.[8]

But negative engagement has the potential to be even more damaging than positive engagement is beneficial. In the aftermath of Hurricane Sandy, for example, two different retailers, The Gap and American Apparel, each sought to promote online sales. American Apparel sent out an e-mail blast to customers on the East Coast, promising 20 percent off all online purchases, "in case you're bored during the storm." The Gap instead relied on Twitter, posting the notice, "Stay safe! We'll be doing lots of Gap.com shopping today. How about you?" In both cases, consumers reacted angrily and rapidly. On Twitter, thousands of them complained that the promotions exhibited "tackiness" and a lack of consideration for the very real threat facing people affected by the storm. The story also made it into mainstream media, prompting the retailers to issue apologies and explanations.[9]

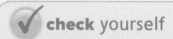

Need help choosing a new lipstick or applying a new makeup trend? Check blogs such as Temptalia.

Courtesy Temptalia.com

✓ check yourself

1. What are the 4Es?
2. What social media elements work best for each of the 4Es?

Next we'll look at the role of various social media tools in shaping the 4E framework for social media.

CATEGORIES OF SOCIAL MEDIA

Consider your own Facebook site. Are all your real-life friends your online friends too? Do you actually know all the friends registered on your online site? In all likelihood, you host online friends you've never met, and your circle of virtual friends may be larger than the number of people you see regularly or talk to personally. Accordingly, the audience for marketers could be bigger on social media sites than through other, more traditional forms of media. Such a huge potential audience has gotten the attention of marketers.

Marketers rely on the three types of social media: social networking sites, media-sharing sites, and thought-sharing sites (or blogs) (see Exhibit 3.3) to achieve three objectives. First, members promote themselves to gain more friends. Second, the sites promote to get more members. Third, outside companies promote their products and services to appeal to the potential consumers who are active on the sites.

▼ **EXHIBIT 3.3** Types of Social Media

Social Network Sites

Social network sites are an excellent way for marketers to create *excitement,* the first of the 4Es. People can interact with friends (e.g., Facebook) or business acquaintances (e.g., LinkedIn). Although the amount of time people spend on such sites varies, research indicates they are widely used, between one and four hours every day.[10]

Forever 21 excites its customers on Facebook.
© Weng lei - Imaginechina via AP Photo

Facebook On this well-known social network platform, more than 1.4 billion monthly active users give companies a forum for interacting with their fans.[11] Thus Facebook not only ensures individual users a way to connect with others, but also gives marketers the ability to target their audience carefully. Companies have access to the same features that regular users do, including a "wall" where they can post company updates, photos, and videos or participate in a discussion board. Only the fans of its page generally have access to such information, so the company can specifically target its fans.

Successful companies on Facebook attempt to excite their customers regularly. On the fan page for the discount clothing retailer Forever 21, for example,[12] when a fan clicks to indicate that he or she "likes" a certain post, the message gets relayed to a news feed. Then every friend of that user sees what he or she likes, creating an exciting and huge multiplier effect.

Display advertising with "Facebook ads" instead targets specific groups of people, according to their profile information, browsing histories, and other preferences. If online users reveal an interest in ski equipment or Burton snowboards, marketers can target both groups. Facebook offers a variation on more traditional forms of promotion, with the promise of more accurate targeting and segmentation. But being effective and relevant on Facebook is not simply a matter of shifting an offline ad into social network sites, as Adding Value 3.2 recognizes.

LinkedIn A professional instead of casual or friendship-based site, LinkedIn allows users to share their professional lives. With more than 347 million users, it is a place where users can post their résumés, network with other professionals, and search for jobs.[13] Users post to question-and-answer forums, job search, and

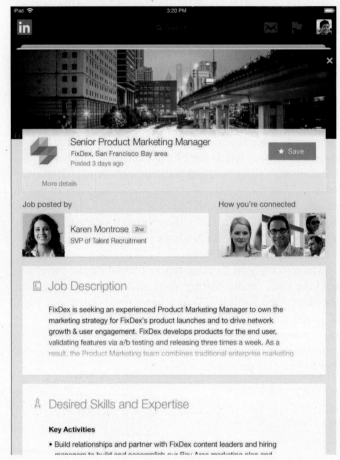

LinkedIn is an excellent place to begin your search for a marketing job.
Courtesy LinkedIn

Adding Value 3.2
Effective Friending[iii]

Sadly, many inexperienced marketers have launched poorly conceived Facebook campaigns with the hope that any strategy that includes social media is "good enough." But good enough is rarely sufficient in a competitive marketplace, and some brands have hurt their images by launching campaigns that are out of step with social media culture.

When a group of industry professionals discussed the ingredients necessary to attract positive attention from Facebook's 1.44 billion users, they agreed that a successful campaign must tell a story. Ideally, the story should involve and engage users in the plotline. Equally important, these creative heavyweights highlighted the need to connect the campaign to the real world.

Clorox's Facebook promotion is designed to educate people about and increase sales of its Green Works products.
© Michelle Pemberton/Rapport Press/ Newscom

Making good use of consumer data available on Facebook can also improve campaign success by giving marketers the ability to home in on target audiences and track consumer response. After months of flat reactions to a Facebook promotion of its environmentally friendly cleaners, Clorox launched new initiatives designed to educate people about and increase sales of its Green Works products. The campaign targeted only those women whose Facebook profiles featured the words *clean* or *green*. At the same time, Clorox aimed to enhance the experience of other potential users by inviting consumers to nominate green heroes in their community to receive a $15,000 grant. In yet another effort, Clorox offered a $3 off coupon to people who connected to the Green Works web page. The result was a record-breaking engagement rate for the company, demonstrating that social media, when used properly, can be valuable marketing tools.

post personal intellectual property, such as presentations they have given.

The professional networking benefits of LinkedIn are particularly beneficial for small-business owners. More than 12 million of LinkedIn's users are small-business owners, making it an excellent resource for entrepreneurs to network with like-minded firms, identify the best vendors, or build brand reputation by participating in LinkedIn's professional association groups.

Google+ With Google+, the company that essentially defined search engines sought to compete in the social media realm. Although it has attracted hundreds of millions of users, most analysts suggest it is not an effective competitor thus far. Even when users register, they do not engage closely with the site; Google+ accounted for a mere 1.28 percent of all social media shares.[14]

Yet it would be risky to ignore Google+ completely. It offers several functions that other social networking sites do not. For example, its "Communities" feature lets people interested in similar topics form their own groups. Unlike Facebook, Google+'s Communities allow brands to join as members—for example, a paddle brand or seller of suntan lotion could easily interact with the members of a group devoted to paddleboarding. Moreover, with Google+'s unique "Hangouts" feature, brands can host discussions or focus groups, as well as post live product demonstrations.[15]

Media-Sharing Sites

The World Wide Web has the ability to connect people more easily and in more ways than have ever been possible before. Media-sharing sites explicitly rely on this capability to enable users to share content they have generated, from videos on YouTube to pictures on Flickr and so on. In terms of the 4E framework, companies use such sites to highlight how consumers can *experience* their goods or services, as well as encourage consumers to *engage* with the firm, its other social media outlets, and other consumers.

YouTube On this video-sharing social media platform with more than 1 billion unique monthly visitors, companies gain a chance to express themselves in a different way than they have in the past. YouTube videos also show up in Google searches, making it an appealing vehicle for retailers.[16] The site's demographics indicate visitors are affluent, of the age range most appealing to retailers, and racially reflective of the wider U.S. population.[17]

Companies can broadcast from their own channel, that is, a YouTube site that contains content relevant only to the company's own products.[18] For example, Home Shopping Network (HSN) offers consumers an interesting vehicle

to utilize the 4E framework. As competition in this field has increased, HSN has added to its communication arsenal an integrated social media component that includes Facebook, Instagram, Twitter, and Pinterest. But perhaps the most powerful tool it has added is its dedicated YouTube channel. Products promoted on HSN are available on YouTube almost immediately after they appear on television. Then HSN marketers can use the information gathered from YouTube to target its direct mail campaigns. For example, it could send jewelry promotions to households that viewed the YouTube video clip for a necklace. Consumer responses get monitored 24/7 and measured against hourly sales goals. There's thus never a dull moment.

Instagram With Instagram, people who have downloaded the app (more than 300 million and counting) can take a photo of themselves or their surroundings.[19] Then they can upload the photo to various social networking sites, including Twitter, Tumblr, or Facebook.

The name of this app evokes the founders' idea of its use: a sort of modern-day, immediate telegram.[20] It has attracted the attention of some of the most famous names in media sharing, including Justin Beiber, Kim Kardashian, and Tony Hawk—which increased its popularity even more. Recognizing the value of a mobile option, Facebook purchased Instagram in 2012. For the first time, the social media giant promised not to absorb its purchase, but to allow Instagram to continue functioning much as it had been all along.[21]

Instagram recently added video-sharing capabilities as well, though another app had beat it to that punch. Vine, which was purchased by Twitter in 2012, lets users capture and share six-second videos. Advertisers already have embraced this option, finding that the short time limit appeals to consumers.

Products promoted on Home Shopping Network (HSN) are available on its dedicated YouTube channel almost immediately after they appear on television.
Courtesy HSN, Inc.

But it also uses Flickr for more serious purposes, such as to post photos related to its Big Knit charity promotion.

People are ready to share a quick video, far more so than a longer commercial, which enhances the chances of a Vine marketing campaign going viral.[22]

Flickr and Other Photo Sites Whereas YouTube allows users to share videos, Flickr, Picasa, TwitPic, Photobucket, and Imgur allow them to share photos. They tend to be less popular as marketing tools, yet some innovative companies have found ways to engage with customers, such as by hosting picture posting competitions or using photos to communicate core tenets and values.[23]

The UK brand Innocent, known for selling pure 100 percent fruit smoothies, uses Flickr to communicate its quirky brand image. Its photo-posting competitions, such as the Funny Shaped Fruit Competition (http://www.flickr.com/groups/funnyshapedfruit/), provide significant entertainment value.

Innocent uses Flickr to post photos for its Big Knit charity promotion.
© John Boud/Alamy

Thought-Sharing Sites

Thought-sharing sites consist of different types of blogs: corporate, professional, personal, and micro. In terms of the 4E framework, blogs are particularly effective at *educating* and *engaging* users, and in many cases enhance their *experience* with the products and services being discussed.

Blogs Originally confined to a journal or diary in a person's room, the **blog** (from "weblog") on the Internet has allowed us to make our thoughts open to the world through thought-sharing websites. For corporations, the comment section allows marketing managers to create a two-way dialogue directly with the end users. Blogs provide firms the opportunity to *educate* their customers about their offers and offerings by explaining their offerings, and to *engage* them by responding to their communications, both positive and negative. The reach that marketers have to their customer from blogs can be categorized by the level of control they offer.

Corporate blogs, which are created by the companies themselves, have the highest level of control because to a large degree, they can control the content posted on them. Of course, blogs also allow customers to respond to posts, so the content can never be completely controlled, but marketing managers have a good opportunity to pepper their blogs with the messages they wish their customers to see. The best corporate blogs illustrate the importance of engaging customers around the core brand tenets without being overly concerned with a hard sell.

The popular regional grocery store chain Wegmans (http://www.wegmans.com/blog/) blogs to generate loyalty and generate sales by sharing employees' ideas about entertaining, nutrition, and recipes. General Electric (http://www.gereports.com/) *educates* customers through its blog by telling entertaining stories geared at getting customers to realize it sells more than just lightbulbs.[24] For Boeing (http://www.boeingblogs.com/randy/), the goal is to *engage* people, even though it produces items that regular consumers are unlikely to encounter or purchase directly. Therefore "Randy's Journal" features travel stories, fun pictures of planes being built, and promises of exciting new innovations from the company.

From a marketing perspective, **professional blogs** are those written by people who review and give recommendations on products and services. Marketers often offer free products or provide modest remuneration to top-rated professional bloggers, in the hopes of getting a good product review. Marketers have less control over professional bloggers than they do their own corporate blogs. But consumers seem to trust professional bloggers' reviews much more than corporate blogs and other more traditional media, like advertising. Such trust may be fleeting, however, as more consumers

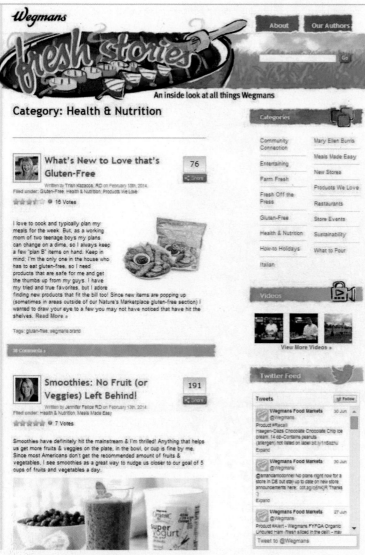

Category: Health & Nutrition

What's New to Love that's Gluten-Free

Written by Trish Klazacos, RD on February 13th, 2014.
Filed under: Gluten-Free, Health & Nutrition, Products We Love

16 Votes

I love to cook and typically plan my meals for the week. But, as a working mom of two teenage boys my plans can change on a dime, so I always keep a few "plan B" items on hand. Keep in mind; I'm the only one in the house who has to eat gluten-free, so I need products that are safe for me and get the thumbs up from my guys. I have my tried and true favorites, but I adore finding new products that fit the bill too! Since new items are popping up (sometimes in areas outside of our Nature's Marketplace gluten-free section) I wanted to draw your eye to a few you may not have noticed that have hit the shelves. Read More »

Tags: gluten-free, wegmans brand

Smoothies: No Fruit (or Veggies) Left Behind!

Written by Jennifer Felice RD on February 13th, 2014.
Filed under: Health & Nutrition, Meals Made Easy

7 Votes

Smoothies have definitely hit the mainstream & I'm thrilled! Anything that helps us get more fruits & veggies on the plate, in the bowl, or cup is fine by me. Since most Americans don't get the recommended amount of fruits & vegetables, I see smoothies as a great way to nudge us closer to our goal of 5 cups of fruits and vegetables a day.

Wegmans' blog is designed to engage customers with healthy and nutritious recipes and interesting food-related ideas and stories.
Courtesy Wegmans

@BestBuy_Deals, @GeekSquad, and @BestBuyNews. Users who tweet the help desk, @Twelpforce, receive an almost instant response from one of Best Buy's 3,000 employees who have signed up to participate on the task force, which further helps showcase the broad spectrum of expertise available through Best Buy.[25]

For small companies with limited marketing budgets, the use of tweeted promotional messages is particularly appealing. A local bakery tweeted "Two new scones: Lemon Blueberry and Chorizo Cheddar!" and received responses from 400 Twitter followers—a huge captive audience for a local entity.

LO 3-3	Understand various motivations for using mobile applications and how they are priced.

GOING MOBILE AND SOCIAL

Of the more than 184 million people who have smartphones in the United States,[26] approximately 60 percent of them make purchases on these devices.[27] About 180 billion apps were downloaded globally in 2015.[28] In the United States alone, almost $10 billion of mobile downloads and in-app revenues were accrued in 2015, even though nearly 93 percent of apps downloaded are free.[29] Mobile app downloads are expected to grow to 286 billion annually by 2017.[30]

realize that professional bloggers are often compensated for positive reviews.

Finally, **personal blogs** are written by people who receive no products or remuneration for their efforts. Thus, of the three types of blogs, marketers have the lowest level of control over this type. However, personal blogs are useful for monitoring what is going on in the marketplace and for responding to customer complaints or compliments.

Microblogs As the name implies, a **microblog** differs from a traditional blog in size—short sentences, short videos, or individual images. The most popular microblogging site, Twitter, provides another option for companies to *educate* their customers by providing corporate and product information, and to *engage* them by providing a platform for two-way communications.

Best Buy hires an army of specialists to manage its Twitter accounts: not just the main account @Best Buy, but also

With more than 500 million downloads, Candy Crush Saga clearly fulfills for many people an important need for unproductive "me time."
© Gabriel Bouys/AFP/Getty Images

showrooming
Customers visit a store to touch, feel, and even discuss a product's features with a sales associate, and then purchase it online from another retailer at a lower price.

▼ **EXHIBIT 3.4** Seven Primary Motivations for Mobile App Usage

Discovery
Seeking news and information

Preparation
Planning for upcoming activities

Accomplishing
Managing finances, health, and productivity

Shopping
Seeking a product or a service

Self-expression
Participating in hobbies and interests

PERCENTAGE OF ALL INTERACTIONS (EXCLUDES E-MAIL, SMS MESSAGES, AND VOICE CALLS)

AVERAGE MINUTES PER MONTH PER USER (METERED)

"Me time"
Seeking relaxation or entertainment (for example, by watching a funny video, reading a gossip website, playing solitaire, or even window shopping for fun)

Socializing
Interacting with other people

Source: "Vision Statement: How People Really Use Mobile," *Harvard Business Review*, January/February 2013, http://www.hbr.org.

Thus, mobile marketing is significant and growing.

As Exhibit 3.4 illustrates, there are seven primary needs that apps meet. They include the need to find "me time," socialize, shop, accomplish, prepare, discover, and self-express.

- The most popular need is all about entertainment and relaxation—that is, "me time." People spend nearly half their time on their smartphones seeking fun, whether by playing Candy Crush Saga or watching *American Horror Story* through their Netflix app.

- Because apps enable people to stay connected with friends, both near and far, specialized entrants are growing to meet people's need to socialize. For example, in China, the social networking app Weixin (pronounced way-SHEEN) allows users to send videos, photos, messages, web

Growing faster than Twitter and Facebook, Weixin has 300 million users, mainly in China, and allows people to send videos, photos, messages, web links, status updates, and news to friends.

© Keepin sh - Imaginechina via AP Photo

links, status updates, and news; it has been released as WeChat in the United States. Weixin has had a faster adoption rate than either Facebook or Twitter, with more than 300 million users in only three years.[31]

- Shoppers want to shop anytime they choose. A process called **showrooming** enables customers to scan a product in a store and instantly compare the prices online to see whether a better deal is available. Using the showrooming Amazon app, if the Amazon price is better, the customer can buy the product online with a single click.

- On the flipside of the need for fun, the need to accomplish means that people seek to manage their finances, improve their health, or become more productive through apps.[32] MyFitnessPal allows users to track their daily exercise, calories, and weight loss, and its social component enables people to post their successes. This app also can interact with Fitbit, Jawbone UP, and iHealth Wireless Scales.

- Calendars, flight trackers, and trip planning apps help consumers meet their need to prepare.[33] For example, Business Calendar helps people plan their day with an interactive

ad-supported app
Apps that are free to download, but place ads on the screen when using the program to generate revenue.

freemium app Apps that are free to download, but include in-app purchases (see also *in-app purchases*).

in-app purchase When a game or app prompts or allows customers to make small "micropurchases" to enhance an app or game.

paid app Apps that charge the customer an up-front price to download the app ($0.99 is the most common), but offer full functionality once downloaded.

paid apps with in-app purchase Apps that require the consumer to pay initially to download the app and then offer the ability to buy additional functionality.

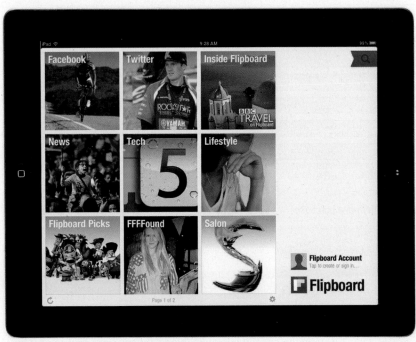

Not only does Flipboard aggregate all of the news important to you in one place, its unique format gives the app the look and feel of a printed magazine.
© Alliance Images/Alamy

app that integrates multiple calendars (e.g., Google Calendar, Outlook Calendar) and allows users to link an event to people in their contacts list and put a daily agenda widget on their smartphone home screen.

- When people seek information, due to their need to discover, they now turn to weather and news apps. Flipboard produces a full-screen magazine, aggregating multiple news and entertainment sources to provide top stories, entertainment, local news, and business news. Its social component allows readers to send selected stories to friends too.

- Finally, people have diverse interests and tastes and thus a need for apps that allow them to express themselves. Tapatalk aggregates tens of thousands of interest groups into a single app, making it easy to connect aficionados of just about any interest or hobby.

As you can see from this discussion, apps can meet several needs at once. Sharing an interesting story with friends via Flipboard can meet the needs of discovery and socialization. Consider the person who purchases Chinese food via

GrubHub's app on her ride home; she's not only shopping, but she's also avoiding making dinner to get some extra me time. With this information in mind, apps (and advertising within those apps) can be designed and targeted in ways that better apply the 4Es.

App Pricing Models

A key decision for firms producing apps is what to charge for them. There are four basic ways of generating revenue from apps—ad-supported apps, freemium apps, paid apps, and paid apps with in-app purchases.

Ad-supported apps are free to download, but place ads on the screen when using the program to generate revenue. Although there are many of these types of apps, the majority of app revenue is generated from the remaining three pricing models, discussed next.

Freemium apps are apps that are free to download but include **in-app purchases** to enhance an app or game. In Candy Crush Saga, you get five lives to play in the game. When you lose a life, it takes 30 minutes in real-life time to get that life back. This is where in-app purchases come in. For just $0.99, you can get all five lives back immediately so you can keep playing.[34] Candy Crush Saga is estimated to earn the developer between $623,000 and $850,000 *a day* in revenue from in-app purchases.[35]

Paid apps charge the customer an upfront price to download the app ($0.99 is the most common), but offer full functionality once downloaded. Similar to the freemium model, **paid apps with in-app purchases** require the consumer to pay initially to download the app and then offer the ability to buy additional functionality.

Which is the best pricing model? Time will tell, but it appears that freemium apps may be the winner. As Exhibit 3.5 shows, free apps with in-app purchases make up the vast majority of revenue from Apple's App Store in 8 of 10 app categories. According to Distimo, a research firm specializing in the mobile app market, 71 percent of apps in Apple's App Store implement a freemium pricing model, and 92 percent of revenues from Apple's App Store and 98 percent from Google's Play App Store come from freemium pricing.[36]

sentiment analysis
A technique that allows marketers to analyze data from social media sites to collect consumer comments about companies and their products.

▼ **EXHIBIT 3.5** Apple App Store Revenue by App Category Pricing Models

% of revenue generated in Apple's App Store from January through November 2013, by app category and pricing model

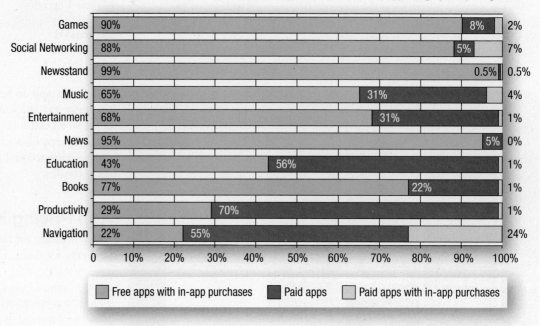

Category	Free apps with in-app purchases	Paid apps	Paid apps with in-app purchases
Games	90%	8%	2%
Social Networking	88%	5%	7%
Newsstand	99%	0.5%	0.5%
Music	65%	31%	4%
Entertainment	68%	31%	1%
News	95%	5%	0%
Education	43%	56%	1%
Books	77%	22%	1%
Productivity	29%	70%	1%
Navigation	22%	55%	24%

Source: Adapted from Christel Schoger, "2013 Year in Review," *Distimo Report,* December 2013, http://www.distimo.com.

✓ check yourself

1. What are the seven types of customer motivations for using mobile apps?
2. What are the four options to price mobile apps?
3. What are some of the most popular types of mobile applications?

LO 3-4 | Recognize and understand the three components of a social media strategy.

HOW DO FIRMS ENGAGE THEIR CUSTOMERS USING SOCIAL MEDIA?

Now that we have an understanding of the various social and mobile media that are at the firm's disposal, it is important to determine how firms should go about engaging customers through social and mobile media. The three-stage process found in Exhibit 3.6 involves *listening* to what customers have to say, *analyzing* the information available through various touch points, and implementing (or *doing*) social media tactics to excite customers.

Listen

From a market research point of view, companies can learn a lot about their customers by listening to (and monitoring) what they say on their social networks, blogs, review sites, and so on. Customers appear willing to provide their opinions on just about anything including their interests and purchases—both their own and their friends'. Writing blogs and providing opinions via polls about such diverse topics as BOTOX treatments, ASICS running shoes, or a particular play of an NFL team during the playoffs all constitute new ways that customers communicate with one another—and with marketers who are paying attention.

Using a technique known as **sentiment analysis**, marketers can analyze the content found on sites like Facebook, Twitter, and online blogs and reviews to assess the favorableness or unfavorableness of the sentiments. Sentiment analysis allows marketers to analyze data from these sources to collect consumer comments about companies and their products. The data are then analyzed to distill customer attitudes and preferences, including reactions to specific products and campaigns.

▼ **EXHIBIT 3.6** Social Media Engagement Process

Listen | Analyze | Do

The NFL blog is one way fans communicate with each other during and after games.
Courtesy NFL Properties, LLC

Scouring millions of sites with sentiment analysis techniques provides new insights into what consumers really think. Companies plugged into this real-time information and these insights can become more nimble, allowing for numerous quick changes such as a product rollout, a new advertising campaign, or reactions to customer complaints.

Several companies specialize in monitoring social media.[37] For example, Salesforce.com offers sentiment analysis and then helps its clients such as GE, Kodak, Microsoft, and PepsiCo engage with their customers.[38] Using sentiment analysis techniques, it processes a constant stream of online consumer opinion from blogs, Facebook, and other networking sites, including 90 million Twitter tweets a day. The Salesforce.com tools for managing consumer sentiment data allow companies to identify opinion trends that might warrant an online corporate response. For instance, Salesforce.com may identify negative consumer sentiment and then provide services to help the client respond. Reacting to attitudes uncovered in sentiment analysis allows companies to counteract negative opinions, maybe influence those perceptions, and perhaps win customer loyalty.[39]

As an example of how a firm like Salesforce.com can help its clients engage their customers, consider the nonprofit New York–based Let's Get Ready that helps low-income high school students get into college.[40] When it decided to compete for American Giving Awards funding, Let's Get Ready needed broader support. Salesforce.com helped the organization find web-based conversations among individuals and groups who might share its educational mission. It further helped Let's Get Ready reach out to potential supporters, share information about its work, and ask for votes. The campaign worked: Let's Get Ready placed second, winning $500,000 from American Giving for free SAT preparation and college admission counseling to motivated students. Sentiment analysis thus is fundamentally transforming how companies interact with and engage their customers.

Salesforce.com's Radian6 website analyzes customer sentiment for its customers, which enables them to identify opinion trends that might warrant an online corporate response.
© copyright salesforce.com, inc. Used with permission.

Analyze

Fortunately, the companies that help facilitate listening also provide analytic tools to assess what customers are saying about the firm and its competitors. There are three main categories of analysis used for understanding data collected from social media.[41]

First, it is important to determine the amount of traffic using their sites, visiting their blogs, or tweeting about them. Measures used for this purpose include **hits** (i.e., total requests for a page), visits to a particular site or page, unique visitors to the site, and **page views** (i.e., the number of times any page gets viewed by any visitor).

Second, while knowing how many people are using a firm's social media is important, it is even more critical to learn who those visitors are, what they are doing, and what engages and excites them. For example, eHarmony works hard to understand what its clients want, both in a service provider and in a mate, as Marketing Analytics 3.1 details. To analyze these factors, social media marketers use metrics such as the **bounce rate**, which refers to the percentage of times a visitor leaves the site almost immediately, such as after viewing only one page. Analyzing which pages are the most frequent entry and exit locations provides direction on how to make a website more effective. In addition, following visitors' **click paths** shows how users proceed through the information—not unlike how grocery stores try to track the way shoppers move through

their aisles. A firm can use this information to provide users with an easier navigation experience through the site so they can more quickly find what they are looking for. The data analysis can also reveal **conversion rates**, a measure that indicates what percentage of visitors or potential customers act as the marketer hopes, whether by clicking, buying, or donating. Click paths and conversion rates can also reveal what users might have wanted, but did not find, at the site.

Third, some companies want to analyze data that come from other sites, such as measuring where people have come from to get to the company's site. Did they search through Google or Amazon? Did they receive a referral from a friend? Which keywords did they use to find the firm? Firms can use **keyword analysis** to determine what keywords people use to search on the Internet for their products and services. With this information, they can refine their websites by choosing keywords to use on their site that their customers use. Then they can assess the return on investment (ROI) made by improving the site. This would be done by calculating the incremental profit increase divided by the investment on the site improvement. For social media, it is more challenging to determine ROI than for more traditional marketing applications because the revenue generated by social media is often not directly related to the expenditure. So, instead of traditional ROI measures, firms often examine questions like: Does having more Twitter followers correlate with having higher sales? Do Facebook fans of the company's buy more than non-fans?[42]

These analyses require well-trained marketing managers, marketing analytic software, and perhaps some help with consulting specialists (e.g., IBM, SAS, PricewaterhouseCoopers). But almost everyone seems to be turning to Google Analytics these days because it offers a sophisticated, in-depth form of analysis, all for free. Not only does Google Analytics track the elements included in Exhibit 3.7, but it also is highly customizable.[43]

Do

Even the greatest analysis has little use if firms fail to implement what they have learned from analyzing their social and mobile media activity. That is, social media may be all about relationships, but ultimately, firms need to use their connections to

▼ **EXHIBIT 3.7** Analytics

Type of Analytic	How It's Used	Competitors Offering Similar Analytics
Content	Understand what's popular and what's not on a firm's website, including page load times and site navigation.	Adobe SiteCatalyst, Clickstream, Coremetrics, IBM SurfAid, Mtracking, VisiStat
Social	Track effectiveness of social media programs, including information on social media referred conversion rates and engagement metrics.	Facebook Insights, Twitter Web Analytics, Webtrends, HootSuite, TweetDeck
Mobile	Track website access from mobile devices, track which ads direct people to a firm's app, and understand what mobile platform performs best.	AppClix, Bango, Flurry, Localytics, Medialets, Webtrends
Conversion	Moving beyond page views and visitor counts, conversion analytics measures sales, downloads, video plays, or any other action important to a firm.	ClickTale, KeyMetric, Latitude
Advertising	Track the effectiveness of social, mobile, and search and display ads and divide ad effectiveness by device, platform, or type.	ad:tech, MediaMelon, MediaCloud, Metronome, Snoobi, Adomic

Source: http://www.google.com/analytics/features/index.html.

Marketing Analytics

Finding a Perfect Match: How eHarmony Leverages Users' Data to Identify Dates—and Their Consumption Patterns[iv]

Some of the same information that enables eHarmony, the online dating service, to connect romantic partners is exactly the same sort of detail that enables eHarmony, the marketer, to communicate most effectively with its clients and prospective customers. The company is upfront in revealing that it collects a lot of data about users—that collection is one of its selling points. By gathering so much insightful information about users, it can better match them with their perfect mate. As a result, it possesses massive amounts of information—approximately 125 terabytes of data, according to one estimate.

To leverage those data for its own benefit, eHarmony switched from an external data analysis service and brought the process in-house. Its sophisticated data analytics enable the firm's seven-person team to determine which communications media sparked responses from which users and when. Whereas previously it struggled to grasp when and why people became loyal customers depending on the channel they used to access its services, today the team gains real-time alerts about whether this person used a smartphone to access its app, or if that person relied on a tablet to visit its website. It carefully calculates the return on its investment in each media buy, according to the lifetime value of each customer, classified according to the route this customer used to access the service, as well as where and when she or he did so.

By enhancing the efficiency of its efforts, eHarmony was able to cut its marketing budget by approximately $5 million. Furthermore, clients' requests for additional information have dropped by around 75 percent, because eHarmony now knows in advance what sorts of details they want and provides it to them predictively.

These data also inform the personalized service the company provides. For example, eHarmony has learned that users who click onto the website through a display ad are more flexible in terms of their requirements in a potential mate. In contrast, if they purchase the service after seeing a televised advertisement, they are much more particular and specific with regard to the range of ages they will consider in a partner. For users who rely on the eHarmony app, the company offers a shorter questionnaire but a wider range of potential dates, because these users tend to be younger and more open-minded when it comes to dating.

Its confidence in its data analytics capabilities is pushing eHarmony's future moves as well. In addition to adding a Spanish-language service, it plans to grow internationally. With a commitment to add one new country each quarter for the next several years, eHarmony is also learning all sorts of new things about its clients. Did you know, for example, that people outside the United States are more willing to date a smoker than are members of the U.S. dating population? eHarmony does.

eHarmony uses its clients' data for matchmaking and more precise target marketing.
Left: © iPhone/Alamy; Right: © The Image Works Archives

Chef Michael Symon and Actress Eva Longoria introduce the Lay's "Do Us A Flavor" crowd-sourced contest winners.
© Diane Bondareff/Invision for Frito-Lay/AP Photo

increase their business.[44] They might launch a new Facebook campaign, actively blog, or provide mobile offers.

What do you do when consumers get tired of the flavors of chips you offer? Instead of developing several new flavors and giving them to focus groups and test markets, in 2013 Lay's took to the Internet. It launched the "Do Us a Flavor" campaign in which customers could suggest new flavor combinations online. After 3.8 million submissions, expert chefs and actor Eva Longoria chose the three finalists: Cheesy Garlic Bread, Chicken & Waffles, and Sriracha. Each of these flavors were developed and sold in stores from February to May and customers were encouraged to try the new flavors and vote for their favorite one. After more than a million votes were tallied on Facebook, Karen Weber-Mendham was given $1 million or 1 percent of the 2013 net sales of her flavor (whichever was higher) for her Cheesy Garlic Bread flavor. The other two finalists received $50,000 each. This campaign was so successful that Lay's launched the contest in several other countries, including the UK, Australia, India, and South Africa, resulting in flavors such as Chili & Chocolate, Late Night Kabob, and Cajun Squirrel. To continue to engage its customers, Lay's launched the "Do Us a Flavor" contest in the United States again in 2014.[45]

To illustrate how firms might go about undertaking such campaigns, consider the steps involved in developing and implementing a Facebook marketing campaign (Exhibit 3.8).[46] These steps are not unlike the steps used in any integrated marketing communications (IMC) program. (See Chapter 17 for more details.) Assume a marketer was developing a Facebook marketing campaign for a new product that they have designed.

1. **Identify strategy and goals.** The firm has to determine exactly what it hopes to promote and achieve through its campaign. Does it want to increase awareness of the product? Is it hoping more potential customers might visit and "like" its Facebook page? Is its focus mainly on increasing sales of the product? Depending on what the company aims to achieve, it might focus on developing a Facebook page, creating a Facebook app, or hosting a Facebook event.

2. **Identify target audience.** The next step is to determine whom the firm is targeting. As Exhibit 3.9 shows, Facebook enables the firm to perform targeting that is based on location, language, education, gender, profession, age, relationship status, likes/dislikes, and friends or connections. The marketer's aim is to find a big enough audience to reach those who might adopt their product without being so big that they end up trying to appeal to someone way outside their target audience.

3. **Develop the campaign: Experiment and engage.** Now that the firm knows who it is targeting, the next step is to develop the communications, including the copy and images. Here again, the process is not very different from any other IMC campaign. There should be a call to action that is clear and compelling. Strong, eye-catching images and designs are important. And the campaign must appeal to the right customers. However, an aspect that is more critical with social media than other forms of IMC is that the images and messages need to be updated almost constantly. Because people expect changing content online, it would be inappropriate to run the same campaign for several months, as the firm might if it was advertising on television, for example.

4. **Develop the budget.** Budgeting is key. Facebook allows advertisers to set a daily budget: Once their costs (usually per click) reach a certain level, the ad disappears for the rest of the day. Of course, this option can be risky if the firm is getting great feedback, and all of a sudden, a compelling ad disappears. Therefore, similar to the campaign content, budgets demand nearly constant review. For example, if a competitor lowers its price significantly, it might be necessary to follow suit to avoid being excluded from customers' consideration sets.

5. **Monitor and change.** The final step is to review the success of the campaign and make changes as necessary. Facebook's Ad Manager offers various metrics and reports, such as number of clicks on ads, audience demographics, and ad performance for specific time periods. ■

▼ **EXHIBIT 3.8** How to Do a Social Media Marketing Campaign

Campaign steps

| 1 Identify strategy & goals | 2 Identify target audience | 3 Campaign: Experiment & engage | 4 Develop budget | 5 Monitor & change |

2. Targeting

Location

Country: (?)   New York

○ Everywhere
○ By State/Province (?)
◉ By City (?)

Demographics

Age: (?)   24 ⬍ — 35 ⬍

Estimated Reach (?)

266,920 people

- who live in the United States
- who live within 50 miles of New York, NY
- between the ages of 24 and 35 inclusive
- who are in the category Cooking

Demographics

Age: (?)   24 ⬍ — 35 ⬍
☐ Require exact age match

Sex: (?) ◉ All   ○ Men   ○

Interests

Precise interests: (?)   Cooking

Switch to Broad Category Targeting (?)

Source: From http://www.facebook.com/business/ads/.

connect Increase your engagement and learning with Connect Marketing.

These Connect activities, available only through your Connect course, have been designed to make the following concepts more meaningful and applicable:

▸ Successfully Using Social Media: Dell Case Analysis

▸ Types of Social Media: Click and Drag Activity

▸ Use of Social Media: GE Video Case

▸ Social Media Metrics: iSeeit! Video

SMARTBOOK™   **iSeeit!**

Chapter four

marketing ethics

Imagine if every time you played Angry Birds or some other game on your mobile phone, personally identifying information—such as your location, the other apps loaded on your phone, your gender, your age, your political leanings, your sexual orientation, and your buying habits—got sent to a massive data repository accessible to various marketers and government agencies. Or don't just imagine it. Read about it in documents leaked by the infamous Edward Snowden.[1] Such information gathering is really nothing new, of course. When people access the web through their computers, they create cookies, or snippets of data that enable marketers to discern where a shopper starts the search process, how he or she proceeds, and where the online encounter ends—as well as what the shopper buys, or doesn't.

A long history of arguments—even before the computer era—debated the acceptability of wiretaps on telephones, whether traditional or mobile, and whether governments had the right to gather specific information (e.g., recordings) or only metadata

LEARNING OBJECTIVES

After reading this chapter, you should be able to:

LO 4-1 Identify the ethical values marketers should embrace.

LO 4-2 Distinguish between ethics and social responsibility.

LO 4-3 Identify the four steps in ethical decision making.

LO 4-4 Describe how ethics can be integrated into a firm's marketing strategy.

LO 4-5 Describe the ways in which corporate social responsibility programs help various stakeholders.

(e.g., general information about the number called, when, and for how long). These debates are becoming increasingly important for marketers as the marketing environment expands to include advanced technology and brand-new methods for collecting data. On one side, the marketing industry has sought to find solutions and self-regulations

continued on p. 68

When you play games like Angry Birds on your mobile phone, personally identifying information may be sent to a massive data repository accessible to various marketers and government agencies.
© MARKA/Alamy

continued from p. 67

to calm customers, avoid the imposition of stronger regulations, and still enable marketing firms to gain access to valuable information about consumer behaviors. But those attempts appear to have stalled, because the online marketing industry simply has not been able to agree about how to police itself. On the other side, legislation introduced by the U.S. Senate attempts to police these activities, mandating the provision of a do-not-track option that would allow computer users to opt out, easily and quickly, from cookie implantations.[2]

Yet cookies might not be the real problem for much longer. In the growing movement toward mobile commerce, marketers can turn to cutting-edge technologies to locate customers through their smartphones and other devices, determine their collective behaviors, and target them with incredibly specific advertisements. For example, Drawbridge maintains partnerships with various advertising platforms and publishers, which create notifications of every visit a user makes to a website or app. These notifications are analyzed to determine which person is using which devices and link them together—as well as determine whether multiple users rely on the same device. For example, if a user visits a travel site through her computer, she might receive an advertisement for rental cars through her phone. However, if her spouse visits a gaming

" Which is the more important corporate objective: making a profit or obtaining, keeping, and protecting customers? "

site instead, Drawbridge knows that it is a different user and personalizes the advertising accordingly.[3]

Rejecting such tactics, many consumers are increasing demands for privacy protections. Online browsers such as Apple's Safari and Mozilla's Firefox have introduced or are working on cookie-blocking technology that might prompt marketers to seek new ways to get around the blocks. Some mobile service providers ask for users' permission to track them. For example, Verizon promised coupons to consumers who agreed to let it share information about their mobile browsing behaviors with advertisers, and AT&T simply announced that it had begun selling aggregated consumer data to advertisers.

The reason for marketers' insistence on using cookies and other tracking technologies, even in the face of customer discontent and legislative threats, is the outstanding value that the information collected can provide. Only by knowing how, when, and where people browse online and through their mobile devices can marketers make sure that they target consumers accurately. These data also represent a major source of revenue for targeted advertising firms that sell consumer data to other advertisers, promising the most accurate information when it comes to selecting who will receive their marketing messages. But they also represent potentially serious intrusions into people's privacy. Thus marketers sit at the heart of modern, international discussions of the efficacy, ethicality, and effectiveness of technological snooping. ■

Which is the more important corporate objective: making a profit or obtaining, keeping, and protecting customers?[4] Although firms cannot stay in business without earning a profit, using profit as the sole guiding light for corporate action can lead to short-term decisions that cause the firm to lose customers in the long run. The balancing act may turn out to be the quest to place the company on the firmest footing possible.

This question leads into the primary ethical dilemma facing managers: how to balance shareholder interests with the needs of society. In our opening example, consumers seek greater protections of their privacy, whereas marketers want access to more and better data about those individual consumers to be able to target them with appealing products at the right time, in the right place, and at the right price—and thereby make more sales.

Other industries face similar ethical dilemmas and seek to find appropriate balances. Since the early 2000s, most

Whole Foods has committed to issuing labels on all GMO-containing foods it sells by 2018.
© Ralph Barrera/MCT/Newscom.

processed foods (e.g., cereals, salad dressings) have contained ingredients made from plants whose DNA has been manipulated in a laboratory. To weather frosts better and produce a greater yield of crops, tomatoes are spliced with salmon genes, for example. Such genetically modified organisms, or GMOs,

appear in a majority of the foods that U.S. consumers eat daily, yet most people remain unaware of their presence because the U.S. Food and Drug Administration does not require GMO food product labeling.[5] The ethical question for food manufacturers is whether they label their products as containing GMOs. On one hand, many consumers express a preference to know and worry about potential negative health effects (though no available scientific evidence has confirmed this threat). On the other hand, genetic modifications increase crop yields and lower production costs, and avoiding a GMO label could help companies sell more of their products. Most food manufacturers seem to be fighting GMO labeling, a choice that can be risky, as Marketing Analytics 4.1 shows. However, in 2014 General Mills decided to make some of its products, such as Cheerios, completely free of GMOs, and Whole Foods has committed to issuing labels on all GMO-containing foods it sells by 2018.[6]

As these examples show, sometimes the ethical dilemma has as much to do with defining our terms as with what the products contain. But even if the question seems to be one of terminology, if customers believe they can no longer trust a company or that the company is not acting responsibly, they will no longer support that company by purchasing its products or services

Marketing Analytics   4.1

How Kellogg's Uses Analytics to Address GMO Concerns[i]

Analytics are a valuable tool for helping manufacturers understand the relationship their customers have with their brands. For example, Kellogg's recently suffered its first sales and profit decreases in decades. The unprecedented drop in these key metrics prompted the company to decide to revamp its brand, cleanly and clearly. But what exactly did it need to change? Using advanced analytics, Kellogg's realized that one of its brands was getting creamed on social media: Reports showed that Kashi, which Kellogg's has promoted as an all-natural option, contained genetically modified organisms (GMOs). Consumers were furious, and they made their opinions clear on various social media.

In response, Kellogg's undertook a complete overhaul in an attempt to redefine its brands' core purpose. It consolidated its 42 separate company websites into a single umbrella site. And it made social media a focal point in its brand overhaul. To manage this social media reinvention, Kellogg's hired a computer whiz to serve as its director of digital and social-media strategy. The strategy first went into effect in the United Kingdom. To encourage trial of its Krave cereal, it released the hashtag "#KravetheSmiler," then awarded prizes to customers who used the hashtag. Throughout the campaign Kellogg's constantly gathered data, including daily summaries of tweets that featured the hashtag, the daily top tweeters, how many tweets per hour they received, and so forth.

The well-planned campaign worked: Kellogg's received more than 35,000 tweets about Krave cereal. Using specially designed algorithms,

Kellogg's could quickly and effectively comb through all the data and award prizes fairly and effectively. Although the campaign improved customer relations, the more important result might have been the way it provided Kellogg's with new insights and data. With this information, Kellogg's is likely to be able to replicate this success in other social media campaigns. For example, it could identify the products in which consumers would be willing to allow GMOs and those in which they absolutely would reject GMOs. Analytics also might show Kellogg's how to seed communication campaigns to give consumers accurate information about GMOs' actual threats and benefits. Thus far, though, its implementation of careful data-based strategies has boosted the return on investment for Kellogg's brands—in some cases, up to six times more than previous methods ever achieved.

Kellogg's used social media to introduce and gather data about its new Krave cereal.
© studiomode/Alamy

or investing in its stock. For marketers, the firm's ability to build and maintain consumer trust by conducting ethical, transparent, clear transactions must be of paramount importance.

In this chapter, we start by examining what marketing ethics is and why behaving ethically is so important to successful marketing and to long-term profits. We then discuss how firms can create an ethical climate among employees and how their individual behavior can affect the ability of the firm to act ethically. To help you make ethical marketing decisions, we provide a framework for ethical decision making and then examine some ethical issues within the context of the marketing plan (from Chapter 2).

THE SCOPE OF MARKETING ETHICS

Business ethics refers to the moral or ethical dilemmas that might arise in a business setting. **Marketing ethics**, in contrast, examines those ethical problems that are specific to the domain of marketing. Firms' attempts to apply sound ethical principles must be a continuous and dynamic process.[7] The nearby cartoon illustrates the importance of making good ethical decisions. Because the marketing profession is often singled out among business disciplines as the root cause of a host of ethical lapses (e.g., unethical advertising, the promotion of shoddy products), anyone involved in marketing must recognize the ethical implications of his or her actions. These can involve societal issues, such as the sale of products or services that may damage the environment; global issues, such as the use of child labor (see Chapter 8 as well); and individual consumer issues, such as deceptive advertising or the marketing of dangerous products. **Deceptive advertising** is a representation, omission, act, or

practice in an advertisement that is likely to mislead consumers acting reasonably under the circumstances.

LO 4-1 | Identify the ethical values marketers should embrace.

Influence of Personal Ethics

Every firm is made up of individuals, each with his or her own needs and desires. Let's start by looking at why people may make *un*ethical decisions and how firms can establish a process for decision making that ensures they choose ethical alternatives instead.

Why People Act Unethically Every individual is a product of his or her culture, upbringing, genes, and various other influences. Yet people also continue to grow emotionally in their understanding of what is and is not ethical behavior. As a six-year-old child, you might have thought nothing of taking your brother's toy and bonking him on the head with it. As an adult, you probably have outgrown this behavior. But all of us vary in the way we view more complex situations, depending on our ethical understandings.

Consider product recalls of toys, for example. How can certain manufacturers engage in such egregious behavior as using lead paint on toys or including magnets that can be swallowed in toys marketed toward young children? What makes people take actions that create so much harm? Are all the individuals who contributed to that behavior just plain immoral? These simple questions have complex answers.

When asked in a survey whether they had seen any unethical behavior among their colleagues, chief marketing officers responded that they had observed employees participating in high-pressure, misleading, or deceptive sales tactics (45 percent); misrepresenting company earnings, sales, and/or revenues (35 percent); withholding or destroying information that could hurt company sales or image (32 percent); and conducting false or misleading advertising (31 percent).[8] Did all the marketers in these situations view their actions as unethical? Probably not. There may have been extenuating circumstances. In marketing, managers often face the choice of doing what is beneficial for them and possibly the firm in the short run and doing what is right and beneficial for the firm and society in the long run.

For instance, a manager might feel confident that earnings will increase in the next few months and therefore believe it benefits himself, his branch, and his employees to exaggerate current earnings just a little. Another manager might feel considerable pressure to increase sales in a retail store, so she brings in some new merchandise, marks it at an artificially high price, and then immediately puts it on sale, deceiving consumers into thinking they are getting a good deal because they viewed the initial price as the real price. These decisions may have been justifiable at the time, but they have serious consequences for the company.

GRANTLAND®

YOUR POSITION MEANS THAT YOU SHOULD TAKE ANY REPORT OF WRONGDOING VERY SERIOUSLY.

YOU MEAN BECAUSE I'M A MANAGER?

YES --

THAT, AND THE POSITION YOU'LL BE IN IF THERE'S AN INVESTIGATION.

WHAT'S THAT?

ALL BY YOURSELF.

Source: Copyright Grantland Enterprises; www.grantland.net.

What is the "real" price? Did the manager bring the T-shirts in at an artificially high level and then immediately mark them down?
© Dennis MacDonald/PhotoEdit.

the serious consideration of "the impact of the company's actions and operating in a way that balances short-term profit needs with society's long-term needs, thus ensuring the company's survival in a healthy environment."[11] This notion goes beyond the individual ethics that we've discussed so far, but for a company to act in a socially responsible manner, the employees of the company must also first maintain high ethical standards and recognize how their individual decisions lead to optimal collective actions of the firm. Firms with strong ethical climates tend to be more socially responsible.

However, it is important to distinguish between ethical business practices and corporate social responsibility programs. Ideally, firms should implement programs that are socially responsible, *and* its employees should act in an ethically responsible manner. (See Exhibit 4.1, upper left quadrant.) Dannon yogurt, for example, has long supported internal research into healthy eating, which supports its ethical commitment to bring "health food to as many people as possible."[12] It is also socially responsible, in that it donates food and money to the hunger-relief charity Feeding America, encourages employees to volunteer in their communities, holds annual Children's Day outreach programs, and reduces its environmental footprints.

To avoid such dire consequences, the short-term goals of each employee must be aligned with the long-term goals of the firm. To align personal and corporate goals, firms need to have a strong ethical climate, explicit rules for governing transactions including a code of ethics, and a system for rewarding and punishing inappropriate behavior. The American Marketing Association (AMA) provides a detailed, multipronged "Statement of Ethics" that can serve as a foundation for marketers,

> " For a company to act in a socially responsible manner, the employees of the company must also first maintain high ethical standards and recognize how their individual decisions lead to optimal collective actions of the firm. "

emphasizing that "As marketers…we not only serve our organizations but also act as stewards of society in creating, facilitating and executing the transactions that are part of the greater economy."[9]

In the next section, we add the concept of corporate social responsibility to our discussion of ethics.

LO 4-2 Distinguish between ethics and social responsibility.

Ethics and Corporate Social Responsibility

Although no single, established definition of the concept exists,[10] **corporate social responsibility (CSR)** generally entails voluntary actions taken by a company to address the ethical, social, and environmental impacts of its business operations and the concerns of its stakeholders. The AMA's definition refers to it as

Dannon yogurt is both ethical and socially responsible. It has an ethical commitment to make healthy food. It is socially responsible since it is involved in many activities and charities that help people.
© Mike Fuentes/The New York Times/Redux Pictures

> # ETHICALLY, HOW DO WE CHARACTERIZE A FIRM THAT OBTAINS ITS PROFITS IN PART THROUGH QUESTIONABLE PRACTICES, THEN DONATES A LARGE PERCENTAGE OF THOSE PROFITS TO CHARITY?

▼ **EXHIBIT 4.1** Ethics versus Social Responsibility

	Socially Responsible	Socially Irresponsible
Ethical	Both ethical and socially responsible	Ethical firm not involved with the larger community
Unethical	Questionable firm practices, yet donates a lot to the community	Neither ethical nor socially responsible

Walmart employees protest low wages.
© Jae C. Hong/AP Photo

Being socially responsible generally means going above and beyond the norms of corporate ethical behavior. For example, a firm's employees may conduct their activities in an ethically acceptable manner, but the firm may still not be considered socially responsible because its activities have little or no impact on anyone other than its closest stakeholders: its customers, employees, and stockholders (Exhibit 4.1, upper right quadrant).

Employees at some firms that are perceived as socially responsible can nevertheless take actions that are viewed as unethical (Exhibit 4.1, lower left quadrant). For instance, a firm might be considered socially responsible because it makes generous donations to charities but is simultaneously involved in questionable sales practices. Walmart was recently ranked as the worst-paying company by the National Employment Law Project, but even as it was underpaying its employees, it was donating more than $1 billion in cash and in-kind items to charitable causes.[13] Ethically, how do we characterize a firm that obtains its profits in part through questionable practices, then donates a large percentage of those profits to charity? The worst situation, of course, is when firms behave both unethically and in a socially unacceptable manner (Exhibit 4.1, lower right quadrant).

Investors express more and more desire to invest in firms that are socially responsible, and consumers increasingly are purchasing services and products from these companies. They also may be willing to pay more if they can be assured the companies truly are ethical.[14] According to a recent poll conducted by *Time* magazine, even in economically constrained settings, 38 percent of U.S. consumers actively tried to purchase from companies they considered responsible. The magazine cites the rise of the "ethical consumer" and the evolution of the social contract "between many Americans and businesses about what goes into making the products we buy."[15]

With such ethical consumers making up more and more of the market, many large companies have recognized that they must be perceived as socially responsible by their stakeholders to earn their business. Other companies began their operations with such a commitment, as Adding Value 4.1 describes.

We cannot expect every member of a firm always to act ethically. However, a framework for ethical decision making can help move people to work toward common ethical goals.

LO 4-3	Identify the four steps in ethical decision making.

A Framework for Ethical Decision Making

Exhibit 4.2 outlines a simple framework for ethical decision making. Let's consider each of the steps.

Step 1: Identify Issues The first step is to identify the issue. For illustrative purposes, we'll investigate the use (or misuse) of data collected from consumers by a marketing

Adding Value 4.1

The Barefoot Entrepreneur[ii]

Blake Mycoskie doesn't just want his customers to buy his shoes; he wants to turn customers into benefactors. In this innovative approach to marketing, his company, TOMS Shoes, does not just engage in charitable acts; the charitable acts are the company. There is no separating TOMS from the social responsibility it embraces.

Mycoskie started out manufacturing a revised version of a traditional Argentinean shoe called alpargatas and selling them to consumers outside their generally impoverished source nation. The combination of the comfortable shoes and the extreme poverty he observed led to a simple code: "You buy a pair of TOMS, and I give a pair to a child on your behalf. One for One." Thus, consumers who buy TOMS Shoes do so because they know that with their purchase, they help donate shoes to people in need. Their choices reflect their desire to make their money count for something.

As the company has grown, it also has added lines of vegan and recycled shoes. Most recently, it expanded into sunglasses, where the One for One philosophy dictates that for every pair sold, TOMS provides eye care, such as medicines, glasses, or surgery, to someone else in the world at risk of losing his or her sight.

But when it comes to procuring other products, finding a socially responsible seller that actively engages in tactics to benefit people and communities might remain challenging for individual shoppers. Therefore, Mycoskie determined that he would bring together sellers and vendors whose work benefited communities onto one online platform. Then shoppers could visit a single site, where they knew that each item they purchased had social, as well as consumption, benefits.

On the TOMS Marketplace website, visitors can search by product line (e.g., apparel, tech, accessories), by their preferred cause (e.g., education, job creation, water), by global region, or by brand. The approximately 200 different products benefit diverse causes: Buying a backpack from Stone + Cloth funds education initiatives in East Africa,

When you buy a pair of TOMS shoes, it gives a pair to a child in need.
© G.M. ANDREWS/The Press-Register/Landov

whereas the purchase of handmade wooden headphones from LSTN means that the company will help restore the hearing of a person with hearing impairment.

Although the TOMS model remains dedicated to a buy one, give one approach, the Marketplace does not require the same commitment from all its 30 or so sellers. Instead, Mycoskie reviews each provider to ensure it "had a mission of improving people's lives baked into its business model." Furthermore, TOMS purchases all the products on the site. In that sense, it functions like a wholesaler that not only procures supply but also takes responsibility for storing, warehousing, shipping, and other logistics.

Detractors argue that TOMS actually may do some harm, in that its provisions might reduce demand for locally produced products. But TOMS already has given away more than 1 million pairs of shoes, so consumers have bought at least that many—at an average price of $55 per pair. Clearly, the value they find in these cloth shoes goes well beyond the simple linen and canvas parts that go into making them.

---

research firm. One of the issues that might arise is the way the data are collected. For instance, are the respondents told about the real purpose of the study? Another issue might be whether the results will be used in a way that might mislead or even harm the public, such as selling the information to a firm to use in soliciting the respondents.

▼ **EXHIBIT 4.2** Ethical Decision-Making Framework

Step 2: Gather Information and Identify Stakeholders In this step, the firm focuses on gathering facts that are important to the ethical issue, including all relevant legal information. To get a complete picture, the firm must identify all the individuals and groups that have a stake in how the issue is resolved.

Stakeholders typically include the firm's employees and retired employees, suppliers, the government, customer groups, stockholders, and members of the community in which the firm operates. Beyond these, many firms now also analyze the needs of the industry and the global community, as well as one-off stakeholders such as future generations and the natural environment itself. In describing its sustainability and transparency efforts, for example, the electronics firm Philips notes that it tries to communicate with and consider "anyone with an interest in Philips."[16]

Step 3: Brainstorm Alternatives
After the marketing firm has identified the stakeholders and their issues and gathered the available data, all parties relevant to the decision should come together to brainstorm any alternative courses of action. In our example, these might include halting the market research project, making responses anonymous, instituting training on the AMA Code of Ethics for all researchers, and so forth. Management then reviews and refines these alternatives, leading to the final step.

Step 4: Choose a Course of Action
The objective of this last step is to weigh the various alternatives and choose a course of action that generates the best solution for the stakeholders, using ethical practices. Management will rank the alternatives in order of preference, clearly establishing the advantages and disadvantages of each. It is also crucial to investigate any potential legal issues associated with each alternative. Of course, any illegal activity should be rejected immediately.

To choose the appropriate course of action, marketing managers will evaluate each alternative by using a process something like the sample ethical decision-making metric in Exhibit 4.3. The marketer's task here is to ensure that he or she has applied all relevant decision-making criteria and to assess his or her level of confidence that the decision being made meets those stated criteria. If the marketer isn't confident about the decision, he or she should reexamine the other alternatives. Using Exhibit 4.3, you can gauge your own ethical response. If your scores tend to be in the "Yes" area (columns 1 and 2), then the situation is not ethically troubling for you. If, in contrast, your scores tend to be in the "No" area (columns 6 and 7), it is ethically troubling, and you know it. If your scores are scattered or are in the "Maybe" area (columns 3, 4, and 5), you need to step back and reflect on how you wish to proceed.

In using such an ethical metric or framework, decision makers must consider the relevant ethical issues, evaluate the alternatives, and then choose a course of action that will help them avoid serious ethical lapses.

Next, let's illustrate how the ethical decision-making metric in Exhibit 4.3 can be used to make ethical business decisions.

Myra Jansen, the head cook at Lincoln High School in Anytown, USA, has had enough. Reports showing that children rarely eat enough vegetables have combined with studies that indicate school kids have a limited amount of time to eat their lunches. The combination has led to increasing obesity rates and troublesome reports about the long-term effects. Myra has therefore decided that the Tater Tots and hot dogs are out. Vegetables and healthy proteins are in.

The problem, of course, is getting the kids to eat raw vegetables, plant proteins, and lean meat. For many teenagers, recommending that they eat healthy food at lunch is akin to calling detention a play date. But Myra has a plan: She's going to reformulate various menu items using different ingredients and just never tell the students. Thus the regular hot dogs will be replaced with turkey or soy dogs. The Tater Tots will contain the

▼ **EXHIBIT 4.3** Ethical Decision-Making Metric

Test	Decision						
	Yes		Maybe			No	
	1	2	3	4	5	6	7
The Publicity Test Would I want to see this action that I'm about to take described on the front page of the local paper or in a national magazine?							
The Moral Mentor Test Would the person I admire the most engage in this activity?							
The Admired Observer Test Would I want the person I admire most to see me doing this?							
The Transparency Test Could I give a clear explanation for the action I'm contemplating, including an honest and transparent account of all my motives, that would satisfy a fair and dispassionate moral judge?							
The Person in the Mirror Test Will I be able to look at myself in the mirror and respect the person I see there?							
The Golden Rule Test Would I like to be on the receiving end of this action and all its potential consequences?							

Source: Adapted from *The Art of Achievement: Mastering the 7 Cs of Business and Life.* © 2002 by Tom Morris, published by Andrews McMeel Publishing LLC, an Andrews McMeel Universal company, Kansas City, Missouri.

more nutrient-dense sweet potatoes instead of the vitamin-deficient regular spuds they used to be made out of. She is convinced she can make such switches for most of the menu items, and none of the children need to know.

Most of the kitchen staff members are onboard with the idea and even have suggested other possible menu switches that would benefit the students by ensuring that they receive a well-balanced meal at school. School board members, when apprised of the idea, got very excited and praised Myra for her innovative thinking. But the community liaison for the school, whose job it is to communicate with parents and other members of the community, is not so sure. Salim Jones is nervous about how students will react when they learn that they have been deceived. He also has two small children of his own, one of whom has a severe wheat allergy. Thus the Joneses are extremely cautious about eating out, always asking for a detailed, specific list of ingredients for anything they order.

Using his training in ethical decision making, Salim sits down to evaluate his alternatives, beginning with identifying possible options available to the school district as well as the various stakeholders who might be affected by the decision. He comes up with the following list:

1. Switch out the food without telling students.

2. Leave menus as they are.

3. Switch out the food ingredients but also tell students exactly what is in each item in the cafeteria.

To make a clear recommendation to the board about what would be the best ethical choice, Salim decides to evaluate each alternative using a series of questions similar to those in Exhibit 4.3.

Question 1: Would I want to see this action described on the front page of the local paper? The school board's reaction caused Salim to think that the larger community would appreciate the effort to improve students' health. Thus, option 1 appears best for these stakeholders, and possibly for society, which may reduce the prevalence of obesity among these students. However, he shudders to think about how angry students might be if they learned they had been tricked. They also likely are accustomed to their menu as it is, and therefore, they would prefer option 2.

Question 2: Would the person I admire most engage in this activity, and would I want him or her to see me engage in this activity? For most of his life, Salim has held up Mahatma Gandhi as his ideal for how to act in the world. For Gandhi, truth was an absolute concept, not something that could be changed depending on the situation. Therefore, Salim believes Gandhi would strongly disapprove of option 1. However, Gandhi also worried about the ethics of eating and avoided food choices that had negative effects on society, so he might reject option 2 as well.

Question 3: Can I give a clear explanation for my action, including an honest account of my motives? In thinking about his children, Salim realizes that he is prioritizing their needs, more so

than the needs of other children, such as those who struggle with weight issues. That is, he worries that his daughter might unknowingly be exposed to wheat in a school cafeteria, so he prefers option 3.

Question 4: Will I be able to look at myself in the mirror and respect what I see? By bringing up the ethics of this decision, even when it seems as if everyone else has agreed with it, Salim feels confident that he has taken the right first step. The option chosen is still important, but it is a group decision, and Salim thinks he is doing his part.

Question 5: Would I want to be on the receiving end of this action and its consequences? Salim struggles most with this question. He remembers the kind of junk foods he chose when he was in college and the 20 pounds he put on as a result. He wishes now that his parents had given him rules to follow about what to eat at school. But he also remembers how rebellious he was and knows that he probably would not have followed those rules. And at the same time, he hates the idea that someone could give him food to eat with falsified ingredients.

On the basis of this exercise, Salim decides that he wants to recommend option 3 to the school board. When he does so, Myra Jansen protests loudly: "This is ridiculous! I know better what kids should be eating, and I know too that some community liaison has no idea what they are willing to eat. You've got to trick them to get them to eat right." Another school board member agrees, noting, "They're just kids. They don't necessarily have the same rights as adults, so we are allowed to decide what's best for them. And hiding the healthy ingredients to get the kids to eat healthy foods is what's best."

So what does the school board decide?

✓ **check** yourself

1. Identify the stages in the ethical decision-making framework.

LO 4-4 Describe how ethics can be integrated into a firm's marketing strategy.

INTEGRATING ETHICS INTO MARKETING STRATEGY

Ethical decision making is not a simple process, though it can get easier as decision makers within the firm become accustomed to thinking about the ethical implications of their actions from a strategic perspective. In this section, we examine how ethical decision making can be integrated into the marketing plan introduced in Chapter 2. The questions vary at each stage of the strategic marketing planning process. For instance, in the

> *Profits from Newman's Own—over $400 million since 1982—have been donated to thousands of charities, especially Newman's Hole in the Wall Gang camps for children with life-threatening diseases.*

planning stage, the firm will decide what level of commitment to its ethical policies and standards it is willing to declare publicly. In the implementation stage, the tone of the questions switches from "can we?" serve the market with the firm's products or services in an ethically responsible manner to "should we?" be engaging in particular marketing practices. The key task in the control phase is to ensure that all potential ethical issues raised during the planning process have been addressed and that all employees of the firm have acted ethically. Let's take a closer look at how ethics can be integrated at each stage of the strategic marketing planning process.

Planning Phase

Marketers can introduce ethics at the beginning of the planning process simply by including ethical statements in the firm's mission or vision statements (recall our discussion of various mission statements in Chapter 2). For instance, the mission statement for natural skin care company Burt's Bees is to "create natural, Earth-friendly personal care products formulated to help you maximize your well-being and that of the world around you,"[17] which reflects not only what is good for its customers but for society in general.

For General Electric, the complexity of its organization and the wealth of ethical issues it faces necessitated an entire booklet, "The Spirit and the Letter." This booklet outlines not only a statement of integrity from the CEO and a code of conduct, but also detailed policies for dealing with everything from international competition laws to security and crisis management to insider trading. In addition, GE publishes an annual citizenship report to determine the scope of its impacts, "produced for the benefit of all stakeholders, including GE employees—the people whose actions define GE every day."[18]

During the planning stage, ethical mission statements can take on another role as a means to guide a firm's SWOT analysis. Newman's Own, for example, has what most would consider a simple but powerful purpose: The company would sell salad dressing (initially; it expanded later to many other product lines) and use the proceeds to benefit charities. This simple idea began in Paul Newman's basement, when he and a friend produced a batch of salad dressing to give as holiday gifts. When they also decided to check with a local grocer to see if it would be interested in the product, they found they could sell 10,000 bottles in two weeks. Thus Newman's Own, a nonprofit organization, quickly grew to include dozens of products. Today, Newman's Own and Newman's Own Organic products are sold in many countries around the world and include more than 100 varieties and dozens of lines, from coffee to popcorn to dog food. Profits from Newman's Own—over $400 million since 1982—have been donated to thousands of charities, especially Newman's Hole in the Wall Gang camps for children with life-threatening diseases.[19]

The unique mission of the company and the entrepreneurial flair of the founders made this nonprofit a smashing, ongoing success. Employees of Newman's Own have the great satisfaction of giving back to society, various charities benefit from the donations, and customers enjoy good food with a clear conscience.

Implementation Phase

In the implementation phase of the marketing strategy, when firms are identifying potential markets and ways to deliver the 4Ps to them, firms must consider several ethical issues. Sometimes a firm's choice of target market and how it pursues it can lead to charges of unethical behavior. For instance, to "like"

Since 1982, Newman's Own has given over $400 million to charities like Newman's Hole in the Wall Gang camps for children with life-threatening diseases.

Left: © FRC Collection/Alamy; Right: © Lamperti Francois-Xavier/Abaca/Newscom

Social & Mobile Marketing 4.1
Who Tweeted Me to Buy a Ford Fiesta?[iii]

Auto manufacturers have long paid celebrities to be spokespeople for their lines of vehicles. But maybe customers really want to hear from people like themselves rather than a celebrity paid millions of dollars to promote a car. Although car companies can save a lot of money by paying normal people less than they pay celebrities, they do not want just anyone to promote their products. They want social media gurus or popular Twitter and blog figures with legions of followers.

Marketing campaigns by Lexus, Ford, and Land Rover all promote their products socially on the web. Ford recruited 100 people with strong online followings to test-drive the Ford Focus and then talk about their experiences online. Ford previously had been successful with its Ford Fiesta campaign, in which anyone who test drove the newly introduced car posted YouTube videos, Flickr photos, and Twitter tweets—adding up to more than 7 million views on YouTube and 4 million mentions on Twitter. As a result, over 130,000 people visited the Ford Fiesta website, 83 percent of whom had never owned a Ford before. The campaign certainly received a lot of attention, though the actual sales conversion has not been disclosed.

Influential online informants also can have negative influences though. Even if a firm pays a blogger or tweeter, no rule can force him or her to write positive reviews. But the likelihood is that a paid blogger will be more positive than an unpaid, disinterested reviewer. Thus the Federal Trade Commission (FTC) has created guidelines for blogging and tweeting, saying that those who post messages must disclose any compensation they may have received for talking about the product. They also must disclose if there is a connection, such as an employee–employer relationship, between the endorser and the marketer of the product that might affect how people evaluate the endorsement.

But such guidelines have little to say about the growing industry available for selling "fake clicks." Whether a thumbs-up on a YouTube

Ford Fiesta's social media campaign draws attention to its traditional media ads.
© Krisztian Bocsi/Bloomberg/Getty Images

video, following a Twitter account, or liking a Facebook page, a click can be bought for as little as half a cent per click. Want 250 Google+ shares? It'll cost you $12.95 from Buy Plus. For 1,000 followers on Instagram, just pay $12 to InstagramEngine.

Originally, these fake click companies designed software bots to generate fake clicks, but social media companies quickly caught on and blocked them. Now click farms have replaced the bots, such that actual people manually click, all day long, every day. These fake clicks are hard to differentiate from genuine user clicks, and the industry is exploding. An estimated $40 million to $360 million was spent buying fraudulent Twitter followers, and more than 14.1 million Facebook accounts are fake.

Grey Poupon's Facebook page consumers would have to apply through their Facebook app. This app would then examine the customer's post history and decide whether the person had "good taste." If they had good taste, they could like the page; if not, then they were not allowed to be part of, as Grey Poupon put it, "the most discerning page on Facebook." Although it may sound fun, there are several privacy issues that made it unethical—users had to allow Grey Poupon to post on their timelines and Grey Poupon got access to their post history.[20] Marketing through social media has some particular ethical concerns associated with it, as Social and Mobile Marketing 4.1 shows.

Once the strategy is implemented, controls must be in place to be certain that the firm has actually done what it has set out to do. These activities take place in the next phase of the strategic marketing planning process.

Control Phase

During the control phase of the strategic marketing planning process, managers must be evaluated on their actions from an ethical perspective. Systems must be in place to check whether each potentially ethical issue raised in the planning process was actually successfully addressed. Systems used in the control phase must also react to change. The emergence of new technologies and new markets ensures that new ethical issues continually arise. In particular, people expect to be able to move normally in public spaces without their location being recorded for subsequent use.[21] Yet marketers regularly collect data on people's location through purchase transactions, and posts on social and mobile sites such as Facebook, Twitter, and Flickr. Additionally, several retailers' credit card systems have been violated, resulting in the theft of consumer data of millions of people, the most egregious of which have been the estimated

110 million at Target and 1.1 million at Neiman Marcus at the end of 2013.[22] Although most experts blame the thefts on U.S.-based credit card companies' reticence to adopt a more secure type of credit card that is used in Europe and elsewhere, the retailers and their customers suffer the consequences.

Many firms have emergency response plans in place just in case they ever encounter an ethical crisis. Ethics thus remains an ongoing crucial component of the strategic marketing planning process and should be incorporated into all the firm's decision making down the road.

check yourself

1. What ethical questions should a marketing manager consider at each stage of the marketing plan?

| LO 4-5 | Describe the ways in which corporate social responsibility programs help various stakeholders. |

CORPORATE SOCIAL RESPONSIBILITY

In 1906, Upton Sinclair published *The Jungle,* his novel exposing the horrific conditions in U.S. meatpacking plants, which prompted President Theodore Roosevelt and Congress to force meat companies to take responsibility for the safety of their products. The notion of societal marketing and corporate social responsibility has changed significantly since then, and recent decades have seen its prevalence increase rapidly. Today, companies are undertaking a wide range of corporate social responsibility initiatives, such as establishing corporate charitable foundations; supporting and associating with existing nonprofit groups; supporting minority activities; and following responsible marketing, sales, and production practices. Exhibit 4.4 provides several illustrations of the CSR programs undertaken by major firms.

For example, FedEx seeks social responsibility in several realms,[23] including:

- *Charitable donations.* Through its "Special Delivery" program, FedEx has donated its services to help various charitable organizations collect and then distribute more than 1 million pounds of food, nearly half a million toys, and a quarter of a million pieces of clothing. More than 90 truckloads, 67 planes, and 15 ocean liners also have carried relief supplies around the globe.

- *Diversity.* FedEx maintains formal groups to ensure it meets global diversity standards. For example, its Corporate Diversity Council develops and promotes diversity programs both within the company and

▼ EXHIBIT 4.4 Sampling of Major Companies' CSR Programs

Company	Illustration of CSR Program
Amazon.com	Developed nonprofit Simple Pay Donation system to help nonprofits raise money easily
BMW	Light Up Hope and BMW Children's Safety programs
Coca-Cola	Spent $102 million through The Coca-Cola Campaign focusing on water stewardship, healthy and active lifestyles, community recycling, and education
FedEx	Transported more than 67 planes' worth of aid to disaster victims
General Electric	Ecomagination campaign, GE Volunteers Foundation
Google	Google.org funds for pro-profit entrepreneurship in Africa, Google China Social Innovation Cup for College Students
McDonald's	99 percent of fish come from MSC-fisheries, transitioning to sustainable food and packaging sources, Ronald McDonald House charities
Procter & Gamble	Live, Learn, and Thrive improves the lives of children worldwide
Southwest Airlines	Employees donate volunteer hours to Ronald McDonald Houses throughout the U.S.
Starbucks	Develops ecologically friendly growing practices, LEED certified stores

Source: Adapted from http://money.cnn.com/magazines/fortune/most-admired/.

throughout the communities in which FedEx operates. Six different affinity groups provide dedicated support to employees who are African American, Hispanic, Asian, women, lesbian, gay, bisexual, or transgender (LGBT), and dealing with cancer.

- *Fuel conservation.* In line with its stated goal to reduce its greenhouse gas emissions by 20 percent, FedEx is in the process of replacing its jets and its delivery trucks with more efficient versions. For example, it operates the largest North American commercial fleet of hybrid vehicles, and its new wide-body planes can use a continuous approach on their descent, which reduces their fuel consumption.

- *Alternative energy sources.* Several of FedEx's domestic hub facilities already rely completely on solar power. It also is seeking to add more such facilities across the world.

> " How does it benefit the company or its shareholders if a company worries about such unquantifiable issues as being a good citizen? "

Some economists and social commentators suggest that CSR is unnecessary and that the goal of any corporation in a capitalist economy is single and simple: make money.[24] The fallout from the recent global economic crisis seems to have pushed economists to repudiate this school of thought. But how does it benefit the company or its shareholders if a company worries about such unquantifiable issues as being a good citizen?

When companies embrace CSR, they appeal not only to their shareholders but also to their key stakeholders (Exhibit 4.5), including their own employees, consumers,

> # IN ONE YEAR, DISNEY GAVE MORE THAN $370 MILLION TO CHARITY, AND ITS EMPLOYEES DONATED 667,013 HOURS OF THEIR TIME THROUGH DISNEY'S VOLUNTEAR PROGRAM. "

▼ **EXHIBIT 4.5** Key CSR Stakeholders

- Employees
- Their families

- Current customers
- Potential customers

| Employees | Customers |
| Marketplace | Society |

- Partners
- Competitors

- Community
- Environment

the marketplace, and society at large. The insurance provider Aflac differentiates its goal "to be a profitable company" from its calling "to be an ethical partner to our stakeholders—one that plays by the rules and demonstrates leadership in the arena of business ethics."[25]

Let's consider each of these stakeholder categories to understand the meaning and effects of corporate social responsibility in the modern marketing arena as well as how CSR ultimately can benefit the firm that undertakes it.

Employees Perhaps the most basic corporate social responsibility to employees is to ensure a safe working environment, free of threats to their physical safety, health, or well-being. In some cases, this basic level of safety seems insufficient to achieve responsibility to workers. Aflac regards its pay-for-performance structure a key element of its responsibility to its employees, with the notion that everyone, from call center operators to the CEO, faces the same compensation standards. In this sense, it ensures equality of treatment and fairness in compensation. In doing so, Aflac earns a reputation as a good place to work and increases the number of people who apply for jobs there. These happy employees also should provide better service to customers, which in turn ensures better outcomes for the firm.

In addition to focusing on employees, more and more firms realize that happy employee families make happy and

productive employees. Consequently, firms are focusing their efforts on outreach programs aimed at their employees' families.

Customers Especially as changes in the marketing environment emerge, firms must consider the effects on the customers who currently patronize them and future customers whom they are targeting. Corporate social responsibility programs must take such shifts and trends into account and react to them quickly. A few of the trends that are receiving the most attention include respecting and protecting privacy in an electronic world and ensuring the healthiness of products, especially those aimed at children. Moreover, CSR often increases consumer awareness of the firm, which can lead to better brand equity and sales in the long run.

Walt Disney often is praised for having one of the best CSR programs in the world. In one year, Disney gave more than $370 million to charity, and its employees donated 667,013 hours of their time through Disney's VoluntEAR program. Partnering with Give Kids the World, these employees renovated 88 vacation villas that the charitable organization offers to the families of children with life-threatening illnesses, so that they can take life-affirming vacations.[26]

Walt Disney's VoluntEAR program is one of the best CSR programs in the world.
© Deshakalyan Chowdhury/Stringer/Getty Images

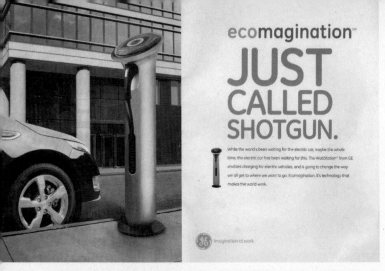

GE is the industry leader in CSR with its ecomagination program.
Courtesy General Electric Company

Marketplace

When one firm in the industry leads the way toward CSR, its partners and competitors often have no choice but to follow—or run the risk of not doing business or being left behind. To address issues such as global warming, water scarcity, and energy, GE uses a program it calls ecomagination, which encompasses a business strategy composed of four commitments: to double investments in clean research and development (R&D), increase revenues from ecomagination products, reduce greenhouse gas emissions, and inform the public about these issues.[27] When confronted with such initiatives, other energy companies are forced to make a decision: continue as they have been doing or adopt more responsible practices themselves. In either case, the initiating firm enjoys an advantage by gaining a reputation for being on the cutting edge of CSR efforts.

Society

Firms expend considerable time and energy engaging in activities aimed at improving the overall community and the physical environment. According to a McKinsey & Co. survey, 95 percent of CEOs believe that society increasingly expects companies to take on public responsibilities.[28] That is, in a broad sense, companies cannot ignore societal demands for

Adding Value 4.2

Walmart Wants to Be the Corporate "Good Guy"[iv]

Walmart is known for its low prices and for driving its vendors nearly to tears to get them. Now it is pressuring its vendors to supply it with environmentally friendly merchandise with labels to prove it. In the future, merchandise sold at Walmart will have the environmental equivalent of nutrition labels, providing information on the product's carbon footprint, the amount of water and air pollution used to produce it, and other environmental issues. To measure how a vendor's products are doing, it has developed a sustainability index that simultaneously takes several issues into consideration. In particular, Walmart required its top 200 factories to cut their energy usage by 20 percent by 2012. Walmart achieved this amazing goal, reducing energy consumption by 2.168 billion kilowatt-hours, or the equivalent amount of energy that would be needed to power 1.46 million homes for a whole year.

It also has committed to buying more of the products it sells in its U.S. stores from U.S. suppliers, in an effort to address high unemployment rates. More directly, it has promised to hire up to 100,000 U.S. veterans, to help address the job challenges many soldiers face upon leaving the military.

Nor has Walmart limited its efforts to the United States. It has sought to increase food safety in China, where the relatively underdeveloped infrastructure can create the danger of contamination of fresh and packaged food products. Walmart created a fleet of customized vans, outfitted with the latest tools for conducting food safety inspections. The vans, staffed by trained specialists, deliver the "China Mobile Labs" to 33 stores throughout Guangzhou, Dongguan, and Shenzhen and ensure the safety and quality of the products they sell.

To reduce the use of plastic bags, and thereby mitigate harm to the environment, Walmart has initiated several campaigns. In particular, plastic bag usage has dropped significantly throughout Asia—by 40 percent in Japan, 86 percent in China, and 90 percent in India.

Why is Walmart attempting to position itself as the retail industry's sustainability leader?
© Walmart Corporation, https://www.flickr.com/photos/ walmartcorporate/5261654374/in/photostream/. Creative Commons license: https://creativecommons.org/licenses/by/2.0/

Walmart has not always been touted as a good corporate citizen, though. In the 1990s, workers at some factories producing clothing for Walmart alleged they had been subjected to inhumane conditions. More recently, two governmental organizations accused Walmart of buying from 15 factories that engage in abuse and labor violations, including child labor, 19-hour shifts, and below-subsistence wages. It and other companies have also been accused of dumping hazardous waste in Oklahoma City.

So why is Walmart attempting to position itself as the retail industry's sustainability leader? The initiatives and related publicity position Walmart as a good corporate citizen and thereby enhance its image. But the retail giant expects its moves to be good for business as well. Its customers, especially younger consumers, are increasingly concerned about how the products they use affect the environment and the people who produce them. Furthermore, Walmart believes that many of these initiatives can help streamline its supply chain processes and therefore provide additional financial benefits to its suppliers and customers.

them to act responsibly. A firm that fails to do so causes damage to all the preceding stakeholders as well as to itself.

For example, reports that the artificial sweeteners in diet sodas might have ill effects, such as long-term weight gain and possible links to developing cancer, have led customers to alter their buying habits. Specifically, sales of diet soda have dropped 6.8 percent in a year, more than three times the decline in regular soda sales. Even though organizations such as the American Diabetic Association and the U.S. Food and Drug Administration have affirmed that diet sodas are safe, the broader shift in societal opinions demands that beverage companies seek new options. In particular, many companies are researching the potential use of stevia, a plant with naturally sweet properties, to replace the artificial versions.[29]

Sustainability

A final category combines considerations of all these stakeholders. According to the U.S. Environmental Protection Agency, "Sustainability is based on a simple principle: Everything that we need for our survival and well-being depends, either directly or indirectly, on our natural environment." Therefore, sustainable actions, including sustainable marketing, allow "humans and nature [to] exist in productive harmony, that permit fulfilling the social, economic and other requirements of present and future generations."[30]

When marketing is truly sustainable, it can benefit the environment, the marketplace, customers, and employees, as Adding Value 4.2 details in relation to Walmart's sustainability efforts. We discuss sustainable, or "green," marketing further in Chapter 5.

check yourself

1. How has corporate social responsibility evolved since the turn of the 21st century?

2. Provide examples of each of the stakeholders that firms should consider in their corporate social responsibility efforts.

---

 connect® Increase your engagement and learning with Connect Marketing.

These Connect activities, available only through your Connect course, have been designed to make the following concepts more meaningful and applicable:

▶ Ethics and Social Responsibility: Newman's Own Video Case

▶ Marketing Practice Ethics Case Analysis

▶ CSR Icebreaker Video Case

▶ Ethical Marketing: iSeeit! Video

Chapter five

analyzing the marketing environment

T ravelers needing a place to grab some shut-eye once knew exactly what to expect when they pulled off the highway to find a hotel chain: a basic room, acceptable bed, relatively Spartan shower, some generic landscape art, and, if they were lucky, a little slightly stale breakfast in the morning. Such expectations are no longer the norm, though, as the hotel industry continues to respond to changing customer needs by transforming itself into one of the most innovative sectors marketing its services today. Consider a few examples aimed at furry travelers in particular.

For modern pet "parents," today's hotel offerings also reflect the increasing belief that pets—especially lovable, drooling, goofy dogs—are part of the family, with the same rights to luxury, comfort, and enjoyment as any human family member. Accordingly, they span a range as broad and varied as the different types of dogs they welcome. At luxury hotels, dogs might be welcomed with a treat bag containing a toy, water dish, and leash (all emblazoned with the hotel's logo, of course). Owners can

LEARNING OBJECTIVES

After reading this chapter, you should be able to:

LO 5-1 Outline how customers, the company, competitors, and corporate partners affect marketing strategy.

LO 5-2 Explain why marketers must consider their macroenvironment when they make decisions.

LO 5-3 Describe the differences among the various generational cohorts.

LO 5-4 Identify various social trends that impact marketing.

request a Ritz-Carlton–branded dog bed to be put in their rooms, or rent a "puppy purse" to carry around their tiny pets.[1]

Beyond product comforts, dog-pertinent service options are remarkably extensive.

continued on p. 84

continued from p. 83

Dog walkers are available to cover daily bathroom chores for busy travelers. Canine pedicures—or (sorry) "peticures"—trim and buff dogs' many nails. Some hotels even offer pet psychics, including one former marketing executive who switched career paths one night after waking up to find her dog talking to her. The range of services is so extensive because people are so passionate about their pets. Marketing research reveals that pet owners seek out offers for their pets that match the offers they prefer for themselves. Thus a weekly visitor to the manicurist is far more likely to seek out someone to take care of her pet's nails too. Furthermore, rather than limiting their canine companions to leisure trips, increasing numbers of business travelers like to bring along a slobbery piece of home, in the form of their best canine friend. While they take business meetings and interact with clients, they can rest assured that their pooch will be shuttled between the hotel and a doggie daycare location, where it can interact with other dogs, for about $299 a day. One hotel chain

To compete effectively, many hotels not only allow pets, but cater to them.
© Christopher Furlong/Getty Images News/Getty Images

estimates that approximately 100,000 pets (99 percent of them dogs) stay in its hotels each year.

These innovative approaches are just the tip of the proverbial iceberg, as the hotel industry actively seeks to speed up and expand its introduction of new products and services, often by testing them in a few locations to gather feedback from travelers. ∎

| LO 5-1 | Outline how customers, the company, competitors, and corporate partners affect marketing strategy. |

A MARKETING ENVIRONMENT ANALYSIS FRAMEWORK

As the opening vignette illustrates, marketers continue to find changes in what their customers demand or expect and adapt their product and service offerings accordingly. By paying close attention to customer needs and continuously monitoring the business environment in which the company operates, a good marketer can identify potential opportunities.

Exhibit 5.1 illustrates factors that affect the marketing environment. The centerpiece, as always, is consumers. Consumers may be influenced directly by the immediate actions of the focal company, the company's competitors, or corporate partners that work with the firm to make and supply products and services to consumers. The firm, and therefore consumers indirectly, is influenced by the macroenvironment, which includes various impacts of culture, demographics, and social, technological, economic, and political/legal factors. We discuss each of these components in detail in this chapter and suggest how they might interrelate.

Because the consumer is the center of all marketing efforts, value-based marketing aims to provide greater value to consumers than competitors offer. Therefore, the marketing firm must consider the entire business process, all from a consumer's point of view.[2] Consumers' needs and wants, as well as their ability to purchase, depend on a host of factors that change and evolve over time. Firms use various tools to keep track of

> " CONSUMERS MAY BE INFLUENCED DIRECTLY BY THE IMMEDIATE ACTIONS OF THE FOCAL COMPANY, THE COMPANY'S COMPETITORS, OR CORPORATE PARTNERS THAT WORK WITH THE FIRM TO MAKE AND SUPPLY PRODUCTS AND SERVICES TO CONSUMERS. "

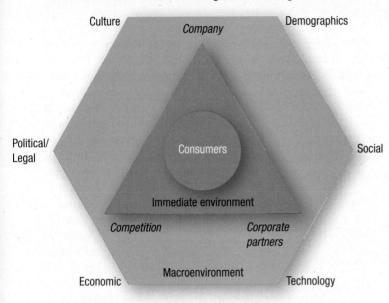

Company Capabilities

In the immediate environment, the first factor that affects the consumer is the firm itself. Successful marketing firms focus on satisfying customer needs that match their core competencies. The primary strength of Corning is its ability to manufacture glass. The company initially made its name by producing the glass enclosure to encase Thomas Edison's lightbulb. But by successfully leveraging its core competency in glass manufacturing while also recognizing marketplace trends toward mobile devices, Corning shifted its focus. As a result, Corning is one of the leading producers of durable, scratch-resistant glass on the faces of smartphones and tablets. More than 1 billion mobile devices feature its Gorilla Glass.[3] Marketers can use analyses of their external environment, like the SWOT analysis described in Chapter 2, to categorize any opportunity as attractive or unattractive. If it appears attractive, they also need to assess it in terms of their existing competencies.

Competitors

Competition also significantly affects consumers in the immediate environment. It is therefore critical that marketers understand their firm's competitors, including their strengths, weaknesses, and likely reactions to the marketing activities that their own firm undertakes.

Watching competitors is a constant effort—and often a serious battle—in many consumer goods categories. No one would want to get caught in the war between the two razor giants, Gillette Co. and Energizer USA, which makes Schick razors, as each manufacturer works to add ever more blades to its disposable razors.[4] Gillette accused Schick of engaging in false and misleading advertising when ads claimed that its Hydro razor

competitors' activities and consumer trends, and they rely on various methods to communicate with their corporate partners. Furthermore, they monitor their macroenvironment to determine how such factors influence consumers and how they should respond to them. Sometimes, a firm can even anticipate trends.

THE IMMEDIATE ENVIRONMENT

Exhibit 5.2 illustrates the factors that affect consumers' immediate environment: the company's capabilities, competitors, and corporate partners.

▼ **EXHIBIT 5.2** Understanding the Immediate Environment

Schick and Gillette are actively engaged in fierce competition for the razor market.
Both photos: © McGraw-Hill Education/Mark Dierker, photographer.

macroenvironmental factors Aspects of the external environment that affect a company's business, such as the culture, demographics, social trends, technological advances, economic situation, and political/regulatory environment.

culture The set of values, guiding beliefs, understandings, and ways of doing things shared by members of a society; exists on two levels: visible artifacts (e.g., behavior, dress, symbols, physical settings, ceremonies) and underlying values (thought processes, beliefs, and assumptions).

would hydrate skin. Schick's parent company countered with the complaint that Gillette's Fusion ProGlide Razor ads attempt to deceive when they assert that the blades are "Gillette's thinnest blades ever." All these efforts represent the companies' recognition of what their closest competitor is doing, as well as their attempts to halt tactics they consider damaging. But at the same time, each razor company touts its benefits over its competitors because the ultimate goal, of course, is to appeal to consumers.

Corporate Partners

Few firms operate in isolation. For example, automobile manufacturers collaborate with suppliers of sheet metal, tire manufacturers, component part makers, unions, transport companies, and dealerships to produce and market their automobiles

> Not only does Nau represent the cutting edge of sustainability and green business, it also clearly demonstrates how "going green" can prompt companies to work more closely with their partners to innovate.

successfully. Parties that work with the focal firm are its corporate partners.

Consider an example that demonstrates the role these partners play and how they work with the firm to create a single, efficient manufacturing system. Unlike most outdoor clothing manufacturers that use synthetic nonrenewable materials, Nau makes modern urban+outdoor apparel from renewable sources such as sustainably harvested eucalyptus and recycled plastic bottles. It was founded by a team of entrepreneurs who left companies such as Nike and Patagonia. To develop rugged and beautiful clothing from sustainable materials, these founders turned to manufacturing partners around the world to develop new fabrics that are performance-driven and technical. One example of an innovative fabric used in Nau's jackets is a blend of recycled polyester and organic cotton that is coated and bonded to recycled polyester knit. The result is a water-resistant, breathable technical soft shell material that is ideal for outdoor activities. To complement the new fabrics, the company uses only organic cotton and wool from "happy sheep," provided by partners in the ranching industry that embrace animal-friendly practices. Not only does Nau represent the cutting edge of sustainability and green business, it also clearly demonstrates how "going green" can prompt companies to work more closely with their partners to innovate.[5]

 check yourself

1. What are the components of the immediate environment?

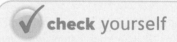 **LO 5-1** | Explain why marketers must consider their macroenvironment when they make decisions.

MACROENVIRONMENTAL FACTORS

In addition to understanding their customers, the company itself, their competition, and their corporate partners, marketers must understand the **macroenvironmental factors** that operate in the external environment. These factors are **c**ulture, **d**emographics, **s**ocial trends, **t**echnological advances, **e**conomic situation, and **p**olitical/regulatory environment, or CDSTEP, as shown in Exhibit 5.3.

Culture

We broadly define **culture** as the shared meanings, beliefs, morals, values, and customs of a group of people.[6] Transmitted by

Nau works with its corporate partners to develop socially responsible outdoor (left) and urban (right) apparel.
Courtesy of Nau International, Inc. Photography by Matthew D'Annunzio.

▼ **EXHIBIT 5.3** The Macroenvironment

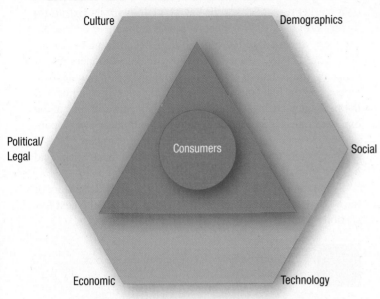

words, literature, and institutions, culture is passed down from generation to generation and learned over time. You participate in many cultures: Your family has a cultural heritage, so perhaps your mealtime traditions include eating rugelach, a traditional Jewish pastry, or sharing corned beef and cabbage to celebrate your Irish ancestry on St. Patrick's Day. In addition, your school or workplace shares its own common culture. In a broader sense, you also participate in the cultural aspects of the town and country in which you live. The challenge for marketers is to have products or services identifiable by and relevant to a particular group of people. Our various cultures influence what, why, how, where, and when we buy. Two dimensions of culture that marketers must take into account as they develop their marketing strategies are the culture of the country and that of a region within a country.

Country Culture

The visible nuances of a country's culture, such as artifacts, behavior, dress, symbols, physical settings, ceremonies, language differences, colors and tastes, and food preferences, are easy to spot. But the subtler aspects of **country culture** generally are trickier to identify and navigate. Sometimes the best answer is to establish a universal appeal within the specific identities of country culture. Disney and other global firms have successfully bridged the cultural gap by producing advertising that appeals to the same target market across countries. The pictures and copy are the same. The only thing that changes is the language.

Regional Culture

The region in which people live in a particular country has its own **regional culture** that affects many aspects of people's lives, including the way they might refer to a particular product category like soft drinks. In the soft drink market, 41 percent of Americans refer to carbonated beverages as "soda," whereas another 38 percent call them "pop," and an additional 15 percent call any such beverage a "Coke,"

country culture
Entails easy-to-spot visible nuances that are particular to a country, such as dress, symbols, ceremonies, language, colors, and food preferences, and subtler aspects, which are trickier to identify.

regional culture The influence of the area within a country in which people live.

Some firms, like Disney, bridge the cultural gap by using the same advertising in different countries. Only the language is different, as illustrated by these two ads for The Avengers. *The left photo is for the Russian market, whereas the right photo is for the Portuguese market.*
Both photos: © Walt Disney Studios Motion Pictures/Courtesy Everett Collection

demographics
Information about the characteristics of human populations and segments, especially those used to identify consumer markets such as by age, gender, income, and education.

generational cohort
A group of people of the same generation—typically have similar purchase behaviors because they have shared experiences and are in the same stage of life.

even when it is Pepsi.[7] Eat lunch in Indiana and you'll have the best luck ordering a "pop" from the midwesterner who owns the restaurant, but if you then head to Atlanta for dinner, you'd better order your "Coke," regardless of the brand you prefer. Head to Massachusetts and the term is "soda," but if you move to Texas, you might be asked if you'd like a Dr Pepper—a generic term for carbonated beverages in the Lone Star state because it was first formulated there in 1885.[8] Imagine the difficulty these firms have in developing promotional materials that transcend these regional differences.

Demographics

Demographics indicate the characteristics of human populations and segments, especially those used to identify consumer markets. Typical demographics such as age (which includes generational cohorts), gender, race, and income are readily available from market research firms such as IRI (formerly SymphonyIRI Group). Many firms undertake their own market research as well. For example, with its ExtraCard loyalty program, CVS collects massive amounts of data about shoppers who visit all its stores. It uses this information to target offers for, say, cosmetics to young female shoppers. But it also uses these data to benefit its communities. When the data gathered show that consumers—especially elderly customers of the pharmacy chain—are not refilling their prescriptions at the expected rate, CVS proactively interacts with these at-risk populations to encourage adherence to their medical plans.[9] Not all firms are quite as effective in their efforts though, as Social and Mobile Marketing 5.1 describes.

Demographics thus provide an easily understood snapshot of the typical consumer in a specific target market, as the next few sections detail.

> **LO 5-3** Describe the differences among the various generational cohorts.

Generational Cohorts Consumers in a **generational cohort**—a group of people of the same generation—have similar purchase behaviors because they have shared experiences and are in the same stage of life. Applying age as a basis to identify consumers is quite useful to marketers,

Social & Mobile Marketing 5.1
Understanding Connections, Both with and by Young Consumers[i]

For marketing executives, choices about where and how much to spend to appeal to consumers should depend mainly on a careful analysis of where those consumers are exposed to marketing messages. But when a generation gap appears between these two groups, advertising choices may reflect marketers' preferences more than consumers'.

A clear manifestation comes from advertising for beauty products. Previous generations of consumers often relied on insights and advice from big, glossy fashion magazines. Lush, expensive, two-page spreads, with glamorous shots of beauty products in use, seemed effective and appropriate. But Millennials (Gen Y) who still read such magazines likely access them online and skip quickly over such long and intrusive ads, with little appreciation for the quality of the shot. Furthermore, recent research shows that such high-quality visual tactics used in print advertisements do not translate particularly well to online product sites. On retail websites, the pretty pictures are largely ineffective because shoppers seek concrete information about their purchase decisions.

According to Forrester Research, 91 percent of Millennials are active Internet users. To reach the web, 59 percent of them use smartphones, 35 percent rely on tablets, and 70 percent employ their laptops. Across these various uses, this younger generation of consumers spends an average of 25 hours online every week.

Their electronic media usage is not the only impressive number describing these consumers: The Millennial market encompasses approximately 105 million consumers, with annual buying power of about $200 billion. Yet even when they recognize and appreciate the size and opportunity that these consumers represent, many marketers—especially those who have reached executive positions after long careers—continue to devote the bulk of their media spending to channels that Millennials simply don't use that much anymore, such as magazines and television.

The main reason for this error might be a somewhat clichéd image of Baby Boomers, confused and overwhelmed by the new options created through technological advances. Faced with a wealth of choices, such as small independent blogs, content-generating sites, and aggregators, these marketing executives retreat to familiar ground. If they aren't sure what each type of site does, they can't determine which is the best option.

Even marketers who embrace technology channels for advertising exhibit a tendency to prefer well-established, widely known spaces, such as Facebook or Google. For young consumers who seek exciting, interactive media content, such options have little chances of success.

▼ **EXHIBIT 5.4** Generational Cohorts

Generational cohort	Gen Z	Gen Y	Gen X	Baby Boomers
Range of birth years	2001–2014	1977–2000	1965–1976	1946–1964
Age in 2015	0–13	14–37	38–49	50–68

Generation Z (Gen Z)
Generational cohort of people born between 2001 and 2014. Also known as *Digital Natives* because people in this group were born into a world that already was full of electronic gadgets and digital technologies, such as the Internet and social networks.

Digital Natives See *Generation Z.*

Generation Y (Gen Y)
Generational cohort of people born between 1977 and 2000; biggest cohort since the original postwar baby boom. Also called *Millennials.*

Millennials See *Generation Y.*

Generation X (Gen X)
Generational cohort of people born between 1965 and 1976.

Baby Boomers
Generational cohort of people born after World War II, between 1946 and 1964.

as long as it is used in conjunction with other consumer characteristics. For example, most media are characterized by the consumers who use them.[10] Age groups can identify appropriate media in which firms should advertise, as discussed in Social and Mobile Marketing 5.1. Although there are many ways to cut the generational pie, we describe four major groups, as listed in Exhibit 5.4.

Members of **Generation Z (Gen Z)** are also known as **Digital Natives** because people in this group were born into a world that already was full of electronic gadgets and digital technologies such as the Internet and social networks.[11] These technologies are being developed and adopted at an unprecedented rate. Whereas it took 38 years for the radio to be adopted by 50 million people and 13 years for television, it only took 2 years for the same number of consumers to sign up for Facebook.

Members of **Generation Y (Gen Y)**, also called **Millennials**, include the more than 60 million people born in the United States between 1977 and 2000. As the children of the Baby Boomers, this group is the biggest cohort since the original postwar World War II boom. It also varies the most in age, ranging from teenagers to adults who have their own families.[12]

The next group, **Generation X (Gen X)**, includes people born between 1965 and 1976 and represents some 41 million Americans. Vastly unlike their Baby Boomer parents, Xers are the first generation of latchkey children (those who grew up in homes in which both parents worked), and 50 percent of them have divorced parents.

After World War II the birthrate in the United States rose sharply, resulting in a group known as the **Baby Boomers**, the 78 million Americans born between 1946 and 1964. Now that the oldest Boomers are collecting Social Security, it is clear that this cohort will be the largest population of 50-plus consumers the United States has ever seen.

Income Income distribution in the United States has grown more polarized—the highest-income groups are growing, whereas many middle- and lower-income groups' real purchasing power keeps declining. Although the trend of wealthy households outpacing both poor and middle classes is worldwide, it is particularly prominent in the United States. For 2013, the average weekly income of the richest 1 to 10 percent of the population was more than $1,917, the average (median) weekly income for the United States as a whole was $827, and the poorest 10 percent of the population earned less than $392 per week. Furthermore, the number of people who earn less than the poverty line ($23,550 for a family of four in 2013) continues to grow.[13] The wealthiest 1 percent control 34.6 percent of Americans' total net worth; the bottom 90 percent control only 26.9 percent in comparison.[14] The increase in wealthy families may

Tweens are always connected.
© Alberto Pomares/E+/Getty Images RF

be due to the maturing of the general population, the increase in dual-income households, and the higher overall level of education. It also may prompt some ethical concerns about the distribution of wealth. However, the broad range in incomes creates marketing opportunities at both the high and low ends of the market.

Although some marketers choose to target only affluent population segments, others have had great success delivering value to middle- and low-income earners. Consider, for example, the toys presented by the specialty retailer Hammacher

or secondary degree accounts for nearly half of all projected job growth in the near future. Moreover, average annual earnings are higher for those with degrees than for those without. Those who did not graduate from high school have an average weekly salary of $468, high school grads earn $648, and those with a bachelor's degree earn $1,216.[17]

For some products, marketers can combine education level with other data such as occupation and income and obtain pretty accurate predictions of purchase behavior. For instance, a full-time college student with a part-time job may have

> THOSE WHO DID NOT GRADUATE FROM HIGH SCHOOL HAVE AN AVERAGE WEEKLY SALARY OF $468, HIGH SCHOOL GRADS EARN $648, AND THOSE WITH A BACHELOR'S DEGREE EARN $1,216.

Schlemmer (HS) versus the mass appeal of Walmart's toy sections. Toy buyers at Walmart are looking for inexpensive products; those at Hammacher Schlemmer go to great lengths to find unusual toys such as the flying Hovercraft, pictured, or the Mind Controlled UFO.[15]

Education

Studies show that higher levels of education lead to better jobs and higher incomes.[16] According to the U.S. Bureau of Labor Statistics, employment that requires a college

This flying Hovercraft, targeted to affluent population segments, is available at Hammacher Schlemmer for only $190,000.
© Splash/Hammacher Schlemmer/Newscom

relatively little personal income but will spend his or her disposable dollars differently than would a high school graduate who works in a factory and earns a similar income. Marketers need to be quite cognizant of the interaction among education, income, and occupation.

Gender

Years ago gender roles appeared clear, but those male and female roles have been blurred. In particular, women today outperform men scholastically, earn higher grades on average, and graduate from both high school and college at greater rates. Perhaps unsurprisingly, recent studies also show that approximately 15 percent of married women in Western economies earn more than their husbands in the workplace.[18] These shifts in status, attitudes, and behaviors affect the way many firms need to design and promote their products and services. More firms are careful about gender neutrality in positioning their products and attempt to transcend gender boundaries, especially through increased interactions with their customers. On the basis of its research with men, for example, the children's stroller company Bugaboo International designed a high-tech, black-and-chrome contraption with dirt bike tires. Several other long-held assumptions about who buys what also are being challenged in today's marketing environment, as Adding Value 5.1 describes.

Ethnicity[19]

Because of immigration and increasing birthrates among various ethnic and racial groups, the United States continues to grow more diverse. Approximately 80 percent of all population growth in the next 20 years is expected to come from African American, Hispanic, and Asian communities. Minorities now represent approximately one-quarter of the population; by 2050 they will represent about 50 percent, and nearly 30 percent of the population will be Hispanic.[20] The United Nations also

Adding Value 5.1

Where Gender Matters—and Where It Doesn't[ii]

In the past, the demographic patterns seemed clear: Women bought personal care products, fragrances, women's clothing, and groceries. Men bought stereo equipment, video games, tires, and men's clothing—if they had to. But in modern-day marketing environments, virtually all of these easy classifications are being challenged by shoppers who have little time to waste with gender stereotypes. And marketers are quickly catching on.

For example, when Urban Outfitters was redesigning its website, it stumbled on what the web designers thought was a brilliant and simple change. They would personalize the site so that female visitors immediately were directed to dresses and blouses, while male visitors saw work shirts and tough-guy jeans. The response was quick—and negative. Female visitors complained that they were the ones buying most of the clothing for the men in their lives. And on top of that, they found the gender-biased marketing offensive.

At the same time, more and more men are in the market for grooming and personal care products. The suggested reasons are many. Maybe the modern generation simply is more accustomed to shopping for themselves. Or perhaps job seekers in a tight economy need any edge they can get, and feeling confident about their personal grooming as they head to interviews might tip the scales in their favor. Regardless of the reason, the conventional wisdom that personal care and fragrance sellers could market just to women has gone out the window.

Overall it appears that men and women have approximately equal influences on households' spending. In a recent survey, 85 percent of

As gender roles shift, more grocery chains are gearing up to better meet the needs of their male customers.
© Fuse/Getty Images RF

women and 84 percent of men agreed that they shared responsibility for shopping decisions.

Such equality of influence is not to say that women and men shop the same way though. As men take on more grocery shopping tasks—a role traditionally assigned to women—some grocery retailers are experimenting with ways to appeal to them. For example, men appear to hate to ask for help, so the stores need to be efficient and clearly laid out with good signage, rather than providing an abundance of customer service.

Best Buy similarly recognized that women are a massive market for electronics, smartphones, and mobile devices. But its stores tended to attract very few female shoppers. Therefore, its recent store design revisions aim to appeal to women with household appliance sections that look more like kitchens than like industrial shipyards and hand sanitizer dispensers placed next to the video game test consoles.

---

estimates that approximately 1 million people per year will emigrate from less developed nations to the United States over the next 40 years.[21] Many foreign-born Americans and recent immigrants tend to concentrate in a handful of metropolitan areas, such as New York, Los Angeles, San Francisco, and Chicago.

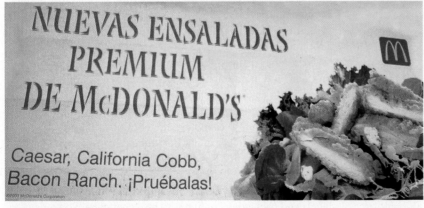

The Hispanic market is so large in some areas of the United States that marketers develop entire marketing programs just to meet their needs.
© Ethel Wolvovitz/The Image Works

LO 5-4 | Identify various social trends that impact marketing.

Among the different groups, Hispanic buying power is projected to reach $1.3 trillion in 2015, a cumulative increase of around 25 percent compared with 2010.[22] The 50 million Hispanic consumers in the United States have increasing influences on mainstream U.S. culture. Many families have been in the United States for multiple generations, and the consumer behavior of these highly acculturated Hispanics differs little from that of other groups of Americans. For example, they use credit cards, are minimally influenced by advertising and product placements, exhibit greater sensitivity to in-store promotions, and are likely to shop online and from catalogs.

The census of 2010 counts 42 million African American U.S. households, who are more affluent and suburban than previous studies suggested. They also tend to be younger, such that 47 percent are between the ages of 18 and 49 years

The United States is like a salad bowl, a mix made up of people from every corner of the world.
© Andrea Laurita/Getty Images RF

This Subway ad speaks directly to the issue of childhood obesity and responds to the new advertising guidelines adopted by marketers. The SUBWAY FRESH FIT FOR KIDS™ meal, which meets the American Heart Association's criteria for a heart-healthy meal, provides a nutritional choice for customers wanting a quick service food alternative for their children.
Courtesy Subway Franchise Advertising Fund Trust.

(i.e., a key age demographic for many marketers). The number of black households earning more than $75,000 has increased by 47 percent since 2005, and by 2015 trends indicate that a majority of black Americans will live in the suburbs.[23] For example, in the Atlanta metropolitan area the city lost 8 percent of its African American households, while the surrounding suburbs gained a remarkable 40 percent.[24] For this demographic segment, especially as it moves increasingly to the suburbs, Home Depot has developed particular appeals featuring national figures such as Tom Joyner and Steve Harvey.

Finally, Asian Americans make up only about 5.6 percent of the U.S. population, but they also represent the fastest-growing minority population, tend to earn more, have more schooling, and be more likely to be professionally employed or own a business.

Social Trends

Various social trends appear to be shaping consumer values in the United States and around the world, including a greater emphasis on health and wellness concerns, greener consumers, and privacy concerns.

Health and Wellness Concerns
Health concerns, especially those pertaining to children, are prevalent, critical, and widespread. In the past 20 years, child obesity has doubled and teenage obesity tripled in the United States, leading to skyrocketing rates of high blood pressure, high cholesterol, early signs of heart disease, and type 2 diabetes among children. The U.S. Centers for Disease Control and Prevention (CDC) also estimates that approximately one-third of U.S. adults are obese, and the incidence of diabetes has reached

8.3 percent—with much higher rates for people still undiagnosed or classified as having prediabetes.[25] It is also increasing at alarming rates in other countries and among consumers who adopt more Western diets.

New advertising guidelines therefore require marketers to produce food in reasonably proportioned sizes. Advertised food items must provide basic nutrients, have less than 30 percent of their total calories from fat, and include no added sweeteners. The advertising also cannot be aired during children's programming, and companies cannot link unhealthy foods with cartoon and celebrity figures. For example, Burger King no longer uses SpongeBob SquarePants to promote burgers and fries.[26] Yet for many consumers, finding the healthiest options using existing labels and packaging continues to be a challenge. Some retailers offer services to help customers with such choices, as Adding Value 5.2 explains.

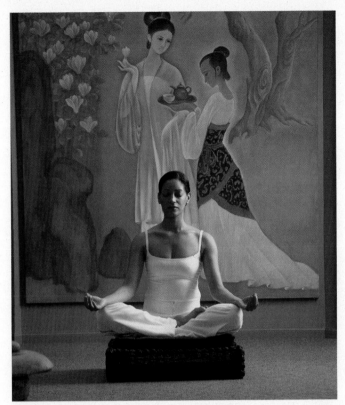

The practice of yoga is growing as more consumers embrace a healthy lifestyle.
© Plush Studios/Blend Images RF

At the same time, consumers' interest in improving their health has opened up several new markets and niches focused on healthy living. For example, consumer spending on yoga classes, mats, and clothing has increased consistently in recent years.[27] Yoga studios actually combine multiple modern trends: As the economy sours, people face increasing stress, which they hope to reduce through yoga. In addition, yoga studios are relatively inexpensive to open and operate, so entrepreneurs and consumers appreciate the value for the money they offer. And of course, Americans remain consistently on the lookout for exercise mechanisms that can help them shed pounds and match media images of athletic prowess and beautiful bodies. Thus competition is growing in this industry, and some studios have begun to combine their basic yoga classes with additional offers to attract clients, such as food services, acupuncture, or massages.[28]

green marketing
Involves a strategic effort by firms to supply customers with environmentally friendly merchandise.

Greener Consumers **Green marketing** involves a strategic effort by firms to supply customers with environmentally friendly, sustainable merchandise and services.[29] As we noted at the end of Chapter 4, sustainability is a critical ethical consideration for marketers. Many consumers, concerned about everything from the purity of air and water to the safety of beef

Adding Value 5.2
Transforming Grocery Stores into Health Providers[iii]

Increasing numbers of supermarkets now feature a new type of employee who floats among aisles, offering advice and suggestions for shoppers. By keeping a registered dietitian on staff, various grocery chains seek to meet their customers' demands for more information about healthy choices, as well as expand their roles in their customers' lives.

Dietitians have long been members of grocery store corporations, but usually they sat in corporate offices and informed executives on product decisions. Moving down the supply chain and into stores, today's dietitian staff advise consumers directly about the products they see on the shelves of their local store. A parent whose child suffers severe food allergies can ask about safe options. A consumer struggling with weight can learn about the best options for reducing calories and fat. And environmentally conscious buyers can determine the difference between "all-natural" and "organic" (the former claim is unregulated; the latter means the product has passed a series of stringent tests).

The Food Marketing Institute recently determined that about one-third of grocery store chains—including Hy-Vee, Safeway, and Wegmans—have added dietitians at the retail level, whereas 86 percent keep one on staff at the corporate level. In addition, predictions suggest that the number of retail dietitians will double in coming years.

Grocery stores, including Coborn's, provide a NuVal ranking from 1 to 100 for each product. Higher scores reflect more nutritious food choices.
© Glen Stubbe/ZUMAPRESS/Minneapolis Star Tribune/Newscom

Much of the advice dietitians offer to shoppers in stores is free, though some stores also offer more extensive consultations for a fee. Furthermore, the stores use their recommendations to promote certain products as "dietitians' picks," highlighted by shelf signs and promotions.

For example, Safeway's new "Simple Nutrition" program highlights 22 separate potential health benefits associated with the various products on its shelves. A third-party organization also has established a NuVal ranking system that assigns each product a nutrition value score, from 1 to 100. The scores reflect more than 30 criteria, such as cholesterol, sugar, and sodium levels, as well as the amount of calcium or protein provided.

greenwashing
Exploiting a consumer by disingenuously marketing products or services as environmentally friendly, with the goal of gaining public approval and sales.

and salmon, believe that each person can make a difference in the environment. For example, nearly half of U.S. adults now recycle their soda bottles and newspapers, and European consumers are even more green. Germans are required by law to recycle bottles, and the European Union does not allow beef raised on artificial growth hormones to be imported.

Demand for green-oriented products has been a boon to the firms that supply them. Marketers encourage consumers to replace older versions of washing machines and dishwashers with water- and energy-saving models and to invest in phosphate-free laundry powder and mercury-free and rechargeable batteries. New markets emerge for recycled building products, packaging, paper goods, and even sweaters and sneakers as well as for more efficient appliances, lighting, and heating and cooling systems in homes and offices. Jumping on the green bandwagon,

Frito-Lay's SunChips line of snack foods uses solar power at one of its eight production facilities to harness the sun's energy to produce its products.[30] Ethical and Societal Dilemma 5.1 examines some of the challenges companies face in making green products.

These green products and initiatives suggest a complicated business model. Are they good for business? Some green options are more expensive than traditional products and initiatives. Are consumers interested in or willing to pay the higher prices for green products? Are firms really interested in improving the environment? Or are they disingenuously marketing products or services as environmentally friendly, with the goal of gaining public approval and sales rather than actually improving the environment? This type of exploitation is common enough that it even has produced a new term: **greenwashing**. Consumers need to question whether a firm is spending significantly more money and time advertising being green and operating with consideration for the environment than actually spending these resources on environmentally sound practices.

> " Demand for green-oriented products has been a boon to the firms that supply them. "

ethical&societal dilemma 5.1

Green Cereal?[iv]

At times it may seem that massive conglomerates are slow to change, but some companies are clearly learning some lessons when it comes to responsible sourcing. Just a few years ago, Nestlé suffered terrible consumer backlash when it agreed to purchase a small amount of palm oil (used in its chocolate candies) from a company that cleared rain forests to access the palms.

Wary of such reactions, General Mills (GM) quickly promised that all the palm oil used in any of its products and packaging would come from responsible, sustainable sources by 2015. Recent estimates suggest that such moves are achieving some success. The rate of Amazonian deforestation in 2012 was lower than at any other point since the Brazilian government started tracking this statistic in 1988. But neither GM nor any of its competitors in the consumer packaged-goods industry have reached the goal of complete sustainability quite yet.

Determined not to limit itself to palm oil, GM also committed to improving the trade

conditions for vanilla farmers that supply the raw material for the traditional, favorite flavor of its Häagen-Dazs ice cream. With a two-year investment of $125 million in Madagascar, GM plans to train small vanilla farmers in sustainable methods that also increase crop quality, such as yield improvements and curing techniques. Ideally, these tactics also will enhance the earnings of local farmers and their communities.

Next, GM helped found—in collaboration with the U.S. Department of Agriculture (USDA) and Environmental Protection Agency (EPA)—the U.S. Food Waste Challenge. This initiative seeks not only to reduce the environmental impacts of waste collected in landfills but also to address spreading food insecurity concerns. By reducing the waste and loss of food products, the collaborators hope to feed more people or at least use the edible remainders for productive uses such as animal feed.

These examples reflect GM's overall sustainability mission and efforts. It has released Global Responsibility Reports annually for more than 40 years. It also touts its efforts widely through its blog, press releases, and other

The demand for palm oil can often lead to rain forests, such as this one, being clear cut.
© Warwick Lister-Kaye/Getty Images RF

communications. In this sense, GM runs the risk that skeptical consumers will come to believe it publicizes its good works to cover up bad behavior. But as the CEO of General Mills has readily acknowledged, "We're finding opportunities to collaborate with business, government and non-governmental organizations on important systemic solutions. While we're proud of our progress, we also know there is still much more to be done. We are committed to continued progress in these areas. Our business requires it and future generations depend on it."

Privacy Concerns More and more consumers worldwide sense a loss of privacy. At the same time that the Internet has created an explosion of accessibility to consumer information, improvements in computer storage facilities and the manipulation of information have led to more and better security and credit check services. Yet controversies still erupt, and some observers suggest hackers are just getting more effective. In 2013, for example, Target suffered a massive security breach that allowed hackers to steal credit and debit card information for 40 million customers, as well as personal information, including phone numbers and addresses, for another 70 million.[31]

Every time a consumer surfs the web and clicks on a site, online marketers can place "cookies" on that user's computer, showing them where he or she starts, proceeds, and ends the online encounter—as well as what he or she buys, and doesn't. For many consumers, such close access to their behaviors is an unacceptable invasion of privacy.

Realizing consumers are upset about this issue, the marketing industry as a whole has sought to find solutions and self-regulations that would calm customers, satisfy cautious regulators, and still enable marketing firms to gain access to invaluable information about consumer behaviors. Those attempts appear to have stalled. The online marketing industry simply has not been able to agree about how to police itself. It looks like it may be up to Congress to address this growing issue.[32]

Technological Advances

Technological advances have accelerated during the past decade, improving the value of both products and services. Consumers have constant access to the Internet everywhere through services such as Wi-Fi, Mobile Hotspots, 4G, and LTE. Smartphones using the iOS and Android systems allow for greater computing, data storage, and communication. Tablet computers, starting with the iPad, have extended mobile computing even further by offering a larger mobile interface in environments that traditionally have limited access.

These examples of advanced technology make consumers increasingly dependent on the help they receive from the providers of the technology. As Marketing Analytics 5.1 details, Netflix relies on its advanced technological capabilities not just to suggest which movies we should watch but also to develop new content that it is confident we will like.

Near field communication technology takes payments, coupons, and loyalty card data from customers as they walk by the scanner. The next broad wave of mobile applications is likely to expand the use of wireless payments, through applications such as Google Wallet, Master Card's Easy Pay, and Isis Mobile Wallet, all of which enable customers' phones to serve as m-wallets.

From the firm's perspective, the technology called radio frequency identification device (RFID) enables it to track an item from the moment it was manufactured, through the distribution system, to the retail store, and into the hands of the final consumer. Because they are able to determine exactly how much of each product is at a given point in the supply chain, retailers can also communicate with their suppliers and collaboratively plan to meet their inventory needs.

Mobile devices enhance the customer's experience by making it easier to interact with the manufacturer or retailer or other customers, and they add a new channel of access, which makes customers more loyal and more likely to spend more with a particular retailer. Walgreens' applications and Web Pickup service allow customers to order prescriptions or review their prescription history, check the in-store inventories, and print photos. As Social and Mobile Marketing 5.2 summarizes, ever more new and exciting technologies seem poised to enter the consumer market.

Economic Situation

Marketers monitor the general **economic situation**, both in their home country and abroad, because it affects the way consumers buy merchandise and spend money. Some major factors that influence the state of an economy include the rate of inflation, foreign currency exchange rates, and interest rates.

Inflation refers to the persistent increase in the prices of goods and services. Increasing prices cause the purchasing power of the dollar to decline; in other words, the dollar buys less than it used to.

In a similar fashion, **foreign currency fluctuations** can influence consumer spending. For instance, in the summer of 2002 the euro was valued at slightly less than US$1. By 2008, it had risen to an all-time high of $1.60, but in early 2015, the euro and the dollar were nearly equivalent.[33] When the euro is more expensive than the dollar, merchandise made in Europe is more costly for Americans, but European shoppers enjoy bargains on U.S. products. When the dollar is worth more than the euro, American-made products become more costly for European consumers, but U.S. buyers can get great deals in Europe.

Interest rates represent the cost of borrowing money. When customers borrow money from a bank, they agree to pay back the loan, plus the interest that accrues. The interest, in effect, is the cost to the customers or the fee the bank charges those customers for borrowing the money. Likewise, if a customer opens a savings account at a bank, he or she will earn

technological advances Macroenvironmental factor that has greatly contributed to the improvement of the value of both products and services in the past few decades.

economic situation Macroeconomic factor that affects the way consumers buy merchandise and spend money, both in a marketer's home country and abroad; see also *inflation, foreign currency fluctuations,* and *interest rates.*

inflation Refers to the persistent increase in the prices of goods and services.

foreign currency fluctuations Changes in the value of a country's currency relative to the currency of another country; can influence consumer spending.

interest rates These represent the cost of borrowing money.

Marketing Analytics

When the Best Is Good Enough: Netflix's Stellar Predictive Analytics[v]

Netflix's data analytics are groundbreaking. In academic circles, its influence has been called a "scientific renaissance" because of the techniques the streaming service has pioneered in its efforts to handle the massive amounts of data it deals in, as well as process payments from across the globe. The power and precision of Netflix's predictive analytics have become such common knowledge that even Netflix pokes fun at itself. In one April Fool's joke, it revised its recommended television and movie categories to include classifications such as "TV Shows Where Defiantly Crossed Arms Mean Business!" Netflix gathers data about every aspect of the viewing process, including not just the basics, such as customer ratings, searches, time of day and week, and location, but also customer behaviors that take place during the movie, such as rewinds, fast-forwards, pauses, and how long they let the credits roll. Going even a step further, Netflix analyzes every hue of color contained in the cover art of the options that it offers and can create a profile of the average color of titles viewed by each customer.

Netflix clearly relies on these customer data to create its hallmark personalized suggestions. But in 2010, Netflix chose not to enhance its ability to personalize any further. In 2009, a team of mathematicians created a new algorithm that would have improved Netflix's personalization by 10 percent, in response to a company-sponsored contest. But Netflix never implemented the improved algorithm. Why? There simply wasn't enough value to be gained from it. Various studies show that, even for the most personal choices, including their love lives, people often forgo what they know already for the thrill of what's new. Thus, Netflix decided that it could deliver more value to its customers by offering something new, rather than a personalized version of what they wanted yesterday. Accordingly, it has

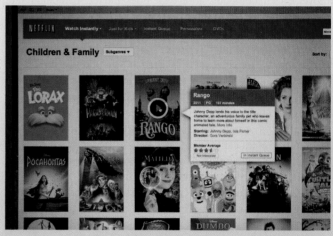

Netflix relies on its advanced technological capabilities not just to suggest which movies we should watch but also to develop new content that it is confident we will like.
© Victor J. Blue/Bloomberg/Getty Images

changed its strategy and its uses of predictive analytics to focus more on creating original content.

Netflix challenges traditional approaches to content development by using data to help make both new show and production decisions. This approach has almost guaranteed the success of the shows, as evidenced by the release of the third season of the award-winning series *House of Cards*. Before this release, the show experienced an unprecedented increase in fans on Facebook and Twitter, approximately double the increase that occurred prior to the Season 2 premier. This jump was especially notable, because a show's social growth usually slows after its first or second season. Even though the third season initially brought some mixed reviews, many viewers already had finished watching the entire season, just a week or so after its release.

interest on the amount saved, which means the interest becomes the fee the consumer gets for loaning the money to the bank. If the interest rate goes up, consumers have an incentive to save more because they earn more for loaning the bank their money; when interest rates go down, however, consumers generally borrow more.

How do these three important economic factors—inflation, foreign currency fluctuations, and interest rates—affect firms' ability to market goods and services? Shifts in the three economic factors make marketing easier for some and harder for others. For instance, when inflation increases, consumers probably don't buy less food, but they may shift their expenditures

> " HOW DO THESE THREE IMPORTANT ECONOMIC FACTORS— INFLATION, FOREIGN CURRENCY FLUCTUATIONS, AND INTEREST RATES—AFFECT FIRMS' ABILITY TO MARKET GOODS AND SERVICES? SHIFTS IN THE THREE ECONOMIC FACTORS MAKE MARKETING EASIER FOR SOME AND HARDER FOR OTHERS. "

U.S. tourists are flocking to other countries like the UK to shop because the value of the dollar is high compared to other currencies like the pound sterling.
© Samir Hussein/Getty Images Entertainment/Getty Images

from expensive steaks to less expensive hamburgers. Grocery stores and inexpensive restaurants win, but expensive restaurants lose. Consumers also buy less discretionary merchandise, though off-price and discount retailers often gain ground at the expense of their full-price competitors. Similarly, the sales of expensive jewelry, fancy cars, and extravagant vacations decrease, but the sale of low-cost luxuries, such as personal care products and home entertainment, tends to increase.

political/regulatory environment Comprises political parties, government organizations, and legislation and laws.

Political/Regulatory Environment

The **political/regulatory environment** comprises political parties, government organizations, and legislation and laws. Organizations must fully understand and comply with any legislation regarding fair competition, consumer protection, or industry-specific regulation. Since the turn of the 20th century,

Social & Mobile Marketing

The News from This Year's CES[vi]

5.2

Every year, the Consumer Electronics Show (CES) in Las Vegas gets bigger and more impressive, hosting the top names in technology and electronics and providing a harbinger of the things to come. The 2014 version was no exception. Some of the main trends emerging from the show are as follows:

1. *Conversational appliances inside connected homes.* Advances in technology promise that not only will our refrigerators tell us when the milk is getting low, but our washing machines will warn us that the rinse cycle is about to start. Bathroom scales will link to online sites to help dieters keep track of their progress. These smart appliances also will have specific recommendations and services for each member of the household, ensuring individual-level targeting.

2. *Really smart, really sharp, really big televisions.* It might seem as if this trend would be covered in the connected homes prediction, but it is so remarkable that it earned its own place on most lists. Televisions are getting bigger than ever, with improved 4K resolution (four times better than the HD televisions currently on the market). The LEDs are getting better too, with an organic version (OLED) that provides better contrast. Finally, the big screens are curving, such that even if viewers have a relatively small room and must sit close to the television, they can still enjoy the full peripheral view.

3. *Fitness, readily on hand.* For a trade show that stereotypically has appealed to tech geeks, fitness was a major theme at CES. The latest innovations make it far easier for consumers to track their exercise rates, times, and distances, then engage with others by uploading the data to shared sites. Enhancing this ease, many of the fitness

apps depend on technology that users can wear, such that they never need to take it off, if they so choose.

4. *The promise of the driverless car.* Automakers including Toyota, Lexus, and Audi announced collaborations with innovators from companies such as Google and Apple in their ongoing effort to devise a car that can drive itself. Others were slightly less ambitious, such as the impending dashboard-mounted weather and music apps from GM. These models also plan to include 4G LTE hotspots within the cars themselves. In a combined effort, Honda, Hyundai, Audi, and GM are working with the chip manufacturer Nvidia and engineers from Google (along with input from the National Highway Traffic Safety Administration) to develop industry standards to define the rules for linked cars and their in-vehicle mobile apps.

Automakers, such as Toyota, are collaborating with companies including Apple and Google to create a self-driving car.
© Karen Bleier/AFP/Getty Images

> ## In a constantly changing marketing environment, the marketers that succeed are the ones that respond quickly, accurately, and sensitively to their consumers.

the government has enacted laws that promote both fair trade and competition by prohibiting the formation of monopolies or alliances that would damage a competitive marketplace, fostering fair pricing practices for all suppliers and consumers.

The government enacts laws focused on ensuring that companies compete fairly with one another. Although enacted in the early part of the 20th century, they remain the backbone of U.S. legislation protecting competition in commerce. These laws include the 1890 Sherman Antitrust Act that prohibits monopolies and other activities that would restrain trade or competition and makes fair trade within a free market a national goal; the 1914 Clayton Act that supports the Sherman Act by prohibiting the combination of two or more competing corporations through pooling ownership of stock and restricting pricing policies such as price discrimination, exclusive dealing, and tying clauses to different buyers; and the 1936 Robinson-Patman Act that specifically outlaws price discrimination toward wholesalers, retailers, or other producers and requires sellers to make ancillary services or allowances available to all buyers on proportionately equal terms. These laws have been specifically used to increase competition, such as the deregulation of the telephone and energy industries, in which massive conglomerates such as Ma Bell, the nickname for AT&T, were broken into smaller, competing companies.

Legislation has also been enacted to protect consumers in a variety of ways. First, regulations require marketers to abstain from false or misleading advertising practices that might mislead consumers, such as claims that a medication can cure a disease when in fact it causes other health risks. Second, manufacturers are required to refrain from using any harmful or hazardous materials (e.g., lead in toys) that might place a consumer at risk. Third, organizations must adhere to fair and reasonable business practices when they communicate with consumers. For example, they must employ reasonable debt collection methods and disclose any finance charges, and they are limited with regard to their telemarketing and e-mail solicitation activities. A summary of the most significant legislation affecting marketing interests appears in Exhibit 5.5.

▼ **EXHIBIT 5.5** Consumer Protection Legislation

Year	Law	Description
1906	Federal Food and Drug Act	Created the Food and Drug Administration (FDA); prohibited the manufacture or sale of adulterated or fraudulently labeled food and drug products.
1914	Federal Trade Commission	Established the Federal Trade Commission (FTC) to regulate unfair competitive practices and practices that deceive or are unfair to consumers.
1966	Fair Packaging and Labeling Act	Regulates packaging and labeling of consumer goods; requires manufacturers to state the contents of the package, who made it, and the amounts contained within.
1966	Child Protection Act	Prohibits the sale of harmful toys and components to children; sets the standard for child-resistant packaging.
1967	Federal Cigarette Labeling and Advertising Act	Requires cigarette packages to display this warning: "Warning: The Surgeon General Has Determined That Cigarette Smoking Is Dangerous to Your Health."
1972	Consumer Product Safety Act	Created the Consumer Product Safety Commission (CPSC), which has the authority to regulate safety standards for consumer products.
1990	Children's Television Act	Limits the number of commercials shown during children's programming.
1990	Nutrition Labeling and Education Act	Requires food manufacturers to display nutritional contents on product labels.
1995	Telemarketing Sales Rule	Regulates fraudulent activities conducted over the telephone. Violators are subject to fines and actions enforced by the FTC.
2003	Controlling the Assault of Non-Solicited Pornography and Marketing Act of 2003 (CAN-SPAM Act)	Prohibits misleading commercial e-mail, particularly misleading subject and from lines.
2003	Amendment to the Telemarketing Sales Rule	Establishes a National Do Not Call Registry, requiring telemarketers to abstain from calling consumers who opt to be placed on the list.
2003	Do Not Spam Law	Laws created to reduce spam or unwarranted e-mails.
2010	Financial Reform Law	Created the Consumer Financial Protection Bureau whose aim is to enforce appropriate consumer-oriented regulations on a number of financial firms, such as banks, mortgage businesses, and payday and student lenders. It also set up the Financial Services Oversight Council to act as an early warning system.

Responding to the Environment

As the examples throughout this chapter show, many companies engage in tactics and marketing strategies that attempt to respond to multiple developments in the wider environment. For example, responding to pressures from the Federal Communications Commission (political and regulatory environment), the economic status of consumers (economic situation), increasing access to faster broadband capabilities (technological advances), and calls for greater social responsibility (social trends), 14 cable companies agreed to provide low-cost Internet access to impoverished families.[34] This remarkable agreement allows the cable companies to promote their social responsibility. But it also ensures that families whose children are eligible for free lunch programs can gain access to the services, opportunities, and options available only online. In a constantly changing marketing environment, the marketers that succeed are the ones that respond quickly, accurately, and sensitively to their consumers. ■

 check yourself

1. What are the six key macroenvironmental factors?
2. Differentiate between country culture and regional culture.
3. What are some important social trends shaping consumer values and shopping behavior?

 Increase your engagement and learning with Connect Marketing.

These Connect activities, available only through your Connect course, have been designed to make the following concepts more meaningful and applicable:

▶ Marketing Mix: Sporting Goods Click and Drag Activity

▶ Analyzing the Environment: Dole Video Case

▶ A New Car for a New Generation: Ford Video Case

▶ Responding to the Marketing Environment: Seventh Generation Case Analysis

▶ Macroenvironmental Factors: iSeeit! Video

Section 2

Chapter SIX

consumer behavior

LEARNING OBJECTIVES

After reading this chapter, you should be able to:

LO 6-1 Articulate the steps in the consumer buying process.

LO 6-2 Describe the difference between functional and psychological needs.

LO 6-3 Describe factors that affect information search.

LO 6-4 Discuss postpurchase outcomes.

LO 6-5 List the factors that affect the consumer decision process.

LO 6-6 Describe how involvement influences the consumer decision process.

In Chapter 1 we described the added value provided by the latest generation of smart devices, from Google Glass to the Nike Fit band. Our focus was on the remarkable strides made with regard to technology and innovation that have allowed users to track their exercise times, sleep patterns, and food intake,[1] or carry the Internet around with them at all times, mounted in the corner of their vision.[2] As we also noted, Google Glass has so appealed to consumers that they have competed to pay around $1,500, just to be able to be among the first to try out the new technological gadget.

What makes people shell out so much to try a virtually untested technology? What keeps others from giving it a go? And why are so many companies introducing some version of wearable technology, despite some warnings that the trend will never take off among regular consumers? The answers to these questions all revolve around consumer behavior, that is, the "dynamic interaction of affect and cognition, behavior, and the environment by which human beings conduct the exchange aspects of their lives."[3]

For wearable technology, the boom appears likely because consumers seek to behave in ways that add value to their lives. Thus they seek to fulfill needs that they recognize, enjoy themselves, impress

continued on p. 102

101

continued from p. 101

others, and so forth. When a skier realizes that it would be helpful to be able to track altitude at each moment of a run, without having to pull a smartphone or other device out of an inner pocket, a need arises. The Recon ski goggles meet this need because they put lots of data within the skier's line of vision automatically, without having to pause the run, and without exposing any fingers to the elements.[4]

Samsung's Galaxy Gear similarly makes data more accessible but slightly less intrusively by providing a watch that syncs with people's smartphones. Rather than needing an extra hand to check the weather, users can simply glance down at their wrists. In addition, this innovation piggybacks off an existing product, namely, wristwatches, so people already are familiar with the notion of having an information tool encircling their wrists, making this version seem far less foreign. Consumers can feel more confident and perceive less risk, and are therefore more likely to purchase it.[5]

Google is partnering with the vision care insurance company VSP to enable users to add their prescription to their Google Glass, and even cover the costs for those who purchase the associated insurance plan.[6] Because the majority of people in the United States wear prescription glasses,[7] Google Glass ultimately might be more popular if people could integrate their prescription into it.

> Generally, people buy one product or service instead of another because they perceive it to be the better value for them.

Noting the potential health care implications of wearable technology, including wrist bands that help people track their fitness goals, Google is also going a step further with its proposed contact lenses. Rather than providing information, these wearable forms of technology would serve to monitor the glucose levels in people's natural tears, enabling diabetics to keep constant track of their critical numbers without any blood or finger pricking.[8]

Ultimately, the success of wearable technology depends on how consumers perceive it and therefore how they behave toward it. If wearable gadgets fulfill enough needs of consumers without creating too many risks or demanding too much cost, we are all likely to be sporting funny-looking glasses, watches, and other gear soon. If instead the prices and threat of looking absurd are too much for people to bear, wearable tech might just fizzle in the market. ∎

Samsung's smart watches sync with its smartphones.
© Guido Mieth/Getty Images

We are all consumers, and we take this status for granted. But we are also complex and irrational creatures who cannot always explain our own choices and actions. This inability makes the vitally important job of marketing managers even more difficult, in that they must be able to explain consumers' behavior to give marketers as clear an understanding of their customers as possible.

To understand consumer behavior, we must ask *why* people buy goods or services. Using principles and theories from sociology and psychology, marketers have been able to decipher many consumer choices and develop basic strategies for dealing with consumers' behavior. Generally, people buy one product or service instead of another because they perceive it to be the better value for them; that is, the ratio of benefits to costs is higher for a particular product or service than for any other.

However, benefits can be subtle and less than rationally assessed, as we shall see. Consider Katie Smith, who is thinking of buying a new outfit for a job interview. She requires something fashionable but professional looking and doesn't want to spend a lot of money. In making the decision about where she should buy the outfit, Katie asks herself:

- Which alternative gives me the best overall value—the most appropriate yet fashionable outfit at the lowest price?

- Which alternative is the best investment—the outfit that I can get the most use of?

Because Katie might have several reasons to choose a particular store or outfit, it is critical for companies such as Banana Republic or Macy's to key in on the specific benefits that are most important to her. Other factors that might influence Katie go beyond her conscious awareness, which means that the retailers need to be even more well versed in her decision process than she is.[9] Only then can they create a marketing mix that will satisfy Katie.

In this chapter, we explore the process that consumers go through when they buy products and services. Then we discuss the psychological, social, and situational factors that influence this consumer decision process. Throughout the chapter, we emphasize what firms can do to influence consumers to purchase their products and services.

an inline six-cylinder motor, something previously available only in BMW automobiles, combined with a stiff aluminum frame. Thus it offers remarkable power on a lightweight bike, enabling it to outperform both the best luxury touring bikes in terms of comfort and serious sporty motorcycles in terms of speed. Of course, not

need recognition
The beginning of the consumer decision process; occurs when consumers recognize they have an unsatisfied need and want to go from their actual, needy state to a different, desired state.

functional needs
Pertain to the performance of a product or service.

> ## " Regardless of the level of your hunger, your desire for ice cream will never be satisfied by any type of salad. "

THE CONSUMER DECISION PROCESS

The consumer decision process model represents the steps that consumers go through before, during, and after making purchases.[10] Because marketers often find it difficult to determine how consumers make their purchasing decisions, it is useful for us to break down the process into a series of steps and examine each individually, as in Exhibit 6.1.

Need Recognition

The consumer decision process begins when consumers recognize they have an unsatisfied need, and they would like to go from their actual, needy state to a different, desired state. The greater the discrepancy between these two states, the greater the **need recognition** will be. For example, your stomach tells you that you are hungry, and you would rather not have that particular feeling. If you are only a little hungry, you may pass it off and decide to eat later. But if your stomach is growling and you cannot concentrate, the *need*—the difference between your actual (hungry) state and your desired (not hungry) state—is greater and you'll want to eat immediately to get to your desired state. Furthermore, your hunger conceivably could be satisfied by a nice healthy salad, but what you really want is a bowl of ice cream. *Wants* are goods or services that are not necessarily needed but are desired.[11] Regardless of the level of your hunger, your desire for ice cream will never be satisfied by any type of salad. Consumer needs like these can be classified as functional, psychological, or both.[12]

everyone in need of solving a transportation function needs the power and speed of a BMW. A bicycle, a motor scooter, or a car can perform this function as well. It just depends on the specific needs of the purchaser.

▼ **EXHIBIT 6.1** The Consumer Decision Process

| LO 6-1 | Articulate the steps in the consumer buying process. |

Functional Needs **Functional needs** pertain to the performance of a product or service. For years, BMW has made functionally superior motorcycles. BMW's K1600 model has

The figure shows the stages: Need recognition → Information search → Alternative evaluation → Purchase → Post-purchase.

"MOST GOODS AND SERVICES SEEK TO SATISFY BOTH FUNCTIONAL AND PSYCHOLOGICAL NEEDS, ALBEIT TO DIFFERENT DEGREES."

What needs does a BMW K1600 satisfy?
© ZUMA Press, Inc./Alamy

As Marketing Analytics 6.1 notes, virtually everyone must pay taxes, and H&R Block seeks to convince taxpayers to let it help them meet this highly functional need.

| LO 6-2 | Describe the difference between functional and psychological needs. |

Psychological Needs **Psychological needs** pertain to the personal gratification consumers associate with a product and/or service.[13] Purses, for instance, provide a functional need—to transport wallets and other personal items and keep them organized and safe. So why would anyone pay more than

$5,000 for a purse that does not perform these tasks any better than a $100 purse? Because they seek to satisfy psychological needs. Each year, Lana Marks produces a single Cleopatra clutch purse valued at $250,000. The purse might be embellished, such as one version that featured more than 1,500 black and white diamonds, 18-carat gold, and alligator skin. The company permits one star each year to bring its purse to the Oscars; recent winners of this informal contest were Charlize Theron and Helen Mirren.[14] Even though these bags are not known for being particularly practical, strong demand for Lana Marks bags persists among women who love exciting (and expensive) purses.

These examples highlight that most goods and services seek to satisfy both functional and psychological needs, albeit to different degrees. Whereas the functional characteristics of a BMW K1600 are its main selling point, it also maintains a fashionable appeal for bikers and comes in several colors to

Do Lana Marks bags, like this one carried by Bingbing Li, satisfy psychological or functional needs?
© Ethan Miller/Staff/Getty Images

match buyers' aesthetic preferences. Lana Marks purses satisfy psychological needs that overshadow the functional needs, though they still ultimately serve the function of carrying personal items.

Successful marketing requires determining the correct balance of functional and psychological needs that best appeal to the firm's target markets.

Search for Information

The second step, after a consumer recognizes a need, is to search for information about the various options that exist to satisfy that need. The length and intensity of the search are based on the degree of perceived risk associated with purchasing the product or service. If the way your hair is cut is important to your appearance and self-image, you may engage in an involved search for the right salon and stylist. Alternatively, an athlete looking for a short buzz cut might go to the closest, most convenient, and cheapest barber shop. Regardless of the required search level, there are two key types of information search: internal and external.

psychological needs Pertain to the personal gratification consumers associate with a product or service.

internal search for information Occurs when the buyer examines his or her own memory and knowledge about the product or service, gathered through past experiences.

external search for information Occurs when the buyer seeks information outside his or her personal knowledge base to help make the buying decision.

Internal Search for Information In an **internal search for information**, the buyer examines his or her own memory and knowledge about the product or service gathered through past experiences. For example, every time Katie wants to eat salad for lunch, she and her friends go to Sweet Tomatoes, but if she's craving dessert, she heads straight to The Cheesecake Factory. In making these choices, she relies on her memory of past experiences when she has eaten at these restaurant chains.

External Search for Information In an **external search for information**, the buyer seeks information outside his or her personal knowledge base to help make the buying decision. Consumers might fill in their personal knowledge

Marketing Analytics
6.1

Tax Time Tactics by H&R Block[i]

Taxes may be among the few certainties in life, but they usually are not considered one of the more fun features. But in an attempt to make the inevitable a little less painful, H&R Block is seeking to make "tax season" a time that regular consumers actually can enjoy, if they do it right. The basis for the claim stems mostly from the company's in-depth analysis of its customer data. An elite analytics team, The Tax Institute at H&R Block, learned by pouring over reams of data that approximately half of the consumers who do their own taxes make mistakes in their returns. Then the team of tax attorneys and CPAs went deeper into the data and determined that about half of those mistaken returns led to people receiving smaller refunds than they actually deserved. In turn, it developed an advertising campaign that promises to "get your billions back" for taxpayers who rely on its professional services.

But H&R Block also acknowledges that more than one-third of U.S. taxpayers continue to do their taxes themselves, so it offers online assistance too. With its software, taxpayers can complete and submit their federal and state income tax returns for less than $10, while still receiving some limited online help from the tax professionals. Although it has been offering the online service for 15 years, its more recent analysis of customer data showed that a $9.99 price would be likely to drive interest while also reinforcing the enjoyable idea of saving money. Moreover, confusion among taxpayers about new laws and regulations (especially those related to the Affordable Care Act) created another opening for H&R Block to attract potential customers, promising that it can help them understand their tax liabilities and

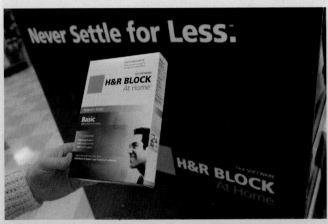

H&R Block uses analytics to make tax preparation more enjoyable, at a price that its customers deem reasonable.
© Paul Sakuma/AP Photo

responsibilities, whether they come in to brick-and-mortar storefronts with all their receipts or aim to complete their paperwork at home.

These moves reflect the tax service's recent adoption of an advanced data analytics platform called Domo, which combines various sources and types of information into a single, straightforward format. According to H&R Block's manager of analytics and operations, "With Domo, we already have alignment on what we are measuring, so we no longer spend time each week discussing the data itself. Instead, we can ask better questions about the business and make decisions based on the information we have."

Katie liked the picture of Reese Witherspoon in jeans that she found in a magazine so much that she navigated to TrueFit.com and purchased them.

© JB Lacroix/WireImage/Getty Images

magazines, television, or radio. Perhaps the most common sources of external information these days are online search engines, such as Google and Bing.

The Internet provides information in various ways.[15] For example, while watching an episode of Fox's *Glee,* Katie saw the character Marley wearing a fantastic outfit that included a flare dress and silver pendant. She pulled her laptop over, went to WornOnTv.net, and found the focal episode, which in turn told her where to purchase the items she loved. The pendant was designed by Baroni and available for $119, and the dress cost $48.[16] But Katie is also a savvy shopper, so when she searched for "Baroni Expressive Pendant" on Bing, she found that she could get it at a lower price from another retailer. Satisfied with that purchase, she began flipping through a magazine and saw Reese Witherspoon wearing a pair of adorable jeans. This time she navigated directly to TrueFit .com, which featured those very jeans, designed by 7 for All Mankind, on its home page.[17] Katie entered her measurements and style preferences, and the website returned recommendations of jeans that would be a good fit for her.

All these examples are external searches for information. Katie used the television show's dedicated site to find a style she liked; she referred to a magazine for additional style tips; and she found jeans that would be a perfect fit for her using the web. All these events took place without Katie ever leaving her home to go to the store or try on dozens of pairs of pants.

Factors Affecting Consumers' Search Processes

It is important for marketers to understand the many factors that affect consumers' search processes. Among them are the following three factors: perceived benefits versus perceived costs of search, the locus of control, and the actual or perceived risk.

> **LO 6-3** Describe factors that affect information search.

The Perceived Benefits versus Perceived Costs of Search Is it worth the time and effort to search for information about a product or service? For instance, most families spend a lot of time researching the housing market in their preferred area before they make a purchase because homes are a very expensive and important purchase with significant safety and enjoyment implications. They likely spend much less time researching which inexpensive dollhouse to buy for the youngest member of the family.[18]

gaps by talking with friends, family, or a salesperson. They can also scour commercial media for unsponsored and (it is hoped) unbiased information, such as that available through *Consumer Reports,* or peruse sponsored media such as

"Is it worth the time and effort to search for information about a product or service?"

The Locus of Control People who have an **internal locus of control** believe they have some control over the outcomes of their actions, in which case they generally engage in more search activities. With an **external locus of control**, consumers believe that fate or other external factors control all outcomes. In that case, they believe it doesn't matter how much information they gather; if they make a wise decision, it isn't to their credit, and if they make a poor one, it isn't their fault. People who do a lot of research before purchasing individual stocks have an internal locus of control; those who purchase mutual funds are more likely to believe that they can't predict the market and probably have an external locus of control. These beliefs have widespread effects. For example, when people believe that they can choose their own consumption goals (internal locus of control), they work harder to achieve them than if those goals feel imposed upon them (external locus of control).[19] Social and Mobile Marketing 6.1 discusses how consumers are gaining a greater internal locus of control over their health by using smartphone apps.

internal locus of control Refers to when consumers believe they have some control over the outcomes of their actions, in which case they generally engage in more search activities.

external locus of control Refers to when consumers believe that fate or other external factors control all outcomes.

Social & Mobile Marketing 6.1
The Future of Health Is Mobile[ii]

A host of new applications and mobile links make it easier than ever for consumers to maintain their own health and well-being with just a few clicks. Whether the condition is chronic or new, these health-related offerings seek to make it easier for health care consumers to understand their options, consider solutions, and recognize when to seek immediate medical care. They also facilitate providers' efforts to stay up to date with the latest treatments and advances. Consider a few examples:

- An award-winning app mySugr turns the tedious task of glucose monitoring into a game for diabetics. They earn points for each data entry they make that helps them tame a monster named Diabetes. The app enables users to record their food consumption and take snapshots of what they have eaten, provides immediate data analyses, produces a summary report that users can send their doctors, and maintains the data in a central location.

- Doctor Mole allows people to take a selfie (i.e., self-portrait) of any suspicious skin growth. Using augmented reality technology, the app applies the well-established criteria for assessing the risk associated with each mole (i.e., asymmetry, borders, color, diameter). Users can determine whether they have a potentially cancerous malignancy or just a new freckle.

- With BurnMed, users draw on a displayed image of a body to indicate the extent of the burn suffered, whether by themselves, a friend, or a patient. This app seeks to target both laypeople and medical practitioners. In a lay setting, users can determine the seriousness of a burn they might have suffered at home. In a medical practice, emergency staff can quickly determine the appropriate treatment when faced with a crisis such as a tanker explosion that burns hundreds of victims.

- The vCath training tool is expressly for medical students who need to learn to insert neurosurgical catheters. In patients this step is critical and risky because students have little leeway for practicing their technique. The app enables them to do so virtually, as many times as they wish, before confronting any patients.

Along with these dedicated apps, various hospitals and doctors are experimenting with software that reminds patients to take their medicine or when their next appointments are. By encouraging positive behaviors, these technology advances should lead to greater consumer health and happiness as well as benefits for society as a whole.

Smartphone apps empower consumers to take control of their health in exciting new ways.
Courtesy mySugr/GmbH. -K. Rose.

performance risk Involves the perceived danger inherent in a poorly performing product or service.

financial risk Risk associated with a monetary outlay; includes the initial cost of the purchase, as well as the costs of using the item or service.

social risk The fears that consumers suffer when they worry others might not regard their purchases positively.

physiological risk The fear of an actual harm should a product not perform properly.

safety risk See *physiological risk.*

psychological risk Associated with the way people will feel if the product or service does not convey the right image.

Actual or Perceived Risk Five types of risk associated with purchase decisions can delay or discourage a purchase: performance, financial, social, physiological, and psychological. The higher the risk, the more likely the consumer is to engage in an extended search.

Performance risk involves the perceived danger inherent in a poorly performing product or service. An example of performance risk is the possibility that Katie Smith's new interview outfit is prone to shrinking when dry cleaned.

Financial risk is risk associated with a monetary outlay and includes the initial cost of the purchase as well as the costs of using the item or service.[20] Katie is concerned not only that her new outfit will provide her with the professional appearance she is seeking but also that the cost of dry cleaning will not be exorbitant. Retailers recognize buying professional apparel can

perform properly. Although physiological risk is typically not an issue with apparel, it can be an important issue when buying other products, such as a car. External agencies and government bodies publish safety ratings for cars to help assuage this risk. Consumers compare the safety records of their various choices because they recognize the real danger to their well-being if the automobile they purchase fails to perform a basic task, such as stopping when the driver steps on the brakes or protecting the passengers in the cabin even if the car flips.

Finally, **psychological risks** are those risks associated with the way people will feel if the product or service does not convey the right image. Katie Smith, thinking of her outfit purchase, read several fashion magazines and sought her friends' opinions because she wanted people to think she looked great in the outfit, and she wanted to get the job!

> " WHEREAS PERFORMANCE RISK INVOLVES WHAT MIGHT HAPPEN IF A PRODUCT DOES NOT PERFORM AS EXPECTED, PHYSIOLOGICAL (OR SAFETY) RISK REFERS TO THE FEAR OF AN ACTUAL HARM SHOULD THE PRODUCT NOT PERFORM PROPERLY. "

be a financial burden and therefore offer guarantees that the products they sell will perform as expected. Their suppliers are also well aware that dry cleaning is expensive and can limit the life of the garment, so many offer easy-to-care-for washable fabrics.

Social risk involves the fears that consumers suffer when they worry others might not regard their purchases positively. When buying a fashionable outfit, consumers like Katie consider what their friends would like. Alternatively, because this job interview is so important, Katie might make a conscious effort to assert a distinctive identity or make a statement by buying a unique, more stylish, and possibly more expensive outfit than her friends would typically buy. She also hopes to impress her prospective boss rather than her pals with her choice.

Physiological risk could also be called **safety risk**. Whereas performance risk involves what might happen if a product does not perform as expected, physiological (or safety) risk refers to the fear of an actual harm should the product not

Recent research suggests that psychological risks might help explain why consumers often think that "bigger is better." In particular, this research helps explain why some enjoy buying large-sized menu items at restaurants. Especially when consumers feel powerless or more vulnerable, they equate larger sizes—whether in televisions, houses, or menu items—with improved status.[21]

Evaluation of Alternatives

Once a consumer has recognized a problem and explored the possible options, he or she must sift through the choices available and evaluate the alternatives. Alternative evaluation often occurs while the consumer is engaged in the process of information search. For example, Katie Smith would rule out various stores because she knows they won't carry the style she needs for the job interview. Once in the store, she would try on lots of outfits and eliminate those that do not fit, do not look good on her, or are not appropriate attire for the occasion. Consumers forgo alternative evaluations altogether when buying habitual (convenience) products; you'll rarely catch a loyal Pepsi drinker buying Coca-Cola.

Attribute Sets Research has shown that a consumer's mind organizes and categorizes alternatives to aid his or her decision process. **Universal sets** include all possible choices for a product category, but because it would be unwieldy for a person to recall all possible alternatives for every purchase decision, marketers tend to focus on only a subset of choices. One important subset is **retrieval sets**, which are those brands or stores that can be readily brought forth from memory. Another is a consumer's **evoked set**, which comprises the alternative brands or stores that the consumer states he or she would consider when making a purchase decision. If a firm can get its brand or store into a consumer's evoked set, it has increased the likelihood of purchase and therefore reduced search time because the consumer will think specifically of that brand when considering choices.

Katie Smith knows that there are a lot of apparel stores (universal set). However, only some have the style that she is looking for, such as Macy's, The Gap, and Banana Republic (retrieval set). She recalls that Macy's is where her mother shops and The Gap is a favorite of her younger sister. But she is sure that Banana Republic and Macy's carry business attire she would like, so only those stores are in her evoked set.

When consumers begin to evaluate different alternatives, they often base their evaluations on a set of important attributes or evaluative criteria. **Evaluative criteria** consist of salient, or important, attributes about a particular product. For example, when Katie is looking for her outfit, she might consider things like the selling price, fit, materials and construction quality, reputation of the brand, and the service support that the retailer offers. At times, however, it becomes difficult to evaluate different brands or stores because there are so many choices,[22] especially when those choices involve aspects of the garment that are difficult to evaluate, such as materials and construction quality.

Consumers use several shortcuts to simplify the potentially complicated decision process: determinant attributes and consumer decision rules. **Determinant attributes** are product or service features that are important to the buyer and on which competing brands or stores are perceived to differ.[23] Because many important and desirable criteria are equal among the various choices, consumers look for something special—a determinant attribute—to differentiate one brand or store from another. Determinant attributes may appear perfectly rational, such as health and nutrition claims offered by certain foods and beverages, or they may be more subtle and psychologically based, such as the red soles on a pair of Christian Louboutin heels. Ethical and Societal Dilemma 6.1 highlights the use of determinant attributes describing food and beverages marketed as natural when in fact they are not.

Macy's is part of the <u>retrieval set</u> *of stores available to women for business apparel, but Banana Republic is in the* <u>evoked set</u> *for young women looking for business apparel.*

Left: © McGraw-Hill Education/Mark Dierker, photographer; Right: Sang Tan/AP Photo

consumer decision rules The set of criteria that consumers use consciously or subconsciously to quickly and efficiently select from among several alternatives.

compensatory decision rule At work when the consumer is evaluating alternatives and trades off one characteristic against another, such that good characteristics compensate for bad ones.

multi-attribute model A compensatory model of customer decision making based on the notion that customers see a product as a collection of attributes or characteristics. The model uses a weighted average score based on the importance of various attributes and performance on those issues.

Consumer Decision Rules **Consumer decision rules** are the set of criteria that consumers use consciously or subconsciously to quickly and efficiently select from among several alternatives. These rules are typically either compensatory or noncompensatory.

Compensatory A **compensatory decision rule** assumes that the consumer, when evaluating alternatives, trades off one characteristic against another, such that good characteristics compensate for bad characteristics.[24] For instance, Hanna Jackson is looking to buy breakfast cereal and is considering several factors such as taste, calories, price, and natural/organic claims. But even if the cereal is priced a little higher than Hanna was planning to spend, a superb overall rating offsets, or compensates for, the higher price.

Although Hanna probably would not go through the formal process of making the purchasing decision based on the **multi-attribute model** described in Exhibit 6.2, this exhibit illustrates how a compensatory model would work.[25] Hanna assigns weights to the importance of each factor. These weights

ethical&societal dilemma   6.1

Wearing the "Healthy" Label: Natural and Organic Foods[iii]

With competition for shelf space always at a premium, today's supermarket aisles are more crowded than ever. Much of the new competition comes from natural and organic foods, which comprised about 10 and 5 percent, respectively, of the more than $700 billion U.S. food industry in 2013.

For a consumer facing a dizzying array of choices, these natural foods offer a unique appeal: They promise to improve personal and planetary health. Organic and natural food companies claim that their foods are safer and more nutritious because they are produced with only natural ingredients.

Consumers generally believe that these claims mean the food contains no artificial or highly processed ingredients. Yet Snapple's "natural" bottled iced tea contains high-fructose corn syrup, a highly processed and controversial form of sugar. In California, most organic strawberry farmers use seeds and plants from nurseries that are not organic, including growers producing fruit for Driscoll Strawberry Associates, the largest berry distributor in the world. The farmers argue that once their plants bear fruit, they halt their use of chemical pesticides

and herbicides, so the berries themselves are still organic. These companies thus might be contradicting consumer expectations, but they are not actually violating federal requirements.

The U.S. Department of Agriculture (USDA) regulates the production of organic foods. Products bearing the USDA Organic label must be grown using organic, not conventional, farming methods. That regulation means using natural fertilizers such as manure or compost, beneficial insects or birds rather than chemical herbicides to control insects, and crop rotation or other manual methods rather than chemical herbicides to control weeds. Animals raised for meat production must be given organic feed and access to the outdoors rather than antibiotics, growth hormones, and other medications.

Yet the USDA's National Organic Program (NOP) regulations do not explicitly govern the production of seeds and planting stock. Advocates who want to see sustainable production methods used throughout the food-growing process have called on the USDA to outlaw the use of chemical fumigants, including methyl bromide, a widely used pesticide and soil sterilizer known to deplete the ozone layer. Furthermore, NOP regulations allow conventional agricultural stock to be used whenever organically grown seeds and plants are not commercially available.

Nor does the USDA regulate the production of foods labeled "natural," except for meats and poultry, which must be minimally processed and free of artificial colors, flavors, sweeteners,

How healthy is Snapple?
© Bloomberg/Contributor/Getty Images

preservatives, and ingredients. No such specifics govern other foods that choose to carry the natural label rather than an organic claim.

For the consumer, the organic and natural food experience is also about perception. Some shoppers may believe these foods deliver healthful benefits, but studies also reveal that simply identifying a grocery item as a healthy food option may affect their eating experience. Specifically, people may perceive that health-oriented foods do not taste good or satisfy their need to curb their appetites. Students given snacks labeled "health bars" reported feeling hungry afterward and craving foods they enjoyed more. In another study, respondents widely perceived "that 'healthy' isn't going to meet enjoyment goals," which likely reflects consumers' assumption that healthy foods won't taste good.

▼ **EXHIBIT 6.2** Compensatory Purchasing Multi-Attribute Model for Buying Cereal

	Taste	Calories	Natural/Organic Claims	Price	Overall Score
Importance Weight	**0.4**	**0.1**	**0.3**	**0.2**	
Cheerios	10	8	6	8	8.2
Post	8	9	8	3	7.1
Kashi	6	8	10	5	7.2

Photos: Michael J. Hruby

noncompensatory decision rule At work when consumers choose a product or service on the basis of a subset of its characteristics, regardless of the values of its other attributes.

conversion rate Percentage of consumers who buy a product after viewing it.

Rent the Runway customers rent haute couture dresses, handbags, and jewelry for a fraction of the purchase price, enjoy them for a few days, and mail them back.
© Web Pix/Alamy

must add up to 1.0. So, for instance, taste is the most important, with a weight of 0.4, and calories are least important, with a weight of 0.1. She assigns weights to how well each of the cereals might perform, with 1 being very poor and 10 being very good. Hanna thinks Cheerios has the best taste, so she assigns it a 10. Then she multiplies each performance rating by its importance rating to get an overall score for each cereal. The rating for Cheerios in this example is the highest of the three cereals [$(0.4 \times 10) + (0.1 \times 8) + (0.3 \times 6) + (0.2 \times 8) = 8.2$)]. This multi-attributes model allows the trade-off between the various factors to be incorporated explicitly into a consumer's purchase decision.

Noncompensatory Sometimes, however, consumers use a **noncompensatory decision rule** in which they choose a product or service on the basis of one characteristic or one subset of a characteristic, regardless of the values of its other attributes.[26] So although Cheerios received the highest overall score of 8.2, Hanna might still pick Kashi because she is particularly sensitive to claims of natural or organic contents, and this brand earned the highest score on this attribute (i.e., a 10). Once a consumer has considered the possible alternatives and evaluated the pros and cons of each, he or she can move toward a purchase decision.

Purchase and Consumption

After evaluating the alternatives, customers are ready to buy. However, they don't always patronize the store or purchase the brand or item on which they had originally decided. It may not be available at the retail store, for example. Retailers therefore

turn to the **conversion rate** to measure how well they have converted purchase intentions into purchases. One method of measuring the conversion rate is the number of real or virtual abandoned carts in the retailer's store or website.

For different types of companies, the conversion rate also refers to rentals (e.g., Netflix) or to outright purchases (e.g., haute couture), though some of these lines appear to be blurring as consumers seek new ways to access the items they want. At Rent the Runway, fashion- and budget-conscious shoppers gain temporary possession of the latest fashions from big names, including Badgley Mischka, Kate Spade, and Vera Wang. As if they were dealing with movies on DVDs, members rent haute couture dresses, handbags, jewelry, and even wedding gowns; pay anywhere between $50 and $400 for their chosen items; receive the glam wear in the mail within a few days; and then return the items after their fabulous affair has ended.[27]

LO 6-4 Discuss postpurchase outcomes.

Postpurchase

The final step of the consumer decision process is postpurchase behavior. Marketers are particularly interested in postpurchase behavior because it entails actual rather than potential customers. Satisfied customers, whom marketers hope to create, become loyal, purchase again, and spread positive word of mouth, so they are quite important. There are three possible postpurchase outcomes, as illustrated in

Exhibit 6.3: customer satisfaction, postpurchase cognitive dissonance, and customer loyalty (or disloyalty).

Customer Satisfaction

Setting unrealistically high consumer expectations of the product through advertising, personal selling, or other types of promotion may lead to higher initial sales, but it eventually will result in dissatisfaction if the product fails to achieve high performance expectations. (For a related discussion about communication gaps, see Chapter 13.) This failure can lead to dissatisfied customers and the potential for negative word of mouth.[28] Setting customer expectations too low is an equally dangerous strategy. Many retailers fail to put their best foot forward. For instance, no matter how good the merchandise and service may be, if a store is not clean and appealing from the entrance, customers are not likely to enter.

Marketers can take several steps to ensure postpurchase satisfaction:

- Build realistic expectations, not too high and not too low.

- Demonstrate correct product use—improper usage can cause dissatisfaction.

- Stand behind the product or service by providing money-back guarantees and warranties.

- Encourage customer feedback, which cuts down on negative word of mouth and helps marketers adjust their offerings.

- Periodically make contact with customers and thank them for their support. This contact reminds customers that the marketer cares about their business and wants them to be satisfied. It also provides an opportunity to correct any problems. Customers appreciate human contact, though it is more expensive for marketers than e-mail or postal mail contacts.

Postpurchase Cognitive Dissonance **Postpurchase cognitive dissonance** is an internal conflict that arises from an inconsistency between two beliefs or between beliefs and behavior. For example, you might have buyer's remorse after purchasing an expensive television because you question whether this high-priced version offers appreciably better quality than a set of similar size but at a lower price—or whether you need a television at all, considering your ability to stream content through your computer. Postpurchase cognitive dissonance generally occurs when a consumer questions the appropriateness of a purchase after his or her decision has been made.

Postpurchase cognitive dissonance is especially likely for products that are expensive, are infrequently purchased, do not work as intended, or are associated with high levels of risk. Marketers direct efforts at consumers after the purchase is made to address this issue.[29] General Electric sends a letter to purchasers of its appliances, positively reinforcing the message that the customer made a wise decision by mentioning the high quality that went into the product's design and production. Some clothing manufacturers include a tag on their garments to offer the reassurance that because of their special manufacturing process, perhaps designed to provide a soft, vintage appearance, there may be variations in color that have no effect on the quality of the item. After a pang of dissonance, satisfaction may then set in.

Let's check back in with our friend Katie to recognize these effects. When Katie purchased her interview outfit at Macy's, she tried it on for some of her friends. Her boyfriend said he loved it, but several of her girlfriends seemed less impressed. Katie thought it made her look more mature. Because of these mixed signals, some dissonance resulted and manifested itself as an uncomfortable, unsettled feeling. To reduce the dissonance, Katie could:

- Take back the outfit.

- Pay attention to positive information, such as looking up ads and articles about this particular designer.

- Seek more positive feedback from friends.

- Seek negative information about outfits made by designers not selected.

Customer Loyalty In the postpurchase stage of the decision-making process, marketers attempt to solidify a loyal relationship with their customers. They want customers to be

▼ **EXHIBIT 6.3** Components of Postpurchase Outcomes

Stores collect customer information for their CRM programs from their loyalty cards.

© Mark Lennihan/AP Photo

satisfied with their purchase and buy from the same company again. Loyal customers will buy only certain brands and shop at certain stores, and they include no other firms in their evoked set. As we explained in Chapter 2, such customers are therefore very valuable to firms, and marketers have designed detailed analytics software and customer relationship management (CRM) programs specifically to acquire and retain them.

Undesirable Consumer Behavior Although firms want satisfied, loyal customers, sometimes they fail to attain them. Passive consumers are those who don't repeat purchase or recommend the product to others. More serious and potentially damaging, however, is negative consumer behavior, such as negative word of mouth and rumors.

Negative word of mouth occurs when consumers spread negative information about a product, service, or store to others. When customers' expectations are met or even exceeded, they often don't tell anyone about it. But when consumers believe that they have been treated unfairly in some way, they usually want to complain, often to many people. The Internet has provided an effective method of spreading negative word of mouth to millions of people instantaneously through personal blogs, Twitter, and corporate websites. In turn, some firms rely on listening software offered by companies like Salesforce.com (as we discussed in Chapter 3), then respond to negative word of mouth through customer service representatives—whether online, on the phone, or in stores—who have the authority to handle complaints. Many companies also allow customers to post comments and complaints to proprietary social media sites.

For example, Whirlpool set up Facebook pages for its appliance brands Maytag, KitchenAid, and Whirlpool. Customers may share their thoughts on these sites without fear that their negative feedback will be deleted from the site. Whirlpool believes that it should keep the bad comments to open up discussions and emphasize the proactive measures the company is taking to remedy service or product failures.[30] If a customer believes that positive action will be taken as a result of the complaint, he or she is less likely to complain to family and friends or through the Internet. (A detailed example of word of mouth appears in Chapter 13.)

negative word of mouth Occurs when consumers spread negative information about a product, service, or store to others.

✓ check yourself

1. Name the five stages in the consumer decision process.
2. What is the difference between a need and a want?
3. Distinguish between functional and psychological needs.
4. What are the various types of perceived risk?
5. What are the differences between compensatory and noncompensatory decision rules?
6. How do firms enhance postpurchase satisfaction and reduce cognitive dissonance?

Whirlpool posts both good and bad comments on Twitter. It believes that posting negative comments opens up discussions and emphasizes the proactive measures the company is taking to remedy service or product failures.
Courtesy Whirlpool

LO 6-5 List the factors that affect the consumer decision process.

FACTORS INFLUENCING THE CONSUMER DECISION PROCESS

The consumer decision process can be influenced by several factors, as illustrated in Exhibit 6.4. First are the elements of the marketing mix, which we discuss throughout this book. Second are psychological factors, which are influences internal to the customer, such as motives, attitudes, perception, and learning. Third, social factors, such as family, reference groups, and culture, also

motive A need or want that is strong enough to cause the person to seek satisfaction.

Maslow's hierarchy of needs A paradigm for classifying people's motives. It argues that when lower-level, more basic needs (physiological and safety) are fulfilled, people turn to satisfying their higher-level human needs (social and personal); see also *physiological, safety, social,* and *personal needs.*

influence the decision process. Fourth, there are situational factors, such as the specific purchase situation, a particular shopping situation, or temporal state (the time of day), that affect the decision process.

Every decision people make as consumers will take them through some form of the consumer decision process. But, like life itself, this process does not exist in a vacuum.

perception, learning, and lifestyle. In this section, we examine how such psychological factors can influence the consumer decision process.[31]

Motives In Chapter 1 we argued that marketing is all about satisfying customer needs and wants. When a need, such as thirst, or a want, such as for a Diet Pepsi, is not satisfied, it motivates us, or drives us, to get satisfaction. So, a **motive** is a need or want that is strong enough to cause the person to seek satisfaction.

People have several types of motives. One of the best-known paradigms for explaining these motive types was developed by Abraham Maslow 45 years ago, called **Maslow's hierarchy of needs**.[32] Maslow categorized five groups of needs, namely,

> ## " EVERY DECISION PEOPLE MAKE AS CONSUMERS WILL TAKE THEM THROUGH SOME FORM OF THE CONSUMER DECISION PROCESS. BUT, LIKE LIFE ITSELF, THIS PROCESS DOES NOT EXIST IN A VACUUM. "

Psychological Factors

Although marketers can influence purchase decisions, a host of psychological factors affect the way people receive marketers' messages. Among them are motives, attitudes,

physiological (e.g., food, water, shelter), safety (e.g., secure employment, health), love (e.g., friendship, family), esteem (e.g., confidence, respect), and self-actualization (people engage in personal growth activities and attempt to meet their intellectual, aesthetic, creative, and other such needs). The pyramid in Exhibit 6.5 illustrates the theoretical progression of those needs.

▼ **EXHIBIT 6.4** Factors Affecting the Consumer Decision Process

- Product
- Price
- Place
- Promotion

- Motives
- Attitudes
- Perceptions
- Learning
- Lifestyle

Marketing mix — Psychological factors — Consumer Decision Process — Social factors — Situational factors

- Family
- Reference groups
- Culture

- Purchase situation
- Shopping situation
- Temporal state

▼ **EXHIBIT 6.5** Maslow's Hierarchy of Needs

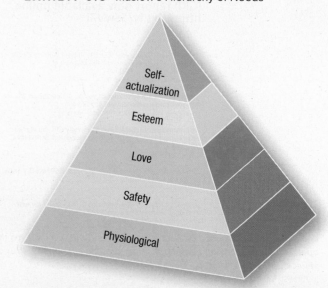

- Self-actualization
- Esteem
- Love
- Safety
- Physiological

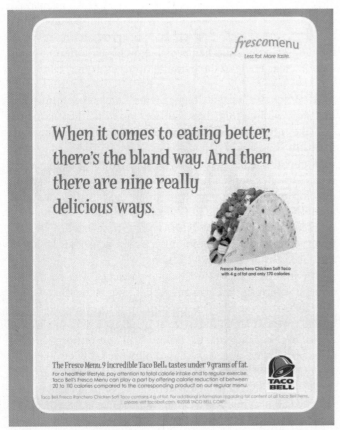

In this ad, Taco Bell satisfies the physiological need of food while letting the consumer know that healthy eating can also be delicious.
Courtesy Taco Bell

Physiological needs deal with the basic biological necessities of life—food, drink, rest, and shelter. Although for most people in developed countries these basic needs are generally met, there are those in both developed and less developed countries who are less fortunate. However, everyone remains concerned with meeting these basic needs.[33] Marketers seize every opportunity to convert these needs into wants by reminding us to eat at Taco Bell, drink milk, sleep on a Beautyrest mattress, and stay at a Marriott.

Safety needs pertain to protection and physical well-being. The marketplace is full of products and services that are designed to make you safer, such as airbags in cars and burglar alarms in homes, or healthier, such as vitamins and organic meats and vegetables.

Love needs relate to our interactions with others. Haircuts and makeup make you look more attractive, and deodorants prevent odor. Greeting cards help you express your feelings toward others.

Esteem needs allow people to satisfy their inner desires. Yoga, meditation, health clubs, and many books appeal to people's desires to grow or maintain a happy, satisfied outlook on life.

Finally, **self-actualization** occurs when you feel completely satisfied with your life and how you live. You don't care what

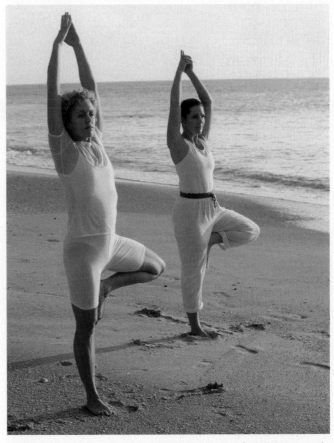

Yoga satisfies esteem needs by helping people satisfy their inner needs.
© Purestock/SuperStock RF

"The marketplace is full of products and services that are designed to make you safer, such as airbags in cars and burglar alarms in homes, or healthier, such as vitamins and organic meats and vegetables."

example. Many of these magazines fulfill several needs simultaneously, of course. Good marketers add value to their products or services by nudging people up the needs hierarchy and offering information on as many of the pyramid of needs as they can.

Attitude We have attitudes about almost everything. For instance, we like this class, but we don't like the instructor. We like where we live, but we don't like the weather. An **attitude** is a person's enduring evaluation of his or her feelings about and behavioral tendencies toward an object or idea. Attitudes are learned and long lasting, and they might develop over a long period of time, though they can also abruptly change. You might like your instructor for much of the semester—until she returns your first exam. The one thing attitudes have in common for everyone is their ability to influence our decisions and actions.

An attitude consists of three components. The **cognitive component** reflects a person's belief system, or what we believe to be true; the **affective component** involves emotions,[35] or what we feel about the issue at hand, including our like or dislike of something; and the **behavioral component** pertains to the actions we undertake based on what we know and feel. For example, Matt and Lisa Martinez see a poster for the latest *Avengers* movie. The ad lists quotes from different movie critics who call it a great and exciting film. Matt and Lisa therefore come to believe that the critics must be correct and that the new *Avengers* movie will be a good movie (cognitive component). Later they catch an interview with Robert Downey Jr., who talks about making the movie and his enjoyment playing Tony Stark (Iron Man). Therefore, Matt and Lisa start to believe the movie will be fun and engaging because they appreciate action adventures and have enjoyed previous Marvel films (affective component). After weighing their various options—which include various other movies, other entertainment options such as attending a concert instead, or just staying home—Matt and Lisa decide to go see the movie (behavioral component).

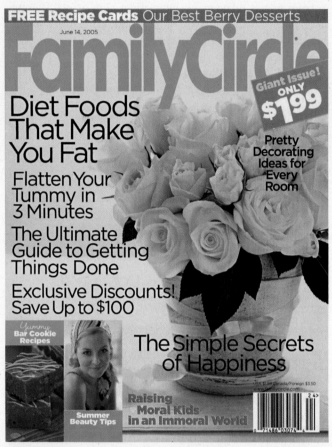

Which category of Maslow's hierarchy of needs does this magazine satisfy?

© AP Photo

others think. You drive a Ford Fusion because it suits the person you are, not because some celebrity endorses it or because you want others to think better of you.

Which of these needs applies when a consumer purchases a magazine? Magazines such as *Men's Health,* for instance, help satisfy physiological needs like how to eat healthy and exercise, but also esteem needs like how to be happy with one's life.[34] Magazines such as *Family Circle* provide tips on how to make the home a safer place to live, and magazines such as *Weddings* help satisfy love and belonging needs because they provide instructions on how to prepare gracious invitations for friends and family, for

> " Attitudes are learned and long lasting, and they might develop over a long period of time, though they can also abruptly change. "

Ideally, agreement exists among these three components. But when there is incongruence among the three—if Matt and Lisa read positive reviews and like action films but do not find Robert Downey Jr. an appealing actor—cognitive dissonance might occur. Matt and Lisa might decide their reviews and their liking of action films will outweigh their dislike of Robert Downey Jr. and go see the movie. If they then find the movie unenjoyable because he is a primary star, they may feel foolish for having wasted their money.

Such dissonance is a terrible feeling that people try to avoid, often by convincing

Based on positive reviews (cognitive component) and positive feelings (affective component), many movie watchers will go see the latest *Avengers* movie (behavioral component) and come away with a positive attitude.
© Photos 12/Alamy

themselves that the decision was a good one in some way.[36] In this example, Matt and Lisa might focus on the special effects and the romantic elements of the movie while mentally glossing over the parts that featured the actor they did not enjoy. In this way, they can convince themselves that the parts they liked were good enough to counterbalance the part they didn't like, and thus, they make their moviegoing experience a positive event overall.

Although attitudes are pervasive and usually slow to change, the important fact from a marketer's point of view is that they can be influenced and perhaps changed through persuasive communications and personal experience. Marketing communication—through salespeople, advertisements, free samples, or other such methods—can attempt to change what people believe to be true about a product or service (cognitive) or how they feel toward it (affective). Because of these effects, marketers have an ethical responsibility to communicate truthfully, as Ethical and Societal Dilemma 6.2 reflects. If the marketing communication is successful, the cognitive and affective components work in concert to affect behavior. Continuing with our example, suppose that prior to viewing the movie ad, Matt and Lisa thought that the new *Fast & Furious* movie would be the next one they would go see, but they had heard such good things about *The Avengers*. The ad positively influenced the cognitive component of their attitude toward *The Avengers,* making it consistent with their affective component.

ethical&societal dilemma   6.2

Can Marketing Be Life Threatening? Allegations of Unethical Practices by Pharmaceutical Firms[iv]

In separate lawsuits brought in Illinois and California, local authorities have charged that five large pharmaceutical firms behaved illegally in promoting painkilling drugs to consumers and health care providers. Specifically, the suits assert that through "aggressive marketing" tactics, the pharmaceutical companies pushed doctors to prescribe powerful opioid drugs to patients whose ailments did not meet the extreme conditions for which these drugs initially were developed. The result, according to the attorneys bringing the suits, has been a vast increase in addiction rates and incalculable damage to society.

Opioid painkillers originally emerged as solutions for patients suffering from extreme, acute pain that could not be relieved by other drugs. These patients were severely disabled by their pain or suffered from serious conditions such as cancer. The prescriptions were intended to be limited, because of the substantial risk of addiction that the painkilling drugs created.

According to the recent lawsuits, though, the pharmaceutical companies put their desire for increased profits ahead of their responsibility to help doctors prescribe their products appropriately. They allege that pharmaceutical sales representatives encouraged doctors to prescribe the drugs for less severe pain and injuries to create a broader market of end users for their products. In addition, the lawsuits argue that some of the companies tried to downplay the risk of addiction in their general marketing communications.

These misleading claims in turn have led to significantly negative implications for society, according to the lawsuits. No one questions the

fact that rates of opioid addiction have increased rapidly in recent years. What is at question is why. According to the City of Chicago and two California counties, these increased rates can be attributed directly to the misleading, irresponsible, and unethical marketing practices of the drug companies. As a result, because taxpayers must pay the millions of dollars in health care costs associated with dealing with drug addiction, even people who are not directly affected by the epidemic suffer. For example, Chicago has asserted that more than 1,000 emergency room visits in one year stemmed from opioid abuse or overdoses. According to one of the district attorneys bringing suit in California, the goal of these legal efforts is not to limit the company's ability to sell but rather to "require these companies to change their conduct and to tell people—to tell the doctors, to tell the patients—tell them that these drugs are dangerous. Tell them they are addictive, and you could overdose on them, and you could die."

perception The process by which people select, organize, and interpret information to form a meaningful picture of the world.

learning Refers to a change in a person's thought process or behavior that arises from experience and takes place throughout the consumer decision process.

lifestyles A component of *psychographics;* refers to the way a person lives his or her life to achieve goals.

Perception Another psychological factor, **perception**, is the process by which we select, organize, and interpret information to form a meaningful picture of the world. Perception in marketing influences our acquisition and consumption of goods and services through our tendency to assign meaning to such things as color, symbols, taste, and packaging. Culture, tradition, and our overall upbringing determine our perception of the world. For instance, Lisa Martinez has always wanted an apartment in the Back Bay neighborhood of Boston because her favorite aunt had one, and they had a great time visiting for Thanksgiving one year. However, from his past experiences Matt has a different perception. Matt thinks Back Bay apartments are small, expensive, and impractical for a couple thinking about having children—though they would be convenient for single people who work in downtown Boston. The city of Boston has worked hard in recent years to overcome the long-standing negative perceptual bias that Matt and many others hold by working with developers to

apparel. Once she was in the store and tried on some outfits, she realized how much she liked the way she looked and felt in them, which involved the affective component. Then she made her purchase, which involved the behavioral component. Each time she was exposed to information about the store or the outfits, she learned something different that affected her perception. Before she tried them on, Katie hadn't realized how easy it would be to find exactly what she was looking for; thus, her perception of Macy's selection of career clothing changed through learning.

Lifestyle **Lifestyle** refers to the way consumers spend their time and money to live. For many consumers, the question of whether the product or service fits with their actual lifestyle (which may be fairly sedentary) or their perceived lifestyle (which might be outdoorsy) is an important one. Some of the many consumers sporting North Face jackets certainly need the high-tech, cold weather gear because they are planning their next hike up Mount Rainier and want to be sure they have sufficient protection against the elements. Others, however, simply like the image that the jacket conveys—the image that they might be leaving for their own mountain-climbing expedition any day now—even if the closest they have come has been shoveling their driveway.

A person's perceptions and ability to learn are affected by his or her social experiences, which we discuss next.

WHEN FAMILIES MAKE PURCHASE DECISIONS, THEY OFTEN CONSIDER THE NEEDS OF ALL THE FAMILY MEMBERS.

create larger, modern, and more affordable apartments and using promotion to reposition the perception of apartments in the Back Bay for young couples.[37]

Learning **Learning** refers to a change in a person's thought process or behavior that arises from experience and takes place throughout the consumer decision process. After Katie Smith recognized that she needed an outfit for her job interview, she started looking for ads and searching for reviews and articles on the Internet. She learned from each new piece of information, so her thoughts about the look she wanted in an outfit were different from those before she had read anything. She liked what she learned about the clothing line from Macy's. She learned from her search, and it became part of her memory to be used in the future, possibly so she could recommend the store to her friends.

Learning affects both attitudes and perceptions. Throughout the buying process, Katie's attitudes shifted. The cognitive component came into play for her when she learned Macy's had one of the most extensive collections of career

Social Factors

The consumer decision process is influenced from within by psychological factors but also by the external, social environment, which consists of the customer's family, reference groups, and culture.[38] (Recall Exhibit 6.4.)

Family Many purchase decisions are made about products or services that the entire family will consume or use. Thus, firms must consider how families make purchase decisions and understand how various family members might influence these decisions.

When families make purchase decisions, they often consider the needs of all the family members. In choosing a restaurant, for example, all the family members may participate in the decision making. In other situations, however, different members of the family may take on the purchasing role. For instance, the husband and teenage child may look through car magazines and *Consumer Reports* to search for information about a new car. But once they arrive at the dealership, the husband and wife,

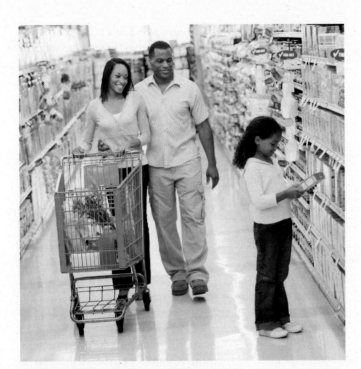
Children influence parents' purchasing decisions.
© Stockbroker/Purestock/SuperStock RF

Gen Xers and Millennials (remember from Chapter 5 that these groups were born anywhere between 1965 and 2000) tend to shop at Target, Kmart, and Walmart and spend more at those stores than other generational groups.[42] Getting these groups to prefer one store, chain, or product over another can make a difference in the bottom line as well as in the chances for survival in a difficult marketplace.

reference group One or more persons whom an individual uses as a basis for comparison regarding beliefs, feelings, and behaviors.

Reference Groups

A **reference group** is one or more persons whom an individual uses as a basis for comparison regarding beliefs, feelings, and behaviors. A consumer might have various reference groups, including family, friends, coworkers, or famous people the consumer would like to emulate. These reference groups affect buying decisions by (1) offering information, (2) providing rewards for specific purchasing behaviors, and (3) enhancing a consumer's self-image.[43]

Reference groups provide information to consumers directly through conversation or indirectly through observation. For example, Katie received valuable information from a friend about where she should shop for her interview outfit. On another occasion, she heard a favorite cousin who is a fashionista praising the virtues of shopping at Macy's, which solidified her decision to go there.

Consumers can identify and affiliate with reference groups to create, enhance, or maintain their self-image. Customers who want to be seen as earthy might buy Birkenstock sandals, whereas those wanting to be seen as high fashion might buy

What reference group is evoked by these Birkenstock sandals?
© Stockdisc/Getty Images RF

not the child, decide which model and color to buy, and the wife negotiates the final deal.[39]

Children and adolescents play an increasingly important role in family buying decisions. Kids in the United States spend over $208 billion a year on personal items such as snacks, soft drinks, entertainment, and apparel. They directly influence the purchase of another $300 billion worth of items such as food, snacks, beverages, toys, health and beauty aids, clothing, accessories, gifts, and school supplies. Their indirect influence on family spending is even higher—$600 billion for items such as recreation, vacations, technology, and the family car.[40] Even grandparents contribute to the economic impact of children in the United States. It is estimated that grandparents spend $10 billion on purchases for grandchildren.[41]

Influencing a group that holds this much spending power is vitally important. Traditional food retailers are already caught in a squeeze between Walmart, which lures low-end customers, and specialty retailers like Whole Foods, which targets the high end. Knowing how children influence food buying decisions is a strategic opportunity for traditional supermarkets and their suppliers to exploit. Currently, the age cohorts referred to as

> " Kids in the United States spend over $208 billion a year on personal items such as snacks, soft drinks, entertainment, and apparel. They directly influence the purchase of another $300 billion worth of items. "

culture The set of values, guiding beliefs, understandings, and ways of doing things shared by members of a society; exists on two levels: visible artifacts (e.g., behavior, dress, symbols, physical settings, ceremonies) and underlying values (thought processes, beliefs, and assumptions).

situational factors Factors affecting the consumer decision process; those that are specific to the situation that may override, or at least influence, psychological and social issues.

Lana Marks bags. If they purchase a gift for someone else and that gift conflicts with their self-image, they also seek to reestablish their preferred affiliation quickly by purchasing something more in line with their identity.[44]

With the increasing popularity of blogs, more and more people are getting recommendations for products from their favorite bloggers. When you follow a blog about kittens, you might notice that the author posts a scathing review of a particular cat tree or strongly recommends a product that encourages kittens to use their litter boxes. Because this blogger offers insights you appreciate, you go out to buy the litter box product but avoid adding that cat tree to your shopping cart. In realizing the vast influence of this reference group, companies today offer prominent bloggers free products and sometimes even pay them to write positive reviews.[45]

Culture

We defined **culture** in Chapter 5 as the shared meanings, beliefs, morals, values, and customs of a group of people. As the basis of the social factors that affect your buying decisions, the culture or cultures in which you participate are not markedly different from your reference groups. That is, your cultural group might be as small as your reference group at school or as large as the country in which you live or the religion to which you belong. Like reference groups, cultures influence consumer

behavior. For instance, the culture at Katie's college is rather fashion conscious. This influences, to some extent, the way she spends, how she dresses, and where she shops.

Situational Factors

Psychological and social factors typically influence the consumer decision process the same way each time. For example, your motivation to quench your thirst usually drives you to drink a Coke or a Pepsi, and your reference group at the workplace coerces you to wear appropriate attire. But sometimes **situational factors**, or factors specific to the situation, override or at least influence psychological and social issues. These situational factors are related to the purchase and shopping situation as well as to temporal states.[46]

Purchase Situation

Customers may be predisposed to purchase certain products or services because of some underlying psychological trait or social factor, but these factors may change in certain purchase situations. For instance, Samantha Crumb considers herself a thrifty, cautious shopper—someone who likes to get a good deal. But her best friend is getting married, and she wants to buy the couple a silver tray. If the tray were for herself, she would probably go to Crate & Barrel or possibly even Walmart. But because it is for her best friend, she went to Tiffany & Co. Why? She wanted to purchase something fitting for the special occasion of a wedding.

> Customers may be predisposed to purchase certain products or services because of some underlying psychological trait or social factor, but these factors may change in certain purchase situations.

Shopping Situation

Consumers might be ready to purchase a product or service but be completely derailed once they arrive in the store. Marketers use several techniques to influence consumers at this choice stage of the decision process, as Adding Value 6.1 describes using one example.[47]

Store Atmosphere Some retailers and service providers have developed unique images that are based at least in part on their internal environment, also known as their atmospherics.[48] Research has shown that, if used in concert with other aspects of a retailer's strategy, music, scent, lighting, and even color can positively influence the decision process.[49] Restaurants such as Outback Steakhouse and The Cheesecake Factory have developed internal environments that are not only pleasant but also consistent with their food and service. Some Wegmans and Whole Foods stores have built bars and restaurants inside their stores, where customers can stop and relax, have a glass of wine or a bite to eat, but still get their shopping done for the week.[50]

Salespeople Well-trained sales personnel can influence the sale at the point of purchase by educating consumers about product attributes, pointing out the advantages of one item over another,

Bloggers can influence their readers to buy or not buy certain products or services.

Courtesy geekygirlreviewsblog.com

Adding Value 6.1

Doing Everything Right— H-E-B Supermarkets[v]

When it comes to consumer behavior, the research is clear: If they want to succeed, companies selling to consumers need to attract consumers' attention, affection, and commitment; put them in a great mood, perhaps by offering them something for nothing; and help people make their decisions easily and in a way that causes them to feel smart and informed. It may be clear, but few companies are applying these lessons as effectively as a regional grocery store chain in Texas, H-E-B.

First, H-E-B gets its regional customers excited and entranced by playing on their shared identity of being from Texas. This option might be less effective in other regions with a weaker sense of identity, but in Texas, the idea that H-E-B is just like its consumers garners it substantial attention and affection. Then once it has people in its stores, it gets them to engage and commit to actually buying by adding tear-off coupons to its displays. Rather than just seeing a sale sign, customers must undertake the action of tearing off a coupon. This action is not particularly strenuous of course, but the simple move increases the chances that shoppers will follow through on their already committed effort by completing the purchase.

Second, H-E-B sets up an appealing and enjoyable atmosphere that seeks to put shoppers in a better mood. In particular, a plethora of coupons give buyers an additional item for free after they purchase. People simply love things for free, so the constant reminder of how much they can get, seemingly at no cost, enhances their moods. As if that were not enough, H-E-B also gives away lots of free samples. In addition to food samples, to keep shoppers' blood sugar levels up it specializes in wine samples. Because alcohol releases dopamine in people's brains, just a small sip of a nice Zinfandel can leave shoppers in a better mood.

Fabio Viviani, Top Chef's *fan favorite, cooks up Italian meatballs at H-E-B.*
© Rachel Denny Clow/AP Photo

Third, the entire operation seeks to make it easier for consumers to buy the products they want and feel pleased with their purchases. H-E-B has avoided loyalty cards and instead simply offers all consumers in the store the same deals on the same items. Thus, shoppers do not need to remember to bring their store coupons or stick their loyalty cards in their wallets before they leave for their grocery run. The fresh food displays also offer obvious highlights of their freshness: a constant smell of rotisserie chicken near the deli display, a guacamole prepping station featuring chefs carving out the avocados right in front of shoppers, and sushi chefs working in the center of the store.

As a result, even though H-E-B remains a regional chain, with limited name recognition outside Texas, its ranking on a recent "consumer delight index" placed it on par with such well-known customer favorites as Trader Joe's and Whole Foods.

and encouraging multiple purchases. Each Apple store features a simple layout that enables shoppers to play with the latest gadgets, though the real key to success is the salespeople. Apple keeps its product lines relatively minimal so salepeople can become familiar with every product in the store. For more technical questions, Apple Geniuses are available and consultations can be scheduled.[51] A training manual recently leaked online shows that the company takes nothing for granted when training its employees, such that it uses role-playing scenarios, lists banned words, and specifies exactly how to communicate with agitated customers. Although technical expertise is a must, Apple also looks for salespeople with "magnetic personalities" and trains them in a five-point selling technique: **a**pproach customers warmly, **p**robe politely to assess their needs, **p**resent solutions the customer can do today, **l**isten and resolve worries the customer may still have, **e**nd by giving the customer a warm goodbye and invite them back.[52] What's that spell?

The Cheesecake Factory has developed atmospherics that are not only pleasant, but consistent with its image, menu, and service.
© Kumar Sriskandan/Alamy

Crowding Customers can feel crowded because there are too many people, too much merchandise, or lines that are too long. If there are too many people in a store, some people become distracted and may even leave.[53] Others have difficulty purchasing if the merchandise is packed too closely together. This issue is a particular problem for shoppers with disabilities.

In-Store Demonstrations The taste and smell of new food items may attract people to try something they normally wouldn't. Similarly, some fashion retailers offer trunk shows, during which their vendors show their whole line of merchandise on a certain day. During these well-advertised events, customers are often enticed to purchase that day because they get special assistance from the salespeople and can order merchandise that the retailer otherwise does not carry.

Promotions Retailers employ various promotional vehicles to influence customers once they have arrived in the store. An unadvertised price promotion can alter a person's preconceived buying plan. Multi-item discounts, such as "buy 1, get 1 free" sales, are popular means to get people to buy more than they normally would.[54] Because many people regard clipping coupons from the newspaper as too much trouble, some stores make coupons available in the store, on the Internet, or on their cell phones. Another form of promotion is offering a free gift with the purchase of a good or service. This type of promotion is particularly popular with cosmetics, and Sephora has worked

> ## MARKETERS SPEND MILLIONS OF DOLLARS DESIGNING AND UPDATING THEIR PACKAGES TO BE MORE APPEALING AND EYE CATCHING. THIS IS WHY PRINGLES KEEPS PACKAGING ITS CHIPS IN TUBES.

In-store demonstrations, such as this one in an Albertson's grocery store, attract consumers to try and buy.
Courtesy Albertson's, Inc.

hard to integrate various elements of its shopping situation to encourage purchase, as Social and Mobile Marketing 6.2 shows.

Packaging It is difficult to make a product stand out in the crowd when it competes for shelf space with several other brands.[55] Customers spend just a few seconds standing in front of products as they decide whether to buy them.[56] This problem is particularly difficult for consumer packaged goods, such as groceries and health and beauty products. Marketers therefore spend millions of dollars designing and updating their packages to be more appealing and eye catching. This is why Pringles keeps packaging its chips in tubes that differ greatly from the formless bags farther down the aisle. But not all product packaging can, or should, remain the same, the way Pringles has. Doublemint Gum undertook its first packaging redesign nearly a century after its 1914 product launch. The move was designed to help the chewing gum appeal to a younger audience, even while it maintained its loyal base of older consumers. Another aging brand, Kraft's Macaroni & Cheese, similarly redesigned its packaging, which it launched originally in 1937.[57]

Temporal State Our state of mind at any particular time can alter our preconceived notions of what we are going to purchase. For instance, some people are morning people, whereas others function better at night. Therefore, a purchase situation may have different appeal levels depending on the time of day and the type of person the consumer is. Mood swings can alter consumer behavior.[58] Suppose Samantha received a parking ticket just prior to shopping at Tiffany & Co. It is likely that she would be less receptive to the salesperson's influence than if she came into the store in

Social & Mobile Marketing 6.2

Ensuring Mobile Dominance through In-Store Promotions[vi]

Some consumers rely on websites to reach their favorite retailers. Others like to head to the stores themselves to check out the options. Still others want a mobile app that enables them to shop quickly and on the go. And increasingly, today's customers demand that retailers offer them all of these options, consistently and constantly, so that they can pick and choose the channel they want to use at any specific time.

This demand is the impetus for the latest developments in the marketing strategy of Sephora, the specialized beauty product retailer. Although it has long maintained a good reputation for its interactive website, the company remains in constant pursuit of a strategy that enables it to reach all its customers through the most channels at the most frequent times. It integrates these efforts with its constantly evolving loyalty program, in an effort to become nearly irresistible to beauty product consumers.

Users of the most recent version of its mobile app, Sephora to Go, can engage in any activities they would pursue in stores. The close alignment across these channels provides a seamless experience. In addition, the app encourages customers to sign up for the loyalty program and create a Beauty Insider account. Once they have done so, they gain a mobile version of their loyalty card. They can check their loyalty points at any time, as well as redeem them however they wish. Downloadable bar codes also are available, which can be scanned in stores.

Simultaneously, Sephora's in-store signage encourages shoppers to sign up for the loyalty program and create a Beauty Insider account. That is, both channels issue similar calls to action. Moreover, the

Sephora engages its customers in the store with its mobile app, Sephora to Go.
© Victor J. Blue/Bloomberg/Getty Images

in-store signs encourage brick-and-mortar shoppers to take advantage of the benefits they can gain from interacting with the retailer, either online or through mobile apps.

As the company recognizes, "The majority of Sephora's clients are cross-channel shoppers," so it wants consumers to go ahead and use their phones while in the stores. In return, Sephora has enjoyed a 150 percent increase in the amount of mobile shopping its customers undertake.

---

a good mood. Her bad mood might even cause her to have a less positive postpurchase feeling about the store. Because retailers cannot affect what happens outside the store very much, they should do everything possible to make sure their customers have a positive shopping experience once they are in the store.

The factors that affect the consumer decision process—the marketing mix, psychological factors, social factors, and situational factors—are all affected by the level of consumer involvement, the subject of the next section.

 check yourself

1. What are some examples of specific needs suggested by Maslow's hierarchy of needs?

2. Which social factors likely have the most influence on
   (a) the purchase of a new outfit for a job interview and
   (b) the choice of a college to attend?

3. List some of the tactics stores can use to influence consumers' decision processes.

LO 6-6 | Describe how involvement influences the consumer decision process.

INVOLVEMENT AND CONSUMER BUYING DECISIONS

Consumers make two types of buying decisions, depending on their level of involvement: extended problem solving or limited problem solving (which includes impulse purchases and habitual decision making). **Involvement** is the consumer's degree of interest in the product or service.[59] Consumers may have different levels of involvement for the same type of product. One consumer behavior theory, the elaboration likelihood model illustrated in Exhibit 6.6, proposes that high- and low-involvement consumers process different aspects of a message or advertisement.

extended problem solving A purchase decision process during which the consumer devotes considerable time and effort to analyzing alternatives; often occurs when the consumer perceives that the purchase decision entails a lot of risk.

limited problem solving Occurs during a purchase decision that calls for, at most, a moderate amount of effort and time.

impulse buying A buying decision made by customers on the spot when they see the merchandise.

If both types of consumers viewed ads for career clothing, the high-involvement consumer (e.g., Katie, who is researching buying an outfit for a job interview) will scrutinize all the information provided (price, fabric quality, construction) and process the key elements of the message more deeply. As an involved consumer, Katie likely ends up judging the ad as truthful and forming a favorable impression of the product, or else she regards the message as superficial and develops negative product impressions (i.e., her research suggests the product is not as good as it is being portrayed).

In contrast, a low-involvement consumer will likely process the same advertisement in a less thorough manner. Such a consumer might pay less attention to the key elements of the message (price, fabric quality, construction) and focus on heuristic elements such as brand name (Macy's I·N·C) or the presence of a celebrity endorser. The impressions of the low-involvement consumer are likely to be more superficial.

Extended Problem Solving

The buying process begins when consumers recognize that they have an unsatisfied need. Katie Smith recognized her need to buy a new outfit for a job interview. She sought information by asking for advice from her friends, reading fashion magazines, and conducting research online. She visited several stores to determine which had the best options for her. Finally, after considerable time and effort analyzing her alternatives, Katie purchased an outfit at Macy's. This process is an example of **extended problem solving**, which is common when the customer perceives that the purchase decision entails a lot of risk. The potential risks associated with Katie's decision to buy the outfit include financial (did I pay too much?) and social (will my potential employer and friends think I look professional?) risks. To reduce her perceived risk, Katie spent a lot of effort searching for information before she actually made her purchase.

Limited Problem Solving

Limited problem solving occurs during a purchase decision that calls for, at most, a moderate amount of effort and time. Customers engage in this type of buying process when they have had some prior experience

▼ **EXHIBIT 6.6** Elaboration Likelihood Model

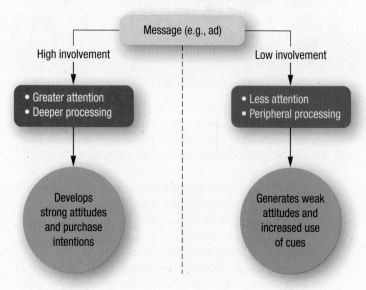

with the product or service and the perceived risk is moderate. Limited problem solving usually relies on past experience more than on external information. For many people, an apparel purchase, even an outfit for a job interview, could require limited effort.

A common type of limited problem solving is **impulse buying**, a buying decision made by customers on the spot when they see the merchandise.[60] When Katie went to the grocery store to do her weekly shopping, she saw a display case of popcorn and Dr Pepper near the checkout counter. Knowing that some of her friends were coming over to watch a movie, she stocked up. The popcorn and soda were an impulse purchase. Katie didn't go through the entire decision process; instead, she recognized her need and jumped directly to purchase without spending any time searching for additional information or evaluating alternatives. The grocery store facilitated this impulse purchase by providing

What type of buying decision does each of these products represent?
Left: © Bill Hogan/MCT/Newscom; Right: Steve Sparrow/Culture/Getty Images

easily accessible cues (i.e., by offering the popcorn and soda in a prominent display, at a great location in the store, and at a reasonable price).

Some purchases require even less thought. **Habitual decision making** describes a purchase decision process in which consumers engage in little conscious effort. On her way home from the grocery store, for example, Katie drove past an In-N-Out Burger and swung into the drive-through for a cheeseburger and Diet Coke. She did not ponder the potential benefits of going to Wendy's instead for lunch. Rather, she simply reacted to the cue provided by the sign and engaged in habitual decision making. Marketers strive to attract and maintain habitual purchasers by creating strong brands and store loyalty (see Chapters 11 and 12) because these customers don't even consider alternative brands or stores. ■

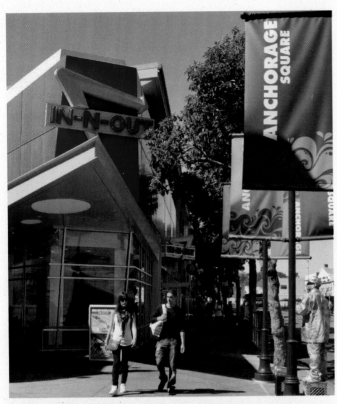

Picking up a hamburger at a drive-through fast-food restaurant like In-N-Out Burger requires little thought. It is a habitual decision.
© K. Rousonelos

 check yourself

1. How do low- versus high-involvement consumers process the information in an advertisement?

2. What is the difference between extended versus limited problem solving?

 connect Increase your engagement and learning with Connect Marketing.

<u>These Connect activities, available only through your Connect course, have been designed to make the following concepts more meaningful and applicable:</u>

▷ Information Search: The Perfect Haircut Click and Drag Activity

▷ Customer Decision Process: Video Streaming Timeline Creation

▷ Customer Behavior: Netflix Video Case

▷ Purchase Decision Process: iSeeit! Video

 SMARTBOOK™   **iSeeit!**

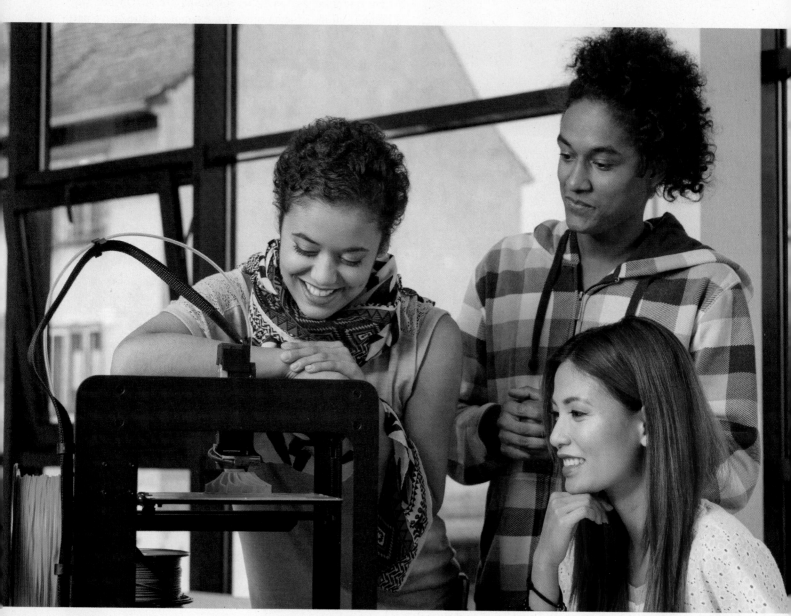

Chapter seven

business-to-business marketing

M anufacturing in the United States is entering a totally new era, and no one company exemplifies the shift better than General Electric (GE). Already the largest U.S. manufacturing firm, GE also is seeking to become the most prolific user of innovative 3D printing. If it succeeds, it seems likely to change virtually every business-to-business (B2B) relationship we find today.

In traditional B2B exchanges, one company, such as a manufacturer, needs to work with another company to obtain the raw materials it needs. So for example, to build parts for the airplane engines it sells, GE would turn to suppliers of titanium, grinding services, and tool manufacturers to provide the necessary materials. Then it would fabricate all the parts of the engine together and sell it to another company, such as an airline.

With its recent purchase of an existing 3D printing company, though, GE is signaling that it aims to cover all—or at least most—of these supply chain steps itself.[1] The 3D printing technology is additive: It

LEARNING OBJECTIVES

After reading this chapter, you should be able to:

LO 7-1   Describe the ways in which business-to-business (B2B) firms segment their markets.

LO 7-2   List the steps in the B2B buying process.

LO 7-3   Identify the roles within the buying center.

LO 7-4   Describe the different types of organizational cultures.

LO 7-5   Detail different buying situations.

builds parts (or toys or virtually anything else) by layering thin sheets of material, in programmed shapes, on top of one another. There is no grinding or removal of any material required, which substantially reduces waste. The promise of 3D printing suggests

continued on p. 128

business-to-business (B2B) marketing The process of buying and selling goods or services to be used in the production of other goods and services, for consumption by the buying organization, or for resale by wholesalers and retailers.

derived demand The linkage between consumers' demand for a company's output and its purchase of necessary inputs to manufacture or assemble that particular output.

continued from p. 127

that someday, GE even could innovate its own processes, such as by printing out the sophisticated tools it might need to install all the various engine parts, which it also has printed.[2]

Thus far, GE uses 3D printing in about 10 percent of its manufacturing efforts, but it hopes to progressively increase this percentage over time. Within two decades, half of all its production is likely to rely, in some way, on its own in-house 3D printing facilities.[3] But at the moment, the actual printers themselves remain out of reach for most companies; even GE does not plan on building its own printers. Furthermore, the materials required for 3D printing, such as high-tech plastics and composites, are more expensive than traditional raw materials.[4]

So, do 3D printers, used throughout supply chains, represent the end of the traditional B2B relationships that GE has enjoyed in the

3D printing is changing the way manufacturing is done in some industries.
© ZUMA Press, Inc./Alamy

past? Not quite. The printers themselves remain expensive and technologically advanced, and manufacturers relying on 3D printers need assistance with them. Furthermore, the capacity of existing printers is not sufficient for GE or any other major manufacturer to use them exclusively. For example, to produce enough airplane engine nozzles to fulfill the orders it currently has in hand, GE would need to maintain about 70 high-capacity 3D printers.[5] Even with its recent purchase of a dedicated 3D printer company, it has access to less than half that amount. ■

Business-to-business (B2B) marketing refers to the process of buying and selling goods or services to be used in the production of other goods and services for consumption by the buying organization and/or resale by wholesalers and retailers. Therefore, a typical B2B marketing transaction involves manufacturers (e.g., GE, Levi's, Siemens, IBM, Ford) selling to wholesalers that, in turn, sell products to retailers. B2B transactions can also involve service firms (e.g., UPS, Oracle, Accenture) that market their services to other businesses but not to the ultimate consumer (e.g., you). The distinction between a B2B and a business-to-consumer (B2C) transaction is not the product or service itself; rather, it is the ultimate user of that product or service. Another key distinction is that B2B transactions tend to be more complex and involve multiple members of both the buying organization (e.g., buyers, marketing team, product developers) and the selling organization (e.g., sellers, R&D support team), whereas B2C often entails a simple transaction between the retailer and the individual consumer.

The demand for B2B sales is often derived from B2C sales in the same supply chain. More specifically, **derived demand** reflects the link between consumers' demand for a company's output and the company's purchase of necessary inputs to manufacture or assemble that particular output. For example, if more customers want to purchase staplers (a B2C transaction), a company that produces them must purchase more metal from its supplier to make additional staplers (a B2B transaction).

Similar to organizations that sell directly to final consumers in B2C transactions, B2B firms focus on serving specific types of customer markets by creating value for those customers. Recognizing the growing demand for ever-increasing smartphone connectivity in cars, both Apple with its CarPlay and

> "The distinction between a B2B and a business-to-consumer (B2C) transaction is not the product or service itself; rather, it is the ultimate user of that product or service."

Apple CarPlay integrates with the dashboard of numerous cars.
Left: © Fabrice Coffrini/AFP/Getty Images; Right: © Kyodo/AP Photo

Google with its Android-based Open Automotive Alliance are making deals to integrate their OSS into cars. Ferrari, Audi, Mercedes-Benz, and Volvo all offer CarPlay in select models and it can also be added as an aftermarket system;[6] Google, on the other hand, has deals with Honda, Hyundai, and General Motors.[7]

Also like B2C firms, many B2B companies find it productive to focus their efforts on key industries or market segments. Although the average large corporation has over 175 social media accounts, small-business owners often struggle to maintain a single social media account on each of the major networks.[8] Enter the B2B firm Constant Contact. This firm provides a centralized dashboard for small businesses to manage their social media accounts, as well as templates for posts and help on creating social media campaigns. Constant Contact could target businesses of any size, but instead it has become one of the leaders in small-business social media management by narrowing its efforts on this key market segment.[9]

In this chapter, we look at the different types of B2B markets and examine the B2B buying process, with an eye toward how it differs from the B2C buying process we discussed in Chapter 6. Several factors influence the B2B buying process, and we discuss these as well.

| LO 7-1 | Describe the ways in which business-to-business (B2B) firms segment their markets. |

B2B MARKETS

The most visible types of B2B transactions are those in which manufacturers and service providers sell to other businesses. However, resellers, institutions, and governments also may be

▼ **EXHIBIT 7.1** B2B Markets

involved in B2B transactions. Therefore, in the next sections we describe each of these B2B organizations (see Exhibit 7.1).

Manufacturers and Service Providers

Manufacturers buy raw materials, components, and parts that allow them to make and market their own goods and ancillary services. For example, the German-based Volkswagen Group, the largest auto manufacturer in Europe, owns and distributes the Audi, Bentley, Bugatti, Lamborghini, Seat, Skoda, Scania VW, and VW Commercial Vehicles brands.[10] Whereas purchasing agents formerly spent 70 percent of their time searching for, analyzing, validating, and forwarding information about parts and components, today they can use VWSupplyGroup.com to communicate with suppliers for all transactions, from procurement to logistics. The VW Group system is used by 45,600 suppliers.[11] Purchasing agents receive product descriptions directly from suppliers online, which means search processes that used to take two hours now require about nine minutes. Users of the system receive alerts of potential parts shortages before they occur and thus can focus on efficiencies instead of redundant paperwork.

IBM provided the consulting services necessary to design the Volkswagen Group's system. IBM, which was once a major manufacturer of computers and related products, now generates 90 percent of its profits from its software, consulting, and financing businesses—all of which are considered services. Like Volkswagen Group, it requires a host of B2B products and services to support these businesses. For instance, the airlines that IBM consultants and service providers rely on to shuttle them around the globe also use a mix of products such as airplanes and fuel as well as consulting, legal, and other services. As Marketing Analytics 7.1 describes, IBM is constantly working to ensure that it can provide the features and capabilities its business customers need.

Resellers

Resellers are marketing intermediaries that resell manufactured products without significantly altering their form. For instance, **wholesalers** and **distributors** buy Xerox products and sell them to retailers (B2B transaction), then retailers

> IBM, WHICH WAS ONCE A MAJOR MANUFACTURER OF COMPUTERS AND RELATED PRODUCTS, NOW GENERATES OVER 90 PERCENT OF ITS PROFITS FROM ITS SOFTWARE, CONSULTING, AND FINANCING BUSINESSES.

resell those Xerox products to the ultimate consumer (B2C transaction). Alternatively, these retailers may buy directly from Xerox. Thus, wholesalers, distributors, and retailers are all resellers. Retailers represent resellers and engage in B2B transactions when they buy fixtures, capital investments, leasing locations, financing operations, and merchandise for their stores.

Institutions

Institutions, such as hospitals, educational organizations, and religious organizations, also purchase all kinds of goods and services. A public school system might have a $40 million annual budget for textbooks alone, which gives it significant buying power and enables it to take advantage of bulk discounts. However, if each school makes its own purchasing decisions, the system as a whole cannot leverage its combined buying power. Public institutions also engage in B2B relationships to fulfill their needs for capital construction, equipment, supplies, food, and janitorial services.

German-based Volkswagen Group, the largest auto manufacturer in Europe, owns and distributes numerous brands.

© Oliver Hardt/AFP/Getty Images/Newscom

Marketing Analytics

Clouding over Computing Power[i]

As their computing power and security demands escalate, few businesses want to maintain their own hardware and servers anymore. Instead, they look to the cloud, where they seek to purchase more computing power, provided at a faster speed, with lower costs.

In response, traditional mainframe providers such as IBM are moving to expand their presence in the cloud. In particular, IBM has devoted billions of dollars to enhancing its cloud capabilities. First, it purchased a cloud company called SoftLayer for $2 billion to add that firm's 13 cloud computing centers to IBM's own 12 data centers. Second, it announced recently that it would allocate an additional $1.2 billion to expanding its cloud computing centers worldwide.

The services provided by these cloud centers will include not just power and data storage but also access to some of IBM's proprietary software and related products. Perhaps most famously, for some of the best IBM clients it will offer access to Watson, IBM's famous *Jeopardy*-winning computer.

The Singaporean bank DBS Group Holdings plans to use Watson to provide up-to-date insights and lessons to its financial planners, who in turn will share that information with high-net-worth clients. With Watson analyzing the massive amounts of financial data available in nearly real time, DBS hopes to improve the customized advising services it provides to wealthy clients, who then may agree to do more of their investing with the bank. To gain this access, DBS will pay around $12 million over three years. It also agreed to share its own data, contributing and updating Watson's knowledge stores constantly.

How did IBM's Watson do on Jeopardy?
© Seth Wenig/AP Photo

Watson's contribution to this shift in emphasis is so notable that IBM has decided to establish a separate "Watson unit." Rather than separating employees responsible for software, hardware, and services, this division will bring together approximately 2,000 employees to address all topics related to Watson. Furthermore, the division has a budget of approximately $100 million to use to fund venture projects that develop apps based on its technology platform.

Government

In most countries, the central government is one of the largest purchasers of goods and services. For example, the U.S. federal government spends about $3.7 trillion annually on procuring goods and services.[12] If you add in the amount state and local governments spend, these numbers reach staggering proportions. Specifically, with its estimated outlay of over $526.6 billion for fiscal year 2014, the Pentagon represents a spending force to be reckoned with,[13] especially when it comes to aerospace and defense (A&D) manufacturers, some of the Pentagon's greatest suppliers of products.

Across these various B2B markets, purchasing methods might vary with the range of options being pursued. As Social and Mobile Marketing 7.1 highlights, iPads are playing increasing roles in educational institutions and businesses, which suggests that institutions need to start making purchasing decisions about them too.

The U.S. government spends over $5 billion a year on aerospace and defense for everything from nuts and bolts to this F-14 Tomcat jetfighter.
© Stocktrek/Getty Images RF

> " The U.S. federal government spends about $3.7 trillion annually on procuring goods and services. "

Social & Mobile Marketing

iPads Go to Work[ii]

Since their introduction, iPads have rocketed into widespread use for gaming, online access, music, videos, and e-mail. Tech-savvy business executives and educators also have noted some advantages of these devices that could make them useful at work, as well as at play. Tablet computers weigh less and cost less than laptop computers. Uploaded e-books can be more up to date and are less expensive than physical textbooks. And in both the classroom and the workplace, the use of iPads extends the enthusiastic adoption of technology that is already occurring naturally in social contexts.

These devices, educators have learned, go beyond delivery of course materials by saving additional funds for schools and increasing the value for students. Students can watch videos or tutorials, take notes, or use interactive programs that demonstrate particular skills. They can scroll effortlessly through documents or between texts to reach a section relevant to the current class discussion. Part-time and distance students can communicate more readily with their classmates, potentially enhancing collaboration and team-based learning. Visual learners, children with autism spectrum disorders or learning disabilities, and students who have grown up using electronic devices in various facets of their lives all can benefit from the interactive nature of iPads. And all students benefit from developing comfort with technology, a vital skill set in tomorrow's workforce.

The iPad is finding fans in the workplace as well. Executives, staff members, and clients at companies as diverse as Wells Fargo Bank, the business management software developer SAP, and Daimler's Mercedes-Benz have adopted the device. Airplane pilots have begun replacing paper binders full of flight manuals, navigation charts, and other materials with iPads. Siemens Energy has equipped some of its wind turbine service technicians with iPads so that they have convenient access to manuals, checklists, and cameras, even from atop a 300-foot tower.

iPad's manufacturer Apple claims that 80 percent of *Fortune* 100 companies are either using the device or have launched pilot projects to try it.

Whether in the classroom or in the workplace, iPads are not without their disadvantages. Schools may save money in textbook costs but will need funding for repairs and wireless infrastructure. Tablets may enhance learning, but they cannot replace teachers or peer-to-peer interactions. Academic and business users find that the virtual keyboard is challenging for composing longer text, sharing applications is burdensome, and multitasking is impossible. Some companies are put off by iPad security breaches; others reject Apple's traditional focus on the consumer market, often at the expense of business sales. Despite these challenges, the iPad has gained a strong foothold in both the classroom and the workplace.

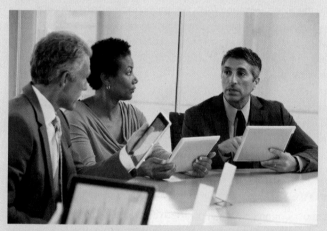

Eighty percent of Fortune 100 companies are either using the iPad or have launched pilot projects to try it.
© Ariel Skelley/Getty Images

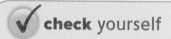

1. What are the various B2B markets?

LO 7-2 | List the steps in the B2B buying process.

THE BUSINESS-TO-BUSINESS BUYING PROCESS

As noted in the previous section, the B2B buying process is unique (Exhibit 7.2): It both parallels the B2C process and differs in several ways. Both start with need recognition, but the information search and alternative evaluation steps are more formal and structured in the B2B process. Typically, B2B buyers specify their needs in writing and ask potential suppliers to submit formal proposals, whereas B2C buying decisions are usually made by individuals or families and do not need formal proposals. Thus, for an individual to buy a tablet computer, all that is required is a trip to the store or a few minutes online and perhaps some preliminary research about iPads versus competitors.

For a school to buy thousands of tablet computers, however, it must complete requisition forms, accept bids from manufacturers, and obtain approval for the expenditure. The final decision rests with a committee, as is the case for most B2B buying decisions, which often demand a great deal of consideration. Finally, in B2C buying situations customers evaluate their purchase decision and sometimes experience postpurchase cognitive dissonance. But formal performance evaluations of the vendor and the products sold generally do not occur, as they do in the B2B setting. Let's examine all six stages in the context of

request for proposals (RFP) A process through which buying organizations invite alternative suppliers to bid on supplying their required components.

web portal An Internet site whose purpose is to be a major starting point for users when they connect to the web.

The first step in the B2B decision process is to recognize that the universities need to purchase 1,200 tablets.
© McGraw-Hill Education/Mark Dierker

a university buying tablets for its incoming first-year students to use as resources.

Stage 1: Need Recognition

In the first stage of the B2B buying process, the buying organization recognizes, through either internal or external sources, that it has an unfilled need. Hypothetical University wants to ensure its students are well educated and able to participate in a technologically connected workforce. It also seeks to grant them affordable access to required educational resources, from textbooks to library access to administrative tasks. The administration of the university also has reviewed research suggesting that portable devices, including tablet computers, can enhance students' in-class learning because they can directly and constantly interact with the materials and take notes in conjunction with the lecture and text, rather than only hearing information or seeing it on a whiteboard. The tablets also support innovative learning methodologies, such as the uses of interactive clickers in lecture-based courses. Using this information, the university has determined

> " Portals can provide tremendous cost savings because they eliminate periodic negotiations and routine paperwork, and they offer the means to form a supply chain that can respond quickly to the buyer's needs. "

it will issue a tablet to each of the 1,200 students entering as its next graduating class.

Stage 2: Product Specification

After recognizing the need and considering alternative solutions, including laptop computers, the university wrote a list of potential specifications that vendors might use to develop their proposals. The school's specifications include screen size, battery life, processor speed, how the device connects to the Internet, and delivery date. In addition, the board of directors of the university has requested that a bundle of educational apps be preloaded on the tablets, that all other apps be removed, and that each tablet come equipped with a screen protector, power cord, cover, stand, keyboard, and headphones. The school hopes to obtain a four-year service contract that includes replacement within 24 hours for any tablets that are returned to the vendor for servicing.

Stage 3: RFP Process

The **request for proposals (RFP)** is a common process through which organizations invite alternative vendors or suppliers to bid on supplying their required components or specifications. The purchasing company may simply post its RFP needs on its website or work through various B2B web portals or inform their preferred vendors directly. Because the university does not have a preferred vendor for tablets yet, it issues an RFP and invites various tablet suppliers, technology companies, and other interested parties to bid on the contract.

Smaller companies may lack the ability to attract broad attention to their requests, so they might turn to a **web portal**, an Internet site whose purpose is to be a major starting point for users when they connect to the web. Although there are general portals such as Yahoo! or MSN, B2B partners connect to specialized or niche portals to participate in online information exchanges and transactions. These exchanges help streamline procurement or distribution processes. Portals can provide tremendous cost savings because they eliminate periodic negotiations and routine paperwork,

▼ **EXHIBIT 7.2** Business-to-Business Buying Process

Need recognition → Product specification → RFP process → Proposal analysis and supplier selection → Order specification → Vendor performance assessment using metrics

> # SOME FIRMS HAVE A POLICY THAT REQUIRES THEM TO NEGOTIATE WITH SEVERAL SUPPLIERS, PARTICULARLY IF THE PRODUCT OR SERVICE REPRESENTS A CRITICAL COMPONENT OR ASPECT OF THE BUSINESS.

and they offer the means to form a supply chain that can respond quickly to the buyer's needs.

Small to medium-sized companies looking for skilled service workers also can use portals such as Guru.com, started to help freelance professionals connect with companies that need their services, whether those services entail graphic design and cartooning or finance and accounting advice. Currently, nearly 1 million professionals list their offerings on this service-oriented professional exchange, and more than 30,000 companies regularly visit the site to post work orders. Guru.com thus provides value to both companies and freelancers by offering not only a site for finding each other but also dispute resolution, escrow for payments, and a means to rate freelancer quality.[14]

Stage 4: Proposal Analysis, Vendor Negotiation, and Selection

The buying organization, in conjunction with its critical decision makers, evaluates all the proposals it receives in response to its RFP. Hypothetical University reviews all proposals it receives, together with the board of directors, representatives from the teachers' union, and members of the student government. Many firms narrow the process to a few suppliers, often those with which they have existing relationships, and discuss key terms of the sale, such as price, quality, delivery, and financing. The university likely considers the bid by the company that installed computers in its library, assuming that provider performed well. Some firms have a policy that requires them to negotiate with several suppliers, particularly if the product or service represents a critical component or aspect of the business. This policy keeps suppliers on their toes; they know that the buying firm can always shift a greater portion of its business to an alternative supplier if it offers better terms.

The university evaluates proposals on the basis of the amount of experience the vendor has with tablet computers and similar technology products, because it wants to make sure that its investment is reliable in the short term and flexible enough to accommodate new apps or updates. In addition, the school wants to be sure the technology will remain relevant in the longer term and not become obsolete. The vendor's ability to meet its specifications also is important because if the processor is too slow, students are unlikely to make use of the devices. The vendor's financial position provides an important indication of whether the vendor will be able to stay in business.

Stage 5: Order Specification

In the fifth stage, the firm places its order with its preferred supplier (or suppliers). The order includes a detailed description of the goods, prices, delivery dates, and, in some cases, penalties for noncompliance. The supplier then sends an acknowledgment that it has received the order and fills it by the specified date. In the case of the school's tablets, the terms are clearly laid out regarding when and how the vendor is expected to perform any preventive maintenance, who the contact person is for any problems with delivery or the tablets themselves, and under what circumstances the vendor will be expected to provide a replacement for a malfunctioning tablet. Issues such as maintenance and replacement are important, because the university does not plan to keep any inventory of extra tablets on hand.

Stage 6: Vendor Performance Assessment Using Metrics

Just as in the consumer buying process, firms analyze their vendors' performance so they can make decisions about their future purchases. The difference is that in a B2B setting, this analysis is typically more formal and objective. Let's consider how Hypothetical University might evaluate the tablet vendor's performance, as in Exhibit 7.3, using the following metrics: delivery (based on promised delivery date), quality, customer service, and issue resolution.

1. The buying team develops a list of issues that it believes are important to consider in the vendor evaluation.

2. To determine the importance of each issue (column 1), the buying team assigns an importance score to each (column 2).

▼ **EXHIBIT 7.3** Evaluating a Vendor's Performance

(1) Key Issues	(2) Importance Score	(3) Vendor's Performance	(4) Importance × Performance (2) × (3)
Customer Service	0.40	5	2.0
Issue Resolution	0.20	4	0.8
Delivery	0.10	5	0.5
Quality	0.30	3	0.9
Total	1.0		4.2

buying center The group of people typically responsible for the buying decisions in large organizations.

initiator The buying center participant who first suggests buying the particular product or service.

influencer The buying center participant whose views influence other members of the buying center in making the final decision.

decider The buying center participant who ultimately determines any part of or the entire buying decision—whether to buy, what to buy, how to buy, or where to buy.

buyer The buying center participant who handles the paperwork of the actual purchase.

user The person who consumes or uses the product or service purchased by the buying center.

gatekeeper The buying center participant who controls information or access to decision makers and influencers.

The more important the issue, the higher its score, but the importance scores must add up to 1. In this case, the buying team believes that customer service and quality are most important, whereas the issue resolution and delivery are comparatively less important.

3. In the third column, the buying team assigns numbers that reflect its judgments about how well the vendor performs. Using a 5-point scale, where 1 equals poor performance and 5 equals excellent performance, the university decides that the tablet vendor performs quite well on all issues except product quality.

4. To calculate an overall performance score in the fourth column, the team combines the importance of each issue and the vendor's performance scores by multiplying them. Because the tablet vendor performed well on the most important issues, when we add the importance/performance scores in column 4, we find that the overall evaluation is pretty good—4.2 on a 5-point scale.

 check yourself

1. Identify the stages in the B2B buying process.
2. How do you perform a vendor analysis?

LO 7-3 | Identify the roles within the buying center.

THE BUYING CENTER

In most large organizations, several people are responsible for buying decisions. These **buying center** participants can range from employees who have a formal role in purchasing decisions (i.e., the purchasing or procurement department) to members of the design team that is specifying the particular equipment or raw material needed for employees who will be using a new machine that is being ordered. All these employees are likely to play different roles in the buying process, which vendors must understand and adapt to in their marketing and sales efforts.

We can categorize six buying roles within a typical buying center (see Exhibit 7.4). One or more people may take on a certain role, or one person may take on more than one of the following roles: (1) **initiator**, the person who first suggests

buying the particular product or service; (2) **influencer**, the person whose views influence other members of the buying center in making the final decision; (3) **decider**, the person who ultimately determines any part of or the entire buying decision—whether to buy, what to buy, how to buy, or where to buy; (4) **buyer**, the person who handles the paperwork of the actual purchase; (5) **user**, the person who consumes or uses the product or service; and (6) **gatekeeper**, the person who controls information or access, or both, to decision makers and influencers.[15]

To illustrate how a buying center operates, consider purchases made by a hospital. Where do hospitals obtain their X-ray machines, syringes, and bedpans? Why are some medical procedures covered in whole or in part by insurance, whereas others are not? Why might your doctor recommend one type of allergy medication instead of another?

▼ **EXHIBIT 7.4** Buying Center Roles

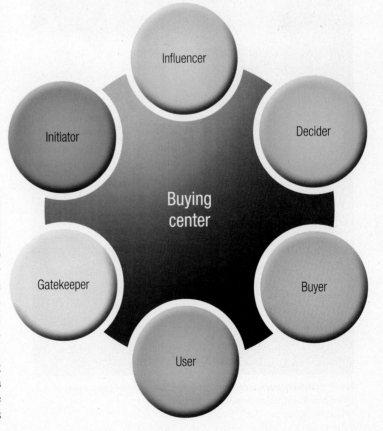

organizational culture Reflects the set of values, traditions, and customs that guide a firm's employees' behavior.

boycott A group's refusal to deal commercially with some organization to protest against its policies.

The Initiator—Your Doctor When you seek treatment from your physician, he or she initiates the buying process by determining the products and services that will best address and treat your illness or injury. For example, say that you fell backward off your snowboard and, in trying to catch yourself, you shattered your elbow. You require surgery to mend the affected area, which includes the insertion of several screws to hold the bones in place. Your doctor promptly notifies the hospital to schedule a time for the procedure and specifies the brand of screws she wants on hand for your surgery.

The Influencer—The Medical Device Supplier, the Pharmacy For years your doctor has been using ElbowMed screws, a slightly higher-priced screw. Her

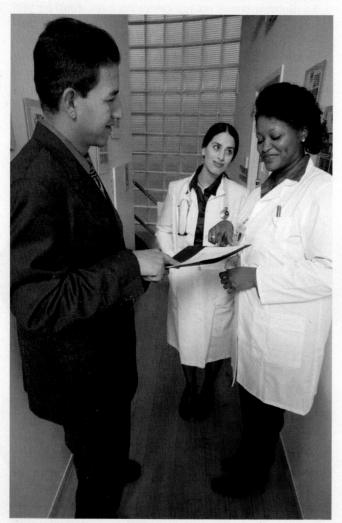

From an ethical perspective, what information should pharmaceutical sales representatives provide to doctors?
© Custom Medical Stock Photo

first introduction to ElbowMed screws came from the company's sales representative, who visited her office to demonstrate how ElbowMed screws were far superior to those of its competition. Your doctor recognized ElbowMed as a good value. Armed with empirical data and case studies, ElbowMed's sales rep effectively influenced your doctor's decision to use that screw.

The Decider—The Hospital Even though your doctor requested ElbowMed screws, the hospital ultimately is responsible for deciding whether to buy ElbowMed screws. The hospital supplies the operating room, instrumentation, and surgical supplies, and, therefore, the hospital administrators must weigh a variety of factors to determine whether the ElbowMed screw is not only best for the patients but also involves a cost that is reimbursable by various insurance providers.

The Buyer The actual buyer of the screw will likely be the hospital's materials manager, who is charged with buying and maintaining inventory for the hospital in the most cost-effective manner. Whereas ElbowMed screws are specific to your type of procedure, other items, such as gauze and sutures, may be purchased through a group purchasing organization (GPO), which obtains better prices through volume buying.

The User—The Patient Ultimately, the buying process for this procedure will be greatly affected by the user, namely you, and your broken elbow. If you are uncomfortable with the procedure or have read about alternative procedures that you prefer, you may decide that ElbowMed screws are not the best treatment.

The Gatekeeper—The Insurance Company Your insurer may believe that ElbowMed screws are too expensive and that other screws deliver equally effective results and therefore refuse to reimburse the hospital in full or in part for the use of the screws.

In the end, the final purchase decision must take into consideration every buying center participant. Ethical and Societal Dilemma 7.1 examines the unethical, illegal, but also international practice of influencing the influencers through expensive gifts and payments.

| LO 7-4 | Describe the different types of organizational cultures. |

Organizational Culture

A firm's **organizational culture** reflects the set of values, traditions, and customs that guide its employees' behavior. The firm's culture often comprises a set of unspoken guidelines that employees share with one another through various work situations. For example, Walmart buyers are not allowed to accept even the smallest gift from a vendor, not even a cup of coffee. This rule highlights its overall corporate culture: It is a low-cost operator whose buyers must base their decisions only on the products' and vendors' merits.

ethical&societal dilemma

7.1

Is It Business or Bribery?[iii]

In some parts of the world, accepting money, offering expensive gifts, or distributing payments to government and business officials to influence business decisions is considered an acceptable business practice. In other nations, these practices are unethical and illegal. As the world moves to a more global economy, pressure is mounting to level the playing field by eliminating bribery. Yet companies that have traditionally relied on business bribery argue that criminalizing this activity will negatively affect their ability to compete. How do executives doing business on an international scale respond when a behavior that could earn them a lucrative contract in one country could earn them jail time in another?

Whenever businesses cooperate with one another or companies intersect with governments, the opportunity exists for bribery. An extravagant gift or economic incentive may mean one contractor lands a lucrative contract. A private exchange of money between an executive and a public official may result in the official driving a new car while the executive's company bypasses a restriction that could hinder its growth. These types of interactions occur behind closed doors and between two people, yet they can have significant repercussions, including unsafe infrastructure, bridges, and buildings, if they occur in the context of large business transactions. Increasingly, players in the world's economies thus are pushing for an end to foreign bribery.

One tactic they are using is a public report by Transparency International that compares corruption rates of countries and industries. This investigation reveals unexpected trends, such as evidence that bribes passing from one business to another are almost as common as bribes slipped to public officials. By highlighting those business sectors or countries perceived as the worst offenders, the Bribery Index also

aims to bring about change, whether through embarrassment or economic repercussions that result when companies refuse to do business in corrupt economies. Finally, this report highlights suggestions for reducing corruption and incentives for improvement.

As summarized in the graph below, the Transparency International Bribery Index reveals that all the world's 28 largest economies engage in bribery; China and Russia emerged as those most likely to be using money and gifts to influence decisions. Both countries have recently begun enforcing legal repercussions for companies and individuals that engage in international business bribery. For example, when reports surfaced that representatives of GlaxoSmithKline (GSK) had bribed doctors, medical practices, and hospitals to prescribe only GSK drugs, China's news media and central government reacted with anger. Calling the drug company a "criminal godfather," Chinese authorities encouraged consumers to boycott its products. A **boycott** is when a group refuses to deal commercially with an organization to protest against its policies. As a result, GSK's business revenues fell by two-thirds in China.

Although in some parts of the world bribes are part of doing business, in the U.S. they are unethical and illegal.
© James Lauritz/Photodisc/Getty Images RF

The Transparency International report also highlights positive results of reduced corruption: A business survey conducted in Europe found that two-thirds of respondents believe that a company with a reputation for ethical behavior enjoys a commercial advantage. Findings such as these, along with improved transparency added to business practices, international anticorruption standards, monitoring and enforcement of anticorruption business policies and laws, and empowerment of whistle-blowers, may also help reduce international bribery rates.

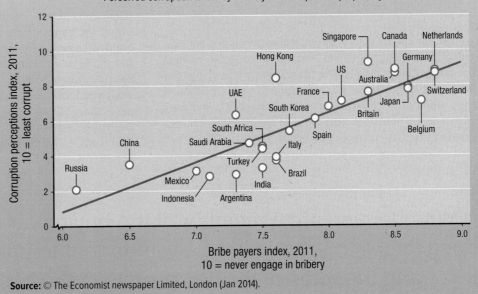

Perceived corruption levels by country and companies' propensity to bribe

Source: © The Economist newspaper Limited, London (Jan 2014).

autocratic buying center A buying center in which one person makes the decision alone, though there may be multiple participants.

democratic buying center A buying center in which the majority rules in making decisions.

consultative buying center A buying center in which one person makes the decision but he or she solicits input from others before doing so.

consensus buying center A buying center in which all members of the team must reach a collective agreement that they can support a particular purchase.

As these examples show, organizational culture can have a profound influence on purchasing decisions. Corporate buying center cultures can be divided into four general types: autocratic, democratic, consultative, and consensus (as illustrated in Exhibit 7.5). Knowing which buying center culture is prevalent in a given organization helps the seller decide how to approach that particular client, how and to whom to deliver pertinent information, and to whom to make sales presentations.

In an **autocratic buying center**, even though there may be multiple participants, one person makes the decision alone, whereas the majority rules in a **democratic buying center**. **Consultative buying centers** use one person to make a decision but solicit input from others before doing so. Finally, in a **consensus buying center**, all members of the team must reach a collective agreement that they can support a particular purchase.[17]

Cultures act like living, breathing entities that change and grow, just as organizations do. Even within some companies, culture may vary by geography, by division, or by functional department. Whether you are a member of the buying center or a supplier trying to sell to it, it is extremely important to understand its culture and the roles of the key players in the buying process. Not knowing the roles of the key players could waste a lot of time and even alienate the real decision maker.

▼ **EXHIBIT 7.5** Organizational Buying Culture

Building B2B Relationships

In B2B contexts there are a multitude of ways to enhance relationships, and these methods seem to be advancing and evolving by the minute.[18] For example, blogs and social media can build awareness, provide search engine results, educate potential and existing clients about products or services, and warm up a seemingly cold corporate culture. An expert who offers advice and knowledge about products increases brand awareness, and a blog is a great medium for this information. Web analytics, such as traffic on the website and the number of comments, can offer tangible evaluations, but a better measure is how often the blog gets mentioned elsewhere, the media

At GE, the culture aims to ensure that members and partners regard B2B as a source of innovation, not a "boring-to-boring" proposition. Rather than lament the relatively less glamorous process of B2B processes, GE has "decided we are geeky and we are proud of it."[16] To promote its offerings, the company thus focuses on how it innovates in B2B settings, and it brings this attitude into its purchasing decisions.

" Whether you are a member of the buying center or a supplier trying to sell to it, it is extremely important to understand its culture and the roles of the key players in the buying process. "

attention it receives, and the interaction, involvement, intimacy, and influence that it promotes.

The LinkedIn.com social network is mainly used for professional networking in the B2B marketplace (see Social and Mobile Marketing 7.2). Twitter, the microblogging site, is also valuable for B2B marketers because they can communicate with other businesses as often as they want. Companies such as HootSuite make it easier for companies using Twitter to manage their followers, update their posts, track analytics, and even schedule tweets, just as they would to manage a traditional marketing campaign.[19]

When executives confront an unfulfilled business need, they normally turn to **white papers** prepared by potential B2B marketers.[20] White papers are a promotional technique used by B2B sellers to provide information about a product or service in an educational context, thereby not appearing like a promotion or propaganda. The goal of white papers is to provide valuable information that a potential B2B buyer can easily understand and that will help the company address its problems with new solutions. For instance, a B2B seller has a technologically advanced solution for an inventory problem. Since the executives of the potential B2B buying

white papers In a B2B context, white papers are a promotional technique used by B2B sellers to provide information about a product or service in an educational context, thereby not appearing like a promotion or propaganda.

Social & Mobile Marketing 7.2
Making the Most of LinkedIn[iv]

Business-to-business (B2B) marketing may seem relatively impersonal, but even in formalized, standardized buying situations personal relationships count. Social media, with a bit of a tweak, play a key role in this setting, just as they do in consumer contexts. Perhaps the best example is LinkedIn, the social media site for business professionals. Launched in 2003, the site has been attracting roughly 1 million members weekly. Its worldwide membership surpassed the 200 million mark. The site is available in over 19 languages and more than 200 countries, which means that it can help B2B interactions overcome geographic boundaries.

In particular, LinkedIn can boast that executives from all the *Fortune* 500 companies have memberships on its site. Accordingly, its promise for networking, whether individually or for the company, is virtually unsurpassed. Such networking entails several key groups:

- *Customers and prospective customers.* LinkedIn allows a firm or its representatives to introduce themselves to possible buyers, using a credible and easily accessible format. The Q&A option on LinkedIn pages also allows customers to ask questions and suppliers to demonstrate their expertise.

- *Investors.* The LinkedIn page offers tangible evidence of the firm's existence and its promise, which is critical information for outsiders who might be willing to invest in its development.

- *Suppliers.* By starting their own group on LinkedIn, B2B buyers might better identify which suppliers in the market are best matched with their needs and most interested in providing the resources they need.

- *Employees and prospective employees.* LinkedIn is a great source for finding employees who are diligent, professional, interested, and qualified. Furthermore, if a firm retains its links to former employees,

LinkedIn is perhaps the best social media site for networking with business professionals.
© Paul Sakuma/AP Photo

it can gain a good source of referrals—assuming those employees left on good terms.

- *Analysts.* The job of an analyst is to find detailed information about a company and then recommend it, or not, to the market. LinkedIn gives firms a means to provide that information in a credible but still firm-controlled context.

The site also provides sophisticated analytics for keeping track of all these networking opportunities. Users can see who visited their pages, which descriptions they viewed, and even compare their LinkedIn performance against competitors' pages.

new buy In a B2B setting, a purchase of a good or service for the first time; the buying decision is likely to be quite involved because the buyer or the buying organization does not have any experience with the item.

firm are not technologically oriented, the B2B seller creates a white paper to explain the solution in non-technological terms so that the buying firm's executives can understand and appreciate the solution before they consider a purchase.

> " Many apparel companies make a significant portion of their revenue through sponsorship deals that grant them the right to sell apparel with popular university logos. "

for their sports teams. Those with successful sports teams have been very successful in managing these relationships, to the benefit of both the team and the company.[21] Large universities that win national championships, such as the University of Alabama or University of Southern California (USC), can solicit sponsorships in exchange for free athletic equipment, whereas less popular teams or smaller schools typically must accept an upfront sponsorship and then agree to buy from that vendor for a specified period of time. In exchange for this sponsorship, the vendors gain the right to sell apparel with the university logo and require the school's team to purchase only their equipment. Many apparel companies make a significant portion of their revenue through sponsorship deals that grant them the right to sell apparel with popular university logos.

In a **new buy** situation, a customer purchases a good or service for the first time,[22] which means the buying decision is likely to be quite involved because the buyer or the buying organization does not have any experience with the item. In the B2B context, the buying center is likely to proceed through all six steps in the buying process and involve many people in the buying decision. Typical new buys might range from capital equipment to components that the firm previously made itself but now has decided to purchase instead. For example, a small college might need to decide which apparel company to approach for a sponsorship. For smaller colleges, finding a company that will sponsor multiple sports teams—such as women's soccer as well as men's basketball—is a priority, though it also

LO 7-5 | Detail different buying situations.

THE BUYING SITUATION

The type of buying situation also affects the B2B decision process. Most B2B buying situations can be categorized into three types: new buys, modified rebuys, and straight rebuys (see Exhibit 7.6). To illustrate the nuances among these three buying situations, consider how colleges and universities develop relationships with some of their suppliers. Most universities negotiate with sports apparel manufacturers, such as Nike, Reebok, and New Balance, to establish purchasing agreements

▼ **EXHIBIT 7.6** Buying Situations

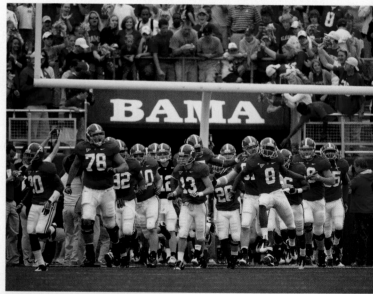

Schools like the University of Alabama negotiate with sports apparel manufacturers, such as Nike, to get free athletic equipment. The manufacturers, in turn, get to sell apparel with the university logo.
© Bob Rosato/Sports Illustrated/Getty Images

must balance other considerations, such as the length of the contract. Some vendors offer perks to attract new buyers; New Balance offers teams that sign up for long-term contracts custom fittings for their players' shoes. Each season, a sales team from New Balance visits the school and custom fits each player to achieve the best fit possible.

With another sort of example, Adding Value 7.1 highlights how HubSpot helps buyers become more informed about products before engaging in the B2B buying process.

Another example of a new buy occurs in the fashion industry, where runway shows offer wholesale buyers an opportunity to inspect new lines of clothing and place orders. Designer sales often occur during private meetings with buyers, both before and after runway shows. Buyers meet with

Adding Value   7.1

Getting Out the Message with Inbound Marketing[v]

Search engines, company web pages, social media sites, and the blogosphere have transformed the way businesses learn about and shop for products and services. Unlike a decade ago, when a prospective customer had little knowledge of a vendor's products at first contact, today's customers have searched the Internet using relevant keywords and reviewed company websites by the time they speak with a vendor. As a result, they are well informed and seriously interested in a purchase, adding new efficiency to B2B transactions. But this development works only if companies have the marketing savvy to use today's technology to their advantage.

Two entrepreneurs noticed that small companies and start-ups without the skills to use these tools effectively get lost in the noise, even if prospective customers are searching for vendors in their niche. Furthermore, companies that enlist marketing firms are disadvantaged if those firms rely solely on traditional best practices, such as print advertising, telemarketing, and trade shows. To help these businesses, the two launched a software marketing program, HubSpot, designed to help companies transform their marketing approach. The idea was to abandon intrusive outbound marketing, which people are increasingly able to screen out, and replace it with **inbound marketing**. Inbound marketing, defined as any marketing tactic that relies on earning customer interest rather than buying it, is built on the understanding that Facebook, Twitter, online user reviews, smartphones, blogs, and websites are the true force behind the way consumers in today's marketplace actually learn and shop.

HubSpot's software contains easy-to-use tools that help companies get noticed, convert website visitors to customers, and analyze the effectiveness of marketing efforts across channels. Among the tools in the first category, for example, is a keyword grader that helps companies create content and a list of relevant keywords to improve search engine odds and ranking. Using the lead conversion tools, marketers without technical skills can create landing pages with customizable lead capture forms, auto-response e-mails, and thank-you pages. These tools can also be used to send customized e-mails to new leads on

a self-selected schedule. The marketing analytics tools allow HubSpot's customers to track competitors, evaluate the impact of a blog, and compare the effectiveness of all marketing channels to provide important insight into the behaviors of customers and the value of each channel to the bottom line.

HubSpot's approach has been successful for both the founders and their customers. The company, launched in June 2006, reached 3,500 customers in four years and is the second-fastest-growing software-as-a-service (SaaS) company in history.

One customer, the nonprofit National Institute for Fitness and Sport (NIFS), wanted to increase its visibility with corporate and retirement fitness centers. After experiencing difficulty driving traffic to the company website—and after an expensive marketing company campaign proved ineffective—NIFS turned to HubSpot. The results were increases in traffic and leads by more than 200 percent and an increase in social media traffic of 16 percent. According to NIFS's director of media, the fitness company "picked up a number of requests for proposals from businesses that never would have paid attention to us initially because we were able to raise where we sit in the search engines."

Companies such as HubSpot are taking advantage of changes that have already occurred in the marketplace to reduce costs and improve the effectiveness of marketing. As technology evolves and more business and individual shoppers use online information to make their purchasing decisions, businesses will have to adapt their marketing strategies to encompass new technologies and new shopping behaviors.

HubSpot helps its customers get noticed on the Internet.
© Hubspot

the designers, discuss the line, and observe a model wearing the clothing. The buyer's challenge then is to determine which items will sell best in the retail stores he or she represents while trying to imagine what the item will look like in regular, as opposed to model, sizes. Buyers must also negotiate purchases for orders that may not be delivered for as much as six months. Buyers can suggest modifications to make the clothing more or less expensive or more comfortable for their customers. Buyers and designers recognize the significant value of this relationship, which occasionally prompts buyers to purchase a few items from a designer, even if those items do not exactly fit the store's core customers' tastes. Doing so ensures that the buyer will have access to the designer's collection for the next season.[23]

In a **modified rebuy**, the buyer has purchased a similar product in the past but has decided to change some specifications, such as the desired price, quality level, customer service level, options, and so forth. Current vendors are likely to have an advantage in acquiring the sale in a modified rebuy situation as long as the reason for the modification is not

These varied types of buying situations call for very different marketing and selling strategies. The most complex and difficult is the new buy because it requires the buying organization to make changes in its current practices and purchases. As a result, several members of the buying center will likely become involved, and the level of their involvement will be more intense than in the case of modified and straight rebuys. In new buying situations, buying center members also typically spend more time at each stage of the B2B buying process, similar to the extended decision-making process that consumers use in the B2C process. In comparison, in modified rebuys the buyers spend less time at each stage of the B2B buying process, similar to limited decision making in the B2C process (see Chapter 6).

In straight rebuys, however, the buyer is often the only member of the buying center involved in the process. Like a consumer's habitual purchase, straight rebuys often enable the buyer to recognize the firm's need and go directly to the fifth step in the B2B buying process, skipping the product specification, RFP process, proposal analysis, and supplier selection steps.

Over the course of a B2B relationship, the type of buying process also can change. The buying process for restaurants appears poised to undergo a significant transformation, because of the potential merger between Sysco and US Foods, the two largest food distributors in the United States. Restaurants that once considered their purchases of hamburger meat a straight rebuy might find that they need to reconsider

> # THESE VARIED TYPES OF BUYING SITUATIONS CALL FOR VERY DIFFERENT MARKETING AND SELLING STRATEGIES.

dissatisfaction with the vendor or its products. The Ohio State University's sports department might ask adidas to modify the specifications for its basketball shoes after noticing some improvements made to the adidas shoes used by the University of Michigan.

Straight rebuys occur when the buyer or buying organization simply buys additional units of products that had previously been purchased. Many B2B purchases are likely to fall in the straight rebuy category. For example, sports teams need to repurchase a tremendous amount of equipment that is not covered by apparel sponsorships, such as tape for athletes' ankles or weights for the weight room. The purchase of bottled water also typically involves a straight rebuy from an existing supplier.

the process. Because the merger would create a single, dominant food supplier, the new company will gain much more power over pricing. In turn, restaurants might need to enter into a modified rebuy (e.g., purchase lower-quality hamburger to cut costs).

Thus, in various ways B2B marketing both differs from and mirrors the consumer behavior (B2C) process we detailed in Chapter 6. The differences in the six stages of the buying process make sense in view of the many unique factors that come into play. The constitution of the buying center (initiator, influencer, decider, buyer, user, and gatekeeper), the culture of the purchasing firm (autocratic, democratic, consultative, or consensus), and the context of the buying situation (new buy, modified rebuy, straight rebuy) all influence the B2B buying process in various ways, which means that sellers must be constantly aware of these factors if they want to be successful in their sales attempts. Finally, just as it has done seemingly everywhere we look, the Internet has radically changed some elements of the B2B world, increasing the frequency of both private electronic exchanges and auctions. ■

✓ **check** yourself

1. What factors affect the B2B buying process?
2. What are the six buying roles?
3. How do new buy, straight rebuy, and modified rebuy differ?

Increase your engagement and learning with Connect Marketing.

These Connect activities, available only through your Connect course, have been designed to make the following concepts more meaningful and applicable:

▶ The Buying Center Click and Drag Activity

▶ The B2B Buying Process: Toyota Timeline Creation

▶ B2B: Dole Video Case

▶ B2B Buying: iSeeit! Video

eight

R eviewing the tumultuous history and modern operations of Coca-Cola in India is like taking a quick survey of global marketing issues. From early failures to notable impacts on local regulations to joint efforts to growth efforts, the story of how this global brand has sought to make its mark in this developing nation is instructive.

When Coke first thought to move into India in the 1970s, it confronted a critical cultural difference between its home base and this foreign market. India was officially closed to foreign investment at the time, which meant that to enter, Coke would have to find an equal, Indian partner. Such a joint venture partnership would have required it to share its famously protected, secret formula for making its carbonated beverage. It was totally unwilling to do so, thus it left for more than 20 years.

But as many developing nations have, India liberalized its economy, opening it to more foreign investments and offering more opportunities for foreign companies to enter. Accordingly, Coca-Cola came back

global marketing

LEARNING OBJECTIVES

After reading this chapter, you should be able to:

LO 8-1 Describe the components of a country market assessment.

LO 8-2 Understand the marketing opportunities in BRIC countries.

LO 8-3 Identify the various market entry strategies.

LO 8-4 Highlight the similarities and differences between a domestic marketing strategy and a global marketing strategy.

in the mid-1990s,[1] but only a few years after its primary rival Pepsi had established a strong base there. To ensure its competitiveness and expand its coverage of the Indian consumer market, Coke bought four local soda brands, so that it gained about 60 percent of the market, far outpacing Pepsi's 30 percent. Yet Coke itself is not the most popular carbonated drink. That

continued on p. 146

continued from p. 145

Coke plans to invest heavily in India to stimulate demand.
© Erica Simone Leeds

distinction belongs to Thums Up, one of the Indian brands Coca-Cola purchased.[2]

Thus, Coke still faces some critical problems in the Indian market. In particular, people just don't drink that much Coke. Whereas the average global consumer drinks 92 bottles of Coke each year, the average Indian consumer drinks only 12 of them (in Brazil, the average consumer drinks around 230 bottles each year).[3] But Coke believes it cannot just ignore this massive and growing consumer market, because it offers one of the few remaining parts of the world that offers such excellent growth opportunities.

Noting this potential, and in its efforts to "stay ahead of the curve," Coke plans to invest approximately $5 billion in India alone in the next few years.[4] With its investments in India and other developing nations, Coca-Cola is taking a very optimistic position: It plans to double its volumes sold and revenues by 2020. That's a pretty tall order for a fizzy drink that already ranks among the top global brands. ◼

Increasing globalization affects not only massive U.S. corporations that actively search out new markets but also small and medium-sized businesses that increasingly depend on goods produced globally to deliver their products and services. Few people think about how globalization affects their daily lives, but take a minute to read the labels on the clothing you are wearing right now. Chances are that most of the items, even if they carry U.S. brand names, were manufactured in another part of the world.

In the United States, the market has evolved from a system of regional marketplaces to national markets to geographically

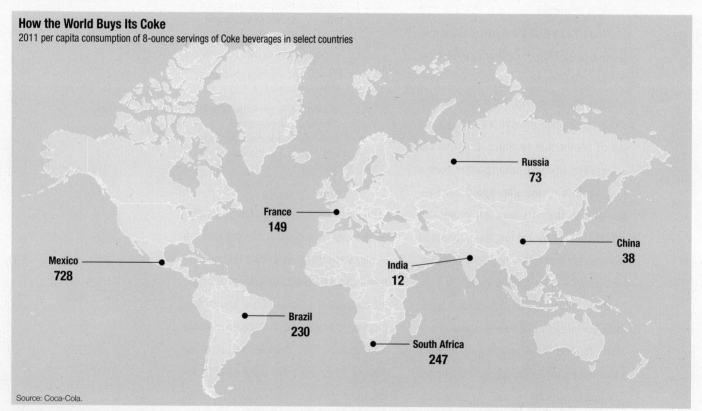

How the World Buys Its Coke
2011 per capita consumption of 8-ounce servings of Coke beverages in select countries

Russia 73
France 149
Mexico 728
India 12
China 38
Brazil 230
South Africa 247

Source: Coca-Cola.

Coke is a top global brand. However, its typical customer in India buys only 12 bottles per year, compared to 728 in Mexico, making India a country with enormous growth potential.

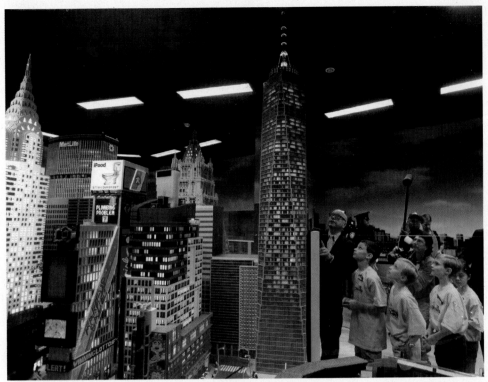

These 25-foot-tall replicas of the New York skyline are made completely out of Legos and have been on display at the Times Square Toys"R"Us in New York City. How do Legos get from their manufacturer in Denmark to toy stores in the United States?
© Dennis Van Tine/Newscom

from Chile in January. Or consider how a $12 digital camera for your keychain, made in Taiwan, could be produced, transported halfway around the world, and sold for so little money at your local Target. These are the questions we will be examining in this chapter.

We begin by looking at how firms assess the potential of a given market, with particular attention to the BRIC countries (Brazil, Russia, India, and China). Next we examine how firms make decisions to go global and choose how and what they will sell globally. Then we explore how to build the marketing mix for global products.

regional markets (e.g., Canada and the United States together) to international markets and finally to global markets. **Globalization** refers to the processes by which goods, services, capital, people, information, and ideas flow across national borders. Global markets are the result of several fundamental changes such as reductions or eliminations of trade barriers by country governments, the decreasing concerns of distance and time with regard to moving products and ideas across countries, the standardization of laws across borders, and globally integrated production processes.[5]

Each of these fundamental changes has paved the way for marketing to flourish in other countries. The elimination of trade barriers and other governmental actions, for instance, allows goods and ideas to move quickly and efficiently around the world, which in turn facilitates the quick delivery of goods to better meet the needs of global consumers.

As a consequence, consumers have easy access to global products and services. When we walk into a toy store we expect to find Lego brand toys from Denmark. In the local sporting goods store we anticipate finding running shoes made in China by the German firm, adidas. In the grocery store we demand out-of-season produce such as blueberries

LO 8-1 Describe the components of a country market assessment.

ASSESSING GLOBAL MARKETS

Because different countries, with their different stages of globalization, offer marketers a variety of opportunities, firms must assess the viability of various potential market entries. As illustrated in Exhibit 8.1, we examine four sets of criteria necessary to assess a country's market: economic analysis, infrastructure and technological analysis, government actions or inactions, and sociocultural analysis. Information about these four areas offers marketers a more complete picture of a country's potential as a market for products and services.

Economic Analysis Using Metrics

The greater the wealth of people in a country, generally, the better the opportunity a firm will have in that particular country. A firm conducting an economic analysis of a country market must

> " The greater the wealth of people in a country, generally, the better the opportunity a firm will have in that particular country. "

trade deficit Results when a country imports more goods than it exports.

trade surplus Occurs when a country has a higher level of exports than imports.

gross domestic product (GDP) Defined as the market value of the goods and services produced by a country in a year; the most widely used standardized measure of output.

gross national income (GNI) Consists of GDP plus the net income earned from investments abroad (minus any payments made to nonresidents who contribute to the domestic economy).

purchasing power parity (PPP) A theory that states that if the exchange rates of two countries are in equilibrium, a product purchased in one will cost the same in the other, expressed in the same currency.

look at three major economic factors using well-established metrics: the general economic environment, the market size and population growth rate, and real income.

Evaluating the General Economic Environment

In general, healthy economies provide better opportunities for global marketing expansions, and there are several ways a firm can use metrics to measure the relative health of a particular country's economy. Each way offers a slightly different view, and some may be more useful for some products and services than for others.

To determine the market potential for its particular product or service, a firm should use as many metrics as it can obtain. One metric is the relative level of imports and exports. The United States, for example, suffers a **trade deficit**, which means that the country imports more goods than it exports.[6] For

U.S. marketers this deficit can signal the potential for greater competition at home from foreign producers. Firms would prefer to manufacture in a country that has a **trade surplus**, or a higher level of exports than imports, because it signals a greater opportunity to export products to more markets.

The most common way to gauge the size and market potential of an economy, and therefore the potential the country has for global marketing, is to use standardized metrics of output. **Gross domestic product (GDP)**, the most widely used of these metrics, is defined as the market value of the goods and services produced by a country in a year. **Gross national income (GNI)** consists of GDP plus the net income earned from investments abroad (minus any payments made to nonresidents who contribute to the domestic economy). In other words, U.S. firms that invest or maintain operations abroad count their income from those operations in the GNI but not the GDP.[7]

Another frequently used metric of an overall economy is the **purchasing power parity (PPP)**, a theory that states that if the exchange rates of two countries are in equilibrium, a product purchased in one will cost the same in the other, if expressed in the same currency.[8] A novel metric that employs PPP to assess the relative economic buying power among nations is *The Economist*'s Big Mac Index, which suggests that exchange rates should adjust to equalize the cost of a basket of goods and services, wherever it is bought around the world. Using McDonald's Big Mac as the market basket, Exhibit 8.2 shows that the cheapest burger is in India, where it costs $1.54, compared with an average American price of $4.62. In Brazil, the same burger costs $5.25. This index thus implies that the Indian rupee is 67 percent undervalued, whereas the Brazilian real is about 13 percent overvalued, in comparison with the U.S. dollar.[9]

These various metrics help marketers understand the relative wealth of a particular country, though they may not give a full picture of the economic

▼ **EXHIBIT 8.1** Components of a Country Market Assessment

- General economic environment
- Market size and population growth
- Real income

- Transportation
- Channels
- Communication
- Commerce

Economic analysis using metrics

Infrastructure and technology

Sociocultural analysis

Government actions

- Power distance
- Uncertainty avoidance
- Individualism
- Masculinity
- Time orientation

- Tariff
- Quota
- Exchange control
- Trade agreement

▼ EXHIBIT 8.2 Big Mac Index

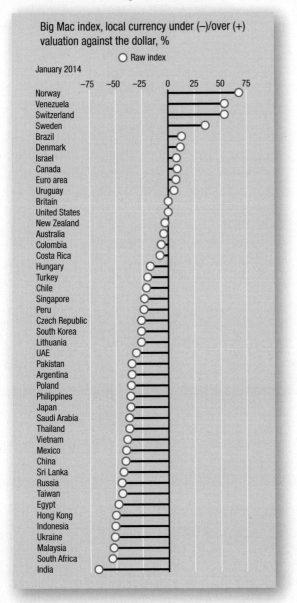

Big Mac index, local currency under (–)/over (+) valuation against the dollar, %

○ Raw index

January 2014

Country		(−75 to 75)
Norway		
Venezuela		
Switzerland		
Sweden		
Brazil		
Denmark		
Israel		
Canada		
Euro area		
Uruguay		
Britain		
United States		
New Zealand		
Australia		
Colombia		
Costa Rica		
Hungary		
Turkey		
Chile		
Singapore		
Peru		
Czech Republic		
South Korea		
Lithuania		
UAE		
Pakistan		
Argentina		
Poland		
Philippines		
Japan		
Saudi Arabia		
Thailand		
Vietnam		
Mexico		
China		
Sri Lanka		
Russia		
Taiwan		
Egypt		
Hong Kong		
Indonesia		
Ukraine		
Malaysia		
South Africa		
India		

Source: © The Economist newspaper Limited, London (Jan 2014).

health of a country because they are based solely on material output. Nor is a weak dollar always a bad thing. For U.S. exporters, a weak dollar means greater demand for their products in foreign countries because they can sell at a lower price.[10] Although an understanding of the macroeconomic environment is crucial for managers facing a market entry decision, of equal importance is the understanding of economic metrics of market size and population growth rate.

Evaluating Market Size and Population Growth Rate

Global population has been growing dramatically since the turn of the 20th century at least. From a marketing perspective, however, growth has never been equally dispersed. Today, less developed nations by and large are experiencing rapid population growth, while many developed countries are experiencing either zero or negative population growth. The countries with the highest purchasing power today may become less attractive in the future for many products and services because of stagnated growth. And the BRIC countries are likely to be the source of most market growth.

In response, consumer goods companies are paying close attention to the strong demand in BRIC nations. Procter & Gamble (P&G), which enjoys a strong advantage in the Chinese market, also is expanding aggressively into India and Brazil and encountering stiff competition. In Brazil oral care is a highly competitive market, with Colgate and P&G competing. In India, big-name Western firms are competing for market share of laundry products.[11]

Another aspect related to market size and population growth pertains to the distribution of the population within a particular region; namely, is the population located primarily in rural or urban areas? This distinction determines where and

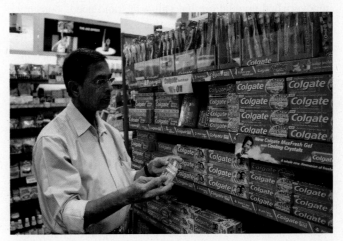

Procter & Gamble is expanding aggressively into India and encountering stiff competition.

© Sebastian D'Souza/Bloomberg/Getty Images

> "TODAY, LESS DEVELOPED NATIONS BY AND LARGE ARE EXPERIENCING RAPID POPULATION GROWTH, WHILE MANY DEVELOPED COUNTRIES ARE EXPERIENCING EITHER ZERO OR NEGATIVE POPULATION GROWTH."

infrastructure The basic facilities, services, and installations needed for a community or society to function, such as transportation and communications systems, water and power lines, and public institutions like schools, post offices, and prisons.

how products and services can be delivered. Long supply chains, in which goods pass through many hands, are often necessary to reach rural populations in less developed countries and therefore add to the products' cost. India's 1.2 billion people live overwhelmingly in rural areas, although the population is moving toward urban areas to meet the demands of the growing industrial and service centers located in major cities such as Bangalore and New Delhi. This population shift, perhaps not surprisingly, is accompanied by rapid growth in the middle class. Furthermore, relatively careful banking policies and minimal dependence on exports have helped protect India from the global financial crisis. The business impacts of these combined trends of increasing urbanization, a growing middle class, a degree of protectionism by the central government, and a youthful populace make India an absolutely enormous market for consumer goods.

Evaluating Real Income Firms can make adjustments to an existing product or change the price to meet the unique needs of a particular country market. Such shifts are particularly common for low-priced consumer goods. In settings in which consumers earn very low wages, the market is known as the "bottom of the pyramid." That is, there is a large, impoverished population that still wants and needs consumer goods but cannot pay the prices that the fewer, wealthier consumers in developed nations can. Thus P&G developed a single-use shampoo packet for consumers who cannot afford an entire bottle at one time. To increase consumption of Coca-Cola in rural India, the company lowered its price to the equivalent of about 10 cents per bottle; Cadbury International introduced Dairy Milk Shots for the equivalent of about 4 cents.[12] Textbook publishers sell paperback versions of U.S. books for a fraction of their U.S. price to countries where students would not otherwise be able to afford a textbook.

But pricing adjustments aren't only for inexpensive products. Fashion and jewelry manufacturers also make downward adjustments to their prices in countries where the incomes of their target markets cannot support higher prices. Nor is price the only factor that companies adjust to appeal to lower income markets. Haier sells washing machines that also have the capacity to wash vegetables to Chinese consumers who confront limited access to resources, such as water and electricity.[13]

Even as multinationals battle for dominance in emerging economies, local marketers are becoming increasingly price competitive in selling their wares. Local marketers already have strong familiarity with their markets, existing distribution channels, and good name recognition. These smaller firms can often exhibit greater flexibility in their pricing to hold on to market

For the Chinese market, Haier sells washing machines that can wash both clothes and vegetables.
© Haier America

share. They also might be able to find a market niche that remained hidden to international firms. In Macau, for example, big international brands have built massive luxury casinos for the gambling public. But a local casino brand offers very low minimum buy-in amounts, so that lower-income gamblers have a place to go.[14] The best outcome for everyone involved is not just a higher share of an existing market but rather the ongoing development of the market for everyone.[15]

Analyzing Infrastructure and Technological Capabilities

The next component of any market assessment is an infrastructure and technological analysis. **Infrastructure** is defined as the basic facilities, services, and installations needed for a community or society to function, such as transportation and communications systems, water and power lines, and public institutions such as schools, post offices, and prisons.

Marketers are especially concerned with four key elements of a country's infrastructure: transportation, distribution channels, communications, and commerce. First, there must be a system to transport goods throughout the various markets and to consumers in geographically dispersed marketplaces—trains, roads, refrigeration. Second, distribution channels must exist to deliver products in a timely manner and at a reasonable cost. Third, the communications system, particularly media access, must be sufficiently developed to allow consumers to find information about the products and services available in the marketplace. Fourth, the commercial infrastructure, which consists of the legal, banking, and regulatory systems, allows markets to function. In the next section, we focus on how issues pertaining to the political and legal structures of a country can affect the risk that marketers face in operating in a given country.

Analyzing Governmental Actions

Governmental actions, as well as the actions of nongovernmental political groups, can significantly influence firms' ability to sell goods and services because they often result in laws or other regulations that either promote the growth of the global market or close off the country and inhibit growth. Some of the effects are difficult to predict in advance, as Ethical and Societal Dilemma 8.1 describes.

> " Marketers are especially concerned with four key elements of a country's infrastructure: transportation, distribution channels, communications, and commerce. "

Tariffs A **tariff**, also called a **duty**, is a tax levied on a good imported into a country. In most cases, tariffs are intended to make imported goods more expensive and thus less competitive with domestic products, which in turn protects domestic industries from foreign competition. In other cases, tariffs might be imposed to penalize another country for trade practices that the home country views as unfair. For example, when the U.S. government determined the prices of solar panels imported from China were artificially low due to illegal subsidies, it imposed a tariff to help domestic firms compete.[16]

Quotas A **quota** designates a minimum or maximum quantity of a product that may be brought into a country during a specified time period. The United States, for instance, has committed to allowing at least 1.23 million tons of sugar to be imported (the quota) without a tariff because the country generally consumes more than

tariff A tax levied on a good imported into a country; also called a *duty*.

duty See *tariff*.

quota Designates the maximum quantity of a product that may be brought into a country during a specified time period.

ethical & societal dilemma 8.1

How Chinese Regulations Change Car-Buying Practices[i]

As the Scottish poet Robert Burns wrote, "The best laid schemes of mice and men/Go often awry." That is, we might have the best intentions to produce beneficial outcomes, but sometimes those plans have a way of leading to the opposite effect. It's a truth that consumer behavior researchers and marketers know only too well.

Consider, for example, the case of China and its latest attempt to limit automobile-induced air pollution. The expansion of China's middle class has created a vast new population of consumers who can now afford cars. The nation's roads, especially in urban centers such as Shanghai, Guangzhou, Guiyang, and Beijing, have become clogged with vehicles. Pollution

levels also have reached critical proportions. And China has moved into the top spot in terms of consumer car purchases, with some estimates suggesting that Chinese consumers will buy 30 million vehicles annually by 2020.

In response to these concerns, Chinese government officials have begun testing a licensing regulation that requires people to enter a lottery for a limited number of car registration tags. Without the license plate, drivers would face severe penalties. Thus, officials hoped to halt the growth in this sector and thereby limit pollution and congestion on the roads. Instead, consumers have taken the threat that the regulations would spread as a great reason to buy a new car immediately. If they might not be able to next year, they had better snag a car right now! In cities in which the regulations are already in place, the lucky license lottery winners also are buying bigger

(i.e., more polluting), more expensive vehicles. As one consumer noted, "Would you want to put a 100,000 yuan plate on a 50,000 yuan car?" Because these consumers already are spending more than they might have planned, just to have the chance to enter the lottery for a license, they feel more justified spending more on the car itself. Average prices paid per car thus have leapt up approximately 88 percent in just two years.

These trends are great news for foreign luxury carmakers like Audi and Mercedes-Benz, whose sales in China have jumped. It is not so great for Chinese carmakers, which have long provided the lower-end, functional vehicles that China's population previously demanded. It also might not be great news for the environment, which was not at all what authorities planned when they implemented these regulations. The best-laid schemes, indeed.

exchange control Refers to the regulation of a country's currency *exchange rate*.

exchange rate The measure of how much one currency is worth in relation to another.

trade agreement Intergovernmental agreement designed to manage and promote trade activities for specific regions.

trading bloc Consists of those countries that have signed a particular trade agreement.

it produces.[17] It then monitors consumption closely to protect domestic sugar farmers. If demand exceeds supply, it increases the quota, but the level depends on annual consumption and production rates.[18]

Tariffs and quotas can have fundamental and potentially devastating impacts on a firm's ability to sell products in another country. Tariffs artificially raise prices and therefore lower demand, and quotas reduce the availability of imported merchandise. Conversely, tariffs and quotas benefit domestically made products because they reduce foreign competition.

Exchange Control
Exchange control refers to the regulation of a country's currency **exchange rate**, the

significantly compared with other important world currencies. When the dollar falls, it has a twofold effect on U.S. firms' ability to conduct global business. For firms that depend on imports of finished products, raw materials that they fabricate into other products, or services from other countries, the cost of doing business goes up dramatically. At the same time, buyers in other countries find the costs of U.S. goods and services much lower than they were before.

Trade Agreements
Marketers must consider the **trade agreements** to which a particular country is a signatory or the **trading bloc** to which it belongs. A trade agreement is an intergovernmental agreement designed to manage and promote trade activities for a specific region, and a trading bloc consists of those countries that have signed the particular trade agreement.[20] Some major trade agreements cover

> " Tariffs artificially raise prices and therefore lower demand, and quotas reduce the availability of imported merchandise. "

measure of how much one currency is worth in relation to another.[19] A designated agency in each country, often the central bank, sets the rules for currency exchange, though in the United States the Federal Reserve sets the currency exchange rates. In recent years the value of the U.S. dollar has changed

two-thirds of the world's international trade: the European Union (EU), the North American Free Trade Agreement (NAFTA), Central America Free Trade Agreement (CAFTA), Mercosur, and the Association of Southeast Asian Nations (ASEAN).[21] These trade agreements are summarized in Exhibit 8.3. The EU represents the highest level of integration across individual nations, whereas the other agreements vary in their integration levels.

▼ **EXHIBIT 8.3** Trade Agreements

Name	Countries
European Union	There are 28 member countries of the EU: Austria, Belgium, Bulgaria, Croatia, Cyprus, Czech Republic, Denmark, Estonia, Finland, France, Germany, Greece, Hungary, Ireland, Italy, Latvia, Lithuania, Luxembourg, Malta, Netherlands, Poland, Portugal, Romania, Slovakia, Slovenia, Spain, Sweden, and the United Kingdom. There are five official candidate countries to join the EU: Macedonia, Serbia, Turkey, Iceland, and Montenegro.
NAFTA	United States, Canada, and Mexico.
CAFTA	United States, Costa Rica, the Dominican Republic, El Salvador, Guatemala, Honduras, and Nicaragua.
Mercosur	Full members: Argentina, Brazil, Paraguay, Uruguay, and Venezuela.
ASEAN	Brunei Darussalam, Cambodia, Indonesia, Laos, Malaysia, Myanmar, Philippines, Singapore, Thailand, and Vietnam.

Source: Information about EU members is from http://europa.eu/about-eu/countries/.

Currency fluctuations enhance or impede tourists.
© J. Hardy/PhotoAlto RF

Analyzing Sociocultural Factors

Understanding another country's culture is crucial to the success of any global marketing initiative. Culture, or the shared meanings, beliefs, morals, values, and customs of a group of people, exists on two levels: visible artifacts (e.g., behavior, dress, symbols, physical settings, ceremonies) and underlying values (thought processes, beliefs, and assumptions).[22] Visible artifacts are easy to recognize, but businesses often find it more difficult to understand the underlying values of a culture and appropriately adapt their marketing strategies to them.[23]

For example, IKEA stores across the globe are open seven days a week—except in France. French law prevents retailers from selling on Sundays, and when IKEA tried to challenge the law by keeping one of its stores open, it provoked a lawsuit

France is the only place on the globe IKEA is not open on Sundays. Notice times for "Dimanche," the French word for Sunday, is absent from the store hours sign.
© PHILIPPE HUGUEN/Getty Images

from a French workers' union. Although IKEA would love to sell over the whole weekend, leaving Sunday as a day of relaxation constitutes a fundamental foundation of French culture. But there is hope for IKEA—the recent slow economic growth and high unemployment of the country is putting pressure on the government to allow retailers to open on Sundays.[24]

For the Swiss, a similar prohibition against Sunday retailing may soon fall to the wayside. If stores remain closed, Switzerland will continue to lose tourism revenues because most foreign visitors, who tend to visit on the weekend, are accustomed to shopping on Sundays. Opening retail stores on Sundays could mean increased consumption and wages for workers who work more hours as well as employment for more people. But the loss of a day traditionally designated for family time and relaxation might be something the country cannot abide.[25] There may be no completely right answer to this dilemma, but global marketers clearly must be aware of the regulations and cultural norms of the countries they enter.

One important cultural classification scheme that firms can use is Geert Hofstede's cultural dimensions concept, which sheds more light on these underlying values. Hofstede initially proposed that cultures differed on four dimensions, but he has added two more dimensions in recent years.[26] Despite some arguments for using other models,[27] Hofstede's cultural dimensions offer a foundation for most research into culture:

1. **Power distance:** willingness to accept social inequality as natural.

2. **Uncertainty avoidance:** the extent to which the society relies on orderliness, consistency, structure, and formalized procedures to address situations that arise in daily life.

3. **Individualism:** perceived obligation to and dependence on groups.

4. **Masculinity:** the extent to which dominant values are male oriented. A lower masculinity ranking indicates that men and women are treated equally in all aspects of society; a higher masculinity ranking suggests that men dominate in positions of power.

5. **Time orientation:** short- versus long-term orientation. A country that tends to have a long-term orientation values long-term commitments and is willing to accept a longer time horizon for, say, the success of a new product introduction.

6. **Indulgence:** the extent to which society allows for the gratification of fun and enjoyment needs or else suppresses and regulates such pursuits.[28]

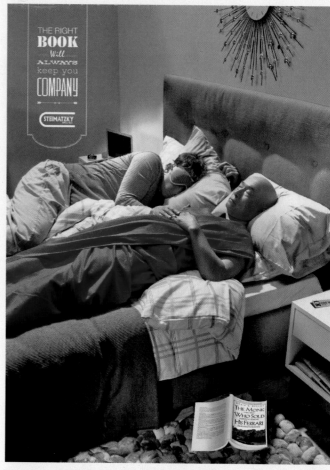

Ads from Steimatzky, the oldest and largest bookstore chain in Israel, illustrate marketing along one of Hofstede's cultural dimensions: one is highly feminine (left) and the other masculine (right).

Both ads: Agency: ACW Grey Tel-Aviv, Israel; Executive Creative Director: Tal Riven; Client Manager: Elad Hermel; Creative Director: Idan Regev; Art Director: Daphne Orner; Copywriter: Kobi Cohen; Planning: Noa Dekel; Supervisor: Mor Pesso; Account Manager: Nataly Rabinovich; Producer: Racheli Zatlawi; Production Company: We Do Production; Photographer: Shai Yehezkelli.

To illustrate two of the six dimensions, consider the data and graph in Exhibit 8.4. Power distance is on the vertical axis and individualism is on the horizontal axis. Several Latin American countries, including Brazil, cluster high on power distance but low on individualism; the United States, Australia, Canada, and the United Kingdom, in contrast, cluster high on individualism but low on power distance. Using this information, firms should expect that if they design a marketing campaign that stresses equality and individualism, it will be well accepted in English-speaking countries, all other factors being equal, but not be as well received in Latin American countries.

Another means of classifying cultures distinguishes them according to the importance of verbal communication.[30] In the United States and most European countries, business relationships are governed by what is said and written down, often through formal contracts. In countries such as China and South Korea, however, most relationships rely on nonverbal cues, so that the situation or context means much more than mere words. For instance, business relationships in China often are formalized by just a handshake, and trust and honor are often more important than legal arrangements.

Overall, culture affects every aspect of consumer behavior: why people buy; who is in charge of buying decisions; and how, when, and where people shop. After marketing managers have completed the four parts of the market assessment, they are better able to make informed decisions about whether a particular country possesses the necessary characteristics to be considered a potential market for the firm's products and services. In the next section, we detail the market entry decision

> Firms should expect that if they design a marketing campaign that stresses equality and individualism, it will be well accepted in English-speaking countries, all other factors being equal, but not be as well received in Latin American countries.

▼ **EXHIBIT 8.4** Country Clusters

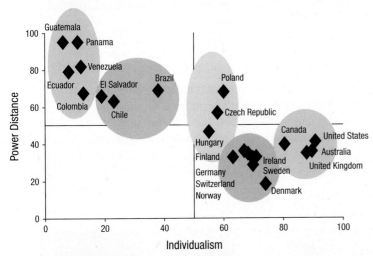

Sources: Geert Hofstede, Geert Jan Hofstede, and Michael Minkov, *Cultures and Organizations, Software of the Mind,* Third Revised Edition, McGraw-Hill 2010, ISBN: 0-07-166418-1. ©Geert Hofstede B.V. quoted with permission.

process, beginning with a discussion of the various ways firms might enter a new global market.

LO 8-2 Understand the marketing opportunities in BRIC countries.

The Appeal of the BRIC Countries

Changes in technology, especially communications, have been a driving force for growth in global markets for decades. The telegraph, radio, television, computer, and Internet have increasingly connected distant parts of the world. Today, communication is instantaneous. Sounds and images from across the globe are delivered to televisions, radios, and computers in real time, which enables receivers in all parts of the world to observe how others live, work, and play.

Like other countries in which McDonald's thrives, Brazil has a strong and growing middle class.
© Bloomberg/Getty Images

increasing promise as a market, but its relatively smaller size leads us to focus on the four BRIC nations, which seem to have the greatest potential for growth. Let's examine each in turn.

Brazil[32] Long a regional powerhouse, Brazil's ability to weather, and even thrive, during the most recent economic storm

> Culture affects every aspect of consumer behavior: why people buy; who is in charge of buying decisions; and how, when, and where people shop.

Perhaps the greatest change facing the global community in recent years has been the growth and expansion of four countries that together have come to be known as the BRIC countries: Brazil, Russia, India, and China. Some commentators suggest adding South Africa, to make BRICS, because of that nation's remarkable transformation into a functioning democracy.[31] The inspiring changes to South Africa suggest its

has transformed it into a global contender. Currently, Brazil is the world's seventh largest economy, but predicted growth rates indicate it will move into the fifth spot within a few years. This growth has been aided by a large, literate population and the impositions of social programs that have allowed more than half of the 201 million Brazilians to enter the middle class. This large South American democracy welcomes foreign investors.

Russia[33] The relations between the United States and Russia are a little more complicated than for Brazil. Since the fall of the former Soviet Union, Russia has undergone multiple upturns and downturns in its economy. However, its overall growth prospects appear promising, especially as a consumer market. Long denied access to consumer goods, the well-educated population of 143 million exhibits strong demand for U.S. products and brands. In particular, the number of Russian Internet users, presently at 67 million, is growing at a rate of approximately 14 percent annually, and is already Europe's largest Internet market.[34] The country also is negotiating to enter the World Trade Organization (WTO) to improve trade relations with other countries. Russia still faces an aging population and low birthrates. If these trends persist, Russia's population could decline by one-third in the next half century. At the same time, corruption is widespread, creating ethical dilemmas for firms trying to market their goods and services.

India[35] With more than 1.2 billion people, or approximately 15 percent of the world's population, together with expanding middle and upper classes, India is one of the world's fastest-growing markets. With a median age of 26.7 years, India has one of the youngest populations in the world. Its young inhabitants increasingly are adopting global attitudes while

In which of the BRIC countries does each of these classic structures reside?

© McGraw-Hill Education/Barry Barker, photographer

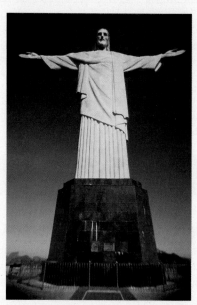

© McGraw-Hill Education/Barry Barker, photographer

© Travelif/iStock Exclusive/Getty Images

© Martin Child/Getty Images

INCREASING LIBERALIZATION IN THE ECONOMY HAS PROMPTED A LARGE INCREASE IN CHINA'S GROSS DOMESTIC PRODUCT (GDP); IT IS NOW THE SECOND-LARGEST ECONOMY AND THE THIRD-LARGEST MARKET FOR U.S. EXPORTS. "

living in growing urban centers and shopping at large malls. The well-educated, modern generation is largely fluent in English, and the highly skilled workforce holds great attraction for firms that hope to expand using local talent, especially in technical fields.

India's retail environment is still dominated by millions of small stores and lacks modern supply chain management facilities and systems.[36] Recent changes by the Indian government, however, have the potential to significantly modernize the retail landscape, as the description in our opening vignette suggested. For example, foreign retailers that carry multiple brands, like Walmart, are now allowed to own up to 51 percent of joint ventures in India, and retailers that carry only their own brand, like Nike, can now own 100 percent of their Indian businesses.

China[37] For most of the 20th century, China experienced foreign occupation, civil unrest, major famine, and a strict one-party Communist regime. However, since 1978, China's

leadership, while maintaining communist political ideals, has embraced market-oriented economic development, which has led to startlingly rapid gains. For many Chinese, recent developments have dramatically improved their living standards and their levels of personal freedom. Increasing liberalization in the economy has prompted a large increase in China's gross domestic product (GDP); it is now the second-largest economy and the third-largest market for U.S. exports. It makes an excellent target for consumer goods, assuming they can be produced at the right price.

Yet the country continues to suffer from drastically unequal economic distribution, which has led to a significant migrant workforce that subsists on part-time, low-paying jobs. These workers were hit hard by the global financial crisis, which reduced demand for Chinese exports for the first time in years. Furthermore, actual growth of the 1.3 billion-strong Chinese population slowed as a result of government population controls that limit each family to one child. Although

The retail landscape in India is changing. Consumers, particularly young ones, are attracted to large modern malls.
© Tashi TOBGYAL/Redux Pictures

Relaxed Indian governmental restrictions now allow foreign retailers that carry their own brand, like Levi's, to own 100 percent of their Indian businesses.
© Aijaz Rahi/AP Photo

Social & Mobile Marketing

The Growth of Social Networking—Brazil's Free Market versus China's Restrictions[ii]

By Facebook CEO Mark Zuckerberg's own admission, Facebook grew exponentially for years without a strategic plan for international growth. As the company has matured, however, Facebook has refocused its attention on global markets. Two countries offer a short course on how that attention must shift with the specific global target.

In Brazil, Facebook already has 65 million members, making the South American nation the second-largest market, behind the United States. It also ranks among the top markets for YouTube, Google, and Twitter. Part of the explanation for this great growth is Brazil's status as one of the most rapidly developing economies in the world. As people gain economic security, they have more resources to spend on social networking gadgets, as well as more leisure time to play with them.

But it also has to do with the culture. Brazil is known for the open, friendly attitudes of its people. For these "hyper-social" consumers, new ways to connect with friends and loved ones represent an important form of need fulfillment. International companies can enter freely, function according to a relatively well-established legal structure, and enjoy a pretty strong infrastructure as well.

In contrast, when companies confront the inherent openness of social networking with China's strict censorship rules, significant challenges arise. Successful entry by social and mobile marketers into China requires a particular blend of timing, skill, cultural understanding, and political savvy. These factors may not be quite in alignment for Facebook. The timing may be wrong because China's autocratic leaders have enforced greater controls on social networking and blogging recently. Nor do Facebook executives appear to have a full grasp of the political and cultural nuances of business in China, despite a good track record of respecting local cultural values, such as when it agreed to block content about Nazism in Germany or drawings of Muhammad in Pakistan. And even if Facebook were to navigate these challenges safely, China has a strong, enduring preference for companies owned and run by its own people.

Censorship issues are highly complex. For instance, how would Facebook respond to retaliation against users who criticize the government? For Google, whose mission statement simply advises "Don't Be Evil," such questions became all too pertinent when hackers in China gained access to the e-mail accounts of prominent human rights activists. When Western companies have cooperated with the Chinese government, some operations have led to the imprisonment of online activists.

In Brazil, the question is how many users the company can encourage to enjoy all the fun of Facebook. In China, a post on Facebook can lead to jail time. Thus, it becomes a question of basic human rights.

CEO Mark Zuckerberg (center) claims that Facebook will employ diplomacy in China, but censorship issues are highly complex.
© Lao Chen/ChinaFotoPress/ZUMAPRESS.com/Newscom

China's median age is slightly younger than that of the United States currently, at 36.3 years, the extended application of the one-child policy means that China is one of the most rapidly aging countries in the world. The central government, concerned about these effects, appears to be reconsidering the policy, but its implications are likely to persist for several generations.

Even as vast numbers of U.S. companies actively target BRIC countries or explore options for entering them, as Social and Mobile Marketing 8.1 highlights, some challenges remain.

 check yourself

1. What metrics can help analyze the economic environment of a country?

2. What types of governmental actions should we be concerned about as we evaluate a country?

3. What are some important cultural dimensions?

4. Why are each of the BRIC countries viewed as potential candidates for global expansion?

158 SECTION 2 | Understanding the Marketplace

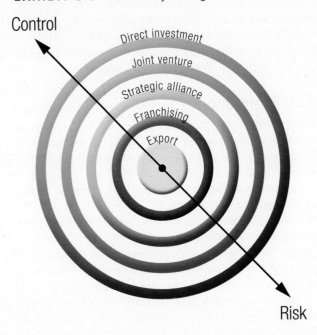

exporting Producing goods in one country and selling them in another.

CHOOSING A GLOBAL ENTRY STRATEGY

When a firm has concluded its assessment analysis of the most viable markets for its products and services, it must then conduct an internal assessment of its capabilities. As we discussed in Chapter 2, this analysis includes an assessment of the firm's access to capital, the current markets it serves, its manufacturing capacity, its proprietary assets, and the commitment of its management to the proposed strategy. These factors ultimately contribute to the success or failure of a market expansion strategy, whether at home or in a foreign market. After these internal market assessments, it is time for the firm to choose its entry strategy.

A firm can choose from many approaches when it decides to enter a new market, which vary according to the level of risk the firm is willing to take. Many firms actually follow a progression in which they begin with less risky strategies to enter their first foreign markets and move to increasingly risky strategies as they gain confidence in their abilities and more control over their operations, as illustrated in Exhibit 8.5. We examine these

> " A firm can choose from many approaches when it decides to enter a new market, which vary according to the level of risk the firm is willing to take. "

different approaches that marketers take when entering global markets, beginning with the least risky.

Exporting

Exporting means producing goods in one country and selling them in another. This entry strategy requires the least financial risk but also allows for only a limited return to the exporting firm. Global expansion often begins when a firm receives an order for its product or service from another country, in which case it faces little risk because it has no investment in people, capital equipment, buildings, or infrastructure.[38] By the same token, it is difficult to achieve economies of scale when everything has to be shipped internationally. The Swiss watchmaker Rolex sells relatively small numbers of expensive watches all over the world. Because its transportation costs are relatively small compared with the cost of the watches, the best way for it to service any market is to export from Switzerland.

▼ **EXHIBIT 8.5** Global Entry Strategies

Control

Direct investment
Joint venture
Strategic alliance
Franchising
Export

Risk

Rolex exports its watches to countries all over the world from its factory in Switzerland.
Courtesy of Rolex USA.

KFC and Pizza Hut are successful global franchisors.
Left: © Yang zheng/AP Photo; Right: © Zhou junxiang/AP Photo

Franchising

Franchising is a contractual agreement between a firm, the **franchisor**, and another firm or individual, the **franchisee**. A franchising contract allows the franchisee to operate a business—a retail product or service firm or a B2B provider—using the name and business format developed and supported by the franchisor. Many of the best-known retailers in the United States are also successful global franchisors, including McDonald's, Pizza Hut, Starbucks, Domino's Pizza, KFC, and Holiday Inn, all of which have found that global franchising entails lower risks and requires less investment than does opening units owned wholly by the firm. However, when it engages in franchising, the firm has limited control over the market operations in the foreign country, its potential profit is reduced because it must be split with the franchisee, and, once the franchise is established, there is always the threat that the franchisee will break away and operate as a competitor under a different name.

Strategic Alliance

Strategic alliances refer to collaborative relationships between independent firms, though the partnering firms do not create an equity partnership; that is, they do not invest in one another. Therefore, when Cisco Systems Inc. of San Jose,

California, and Tata Consultancy Services of Mumbai, India, entered into their strategic alliance, they both continued to develop market-ready infrastructure and network solutions for customers, but they relied on each other to provide the training and skills that one or the other might have lacked. At the same time, Cisco maintains alliances with various other companies, including Microsoft, Nokia, IBM, and Accenture.

Joint Venture

A **joint venture** is formed when a firm entering a market pools its resources with those of a local firm. As a consequence, ownership, control, and profits are shared. In addition to sharing financial burdens, a local partner offers the foreign entrant greater understanding of the market and access to resources such as vendors and real estate.

Some countries require joint ownership of firms entering their domestic markets, as is the case with the new regulations affecting multi-line retailers entering India, though many of these restrictions have loosened as a result of WTO negotiations and ever-increasing globalization pressures. Problems with this entry approach can arise when the partners disagree or if the government places restrictions on the firm's ability to move its profits out of the foreign country and back to its home country.

Lenovo actively promotes its products in Brazil.
© Lenovo

Yet joint ventures also can provide highly promising insights and benefits for all the partners, as Adding Value 8.1 suggests.

Direct Investment

Direct investment requires a firm to maintain 100 percent ownership of its plants, operation facilities, and offices in a foreign country, often through the formation of wholly owned subsidiaries. This entry strategy requires the highest level of investment and exposes the firm to significant risks, including the loss of its operating and/or initial investments. A dramatic economic downturn caused by a natural disaster, war, political instability, or changes in the country's laws can increase a foreign entrant's risk considerably. Many firms believe that in certain

Adding Value   8.1

Tata Starbucks and the Indian Coffee Culture[iii]

Starbucks traditionally has relied on a franchising model to expand internationally. But when it came to India, the coffee chain took another approach. It allied with Tata Group, another huge, international name, to create the Tata Starbucks Limited joint venture. The two conglomerates are equal partners in the venture—which celebrated its first anniversary not with champagne but by

releasing a new coffee blend: India Estates, comprised of only Indian-sourced coffee.

Since its initial launch with one store in October 2012, the joint venture has grown exponentially. Its store count reached 25 within a year, with stores in Delhi, Pune, and Mumbai. It also promises frequent new openings, including greater spread throughout the nation and localized offerings. For example, when the first store opened in Bangalore, in southern India, it offered more food options containing specific local flavors.

But it remains an international joint venture, and some marketing appeals span virtually every culture. Thus in autumn, Salted Caramel Mochas rolled out in India, just as they have done throughout the world for the past several years.

Starbucks is growing by leaps and bounds in India.
© Peter Horree/Alamy

markets, these potential risks are outweighed by the high potential returns. With this strategy, none of the potential profits must be shared with other firms. In addition to the high potential returns, direct investment offers the firm complete control over its operations in the foreign country.

Although we often tend to think of direct investment flowing from more to less developed economies, the dynamic international market means that sometimes it goes the other way. The computer maker Lenovo started in China but has since expanded its operations. In addition to purchasing IBM's PC division and Motorola's handset business unit, it established parallel headquarters in both Beijing and North Carolina. When it entered Brazil, it quickly established separate manufacturing plants to keep its costs low.[39]

As we noted, each of these entry strategies entails different levels of risk and rewards for the foreign entrant. But even after a firm has determined how much risk it is willing to take, and therefore how it will enter a new global market, it still must establish its marketing strategy, as we discuss in the next section.

✓ check yourself

1. Which entry strategy has the least risk and why?
2. Which entry strategy has the most risk and why?

LO 8-4 Highlight the similarities and differences between a domestic marketing strategy and a global marketing strategy.

CHOOSING A GLOBAL MARKETING STRATEGY

Just like any other marketing strategy, a global marketing strategy includes two components: determining the target markets to pursue and developing a marketing mix that will sustain a competitive advantage over time. In this section, we examine marketing strategy as it relates specifically to global markets.

Target Market: Segmentation, Targeting, and Positioning

Global segmentation, targeting, and positioning (STP) are more complicated than domestic STP for several reasons. First, firms considering a global expansion have much more difficulty understanding the cultural nuances of other countries. Second, subcultures within each country

also must be considered. Third, consumers often view products and their role as consumers differently in different countries.[40] A product, service, or even a retailer often must be positioned differently in different markets.

Even when an STP strategy appears successful, companies must continually monitor economic and social trends to protect their position within the market and adjust products and marketing strategies to meet the changing needs of global markets. In this sense, global marketing is no different from local or national marketing.

Segments and target markets can and should be defined by more than just geography. For example, when Yahoo! determines its segmentation and positioning strategies, it relies on research into a segment familiar throughout the world: moms. By working with a global market research firm, Yahoo! investigates how moms in Russia, Colombia, China, the United States, Mexico, India, the United Kingdom, Argentina, and France understand and use social media and other modern technologies. This study of global moms also aims to determine how digital technology affects family interactions, such as mealtimes, special occasions, and scheduling.[41] Looking on with great interest is the global product brand Procter & Gamble, which has run a global "Proud Sponsor of Moms" campaign during each recent iteration of the Olympic Games.[42]

When any firm identifies its positioning within the market, it then must decide how to implement its marketing strategies using the marketing mix. Just as firms adjust their products and services to meet the needs of national target markets, they must alter their marketing mix to serve the needs of global markets.

Global Product or Service Strategies There are three potential global product strategies: (1) sell the same product

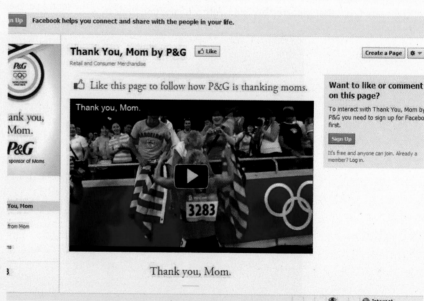

Procter & Gamble targeted moms on a global basis with its "Proud Sponsor of Moms" campaign, which ran during the 2012 Summer Olympics.
© The Procter & Gamble Company. Used by permission.

or service in both the home country market and the host country; (2) sell a product or service similar to that sold in the home country but include minor adaptations; and (3) sell totally new products or services. The strategy a firm chooses depends on the needs of the target market. The level of economic development, as well as differences in product and technical standards, helps determine the need for and level of product adaptation. Cultural differences such as food preferences, language, and religion also play a role in product strategy planning.

Same Product or Service The most typical method of introducing a product outside the home country is to sell the same product or service in other countries. Ford Motor Co., for example, envisions a world car that will sell everywhere, as we discuss in Adding Value 8.2. However, in **reverse innovation**, companies initially develop products for niche or underdeveloped markets and then expand them into their original or home

markets. For example, General Electric realized that adapting medical diagnostic equipment that had been developed in the United States to sell it in India was ineffective. Few Indian medical providers had sufficient resources to pay $20,000 for the massive machinery. Therefore, GE undertook innovation specific to the Indian market to develop a battery-operated, portable EKG (electrocardiogram) machine for $500. Then it realized that the small, affordable machines would appeal as well to U.S. emergency medical personnel in the field and therefore globalized its offer.[43]

Similar Product or Service with Minor Adaptations Campbell Soup discovered that even though Russia and China are two of the largest markets for soup in the world, cooks in

reverse innovation
When companies initially develop products for niche or underdeveloped markets, and then expand them into their original or home markets.

Adding Value 8.2

Ponying Up the Latest Ford Mustang[iv]

When the 2015 model of the classic American muscle car hit the streets, it wasn't only on Route 66. Instead, Ford's latest iteration of its iconic car was introduced simultaneously in six global cities, spanning four continents. The worldwide move aims to both acknowledge the car's 50-year history and expand its appeal to a broader market in the future.

In keeping with its tradition, the redesign retains most of the visual features that consumers have come to associate with the Mustang: blunt-nosed and stylish, with a substantial grille and a profile low to the ground. Despite some buzz that Ford would completely redesign the look (and apparently there was some debate about doing so inside the company), ultimately it chose to keep things visually similar.

In contrast, another recent version of a storied muscle car, the Chevy Camaro, broke with its historical look to adopt a more angular profile. This change seems popular. In the head-to-head-to-head competition among the Mustang, the Camaro, and the Dodge Charger, the Camaro seems to be pulling out ahead. Not only is the Camaro tops in sales among pony cars, but it also attracts a greater percentage of female drivers and a younger demographic than either of the other two options.

Ford's response was to introduce the newest Mustang as a global car, not just an American one. Along with its simultaneous grand release events in far-flung places such as Shanghai, Barcelona, and Sydney, Ford undertook a social media blitz, mostly targeting Mustang fan clubs and car groups worldwide. Even if it predicts that international sales will be responsible for only about 10 percent of revenues, Ford hopes the Mustang will serve as a sort of "ambassador," opening parking spaces and garages to other Ford models.

Chevrolet redesigned its classic Camaro (a 1969 version is pictured on the left) to have a more angular profile (right), making it popular with female and younger car buyers.
Left: © Ken Babione/Getty Images; Right: © AP Photo/Imaginechina

those countries have unique demands. Chinese consumers drink 320 billion bowls of soup each year, and Russian buyers consume 32 billion servings, compared with only 14 billion bowls of soup served in the United States. However, Chinese cooks generally refuse to resort to canned soup; the average Chinese consumer eats soup five times each week, but he or she also takes great pride in preparing it personally with fresh ingredients. In contrast, Russian consumers, though they demand very high quality in their soups, had grown tired of spending hours preparing their homemade broths. To identify opportunities in these markets, Campbell sent teams of social anthropologists to study how Chinese and Russian cooks prepare and consume soup. When it faced further hurdles, it entered into a joint venture with the Swire soup company in China. But its efforts in Russia never panned out, forcing Campbell to withdraw after around four years. That is, even with extensive, devoted efforts by an industry giant, global marketing remains a challenge.[44]

Referred to as **glocalization**, some firms also standardize their products globally but use different promotional campaigns to sell them. The original Pringles potato chip product remains the same globally, as do the images and themes of the promotional campaign, with limited language adaptations for the local markets, although English is used whenever

Campbell's research found that Russians eat a lot of soup, and they want time-saving preparation help. So it developed broths to enable cooks to prepare soups with their own flair.
© Courtesy Campbell Soup Company.

Pringles sometimes changes flavors to reflect local tastes and demand, for example, these paprika-flavored chips sold in Italy and Germany.
© WHITEBOX MEDIA/Mediablitzimages/ Alamy

possible. However, the company changes Pringles' flavors in different countries, including paprika-flavored chips sold in Italy and Germany.[45]

Totally New Product or Service The level of economic development and cultural tastes also affects global product strategy because it relates directly to consumer behavior. For example, although you are likely to know Heinz for its tomato ketchup, as you traveled the globe you would find they sell many unique products in different countries. If you taste the ketchup in the Philippines, you'll be surprised to find its made with bananas instead of tomatoes (and sold under Heinz's Jufran label). In many East Asian countries Heinz competes by selling soy sauce. The size of the package varies by country as well. Whereas in the United States big bottles of condiments are sold, in poorer countries, such as Indonesia, condiments (e.g., soy sauce) are sold in single-serve packets for a few pennies.[46]

Global Pricing Strategies Determining the selling price in the global marketplace is an extremely difficult task.[47] Many countries still have rules governing the competitive marketplace, including those that affect pricing. For example, in parts of Europe, including Belgium, Italy, Spain, Greece, and France, sales are allowed only twice a year, in January and June or July. In most European countries retailers can't sell below cost, and in others they can't advertise reduced prices in advance of sales or discount items until they have been on the shelves more than a month. For firms such as Walmart and other discounters, these restrictions threaten their core competitive positioning as the lowest-cost provider in the market. Other issues, such as tariffs, quotas, antidumping laws, and currency exchange policies, can also affect pricing decisions.[48]

> " Chinese consumers drink 320 billion bowls of soup each year, and Russian buyers consume 32 billion servings, compared with only 14 billion bowls of soup served in the United States. "

> ## THE NUMBER OF FIRMS WITH WHICH THE SELLER NEEDS TO DEAL TO GET ITS MERCHANDISE TO THE CONSUMER DETERMINES THE COMPLEXITY OF A CHANNEL.

Competitive factors influence global pricing in the same way they do home country pricing, but because a firm's products or services may not have the same positioning in the global marketplace as they do in their home country, market prices must be adjusted to reflect the local pricing structure. Spain's fashion retailer Zara, for instance, is relatively inexpensive in the EU but is priced about 40 percent higher in the United States, putting it right in the middle of its moderately priced competition.[49] Zara is dedicated to keeping production in Spain, but it also must get its fashions to the United States quickly, so it incurs additional transportation expenses, which it passes on to its North American customers. Finally, as we discussed previously in this chapter, currency fluctuations affect global pricing strategies.

Global Distribution Strategies Global distribution networks form complex value chains that involve middlemen, exporters, importers, and different transportation systems.

Zara attracts fast fashion customers by offering great prices.
© Inditex

These additional middlemen typically add cost and ultimately increase the final selling price of a product. As a result of these cost factors, constant pressure exists to simplify distribution channels wherever possible.

The number of firms with which the seller needs to deal to get its merchandise to the consumer determines the complexity of a channel. In most developing countries, manufacturers must go through many types of distribution channels to get their products to end users, who often lack adequate transportation to shop at central shopping areas or large malls. Therefore, consumers shop near their homes at small, family-owned retail outlets. To reach these small retail outlets, most of which are located far from major rail stations or roads, marketers have devised a variety of creative solutions. Unilever's strategy in India is a prime example of how a global company can adapt its distribution network to fit local conditions. Unilever trained 45,000 Indian women to serve as distributors, who in turn extended Unilever's reach to nearly 100,000 villages and their 3 million residents all across India. The program generates $250 million each year just in villages that otherwise would be too costly to serve.[50]

Global Communication Strategies The major challenge in developing a global communication strategy is identifying the elements that need to be adapted to be effective in the global marketplace. For instance, literacy levels vary dramatically across the globe. Consider again the BRIC nations: In India, approximately 38 percent of the adult population is illiterate (and for Indian women, the illiteracy rate surpasses 50 percent), compared with 10 percent in Brazil, less than 5 percent in China, and less than 1 percent in Russia.[51] Media availability also varies widely; some countries offer only state-controlled media. Advertising regulations differ too. In an attempt at standardization, the EU recently recommended common guidelines for its member countries regarding advertising to children and is currently initiating a multiphase ban on junk food advertising.[52]

Differences in language, customs, and culture also complicate marketers' ability to communicate with customers in various countries. Language can be particularly vexing for advertisers. For example, in the United Kingdom a thong is only a sandal, whereas in the United States it can also be an undergarment. To avoid the potential embarrassment that language confusion can cause, firms spend millions of dollars to develop brand names that have no preexisting meaning in any known language, such as Accenture (a management consulting firm) or Avaya (a subsidiary of Lucent Technologies, formerly Bell Labs).

Nike's Chinese brand name is pronounced "nai ke," which is very similar to the English pronunciation, and means "Enduring and Persevering."
© Shiho Fukada/Redux Pictures

Within many countries there are multiple variants on a language or more than one language. For example, China has three main languages; the written forms produce meaning through the characters used but the spoken forms depend on tone and pronunciation. Some firms choose names that sound similar to their English-language names, such as Nike, whose Chinese brand name is pronounced *nai-ke*. Others focus on the meanings of the characters, such that Citibank is known as *hui-qi-yinhang*, which means "star-spangled banner bank." Still other firms, such as Mercedes-Benz, have adapted their names for each language: *peng-zee* in Cantonese for Hong Kong, *peng-chi* in Mandarin for Taiwan, and *ben-chi* in Mandarin for mainland China. Naming is a constant challenge in China, especially to avoid the threat that a brand name evokes unwanted connotations, such as when Microsoft realized that the sound of its search engine name, Bing, meant "virus" in China—not the best image for an online company![53]

Noting the growth of luxury consumption, the *New York Times* began offering the option for luxury brands to purchase their own pages on its online version for China, with appropriate translations and links to dedicated sites. Because the site uses a simplified, traditional version of the Chinese language, it is accessible to all readers. The luxury brand advertisers—including Ferragamo, Cartier, and Bloomingdale's—then choose the content of the links. Whereas Cartier sends readers who click to its dedicated Cartier China site, Bloomingdale's provides a listing of its top 10 brands for the week, in English.[54]

Even with all these differences, many products and services serve the same needs and wants globally with little or no adaptation in their form or message. Firms with global appeal can run global advertising campaigns and simply translate the wording in the advertisements and product labeling.

Other products require a more localized approach because of cultural and religious differences. In a classic advertisement for Longines watches, a woman's bare arm and hand appear, with a watch on her wrist. The advertisement was considered too risqué for Muslim countries, where women's bare arms are never displayed in public, but the company simply changed the advertisement to show a gloved arm and hand wearing the same watch.

Even among English speakers, there can be significant differences in the effectiveness of advertising campaigns. Take the popular "What Happens in Vegas Stays in Vegas" advertising campaign, which has been very successful and spawned numerous copycat slogans in the United States. Essentially, the U.S. mass market thought the provocative campaign pushed the envelope, but just far enough to be entertaining. However, when the Las Vegas tourism group extended its advertising to the United Kingdom, it found that the ad campaign was not nearly as effective. After conducting focus groups, the group found that British consumers did not find the advertisements edgy enough for their more irreverent British tastes. In response, the advertising agency began studying British slang and phrases to find ways to make the campaign even sexier and more provocative.[55] ▪

 check yourself

1. What are the components of a global marketing strategy?
2. What are the three global product strategies?

Increase your engagement and learning with Connect Marketing.

These Connect activities, available only through your Connect course, have been designed to make the following concepts more meaningful and applicable:

- Global Marketing: Kraft Video Case
- Global Market Entry: Timeline Creation
- Market Assessment: Under Armour Click and Drag Activity
- Global Entry Strategies: iSeeit! Video

SMARTBOOK™   **iSeeit!**

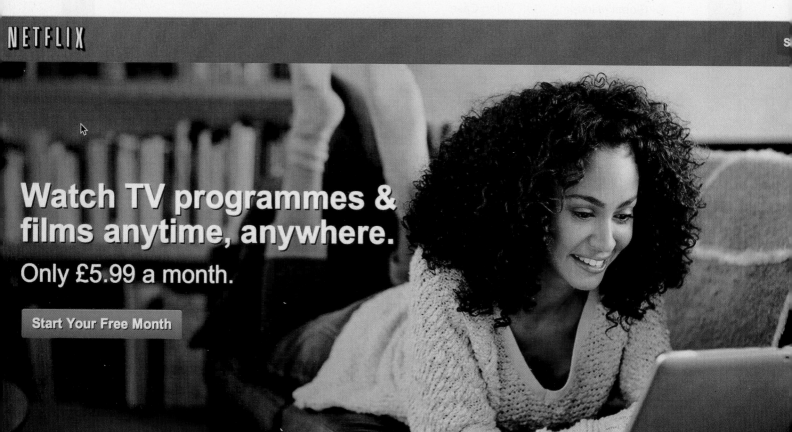

NETFLIX

**Watch TV programmes &
films anytime, anywhere.**

Only £5.99 a month.

Start Your Free Month

Chapter nine

segmentation, targeting, and positioning

Netflix, the movie rental company, has become one of the most popular and successful streaming content providers.[1] Through careful analysis of its millions of viewers and how they watched shows, it realized that they liked the actor Kevin Spacey, the director David Fincher, and a British political thriller called *House of Cards*. Putting those three elements together meant that Netflix could produce a show that was nearly guaranteed to appeal to a wide range of viewers.

But even as it recognized the widespread appeal of the show, Netflix made sure to target advertisements for it to each specific segment. That is, fans of Spacey's, viewing *The Usual Suspects* one more time on Netflix, saw advertisements for *House of Cards* that featured his powerful character. Female subscribers who had given top ratings to movies starring strong female leads instead got a preview of Robin Wright and her powerful lead role. For serious cinemaphiles, the marketing centered on Fincher's risk-taking and daring oeuvre.

LEARNING OBJECTIVES

After reading this chapter, you should be able to:

LO 9-1   Outline the different methods of segmenting a market.

LO 9-2   Describe how firms determine whether a segment is attractive and therefore worth pursuing.

LO 9-3   Articulate the differences among targeting strategies: undifferentiated, differentiated, concentrated, or micromarketing.

LO 9-4   Determine the value proposition.

LO 9-5   Define positioning, and describe how firms do it.

Part of the reason Netflix was able to establish such clear appeals for different segments of customers stemmed from the categorization it already had in place. To help recommend movies to its customers, Netflix has created approximately 79,000

continued on p. 170

continued from p. 169

categories of movie types—not just "New Releases" but also "Witty Romantic Independent Comedies," "Dark Thrillers Based on Books," or "Understated Movies."

Netflix also knows that its adult consumers can be fickle. When faced with something they don't like, adults just switch to another entertainment offering. Children, in contrast, have fewer options and less room to switch. Hence, Netflix's original content also features an offering developed in cooperation with DreamWorks Animation to target youthful audiences explicitly.

The *Turbo: F.A.S.T.* television series will air following the release of an animated film about the same character (a snail who gains super speed after being exposed to a freak accident). The deal also comes after another agreement between DreamWorks and Netflix, in which Netflix purchased the rights to show some of DreamWorks'

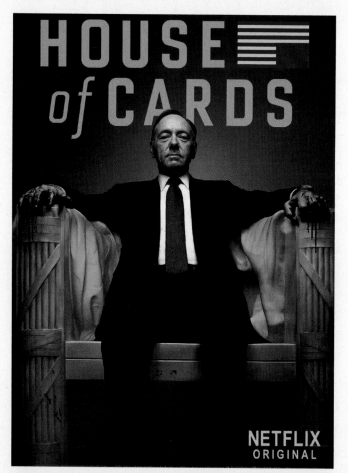

Netflix analyzed data from its millions of viewers to help design the wildly successful political thriller, House of Cards, starring Kevin Spacey. It then used different advertisements for the series to target various Netflix customer segments.
© AF archive/Alamy

most well-known titles. Around the same time, it also inked an agreement with Disney to access its library—including its recently acquired set of Lucasfilm movies.[2]

By appealing to children and their families, Netflix believes it can achieve new levels of customer loyalty. The children themselves are unlikely to switch because Netflix offers them easy access through their parents' iPads or their Wii consoles. Furthermore, few parents are willing to incur their children's wrath by canceling their Netflix subscription, when Netflix offers those children some of their favorite shows and movies. ■

In Chapter 1, we learned that marketing is about satisfying consumers' wants and needs. Chapter 2 noted how companies analyze their markets to determine the different kinds of products and services people want. But it is not sufficient just to produce such an offering. Firms must also position their offerings in the minds of customers in their target market in such a way that these consumers understand why the thing the company is providing meets their needs better than other, competitive offerings.

This process requires a marketing plan, as we discussed in Chapter 2. You should recall that the third step of this plan is to identify and evaluate opportunities by performing an STP (segmentation, targeting, and positioning) analysis. This chapter focuses on that very analysis.

| LO 9-1 | Outline the different methods of segmenting a market. |

THE SEGMENTATION, TARGETING, AND POSITIONING PROCESS

In this chapter, we discuss how a firm conducts a market segmentation or STP analysis (see Exhibit 9.1). We first outline a firm's overall strategy and objectives, methods of segmenting the market, and which segments are worth pursuing. Then we discuss how to choose a target market or markets by evaluating each segment's attractiveness and, on the basis of this evaluation, choose which segment or segments to pursue. Finally, we describe how a firm develops its positioning strategy.

Although the STP process in Exhibit 9.1 implies that the decision making is linear, this need not be the case. For instance, a firm could start with a strategy but then modify it as it gathers more information about various segments' attractiveness.

Step 1: Establish the Overall Strategy or Objectives

The first step in the segmentation process is to articulate the vision or objectives of the company's marketing strategy

EXHIBIT 9.1 The Segmentation, Targeting, and Positioning Process

Step 1: Establish strategy or objectives

Step 2: Use segmentation methods

Segmentation

Step 3: Evaluate segment attractiveness

Step 4: Select target market

Targeting

Step 5: Identify and develop positioning strategy

Positioning

clearly. The segmentation strategy must be consistent with and derived from the firm's mission and objectives as well as its current situation—its strengths, weaknesses, opportunities, and threats (SWOT). Coca-Cola's objective, for instance, is to increase sales in a mature industry. The company knows its strengths are its brand name and its ability to place new products on retailers' shelves, but its primary weakness is that it may not have a product line for newer market segments. Identifying this potentially large and profitable market segment, before many of its mainstream competitors can do so, offers a great opportunity. However, following through on that opportunity could lead to a significant threat: competitive retaliation. Coca-Cola's recent choice to pursue health-conscious men with products such as Coke Zero is consistent with its overall strategy and objectives.

Now let's take a look at methods for segmenting a market.

Coke Zero targets health-conscious men.
© Michael J. Hruby

Step 2: Use Segmentation Methods

The second step in the segmentation process is to use a particular method or combination of methods to segment the market. This step also develops descriptions of the different segments, which helps firms better understand the customer profiles in each segment. With this information, they can distinguish customer similarities within a segment and dissimilarities across segments. Marketers use geographic, demographic, psychographic, benefits, and behavioral segmentation methods, as Exhibit 9.2 details.

Soft drink marketers, for instance, divide the carbonated beverage landscape into caffeinated or decaffeinated, regular (with sugar) or diet, and cola versus something else. This segmentation method is based on the *benefits* that consumers derive from the products.

Geographic Segmentation **Geographic segmentation** organizes customers into groups on the basis of where they live. Thus, a market could be grouped by country, region (northeast, southeast), or areas within a region (state, city,

> ## "The first step in the segmentation process is to articulate the vision or objectives of the company's marketing strategy clearly."

demographic segmentation The grouping of consumers according to easily measured, objective characteristics such as age, gender, income, and education.

psychographic segmentation A method of segmenting customers based on how they spend their time and money, what activities they pursue, and their attitudes and opinions about the world in which they live.

neighborhoods, zip codes). Not surprisingly, geographic segmentation is most useful for companies whose products satisfy needs that vary by region.

Firms can provide the same basic goods or services to all segments even if they market globally or nationally, but better marketers make adjustments to meet the needs of smaller geographic groups.[3] A national grocery store chain such as Safeway or Kroger runs similar stores with similar assortments in various locations across the United States. But within those similar stores, a significant percentage of the assortment of goods will vary by region, city, or even neighborhood, depending on the different needs of the customers who surround each location.

Demographic Segmentation
Demographic segmentation groups consumers according to easily measured, objective characteristics such as age, gender, income, and

education. These variables represent the most common means to define segments because they are easy to identify and demographically segmented markets are easy to reach. Kellogg's uses age segmentation for its breakfast cereals: Cocoa Krispies and Fruit Loops are for kids; Special K and All-Bran are for adults. It also tends to adopt a gender-based segmentation, such that marketing communications about Special K almost exclusively appeal to women.

Gender plays a very important role in how most firms market products and services.[4] For instance, TV viewing habits vary significantly between men and women. Men tend to channel surf—switching quickly from channel to channel—and watch prime-time shows that are action oriented and feature physically attractive cast members. Women, in contrast, tend to view shows to which they can personally relate through the situational plot or characters and those recommended by friends. Print media are similar: A company such as Proactiv, which seeks to appeal to both men and women worried about the condition of their skin, therefore carefully considers the gender-based appeal of different magazines when it purchases advertising space.

However, demographics may not be useful for defining the target segments for other companies. They are poor predictors of the users of activewear, such as jogging suits and athletic shoes. At one time, firms such as Nike assumed that activewear would be purchased exclusively by young, active people, but the health and fitness trend has led people of all ages to buy such merchandise. Even relatively inactive consumers of all ages, incomes, and education find activewear more comfortable than traditional street clothes.

Rethinking some stereotypical ideas about who is buying thus has become a relatively common trend among firms that once thought their target market was well defined. As Social and Mobile Marketing 9.1 shows, even some of the most well-known companies in the world must continually reconsider the true identity of their prime targets.

Psychographic Segmentation
Of the various methods for segmenting, or breaking down, the market, **psychographic segmentation** is the one that delves into how consumers actually describe themselves. Usually marketers

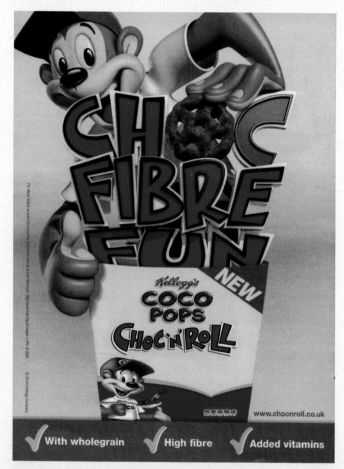

Kellogg's uses this packaging in the UK for its Coco Pops cereal. What segmentation methods are Kellogg's using?
Image Courtesy of The Advertising Archives

Social & Mobile Marketing

9.1

Is Facebook Over?[i]

According to a recent study funded by the European Union, the terms that UK teens (16–18 years of age) use to describe Facebook include *embarrassing, old,* and *dead and buried.* These are not exactly the sorts of images that a company that revolutionized social media prefers to embrace. So what has led Facebook, once the social media home base of teens, to become the last place they want to be seen?

Most analyses suggest the main problem was its growing popularity—and more specifically, its growing popularity among their parents' generation. As mom, dads, aunts, uncles, and even grandparents joined the network, teens quickly became less willing to share quite so much. Humor sites collect various awkward moments when a teenager rails against an unfair parent on Facebook, only to have that parent respond with deeply embarrassing accounts of the teen's behavior or the imposition of a new punishment.

Beyond these direct contacts, teens tend to assume that anything their parents like cannot be cool for them as well. If their grandmother posts pictures of her vacation to Facebook, seemingly by definition the site cannot be cool anymore.

As challenging as these trends are for Facebook, it could always re-brand itself as the social media location for middle-aged users who want to share their thoughts about their children or grandchildren. The larger question is where teens will go next to get their social media fix. The growing popularity of Snapchat implies that teens might begin preferring temporary, ephemeral sharing, possibly in reaction to the lessons learned when Facebook posts remain accessible to employers and school administrators. Moreover, teens seemingly use various sites for different purposes: Twitter for wide broadcasts, Instagram for visual sharing, WhatsApp for more personal interactions.

The variety suggests a gap in the market, waiting for some innovative entrepreneur to devise the next big thing, a site that teens consider cool and compelling—until their parents find it and ruin it too, of course.

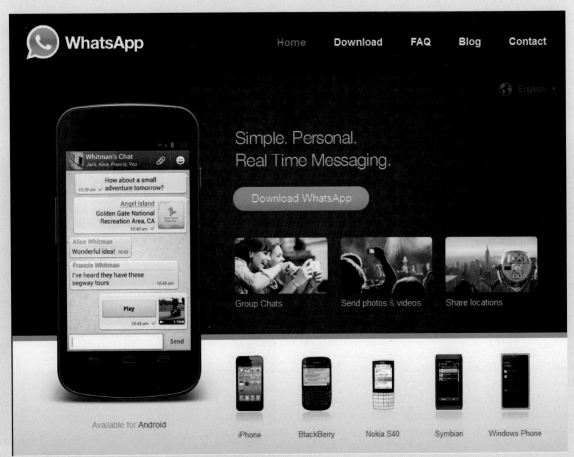

Have you used WhatsApp to do real-time messaging?
© WhatsApp

Such tactics need to balance the ideal with the realistic. Advertisements for men's underwear tend to feature salacious shots of incredibly cut men, usually with shaved chests. But in making this appeal to women who might purchase briefs, boxers, and T-shirts for their husbands or partners, underwear marketers forgot about men as their underlying target market. And these male shoppers have long felt uncomfortable in stores, reaching for a box featuring a nearly naked man. Rather than being aspirational, the models had become so outside the norm that they seemed like a cruel taunt. Thus a recent advertising campaign by the men's underwear brand 2(x)ist features a handsome but not "perfect" model, wearing a robe that covers most of his body. The Mack Wheldon brand offers up another handsome but slightly goofy model, who trips while trying to take off his pants to reveal his underwear.[7]

Lifestyles, the third component of people's psychographic makeup, are the way we live.[8] If values provide an end goal and

determine (through demographics, buying patterns, or usage) into which segment an individual consumer falls. **Psychographics** studies how people self-select, as it were, based on the characteristics of how they choose to occupy their time (behavior) and what underlying psychological reasons determine those choices.[5] For example, a person might have a strong need for inclusion or belonging, which motivates him or her to seek out activities that involve others, which in turn influences the products he or she buys to fit in with the group. Determining

> A PERSON WHO HAS A GOAL TO BELONG MAY SEE, OR WANT TO SEE, HIMSELF AS A FUN-LOVING, GREGARIOUS TYPE WHOM PEOPLE WISH TO BE AROUND.

psychographics involves knowing and understanding three components: self-values, self-concept, and lifestyles.

Self-values are goals for life, not just the goals one wants to accomplish in a day. They are the overriding desires that drive how a person lives his or her life. Examples might be the need for self-respect, self-fulfillment, or a specific sense of belonging. This motivation causes people to develop self-images of how they want to be and then images of a way of life that will help them arrive at these ultimate goals. From a marketing point of view, self-values help determine the benefits the target market may be looking for from a product. The underlying, fundamental, personal need that pushes a person to seek out certain products or brands stems from his or her desire to fulfill a self-value.

People's self-image, or **self-concept**, is the image people ideally have of themselves.[6] A person who has a goal to belong may see, or want to see, himself as a fun-loving, gregarious type whom people wish to be around. Marketers often make use of this particular self-concept through communications that show their products being used by groups of laughing people who are having a good time. The connection emerges between the group fun and the product being shown and connotes a lifestyle that many consumers seek.

Marketers like Benetton want their ads to appeal to people's self-concepts: "I'm like them (or I want to be like them), so I should buy their products."

© Benetton Group SPA; Photo by: Oliviero Toscani.

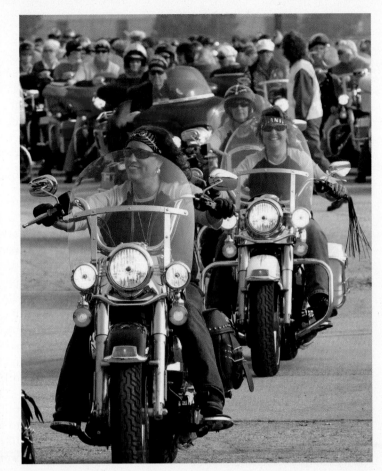

Using lifestyle segmentation, Harley-Davidson has four main target markets: On the left is its core segment consisting of men older than 35 years. On the right are women older than 35 years.
Left: © Bloomberg/Getty Images; Right: © Jeffrey Phelps/AP Photo

self-concept is the way one sees oneself in the context of that goal, lifestyles are how we live our lives to achieve goals.

One of the most storied lifestyles in American legend is the Harley way of life. The open road, wind in your hair, rebelling against conventions—the image nearly always depicted men like Dennis Hopper in *Easy Rider*. But the notions of freedom, rebellion, and standing out from a crowd vastly appeal to all sorts of people. In response, Harley-Davidson has shifted its STP methods to define four main target markets: core (men older than 35 years), young adults (both genders, 18–34 years), women (older than 35 years), and diverse (men and women, African American and Hispanic, older than 35 years).[9]

For women, for example, it encourages lifestyle events such as Garage Parties, women's-only social gatherings hosted in the evenings at dealerships to teach women the basics of motorcycling. The company publication *We Ride* focuses solely on female Hogs, and the HD-1 Customization website offers a separate process for women to build their cycles to match their build, power preferences, and color desires.[10]

> "Consumers buy products and services because of their primary motivations—that is, how they see themselves in the world and how that self-image governs their activities."

The most widely used tool to support such psychographic segmentation efforts is owned and operated by Strategic Business Insights (SBI).[11] Consumers can be classified into the eight segments shown in Exhibit 9.3 based on their answers to the questionnaire (http://www.strategicbusinessinsights.com/vals/presurvey.shtml). The vertical dimension of the VALS framework indicates level of resources, including income, education, health, energy level, and degree of innovativeness. The upper segments have more resources and are more innovative than those on the bottom.

The horizontal dimension shows the segments' primary psychological motivation for buying. Consumers buy products and services because of their primary motivations—that is, how they see themselves in the world and how that self-image governs their activities. The three primary motivations of U.S. consumers are ideals, achievement, and self-expression. People who are primarily motivated by ideals are guided by knowledge and principles. Those who are motivated by achievement look for products and services that

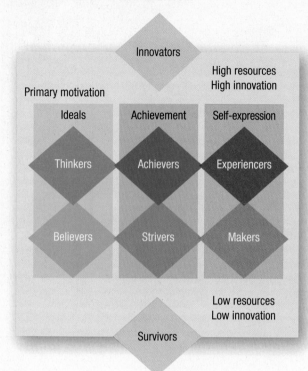

Innovators

High resources
High innovation

Primary motivation

Ideals · Achievement · Self-expression

Thinkers · Achievers · Experiencers

Believers · Strivers · Makers

Low resources
Low innovation

Survivors

Source: Reprinted with permission of Strategic Business Insights (SBI); http://www.strategicbusinessinsights.com/VALS.

demonstrate success to their peers. Consumers who are primarily motivated by self-expression desire social or physical activity, variety, and risk.

VALS enables firms to identify target segments and their underlying motivations. It shows correlations between psychology and lifestyle choices. For instance, a European luxury automobile manufacturer used VALS to identify online, mobile applications that would appeal to affluent, early-adopter consumers within the next five years.[12] The VALS analysis enabled the company to prioritize the most promising applications to develop. In another case, VALS was used to help a medical center identify customers most interested and able to afford cosmetic surgery. Based on the underlying motivations of its target customers, the center and its ad agency developed an ad campaign so successful that it had to be pulled early to avoid overbooking at the surgical center.

Firms are finding that psychographic segmentation schemes like VALS are often more useful for predicting consumer behavior than are demographics. This is because people who share demographics often have very different psychological traits. Take, for example, Jack and John, both 30-year-old, married college graduates. Demographically they are the same, but Jack is risk-averse and John is a risk taker. Jack is socially conscious and John is focused on himself. Lumping Jack and John together as a target does not make sense because the ways they think and act are totally different.

There are limitations to using psychographic segmentation, however. Psychographics are more expensive as a means to identify potential customers. With demographics, a firm like Nike can easily identify its customers as, say, men or women and then direct its marketing strategies to each group differently. The problem is that not all men are alike, as we saw with Jack and John. Women are not all alike either! To identify VALS Thinkers or Makers, companies use the VALS questionnaire in surveys or focus groups. Then VALS provides robust segment descriptions, linkages with consumer product and media–use data, and communication tools to create consistent messages that build brand awareness and customer loyalty.[13]

It is just as easy to identify Thinkers (left) as it is Makers (right). A person is given the VALS questionnaire, and the VALS program at SBI runs the answers through the computer for scoring to determine the VALS type.
Left: © Sam Edwards/Getty Images RF; Right: © Huntstock/Getty Images RF

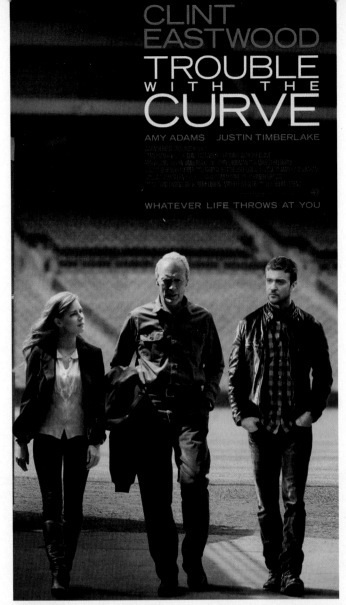

What emotions are evoked by the movie Trouble with the Curve *and its stars?*

© AF archive/Alamy

Benefit Segmentation
Benefit segmentation groups consumers on the basis of the benefits they derive from products or services. Because marketing is all about satisfying consumers' needs and wants, dividing the market into segments whose needs and wants are best satisfied by the product benefits can be a very powerful tool.[14] It is effective and relatively easy to portray a product's or service's benefits in the firm's communication strategies.

Hollywood in particular is a constant and effective practitioner of benefit segmentation. Although all movies may seem to provide the same service—entertainment for a couple of hours—film producers know that people visit the theater or rent films to obtain a vast variety of benefits, and market them accordingly. Need a laugh? Try the latest comedy from Adam Sandler or Melissa McCarthy. Want to cry and then feel warm and fuzzy? Go see *Trouble with the Curve,* starring Clint Eastwood, Amy Adams, and Justin Timberlake, for by the time you leave the theater, you are likely to feel quite happy: The lead characters will have faced obstacles, overcome them, and ultimately found love.

Behavioral Segmentation
Behavioral segmentation divides customers into groups on the basis of how they use the product or service. Some common behavioral measures include occasion and loyalty.

Occasion Behavioral segmentation based on when a product or service is purchased or consumed is called **occasion segmentation**. Men's Wearhouse uses this type of segmentation to develop its merchandise selection and its promotions. Sometimes men need a suit for their everyday work, but other suits are expressly for special occasions such as a prom or a wedding. Snack food companies such as Frito-Lay also make and promote snacks for various occasions—individual servings of potato chips for a snack on the run but 16-ounce bags for parties.

Loyalty Firms have long known that it pays to retain loyal customers. Loyal customers are those who feel so strongly that the firm can meet their relevant needs best that any competitors are virtually excluded from their consideration; that is, these customers buy almost exclusively from the firm. These loyal customers are the most profitable in the long term.[15] In light of the high cost of finding new customers and the profitability of loyal customers, today's companies are using **loyalty segmentation** and investing in retention and loyalty initiatives to retain their most profitable customers. From simple, "buy 10 sandwiches, get the 11th free" punchcards offered by local restaurants to the elaborate travel-linked programs run by hotel and

> Because marketing is all about satisfying consumers' needs and wants, dividing the market into segments whose needs and wants are best satisfied by the product benefits can be a very powerful tool.

Restaurants offer loyalty programs because it is less expensive to retain customers than to attract new ones.

© Eric Audras/Onoky/SuperStock RF

airline affiliates, such loyalty segmentation approaches are ubiquitous. Starbucks is using its loyalty programs and mobile apps to enhance value for its customers, as highlighted in Marketing Analytics 9.1.

Using Multiple Segmentation Methods Although all segmentation methods are useful, each has its unique advantages and disadvantages. For example, segmenting by demographics and geography is easy because information about who the customers are and where they are located is readily available, but these characteristics don't help marketers determine their customers' needs. Knowing what benefits customers are seeking or how the product or service fits a particular lifestyle is important for designing an overall marketing strategy, but such segmentation schemes present a problem for marketers attempting to identify specifically which customers are seeking these benefits. Thus, firms often employ a combination of

Marketing Analytics

9.1

A Complete Ecosystem for Coffee Drinkers: The Starbucks Mobile Plan[ii]

When it comes to mobile marketing, few brands are more successful than Starbucks. Reportedly, Starbucks customers make payments using a mobile device 7 million times per week, accounting for 16 percent of all transactions. These staggering numbers far exceed any of Starbucks' competitors, indicating that it has overcome one of the biggest hurdles in mobile marketing—namely, getting customers to engage frequently with it on their mobile devices. One observer attributes this level of success to Starbucks' creation of "a digital ecosystem that entwines the payment platform with their rewards program."

The loyalty program, My Starbucks Rewards, allows members to pay via their mobile device and earn points toward discounts and free offers. The integration of My Starbucks Rewards with the mobile app has been crucial to the app's success, because the moment customers use their mobile payment operation, Starbucks can gather the purchase behavior data, appropriately segment that customer, and offer customers deals immediately. Previously it would have taken at least a week for the company to even receive the purchase information. In the past year, Starbucks also introduced another way for customers to engage with the loyalty program: When they buy packages of Starbucks coffee in grocery stores, they can earn rewards points toward drinks and snacks in Starbucks stores. This feature has helped increase the My Starbucks Rewards program membership to over 9 million people.

Looking ahead, Starbucks has plans to increase its rewards program membership even further by improving the integration of the mobile app and the in-store experience. It will unveil a mobile ordering feature to reduce wait times in stores and improve the overall Starbucks experience. The introduction of this feature should spark a sizable increase in the number of loyalty members. With all these data collected about its My Starbucks Rewards customers, it can shape its marketing tactics, promotions, and store locations in optimal ways.

Starbucks is using its loyalty programs and mobile apps to enhance value for its customers.

© Kevin Schafer/Moment Mobile ED/Getty Images

segmentation methods, using demographics and geography to identify and target marketing communications to their customers, then using benefits or lifestyles to design the product or service and the substance of the marketing message.

One very popular mixture of segmentation schemes is geodemographic segmentation. Based on the adage "birds of a feather flock together," **geodemographic segmentation** uses a combination of geographic, demographic, and lifestyle characteristics to classify consumers. Consumers in the same neighborhoods tend to buy the same types of cars, appliances, and apparel and shop at the same types of retailers.

One widely used tool for geodemographic market segmentation is the Tapestry™ Segmentation system developed and marketed by ESRI.[16] Tapestry Segmentation classifies all U.S. residential neighborhoods into 65 distinctive segments based on detailed demographic data and lifestyles of people who live in each U.S. block tract (zip code + 4).[17] Each block group then can be analyzed and sorted by many characteristics, including income, home value, occupation, education, household type, age, and several key lifestyle characteristics. The information in Exhibit 9.4 describes three Tapestry segments.

Geodemographic segmentation can be particularly useful for retailers because customers typically patronize stores close to their neighborhood. Thus, retailers can use geodemographic segmentation to tailor each store's assortment to the preferences

> Knowing what benefits customers are seeking or how the product or service fits a particular lifestyle is important for designing an overall marketing strategy, but such segmentation schemes present a problem for marketers attempting to identify specifically which customers are seeking these benefits.

geodemographic segmentation The grouping of consumers on the basis of a combination of geographic, demographic, and lifestyle characteristics.

▼ **EXHIBIT 9.4** Examples of Tapestry

	Segment 01 - *Top Rung*	Segment 18 - *Cozy and Comfortable*	Segment 52 - *Inner City Tenants*
LifeMode Summary Group	L1 *High Society*	L2 *Upscale Avenues*	L8 *Global Roots*
Urbanization Summary Group	U3 *Metro Cities I*	U8 *Suburban Periphery II*	U4 *Metro Cities II*
Household Type	Married-Couple Families	Married-Couple Families	Mixed
Median Age	44.6	41.7	28.8
Income	High	Upper Middle	Lower Middle
Employment	Prof/Mgmt	Prof/Mgmt	Srvc/Prof/Mgmt/Skilled
Education	Bach/Grad Degree	Some College	No HS Diploma; HS; Some Coll
Residential	Single Family	Single Family	Multiunit Rentals
Race/Ethnicity	White	White	White; Black; Hispanic
Activity	Participate in public/civic activities	Dine out often at family restaurants	Play football, basketball
Financial Activity	Own stock worth $75,000+	Have personal line of credit	Have personal education loan
Activity	Vacation overseas	Shop at Kohl's	Go dancing
Media	Listen to classical, all-news radio	Listen to sporting events on radio	Read music, baby, fashion magazines
Vehicle	Own/Lease luxury car	Own/Lease minivan	Own/Lease Honda

Source: Esri, "Tapestry Segmentation: The Fabric of America's Neighborhoods

ethical&societal dilemma

9.1

Congressional Hearings and the Ethical Considerations for Modern Loyalty Programs[iii]

Loyalty programs are so widespread, spanning so many industries, that they may seem unquestionable. But recent hearings held by the U.S. Congress Commerce Committee created some challenging questions, especially for the data warehouses that help companies target their ideal markets.

Part of the impetus for this questioning is the increased insights that marketers gain about their customers using technologically advanced data gathering methods. Especially when consumers opt in to a loyalty program,

they grant data brokers access to vast amounts of information about them. These brokers, including Experian, Acxiom, and Epsilon, earn their revenues by gathering and warehousing these massive amounts of consumer data, and then selling selected slices to companies that want to target a particular audience.

The chair of the hearings, Democratic senator John Rockefeller of West Virginia, voiced concerns that the practices of the data brokers were shrouded in secrecy, such that there was insufficient oversight of how they collected and used information about consumers. But his challenges also extended to some central tactics embraced by marketers.

By segmenting populations by gender, race, ethnicity, and income, Rockefeller asserted, data gatherers were inherently discriminatory. Predatory lenders who identify a population of lower-income, less educated consumers might target them unfairly, such as by promising loans but only at very high

interest rates. A list of people suffering from a genetic disease might attract the attention of unethical peddlers of "miracle cures." Because so many personal data are now available online, oversight of the uses of the data becomes even more difficult.

Rockefeller also objected to the defining feature of loyalty programs, namely, the provision of benefits to customers that the provider deems "better." Using the example of airlines, the hearing noted that in the aftermath of a cancellation, airlines often give priority to their best customers to help them find another route to their destination. Such practices in turn make the industry more frustrating and less serviceable for occasional or infrequent fliers. Overall, then, the harms to the broader society might outweigh the benefits to the individual or the firm.

Or perhaps the problem is merely unethical implementation, and the segmentation and targeting that Rockefeller decries is merely part of doing business.

---

of the local community. If a toy store discovers that one of its stores is surrounded by Inner City Tenants (Exhibit 9-4), it might adjust its offering to include less expensive toys. Stores surrounded by Top Rung (Exhibit 9-4) would warrant a more expensive stock selection.

This kind of segmentation is also useful for finding new locations; retailers identify their best locations and determine what types of people live in the area surrounding those stores, according to the geodemographic clusters. They can then find other potential locations where similar segments reside.

However, such treasure troves of data introduce a host of ethical concerns, as highlighted in Ethical and Societal Dilemma 9.1.

> 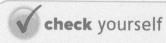 **check yourself**
>
> 1. What are the various segmentation methods?

LO 9-2 Describe how firms determine whether a segment is attractive and therefore worth pursuing.

Step 3: Evaluate Segment Attractiveness

The third step in the segmentation process involves evaluating the attractiveness of the various segments. To undertake this

evaluation, marketers first must determine whether the segment is worth pursuing, using several descriptive criteria: Is the segment identifiable, substantial, reachable, responsive, and profitable (see Exhibit 9.5)?

Identifiable Firms must be able to identify who is within their market to be able to design products or services to meet their needs. It is equally important to ensure that the segments are distinct from one another, because too much overlap between segments means that distinct marketing strategies aren't necessary to meet segment members' needs. Thus, people who follow the men's fashion blog *An Affordable Wardrobe* tend to be distinct from people who follow the women's fashion blog *Fabsugar*.

Substantial Once the firm has identified its potential target markets, it needs to measure their sizes. If a market is too small or its buying power insignificant, it won't generate sufficient profits or be able to support the marketing mix activities. As China's economy started growing, there were not enough middle-class car buyers to push foreign automakers to design an entry-level vehicle. It was only after that number grew substatially that it became worthwhile for them to market to these identified consumers.

Reachable The best product or service cannot have any impact, no matter how identifiable or substantial the target market is, if that market cannot be reached (or accessed) through persuasive communications and product distribution.

The consumer must know the product or service exists, understand what it can do for him or her, and recognize how to buy it. If Victoria's Secret fails to tell women that it is offering some less luxurious, more affordable options, shoppers will just walk right past the store and buy basic bras from the Macy's store in the same mall.

Responsive

For a segmentation strategy to be successful, the customers in the segment must react similarly and positively to the firm's offering. If, through the firm's

If you are looking for a luxury SUV, General Motors hopes you will choose a Cadillac.
© Zhang yingnan/AP Photo

distinctive competencies, it cannot provide products or services to that segment, it should not target it. For instance, the Cadillac division of General Motors (GM) has introduced a line of cars to the large and very lucrative luxury car segment. People in this market typically purchase Porsches, BMWs, Audis, and Lexuses. In contrast, GM has been somewhat successful competing for the middle-priced family-oriented car and light truck segments. Thus, even though the luxury car segment meets all the other criteria for a successful segment, GM took a big risk in attempting to pursue this market.

Profitable

Marketers must also focus their assessments on the potential profitability of each segment, both current and future. Some key factors to keep in mind in this analysis include market growth (current size and expected growth rate), market competitiveness (number of competitors, entry barriers, product substitutes), and market access (ease of developing or accessing distribution channels and brand familiarity). Some straightforward calculations can help illustrate the profitability of a segment:

$$\text{Segment profitability} = (\text{Segment size} \\ \times \text{Segment adoption percentage} \times \text{Purchase behavior} \\ \times \text{Profit margin percentage}) - \text{Fixed costs}$$

where

Segment size = Number of people in the segment

Segment adoption percentage = Percentage of customers in the segment who are likely to adopt the product/service

Purchase behavior = Purchase price × number of times the customer would buy the product/service in a year

Profit margin percentage = (Selling price − variable costs) ÷ selling price

Fixed costs = Advertising expenditure, rent, utilities, insurance, and administrative salaries for managers

To illustrate how a business might determine a segment's profitability, consider Camillo's start-up lawn service. He is trying to determine whether to target homeowners or businesses in a small midwestern town. Exhibit 9.6 estimates the profitability of the two segments. The homeowner segment is much larger than the business segment, but there are already several lawn services with established customers. There is much less competition in the business segment. So, the segment adoption rate for the homeowner segment is only 1 percent, compared with 20 percent for the business segment. Camillo can charge a much higher price to businesses, and they use lawn services more frequently. The profit margin for the business segment is higher as well because Camillo can use large equipment to cut the grass and therefore save on variable labor costs. However, the fixed costs for purchasing and maintaining the large equipment are much higher for the business segment. Furthermore, he needs to spend more money obtaining and maintaining the

	Homeowners	Businesses
Segment size	75,000	1,000
Segment adoption percentage	1%	20%
Purchase behavior		
Purchase price	$100	$500
Frequency of purchase	12 times	20 times
Profit margin percentage	60%	80%
Fixed costs	$400,000	$1,000,000
Segment profit	$140,000	$600,000

business customers, whereas he would use less expensive door-to-door flyers to reach household customers. On the basis of these informed predictions, Camillo decides the business segment is more profitable for his lawn service.

This analysis provides an estimate of the profitability of two segments at one point in time. It is also useful to evaluate the profitability of a segment over the lifetime of one of its typical customers. To address such issues, marketers consider factors such as how long the customer will remain loyal to the firm, the defection rate (percentage of customers who switch on a yearly basis), the costs of replacing lost customers (advertising, promotion), whether customers will buy more or more expensive merchandise in the future, and other such factors.

Now that we've evaluated each segment's attractiveness (Step 3), we can select the target markets to pursue (Step 4).

LO 9-3 Articulate the differences among targeting strategies: undifferentiated, differentiated, concentrated, or micromarketing.

Step 4: Select a Target Market

The fourth step in the STP process is to select a target market. The key factor likely to affect this decision is the marketer's ability to pursue such an opportunity or target segment. Thus, as we mentioned in Chapter 2, a firm assesses both the attractiveness of the target market (opportunities and threats based on the SWOT analysis and the profitability of the segment) and its own competencies (strengths and weaknesses based on the SWOT analysis) very carefully.

Determining how to select target markets is not always straightforward, especially when the firms consider certain markets to be too old to be worthwhile as Adding Value 9.1 explains.

Adding Value   9.1

Are Baby Boomers Too Old for TV? Some Networks Seem to Think So[iv]

The western mystery show *Longmire,* aired on the A&E cable network, had a lot going for it. It was based on a series of bestselling books, featured an appealing hero, and attracted an average of 5.6 million viewers per show—quite a substantial number for a basic cable channel. And yet A&E canceled the show, refusing to renew it for a fourth season, citing as one of its reasons that its primary audience, which had a median age of 60 years, simply did not reflect its target market of 18- to 45-year-old viewers.

The 18–45 demographic is famously appealing to television networks, because this age group appeals most to advertisers. Thus virtually every network, whatever its general theme or concept, aims to attract viewers whose ages fall within this three-decade range. To do so, they often pursue shows that offer edgy, controversial, or exciting content.

Longmire had none of those traits. A relatively straightforward procedural, its titular main character was a traditional hero, rather than a tormented antihero. As the show's executive producer readily noted, "This is not a cynical show." Possibly as a result, it was very popular among older audiences, who enjoyed the linear narrative and appealingly clever lead detective.

Such audiences may find themselves with less and less to watch though, because *Longmire* is not the only show A&E canceled despite its

A&E canceled its successful western show, Longmire, *because its primary audience was too old.*
Ursula Coyote/©A&E/courtesy Everett Collection

high ratings among older viewers. It also gave the ax to *The Glades,* another option that viewers older than 60 years tended to tune in to watch. Nor is A&E the only network to avoid targeting a Baby Boomer audience; even when its show *Harry's Law* garnered strong ratings among this cohort, NBC canceled it after just a couple of seasons.

Without generalizing too broadly about older viewers, they appear less interested in unscripted or reality shows, which may leave them out of luck. The latter are far less expensive to produce than scripted dramas and thus continue to spread across networks, including A&E, which hosts the reality show *Duck Dynasty*.

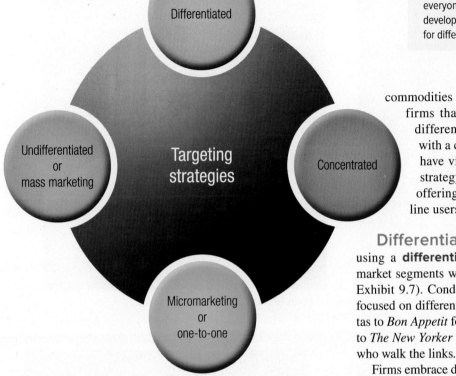

undifferentiated targeting strategy (mass marketing) A marketing strategy a firm can use if the product or service is perceived to provide the same benefits to everyone, with no need to develop separate strategies for different groups.

differentiated targeting strategy A strategy through which a firm targets several market segments with a different offering for each.

commodities such as salt or sugar. However, even those firms that offer salt and sugar now are trying to differentiate their products. Similarly, everyone with a car needs gasoline. Yet gasoline companies have vigorously moved from an undifferentiated strategy to a differentiated one by targeting their offerings to low-, medium-, and high-octane gasoline users.

Differentiated Targeting Strategy Firms using a **differentiated targeting strategy** target several market segments with a different offering for each (again see Exhibit 9.7). Condé Nast has more than 20 niche magazines focused on different aspects of life—from *Vogue* for fashionistas to *Bon Appetit* for foodies to *GQ* for fashion-conscious men to *The New Yorker* for literature lovers to *Golf Digest* for those who walk the links.

Firms embrace differentiated targeting because it helps them obtain a bigger share of the market and increase the market for their products overall. Readers of *Golf Digest* probably are unlike readers of *Architectural Digest* in their interests, as well as in their demographics, such as gender, age, and income. Providing products or services that appeal to multiple segments helps diversify the business and therefore lowers the company's (in this case, Condé Nast's) overall risk. Even if one magazine suffers a circulation decline, the impact on the firm's profitability can be offset by revenue from another publication that

Exhibit 9.7 illustrates several targeting strategies, which we discuss in more detail next.

Undifferentiated Targeting Strategy, or Mass Marketing
When everyone might be considered a potential user of its product, a firm uses an **undifferentiated targeting strategy (mass marketing)**. (See Exhibit 9.7.) Clearly, such a targeting strategy focuses on the similarities in needs of

> " If the product or service is perceived to provide similar benefits to most consumers, there simply is little need to develop separate strategies for different groups. "

the customers as opposed to the differences. If the product or service is perceived to provide similar benefits to most consumers, there simply is little need to develop separate strategies for different groups.

Although not a common strategy in today's complex marketplace, an undifferentiated strategy is used for many basic

continues to do well. But a differentiated strategy is likely to be more costly for the firm.

Concentrated Targeting Strategy
When an organization selects a single, primary target market and focuses all its energies on providing a product to fit that market's needs,

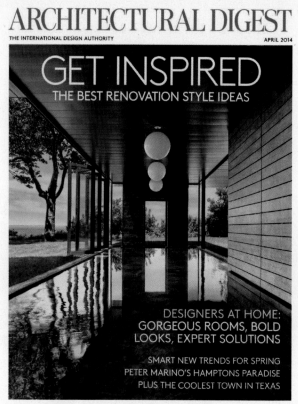

Condé Nast has more than 20 niche magazines focused on different aspects of life.
Left: © Peter Yang/Golf Digest; Right: © Bjorn Wallander/Architectural Digest.

it is using a **concentrated targeting strategy**. Entrepreneurial start-up ventures often benefit from using a concentrated strategy, which allows them to employ their limited resources more efficiently. Newton Running, for instance, has concentrated its targeting strategy to runners—but not all runners. It focuses only on those who prefer to land on their forefeet while running, a style that recently has been suggested as more natural, efficient, and less injury-prone than the style encouraged by more traditional running shoes with their heel-first construction and substantial cushioning. In comparison, though it also is known for its running shoes, Nike uses a differentiated targeting strategy (recall the opening vignette about Nike in Chapter 2). It makes shoes for segments that include basketball and football players and skateboarders as well as fashion-conscious white-collar workers with its subsidiary brand Cole Haan.

Micromarketing[18] Take a look at your collection of belts. Have you ever had one made to match your exact specifications? (If you're interested, try http://www.leathergoodsconnection.com.) When a firm tailors a product or service to suit an individual customer's wants or needs, it is undertaking an extreme form of segmentation called **micromarketing** or **one-to-one marketing**.

Such small producers and service providers generally can tailor their offerings to individual customers more easily. But it is far more difficult for larger companies to achieve this degree of segmentation. Major players such as Dell (computers) and Lands' End (shirts) tried to capitalize on Internet technologies to offer custom products. Lands' End let customers choose from a variety of options in the fabric, type of collar, sleeve,

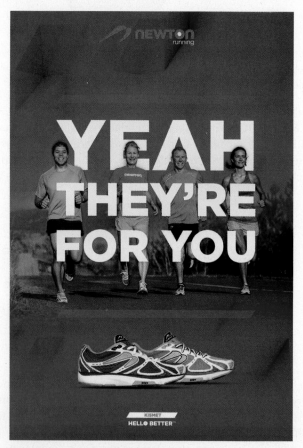

Which segment is being targeted?
© Newton Running

shape, and based on the customer's specific measurements—but it halted this service when it could not manage to achieve profitable sales. Dell allowed customers to choose the size, color, and speed of their laptops, though it has backed off its promotions and limits the choice of software included. These adjustments demonstrate the difficulty of micromarketing.

The Internet clearly helps facilitate such a segmentation strategy. Companies can cater to very small segments, sometimes as small as one customer at a time, relatively efficiently and inexpensively (e.g., mortgage and insurance sites provide personalized quotes). An Internet-based company can offer one-to-one service more inexpensively than can other venues, such as retail stores or telephone-based businesses. For example, frequent fliers of American Airlines can check prices and choose special services online at a fraction of the cost that the company would incur for a phone consultation with a ticket agent.

The Internet also simplifies customer identification, in ways that are constantly changing, as we discussed in the opening vignette for Chapter 4. **Cookies**, or small text files a website stores in a visitor's browser, provide a unique identification of each potential customer who visits and details how the customer has searched the site. In turn, advertisers using retargeting technologies can link their advertisements to the browsing history of any individual user. For example, Twitter's Tailored Audiences service helps corporate clients advertise their products to any Twitter subscriber who has shown any interest in the brand through her or his online activities.[19]

Marketers also can ask visitors to fill out an online registration form. Using such information, the company can make a variety of recommendations to customers. Amazon.com is renowned for the algorithms it uses to provide recommendations for related products to customers as they browse the site, which match customer profiles to those of other customers. The marketing strategy therefore is customized in real time, using known and accurate data about the customer. Staples offers merchandise at different prices in different parts of the country—simply by asking customers to enter their zip codes.

Customers can even do the work themselves, both to create items for themselves and to find the perfect gifts for others.[20] Mars Chocolate North America's MY M&M's Brand site (http://www.mymms.com) lets customers customize their own M&M's Chocolate Candies with personalized greetings, including messages for birthday parties, sporting events, graduations, and weddings—as well as wedding proposals! Both online and in stores, Build-A-Bear lets young (or not so young) customers design their very own stuffed furry friend with unique clothes, accessories, sounds, and the name printed on its birth certificate.

Some consumers appreciate such custom-made goods and services because they are made especially for them, which means they'll meet the person's needs exactly. If a tailor measures you first and then sews a suit that fits your shoulders, hips, and leg length exactly, it probably will fit better than an off-the-rack suit that you pick up at a department store. But such products and services are typically more expensive than ready-made offerings and often take longer to obtain. You can purchase a dress shirt in your size at Macy's and wear it out of the store. Ordering a tailored shirt from an online site that allows you to enter in your measurements might

> *Amazon.com is renowned for the algorithms it uses to provide recommendations for related products to customers as they browse the site, which match customer profiles to those of other customers.*

www.mymms.com allows customers to customize their candy.
© Mars, Inc.

market positioning
Involves the process of defining the marketing mix variables so that target customers have a clear, distinctive, desirable understanding of what the product does or represents in comparison with competing products.

value proposition
The unique value that a product or service provides to its customers and how it is better than and different from those of competitors.

Build-A-Bear lets customers design their own stuffed furry friend with unique clothes, accessories, sounds, and the name printed on its birth certificate.

© Build-A-Bear Workshop, Inc.

take five to six weeks to receive delivery. And if you visited an old-fashioned tailor, the processes of measuring you, ordering the material, and sewing the pants might take several months— at a much higher cost.

LO 9-4 Determine the value proposition.

Step 5: Identify and Develop Positioning Strategy

The last step in developing a market segmentation strategy is positioning. **Market positioning** involves a process of defining the marketing mix variables so that target customers have a clear, distinctive, desirable understanding of what the product does or represents in comparison with competing products.

The positioning strategy can help communicate the firm's or the product's **value proposition**, which communicates the customer benefits to be received from a product or service and thereby provides reasons for wanting to purchase it.

To visualize the value proposition, examine the Circles for a Successful Value Proposition framework in Exhibit 9.8A.[21] The first circle represents the customer needs and wants, the second circle represents the benefits that the company provides (i.e., its capabilities), and the final circle represents the benefits provided by competitors. The best situation is if a firm's product or service offering overlaps with customer needs and wants but suffers no overlap with competitors' offerings (Exhibit 9.8A). The shaded portion reflects the value proposition, or the intersection of what the customer needs and wants with what the firm can offer. Unfortunately, even if the situation depicted in Exhibit 9.8A existed, the product or service then would be

▼ **EXHIBIT 9.8** Circles for a Successful Value Proposition

A. No overlap with competition

#1: Firm's value proposition.
#2: Customer's unmet needs (marketing opportunity).
#3: Firm's benefits that are not required—educate customer or redesign product.
#4: Key benefits that both the firm and competitor provide that customers require—carefully monitor performance relative to competitor on these benefits.
#5: Competitor's value proposition—monitor and imitate if needed.
#6: Benefits both firms provide that customers do not appear to need.
#7: Competitor benefits that are not required.

B. Determining the value proposition

successful, so it likely would not be sustainable because competitors would attempt to copy the important product or service attributes and therefore begin to encroach on the firm's value proposition. Maintaining a unique value proposition can be sustained in the long term only in monopoly situations or possibly monopolistic competition situations.

In Exhibit 9.8B, the intersection of customer needs, the benefits provided by our focal firm, and the benefits provided by a competing firm reveal seven specific spaces where a product or service might be located. Let's look at each one in turn, using the offerings of the airline industry as hypothetical examples to understand each space.

Space 1. Representing the firm's value proposition, this space reveals which customer needs are effectively met by the benefits that the firm provides but not by the benefits provided by competitors. That is, there is no overlap between competitors. When airline customers prefer a cattle-call approach to seating, which allows them to choose their own seats on the plane as long as they get an early check-in, they turn to Southwest, and Southwest alone, for their flights.

Space 2. These customer needs are unmet. It represents an important marketing opportunity in that the firm could create new products or augment existing services to satisfy these needs better. A direct route between two cities that currently are not connected by any airline represents a prime example of such a space.

Space 3. Customers express little need or desire for these company benefits. The firm thus has several options. It might educate customers about the importance and benefits that it provides with this space, to encourage customers to develop a sense of their need. Alternatively, it could reengineer its approach to stop providing these unwanted benefits, which likely would enable it to save money. For example, when airlines realized that passengers cared little about the appearance of a piece of lettuce underneath the in-flight sandwiches they were served, they saved millions of dollars they had previously spent on unwanted produce.

Space 4. These needs are being met by the benefits of the firm as well as by competitors. Many customers make frequent trips between major cities, like New York and Washington, DC, and many airlines offer multiple direct flights each day between these hubs. Each firm therefore works to compete effectively, such as by offering convenient flight times or striving to increase its on-time rates to make it easier for customers to compare firms on these specific features.

Space 5. This space constitutes the competitor's value proposition: the needs of customers that are met by benefits a competitor provides but not by the benefits provided by our focal firm. For example, only a few airlines host separate lounges for their best customers; a lower-cost airline cannot compete in this space. However, if more and more customers start to make demands for these benefits, the focal firm needs to monitor developments carefully and match some benefits if possible.

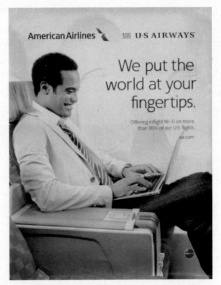

A firm's value proposition is represented by the benefits that a firm provides but not by the benefits provided by competitors. Airline customers that are looking for a good value and will therefore tolerate a cattle-call approach to seating, which allows them to choose their own seats on the plane as long as they get an early check-in, turn to Southwest for their flights (left). Alternatively, customers that are looking for lots of world-wide flight options will turn to American Airlines/US Airways (right).
Left: © Buskirk Services, Inc./PhotoEdit; Right: © Ashok Saxena/Alamy

value Reflects the relationship of benefits to costs, or what the consumer *gets* for what he or she *gives*.

Space 6. Although both the focal firm and its competitors provide these benefits, they somehow are not meeting customer needs. The stringent security screening requirements aim to increase passenger safety, but they also represent a significant inconvenience that many fliers associate with airlines rather than federal regulators. Expending significant efforts to educate customers by the focal firm about these needs would also benefit competitors, so they likely are lower in the priority list of spending.

Space 7. Finally, some competitor benefits are either undesired or unnecessary among customers. Similar to Space 3, the competitor could invest money to educate customers about the importance of these benefits and highlight their needs through advertising and promotional campaigns. If so, the focal firm should recognize that this need is moving to Space 5. Alternatively, the competitor could reengineer its products to eliminate these benefits, in which case it requires no response from the focal firm.

Regardless of their existing space, firms must constantly and closely monitor their competitors' offerings. If competitors offer features that the firm does not, it is important to determine their importance to customers. Important attributes should be considered for inclusion in the firm's offering—or else they will provide a unique value proposition for competitors.

In Exhibit 9.9, we highlight the elements of developing and communicating a firm's value proposition. The main value proposition components are:

1. Target market
2. Offering name or brand
3. Product/service category or concept
4. Unique point of difference/benefits

Let's focus on a couple of well-known products, Gatorade and 7-Up, and their potential value propositions (brackets are added to separate the value proposition components):

- **Gatorade:**[22] To [athletes around the world] [Gatorade] is the [sports drink] [representing the heart, hustle, and soul of athleticism and gives the fuel for working muscles, fluid for hydration, and electrolytes to help replace what is lost in sweat before, during, and after activity to get the most out of your body].

▼ **EXHIBIT 9.9** Value Proposition Statement Key Elements

	Gatorade	7-Up
Target market:	Athletes around the world	Non-cola consumers
Offering name or brand:	Gatorade	7-Up
Product/service category or concept:	Sports drink	Non-caffeinated soft drink
Unique point of difference/benefits:	Representing the heart, hustle, and soul of athleticism and gives the fuel for working muscles, fluid for hydration, and electrolytes to help replace what is lost in sweat before, during, and after activity to get the most out of your body.	Light, refreshing, lemon-lime flavored, and has a crisp, bubbly, and clean taste.

What are the value propositions for Gatorade and 7-UP?
© Michael J. Hruby

- **7UP:**[23] To [non-cola consumers] [7-Up] is a [non-caffeinated soft drink] that is [light, refreshing, lemon-lime flavored, and has a crisp, bubbly, and clean taste].

LO 9-5 Define positioning, and describe how firms do it.

Positioning Methods

Firms position products and services based on different methods such as the value proposition, salient attributes, symbols, and competition. Thus, firms position their products and services according to value and salient attributes. **Value** is a popular positioning method because the relationship of price to quality is among the most important considerations for consumers when they make a purchase decision.

Remember that value does not necessarily mean low priced. For Louis Vuitton, appealing to its target market means making its offerings even more rare and expensive. Much of its recent revenues have come from lower margin products, such as perfume, so it introduced a new ultra-luxury line to appeal to its target market of the wealthiest customers. New offerings include clothing made of vicuna wool or lotus fibers—that is, extremely rare and difficult to harvest materials.[24] Other brands promote an idea of luxury being valuable because it lasts for generations, as exemplified by Patek Phillipe, Hermès, and Chanel.

Another common positioning strategy focuses on the product attributes that are most important to the target market. With its all-wheel-drive Quattro, Audi has positioned itself on

French retailer Hermès is positioned as a luxury brand, which makes its customers less price-sensitive for its products like this handmade Birkin bag which retails for $9,000.
© Tiffany Rose/Getty Images

Audi has positioned itself as an uncompromising high-performance car.
© Jeff Morgan 16/Alamy

performance and handling. Targeting a different market, Subaru positions its all-wheel drive slightly differently, instead focusing on safety and handling.

A well-known symbol can also be used as a positioning tool. What comes to mind when you think of Colonel Sanders, the Jolly Green Giant, the Gerber Baby, or Tony the Tiger? Or consider the Texaco star, the Nike swoosh, or the Ralph Lauren polo player? These symbols are so strong and well known that they create a position for the brand that distinguishes it from its competition. Many such symbols are registered trademarks that are legally protected by the companies that developed them.

Firms can choose to position their products or services against a specific competitor or an entire product/service classification. For instance, although most luggage companies focus on building lightweight and functional designs, Saddleback Leather focuses on rugged durability and a classic look. Offering a 100-year guarantee on its products, the owner Dave positions his bags as something "your grandkids will fight over." This craftsmanship comes at a cost—its suitcases sell for more than $1,000.

Marketers must be careful, however, that they don't position their product too closely to their competition. If, for

How does Saddleback Leather position itself?
© Saddleback Leather Company

instance, their package or logo looks too much like a competitor's, they might be opening themselves up to a trademark infringement lawsuit. Many private-label and store brands have been challenged for using packaging that appears confusingly similar to that of the national brand leaders in a category. Similarly, McDonald's sues anyone who uses the *Mc* prefix, including McSleep Inns and McDental Services, even though in the latter case there was little possibility that consumers would believe the fast-food restaurant company would branch out into dental services.

Positioning Using Perceptual Mapping

Now that we have identified the various methods by which firms position their products and services, we discuss the actual steps they go through to establish that position. When developing a positioning strategy, firms go through six important steps. But before you read about these steps, examine Exhibit 9.10 (Charts A–D), a hypothetical perceptual map of the soft drink industry. A **perceptual map** displays, in two or more dimensions, the position of products or brands in the consumer's mind. We have chosen two dimensions for illustrative purposes: sweet versus light taste (vertical) and less natural versus healthy (horizontal). Also, though this industry is quite complex, we have simplified the diagram to include only a few players in the market. The position of each brand is denoted by a small circle, except for the focal brand, Gatorade, whch is denoted by a star. The numbered circles denote consumers' **ideal points**—where a particular market segment's ideal product would lie on the map. The larger the numbered circle, the larger the market size.

To derive a perceptual map such as shown in Exhibit 9.10, marketers follow six steps.

1. **Determine consumers' perceptions and evaluations of the product or service in relation to competitors'.** Marketers determine their brand's position by asking consumers a series of questions about their and competitors' products. For instance,

Gatorade and Powerade are positioned similarly and compete with each other for customers who seek healthy sweet drinks.
© Rachel Epstein/
PhotoEdit

> GATORADE ALSO RECOGNIZES A MARKET OF CONSUMERS WHO WOULD PREFER A LESS SWEET, LESS CALORIE-LADEN DRINK THAT OFFERS THE SAME REJUVENATING PROPERTIES AS GATORADE. CURRENTLY, NO PRODUCT IS ADEQUATELY SERVING MARKET 4.

▼ **EXHIBIT 9.10A** Perceptual Maps

Chart A

```
                    Sweet taste
        ┌──────────────┬──────────────┐
        │              │              │
        │  ○ Pepsi     │  ○ Powerade  │
        │              │  ✛ Gatorade  │
  Less  │              │              │ Healthy
 natural├──────────────┼──────────────┤
        │              │ ○ Propel Fitness
        │              │   Water      │
        │              │ ○ Bottled water
        │              │              │
        └──────────────┴──────────────┘
                    Light taste
```

they might ask how the consumer uses the existing product or services, what items the consumer regards as alternative sources to satisfy his or her needs, what the person likes or dislikes about the brand in relation to competitors, and what might make that person choose one brand over another. Exhibit 9.10A depicts the six products using two dimensions (light taste–sweet taste; and less natural–healthy).

2. **Identify the market's ideal points and size.** On a perceptual map, marketers can represent the size of current and potential markets. For example, Exhibit 9.10B uses differently sized ovals that correspond to the market size. Ideal point 1 represents the largest market, so if the firm does not already have a product positioned close to this point, it should consider an introduction. Point 3 is the smallest market, so there are relatively few customers who want a healthy, light-tasting drink. This is not to suggest that this market should be ignored; however, the company might want to consider a niche, rather than mass, market strategy for this group of consumers.

3. **Identify competitors' positions.** When the firm understands how its customers view its brand relative to competitors', it must study how those same competitors position themselves. For instance, Powerade positions itself closely to Gatorade, which means they appear next to each other on the perceptual map and appeal to target market 2 (see Exhibit 9.10C). They are also often found next to each other on store shelves, are similarly priced, and are viewed by customers as sports drinks. Gatorade also knows that its sports drink is perceived to be more like Powerade than like its own Propel Fitness Water (located near target market 3) or Coke (target market 1).

4. **Determine consumer preferences.** The firm knows what the consumer thinks of the products or services in the marketplace

▼ **EXHIBIT 9.10B** Perceptual Maps

Chart B

```
                    Sweet taste
        ┌──────────────┬──────────────┐
        │              │              │
        │   ( 1 )      │    ( 2 )     │
        │              │              │
  Less  │              │      ( 4 )   │ Healthy
 natural├──────────────┼──────────────┤
        │              │   ( 3 )      │
        │              │              │
        │              │              │
        └──────────────┴──────────────┘
                    Light taste
```

◯ Target market size indicated by size of oval

and their positions relative to one another. Now it must find out what the consumer really wants, that is, determine the ideal product or service that appeals to each market. For example, a huge market exists for traditional Gatorade, and that market is shared by Powerade. Gatorade also recognizes a market, depicted as the ideal product for segment 4 on the perceptual map, of consumers who would prefer a less sweet, less calorie-laden drink that offers the same rejuvenating properties as Gatorade. Currently, no product is adequately serving market 4.

5. **Select the position.** Continuing with the Gatorade example, the company has some choices to appeal to the "less sweet sports drink" target market 4. It could develop a new product to meet the needs of market 4 (see Exhibit 9.10D, option 1).

▼ **EXHIBIT 9.10C** Perceptual Maps

Chart C

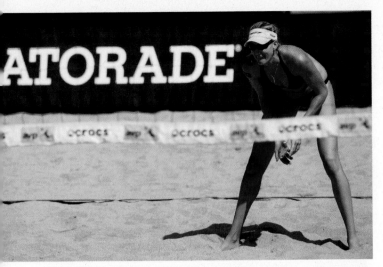

Gatorade uses athletes to compete for target markets in Exhibit 9.10.
© Jed Jacobsohn/Getty Images

Alternatively, it could adjust or reposition its marketing approach—its product and promotion—to sell original Gatorade to market 4 (option 2). Finally, it could ignore what target market 4 really wants and hope that consumers will be attracted to the original Gatorade because it is closer to their ideal product than anything else on the market.

6. **Monitor the positioning strategy.** Markets are not stagnant. Consumers' tastes shift, and competitors react to those shifts. Attempting to maintain the same position year after year can spell disaster for any company. Thus, firms must always view the first three steps of the positioning process as ongoing, with adjustments made in step four as necessary.

Despite the apparent simplicity of this presentation, marketers should recognize that changing their firm's positioning is never an easy task. ■

✓ **check** yourself

1. What is a perceptual map?
2. Identify the six positioning steps.

Mc Graw Hill Education **connect®** Increase your engagement and learning with Connect Marketing.

These Connect activities, available only through your Connect course, have been designed to make the following concepts more meaningful and applicable:

▶ Segmentation: Case Analysis on the College Food Industry

▶ Methods for Segmenting Markets: Click and Drag Activity

▶ Segmentation, Targeting, and Positioning: McDonald's Video Case

▶ Effective Market Segmentation: Thermos Video Case

▶ The Segmentation Process: iSeeit! Video

Mc Graw Hill Education **SMARTBOOK™**   Mc Graw Hill Education **iSeeit!**

marketing research

LEARNING OBJECTIVES

After reading this chapter, you should be able to:

LO 10-1 Identify the five steps in the marketing research process.

LO 10-2 Describe the various secondary data sources.

LO 10-3 Describe the various primary data collection techniques.

LO 10-4 Summarize the differences between secondary data and primary data.

LO 10-5 Examine the circumstances in which collecting information on consumers is ethical.

When we discussed Disney as an example of a stellar customer service provider in Chapter 2, we noted how it personalizes the experience for every visitor. To offer such remarkable personalization and service, Disney needs information: about who customers are, what they like, where they are going, and so on.

It has long engaged in observational research, by watching how people move through its parks. Such research helped it determine just how far apart each trash can should be, for example, to ensure that anytime a visitor was ready to throw away a wrapper, he or she had a ready receptacle in which to toss it.

Disney also combines the data it collects from guests at its hotels, information provided when people buy theme park tickets online, and other such purchasing details. Thus it can determine how many families are staying, but also how many couples are using Disney for their honeymoon. In turn, it can distribute its attractions according to its target market: plenty of rides for kids, as well as romantic sites for couples to enjoy the weather and their time alone.

A more recent initiative relies on a wristband, called My Magic+. The wristband represents hotel guests' room key and credit card, so simply by swiping it they can access their rooms or charge their poolside lunch to their room account. For

continued on p. 194

continued from p. 193

day visitors to the parks, the bands enable them to check in for rides, make dinner reservations, or purchase souvenirs, charged to a linked credit card.[1]

These are the benefits the wristbands offer for customers. For Disney, they offer remarkable access to real-world data about how visitors and guests actually make purchase decisions. By tracking the timing of their ride choices, Disney learns when and where it needs to increase staffing, to ensure a smooth traffic flow. Even inventory decisions are informed by far more detailed information, such as whether customers seem to prefer picking up a princess dress near Cinderella's castle or somewhere else in the park.

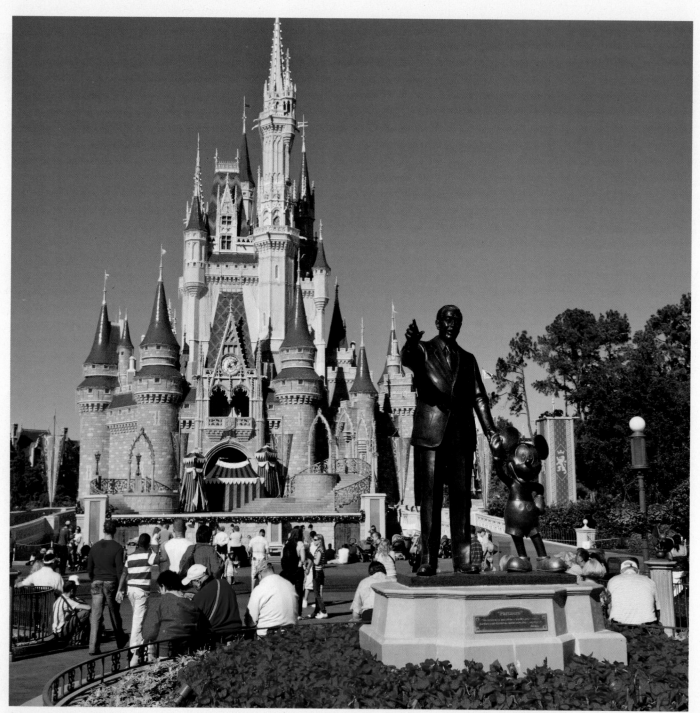

Disney collects information on its customers using conventional and not-so-conventional methods.
© Ron S Buskirk/Alamy

On a more personalized level, willing park visitors with a Magic band might agree to receive notifications about when they should hurry over to a popular ride, because the lines are relatively short. Such communications would not only appeal to customers but also could help Disney even out its ride capacity better. In this sense, Disney happily reported that soon after the introduction of the new system, it was able to accommodate approximately 3,000 more visitors during the holiday season than it had the previous year.[2]

Disney has started marketing the bands themselves as souvenirs—a collectible that people can take home to remember their visit, but also potentially a way for Disney to keep track of them. Such access has, perhaps not surprisingly, created some backlash among privacy experts and some consumers. Especially because so much of Disney's target market consists of children, these ethical questions are salient. Should a massive corporation have access to a child's name, favorite princess, and birthdate, for example? ■

oriented because they build their strategies by using customer input and continual feedback. Third, by constantly monitoring their competitors, firms can anticipate and respond quickly to competitive moves.

marketing research
A set of techniques and principles for systematically collecting, recording, analyzing, and interpreting data that can aid decision makers involved in marketing goods, services, or ideas.

If you think market research is applicable only to corporate ventures though, think again. Nonprofit organizations and governments also use research to serve their constituencies better. The political sector has been slicing and dicing the voting public for decades to determine relevant messages for different demographics. Politicians desperately want to understand who makes up the voting public to determine how to reach them. But not only do they want to know your political views, they also want to understand your media habits, such as what magazines you subscribe to, so they can target you more effectively.

To do so, they rely on the five-step marketing research process we outline in this chapter. We also discuss some of the ethical implications of using the information that these databases can collect.

> WHEN MARKETING MANAGERS ATTEMPT TO DEVELOP THEIR STRATEGIES, MARKETING RESEARCH CAN PROVIDE VALUABLE INFORMATION THAT WILL HELP THEM MAKE SEGMENTATION, POSITIONING, PRODUCT, PLACE, PRICE, AND PROMOTION DECISIONS.

Marketing research is a prerequisite of successful decision making. It consists of a set of techniques and principles for systematically collecting, recording, analyzing, and interpreting data that can aid decision makers involved in marketing goods, services, or ideas. When marketing managers attempt to develop their strategies, marketing research can provide valuable information that will help them make segmentation, positioning, product, place, price, and promotion decisions.

Firms invest billions of dollars in marketing research every year. The largest U.S.-based marketing research firm, the Nielsen Company, earns annual worldwide revenues of over $5 billion.[3] Why do marketers find this research valuable? First, it helps reduce some of the uncertainty under which they currently operate. Successful managers know when research might help their decision making and then take appropriate steps to acquire the information they need. Second, marketing research provides a crucial link between firms and their environments, which enables them to be customer

THE MARKETING RESEARCH PROCESS

Managers consider several factors before embarking on a marketing research project. First, will the research be useful; will it provide insights beyond what the managers already know and reduce uncertainty associated with the project? Second, is top management committed to the project and willing to abide by the results of the research? Related to both of these questions is the value of the research. Marketing research can be very expensive, and if the results won't be useful or management does not abide by the findings, it represents a waste of money. Third, should the marketing research project be small or large? A project might involve a simple analysis of data that the firm already has, or it could be an in-depth assessment that costs hundreds of thousands of dollars and takes months to complete.

The marketing research process itself consists of five steps (see Exhibit 10.1). Although we present the stages of the

Step 1: Defining the objectives and research needs

Step 2: Designing the research

Step 3: Collecting the data

Step 4: Analyzing the data and developing insights

Step 5: Developing and implementing an action plan

and preliminary analysis. If they uncover new information during the collection step or if the findings of the analysis spotlight new research needs, they might redefine their objectives and begin again from a new starting point. Another important requirement before embarking on a research project is to plan the entire project in advance. By planning the entire research process prior to starting the project, researchers can avoid unnecessary alterations to the research plan as they move through the process.

LO 10-1	Identify the five steps in the marketing research process.

Marketing Research Process Step 1: Defining the Objectives and Research Needs

Because research is both expensive and time-consuming, it is important to establish in advance exactly what problem needs to be solved. For example, as Adding Value 10.1 outlines, McDonald's is considering ways to address a deeply troubling concern, namely, breakfast service that ends before noon. In general, marketers must clearly define the objectives of their marketing research project.

Consider a scenario: McDonald's wants a better understanding of its customers' experience. It also needs to understand how customers view the experience at Wendy's, a main competitor. Finally, McDonald's hopes to gain some insight into how it should set a price for and market its latest combo meal of a hamburger, fries, and drink. Any one of these questions could initiate a research project. The complexity of the project that the company eventually undertakes depends on how much time and resources it has available, as well as the amount of in-depth knowledge it needs.

Researchers assess the value of a project through a careful comparison of the benefits of answering some of their questions and the costs associated with conducting the research. When researchers have determined what information they need to address a particular problem or issue, the next step is to design a research project to meet those objectives.

Marketing Research Process Step 2: Designing the Research

The second step in the marketing research project involves design. In this step, researchers identify the type of data needed and determine the research necessary to collect them. Recall that the objectives of the project drive the type of data needed, as outlined in Step 1.

Let's look at how this second step works, using the McDonald's customer experience. McDonald's needs to ask its customers about their McDonald's experience. However, because people don't always tell the whole truth in surveys, the company also may want to observe customers to see how they

marketing research process in a step-by-step progression, of course research does not always, or even usually, happen that way. Researchers go back and forth from one step to another as the need arises. For example, marketers may establish a specific research objective, which they follow with data collection

Adding Value 10.1

A Key Motivation for Waking Teens Early on Weekends Disappears—McDonald's Hints at Breakfast All Day[i]

Once upon a time, McDonald's did not offer any breakfast: no pancakes, no links, no nothing. Then in 1973 it introduced the Egg McMuffin, and today it generates almost a quarter of its revenues from its breakfast offerings. But since that introduction, there has been one persistent problem suffered by night owls and morning laggards: Breakfast stops at 10:30 a.m. sharp. After this time, hungry diners must select a burger or wrap to wake them up, because no restaurants allow them to purchase traditional morning fare.

All that may be about to change. McDonald's has started testing, in limited regions, a "Breakfast After Midnight" menu in some of its 24-hour restaurants. This expansion has been relatively secretive, in that customers have to be in the local store at 2:00 a.m. to learn whether they can get their fix of egg, cheese, sausage, and biscuit. Some reports suggest the test markets appear already in Texas, Delaware, and Illinois (the site of McDonald's corporate headquarters). In addition, some overseas stores already have the all-day breakfast in place.

For late-morning risers everywhere else, the real excitement came when McDonald's CEO Don Thompson acknowledged, on a national news segment, that expanding the breakfast menu to make it available all day was a real possibility. The demand is clearly there, in that

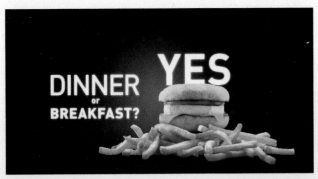

McDonald's has started testing a "Breakfast After Midnight" menu in some of its 24-hour restaurants to provide its customers what they want, when they want it.
© McDonalds Corporation

observers have identified breakfast as the biggest potential growth category for the brand, as well as its competitors.

The challenge is capacity. According to one franchise owner, because McDonald's continues to ask employees to use toasters and griddles to prepare its fast-food offerings—rather than faster options such as microwaves—selling both breakfast and dinner items simultaneously would strain the preparation capabilities of stores. Furthermore, McDonald's has already expanded its menu into other categories, such as wraps and salads. Perhaps adding another entire category of items would overly tax the busy employees.

But for young adults rolling out of bed at noon on a Saturday, such arguments likely have little weight. Ultimately, McDonald's may be forced to provide what its customers want, exactly when and where they want it.

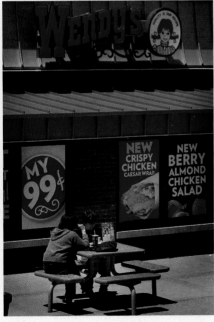

If McDonald's were to do research to better understand its customers' experience, it would study both the McDonald's experience and that of its major competitors, like Wendy's.
Left: © McGraw-Hill Education/John Flournoy, photographer; Right: © Scott Olson/Getty Images

actually enter the stores, interact with employees, and consume the product. The project's design might begin with available data, such as information that shows many customers arrive at 10:45 asking for breakfast or that people with children often come into the restaurants at lunchtime and order Happy Meals. Then McDonald's marketing researchers can start to ask customers specific questions about their McDonald's experience.

Marketing Research Process Step 3: Collecting the Data

Data collection begins only after the research design process. Based on the design of the project, data can be collected from secondary or primary data sources. **Secondary data** are pieces of information that have been collected prior to the start of the focal research project. Secondary data include both external and internal data sources. **Primary data**, in contrast, are those data collected to address specific research needs. Some common primary data collection methods include focus groups, in-depth interviews, and surveys.

For our hypothetical fast-food scenario, McDonald's may decide to get relevant secondary data from external providers

> " Some common primary data collection methods include focus groups, in-depth interviews, and surveys. "

such as National Purchase Diary Panel and Nielsen. The data might include the prices of different ingredients, sales figures, growth or decline in the category, and advertising and promotional spending. McDonald's is likely to gather pertinent data about sales from its franchisees. However, it also wants competitor data, overall food consumption data, and other information about the quick-service restaurant category, which it likely obtains from appropriate syndicated data providers. Based on the data, it might decide to follow up with some primary data using a survey.

No company can ask every customer his or her opinions or observe every customer, so researchers must choose a group of customers who represent the customers of interest, or a **sample**, and then generalize their opinions to describe all customers with the same characteristics. They may choose the sample participants at random to represent the entire customer market. Or they may choose to select the sample on the basis of some characteristic, such as their age, so they can research how seniors experience buying Value Meals.

Marketing researchers use various methods of asking questions to measure the issues they are tackling. In our hypothetical McDonald's scenario, assume the research team has developed a questionnaire (see Exhibit 10.2), using a few different types of questions. Section A measures the customer's experience in McDonald's, Section B measures the customer's experience in Wendy's, Section C measures the customer's habits at McDonald's, and Section D measures customer demographics.[4]

Marketing Research Process Step 4: Analyzing the Data and Developing Insights

The next step in the marketing research process—analyzing and interpreting the data—should be both thorough and methodical. To generate meaningful information, researchers analyze and make use of the collected data. In this context, **data** can be defined as raw numbers or other factual information that, on their own, have limited value to marketers. However, when the data are interpreted, they become **information**, which results from organizing, analyzing, and interpreting data and putting them into a form that is useful to marketing decision makers. For example, a checkout scanner in the grocery store collects sales data about individual consumer purchases. Not until those data are categorized and examined do they provide information about which products and services

McDonald's assesses its customers' market experience by examining available data and then asks customers about their experience with products such as Value Meals.
© Michael J. Hruby

▼ **EXHIBIT 10.2** A Hypothetical Fast-Food Survey

Please Evaluate Your Experience at McDonald's

A. McDonald's

	Strongly Disagree 1	Disagree 2	Neither Agree nor Disagree 3	Agree 4	Strongly Agree 5
McDonald's food tastes good	☐	☐	☐	☑	☐
McDonald's is clean	☐	☐	☐	☑	☐
McDonald's has low prices	☐	☐	☐	☑	☐

B. Wendy's

	Strongly Disagree 1	Disagree 2	Neither Agree nor Disagree 3	Agree 4	Strongly Agree 5
Wendy's food tastes good	☐	☐	☐	☑	☐
Wendy's is clean	☐	☐	☐	☑	☐
Wendy's has low prices	☐	☐	☐	☑	☐

C. McDonald's

	Never	1–2 times	3–4 times	More than 5 times
In the last month, how many times have you been to McDonald's?	☐	☐	☐	☑
In the last month, how often did you order breakfast items at McDonald's?	☐	☐	☐	☐
If McDonald's offered breakfast items all the time, how often would you order them outside of normal breakfast times in a typical month?	☐	☐	☐	☐

On average, how much do you spend each visit at McDonald's? $_____

What is your favorite item at McDonald's? _____

D. Please tell us about yourself

	Under 16	17–24	25–35	36+
What is your age?	☐	☐	☐	☐

	Male	Female		
What is your gender?	☐	☐		

were purchased together or how an in-store promotional activity translated into sales.

For the McDonald's example, we can summarize the results of the survey (from Exhibit 10.2) in Exhibit 10.3. Both McDonald's and Wendy's scored the same on the cleanliness of their restaurants, but McDonald's had lower prices, whereas Wendy's food tasted better. McDonald's may want to improve the taste of its food, without raising prices too much, to compete more effectively with Wendy's.

Marketing Research Process Step 5: Developing and Implementing an Action Plan

In the final phase in the marketing research process, the analyst prepares the results and presents them to the appropriate decision makers, who undertake appropriate marketing strategies. A typical marketing research presentation includes an executive summary, the body of the report (which discusses the research objectives, methodology used, and detailed findings), the conclusions, the limitations, and appropriate supplemental tables, figures, and appendixes.[5]

In the McDonald's hypothetical scenario, according to the research findings, the company is doing fine in terms of cleanliness (comparable to its competitors) and is perceived to have lower prices, but the taste of its food could be improved. It also found that of those customers that purchased breakfast items relatively frequently (at least three times per month), 35 percent would go for breakfast outside the normal breakfast times frequently. Also, of those that never ordered breakfast items, 25 percent would order breakfast items outside the normal breakfast times occasionally (at least once a month). Using this analysis and the related insights gained, McDonald's might consider hiring some gourmet chefs as consultants to improve the menu and offerings, and offer breakfast items 24/7 on a trial basis.[6] It then could highlight its efforts to improve the taste of the food and add desired offerings (e.g., breakfast items) through marketing communications and promotions. McDonald's also should consider undertaking additional pricing research to determine whether its lower prices enhance sales and profits or whether it could increase its prices and still compete effectively with Wendy's.

Now let's take a closer look at sources of secondary and primary data.

 check yourself

1. What are the steps in the marketing research process?
2. What is the difference between data and information?

> Secondary data might come from free or very inexpensive external sources such as census data, information from trade associations, and reports published in magazines.

McDonald's marketing research will show how to better compete against Wendy's.
© Michael Neelon(misc)/Alamy

LO 10-2 | Describe the various secondary data sources.

SECONDARY DATA

A marketing research project often begins with a review of the relevant secondary data. Secondary data might come from free or very inexpensive external sources such as census data, information from trade associations, and reports published in magazines. Although readily accessible, these inexpensive sources may not be specific or timely enough to solve the marketer's research needs and objectives. Firms also can purchase more specific or applicable secondary data from specialized research firms. Finally, secondary sources can be accessed through internal sources, including the company's sales invoices, customer lists, and other reports generated by the company itself.

In political settings, such secondary data can be critical for candidates running for office. Both major political parties thus have developed proprietary databases that contain vast information about voters, broken down by demographic and geographic

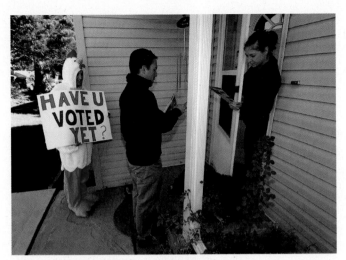

Secondary data are useful to politicians so they know who they are talking to before they knock on their door.
© AP Photo/Cathleen Allison

information. Before a local politician, canvasser, or poll taker even knocks on doors in a neighborhood, he or she likely knows which houses are inhabited by retirees, who has a subscription to the *Wall Street Journal* or *New York Times,* for whom the residents said they voted in the last election, or whether they served in the military. All these traits can give hints about the voters' likely concerns, which a good politician can address immediately upon knocking on the door. Such research also can dictate tactics for designing broader campaign materials or to zero in on very specific issues. Social media campaigns are a growing mechanism used to interact with potential voters in a more timely manner than more traditional methods. Monitoring tweets after a major address by a candidate, for instance, would provide instant feedback and direction for future communications.

Inexpensive External Secondary Data

Some sources of external secondary data can be quickly accessed at a relatively low cost. The U.S. Bureau of the Census (http://www.census.gov), for example, provides data about businesses by county and zip code. If you wanted to open a new location of a business you are already operating, these data might help you determine the size of your potential market.

Often, however, inexpensive data sources are not adequate to meet researchers' needs. Because the data initially were acquired for some purpose other than the research question at hand, they may not be completely relevant or timely. The U.S. Census is a great source of demographic data about a particular market area, and it can be easily accessed at a low cost. However, the data are collected only at the beginning of every decade, so they quickly become outdated. If an entrepreneur wanted to open a retail flooring store in 2016, for example, the data would already be six years old, and the housing market likely would be stronger than it was in 2010. Researchers must also pay careful attention to how other sources of inexpensive

secondary data were collected. Despite the great deal of data available on the Internet, easy access does not ensure that the data are trustworthy.

syndicated data Data available for a fee from commercial research firms such as Information Resources Inc. (IRI), National Purchase Diary Panel, and Nielsen.

Syndicated External Secondary Data

Although the secondary data described previously are either free or inexpensively obtained, marketers can purchase external secondary data called **syndicated data**, which are available for a fee from commercial research firms such as IRI, the National Purchase Diary Panel, and Nielsen. Exhibit 10.4 contains information about various firms that provide syndicated data.

Consumer packaged-goods firms that sell to wholesalers often lack the means to gather pertinent data directly from

▼ **EXHIBIT 10.4** Syndicated Data Providers and Some of Their Services

Name	Services Provided
Nielsen (http://www.nielsen.com)	With its *Market Measurement Services,* the company tracks the sales of consumer packaged goods, gathered at the point of sale in retail stores of all types and sizes.
IRI (http://www.iriworldwide.com)	*InfoScan* store tracking provides detailed information about sales, share, distribution, pricing, and promotion across a wide variety of retail channels and accounts.
J.D. Power and Associates (http://www.jdpower.com)	Widely known for its automotive ratings, it produces quality and customer satisfaction research for a variety of industries.
Mediamark Research Inc. (http://www.mediamark.com)	Supplies multimedia audience research pertaining to media and marketing planning for advertised brands.
National Purchase Diary Panel (http://www.npd.com)	Based on detailed records consumers keep about their purchases (i.e., a diary), it provides information about product movement and consumer behavior in a variety of industries.
NOP World (http://www.nopworld.com)	The *mKids US* research study tracks mobile telephone ownership and usage, brand affinities, and entertainment habits of American youth between 12 and 19 years of age.
Research and Markets (http://www.researchandmarkets.com)	Promotes itself as a one-stop shop for market research and data from most leading publishers, consultants, and analysts.
Roper Center for Public Opinion Research (http://www.ropercenter.uconn.edu)	The *General Social Survey* is one of the nation's longest running surveys of social, cultural, and political indicators.
Simmons Market Research Bureau (http://www.smrb.com)	Reports on the products American consumers buy, the brands they prefer, and their lifestyles, attitudes, and media preferences.
Yankelovich (http://thefuturescompany.com/new-us-monitor/)	The *MONITOR* tracks consumer attitudes, values, and lifestyles shaping the American marketplace.

scanner data A type of syndicated external secondary data used in quantitative research that is obtained from scanner readings of UPC codes at check-out counters.

panel data Information collected from a group of consumers.

the retailers that sell their products to consumers, which makes syndicated data a valuable resource for them. Some syndicated data providers also offer information about shifting brand preferences and product usage in households, which they gather from scanner data, consumer panels—and several other cutting-edge methods, as detailed in Social and Mobile Marketing 10.1.

Scanner data are used in quantitative research obtained from scanner readings of Universal Product Code (UPC) labels at checkout counters. Whenever you go into your local grocery store, your purchases are rung up using scanner systems. The data from these purchases are likely to be acquired by leading marketing research firms, such as IRI or Nielsen, which use this information to help leading

> " Some syndicated data providers also offer information about shifting brand preferences and product usage in households, which they gather from scanner data, consumer panels, and several other cutting-edge methods. "

consumer packaged-goods firms (e.g., Kellogg's, Pepsi, Kraft) assess what is happening in the marketplace. For example, a firm can use scanner data to determine what would happen to its sales if it reduced the price of its least popular product by 10 percent in a given month. In the test market in which it lowers the price, do sales increase, decrease, or stay the same?

Panel data are information collected from a group of consumers, organized into panels, over time. Data collected from panelists often include their records of what they have purchased (i.e., secondary data) as well as their responses to survey questions that the client gives to the panel firm to ask the panelists (i.e., primary data). Secondary panel data thus might show that when Diet Pepsi is offered at a deep discount, 80 percent of usual Diet Coke consumers switch to Diet Pepsi. Primary panel data could give insights into what they think of each option. We discuss how marketing researchers use scanner and panel data to answer specific research questions further in the primary data section.

Social & Mobile Marketing 10.1
Nielsen Seeks to Track Viewership, regardless of the Media People Use to Watch[ii]

As television viewers have changed their practices—such that more and more people catch the latest shows on their tablets or smartphones rather than home-based television screens—marketing researchers have unfortunately failed to keep up. For example, Nielsen, the most famous provider of ratings that reflect people's viewing patterns, maintained two separate measures: one for regular television and one for online viewing. It had no metric for views through other forms of streaming media.

That gap may be about to disappear, though. In the immediate future, Nielsen plans to introduce a Twitter-based measure that will assess the number of tweets about a show as a measure of popularity. Its initial metric suggests that every tweet represents about 50 people watching the show, regardless of where or how.

Then next year it plans to introduce a mobile-linked measurement system. With this proprietary method, Nielsen will enable the networks to issue their content through mobile applications that contain a preexisting link back to Nielsen's data collection methods. When a viewer downloads the app with the content, Nielsen knows it and can add that viewership to the show's and its network's ratings.

Such measures are critical for content providers, because ratings determine advertising sales and rates. A show or network with higher ratings attracts more potential advertisers and can charge them more. In recent months, when the traditional ratings formats showed that viewership was declining, advertisers grew concerned. At the same time, the networks protested loudly that the ratings were undercutting the extent of their true market by ignoring the people watching on their tablets.

Nielsen's moves seek to address those complaints, but they also have sparked some new concerns. In particular, insufficient evidence exists to confirm whether Twitter numbers are really a good representation of viewership. Without strong support for the link between tweets and the actual popularity of a show, the new measure might be meaningless. In addition, the mobile system is not slated to be ready for at least another year. Even when it appears, some observers suggest that it could be blocked by security features in Apple operating systems that prevent metering software from running simultaneously with other programs.

Thus marketing researchers face a problem without a ready solution. They know that consumers are moving away from their televisions, but they have no idea how to measure what they do after those viewers move.

data warehouses
Large computer files that store millions and even billions of pieces of individual data.

data mining The use of a variety of statistical analysis tools to uncover previously unknown patterns in the data stored in databases or relationships among variables.

Syndicated external secondary data are acquired from scanner data obtained from scanner readings of UPC codes at checkout counters (left) and from panel data collected from consumers that electronically record their purchases (right).
Left: © Glow Images, Inc/Getty Images; Right: Courtesy The Nielsen Co. © Stephen Barnes/Bowline Images/Alamy

> " OVERALL, BOTH PANEL AND SCANNER DATA, AS WELL AS THEIR MORE ADVANCED ITERATIONS GATHERED THROUGH SOCIAL MEDIA AND ONLINE USAGE PATTERNS, PROVIDE FIRMS WITH A COMPREHENSIVE PICTURE OF WHAT CONSUMERS ARE BUYING OR NOT BUYING. "

Overall, both panel and scanner data, as well as their more advanced iterations gathered through social media and online usage patterns, provide firms with a comprehensive picture of what consumers are buying or not buying. The key difference between scanner research and panel research is how the data are aggregated. Scanner research typically focuses on weekly consumption of a particular product at a given unit of analysis (e.g., individual store, chain, region); panel research focuses on the total weekly consumption by a particular person or household.

Internal Secondary Data

Internally, companies also generate a tremendous amount of secondary data from their day-to-day operations. One of the most valuable resources such firms have at their disposal is their rich cache of customer information and purchase history. However, it can be difficult to make sense of the millions and even billions of pieces of individual data, which are stored in large computer files called **data warehouses**. For this reason, firms find it necessary to use data mining techniques to extract valuable information from their databases.

Data mining uses a variety of statistical analysis tools to uncover previously unknown patterns in the data or relationships among variables. Some retailers try to customize their product and service offerings to match the needs of their customers. For instance, the UK grocer Tesco uses its loyalty card to collect massive amounts of information about its individual customers. Every time a loyalty card member buys something, the card is scanned and the store captures key purchase data specific to that member. But these specific data are basically useless until Tesco mines and analyzes them to identify three income groups: upscale, middle income, and less affluent. With this mined information, Tesco has been able to create appealing private-label product offerings for each group, according to their preferences, and began targeting promotions to each customer according to his or her income classification.

Marketers use data mining techniques to determine what items people buy at the same time so they can be promoted and displayed together.
© B2M Productions/Photographer's Choice/Getty Images

Data mining can also enable a home improvement retailer such as Lowe's to learn that 25 percent of the time its customers buy a garden hose, they also purchase a sprinkler. With such information, the retailer may decide to put the garden hoses next to the sprinklers in the store. Outside the retail realm, an investment firm might use statistical techniques to group clients according to their income, age, type of securities purchased, and prior investment experience. This categorization identifies different segments to which the firm can offer valuable packages that meet their specific needs. The firm also can tailor separate marketing programs to each of these segments.

By analyzing the enormous amount of information that they possess about customers, companies have developed statistical models that help identify when a customer is dissatisfied with his or her service. Once the company identifies an unhappy customer, it can follow up and proactively address that customer's issues. By mining customer data and information, the company also reduces its churn levels. **Churn** is the number of participants who discontinue use of a service, divided by the average number of total participants. With this knowledge, the company can focus on what it does best. Overall, firms hope to use data mining to generate customer-based analytics that they can apply to their strategic decision making and thereby make good customers better and better customers their best.

Big Data The field of marketing research has seen enormous changes in the last few years because of (1) the increase in the amounts of data to which retailers, service providers, and manufacturers have access; (2) their ability to collect these data from transactions, customer relationship management (CMR) systems, websites, and social media platforms that firms increasingly use to engage with their customers;[7] (3) the ease of collecting and storing these data; (4) the computing ability readily available to manipulate data in real time; and (5) access to in-house or available software to convert the data into valuable decision-making insights using analytic dashboards.

To specify this explosion of data, which firms have access to but cannot handle using conventional data management and data mining software, the term **big data** has arisen in the popular media. Leading firms already are converting their big data into customer insights, such as Amazon, Netflix, Google, Nordstrom, Kroger, Tesco, Macy's, American Express, and Walmart—though this list also keeps growing.[8]

Amazon may be the poster child for big data. Any Amazon shopper is familiar with its recommendation engine, which notes what the consumer is purchasing, analyzes purchase patterns by similar customers, and suggests other items the customer might enjoy, as well as what other people who bought the focal item also added to their shopping carts.[9] With more than 200 million active customers and billions of pieces of shopping data,[10] Amazon certainly qualifies as a big data user; its item-to-item collaborative filtering helps it determine which relevant products to suggest, generating almost one-third of its sales.[11]

The UK grocery retailer Tesco processes its data at a rate of approximately 100 customer baskets per second, to cover its 6 million daily transactions.[12] Furthermore, each purchased product can feature up to 45 data attributes: Is it Tesco's own brand, an ethnic recipe, exotic (e.g., star fruit) or basic (e.g., apple), and so on? On the basis of the attributes of the items customers purchase, Tesco filters them to define who they are, who else lives in their household, and what hobbies they have, then provides specific incentives that match these characteristics.[13]

To enable these efforts, firms such as SAP, Splunk, and GoodData offer a host of software solutions to help firms better integrate their data, visualize them, and then move from data to real-time insights.[14] The suite of options previously were available only to the largest firms, but with costs falling they are now more accessible to smaller firms.

Marketing Analytics

Google Analytics Promises Movie Studios the Ability to Predict Performance, Weeks Prior to Opening[iii]

When a lot of movie watchers search for the trailer for a film in the month before the movie opens, it promises a bigger opening weekend. Such a claim might seem somewhat self-evident, but Google has announced that it has the means to quantify this effect and thereby help movie studios predict their profits, up to a month prior to the opening day.

More precisely, Google asserts that search volume for the movie title (combined with a few other metrics, such as the season and whether the movie is a franchise) offers a 94 percent accurate prediction of box office performance.

Other proprietary information that Google can use to predict success includes the volume of clicks on search ads. If, for example, one movie prompted 20,000 more paid clicks than another film, it will bring in approximately $7.5 million more in revenues during its opening weekend. Furthermore, the search effects are not limited to Google; YouTube searches reveal similar predictive information. From its analysis, Google recommends that studios need to go beyond just a one-week window, because studying the search and click trends for a month increases the accuracy and power of its predictions significantly.

Moving beyond the implications for opening weekend, Google asserts that weekday searches in the weeks leading up to the release offer better predictors of continued revenues. That is, if a film fan searches for a movie title on a Tuesday, she or he is more likely to hold off on seeing the movie, rather than rushing out during opening weekend. On a related note, Google notes that nearly half of all moviegoers choose the film they will see that night on the same day. Thus, studios need to maintain a marketing presence far past opening day, to be sure to catch the laggard customers' attention.

But unless the movie is a big name, an anticipated release, or a franchise, most people have no idea of what is coming to their local Cineplex. Instead, during weeks without a major movie release, Google

Google analytics are increasingly used to predict the success of movies.
© Frazer Harrison/Getty Images

notes that consumers undertake more generic searches to gather information about what new movies might be available. On average, these film buffs consider 13 sources of information before they select a specific film to watch.

The big data explosion also stems from the growth of online and social media. In response, Google, Facebook, and Twitter all provide analytic dashboards designed to help their customers understand their own web traffic. In particular, Google has developed tremendous marketing analytical capabilities that it makes available to partner firms. Google helps firms attract customer traffic to their sites through the use of more relevant keywords, the purchase of Google AdWords, and better conversion methods.[15] Using Google Analytics, Puma has gained insights into which online content and products most engaged its web visitors, while also defining where these visitors lived. With these visitor behavioral data in hand, Puma has revised its website to be more dynamic (http://www.Puma.com) and has created unique identifiers for its various product categories (e.g., PUMA Golf), targeting them in accordance with the home region of the visitor.[16]

As Marketing Analytics 10.1 explains, sometimes the "internal" data can be gathered by a partner firm too, providing deeper insights than an individual firm can derive.

qualitative research
Informal research methods, including observation, following social media sites, in-depth interviews, focus groups, and projective techniques.

quantitative research
Structured responses that can be statistically tested to confirm insights and hypotheses generated via qualitative research or secondary data.

observation An exploratory research method that entails examining purchase and consumption behaviors through personal or video camera scrutiny.

check yourself

1. What is the difference between internal and external secondary research?

LO 10-3 | Describe the various primary data collection techniques.

PRIMARY DATA COLLECTION TECHNIQUES

In many cases, the information researchers need is available only through primary data or data collected to address specific research needs. Depending on the nature of the research problem, the primary data collection method can employ a *qualitative* or a *quantitative* research method.

As its name implies, **qualitative research** is used to understand the phenomenon of interest through broad, open-ended responses. It provides initial information that helps the researcher more clearly formulate the research objectives. Qualitative research is more informal than quantitative research methods and includes observation, following social media sites, in-depth interviews, and focus groups (see Exhibit 10.5, left side).

Once the firm has gained insights from doing qualitative research, it is likely to engage in **quantitative research**, which

are structured responses that can be statistically tested. Quantitative research provides information needed to confirm insights and hypotheses generated via qualitative research or secondary data. It also helps managers pursue appropriate courses of action. Formal studies such as specific experiments, scanner and panel data, or some combination of these are quantitative in nature (see Exhibit 10.5, right side). We now examine each of these primary data collection techniques in order.

Observation **Observation** entails examining purchase and consumption behaviors through personal or video camera scrutiny, or by tracking customers' movements electronically as they move through a store. For example, researchers might observe customers while they shop or when they go about their daily lives, during which processes they use a variety of products. Observation can last for a very brief period of time (e.g., two hours watching teenagers shop for clothing in the mall), or it may take days or weeks (e.g., researchers live with families to observe their use of products). When consumers are unable to articulate their experiences, observation research becomes particularly useful; how else could researchers determine which educational toys babies choose to play with or confirm details of the buying process that consumers might not be able to recall accurately?

Although traditionally firms might videotape customers' movements, Microsoft's Kinect sensors are providing a less intrusive option. Discretely embedded in aisles of retail stores, the sensors provide three-dimensional spatial recognition. Thus retailers and their suppliers can unobtrusively track the amount of time people spend in front of a shelf, which products they touch or pick up, the products they return to shelves, and finally what they add to their carts and purchase.[17] The data gathered can be used to improve store layouts because they can identify causes of slow-selling merchandise, such as poor shelf placement. By studying customers' movements, marketers can also

> Qualitative research is more informal than quantitative research methods and includes observation, following social media sites, in-depth interviews, and focus groups.

▼ **EXHIBIT 10.5** Qualitative versus Quantitative Data Collection

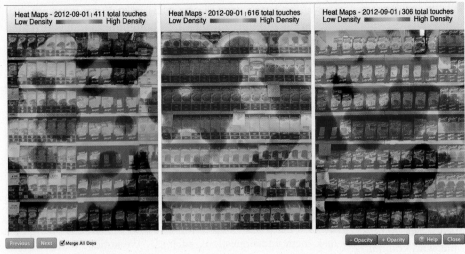

Heat Maps - 2012-09-01 | 411 total touches
Low Density ▬▬▬▬▬ High Density

Heat Maps - 2012-09-01 | 616 total touches
Low Density ▬▬▬▬▬ High Density

Heat Maps - 2012-09-01 | 306 total touches
Low Density ▬▬▬▬▬ High Density

Using Microsoft Kinect sensors, firms like Shopperception create heatmaps of shopper interactions with the products (touches, pickups, and returns). The red represents the hot zones where shoppers touch the most, yellow less, and blue not at all.
Courtesy Shopperception

the poorest consumers were interested only in functionality of a product—how to get hair clean. One woman struggled to find ways to wash her long hair effectively, even in the face of severe water shortages, rather than cut off what she considered the source of her beauty. Based on its research, P&G has added value by selling Rejoice shampoo inexpensively ($1.50) to a market that was using alternative options such as laundry detergent. Other observations pushed P&G to develop a more skin-sensitive laundry detergent after noting how many people in developing markets wash their clothes by hand.[18] These insights might be helpful, both for the company that gathers them and for consumers who ultimately benefit from better products.

learn where customers pause or move quickly or where there is congestion. This information can help them decide if the layout and merchandise placement is operating as expected, such as whether new or promoted merchandise is getting the attention it deserves.

Observation may be the best—and sometimes the only—method to determine how customers might use a product; therefore it is useful for designing and marketing products. By watching women wash their hair in a rural town in China, Procter & Gamble recognized the fallacy of its assumption that

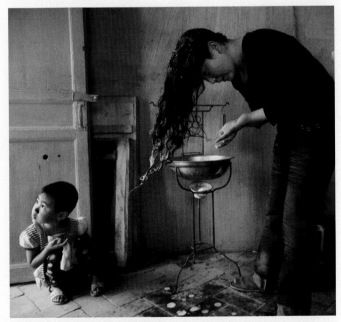

By watching women in rural China wash their hair, Procter & Gamble learned that even their poorest customers wanted beautiful hair, but it has to be packaged affordably.
© Benjamin Lowy/Getty Images

Social Media

Social media sites are a booming source of data for marketers. Marketers have realized that social media can provide valuable information that could aid their marketing research and strategy endeavors. In particular, contributors to social media sites rarely are shy about providing their opinions about the firm's own products or its competitors' offerings. If companies can monitor, gather, and mine these vast social media data, they can learn a lot about their customers' likes, dislikes, and preferences. They then might cross-reference such social media commentary with consumers' past purchases to derive a better sense of what they want. Customers also appear keen to submit their opinions about their friends' purchases, interests, polls, and blogs.

Blogs in particular represent valuable sources of marketing research insights. Marketers are paying attention to online reviews about everything from restaurants to running shoes to recycling. *The Truth About Cars* blog is known for its unflinchingly objective reviews of various makes and models as well as

When Kraft considered the launch of its South Beach product line, it created a virtual community of health and wellness opinion leaders and women who wanted to lose weight.
© Michael J. Hruby

virtual community
Online networks of people who communicate about specific topics.

sentiment mining
Data gathered by evaluating customer comments posted through social media sites such as Facebook and Twitter.

in-depth interview
An exploratory research technique in which trained researchers ask questions, listen to and record the answers, and then pose additional questions to clarify or expand on a particular issue.

discussions about the industry as a whole, marketing tactics, and global competition, among other topics.[19] Analyzing the content of this blog, and others like it, provides an excellent source of ideas and information for auto industry executives. Another creative use of social media for market research involves building online communities for companies. When it considered the launch of its South Beach product line, Kraft hired Communispace to create a **virtual community** (an online network of people who communicate about specific topics) of target consumers: 150 health and wellness opinion leaders and 150 women who wanted to lose weight became a virtual community. The participants openly shared their frustrations and difficulties managing their weight because the community environment prompted them to sense that everyone else on the site struggled with similar issues and concerns. By monitoring the community, Kraft learned that it would need to educate consumers about the South Beach Diet and offer products that could address cravings throughout the day, not just at mealtimes. Six months after the line's introduction, Kraft had earned profits of $100 million.[20]

Noting these various opportunities and marketing research sources online, many companies—including Ford Motor Co., PepsiCo, Coca-Cola, and Southwest Airlines—have added heads of social media to their management teams. These managers take responsibility for scanning the web for blogs, postings, tweets, or Facebook posts in which customers mention their experience with a brand. By staying abreast of this continuous stream of information, companies can gather the most up-to-date news about their company, products, and services as well as their competitors. These social media searches allow companies to learn about customers' perceptions and resolve customer complaints they may never have heard about through other channels.

The data gathered through the searches also undergo careful analyses: Are customer sentiments generally positive, negative, or neutral? What sort of intensity or interest levels do they imply? How many customers are talking about the firm's products, and how many focus instead on competitors'? This data analysis is understandably challenging, considering the amount of data available online. However, monitoring consumer sentiments has grown easier with the development of social media monitoring platforms.

Using a technique known as **sentiment mining**, firms collect consumer comments about companies and their products on social media sites such as Facebook, Twitter, and online blogs. The data are then analyzed to distill customer attitudes toward and preferences for products and advertising campaigns. Scouring millions of sites by combining automated online search tools with text analysis techniques, sentiment mining yields qualitative data that provide new insight into what consumers really think. Companies plugged into this real-time information can become more nimble, allowing for quick changes in a product rollout or a new advertising campaign.[21]

In-Depth Interviews

In an **in-depth interview**, trained researchers ask questions and listen to and record the answers, and then pose additional questions to clarify or expand on a particular issue. For instance, in addition to simply watching teenagers shop for apparel, interviewers might stop them one at a time in the mall to ask them a few questions, such as: "We noticed that you went into and came out of Abercrombie & Fitch very quickly without buying anything. Why was that?" If the subject responds that no one had bothered to wait on her, the interviewer might ask a follow-up question like, "Oh? Has that happened to you before?" or "Do you expect more sales assistance there?"

Although relatively expensive, in-depth interviews can reveal information that would be difficult to obtain with other methods.
© Spencer Grant/PhotoEdit

focus group interview
A research technique in which a small group of persons (usually 8 to 12) comes together for an intensive discussion about a particular topic, with the conversation guided by a trained moderator using an unstructured method of inquiry.

survey A systematic means of collecting information from people that generally uses a *questionnaire*.

questionnaire A form that features a set of questions designed to gather information from respondents and thereby accomplish the researchers' objectives; questions can be either unstructured or structured.

unstructured questions Open-ended questions that allow respondents to answer in their own words.

structured questions Closed-ended questions for which a discrete set of response alternatives, or specific answers, is provided for respondents to evaluate.

In-depth interviews provide insights that help managers better understand the nature of their industry as well as important trends and consumer preferences, which can be invaluable for developing marketing strategies. Specifically, they can establish a historical context for the phenomenon of interest, particularly when they include industry experts or experienced consumers. They also can communicate how people really feel about a product or service at the individual level. Finally, marketers can use the results of in-depth interviews to develop surveys.

In-depth interviews are, however, relatively expensive and time-consuming. The interview cost depends on the length of the interaction and the characteristics of the people included in the sample. If the sample must feature medical doctors, for example, the costs of getting sufficient interviews will be much higher than the costs associated with intercepting teenagers in a mall.

Focus Group Interviews

In **focus group interviews**, a small group of persons (usually 8 to 12) come together for an intensive discussion about a particular topic. Using an unstructured method of inquiry, a trained moderator guides the conversation, according to a predetermined, general outline of topics of interest. Researchers usually record the interactions by videotape or audiotape so they can carefully comb through the interviews later to catch any patterns of verbal or nonverbal responses. In particular, focus groups gather qualitative data about initial reactions to a new or existing product or service, opinions about different competitive offerings, or reactions to marketing stimuli, like a new ad campaign or point-of-purchase display materials.[22]

To obtain new information to help it continue its innovative success derived from its introduction of low-sodium choices, Campbell Soup conducted extensive focus groups with female shoppers who indicated they would buy ready-to-eat soups. The groups clearly revealed the women's top priorities: a nutritious soup that contained the ingredients they would use if they made soup. They wanted, for example, white meat chicken, fresh vegetables, and sea salt. In addition, focus group participants were equally clear about what they did *not* want, like high fructose corn syrup, MSG, and other stuff whose names they could not even pronounce.[23]

The growth of online technology, as well as computer and video capabilities, have provided tremendous benefits for focus group research, which now often takes place online. Online focus group firms offer a secure site as a platform for companies to listen in on focus groups and even interact with consumers, without anyone having to travel. The client company not only saves costs but also gains access to a broader range of potential customers who live in various neighborhoods, states, or even countries.

✓ check yourself

1. What are the types of qualitative research?

Survey Research

Arguably the most popular type of quantitative primary collection method is a **survey**—a systematic means of collecting information from people using a questionnaire. A **questionnaire** is a document that features a set of questions designed to gather information from respondents and thereby accomplish the researchers' objectives. Individual questions on a questionnaire can be either unstructured or structured. **Unstructured questions** are open ended and allow respondents to answer in their own words. An unstructured question like "What are the most important characteristics for choosing a brand of shampoo?" yields an unstructured response. However, the same question could be posed to respondents in a structured format by providing a fixed set of response categories, such as price, fragrance, ability to clean, or dandruff control, and then asking respondents to rate the importance of each. **Structured questions** are closed-ended questions for which a discrete set of response alternatives, or specific answers, is provided for respondents to evaluate (see Exhibit 10.6).

Developing a questionnaire is part art and part science. The questions must be carefully designed to address the specific set

> FOCUS GROUPS GATHER QUALITATIVE DATA ABOUT INITIAL REACTIONS TO A NEW OR EXISTING PRODUCT OR SERVICE, OPINIONS ABOUT DIFFERENT COMPETITIVE OFFERINGS, OR REACTIONS TO MARKETING STIMULI.

▼ EXHIBIT 10.6 Structured versus Unstructured Response

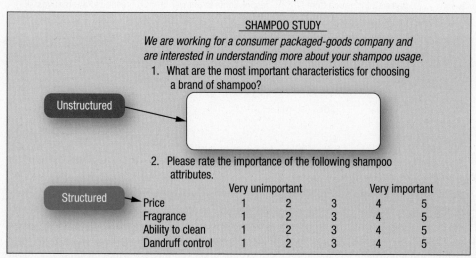

SHAMPOO STUDY

We are working for a consumer packaged-goods company and are interested in understanding more about your shampoo usage.

1. What are the most important characteristics for choosing a brand of shampoo?

Unstructured

2. Please rate the importance of the following shampoo attributes.

	Very unimportant			Very important	
Structured					
Price	1	2	3	4	5
Fragrance	1	2	3	4	5
Ability to clean	1	2	3	4	5
Dandruff control	1	2	3	4	5

market. Web surveys have steadily grown as a percentage of all quantitative surveys. Online surveys have a lot to offer marketers with tight deadlines and small budgets.[25]

In particular, the response rates for online surveys are relatively high. Typical response rates run from 1 to 2 percent for mail and 10 to 15 percent for phone surveys. For online surveys, in contrast, the response rate can reach 30 to 35 percent or even higher in business-to-business research. It also is inexpensive. Costs likely will continue to fall as users become more familiar with the online survey process. Results are processed and received quickly.

of research questions. Moreover, for a questionnaire to produce meaningful results, its questions cannot be misleading in any fashion (e.g., open to multiple interpretations), and they must address only one issue at a time. They also must be worded in vocabulary that will be familiar and comfortable to those being surveyed. The questions should be sequenced appropriately: general questions first, more specific questions next, and demographic questions at the end. Finally, the layout and appearance of the questionnaire must be professional and easy to follow, with appropriate instructions in suitable places. For some tips on what to avoid when designing a questionnaire, see Exhibit 10.7.[24]

Similar to focus groups, marketing surveys can be conducted either online or offline, but online marketing surveys offer researchers the chance to develop a database quickly with many responses, whereas offline marketing surveys provide a more direct approach that includes interactions with the target

Survey research uses questionnaires to collect primary data. Questions can be either unstructured or structured.
© Kayte Deioma/PhotoEdit

▼ EXHIBIT 10.7 What to Avoid When Designing a Questionnaire

Issue	Good Question	Bad Question
Avoid questions the respondent cannot easily or accurately answer.	When was the last time you went to the grocery store?	How much money did you spend on groceries last month?
Avoid sensitive questions unless they are absolutely necessary.	Do you take vitamins?	Do you dye your gray hair?
Avoid double-barreled questions, which refer to more than one issue with only one set of responses.	1. Do you like to shop for clothing? 2. Do you like to shop for food?	Do you like to shop for clothing and food?
Avoid leading questions, which steer respondents to a particular response, irrespective of their true beliefs.	Please rate how safe you believe a BMW is on a scale of 1 to 10, with 1 being not safe and 10 being very safe.	BMW is the safest car on the road, right?
Avoid one-sided questions that present only one side of the issue.	To what extent do you believe fast food contributes to adult obesity using a five-point scale? 1: Does not contribute 5: Main cause	Fast food is responsible for adult obesity: Agree/Disagree

Source: Adapted from A. Parasuraman, Dhruv Grewal, and R. Krishnan, *Marketing Research,* 2nd ed. (Boston: Houghton Mifflin, 2007), Ch. 10.

Walmart's UK subsidiary Asda uses an 18,000-customer panel, which it calls "Pulse of the Nation," to help determine which products to carry.
© David Levenson/Alamy

Reports and summaries can be developed in real time and delivered directly to managers in simple, easy-to-digest reports, complete with color, graphics, and charts. Traditional phone or mail surveys require laborious data collection, tabulation, summary, and distribution before anyone can grasp their results.

Diverse online survey software, such as Qualtrics, Survey-Monkey, and Zoomerang, make it very easy to draft an online survey using questions from existing survey libraries. A survey link can be sent easily in an e-mail to potential respondents or panelists as well as posted on specific sites that are likely to attract the target audience or people who are willing to perform online work (e.g., Amazon's Mechanical Turk Site).

Panel- and Scanner-Based Research

As discussed previously, panel and scanner research can be either secondary or primary. In this section, we consider the use of a panel to collect primary data. Walmart's UK subsidiary Asda uses an 18,000-customer panel, which it calls Pulse of the Nation, to help determine which products to carry. Asda sends e-mails to each participant with product images and descriptions of potential new products. The customers' responses indicate whether they think each product should be carried in stores. As an incentive to participate, Asda enters respondents automatically in a drawing for free prizes.[26]

Experimental Research

Experimental research (an **experiment**) is a type of quantitative research that systematically manipulates one or more variables to determine which variables have a causal effect on other variables. For example, in our earlier scenario, one thing the hypothetical McDonald's research team was trying to determine was the most profitable price for a new menu combo item (hamburger, fries, and drink). Assume that the fixed cost of developing the item is $300,000 and the variable cost, which is primarily composed of the cost of the food itself, is $2. McDonald's puts the item on the menu at four prices in four markets. (See Exhibit 10.8.) In general, the more expensive the item, the less it will sell. But by running this experiment, the restaurant chain determines that the most profitable price is the second least expensive ($5). These findings suggest some people may have believed the most expensive item ($7) was too expensive, so they refused to buy it. The least expensive item ($4) sold fairly well, but McDonald's did not make as much money on each item sold. In this experiment, the changes in price likely caused the changes in quantities sold and therefore affected the restaurant's profitability.

Firms are also actively using experimental techniques on Facebook. Once a firm has created its Facebook page, it can devise advertisements and rely on Facebook's targeting options to deliver those ads to the most appropriate customer segments. To make sure the communication is just right, companies can

▼ **EXHIBIT 10.8** Hypothetical Pricing Experiment for McDonald's

	1	2	3	4	5
Market	Unit Price	Market Demand at Price (in Units)	Total Revenue (Col. 1 × Col. 2)	Total Cost of Units Sold ($300,000 Fixed Cost + $2.00 Variable Cost)	Total Profits (Col. 3 − Col. 4)
1	$4	200,000	$800,000	$700,000	$100,000
2	5	150,000	750,000	600,000	150,000
3	6	100,000	600,000	500,000	100,000
4	7	50,000	350,000	400,000	(50,000)

Using an experiment, McDonald's would test the price of new menu items to determine which is the most profitable.
© AP Photo/Mary Altaffer

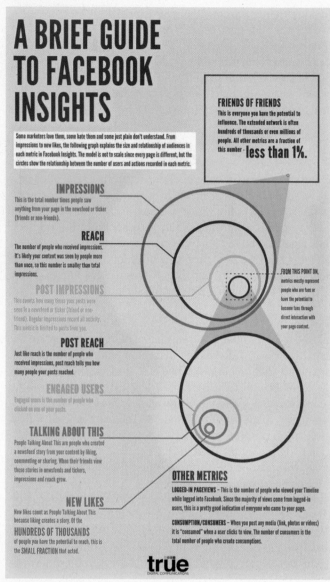

A BRIEF GUIDE TO FACEBOOK INSIGHTS

Some marketers love them, some hate them and some just plain don't understand. From impressions to new likes, the following graph explains the size and relationship of audiences in each metric in Facebook Insights. The model is not to scale since every page is different, but the circles show the relationship between the number of users and actions recorded in each metric.

FRIENDS OF FRIENDS
This is everyone you have the potential to influence. The extended network is often hundreds of thousands or even millions of people. All other metrics are a fraction of this number **less than 1%.**

IMPRESSIONS
This is the total number times people saw anything from your page in the newsfeed or ticker (friends or non-friends).

REACH
The number of people who received impressions. It's likely your content was seen by people more than once, so this number is smaller than total impressions.

POST IMPRESSIONS
This counts how many times your posts were seen in a newsfeed or ticker (friend or non-friend). Regular impressions record all activity. This metric is limited to posts from you.

POST REACH
Just like reach is the number of people who received impressions, post reach tells you how many people your posts reached.

ENGAGED USERS
Engaged users is the number of people who clicked on one of your posts.

TALKING ABOUT THIS
People Talking About This are people who created a newsfeed story from your content by liking, commenting or sharing. When their friends view those stories in newsfeeds and tickers, impressions and reach grow.

NEW LIKES
New likes count as People Talking About This because liking creates a story. Of the **HUNDREDS OF THOUSANDS** of people you have the potential to reach, this is the **SMALL FRACTION** that acted.

FROM THIS POINT ON, metrics mostly represent people who are fans or have the potential to become fans through direct interaction with your page content.

OTHER METRICS

LOGGED-IN PAGEVIEWS – This is the number of people who viewed your Timeline while logged into Facebook. Since the majority of views come from logged-in users, this is a pretty good indication of everyone who came to your page.

CONSUMPTION/CONSUMERS – When you post any media (link, photos or videos) it is "consumed" when a user clicks to view. The number of consumers is the total number of people who create consumptions.

trüe
DIGITAL COMMUNICATIONS

Facebook analytics help firms increase customer engagement.
Source: truedigital.com.
Courtesy of True Digital Communications

experiment with alternative versions and identify which advertisement is most effective. State Bicycle Co., a manufacturer in Arizona, needed to determine what other interests its customers had, as well as who its main competitors were. Therefore, it tested a range of ads, targeting customers who searched for different bands (e.g., did more Arcade Fire or Passion Pit fans click their link?) and other bicycle manufacturers. With this information, it devised new contests and offerings on its own homepage to attract more of the visitors who were likely to buy.[27] Facebook tries to help its corporate clients enhance their own customers' engagement and influence through a variety of options: check-ins, asking for customer comments, sharing information with friends, and so on.[28] It measures all these forms of data, contributing even further to the information businesses have about their page visitors.

> **LO 10-4** Summarize the differences between secondary data and primary data.

Advantages and Disadvantages of Primary and Secondary Research

Now that we have discussed the various secondary and primary data collection methods, think back over our discussion and ask yourself what seem to be the best applications of each and when you would want to go to secondary sources or use primary collection methods. We can see that both primary data and secondary data have certain inherent and distinct advantages and disadvantages. For a summary of the advantages and disadvantages of each type of research, see Exhibit 10.9.

> **check** yourself
>
> 1. What are the types of quantitative research?
> 2. What are the advantages and disadvantages of primary and secondary research?

▼ **EXHIBIT 10.9** Advantages and Disadvantages of Secondary and Primary Data

Type	Examples	Advantages	Disadvantages
Secondary research	☐ Census data ☐ Sales invoices ☐ Internet information ☐ Books ☐ Journal articles ☐ Syndicated data	☐ Saves time in collecting data because they are readily available ☐ Free or inexpensive (except for syndicated data)	☐ May not be precisely relevant to information needs ☐ Information may not be timely ☐ Sources may not be original, and therefore usefulness is an issue ☐ Methodologies for collecting data may not be appropriate ☐ Data sources may be biased
Primary research	☐ Observed consumer behavior ☐ Focus group interviews ☐ Surveys ☐ Experiments	☐ Specific to the immediate data needs and topic at hand ☐ Offers behavioral insights generally not available from secondary research	☐ Costly ☐ Time-consuming ☐ Requires more sophisticated training and experience to design study and collect data

THE ETHICS OF USING CUSTOMER INFORMATION

As we noted in Chapter 4, upholding strong business ethics requires more than a token nod to ethics in the mission statement. A strong ethical orientation must be an integral part of a firm's marketing strategy and decision making. It is particularly important for marketers to adhere to ethical practices when conducting marketing research. The American Marketing Association provides three guidelines for conducting marketing research: (1) It prohibits selling or fund-raising under the guise of conducting research, (2) it supports maintaining research integrity by avoiding misrepresentation or the omission of pertinent research data, and (3) it encourages the fair treatment of clients and suppliers.[29] Numerous codes of conduct written by various marketing research societies all reinforce the duty of researchers to respect the rights of the subjects in the course of their research. The bottom line: Marketing research should be used only to produce unbiased, factual information.

As technology continues to advance, the potential threats to consumers' personal information grow in number and intensity. Ethical and Societal Dilemma 10.1 discusses an interesting example of how retailers are using mannequins with hidden cameras to monitor shoppers. Marketing researchers must be vigilant to avoid abusing their access to these data. Security breaches at some of the United States' largest retailers, banks,

ethical&societal dilemma

10.1

Oh, Say, Can You See? The Implications of Mannequins That Capture Shoppers' Demographic Data[iv]

The basic elements of a new data-gathering tool for retailers are not in any real contention. By spending about $5,000 to purchase an Eye-See mannequin from a provider called Almax, retailers gain not only a place to display clothing but also a discreet recording tool that indicates the genders, ages, and ethnicities of the customers who walk by the display.

Rather more controversial are the implications of this innovation. On one side, consumer privacy advocates complain that the mannequins obtain information about shoppers without their permission. Although Almax asserts that the technology embedded in the displays does not actually record the information, these commentators worry that the mannequins could be used to survey shoppers solely for the benefit of the retailer. Because the mannequins do not look any different from regular mannequins, shoppers have no way of knowing whether someone (or something) is watching them as they walk through the store.

Furthermore, consumers have no control over what retailers do with the aggregated data.

On the other side, retailers note that because the mannequins do not record, their use is no different from that of a closed-circuit system. Furthermore, some commentators argue that consumers should have no expectation of privacy in public spaces. Certainly, a staffer could similarly mark down people's ages, races, and genders as they walk through the shop doors. The electronic form simply does this work better and more accurately.

In implementing the new technology, one retailer recognized the predominance of Asian shoppers after about 4:00 p.m., so it hired more Chinese-speaking staffers to put on the floor to assist them. Another retailer realized that a lot of children were walking through its stores, so it added an entirely new children's clothing line to its offerings. Buoyed by its early successes, Almax also plans to add a function that would capture shoppers' conversations as they pass by the mannequins.

Current legislation allows retailers to maintain cameras and record customers for security purposes as long as they post warnings that customers might be recorded. However, the use of the mannequins is clearly for marketing purposes, not security. And most retailers seem to prefer to keep their usage of the new technology under wraps. Almax has not officially released the names of any of its

EyeSee mannequins do not record or store any images, so the privacy of the customer is protected.
© Almax S.p.A.

clients—perhaps somewhat ironically, citing their need for privacy.

From your perspective as a consumer, do you believe that mannequins that record your movements, image, and possibly conversations in a store invade your privacy? If so, would you avoid stores that use this technology?

credit-reporting services, and peer-to-peer networks have shown just how easily stored data can be abused.[30] From charitable giving to medical records to Internet tracking, consumers are more anxious than ever about preserving their fundamental right to privacy. They also demand increasing control over the information that has been collected about them.

Many firms voluntarily notify their customers that any information provided to them will be kept confidential and not given

gender, and attention level.[32] The resulting communication is precisely targeted, which should make the advertisement more interesting to the consumer walking by—though it also could lead to embarrassing encounters. Imagine, for example, a teenager with skin problems having a billboard loudly broadcast an acne product ad as he walks by!

Several organizations, including the Center for Democracy & Technology (CDT) and the Electronic Privacy Information Center (EPIC), have emerged as watchdogs over data mining of consumer information. In addition, national and

> ## Companies will have to deal with adherence to a complex patchwork of different privacy regulations across the country, making business on the Internet harder to conduct.

or sold to any other firm. As more firms adopt advanced marketing research technology, such as neuromarketing and facial recognition software, they also are working to ensure they receive permission from consumers. For example, Coca-Cola's neuromarketing experiments will record participants' faces as they watch advertisements or prototypes, then assess how their eyes moved, when they smiled or frowned, and so on—but only after those participants have agreed to be recorded.[31]

In contrast, consumers have little control over facial recognition software that allows companies to detect demographic information based on their appearances. For example, digital billboards embedded with such software can identify passersby and then display ads targeted to them based on their age,

state governments in the United States play a part in protecting privacy. Companies are legally required to disclose their privacy practices to customers on an annual basis.[33] As the U.S. federal government has failed to enact comprehensive privacy laws for the Internet, several states are starting to consideration legislation. While this may be good for the consumer, companies will have to deal with adherence to a complex patchwork of different privacy regulations across the country, making business on the Internet harder to conduct.[34]

On Facebook, facial detection software applied to photographs eliminates the need for users to continue to tag the same people multiple times. It also stores all users' biometric data. **Biometric data** include one or more physical traits such as

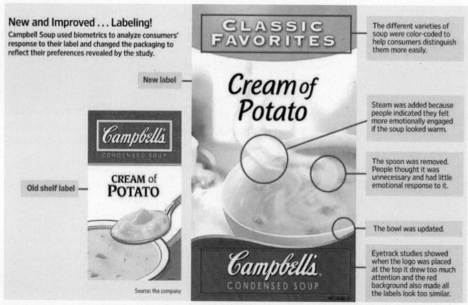

Campbell's redesigned its cans based on information it obtained through neuromarketing studies.
Source: Campbell Soup Company.

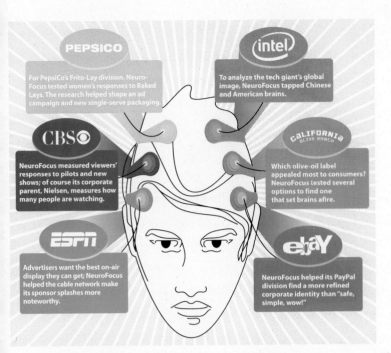

PEPSICO For PepsiCo's Frito-Lay division, Neuro-Focus tested women's responses to Baked Lays. The research helped shape an ad campaign and new single-serve packaging.

(intel) To analyze the tech giant's global image, NeuroFocus tapped Chinese and American brains.

CBS NeuroFocus measured viewers' responses to pilots and new shows; of course its corporate parent, Nielsen, measures how many people are watching.

CALIFORNIA OLIVE RANCH Which olive-oil label appealed most to consumers? NeuroFocus tested several options to find one that set brains afire.

ESPN Advertisers want the best on-air display they can get; NeuroFocus helped the cable network make its sponsor splashes more noteworthy.

ebay NeuroFocus helped its PayPal division find a more refined corporate identity than "safe, simple, wow!"

Findings from neuromarketing studies by NeuroFocus.

facial characteristics, iris scans, or fingerprints. Facebook users can turn off the facial detection function, but their biometric data are still collected. In Germany, with its strict privacy laws, regulators have demanded that Facebook stop collecting any biometric data.

Going even deeper than using biometric data, *neuromarketing* claims the ability to read consumers' minds using wireless electroencephalogram (EEG) scanners that measure the involuntary brain waves that occur when they view a product, advertisement, or brand images.[35] Such insights would be invaluable for marketers to discover what truly appeals to consumers. For example, based on results of a series of neuromarketing studies, Campbell's has recently changed its soup labels by shrinking the logo and emphasizing the soup to increase customers' emotional responses to the cans.[36] But as anyone who has ever seen a science fiction movie can imagine, the potential for abuses of such tools are immense. And a key question remains: Do any consumers want marketers reading their brain waves and marketing goods and services to them in a manner that bypasses their conscious thoughts? One firm, NeuroFocus, used neuromarketing techniques with several global firms to garner customer information that would be difficult, if not impossible, to obtain using more traditional research methods. ■

Chapter eleven

product, branding, and packaging decisions

To convey its brand of unconscious cool and radical adventure, Red Bull embraces daredevil stunts but also seeks to avoid making it look as if it is trying too hard to promote itself in so doing. Thus its branding operations walk a delicate line: Make a name for the brand but without appearing to do so.

Consider the Red Bull Stratos project. Over a period of approximately five years, Red Bull bankrolled the experimental development of a flight suit that would enable daredevil and skydiver Felix Baumgartner to free fall from 24 miles up, break the sound barrier, and still survive his jump from space.[1]

A camera mounted on his helmet recorded the entire experience, including the early moments, when he spun out of control in the thin stratosphere, until nearly five minutes later, when he landed. Approximately 8 million people watched the jump live.

The company has continually sought to reinforce its image as a cutting-edge, danger-seeking, boundary-pushing entity. The data gathered through the Stratos project are being made available to pilots and astronauts who might need to bail out

LEARNING OBJECTIVES

After reading this chapter, you should be able to:

LO 11-1 Describe the components of a product.

LO 11-2 Identify the types of consumer products.

LO 11-3 Explain the difference between a product mix's breadth and a product line's depth.

LO 11-4 Identify the advantages that brands provide firms and consumers.

LO 11-5 Explain the various components of brand equity.

LO 11-6 Determine the various types of branding strategies used by firms.

LO 11-7 Distinguish between brand extension and line extension.

LO 11-8 Indicate the advantages of a product's packaging and labeling strategy.

continued on p. 218

product Anything that is of value to a consumer and can be offered through a voluntary marketing exchange.

core customer value The basic problem-solving benefits that consumers are seeking.

continued from p. 217

of a disabled aircraft. The newly designed space suit also revealed that it could protect the human body against the extreme conditions in the stratosphere.

Pushing the envelope is just what Red Bull wants its brand to be known for doing. By sponsoring events such as the space jump or even its annual Flugtag competition, Red Bull brands itself as fun, a little crazy, and ready for anything. But by letting the events speak largely for themselves rather than promoting its participation in a traditional sense, it also maintains an image of slightly detached cool. It hopes that consumers who would like to think of themselves the same way will find this branding deeply compelling. ■

As a key element of a firm's marketing mix (the four Ps), product strategies are central to the creation of value for the consumer. A **product** is anything that is of value to a consumer and can be offered through a voluntary marketing exchange. In addition to goods, such as soft drinks, or services, such as a stay in a hotel, products might be places (e.g., Six Flags theme parks), ideas (e.g., stop smoking), organizations (e.g., MADD), people (e.g., Oprah Winfrey), or communities (e.g., Facebook) that create value for consumers in their respective competitive marketing arenas.

This chapter begins with a discussion of the complexity and types of products. Next we examine how firms adjust their product lines to meet and respond to changing market conditions. Then we turn our attention to branding—why are brands valuable to the firm, and what are the different branding strategies firms use? We also never want to underestimate the value of a product's package and label. These elements should send a strong message from the shelf: Buy me! The final section of this chapter examines packaging and labeling issues.

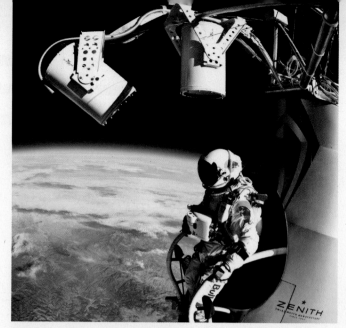

Red Bull's Stratos project bankrolled the development of a flight suit that would enable skydiver Felix Baumgartner to free fall from 24 miles up, breaking the sound barrier.
© Jay Nemeth/ZUMA Press/Newscom

LO 11-1	Describe the components of a product.

COMPLEXITY AND TYPES OF PRODUCTS

Complexity of Products

There is more to a product than its physical characteristics or its basic service function. Marketers involved with the development, design, and sale of products think of them in an interrelated fashion, as depicted in Exhibit 11.1. At the center is the **core customer value**, which defines the basic problem-solving benefits that consumers are seeking. When Mars manufactures M&M's, Snickers, and other confectionary products, or when Trek designs bicycles, each company's core question is, what are customers looking for? With Mars, is it a sweet, great tasting

▼ **EXHIBIT 11.1** Product Complexity

© Photodisc/Getty Images RF

Actual product
Brand name   Packaging
Quality level   Features/Design

Core customer value

Associated services
Financing
Product warranty
Product support

© Michael Blann/Getty Images RF

snack, or is it an energy boost? With Trek, is the bike being used for basic green transportation (a cruiser), or is it for speed and excitement (a road, hybrid, or mountain bike)?

Marketers convert core customer value into an **actual product**. Attributes such as the brand name, features/design, quality level, and packaging are important, but the level of their importance varies, depending on the product. The Trek Madone 7 Series, for instance, is positioned as "see how fastest feels."[2] It features a carbon frame that is light, stiff, and comfortable; an advanced shifting system; and other high-tech features. Not only is it beautiful to look at, but customers can choose from three fits—pro, performance, and touring.

The **associated services** in Exhibit 11.1, also referred to as the **augmented product**, include the nonphysical aspects of the product, such as product warranties, financing, product support, and after-sale service. The amount of associated services also varies with the product. The associated services for a package of M&M's may include only a customer complaint line, which means they are relatively less important than the associated services for a Trek bicycle. The frame of the Madone 7 Series bicycle is guaranteed for the lifetime of the original owner. Trek sells its bikes only in shops that have the expertise to service them properly. Every possible consumer question is answered on Trek's comprehensive website. Trek even has a financing program that allows customers to purchase a new bike on credit.

When developing or changing a product, marketers start with the core customer value to determine what their potential customers are seeking. Then they make the actual physical product and add associated services to round out the offering.

actual product The physical attributes of a product including the brand name, features/design, quality level, and packaging.

associated services (also called augmented product) The nonphysical attributes of the product including product warranties, financing, product support, and after-sale service.

augmented product See *associated services*.

LO 11-2 | Identify the types of consumer products.

Types of Products

Marketers consider the types of products they are designing and selling because these types affect how they will promote, price, and distribute their products. There are two primary categories

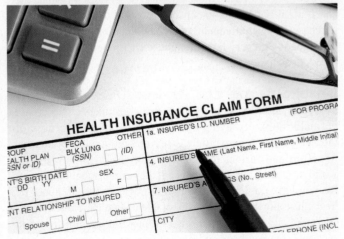

A medical professional is a specialty service. Apparel is a shopping product. Soda is a convenience product. Insurance is an unsought service.

Top left: © Comstock Images/SuperStock RF; Top right: © Big Cheese Photo/SuperStock RF; Bottom left: © McGraw-Hill Education/Jill Braaten; Bottom right: © numbeos/E-plus/Getty Images RF

consumer product Products and services used by people for their personal use.

specialty products/services Products or services toward which the customer shows a strong preference and for which he or she will expend considerable effort to search for the best suppliers.

shopping products/services Those for which consumers will spend time comparing alternatives, such as apparel, fragrances, and appliances.

convenience products/services Those for which the consumer is not willing to spend any effort to evaluate prior to purchase.

unsought products/services Products or services consumers either do not normally think of buying or do not know about.

product mix The complete set of all products offered by a firm.

product lines Groups of associated items, such as those that consumers use together or think of as part of a group of similar products.

breadth Number of product lines offered by a firm; also known as variety.

depth The number of categories within a product line.

of products and services that reflect who buys them: consumers or businesses. Chapter 7 discussed products for businesses. Here we discuss consumer products.

Consumer products are products and services used by people for their personal use. Marketers further classify consumer products by the way they are used and how they are purchased.

Specialty Products/Services
Specialty products/services are those for which customers express such a strong preference that they will expend considerable effort to search for the best suppliers. Road bike enthusiasts, like those interested in the Trek Madone 7 Series, devote lots of time and effort to selecting just the right one. Other examples might include luxury cars, legal or medical professionals, or designer apparel.

Shopping Products/Services
Shopping products/services are products or services for which consumers will spend a fair amount of time comparing alternatives, such as furniture, apparel, fragrances, appliances, and travel alternatives. When people need new sneakers, for instance, they often go from store to store shopping—trying on shoes, comparing alternatives, and chatting with salespeople.

Convenience Products/Services
Convenience products/services are those products or services for which the consumer is not willing to expend any effort to evaluate prior to purchase. They are frequently purchased commodity items, usually bought with very little thought, such as common beverages, bread, or soap.

Unsought Products/Services
Unsought products/services are products or services that consumers either do not normally think of buying or do not know about. Because of their very nature, these products/services require lots of marketing effort and various forms of promotion. When new-to-the-world products are first introduced, they are unsought products. Do you have cold hands and don't know what to do about it? You must not have heard yet of HeatMax HotHands Hand Warmers, air-activated packets that provide warmth for up to 10 hours. Do you have an internship in a less developed country and your regular insurance cannot give you the coverage you may need in case of an emergency? You now can turn to a Medex insurance policy.

✓ **check** yourself

1. Explain the three components of a product.
2. What are the four types of consumer products?

LO 11-3 Explain the difference between a product mix's breadth and a product line's depth.

PRODUCT MIX AND PRODUCT LINE DECISIONS

The complete set of all products and services offered by a firm is called its **product mix**. An abbreviated version of BMW's product mix appears in Exhibit 11.2. The product mix typically consists of various **product lines**, which are groups of associated items that consumers tend to use together or think of as part of a group of similar products or services. BMW's product lines (brands) include BMW, cars targeted at middle-aged professionals;

▼ **EXHIBIT 11.2** Abbreviated List of BMW Product Mix

Product Lines			
BMW	**MINI**	**Rolls-Royce**	**Motorrad**
2 Series	Clubman	Ghost	C Series
3 Series	Convertible	Phantom	F Series
4 Series	Countryman	Wraith	G Series
5 Series	Coupe		K Series
6 Series	Hardtop		R Series
7 Series	John Cooper Works		S Series
X Series	Paceman		
Z4 Series	Roadster		
M Series			
BMW i			
Hybrid			

the MINI, cars targeted to the young adult market; Rolls-Royce, cars targeted at the ultra-wealthy market; and BMW Motorrad, its motorcycle line.

The product mix reflects the breadth and depth of the company's product lines. A firm's product mix **breadth** represents a count of the number of product lines offered by the firm; BMW has four, as indicated by the four columns in Exhibit 11.2. Product line **depth**, in contrast, equals the number of products within a product line. Within BMW's Rolls-Royce brand, for example, it offers Phantom, Wraith, and Ghost models.

However, adding unlimited numbers of new products can have adverse consequences. Too much breadth in the product mix becomes costly to maintain, and too many brands may weaken the firm's reputation.[3] With more products and product lines, the firm must keep track of trends and developments in various industries, which might tax its resources. Marketing Analytics 11.1 describes how Macy's uses advanced methods to fine-tune its product lines. When it realized just how dynamic and changing the global PC market had become, Sony made the strategic choice to sell off, or divest itself of, any PC business. In so doing, it gained more flexibility and could assign more resources and attention to its smartphone and tablet product lines.[4]

BMW's MINI product line targets young adults.
© BMW AG

Marketing Analytics 11.1

How Macy's Defines Its Assortment through Analytics[i]

In the current marketing landscape, it is critical that retailers have a well-developed understanding of their customers. Macy's is using predictive analytics to gain more insight into its customers and improve the buying experience across all channels. For years, Macy's has been collecting data to create a customer-centric in-store experience. Specifically, Macy's uses predictive analytics to create its assortment. The retailer collects data on details such as out-of-stock rates, price promotions, and sell-through rates, then combines those data with stock-keeping unit (SKU)–information from each location to segment customers and create personalized store assortments.

As sales continue to shift to digital platforms, Macy's also uses predictive analytics to create an engaging online experience through Macys.com. The company analyzes visit frequency, style preferences, and shopping motivations in its website data, then seeks to apply the insights to ensure that every customer has an enjoyable, effortless shopping experience. Macys.com does more than just use predictive analytics to create personalized purchase suggestions, though. It calculates the likelihood that each customer will spend a specific amount in a particular product category, then uses that information to present the customer with personalized offers on the checkout page. Furthermore, analytics enable Macy's to send registered users of Macys.com even more personalized e-mail offers. For example, it can send up to 500,000 unique versions of the same mailing.

Macy's already has enjoyed significant success as a result of its implementation of advanced predictive analytics. It has continued to experience increases in

Macys.com analyzes visit frequency, style preferences, and shopping motivations in its website data to develop promotions like the one pictured.
Courtesy Macy's

store sales and online sales, at least partially due to its targeted e-mails. Looking to the future, Macy's plans to improve its online and mobile shopping experiences even further while enhancing the integration of these various shopping platforms to create a seamless experience, with just the right product mix.

Product Line A	Product Line B	Product Line C	Product Line D
ENERGY DRINK	VITAMIN WATER	PROTEIN-BAR	YOGURT
A1	B1	(C1)	(D1)
A2	B2	(C2)	D2
A3	B3		D3
(A4)	B4		(D4)
	(B5)		
	(B6)		

| Added depth: New product (A4) | Decreased depth: Dropped B5 & B6 | Decreased breadth: Dropped product line C (C1 & C2) | Added breadth: New line (D1, D2, D3, & D4) |

So why do firms change their product mix's breadth or depth?[5]

Increase Depth Firms might add items to address changing consumer preferences or to preempt competitors while boosting sales (see the addition of product A4 in Exhibit 11.3). At Taco Bell, the addition of new varieties of its Doritos Locos Tacos enable it to appeal better to consumers who enjoy spicy foods or love Cool Ranch flavor. The tacos still contain the same ingredients, but the availability of 123 different Doritos flavors significantly increases the product line's depth.[6] Social and Mobile Marketing 11.1 describes another extension in a product market, as Axe expands its fragrance product line to create a version for women.

Decrease Depth From time to time, it is also necessary to delete products within a product line to realign the firm's resources (see the deletion of products B5 and B6 in Exhibit 11.3). The decision is never taken lightly. Generally, substantial investments have been made to develop and manufacture the products. Yet firms often must prune their product lines to eliminate unprofitable or low margin items and refocus their marketing efforts on their more profitable items. Procter & Gamble (P&G) introduced Tide Basic as an extension of its Tide line—probably the best-known detergent brand and a product that enjoys a reputation as an innovative, high-end brand. Tide Basic was priced 20 percent cheaper than regular Tide, but P&G deleted the extension less than a year after introducing it, worried that an inexpensive, less effective version simply undermined its brand rather than offering an appealing alternative.[7]

Decrease Breadth Sometimes it is necessary to delete entire product lines to address changing market conditions or meet internal strategic priorities (e.g., deleting product line C in Exhibit 11.3). Thus, the firm drops its line of protein bars and focuses its attention on its energy drinks and vitamin water (product lines A and B).

Increase Breadth Firms often add new product lines to capture new or evolving markets and increase sales (e.g., product line D in Exhibit 11.3). The firm adds a whole new line of yogurt.

 check yourself

1. What is the difference between product mix breadth and product line depth?
2. Why change product mix breadth?
3. Why change product line depth?

> " The tacos still contain the same ingredients, but the availability of 123 different Doritos flavors significantly increases the product line's depth. "

Social & Mobile Marketing

Axe Brand's Anarchy Fragrance and Graphic Novel[ii]

11.1

Axe body spray already owned 75 percent of the men's fragrance market, so when its owner, Unilever, wanted to grow the brand, it needed to expand its product depth. Thus came Axe Anarchy, a scent offered in both male and female versions, to exploit the promise of irresistible sexuality that has proven successful so far.

In a decade's worth of controversial Axe commercials, average guys drew very attractive women to them simply by spraying themselves with the scent. The Anarchy message is even edgier. As the name suggests, the product promises the notion of sexual energy that goes slightly out of control. An early commercial depicts a chaotic series of events, including a car pileup, in which a man and a woman remain oblivious to the havoc but gravitate toward each other until they are just inches apart. "Unleash the chaos," the screen recommends, as the video cuts to shots of the two actors spraying themselves. "New Axe Anarchy for him and for her."

Noting its youthful target market, Unilever also wanted to ensure that the advertising medium for Anarchy fit the brand extension, so the company unleashed an interactive digital campaign in the form of an online graphic novel. The serialized, comic book fantasy about the chaotic exploits of the Anarchy Girls would evolve in real time, in response to viewer input. *X-Men* writers hired to create the narrative in collaboration with any of the 2.3 million fans who registered on YouTube, Facebook, Twitter, and Axe's other social channels to help shape the story.

The marketing subtext was clear: Break the narrative and break through sexually, which seemed to offer a potent message for young women. But some observers remain unconvinced that Axe's bold, crowd-sourced digital venture will help the brand make the crossover into the women's body spray market. Could graphic novels, with their traditionally young male audience, really connect with young women? Do the Anarchy Girls—with their revealing clothing and unrealistic bodies—really empower, or do they just objectify women? Would Axe's explosive brand expansion strategy actually alienate the very audience that built its body spray brand—that is, average-guy male teens trying to attract a special girl? Would advertising to girls make Axe lose credibility among boys?

To promote the Axe Anarchy fragrance to young men and women, Unilever created a comic book fantasy about "Anarchy Girls," available in real time on YouTube and other social media.

Unilever

BRANDING

A company lives or dies based on brand awareness. Consumers cannot buy products that they don't know exist. Even if the overall brand name is familiar, it won't help sales of individual products unless consumers know what products are available under that name. Sports fans have long been familiar with the rallying cry for Under Armour and its line of athletic gear: "Protect this house." But when the company chose to refresh its tagline, it undertook a massive ad campaign to introduce its new slogan, "I will." In addition to extensive online and outdoor advertising, Under Armour intensified its branding efforts during the NBA All-Star Weekend, when television ads flooded the airwaves, promising new technology introductions and working to expand its appeal to both male and female sportswear consumers.[8]

Branding also provides a way for a firm to differentiate its product offerings from those of its competitors. Both Snapple and Tropicana make and sell fruit drinks, yet consumers may choose one over the other because of the associations that the brands invoke. As we discuss in more detail subsequently, brand names, logos, symbols, characters, slogans, jingles, and even distinctive packages constitute the various brand elements firms use,[9] which they usually choose to be easy for consumers to recognize and remember. Most consumers know the Nike swoosh and would recognize it even if the word *Nike* did not

▼ **EXHIBIT 11.4** What Makes a Brand?

Brand Element	Description
Brand name	The spoken component of branding, it can describe the product or service characteristics and/or be composed of words invented or derived from colloquial or contemporary language. Examples include Comfort Inn (suggests product characteristics), Apple (no association with the product), or Zillow.com (invented term).
URLs (uniform resource locators) or domain names	Locations of pages on the Internet, which often substitute for the firm's name, such as Toyota (http://www.toyota.com).
Logos and symbols	Visual branding elements that stand for corporate names or trademarks. Symbols are logos without words. Examples include the McDonald's arch.
Characters	Brand symbols that could be human, animal, or animated. Examples include the Energizer Bunny and Rice Krispies' Snap, Crackle, and Pop.
Slogans	Short phrases used to describe the brand or persuade consumers about some characteristics of the brand. Examples include State Farm's "Like A Good Neighbor" and Dunkin' Donuts' "America Runs On Dunkin'."
Jingles/Sounds	Audio messages about the brand that are composed of words or distinctive music. An example is Intel's four-note sound signature that accompanies the Intel Inside slogan.

Source: Adapted from Kevin Lane Keller, *Strategic Brand Management,* 4th ed. (Upper Saddle River, NJ: Prentice Hall, 2012).

appear on the product or in an advertisement. Exhibit 11.4 summarizes some of these brand elements.

LO 11-4	Identify the advantages that brands provide firms and consumers.

Value of Branding for the Customer

Brands add value to merchandise and services, for both consumers and sellers, beyond physical and functional characteristics or the pure act of performing the service.[10] Let's examine some ways in which brands add value for both customers and the firm.

Brands Facilitate Purchases Brands are often easily recognized by consumers, and because they signify a certain quality level and contain familiar attributes, brands help consumers make quick decisions, especially about their purchases.[11] The cola market is a particularly strong example of this benefit. Some people think cola is cola, such that one brand is not too different from another. But branding has made it easy for Pepsi drinkers to find the familiar logo on the store shelf and more likely that they simply buy one of Pepsi's other products,

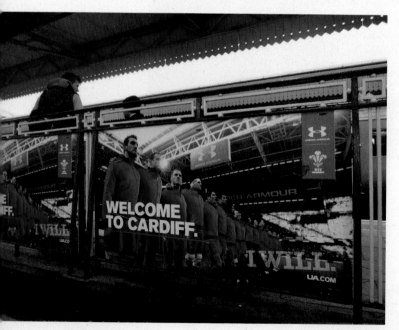

Using its new slogan, "I will," Under Armour sponsors the WRU Welsh Rugby Team.
© Kathy deWitt/Alamy

Characters like Rice Krispies' Snap, Crackle, and Pop help build a brand.
© Michael Neelon(misc)/Alamy

Brands Protect from Competition and Price Competition
Strong brands are somewhat protected from competition from other firms and price competition. Because such brands are more established in the market and have a more loyal customer base, neither competitive pressures on price nor retail-level competition is as threatening to the firm. Lacoste is widely known for its cotton knit shirts. Although many similar brands are available and some retailers offer their own brands, Lacoste is perceived to be of superior quality, garners a certain status among its users, and therefore can command a premium price.

Brands Are Assets
For firms, brands are also assets that can be legally protected through trademarks and copyrights and thus constitute a unique form of ownership. Firms sometimes have to fight to ensure their brand names are not being used, directly or indirectly, by others.

LO 11-5	Explain the various components of brand equity.

Brands Affect Market Value
Having well-known brands can have a direct impact on the company's bottom line. The value of a company is its overall monetary worth, comprising

should they decide to switch to a diet soda or a flavored version. From promotions, past purchases, or information from friends and family, they recognize the offering before they even read any text on the label, and they likely possess a perception of the brand's level of quality, how it tastes, whether it is a good value, and, most important, whether they like it and want to buy it. Brands enable customers to differentiate one firm or product from another. Without branding, how could we easily tell the difference between Coca-Cola and Pepsi before tasting them?

Brands Establish Loyalty
Over time and with continued use, consumers learn to trust certain brands. They know, for example, that they wouldn't consider switching brands and, in some cases, feel a strong affinity to certain brands. Amazon .com has a loyal following because its reputation for service prompts customers to turn to it first. A customer whose $500 PlayStation 3 was apparently stolen during delivery received another PlayStation 3, without even having to pay additional shipping costs. Amazon lost $500, plus shipping, on a mistake that was not its fault, but it also gained a reputation for service with this customer, who would not only buy more electronics from Amazon but also tell everyone he could think of about this extraordinary example of customer service and choose Amazon's brand extension into the Kindle offerings before similar options provided by other brands.[12]

Lacoste has a superior-quality image that helps protect it from competition and enables it to command relatively high prices.
© Bryn Colton/Bloomberg/Getty Images.

brand equity The set of assets and liabilities linked to a brand that add to or subtract from the value provided by the product or service.

brand awareness Measures how many consumers in a market are familiar with the brand and what it stands for; created through repeated exposures of the various brand elements (brand name, logo, symbol, character, packaging, or slogan) in the firm's communications to consumers.

a vast number of assets. When the brand loses value, it also threatens other assets. For RadioShack, once the first destination for consumers seeking a Walkman or boom box, the loss of brand value as it has struggled to maintain relevance as a provider of modern, cutting-edge technology ultimately led to its demise in bankruptcy.

The value of a brand can be defined as the earning potential of that brand over the next 12 months.[13] The world's 10 most valuable brands for 2013 appear in Exhibit 11.5.

Brand Equity for the Owner

The value of a brand translates into **brand equity**, or the set of assets and liabilities linked to a brand that add to or subtract from the value provided by the product or service.[14] Like the physical possessions of a firm, brands are assets a firm can build, manage, and harness over time to increase its revenue, profitability, and overall value. For example, firms spend millions of dollars on promotion, advertising, and other marketing efforts throughout a brand's life cycle. Marketing expenditures allocated carefully can result in greater brand recognition, awareness, perceived value, and consumer loyalty for the brand, which all enhance the brand's overall equity. Such benefits can be particularly strong if the brand markets itself ethically, as Ethical and Societal Dilemma 11.1 notes.

> ## " When the brand loses value, it also threatens other assets. "

IBM is one of the world's most valuable brands.
Image Courtesy of The Advertising Archives.

How do we know how good a brand is, or how much equity it has? Experts look at four aspects of a brand to determine its equity: brand awareness, perceived value, brand associations, and brand loyalty.

Brand Awareness
Brand awareness measures how many consumers in a market are familiar with the brand and what it stands for and have an opinion about it. The more aware or familiar they are, the easier their decision-making process is, which improves the chances of purchase. Familiarity matters most for products that are bought without much thought, such as soap or chewing gum, but brand awareness

▼ **EXHIBIT 11.5** The World's 10 Most Valuable Brands

2013 Rank	2012 Rank	Brand	Country	Sector	Brand Value (in $ Billions)
1	2	Apple	United States	Technology	$98.3
2	4	Google	United States	Technology	93.2
3	1	Coca-Cola	United States	Beverages	79.2
4	3	IBM	United States	Business Services	78.8
5	5	Microsoft	United States	Technology	59.5
6	6	GE	United States	Diversified	46.9
7	7	McDonald's	United States	Restaurants	41.9
8	9	Samsung	South Korea	Technology	39.6
9	8	Intel	United States	Technology	37.3
10	10	Toyota	Japan	Automotive	35.3

Source: From Interbrand.com, http://www.interbrand.com/best_global_brands.aspx.

is also critical for infrequently purchased items or those the consumer has never purchased before. If the consumer recognizes the brand, it probably has attributes that make it valuable.[15] For those who have never purchased a Toyota, the simple awareness that it exists can help facilitate a purchase. Marketers create brand awareness through repeated exposures of the various brand elements (brand name, logo, symbol, character, packaging, or slogan) in the firm's communications to consumers through advertising, publicity, or other methods (see Chapters 17–19).

Certain brands gain such predominance in a particular product market over time that they become synonymous with the product itself; that is, the brand name starts being used as the generic product category. Examples include Kleenex tissues, Clorox bleach, Band-Aid adhesive bandages, and the Google search engine. Companies must be vigilant in protecting their brand names because if they are used so generically, over time the brand itself can lose its trademark status. For competitors, this trend similarly is destructive: If everyone with an upset stomach asks for Pepto-Bismol and never considers any alternatives, brands such as Activia suffer smaller chances of making it into customers' shopping baskets. To counteract such concerns, Activia uses well-known celebrities such as Shakira in its advertisements, to make sure it is recognizable and prominent.[16]

These brands are so strong that they have become synonymous with the product itself.
© McGraw-Hill Education

Perceived Value The **perceived value** of a brand is the relationship between a product's or service's benefits and its cost. Customers usually determine the offering's value in relationship to that of its close competitors. If they believe a less

ethical&societal dilemma   11.1

(Not) Marketing Sugary Drinks to Kids[iii]

Obesity rates are often highest in the nations and regions that drink the most soda. The sugary, high-calorie versions of popular carbonated beverage brands in turn have been widely blamed for the growing rates of obesity, especially among children. Those complaints also are growing as brands expand outside the United States and potentially threaten the long-term health of kids across the globe.

Even as it strongly maintains that sodas are not the main culprit in rising obesity rates, Coca-Cola has acknowledged its own limited responsibility and therefore vowed not to advertise in settings in which children make up more than 35 percent of the anticipated audience (previously, it set this standard at 50 percent). Thus Coke ads have disappeared from cartoon networks and youth-oriented shows, children's magazines, and so forth.

In addition to its commitment not to advertise directly to children younger than 12 years of age, Coke has invested in initiatives to promote more physical activity and to encourage consumers to consider lower calorie alternatives, whether Diet Coke or Minute Maid juices (which Coca-Cola also owns). Beyond advertising, Coke's new product development efforts are largely focused on identifying and integrating natural low-calorie sweeteners. In some countries, its packaging also will feature more prominent information about calorie contents.

Yet critics point out that even as Coke promises to stop targeting children, it has confirmed that it has no plans to stop relying on its popular polar bear advertisements during the holiday season, nor will it eliminate images of children enjoying Coke in its ads. Thus while Coca-Cola might be working to reduce the amount of marketing children might see during their favorite programs, it certainly does not plan to stop appealing to young consumers altogether.

Should Coca-Cola and other consumer packaged-goods companies be allowed to advertise to children?
© GL Archive/Alamy

expensive brand is about the same quality as a premium brand, the perceived value of that cheaper choice is high. Merchandise sold by Target and Kohl's is not always perceived to be the highest quality, nor is the apparel the most fashion-forward. But not every customer needs to show up at school looking like they came from a fashion show runway. At the same time, these retailers hire high-fashion designers to create reasonably priced lines to feature in their stores—as Target did with Lilly Pulitzer and Altuzarra to create well-designed pieces at Target-level prices.

Brand Associations

Brand associations reflect the mental and emotional links that consumers make between a brand and its key product attributes, such as a logo and its color, slogan, or famous personality. These brand associations often result from a firm's advertising and promotional efforts. Toyota's hybrid car, the Prius, is known for being economical, a good value, stylish, and good for the environment. But firms also attempt to create specific associations with positive consumer emotions such as fun, friendship, good feelings, family gatherings, and parties. Jingles can establish particularly strong associations, especially when they are catchy and get stuck in consumers' heads. State Farm Insurance continues to rely on the jingle that Barry Manilow wrote for it in the 1970s: In modern advertisements, young customers in trouble sing the phrase

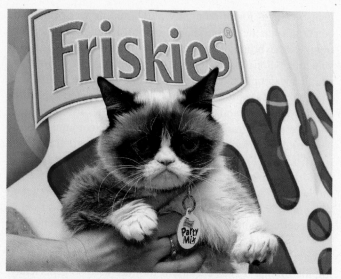

Friskies cat food is associated with its famous "spokesperson," Grumpy Cat.
© Robin Marchant/Getty Images

"like a good neighbor, State Farm is there," and an agent magically appears on scene.[17]

Because of his vast viral popularity, Grumpy Cat (real name: Tardar Sauce) has been approached by several brands that seek to be associated with him, to benefit from his entertaining, satirical, and hip image. The feline's naturally unhappy looking mouth now appears across Friskies' product line. Mashable featured Grumpy Cat in its tent at South by Southwest, and a bidding process led to the promise of an upcoming Grumpy Cat movie.[18]

Brand Loyalty

Brand loyalty occurs when a consumer buys the same brand's product or service repeatedly over time rather than buy from multiple suppliers within the same category.[19] Therefore, brand-loyal customers are an important source of value for firms. First, firms such as airlines, hotels, long-distance telephone providers, credit card companies, and retailers reward loyal consumers with loyalty or customer relationship management (CRM) programs, such as points customers can redeem for extra discounts or free services, advance notice of sale items, and invitations to special events sponsored by the company. Second, the marketing costs of reaching loyal consumers are much lower because the firm does not have to spend money on advertising and promotion campaigns to attract these customers. Loyal consumers simply do not need persuasion or an extra push to buy the firm's brands. Third, loyal customers tend to praise the virtues of their favorite products, retailers, or services to others. This positive word of mouth reaches potential customers and reinforces the perceived value of current customers, all at no cost to the firm. Fourth, a high level of brand loyalty insulates the firm from competition because, as we noted in Chapter 2, brand-loyal customers do not switch to competitors' brands, even when provided with a variety of incentives.

Target teamed up with high-fashion designer Lilly Pulitzer to create reasonably priced, yet very fashionable apparel.
Neil Rasmus/BFAnyc.com/SIPPL Sipa USA/AP Photo

LO 11-6 | Determine the various types of branding strategies used by firms.

BRANDING STRATEGIES

Firms institute a variety of brand-related strategies to create and manage key brand assets, such as the decision to own the brands, establishing a branding policy, extending the brand name to other products and markets, cooperatively using the brand name with that of another firm, and licensing the brand to other firms.

Brand Ownership

Brands can be owned by any firm in the supply chain, whether manufacturers, wholesalers, or retailers. There are two basic brand ownership strategies: manufacturer brands and retailer/store brands, as Exhibit 11.6 shows. Additionally, the brands can be marketed using a common/family name or as individual brands.

> The majority of the brands marketed in the United States are manufacturer brands, and manufacturing firms spend millions of dollars each year to promote their brands.

Manufacturer Brands

Manufacturer brands, also known as **national brands**, are owned and managed by the manufacturer. Some famous manufacturer brands are Nike, Coca-Cola, KitchenAid, and Sony. With these brands, the manufacturer develops the merchandise, produces it to ensure consistent quality, and invests in a marketing program to establish an appealing brand image. The majority of the brands marketed in the United States are manufacturer brands, and manufacturing firms spend millions of dollars each year to promote their brands. By owning their brands, manufacturers retain more control over their marketing strategy, are able to choose the appropriate market segments and positioning for the brand, and can build the brand and thereby create their own brand equity.

Retailer/Store Brands Retailer/store brands, also called **private-label brands**, are products developed by retailers. In some cases, retailers manufacture their own products, whereas in other cases they

manufacturer brands (national brands) Brands owned and managed by the manufacturer.

retailer/store brands Products developed by retailers. Also called *private-label brands.*

private-label brands Brands developed and marketed by a retailer and available only from that retailer; also called *store brands.*

▼ **EXHIBIT 11.6** Who Owns the Brand?

Who Owns the Brand?		Manufacturer/National Brand	Retailer/Store Brand
Common Name or Not?	Family Brands	Kellogg's family line	Kroger's line
	Individual Brands	Kellogg's individual brand	Kroger's individual brand

(top left, top right & and bottom left) © McGraw-Hill Education, (bottom right) © Food Collection/Alamy

develop the design and specifications for their retailer/store brands and then contract with manufacturers to produce those products. Some national brand manufacturers work with retailers to develop a special version of their standard merchandise offering to be sold exclusively by the retailer.

In the past, sales of store brands were limited. But in recent years, as the size of retail firms has increased through growth and consolidation, more retailers have the scale economies to develop private-label merchandise and use this merchandise to establish a distinctive identity. In addition, manufacturers are more willing to accommodate the needs of retailers and develop co-brands for them.[20] At Stop & Shop, 40 percent of sales in some stores come from store brand options.[21] Both Costco and Trader Joe's have based their brand identities around their store brands.

Naming Brands and Product Lines

Although there is no simple way to decide how to name a brand or a product line, the more the products vary in their usage or performance, the more likely it is that the firm should use individual brands. For example, General Motors uses several individual brands (Cadillac, Chevrolet, and GMC), each catering to very different target markets and meeting different needs. Hyundai, on the other hand, uses only one brand since usage and level of performance are relatively homogeneous.

Family Brands
A firm can use its own corporate name to brand all its product lines and products; for example, Kellogg's incorporates the company name into the brand name of Kellogg's Rice Krispies (refer to Exhibit 11.6). When all products are sold under one **family brand**, the individual brands benefit from the overall brand awareness associated with the family name. Kellogg's uses its family brand name prominently on its cereal brands (e.g., Kellogg's Special K, Kellogg's Froot Loops, Kellogg's Rice Krispies).

Kellogg's uses a family branding strategy in which several product lines are sold under one name.
Michael J. Hruby

Kellogg's also uses an individual branding strategy since Keebler, Cheez-It, Morningstar, and Famous Amos are all marketed using separate names.
Michael J. Hruby

Individual Brands
A firm can use **individual brand** names for each of its products. For example, while Kellogg's makes good use of the family branding strategy, it also allows other products, such as Morningstar Farms, Famous Amos cookies, Keebler cookies, and Cheez-Its (Exhibit 11.6), to keep individual identities not readily seen as being under the Kellogg's umbrella.[22]

| LO 11-7 | Distinguish between brand extension and line extension. |

Brand and Line Extensions[23]

A **brand extension** refers to the use of the same brand name in a different product line. It is an increase in the product mix's breadth.[24] The dental hygiene market, for instance, is full of brand extensions; Colgate and Crest sell toothpaste, toothbrushes, and other dental hygiene products, even though their original product line was just toothpaste. A **line extension** is the use of the same brand name within the same product line and represents an increase in a product line's depth.

There are several advantages to using the same brand name for new products. First, because the brand name is already well established, the firm can spend less in developing consumer brand awareness and brand associations for the new product.[25] Kellogg's has branched out from the cereal company it once was. Its strategy of branding the corporate name into the product name has allowed it to introduce new products quicker and more easily. Kellogg's Eggo Syrup was a natural extension to its product line of breakfast foods.

Second, if either the original brand or the brand extension has strong consumer acceptance, that perception will carry over to the other product. Consumers who had not used the Neutrogena brand before trying the brand extension Neutrogena Wave power cleanser might be encouraged to try Neutrogena's core product line of cleansers and moisturizing

Using a brand extension strategy, Frito-Lay markets both chips and dips under its Frito-Lay and Tostitos brand names.

Michael J. Hruby

lotions, especially if their experience with the Wave has been positive.[26]

Third, when brand extensions are used for complementary products, a synergy exists between the two products that can increase overall sales. For example, Frito-Lay markets both chips and dips under its Frito-Lay and Tostitos brand names. When people buy the chips, they tend to buy the dips as well.

Not all brand extensions are successful, however. Some can dilute brand equity.[27] **Brand dilution** occurs when the brand extension adversely affects consumer perceptions about the attributes the core brand is believed to hold.[28] Here are some examples of unsuccessful brand extensions:[29]

- Cheetos Lip Balm was based on the idea that if you like Cheetos, you would want to wipe it all over your lips.

- Lifesavers Soda did well in prelaunch taste tests but didn't in subsequent sales.

- Colgate Kitchen Entrees were microwavable frozen dinner entrees that shared the name with the famous toothpaste.

- Bic thought that since people wanted their disposable lighters and razors, they would also want disposable underwear. They were wrong.

Lifesavers unsuccessfully attempted a brand extension strategy with its line of soda.

GfK Custom Research

To prevent the potentially negative consequences of brand extensions, firms consider the following:

- Marketers should evaluate the fit between the product class of the core brand and that of the extension.[30] If the fit between the product categories is high, consumers will consider the extension credible, and the brand association will be stronger for the extension. Thus, when Starbucks introduced its line of instant coffee, VIA, it made sense to its customers.

- Firms should evaluate consumer perceptions of the attributes of the core brand and seek out similar attributes for the extension because brand-specific associations are very important for extensions.[31] For example, if HP printers were associated with reliability, performance, and value, consumers would expect the same brand-specific attributes in other products that carried the HP brand name.

- Firms should refrain from extending the brand name to too many products and product categories to avoid diluting the brand and damaging brand equity. Zippo, the company famous for its lighters, failed when it introduced a perfume in a lighter look-a-like container.[32]

- Firms should consider whether the brand extension will be distanced from the core brand, especially if the firm wants to use some but not all of the existing brand associations. Marriott has budget, midtier, and luxury hotels. Its luxury hotels, including the Ritz-Carlton, Edition, and Renaissance, do not use the name Marriott at all.[33]

Co-Branding

Co-branding is the practice of marketing two or more brands together on the same package, promotion, or store. Co-branding can enhance consumers' perceptions of product quality by signaling unobservable product quality through links between the firm's brand and a well-known quality brand. For example, Yum! Brands frequently combines two or more of its restaurant chains, including A&W, KFC, Long John Silver's, Pizza Hut, and Taco Bell, into one store space. This co-branding strategy is designed to appeal to diverse market segments and extend the hours in which each restaurant attracts customers. Yet co-branding also creates risks, especially when the customers of each of the brands turn out to be vastly different. For example, the Burger King and Häagen-Dazs co-branding strategy failed because the customer profiles for each brand were too different.[34] Co-branding may also fail when there are disputes or conflicts of interest between the co-brands.

Brand Licensing

Brand licensing is a contractual arrangement between firms whereby one firm allows another to use its brand name, logo, symbols, and/or characters in exchange for a negotiated fee.[35]

brand dilution Occurs when a brand extension adversely affects consumer perceptions about the attributes the core brand is believed to hold.

co-branding The practice of marketing two or more brands together, on the same package or promotion.

brand licensing A contractual arrangement between firms, whereby one firm allows another to use its brand name, logo, symbols, or characters in exchange for a negotiated fee.

brand repositioning
A strategy in which marketers change a brand's focus to target new markets or realign the brand's core emphasis with changing market preferences.

rebranding See *brand repositioning.*

primary package
The packaging the consumer uses, such as the toothpaste tube, from which he or she typically seeks convenience in terms of storage, use, and consumption.

secondary package
The wrapper or exterior carton that contains the primary package and provides the UPC label used by retail scanners; can contain additional product information that may not be available on the primary package.

Brand licensing is common for toys, apparel, accessories, and entertainment products such as video games. The firm that provides the right to use its brand (licensor) obtains revenues through royalty payments from the firm that has obtained the right to use the brand (licensee). These royalty payments may take the form of an upfront, lump-sum licensing fee or be based on the dollar value of sales of the licensed merchandise.

One very popular form of licensing is the use of characters created in books and other media. Such entertainment licensing has generated tremendous revenues for movie studios. Disney, for instance, flooded retail stores with products based on its *Frozen* movie. *Star Wars* memorabilia has continued to be successful since the first film was released in the 1970s. A long-standing staple of licensing has been major league sports teams that play in the NBA, NFL, or NHL as well as various collegiate sports teams.

Licensing is an effective form of attracting visibility for the brand and thereby building brand equity while also generating additional revenue. There are, however, some risks associated with it. For the licensor, the major risk is the dilution of its brand equity through overexposure of the

brand, especially if the brand name and characters are used inappropriately.[36]

Brand Repositioning

Brand repositioning or **rebranding** refers to a strategy in which marketers change a brand's focus to target new markets or realign the brand's core emphasis with changing market preferences.[37] Although repositioning can improve the brand's fit with its target segment or boost the vitality of old brands, it is not without costs and risks. Firms often need to spend tremendous amounts of money to make tangible changes to the product and packages as well as intangible changes to the brand's image through various forms of promotion, as Adding Value 11.1 details. These costs may not be recovered if the repositioned brand and messages are not credible to consumers or if the firm has mistaken a fad for a long-term market trend. Examples of recent rebranding efforts that have provoked consumers' disdain include Olive Garden, The Gap, and Tropicana.[38]

✓ **check yourself**

1. What are the differences between manufacturer and private-label brands?

2. What is co-branding?

3. What is the difference between brand extension and line extension?

4. What is brand repositioning?

LO 11-8 | Indicate the advantages of a product's packaging and labeling strategy.

PACKAGING

Packaging is an important brand element with more tangible or physical benefits than other brand elements. Packages come in different types and offer a variety of benefits to consumers, manufacturers, and retailers. The **primary package** is the one the consumer uses, such as the toothpaste tube. From the primary package, consumers typically seek convenience in terms of storage, use, and consumption.

The **secondary package** is the wrapper or exterior carton that contains the primary package and provides the UPC label used by retail scanners. Consumers can use the secondary package to find additional product information that may not be available on the primary package. Like primary packages, secondary packages add consumer value by facilitating the convenience of carrying, using, and storing the product.

Whether primary or secondary, packaging plays several key roles: It attracts the consumers' attention. It enables products to

The NFL licenses products like these jerseys to a manufacturer in exchange for a negotiated fee.
© Ira Berger/Alamy

Adding Value   11.1

The Global Appeal and Rebranding Efforts of American Airlines[iv]

For more than 40 years, American Airlines had used the same logo: a pair of capital *A*s, one red and one blue, surrounding the silhouette of a diving eagle. When the airline purchased 550 new planes, made from a new composite material, it had to change the look of the finish, so it decided to change its look altogether, including a new logo, new designs for the plane interiors, a new website, and new kiosk interfaces in terminals.

The most visible element thus far is the new logo, which removes the double *A* and offers a more abstract version of an eagle. The abstract image is oriented more horizontally, rather than vertically downward. On the new planes, this eagle logo will appear near the front, as if pointing the direction for the flight. Furthermore, the tails of each airplane will feature another abstract image, evocative of the U.S. flag with blue and red stripes (but no stars).

The abstraction of the images reflects American Airlines' goals for the rebranding, namely, to emphasize the "American spirit" without evoking negative images of the United States in global markets. Futurebrand, the agency that American Airlines hired to assist it with its efforts, polled consumers around the world to identify positive traits they associated with the United States. The effort sought to determine not just how people view American products and services but also how they view America in a global age.

The results highlighted images of progress, technology, and entertainment, but they also cautioned against any implication of attack or aggression. Therefore the downward-diving eagle needed to go because it was likely to be interpreted as attacking. A direct representation of the U.S. flag might have been perceived as jingoistic, whereas the abstracted version simply provides a more neutral identifying hint.

In eliminating a widely familiar logo along with its well-known letter typeface, American Airlines clearly is taking a risk that it will lose brand recognition among customers who unconsciously seek the same look they have always seen at the airport. But in a global economy, a company with an American identity, in all senses of the term, needs to take care to emphasize the positives while avoiding more controversial elements.

American Airlines' new logo is an abstract version of an eagle. The tails of each plane feature an abstraction of the U.S. flag.
© Kevin Clark/Alamy RF

stand out from their competitors. It offers a promotional tool (e.g., "NEW" and "IMPROVED" promises on labels). Finally, it allows for the same product to appeal to different markets with different sizes, such that convenience stores stock little packages that travelers can buy at the last minute, whereas Costco sells extra large versions of products.

Firms occasionally change or update their packaging as a subtle way of repositioning the product. A change can be used to attract a new target market and/or appear more up to date to its current market. For instance, the Morton Salt umbrella girl has significantly changed since it was first introduced in 1914, but the slogan "when it rains it pours" endures today. Changes also can make consumers feel like they are receiving something tangible in return for paying higher prices, even when the product itself remains untouched. Whether true or not, consumers see new packaging and tend to think that the "new" product may be worth trying. In honor of its 100th birthday, Morton has redesigned the packaging of over 100 individual items to give a clean, modern feel.[39]

Morton Salt changed its packaging to celebrate its 100th anniversary.
© Mike Mozart, https://www.flickr.com/photos/jeepersmedia/14116495271. Creative Commons license: https://creativecommons.org/licenses/by/2.0/

Daisy Brand simplified its cottage cheese containers and added colored lids to make them more recognizable.
© Daisy Brand

L'eggs pantyhose packaging forgoes retailer and manufacturer convenience for its iconic egg shape.
© McGraw-Hill Education

Some packaging changes are designed to make the product more recognizable, such as L'eggs pantyhose iconic egg shape container and Daisy Brand's redesign of its cottage cheese containers. Known for using no more than four ingredients in any of its cottage cheese products, the redesign has taken a simple, Spartan look and paired it with blue lids. The color blue of the lid varies by the fat content of the cottage cheese. Combining a simple container and varying colored lids, Daisy Brand expects its new containers will grab consumers' attention in the dairy case and increase sales.[40]

An interesting recent development in packaging is a move to "sustainable packaging." **Sustainable packaging** is product packaging that is ecologically responsible. Leaders in this area of innovation include Coca-Cola, Microsoft, Waste Management, Aveda, and Zappos. These firms host a sustainable packaging conference that brings together more than 250 firms to discuss new methods to produce environmentally responsible packaging that is also cost effective. Ideas from this conference include returnable packaging, use of 3D printing, and flexible packaging. They have also set up a website with information on future conferences and information for the industry at http://www.sustainability-in-packaging.com.[41]

ethical&societal dilemma 11.2

Calories 0, Vitamins 0: How Much Information Can Water Labels Provide?[v]

Water, water everywhere. Especially in developed countries, consumers everywhere can simply turn on the tap, and there it is. And yet firms have been successful in packaging this almost free natural resource, creating some cachet for it, and selling it.

Bottled water enjoyed double-digit growth, year to year, as U.S. consumers doubled the amount they drank from 13.4 to 29.3 gallons per year. The popularity and growth of the industry has attracted attention, though. Bottled and tap water companies operate under different regulations. Yet many observers and government agencies argue the rules should be the same, with water bottle labeling subject to regulations as detailed as those that the tap water companies experience.

Bottled water, as a food product, currently is regulated by the Food and Drug Administration (FDA), so it lists nutrition information and

Would more comprehensive labels on bottled water change your water consumption behavior?
© Michael J. Hruby

ingredients on the labels (i.e., 0 percent of most nutrients; contents: water). In contrast, municipal water is controlled by the Environmental Protection Agency (EPA), which has more authority to enforce quality standards. The result may be misinformed consumers, many of whom believe bottled water is safer and healthier than tap water. And yet according to the U.S. Government Accounting Office (GAO), the FDA lacks the authority to require water bottlers to use certified water quality tests or report those test results. Also, the existing requirements to ensure safe bottled water, both state and federal, are less comprehensive than the rules about safeguarding tap water.

Even without such regulations, consumers may be changing their attitudes. The bottled water industry recently has experienced flat growth. The cause may be the economic downturn, which has forced consumers to cut costs wherever possible. Environmental concerns may be another factor since bottled water creates significant waste. Perhaps better labeling of products will mean even less ambiguity about the value of bottled versus tap water, which could offer opportunities for differentiation among bottled water brands that adopt different bottling and labeling methods.

Would more comprehensive labels on bottled water change your water consumption behavior? Is bottled water better than tap water? Is buying bottled water an ecologically sound purchase decision?

Packaging can also be used in a far subtler way, namely, to help suppliers save costs. When the costs of producing a product rise significantly, manufacturers are faced with either raising prices—something customers don't usually like—or reducing the amount of product sold in a package. Chobani reduced the size of its Greek yogurt containers by 12 percent. When customers noticed the decrease, they took to Twitter and Facebook to complain about the change.[42]

Product Labeling

Labels on products and packages provide information the consumer needs for his or her purchase decision and consumption of the product. In that they identify the product and brand, labels are also an important element of branding and can be used for promotion. The information required on them must comply with general and industry-specific laws and regulations, including the constituents or ingredients contained in the product, where the product was made, directions for use, and/or safety precautions.

Many labeling requirements stem from various laws, including the Federal Trade Commission Act of 1914, the Fair Packaging and Labeling Act of 1967, and the Nutrition Labeling Act of 1990. Several federal agencies, industry groups, and consumer watchdogs carefully monitor product labels. The Food and Drug Administration is the primary federal agency that reviews food and package labels and ensures that the claims made by the manufacturer are true. Ethical and Societal Dilemma 11.2 illustrates the problems associated with the different regulations that apply to various edible products as well as some associated labeling concerns.

A product label is much more than just a sticker on the package; it is a communication tool. Many of the elements on the label are required by laws and regulations (i.e., ingredients, fat content, sodium content, serving size, calories), but other elements remain within the control of the manufacturer. How manufacturers use labels to communicate the benefits of their products to consumers varies by the product. Many products highlight specific ingredients, vitamin content or nutrient content (e.g., iron), and country of origin. This focus signals to consumers that the product offers these benefits. The importance of the label as a communication tool should not be underestimated. ∎

 Increase your engagement and learning with Connect Marketing.

<u>These Connect activities, available only through your Connect course, have been designed to make the following concepts more meaningful and applicable:</u>

▶ How to Build on the Value of the Brand: Band-Aid Case Analysis

▶ Branding Strategies: Click and Drag Activity

▶ Frito Lay: Doritos Branding Video Case

▶ Brand Equity: iSeeit! Video

twelve

developing
new products

In Chapter 7, we discussed how 3D printing is changing the interactions between businesses in business-to-business markets. But those are secondary effects, in a way. The most prominent and talked about revolution brought about by 3D printing and the increasing availability of 3D printers pertains to the innovative new products that companies and individual consumers might create with them.

In the fashion industry, 3D printing created a corset and wings worn by models in a Victoria's Secret Fashion Show.[1] The massive wings represented a creative innovation; had they been produced with traditional methods, their weight would never have allowed the model to carry them down the runway. Fashion designers in various realms are investigating how they can adapt the technology to enable consumers to order and purchase clothing with exactly tailored fit. The production process also becomes notably faster, which constitutes a significant appeal in the rapidly changing world of fashion, where getting to market first is usually a notable benefit. The

LEARNING OBJECTIVES

After reading this chapter, you should be able to:

LO 12-1 Identify the reasons firms create new products.

LO 12-2 Describe the different groups of adopters articulated by the diffusion of innovation theory.

LO 12-3 Describe the various stages involved in developing a new product or service.

LO 12-4 Explain the product life cycle.

printers even enable clothing manufacturers to experiment with new combinations of materials.

As more companies and consumers seek out the printers, their prices have dropped precipitously. The technology keeps improving, and the machines seem poised to take off, such that some prognosticators claim that 3D printers will become as ubiquitous as regular ink printers in

continued on p. 238

continued from p. 237

people's homes.[2] Other observers question whether they will really follow a traditional diffusion throughout the market.[3] Citing reasons such as the continued sophistication of the process, these critics argue that 3D printers have not yet become easy enough to use for an everyday consumer to adopt. In addition, different printers would be needed to print items out of different materials. For example, if someone wanted to print a wooden frame for the family portrait, plastic bumpers to protect the walls from the corners of the picture, and nickel nails to hang it, he or she would need three separate printers.

A separate question involves what happens if an art lover, rather than hanging a family portrait, programs a 3D printer to reproduce a famous sculpture or trademarked item. If it is possible for parents to print out new LEGO sets identical to those they might buy in the store, are they engaging in theft or trademark infringement?[4]

Maybe the biggest controversy—and the greatest promise—comes about when we consider one more possibility for 3D printing: food. The Chef Jet printer can take extrusions of edible items and print them out in various shapes, colors, and sizes. Some applications seem less likely to work; diners cannot get a steak from a printer. Furthermore, people who worry about artificial-seeming foods might never warm up to the idea. But the printers can combine multiple vegetables together into a single paste, enabling parents to sneak broccoli and kale to their kids by adding in another flavor and printing it in the shape of a train or cool toy.[5] Though important, for most consumers that's not even the best idea. The best notion is the one in which they can get chocolate, without ever leaving their homes, in the flavor, density, and amount they want, even if the chocolate craving hits at 3:00 a.m.[6] ■

3D printing created a corset and wings worn by models in a Victoria's Secret Fashion Show.
© Jamie McCarthy/Getty Images

Few three-letter words are more exciting than *new*. It brings forth an image of freshness, adventure, and excitement. Yet *new* also is a complex term when it comes to market offerings because it might mean adding something new to an existing product, introducing a flavor never offered before, or relying on different packaging that provides added value. But the most exhilarating type of new product is something never seen before. Thousands of patent applications pursue this elusive prize: a successful and truly innovative new product.

Imagine living 200 years ago: You cook meals on a stove fueled by coal or wood; you write out homework by hand (if you are lucky enough to attend school) and by candlelight. To get to school, you hike along unpaved roads to reach a small, cold, basic classroom with just a few classmates who listen to a lecture from a teacher writing on a blackboard.

Today, you finish your homework on a laptop computer with word processing software that appears to have a mind of its own and can correct your spelling automatically. Your

"THE MOST EXHILARATING TYPE OF NEW PRODUCT IS SOMETHING NEVER SEEN BEFORE. THOUSANDS OF PATENT APPLICATIONS PURSUE THIS ELUSIVE PRIZE: A SUCCESSFUL AND TRULY INNOVATIVE NEW PRODUCT."

climate-controlled room has ample electric light. While you work on your laptop, you also talk with a friend using the hands-free headset of your wireless phone. As you drive to school in your car, you pick up fast food from a convenient drive-through window while browsing and listening to your personal selection of songs playing through your car speakers, connected wirelessly to your iPad. Your friend calls to discuss a slight change to the homework, so you pull over to grab your iPhone, make the necessary change to your assignment, and e-mail it from your smartphone to your professor. When you arrive at school, you sit in a 200-person classroom, where you can plug in your laptop, take notes on your iPad, or digitally record the lecture. The professor adds notes on the day's PowerPoint presentations using her tablet computer. You have already downloaded the PowerPoint presentations and add similar notes through your own laptop. After class, to complete your planning for a last-minute party, you send out a Facebook invitation to your friends and ask for responses to get a head count. You then text your roommate, telling her to get food and drinks for the right number of people, which she orders through an online grocer that will deliver later in the day.

Our lives are defined by the many new products and services developed through scientific and technological advances and by the added features included in products that we have always used. In this second chapter dealing with the first P in the marketing mix (product), we continue our discussion from the preceding chapter and explore how companies add value to product and service offerings through innovation. We also look at how firms develop new products and services on their own. We conclude the chapter with an examination of how new products and services get adopted by the market and how firms can change their marketing mix as the product or service moves through its life cycle.

> It is more useful to think of the degree of newness or innovativeness on a continuum from truly new-to-the-world to slightly repositioned.

| LO 12-1 | Identify the reasons firms create new products. |

WHY DO FIRMS CREATE NEW PRODUCTS?

New market offerings provide value to both firms and customers. But the degree to which they do so depends on how new they really are. When we say a "new product/service," we don't necessarily mean that the market offer has never existed before. Completely new-to-the-market products represent fewer than 10 percent of all new product introductions each year. It is more useful to think of the degree of newness or innovativeness on a continuum from truly

Kraft's Capri Sun packages have gotten bigger.
© McGraw-Hill Education

innovation The process by which ideas are transformed into new products and services that will help firms grow.

new-to-the-world—as Wi-Fi was a few years ago—to slightly repositioned, such as when Kraft's Capri Sun brand of ready-to-drink beverages were repackaged in a bigger pouch to appeal to teens.

Regardless of where on the continuum a new product lies, firms have to innovate. **Innovation** refers to the process by which ideas are transformed into new offerings, including products, services, processes, and branding concepts that will help firms grow. Without innovation and its resulting new products and services, firms would have only two choices: continue to market current products to current customers or take the same product to another market with similar customers.

Although innovation strategies may not always work in the short run—some estimates indicate that only about 3 percent of new products actually succeed—various overriding and long-term reasons compel firms to continue introducing new products and services, as the following sections describe.

Changing Customer Needs

When they add products, services, and processes to their offerings, firms can create and deliver value more effectively by satisfying the changing needs of their current and new customers or by keeping customers from getting bored with the current product or service offering. Sometimes companies can identify problems and develop products or services that customers never knew they needed. For example, moving can be stressful; among other things, having to buy, build, and dispose of moving boxes is a hassle, expensive, and not very good for the environment. Canadian firm Frogbox rents out reusable plastic moving boxes. It delivers them to customers and picks them up at the new address when they are finished. The boxes stack neatly inside each other and don't require assembly, eliminating the time-consuming task of building and breaking down boxes. The firm is called Frogbox because it donates 1 percent of sales to frog habitat restoration.[7] Adding to its sustainability efforts, it uses solar energy to power its website and waste-generated biodiesel to fuel its trucks.

In other cases, customers enter new stages in their lives that intensify their demand for such innovations. Technology advances are obvious examples: Waterproof phone cases were

Moving? Rent Frogbox reusable plastic boxes and spare the landfills.
Courtesy FROGBOX, Inc.

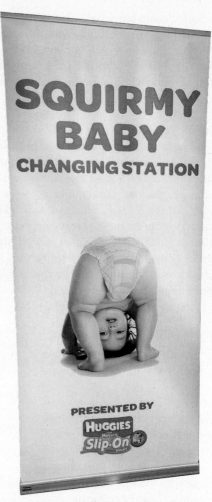

Huggies Little Movers Slip-On diapers are designed to make life easier for parents.
© Jemal Countess/Getty Images

rarely a necessity until people started carrying their smartphones everywhere, including near the kitchen sink, into the bathroom, and poolside. For parents of infants, the market is relatively stable, in the sense that most products have been around for years. But Huggies also recognized that parents of toddlers often struggled to get their wriggly babies to stay still for diaper changes, so it introduced Little Movers Slip-Ons, to help make the change a fun game rather than a frustrating struggle. The per-diaper price is about 16 cents more than a regular diaper, but Huggies also knows that if it can appeal to the relatively loyal parent segment (approximately 55 percent of whom nearly always buy their preferred brand), its innovation can help it maintain market share.[8]

Market Saturation

The longer a product exists in the marketplace, the more likely it is that the market will become saturated. Without new products or services, the value of the firm will ultimately decline.[9] Imagine, for example, if car companies simply assumed and expected that people would keep their cars until they stopped running. If that were the case, there would be no need to come up with new and innovative models; companies could just stick with the models that sell well. But few consumers actually keep the same car until it stops running. Even those who want to stay with the same make and model often want something new, just to add some variety to their lives. Therefore, car companies revamp their models every year, whether with new features like advanced GPS or a more powerful engine or by redesigning the entire look of the vehicle. The firms sustain their growth by getting consumers excited by the new looks and new features, prompting many car buyers to exchange their old vehicle years

> Imagine if car companies simply assumed and expected that people would keep their cars until they stopped running.

Adding Value 12.1

Carmakers Look for an Edge, above and below the Hood[i]

The competition and new partnerships generated by the global car market have yielded a wealth of new product approaches, both above and below the hood, as automakers strive to meet an international aesthetic while also responding to near-universal demand for more fuel-efficient cars. In particular, U.S. carmakers can no longer simply appeal to American tastes, with tailfins, boxy SUVs, and little concern about fuel economy. Car design must meet the demands of drivers overseas. General Motors recently introduced a new concept car, the Chevrolet Tru 140S, an "affordable exotic" model that gets 40 miles per gallon. Another Chevrolet concept, Code 130R, takes elements from the BMW 1 Series, the 1960s Ford Anglia from Europe, and Japanese subcompact car models.

While crafting new looks, GM also is looking for designs that will survive shifting trends. The Cadillac ATS sedan, which aims to compete with the BMW 3 Series, is not nearly as distinctive as classic Cadillac models from the past. But its understated style may enable the ATS to age more gracefully and require fewer, less frequent redesigns. Ford hired European designers to come up with many of its most successful recent models, including the Focus and the Fiesta. These small, quick, sporty cars appeal to the worldwide market. Chrysler's new owner Fiat has added Italian elements to make the U.S. brand appear more global in its design.

Automakers also are relying heavily on new engineering to meet global demand. Tighter fuel-efficiency standards and shifting buyer preferences are forcing carmakers to develop lighter, smaller-cylinder cars, more electrics and hybrids, and new turbocharged engines that couple with electric motors. Even luxury cars are becoming lighter. Mercedes-Benz has spent seven years developing the aluminum body of its new SL

The 2015 Cadillac ATS is less distinctive than earlier models. As a result its understated style may require fewer redesigns.
© Stan Honda/Getty Images

550, which is 308 pounds lighter than the previous model yet still offers unparalleled torsion resistance.

Smaller engines are getting a second look too: For the first time in 20 years, Cadillac is offering a four-cylinder engine to deliver fuel efficiency in its ATS. The appeal of these smaller, powerful engines is vast. Ford's new Fusion Hybrid couples a new, lighter lithium ion battery with a lighter four-cylinder engine to deliver six more miles per gallon in fuel efficiency. Plug-in hybrids are entering the market, including Ford's Fusion Energi, which competes with the Chevy Volt and models influenced by Toyota's Prius.

While redesigning its cars for more European tastes, Fiat-owned Chrysler has revived some of the engineering that made its Dodge Dart compact so efficient. And GM has used its globally successful small-car platform as the basis for both its Chevrolet Sonic subcompact and the Buick Encore crossover. With design oriented to global tastes and engineering focused on a newer, more efficient bottom line, automakers worldwide are hoping drivers will like what they see.

---

before its functional life is over. Adding Value 12.1 notes some other innovations that carmakers are trying.

Saturated markets can also offer opportunities for a company that is willing to adopt a new process or mentality. At one point in time, mass marketers would not even consider entering a market that they believed would not earn at least $50 million. But General Mills is looking to niche markets for its future growth. Whereas only 1 percent of the U.S. population suffers from celiac disease—a condition in which ingested gluten damages the digestive system—a much higher percentage of U.S. consumers say they want to reduce or eliminate gluten, a wheat protein, from their diet. As awareness increases, those percentages are growing, such that the U.S. market for gluten-free products could be broadly worth up to $10 billion.[10] General Mills has created more than 300 gluten-free products, including both variations on its regular offerings, like Chex cereals, and brand-new concepts, such as gluten-free desserts and pancake mixes.[11]

General Mills provides a number of gluten-free options at http://www.chex.com/recipes/gluten-free.
© Bruce Bisping/ZUMAPRESS/Newscom

The Keebler line's risk is lessened by offering many variations of its basic product, cookies.
© Michael J. Hruby

Managing Risk through Diversity

Through innovation, firms often create a broader portfolio of products, which help them diversify their risk and enhance firm value better than a single product can.[12] If some products in a portfolio perform poorly, others may do well. Firms with multiple products can better withstand external shocks, including changes in consumer preferences or intensive competitive activity. For this reason, firms such as 3M demand that a specific percentage of their sales each year must come from new products introduced within the previous few years. In the cookie aisle, Keebler offers many variations of its basic product, cookies, including Animals, Chips Deluxe, E.L. Fudge, Gripz, Sandies, Vanilla Wafers, and Vienna Fingers. This diversification enables Keebler to enjoy more consistent performance than it would with just one kind of cookie.

Fashion Cycles

In industries that rely on fashion trends and experience short product life cycles—including apparel, arts, books, and software markets—most sales come from new products. For example, a motion picture generates most of its theater, DVD, and cable TV revenues within a year of its release. If the same selection of books were always for sale, with no new titles, there would be no reason to buy more. Consumers of computer software and video games

To generate sales, apparel fashion designers produce entirely new product selections a few times per year.
© Caroline Bittencourt/
LatinContent/Getty Images

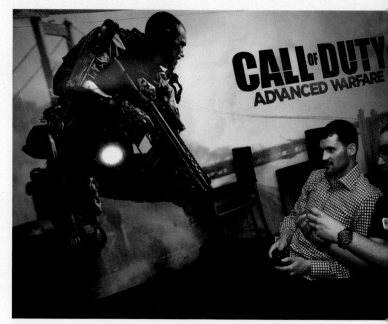

Video games like Call of Duty Advanced Warfare are "fashionable" because consumers demand new versions. Once they have "beat" the game, they want to be challenged with a new experience.
© Imeh Akpanudosen/Getty Images

demand new offers because once they have beaten the game, they want to be challenged by another game or experience the most recent version, as the remarkable sales of successive versions of the Call of Duty game exemplify.[13] In the case of apparel, fashion designers produce entirely new product selections a few times per year.

Improving Business Relationships

New products do not always target end consumers; sometimes they function to improve relationships with suppliers. For example, Kraft, the maker of Capri Sun, found that its lemonade flavor was selling poorly. Through a little market research, it realized that the reason was the placement of the packages in pallets. Because it was placed at the bottom of the stack in pallets, lemonade was the last flavor retailers would sell. By changing and innovating its pallet, Kraft offered chimney stacks for each flavor, enabling the retail stockers to reach whichever flavor they needed easily. Sales of Capri Sun's lemonade improved by 162 percent.[14]

Even if they succeed in innovating and creating new products, new-to-the-world products are not adopted by everyone at the same time. Rather, they diffuse or spread through a population in a process known as *diffusion of innovation*, which will be discussed next.

✓ check yourself

1. What are the reasons firms innovate?

DIFFUSION OF INNOVATION

The process by which the use of an innovation—whether a product, a service, or a process—spreads throughout a market group, over time and across various categories of adopters, is referred to as **diffusion of innovation**.[15] The theory surrounding diffusion of innovation helps marketers understand the rate at which consumers are likely to adopt a new product or service. It also gives them a means to identify potential markets for their new products or services and predict their potential sales, even before they introduce the innovations.[16]

Truly new product introductions, that is, new-to-the-world products that create new markets, can add tremendous value to firms. These new products, also called **pioneers** or **breakthroughs**, establish a completely new market or radically change both the rules of competition and consumer preferences in a market.[17] The Apple iPod is a pioneer product. Not only did it change the way people listen to music but it also created an entirely new industry devoted to accessories such as cases, ear buds, docking stations, and speakers. Although Apple offers many of these accessories itself, other companies have jumped on the bandwagon, ensuring that you can strap your iPod to your arm while on the move or insert it into the base of a desk lamp equipped with speakers to get music and light from your desk. And don't forget: The iPod also launched perhaps the most notable other recent pioneer, the iPhone, along with the innovative iTunes service, the iPod Touch, and even the iPad.[18]

Pioneers have the advantage of being **first movers**; as the first to create the market or product category, they become readily recognizable to consumers and thus establish a commanding and early market share lead. Studies also have found that market pioneers can command a greater market share over a longer time period than later entrants can.[19]

Yet not all pioneers succeed. In many cases, imitators capitalize on the weaknesses of pioneers and subsequently gain advantage in the market. Because pioneering products and brands face the uphill task of establishing the market alone, they pave the way for followers, who can spend less marketing effort creating demand for the product line and focus directly on creating demand for their specific brand. Also, because the pioneer is the first product in the market, it often has a less sophisticated design and may be priced relatively higher, leaving room for better and lower-priced competitive products.

diffusion of innovation The process by which the use of an innovation, whether a product or a service, spreads throughout a market group over time and over various categories of adopters.

pioneers New product introductions that establish a completely new market or radically change both the rules of competition and consumer preferences in a market; also called *breakthroughs*.

breakthroughs See *pioneers*.

first movers Product pioneers that are the first to create a market or product category, making them readily recognizable to consumers and thus establishing a commanding and early market share lead.

Apple has released several pioneer products in recent years, including the iPhone.
© Stephen Lam/Reuters/Corbis

K-Cup Packs were a pioneer coffee delivery method that created a new coffee market.
© Green Mountain Coffee Roasters, Inc.

Clairol's Touch of Yogurt Shampoo failed because consumers didn't like the idea of washing their hair with yogurt.
© GfK Custom Research, LLC.

An important question to ask is, Why is the failure rate for new products so high? One of the main reasons is the failure to assess the market properly by neglecting to do appropriate product testing, targeting the wrong segment, and/or poor positioning.[20] Firms may also overextend their abilities or competencies by venturing into products or services that are inconsistent with their brand image and/or value proposition. We discuss some infamous product failures in Exhibit 12.1.

As the diffusion of innovation curve in Exhibit 12.2 shows, the number of users of an innovative

▼ **EXHIBIT 12.2** Diffusion of Innovation Curve

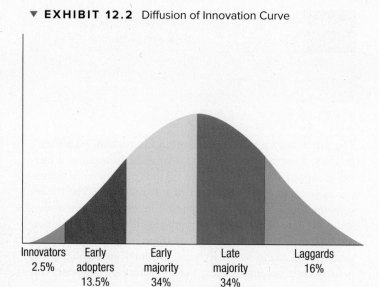

| Innovators 2.5% | Early adopters 13.5% | Early majority 34% | Late majority 34% | Laggards 16% |

Time of adoption of the innovation

Source: Adapted from Everett M. Rodgers, *Diffusion of Innovation* (New York: Free Press, 1983).

▼ **EXHIBIT 12.1** Illustrative Product Failures

Product	Concept	Why It Failed
New Coke	In response to growing market pressure, Coca-Cola launched a reformulated version of its classic cola in 1985 that was so hated it was pulled from shelves three months later.	Coke underestimated the consumers' affinity to the original formulation and their unwillingness to change.
Sony Betamax	In 1975, Sony bet big on the Betamax, one of the first ever mass-produced home video recording systems.	Unfortunately, the next year, JVC launched the VHS player, ensuring a format war similar to the Blu-ray and HD-DVD format wars of 2006.
Harley-Davidson Perfume	After being successful with lighters and T-shirts bearing the Harley logo, Harley-Davidson branched out into its own line of perfumes associated with the motorcycle lifestyle.	Although lighters and T-shirts may resonate with the Harley image, customers were not as attracted to smelling like a motorcycle.
Bic Underwear	Bic is well known for its disposable products: pens, lighters, and razors. Capitalizing on its ability to cross product categories, Bic began producing underwear.	The concept of buying underwear from a company well known for disposable pens was confusing and off-putting to consumers.
Bottled Water for Pets	Trying to capitalize on the pet pampering craze, makers of *Thirsty Cat!* and *Thirsty Dog!* launched a line of bottled water for cats and dogs. No longer did owners need to give their pet tap water; instead they could give them a daily pet drink in flavors such as Crispy Beef, Tangy Fish, and Grilled Chicken.	Although people do indeed desire to pamper their pets, the idea of purchasing bottled water for them never caught on. The associations generated by their flavors, such as tangy fish-tasting water, probably did not help either.
Frito-Lay Lemonade	To Frito-Lay, lemonade seemed like a reasonable enough brand extension. After all, the high salt content of corn chips often leads consumers to search out something to quench their thirst.	Associating a salty snack with a supposed thirst quencher did not go over well.
Kellogg's Breakfast Mates	Capitalizing on the convenience market, Kellogg's Breakfast Mates launched a line of cereal products in 1998 that came with cereal, spoon, and milk.	Sometimes a good idea is poorly executed. The milk was usually warm because it did not require refrigeration and the product was not child-friendly, making its appeal very limited.
Apple Newton	Launched in 1993 with a price tag of more than $700, the Apple Newton was one of the first PDAs, which then led the way for the Palm Pilot, BlackBerry, and iPad.	The Newton concept was ahead of its time. Unfortunately due to its bulky size and ridicule by comedians, the Newton lasted only until 1998.
Colgate Kitchen Entrees	Colgate launched a line of frozen dinners. Apparently the idea was that consumers would enjoy eating a Colgate meal and then using Colgate on their toothbrush afterward.	The association of toothpaste with a chicken stir-fry was something customers did not find appetizing.
Clairol's Touch of Yogurt Shampoo	Clairol marketed a shampoo with a touch of yogurt to improve hair quality.	Consumers were not enticed with the idea of washing their hair with yogurt, something Clairol should have known after its Look of Buttermilk failed in test markets a few years earlier.

Source: DailyFinance.com, "Top 25 Biggest Product Flops of All Time," http://www.dailyfinance.com/photos/top-25-biggest-product-flops-of-all-time/3662621.

product or service spreads through the population over a period of time and generally follows a bell-shaped curve. A few people buy the product or service at first, then more buy, and finally fewer people buy as the degree of the diffusion slows. These purchasers can be divided into five groups according to how soon they buy the product after it has been introduced.

Innovators

Innovators are those buyers who want to be the first on the block to have the new product or service. These buyers enjoy taking risks and are regarded as highly knowledgeable. You probably know someone who is an innovator—or perhaps you are one for a particular product or service category. For example, the person who stood in line overnight to be sure to get a ticket for the very first showing of the latest superhero movie is an innovator in that context. Those consumers who already have 3D printers at their homes are likely innovators too. Firms that invest in the latest technology, either to use in their products or services or to make the firm more efficient, also are considered innovators. Typically, innovators keep themselves very well informed about the product category by subscribing to trade and specialty magazines, talking to other

them go ahead and purchase because early adopters tend to enjoy novelty and often are regarded as the opinion leaders for particular product categories.

This group, which represents about 13.5 percent of all buyers in the market, spreads the word. As a result, early adopters are crucial for bringing the other three buyer categories to the market. If the early adopter group is relatively small, the number of people who ultimately adopt the innovation likely will also be small.

Early Majority

The **early majority**, which represents approximately 34 percent of the population, is crucial because few new products and services can be profitable until this

> ## YOU PROBABLY KNOW SOMEONE WHO IS AN INNOVATOR—OR PERHAPS YOU ARE ONE FOR A PARTICULAR PRODUCT OR SERVICE CATEGORY.

experts, visiting product-specific blogs and forums that describe the coolest new products,[21] and attending product-related forums, seminars, and special events. Yet innovators represent only about 2.5 percent of the total market for any new product or service.

These innovators are crucial to the success of any new product or service, though, because they help the product gain market acceptance. Through talking about and spreading positive word of mouth about the new product, they prove instrumental in bringing in the next adopter category, known as early adopters.[22]

Early Adopters

The second subgroup that begins to use a product or service innovation is **early adopters**. They generally don't like to take as much risk as innovators do but instead wait and purchase the product after careful review. Thus, this market waits for the first reviews of the latest movie before purchasing a ticket, though they likely still go a week or two after it opens. They do not stand in line to grab the first Samsung 4K televisions; only after reading the innovators' complaints and praises do they decide whether the new technology is worth the cost.[23] But most of

Users of Gillette's Fusion Proglide are early adopters.
© Aynsley Floyd/Invision for Gillette/AP Photo

large group buys them. If the group never becomes large enough, the product or service typically fails.

The early majority group differs in many ways from buyers in the first two stages. Its members don't like to take as much risk and therefore tend to wait until the bugs are worked out of a particular product or service. This group probably rents the latest *Hunger Games* movie during the first week it comes out on video. Thus, early majority members experience little risk because all the reviews are in, and their costs are lower because they're renting the movie instead of going to the theater. When early majority customers enter the market, the number of competitors in the marketplace usually also has reached its peak, so these buyers have many price and quality choices.

Late Majority

At 34 percent of the market, the **late majority** is the next group of buyers to enter a new product market. When they do, the product has achieved its full market potential. Perhaps these movie watchers wait until the newest movie is easy to find at Red Box or put it low on their Netflix queue, to be delivered after the other consumers interested in watching it have already seen it. By the time the late majority enters the market, sales tend to level off or may be in decline.

Laggards

Laggards make up roughly 16 percent of the market. These consumers like to avoid change and rely on traditional products until they are no longer available. In some cases, laggards may never adopt a certain product or service. When the sequel to *The Hunger Games*: *Catching Fire* eventually shows up on their regular television networks, they are likely to watch it.

Using the Diffusion of Innovation Theory

Using the diffusion of innovation theory, firms can predict which types of customers will buy their new product or service immediately after its introduction as well as later as the product is more and more accepted by the market. With this knowledge, the firm can develop effective promotion, pricing, and other marketing strategies to push acceptance among each customer group. Let's consider an example of some everyday products that nearly all of us use at some point.

Although they are not as flashy as Google Glass or the latest iPhone, cleaning supplies are used by everyone. Oftentimes the innovators who adopt new cleaning products are the ones who are the most fanatical about cleaning. Firms conduct in-depth research into how people clean their homes to identify such segments. This research finds that some people are so obsessive about cleaning that they spend nearly 20 hours every week doing it, while others are so reluctant that they avoid cleaning as much as they can; their average weekly cleaning time is about 2.5 hours.[24] Their options with regard to the products to

REMEMBER WHO THE ENEMY IS

THE HUNGER GAMES:
CATCHING FIRE

NOVEMBER 22
EXPERIENCE IT IN IMAX

Early majority members would probably rent the latest Hunger Games *movie rather than see it in theaters when it first comes out. They can assess the movie from its reviews, and the cost of a rental is lower than at the theater. Overall these consumers experience little risk.*
© Lionsgate/Photos 12/Alamy

> " By the time the late majority enters the market, sales tend to level off or may be in decline. "

Consumers who are fixated on cleaning will spend substantial amounts for the most technologically advanced machines, like this Dyson Ball Vacuum.
© Hugh Threlfall/Alamy

purchase to assist them in their cleaning tasks are vast, from scrubbers to sprays to vacuums to dusters. Thus, in the vacuum cleaner market, manufacturers recognize that the segment of consumers who will spend substantial amounts for the most technologically advanced, powerful, easy-to-maneuver machines, such as the latest Dyson model, are likely to be the segment of consumers that is most fixated on cleaning.[25] But another segment just wants some basic suction to get the grit out of their rugs.

Relative Advantage
If a product or service is perceived to be better than substitutes, then the diffusion will be relatively quick. As advertising for Swiffer products emphasizes, its mops and dusters promise to make cleaning faster, easier, and more efficient. In featuring real families, it seeks to highlight the relative advantage for all types of cleaners. Older people who might once have gotten on their hands and knees to scrub the floor can now rely on the design of the cleaning pads on the end of the mop to get the job done. Their children, who have never been very good at cleaning, can swipe a few surfaces and get the house looking clean before their parents visit. And a man who has lost an arm to cancer can still help his family keep the house clean, because the duster does not require him to use a spray or climb a ladder to dust the ceiling fan.[26]

Compatibility
A diffusion process may be faster or slower, depending on various consumer features, including international cultural differences. Electrolux's latest bagless vacuums offer a key innovation: They solve the age-old problem of how to empty the chamber without having a cloud of particles fly out: compact the dirt into a "pellet." To make the product more compatible with the needs of people in different cultures, it is made in various sizes. The U.S. version offers a carpet

nozzle with a motor, to deal with the dirt accumulated in Americans' larger, often carpeted homes. Because in many Asian "megacities" consumers live in tiny apartments, Electrolux has introduced a smaller version that is also very quiet.[27]

Observability
When products are easily observed, their benefits or uses are easily communicated to others, which enhances the diffusion process. To demonstrate to consumers why they should spend $400 on a blender, Blendtec launched an extensive YouTube campaign titled "Will It Blend?" to demonstrate the effectiveness of the blender. In each video, a spokesperson in a white lab coat blends a different product in the Blendtec—from iPads to baseballs to Justin Bieber's autobiography—and gives visible proof to consumers of the quality of the product. The humor and innovativeness of this product demonstration has caused these videos to go viral, with over 230 million views and 700,000 subscribers.[28] Yet some cleaning products face a serious challenge in making their innovations widely observable, because few consumers spend a lot of time talking about the products that are of a more personal nature, such as what they use to clean their toilets. Even a great product might diffuse more slowly if people feel uncomfortable talking about what they perceive to be involved in their personal care.

Electrolux revolutionizes the vacuum market with a bagless vacuum cleaner.
© Electrolux

> " A diffusion process may be faster or slower, depending on various consumer features, including international cultural differences. "

Complexity and Trialability
Products that are relatively less complex are also relatively easy to try. These products will generally diffuse more quickly and lead to greater/faster adoption than those that are not so easy to try. In the cleaning products range, it is far easier to pick up a new spray cleaner at the grocery store to try at home than it is to assess and test a new vacuum. In

Idea generation	Concept testing	Product development	Market testing	Product launch	Evaluation of results
Development of viable new product ideas.	Testing the new product idea among a set of potential customers.	Development of prototypes and/or the product.	Testing the actual products in a few test markets.	Full-scale commercialization of the product.	Analysis of the performance of the new product and making appropriate modifications.

response, manufacturers seek ways to help people conduct trials. For example, Dyson's displays in national retailers such as Bed, Bath, & Beyond often include floor space that allows shoppers to run the machine to see how well the roller ball works or watch it pick up dirt.

The diffusion of innovation theory thus comes into play in the immediate and long-term aftermath of a new product or service introduction. But before the introduction, firms must actually develop those new offerings. In the next section, we detail the process by which most firms develop new products and services and how they introduce them into the market.

check yourself

1. What are the five groups on the diffusion of innovation curve?
2. What factors enhance the diffusion of a good or service?

LO 12-3 Describe the various stages involved in developing a new product or service.

HOW FIRMS DEVELOP NEW PRODUCTS

The new product development process begins with the generation of new product ideas and culminates in the launch of a new product and the evaluation of its success. The stages of the new product development process, along with the important objectives of each stage, are summarized in Exhibit 12.3.

Idea Generation

To generate ideas for new products, a firm can use its own internal research and development (R&D) efforts, collaborate with other firms and institutions, license technology from research-intensive firms, brainstorm, research competitors' products and services, and/or conduct consumer research; see Exhibit 12.4. Firms that want to be pioneers rely more extensively on R&D efforts, whereas those that tend to adopt a follower strategy are more likely to scan the market for ideas. Let's look at each of these idea sources.

Internal Research and Development Many firms have their own R&D departments, in which scientists work to solve complex problems and develop new ideas. Historically, firms such as IBM in the computer industry, Black and Decker in the consumer goods industry, 3M in the industrial goods industry, and Merck and Pfizer in the pharmaceuticals industry have relied on R&D development efforts for their new products. In other industries, such as software, music, and motion pictures, product development efforts also tend to come from internal ideas and R&D financial investments. According to Marketing Analytics 12.1, General Motors is leveraging the data it gathers from customers as a sort of internal research source to support its designs.

The product development costs for these firms are quite high, and the resulting new product or service has a good chance of being a technological or market breakthrough. Firms expect such products to generate enough revenue and profits to make the

▼ **EXHIBIT 12.4** Sources of New Product Ideas

Source of ideas: Internal R&D, R&D consortia, Licensing, Brainstorming, Outsourcing, Competitors' products, Customer input

Marketing Analytics

Data That Help the Brand and the Customer: GM's Big Data Use[ii]

With its famous brands, such as Chevrolet and Cadillac, General Motors (GM) is a staple in the U.S. car industry. It also was one of the companies hit the hardest by the 2008 recession, following which it filed for bankruptcy and received a government bailout. In 2012, GM announced a new business strategy, a major component of which was more efficient and effective uses of big data. The importance of analytics again came to center stage in 2013, when the company faced legal allegations regarding the recall of the Chevy Cobalt. After the crisis, GM restressed the importance of big data even more and promised that analytics would be at the heart of all its future product development.

In particular, data analytics at GM support the development of new cars. Through GM's newly centralized data warehouse, it can analyze trends in both production and customer behavior. Furthermore, GM manufacturer data can be segmented at the individual vehicle identification number (VIN) level and then analyzed to improve quality and safety. For example, manufacturer data analytics helped GM develop tools that reduced the complexity associated with the mechanics of vehicle design. General Motors also is collecting data about its sales and dealerships and uses these data to create detailed customer profiles. The level of customer insight that these profiles provide enables GM to develop new products that then grant customers sufficient value. For example, GM's applied market information influenced its development of high-efficiency products, which help reduce pollution.

All this is just the start. New "connected cars" are generating even more data for the car industry, and the analyses of these data will likely define the

General Motors uses its Onstar system for remote communication with customers and diagnoses of problems. It analyzes the data it collects from its Onstar database to support the development of new cars.
© Bloomberg/Getty Images

cars found on the roads of the future. Connected cars communicate with the manufacturers directly through 4G or LTE. Currently, there are 9 million of these cars on the road, with 35 million projected by 2020. With its subscription-based, in-car security system OnStar, GM has an advantage in this effort: It already uses OnStar for remote communication and diagnoses of problems. Thus it gains real-time information, which GM can use to improve its future car designs, even as the predictive diagnosis and preventive maintenance offer customers value by saving them money or preventing them from being stranded by a car that won't start.

costs of R&D worthwhile. R&D investments generally are considered continuous investments, so firms may lose money on a few new products. In the long run, though, these firms are betting that a few extremely successful new products, often known as blockbusters, can generate enough revenues and profits to cover the losses from other introductions that might not fare so well.

Some global firms also are taking an approach called reverse innovation, as we discussed in Chapter 7. They turn to subsidiaries in less developed markets for new product ideas. From its Shanghai research center, Coca-Cola developed Minute Maid Pulpy, a juice drink that the corporation has moved into 19 countries and is now worth more than $1 billion. Levi's Denizen brand got its start in India and China, where the company worked on ideas for producing more affordable jeans. In the U.S. market, Denizen jeans sell for about half the cost of a pair of regular Levi's and are available exclusively at Target.[29]

R&D Consortia In recent years, more and more firms have been joining consortia, or groups of other firms and institutions, possibly including government and educational

Where do you think Fujitsu derived the idea for a waterproof tablet? Internal R&D, R&D consortia, licensing, brainstorming, outsourcing, competitor's products, customer input, or a combination?
© Odd Andersen/AFP/Getty Images

IN MANY CASES, THE CONSORTIA INVOLVE PHARMACEUTICAL OR HIGH-TECH MEMBERS, WHOSE RESEARCH COSTS CAN RUN INTO THE MILLIONS—TOO MUCH FOR A SINGLE COMPANY TO BEAR.

institutions, to explore new ideas or obtain solutions for developing new products. Here, the R&D investments come from the group as a whole, and the participating firms and institutions share the results.

In many cases, the consortia involve pharmaceutical or high-tech members, whose research costs can run into the millions—too much for a single company to bear. The National Institutes of Health (NIH) sponsors medical foundations to conduct research to treat rare diseases. The research is then disseminated to the medical community, thus encouraging the development of drugs and therapies more quickly and at a lower cost than would be possible if the research were privately funded. The U.S. cable industry has initiated its CableLabs–Energy Lab consortium to find ways to improve the energy efficiency of cable set-top boxes and develop more advanced cable services, such as better sleep settings, to promote other forms of energy conservation.[30]

Licensing

For many other scientific and technological products, firms buy the rights to use the technology or ideas from other research-intensive firms through a licensing agreement. This approach saves the high costs of in-house R&D, but it means that the firm is banking on a solution that already exists but has not been marketed. Some of the largest recent licensing deals in the pharmaceutical industry are for potential weight-loss solutions. In separate deals, one worth $1.4 billion and another worth $1.1 billion, two big pharmaceutical firms licensed the marketing rights for new products developed by small biotechnology firms to combat obesity.[31] Yet neither drug had received FDA approval at the time of the deals!

Brainstorming

Firms often engage in brainstorming sessions during which a group works together to generate ideas. One of the key characteristics of a brainstorming session is that no idea can be immediately accepted or rejected. The moderator of the session may channel participants' attention to specific product features and attributes, performance expectations, or packaging. Only at the end of the session do the members vote on the best ideas or combinations of ideas. Those ideas that receive the most votes are carried forward to the next stage of the product development process.

Outsourcing

In some cases, companies have trouble moving through these steps alone, which prompts them to turn to outside firms such as IDEO, a design firm based in Palo

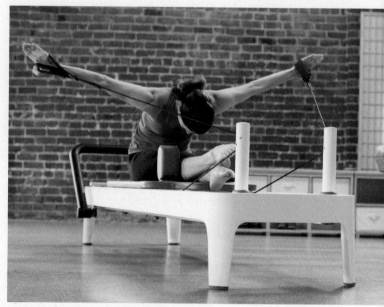

Balance Body partnered with IDEO to develop a less-intimidating, more-user-friendly reformer to be used with Pilates.
© Courtesy Balanced Body, Inc

Alto, California. IDEO does not offer products but rather a stellar service that helps clients generate new product and service ideas in industries such as health care, toys, and computers. IDEO employs anthropologists, graphic designers, engineers, and psychologists whose special skills help foster creativity and innovation. As exercise is becoming more and more popular, companies are looking for ways to capitalize on the beginner's market. Balanced Body is a company that makes and sells reformers to be used with Pilates. A reformer is a device that helps Pilates participants develop good alignment, core strength, and flexibility. When Balanced Body did research and found that people starting Pilates found the reformers that were currently on the market to be too intimidating, it partnered with IDEO to develop a reformer that had better user experience while maintaining the high level of functionality its products engender.[32] In an eight-week period, IDEO created a redesigned model with fewer wheels while improving functionality and adjustability of the product and reducing the cost of the machine.

Competitors' Products

A new product entry by a competitor may trigger a market opportunity for a firm, which can use reverse engineering to understand the competitor's product and then bring an improved version to market. **Reverse engineering** involves taking apart a product, analyzing it, and creating an improved product that does not infringe on the competitor's patents, if any exist. This copycat approach to new product development is widespread and practiced by even the most research-intensive firms. Copycat consumer goods show up in apparel, grocery, and drugstore products as well as in technologically more complex products such as automobiles and computers, as Social and Mobile Marketing 12.1 notes.

Customer Input
Listening to the customer in both B2B and B2C markets is essential for successful idea generation.[33] Because customers for B2B products are relatively few, firms can follow their use of products closely and solicit suggestions and ideas to improve those products either by using a formal approach, such as focus groups, interviews, or surveys, or through more informal discussions. The firm's design and development team then works on these suggestions, sometimes in consultation with the customer. This joint effort between the selling firm and the customer significantly increases the probability that the customer eventually will buy the new product.

Customer input in B2C markets comes from a variety of sources, though increasingly through social media. By monitoring online feedback, whether requested by the firm or provided voluntarily in customer reviews, companies can get better ideas about new products or necessary changes to existing ones. The recent introduction of Green Giant snack chips provides a good example of using inputs from various types of partners. General Mills (which owns the Green Giant brand) heard a pitch for a new vegetable-based snack chip from its supplier Shearer's Chips. The chip manufacturer developed 10 options for its business customer, General Mills. Then General Mills solicited input from its end consumers to find out which flavors they might like best. Online reviews suggested the need for a much zestier

reverse engineering
Involves taking apart a competitor's product, analyzing it, and creating an improved product that does not infringe on the competitor's patents, if any exist.

Social & Mobile Marketing 12.1
When Microsoft Plays Catch-Up[iii]

Microsoft is one of the most innovative companies of all time. After revolutionizing the home computer industry, it set out to be a leader in the information-technology home-entertainment fields. It seems like not a year ever goes by without something new from the brainchild of Bill Gates.

But one area in which Microsoft has been behind the curve is the search engine market. Google, with its nearly 70 percent market share and massive name recognition, does not appear to be in any real danger from competitors, including Microsoft's Bing.com. But Bing already has outpaced Yahoo.com for the remainder of the market, and its market share has been growing, slowly but surely. Perhaps most important, it is distinguishing itself by providing more frequent updates and feature additions than the other search engines. Consumers benefit overall because Bing is forcing competitors to improve their offering to keep pace with Microsoft or prevent it from stealing market share from them.

Its efforts have paid off somewhat: Bing now attracts an approximately 18 percent market share among U.S. users, whereas Yahoo! accounts for only about 10 percent. Google maintains a remarkably high share, though that level has decreased in recent years. Despite these seeming successes, the costs of its copycat efforts have meant that the division responsible for Bing lost $2.56 billion in one recent fiscal year.

To differentiate itself better, Bing is being promoted as a decision engine rather than a search engine. It integrates Foursquare, a location-based phone application, into Bing Maps results. Users can focus on a particular area, such as South Boston, which means Bing can act like an integrative day planner and list the best things to do in that area. It is working on developing a desktop application, and Bing links seamlessly with Facebook to show users which search outcome their friends like best. Despite Microsoft's problems developing search engines, Bing suggests it intends to stay aggressive in this market.

Microsoft's Bing competes with Google in the search engine market.
© M4OS Photos/Alamy

version of the roasted vegetable tortilla chips, which ultimately appeared on store shelves.[34]

In some cases, consumers may not expressly demand a new product, even though their behavior demonstrates their desire for it. For example, Home Depot conducted some in-home research with consumers to see where they might have unexpressed needs. Although they never mentioned their need, the researchers realized that women engaged in heavy-duty gardening tasks wound up struggling with the bulky, heavy buckets they were using to transport dirt and fertilizer to different areas of the yard. In partnership with a design firm, it thus developed the Big Gripper bucket with a more ergonomic handle, a secondary grip on the side (to make it easier to tip the bucket), and another grip on the bottom. In this case, Home Depot has improved on a product that has not changed notably in decades, by observing how people use it.[35]

Another particularly successful customer input approach is to analyze **lead users**, those innovative product users who

Innovative customers called lead users are especially influential in the fashion industry because designers frequently change their designs based on trends they see on the street.
© Big Cheese Photo/Superstock RF

modify existing products according to their own ideas to suit their specific needs.[36] If lead users customize a firm's products, other customers might wish to do so as well. Thus, studying lead users helps the firm understand general market trends that might be just on the horizon. Manufacturers and retailers of fashion products often spot new trends by noticing how innovative trendsetters have altered their clothing and shoes. Designers of high-fashion jeans distress their products in different ways depending on signals they pick up on the street. One season jeans appear with whiskers, the next season they have holes, the next, paint spots.

At the end of the idea-generation stage, the firm should have several ideas that it can take forward to the next stage: concept testing.

Concept Testing

An idea with potential is developed further into a **concept**, which in this context refers to a brief written description of the product; its technology, working principles, and forms; and what customer needs it would satisfy.[37] A concept might also include visual images of what the product would look like.

Concept testing refers to the process in which a concept statement is presented to potential buyers or users to obtain their reactions. These reactions enable the developer to estimate the sales value of the product or service concept, possibly make changes to enhance its sales value, and determine whether the idea is worth further development.[38] If the concept fails to meet customers' expectations, it is doubtful it would succeed if it were to be produced and marketed. Because concept testing occurs very early in the new product introduction process, even before a

By listening to consumers' input, the Big Gripper bucket was designed to make it easier to handle.
© Leaktite Corporation

real product has been made, it helps the firm avoid the costs of unnecessary product development.

The concept for an electric scooter might be written as follows:

> The product is a lightweight electric scooter that can be easily folded and taken with you inside a building or on public transportation. The scooter weighs 25 pounds. It travels at speeds of up to 15 miles per hour and can go about 12 miles on a single charge. The scooter can be recharged in about two hours from a standard electric outlet. The scooter is easy to ride and has simple controls—just an accelerator button and a brake. It sells for $299.[39]

Concept testing progresses along the research techniques described in Chapter 10. The firm likely starts with qualitative research, such as in-depth interviews or focus groups, to test the concept, after which it can undertake quantitative research through Internet or mall-intercept surveys. Video clips on the Internet might show a virtual prototype and the way it works so that potential customers can evaluate the product or service. In a mall-intercept survey, an interviewer would provide a description of the concept to the respondent and then ask several questions to obtain his or her feedback.

The most important question pertains to the respondent's purchase intentions if the product or service were made available. Marketers also should ask whether the product would satisfy a need that other products currently are not meeting. Depending on the type of product or service, researchers might also ask about the expected frequency of purchase, how much customers would buy, whether they would buy it for themselves or as a gift, when they would buy, and whether the price information (if provided) indicates a good value. In addition, marketers usually collect some information about the customers so they can analyze which consumer segments are likely to be most interested in the product.

Some concepts never make it past the concept testing stage, particularly if respondents seem uninterested. Those that do receive high evaluations from potential consumers, however, move on to the next step, product development.

Product Development

Product development or **product design** entails a process of balancing various engineering, manufacturing, marketing, and economic considerations to develop a product's form and features or a service's features. An engineering team develops a product prototype that is based on research findings from the previous concept testing step as well as their own knowledge about materials and technology. A

prototype is the first physical form or service description of a new product, still in rough or tentative form, which has the same properties as a new product but is produced through different manufacturing processes—sometimes even crafted individually.[40]

Product prototypes are usually tested through alpha and beta testing. In **alpha testing**, the firm attempts to determine whether the product will perform according to its design and whether it satisfies the need for which it was intended.[41] Rather than use potential consumers, alpha tests occur in the firm's R&D department. For instance, Ben & Jerry's Ice Cream alpha tests all its proposed new flavors on its own (lucky) employees at its corporate headquarters in Vermont.

Many people, consumer groups, and governmental agencies are concerned when alpha testing involves tests on animals, particularly when it comes to pharmaceuticals and cosmetics.

Is Ben & Jerry's Ice Cream doing alpha or beta testing?
© Nick Wass/AP Photo

> "If the concept fails to meet customers' expectations, it is doubtful it would succeed if it were to be produced and marketed."

Ethical and Societal Dilemma 12.1 discusses these concerns in the United States, the European Union, and China.

In contrast, **beta testing** uses potential consumers, who examine the product prototype in a real-use setting to determine its functionality, performance, potential problems, and other issues specific to its use. The firm might develop several prototype products that it gives to users, then survey those users to determine whether the product worked as intended and identify any issues that need resolution.

ethical&societal dilemma 12.1

Should Firms Test on Animals?[iv]

Product testing on animals has been a primary issue for animal rights activists for years. As public opposition to animal testing increases, so do many companies' declarations that they do not test products on animals. However, such statements can be misleading because even though the whole product may not have been tested on animals, the individual ingredients may have been. To help clarify any confusion, companies can apply to the Coalition for Consumer Information on Cosmetics (CCIC), a national group formed by eight animal welfare group members such as the United States Humane Society and the Doris Day Animal League, and be certified as cruelty free. They then can purchase the trademarked Leaping Bunny Logo from CCIC for use on their labels.

One of the founding principles of The Body Shop, and one that has resonated well with its customers, is that its products are free of animal testing. Another major cosmetics manufacturer, Procter & Gamble, has eliminated animal testing on more than 80 percent of its products. It uses a combination of in vitro testing, computer modeling, and historical data to determine the safety of new products and ingredients. These methods are more expensive than more traditional methods, but P&G claims that the results are better. If performed correctly, new chemicals can either be dropped from consideration or pushed forward in as little as three days compared to the six months previously required for animal testing.

However, animal welfare groups continue to push P&G and other firms to stop the use of animal testing altogether. People for the Ethical Treatment of Animals (PETA) publicly cites companies it accuses of engaging in animal testing and other activities considered to be inhumane

Activists from the People for the Ethical Treatment of Animals (PETA) participate in a protest against animal slaughter near a mall where Hermès—the French luxury goods company— has a store in Jakarta, Indonesia. PETA demanded Hermès stop selling exotic animal skin products and released gruesome videos of reptiles being skinned alive in Indonesia.
© Money Sharma/EPA/Newscom

and praises those that do not. PETA's efforts have caused firms like Hugo Boss, H&M, and Liz Claiborne to stop buying their wool from Australia because some Australian sheep farmers shear their sheep's wool in inhumane ways.

The European Union has passed a ban on animal testing altogether. Beginning in 2009 and finalized in 2013, any cosmetic tested on animals, even in other parts of the world, cannot be sold in the European Union. However, the cosmetics industry is worried that this ban will affect not only their companies' sales but also their customers' ability to find the products they want. The EU cosmetics industry successfully lobbied for an extension on certain areas of toxicity testing to provide more time to find alternatives. The cosmetics industry believes it will be difficult to find alternative testing methods in time, and if it cannot, it will have fewer ingredients to make the products consumers want.

In contrast, China requires animal testing on cosmetics products before they may be sold in that nation. To avoid the risk that Chinese authorities will test their products, some companies choose not to enter the market. However, such a stance might not be viable in the long term, as the already massive Chinese market—especially for cosmetics—grows.

The issues involved in animal testing are complex. At the broadest level, should firms be allowed to develop products that customers want, even if there is some potential harm to the environment or to those animals that share the environment with humans? More specifically, should firms be allowed to test products on animals, even when those products are not specifically designed to improve the health and well-being of their human users? Does the testing that is performed endanger the lives or health of the animals?

The advent of the Internet has made recruiting beta testers easier than ever. Through sites such as OnlineBeta (http://www.onlinebeta.com), everyday people can sign up to become beta testers for products from companies such as Dell, Kodak, and TomTom. To further automate the beta testing process, YouEye is developing eye tracking technology that works with an individual's webcam. Instead of needing to spend thousands of dollars on eye tracking equipment and having customers come into labs, firms will be able to utilize everyday webcams to track not only what a person attends to on a computer screen but also his or her emotional reactions to these products.[42]

Market Testing

The firm has developed its new product or service and tested the prototypes. Now it must test the market for the new product with a trial batch of products. These tests can take two forms: premarket testing and test marketing.

Premarket Tests
Firms conduct **premarket tests** before they actually bring a product or service to market to determine how many customers will try and then continue to use the product or service according to a small group of potential consumers. One popular proprietary premarket test version is called Nielsen BASES. During the test, potential customers are exposed to the marketing mix variables, such as the advertising, then surveyed and given a sample of the product to try.[43] After some period of time, during which the potential customers try the product, they are surveyed about whether they would buy/use the product again. This second survey provides an estimation of the probability of a consumer's repeat purchase. From these data, the firm generates a sales estimate for the new product that enables it to decide whether to introduce the product, abandon it, redesign it before introduction, or revise the marketing plan. An early evaluation of this sort—that is, before the product is introduced to the whole market—saves marketers the costs of a nationwide launch if the product fails.

Sometimes firms simulate a product or service introduction, in which case potential customers view the advertising of various currently available products or services along with advertising for the new product or service. They receive money to buy the product or service from a simulated environment, such as a mock web page or store, and respond to a survey after they make their purchases. This test can determine the effectiveness of a firm's advertising as well as the expected trial rates for the new product.

Test Marketing
A method of determining the success potential of a new product, **test marketing** introduces the offering to a limited geographical area (usually a few cities) prior to a national launch. Test marketing is a strong predictor of product success because the firm can study actual purchase behavior, which is more reliable than a simulated test. A test marketing effort uses all the elements of the marketing mix: It includes promotions such as advertising and coupons, just as if the product were being introduced nationally, and the product appears in targeted retail outlets, with appropriate pricing. On the basis of the results of the test marketing, the firm can estimate demand for the entire market.

Test marketing costs more and takes longer than premarket tests, which may provide an advantage to competitors that could get a similar or better product to market first without test marketing. For this reason, some firms might launch new products without extensive consumer testing and rely instead on intuition, instincts, and guts.[44]

Product Launch

If the market testing returns with positive results, the firm is ready to introduce the product to the entire market. This most critical step in the new product introduction requires tremendous financial resources and extensive coordination of all aspects of the marketing mix. For any firm, if the new product launch is a failure, it may be difficult for the product—and perhaps the firm—to recover. For example, though the number of 3D movie theaters continues to grow, ticket sales for these offerings first leveled off and now have started to decline. The introduction of the new technology was popular enough that sellers invested heavily in building more than 15,000 3D screens, and Hollywood promised a wider range of 3D film options. But if—as appears to be the case—moviegoers have decided that the realistic, three-dimensional images are not worth the higher ticket price, such investments might be painful for both movie studios and movie theaters.[45]

So what does a product launch involve? First, on the basis of the research it has gathered on consumer perceptions, the tests it has conducted, and competitive considerations, the firm

Is the 3D experience worth the price?
© Jasper White CM/Image Source RF

product life cycle
Defines the stages that new products move through as they enter, get established in, and ultimately leave the marketplace and thereby offers marketers a starting point for their strategy planning.

introduction stage
Stage of the product life cycle when innovators start buying the product.

growth stage Stage of the product life cycle when the product gains acceptance, demand and sales increase, and competitors emerge in the product category.

maturity stage Stage of the product life cycle when industry sales reach their peak, so firms try to rejuvenate their products by adding new features or repositioning them.

decline stage Stage of the product life cycle when sales decline and the product eventually exits the market.

confirms its target market (or markets) and decides how the product will be positioned. Then the firm finalizes the remaining marketing mix variables for the new product, including the marketing budget for the first year.[46]

The timing of the launch may also be important, depending on the product.[47] Hollywood studios typically release movies targeted toward general audiences (i.e., those rated G or PG) during the summer when children are out of school. New automobile models traditionally are released for sale during September, and fashion products are launched just before the season of the year for which they are intended.

Evaluation of Results

After the product has been launched, marketers must undertake a critical postlaunch review to determine whether the product and its launch were a success or failure and what additional resources or changes to the marketing mix are needed, if any. Many firms use panel data to improve the probability of success during the test marketing phase of a new product introduction. The consumer panel data are collected by panelists scanning in their receipts using a home scanning device. This information is used to measure individual household first-time trials and repeat purchases. Through such data, market demand can be estimated, so the firm can figure out how best to adjust its marketing mix. Some products never make it out of the introduction stage, especially those that seem almost laughable in retrospect. Bottled water for pets? Harley-Davidson perfume?[48]

For those products that do move on, firms can measure the success of a new product by three interrelated factors: (1) its satisfaction of technical requirements, such as performance; (2) customer acceptance; and (3) its satisfaction of the firm's financial requirements, such as sales and profits.[49] If the product is not performing sufficiently well, poor customer acceptance will result, which in turn leads to poor financial performance.

The new product development process, when followed rationally and sequentially, helps avoid such domino-type failures. The product life cycle, discussed in the next section, helps marketers manage their products' marketing mix during and after introduction.

LO 12-4 | Explain the product life cycle.

THE PRODUCT LIFE CYCLE

The **product life cycle** defines the stages that products move through as they enter, get established in, and ultimately leave the marketplace. It thereby offers marketers a starting point for their strategy planning. The stages of the life cycle often reflect marketplace trends, such as the healthy lifestyle trend that today places organic and green product categories in their growth stages. Exhibit 12.5 illustrates a typical product life cycle, including the industry sales and profits over time. In their life cycles, products pass through four stages: introduction, growth, maturity, and decline. When the product category first launches, its products initiate the **introduction stage**. In the **growth stage**, the product gains acceptance, demand and sales increase, and more competitors emerge in the product category. In the **maturity stage**, industry sales reach their peak, so firms try to rejuvenate their products by adding new features or repositioning them. If these efforts succeed, the product achieves new life.[50] If not, it goes into the **decline stage** and eventually exits the market.

Not every product follows the same life cycle curve. Many products, such as home appliances, stay in the maturity stage for a very long time. Manufacturers may add features to dishwashers and washing machines, but the mature product category remains essentially the same and seems unlikely to enter the decline stage unless some innovative, superior solution comes along to replace them.

The product life cycle offers a useful tool for managers to analyze the types of strategies that may be required over the life

> "Firms can measure the success of a new product by three interrelated factors: (1) its satisfaction of technical requirements, such as performance; (2) customer acceptance; and (3) its satisfaction of the firm's financial requirements."

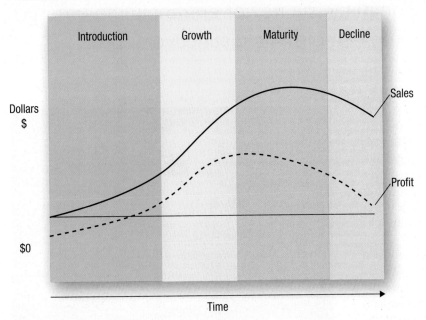

of their products. Even the strategic emphasis of a firm and its marketing mix (four Ps) strategies can be adapted from insights about the characteristics of each stage of the cycle, as we summarize in Exhibit 12.6.

Let's look at each of these stages in depth.

Introduction Stage

The introduction stage for a new, innovative product or service usually starts with a single firm, and innovators are the ones to try the new offering. Some new-to-the-world products and services that defined their own product category and industry include the telephone (invented by Alexander Graham Bell in

1876), the transistor semiconductor (Bell Laboratories in 1947), the Walkman portable cassette player (Sony in 1979), the Internet browser (Netscape in 1994), personal digital assistant (Palm in 1996), iTunes (Apple in 2001), Facebook (2004), Blu-ray (Sony in 2006), iPad (Apple in 2010), and smartwatches (Pebble in 2013). Sensing the viability and commercialization possibilities of some market-creating new product, other firms soon enter the market with similar or improved products at lower prices. The same pattern holds for less innovative products such as apparel, music, and even a new soft drink flavor. The introduction stage is characterized by initial losses to the firm due to its high start-up costs and low levels of sales revenue as the product begins to take off. If the product is successful, firms may start seeing profits toward the end of this stage.

Growth Stage

The growth stage of the product life cycle is marked by a growing number of product adopters, rapid growth in industry sales, and increases in both the number of competitors and the number of available product versions.[51] The market becomes more segmented and consumer preferences more varied, which increases the potential for new markets or new uses of the product or service.[52]

Also during the growth stage, firms attempt to reach new consumers by studying their preferences and producing different product variations—varied colors, styles, or features—which enable them to segment the market more precisely. The goal of this segmentation is to ride the rising sales trend and firmly establish the firm's brand, so as not to be outdone by competitors. For example, many food manufacturers are

> " THE INTRODUCTION STAGE IS CHARACTERIZED BY INITIAL LOSSES TO THE FIRM DUE TO ITS HIGH START-UP COSTS AND LOW LEVELS OF SALES REVENUE AS THE PRODUCT BEGINS TO TAKE OFF. "

▼ EXHIBIT 12.6 Characteristics of Different Stages of the Product Life Cycle

	Introduction	Growth	Maturity	Decline
Sales	Low	Rising	Peak	Declining
Profits	Negative or low	Rapidly rising	Peak to declining	Declining
Typical consumers	Innovators	Early adopters and early majority	Late majority	Laggards
Competitors (number of firms and products)	One or few	Few but increasing	High number of competitors and competitive products	Low number of competitors and products

working hard to become the first brand that consumers think of when they consider organic products. Del Monte was the first of the major canned vegetable sellers to go organic. The cans feature bold "organic" banners across the front and promise that no pesticides were used to produce the food items. Even though Del Monte products have been around for over 100 years, in this growth category the company is a newer entrant in the organic market, so it must work to establish its distinctive appeal.[53]

As firms ride the crest of increasing industry sales, profits in the growth stage also rise because of the economies of scale associated with manufacturing and marketing costs, especially promotion and advertising. At the same time, firms that have not yet established a stronghold in the market, even in narrow segments, may decide to exit in what is referred to as an industry shakeout.

Maturity Stage

The maturity stage of the product life cycle is characterized by the adoption of the product by the late majority and intense competition for market share among firms. Marketing costs (e.g., promotion, distribution) increase as these firms vigorously defend their market share against competitors. They also face intense competition on price as the average price of the product falls substantially compared with the shifts during the previous two stages of the life cycle. Lower prices and increased marketing costs begin to erode the profit margins for many firms. In the later phases of the maturity stage, the market has become quite saturated, and practically all potential customers for the product have already adopted the product. Such saturated markets are prevalent in developed countries.

In the United States, most consumer packaged goods found in grocery and discount stores are already in the maturity stage. For example, in the well-established hair care product market, consumer goods companies constantly search for innovations to set themselves apart and extend the time in which they maintain their position in the maturity stage. Observing the popularity of new skin care products, hair care manufacturers have integrated similar product benefits to their products. These companies have introduced antiaging shampoos and conditioners, prewash hair masks, serums, and multiple-step solutions that go beyond the old mantra of wash, rinse, and repeat.[54]

Firms pursue various strategies during this stage to increase their customer base and/or defend their market share. Other tactics include entry into new markets and market segments and developing new products.

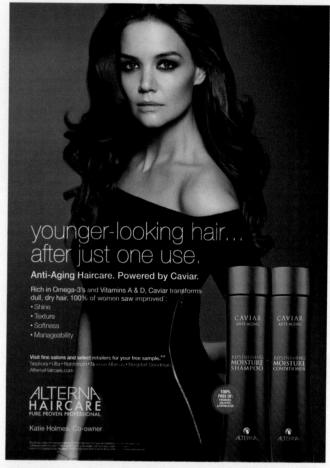

Recognizing that shampoo is a mature product category, Alterna and other manufacturers have introduced antiaging hair products.
© Alterna Haircare

Entry into New Markets or Market Segments

Because a market is saturated, firms may attempt to enter new geographical markets, including international markets (as we discussed in Chapter 8), that may be less saturated. For example, pharmaceutical companies are realizing that they need to turn to BRIC countries for continued growth in the coming years. While the U.S. and European markets are fairly saturated, it is predicted that BRIC countries will go from representing 5 percent of the total pharmaceutical market in 2005 to 30 percent by 2016.[55]

However, even in mature markets, firms may be able to find new market segments. Apple is well known for releasing new versions of its iPhone and iPad yearly, and development cycles are getting even shorter. Although people still two-year contract. To expand to these lower-income market segments, Apple doesn't get rid of its older devices when a new one comes along. Instead, it reduces the price on the older versions that are cheaper to produce. As a result, it is able to reach customers that would never be able to afford the latest iPhone model.

Development of New Products Despite market saturation, firms continually introduce new products with improved features or find new uses for existing products because they need constant innovation and product proliferation to defend market share from intense competition. Firms continually introduce new products to ensure that they are able to retain or grow their respective market shares. Hallmark, which has been the hallmark name for greeting cards for a long time, is trying a variety of innovations. They include customizable greeting cards, plates, and interactive storybooks that can be personalized for various recipients, as well as greeting applications that are available for both iPod and iPad users.[57]

Decline Stage

Firms with products in the decline stage either position themselves for a niche segment of diehard consumers or those with special needs or they completely exit the market. The few laggards who have not yet tried the product or service enter the market at this stage. Take vinyl long-playing records (LPs), for example. In an age of Internet-downloaded music files, it may seem surprising that vinyl records are still made and sold. Sales of vinyl LPs had long been declining, but they have enjoyed a resurgence in just the past few years as diehard music lovers demand the unique sound of a vinyl record rather than the digital sound of CDs and music files. Still, the 5.5 million LPs sold in the United States per year pales in comparison with the 1.26 billion digital downloads.[58] The grooves in vinyl records create sound waves that are similar to those of a live performance, however, which means

To reach new market segments Apple reduces the price of older versions of its products when new ones are released.
© McGraw-Hill Education/Mark Dierker, photographer

get excited over these new products, they are also beginning to suffer from "device exhaustion," in which they are becoming progressively less likely to continue to upgrade their phones and tablets. As a result, it is predicted by 2015 the smartphone and tablet market will be mature.[56] Although the market may be maturing, for many people these new versions are prohibitively expensive, even when signing a

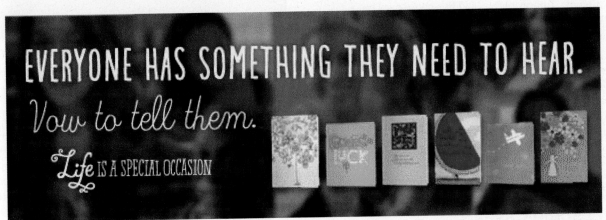

Hallmark's "Life Is a Special Occasion" campaign moves beyond the idea that cards are only for holidays or birthdays. It encourages consumers to connect with loved ones all the time.
© Hallmark online ad courtesy of Hallmark Cards, Inc

they provide a more authentic sound, which in turn means nightclub DJs, discerning music listeners, and collectors will always prefer them.[59]

Aiding this continued demand is the fact that there are simply too many albums of music from the predigital era that are available only on vinyl. It may take many years, maybe even decades, for all the music from earlier generations to be digitized. Until that time, turntable equipment manufacturers, small record-pressing companies such as Music Connection in Manhattan, and new and emerging record companies such as Premier Crue Music continue to have a market that demands their LPs.[60]

implement during each stage of the life cycle of a product, this tool must be used with care. The most challenging part of applying the product life cycle concept is that managers do not know exactly what shape each product's life cycle will take, so there is no way to know precisely what stage a product is in. If, for example, a product experiences several seasons of declining sales, a manager may decide that it has moved from the growth stage to decline and stop promoting the product. As a result, of course, sales decline further. The manager then believes he or she made the right decision because the product continues to follow a predetermined life cycle. But what if the original sales decline was due to a poor

> ## NEW PRODUCTS AND SERVICES THAT CONSUMERS ACCEPT VERY QUICKLY HAVE HIGHER CONSUMER ADOPTION RATES VERY EARLY IN THEIR PRODUCT LIFE CYCLES AND MOVE FASTER ACROSS THE VARIOUS STAGES.

The Shape of the Product Life Cycle Curve

In theory, the product life cycle curve is bell shaped with regard to sales and profits. In reality, however, each product or service category has its own individual shape; some move more rapidly through their product life cycles than others, depending on how different the category is from offerings currently in the market and how valuable it is to the consumer. New products and services that consumers accept very quickly have higher consumer adoption rates very early in their product life cycles and move faster across the various stages.

For example, Blu-ray players and Blu-rays moved much faster than DVDs across the life cycle curve and have already reached the maturity stage, likely because consumers who already owned DVDs were accustomed to playing prerecorded movies and TV shows. It also was easy to switch DVD customers to Blu-ray technology because DVDs played on Blu-ray players, and Blu-rays had better video and audio quality than DVDs. With the advent of 4K televisions that offer resolutions four times higher than current 1080p HD TVs, it is likely we may see another fast adoption of a new video format, such as 4K Blu-ray.

Strategies Based on Product Life Cycle: Some Caveats

Although the product life cycle concept provides a starting point for managers to think about the strategy they want to

DVD customers quickly switched to Blu-rays because of the enhanced picture and sound quality.
© Leon Neal/Alamy

strategy or increased competition—issues that could have been addressed with positive marketing support? In this case, the product life cycle decision became a self-fulfilling prophecy, and a growth product was doomed to an unnecessary decline.[61] Fortunately, new research, based on the history of dozens of consumer products, suggests that the product life cycle concept is indeed a valid idea, and new analytical tools now provide rules for detecting the key turning points in the cycle.[62] ■

connect Increase your engagement and learning with Connect Marketing.

These Connect activities, available only through your Connect course, have been designed to make the following concepts more meaningful and applicable:

▶ The Product Life Cycle: Click and Drag Activity

▶ New Product Development: Sara Lee Video Case

▶ New Product Development: Red Mango Video Case

▶ Understanding Product Development: iSeeit! Video

SMARTBOOK™   **iSeeit!**

thirteen

services: the intangible product

When Amazon first introduced its Prime service, its goal was to build customer loyalty. For $79 per year (now $99 per year), membership guaranteed unlimited two-day shipping on all products purchased on the site. The innovation was an immediate success. Millions of Amazon's customers signed up, and they were less likely to purchase from anywhere else.

The program played directly on their consumer psychology: Customers realize that they earn more from the program when they use it more, at no extra cost to them. For example, 10 products purchased on Amazon with two-day shipping likely pay for the $79 membership. If they go on to buy 100 or 1,000 products, still for just $79, customers feel like they have put one over on the company. In a sense, they have. Amazon has demonstrated its willingness to lose significant profits to develop its program and build unparalleled customer loyalty.

Over time, Amazon added many new features to Prime, and the cost remained

LEARNING OBJECTIVES

After reading this chapter, you should be able to:

LO 13-1   Describe how the marketing of services differs from the marketing of products.

LO 13-2   Discuss the four gaps in the Service Gaps Model.

LO 13-3   Examine the five service quality dimensions.

LO 13-4   Explain the zone of tolerance.

LO 13-5   Identify three service recovery strategies.

the same for nearly a decade. But ultimately, noting estimates that it lost approximately $11 per Prime customer each year, Amazon realized that the service was dampening its profits due to its higher operating expenses. Accordingly, at the start of 2014 it announced the price of Prime memberships

continued on p. 264

service Any intangible offering that involves a deed, performance, or effort that cannot be physically possessed; intangible customer benefits that are produced by people or machines and cannot be separated from the producer.

customer service Specifically refers to human or mechanical activities firms undertake to help satisfy their customers' needs and wants.

continued from p. 263

would increase to $99 per year. Despite negative reactions from existing Prime members who hate the idea of paying $20 more for their benefits, Amazon believes the move ultimately will be profitable because it continues to add to the services it offers.

For example, Amazon offers a book-lending service for Prime customers who own the Kindle Fire,

entertainment. That is, though some existing members may drop Prime, rebelling against the price increase, others continue to find the service highly valuable.[1] ■

Whereas a **service** is any intangible offering that involves a deed, performance, or effort that cannot be physically possessed,[2] **customer service** specifically refers to human or mechanical activities firms undertake to help satisfy their customers' needs and wants. By providing good customer service, firms add value to their products.

Exhibit 13.1 illustrates the continuum from a pure service to a pure good. Most offerings, like those of Samsung, lie somewhere in the middle and include some service and some good (i.e., a hybrid of the two). Even those firms that are engaged primarily in

> ## Most offerings lie somewhere in the middle and include some service and some good.

such that they may read one free e-book each month. Furthermore, Prime members gain free access to approximately 40,000 movies and television programs through Amazon's streaming services. As Amazon adds more products to its retail site, customers also might find the Prime service even more valuable because they can get their groceries shipped for free, not just their reading

Is Amazon Prime worth $99 a year?
© Web Pix/Alamy

selling a good, such as an apparel store, typically view service as a method to maintain a sustainable competitive advantage. This chapter moves on to take an inclusive view of services as anything from pure service businesses, such as Twitter, to a business that uses service as a differentiating tool to help it sell physical goods.

Economies of developed countries such as of the United States have become increasingly dependent on services. Services account for 76 percent of the U.S. gross domestic product (GDP), a much higher percentage than they did 50, 20, or even 10 years ago. In turn, the current list of *Fortune* 500 companies contains more service companies and fewer manufacturers than in previous decades.[3] This dependence and the growth of service-oriented economies in developed countries have emerged for several reasons.

First, it is generally less expensive for firms to manufacture their products in less developed countries. Even if the goods are finished in the United States, some of their components likely were produced elsewhere. In turn, the proportion of service production to goods production in the United States and other similar economies has steadily increased over time.

Second, people place a high value on convenience and leisure. For instance, household maintenance activities, which many people performed themselves in the past, have become more popular and quite specialized. Food preparation, lawn maintenance, house cleaning, pet grooming, laundry and dry cleaning, hair care, and automobile maintenance are all often performed by specialists.

Third, as the world has become more complicated, people are demanding more specialized services—everything from

▼ EXHIBIT 13.1 The Service–Product Continuum

Doctor   Hotel   Dry cleaners   Restaurant   Apparel specialty store   Grocery store

Service dominant   Product dominant

(Doctor): © Dynamic Graphics/JupiterImages RF, (Hotel): © Jose Fuste Raga/Corbis, (Dry cleaners): © McGraw-Hill Education/Andrew Resek, photographer, (Restaurant): © John A. Rizzo/Getty Images RF, (Apparel): © Charles Bowman/Alamy RF, (Grocery store): © Photodisc/Getty Images RF

plumbers to personal trainers, from massage therapists to tax preparation specialists, from lawyers to travel and leisure specialists and even to health care providers. The aging population in particular has increased the need for health care specialists, including doctors, nurses, and caregivers in assisted living facilities and nursing homes, and many of those consumers want their specialists to provide personalized, dedicated services.

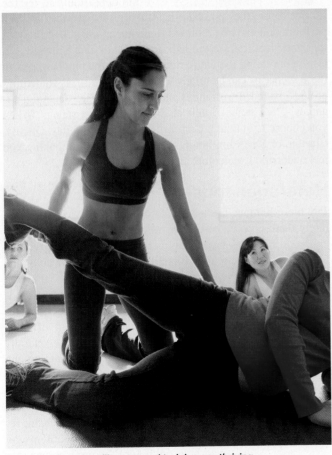

Specialized services like personal training are thriving.
© John Lund/Drew Kelly/Blend Images RF

| LO 13-1 | Describe how the marketing of services differs from the marketing of products. |

SERVICES MARKETING DIFFERS FROM PRODUCT MARKETING

The marketing of services differs from product marketing because of the four fundamental differences involved in services: Services are intangible, inseparable, heterogeneous, and perishable.[4] (See Exhibit 13.2.) This section examines these differences and discusses how they affect marketing strategies.

Since it is difficult to show a service, Six Flags evokes images in its advertising of happy families and friends enjoying a ride at one of its amusement parks.
© Ken James/Bloomberg/Getty Images

▼ **EXHIBIT 13.2** Core Differences between Services and Goods

A service that cannot be shown directly to potential customers also is difficult to promote. Marketers must creatively employ symbols and images to promote and sell services, as Six Flags does in using its advertising to evoke images of happy families and friends enjoying a roller coaster ride. Professional medical services provide appropriate images of personnel doing their jobs in white coats surrounded by high-tech equipment.

Some services have found excellent ways to make their offerings more tangible to their customers, as Adding Value 13.1 notes.

Inseparable Production and Consumption

Unlike a pair of jeans that may have been made halfway around the world six months prior to their purchase, services are produced and consumed at the same time; that is, service and consumption are **inseparable**. When getting a haircut, the customer is not only present but also may participate in the service process. Furthermore, the interaction with the service provider may have an important impact on the customer's perception of the service outcome. If the hairstylist appears to be having fun while cutting hair, it may affect the experience positively.

Because the service is inseparable from its consumption, customers rarely have the opportunity to try the service before they purchase it. And after the service has been performed, it can't be returned. Imagine telling your hairstylist that you want to have the hair around your ears trimmed as a test before doing the entire head. Because the purchase risk in these scenarios can be relatively high, service firms sometimes provide extended warranties and 100 percent satisfaction guarantees. The Choice Hotels chain, for instance, states: "When you choose to stay at a Comfort Inn, Comfort Suites, Quality, Clarion, or Sleep Inn hotel, we are committed to making you feel understood, welcome, and important."[5]

Intangible

As the title of this chapter implies, the most fundamental difference between a product and a service is that services are **intangible**—they cannot be touched, tasted, or seen like a pure product can. When you get a physical examination, you see and hear the doctor, but the service itself is intangible. This intangibility can prove highly challenging to marketers. For instance, it makes it difficult to convey the benefits of services—try describing whether the experience of visiting your dentist was good or bad and why. Service providers (e.g., physicians, dentists) therefore offer cues to help their customers experience and perceive their service more positively, such as a waiting room stocked with television sets, beverages, and comfortable chairs to create an atmosphere that appeals to the target market.

> "Because the service is inseparable from its consumption, customers rarely have the opportunity to try the service before they purchase it. And after the service has been performed, it can't be returned."

Heterogeneous

The more humans are needed to provide a service, the more likely there is to be **heterogeneity** or variability in the service's quality. A hairstylist may give bad haircuts in the morning because he or she went out the night before. Yet that stylist still may offer a better service than the undertrained stylist working in the next station over. A restaurant, which offers a mixture of services and products, generally can control its food quality but not the variability in food preparation or delivery. If a consumer has a problem with a product, it can be replaced, redone, destroyed, or, if it is already in the supply chain, recalled. In many cases, the problem can even be fixed before the product gets into consumers' hands. An inferior service

Adding Value 13.1

Carbonite's Secure Online Backup[i]

The prospect of losing data haunts virtually every computer user. And for good reason, especially among business users: The Federal Emergency Management Agency says 40 to 60 percent of small businesses fail to reopen after they suffer a severe data disruption. To address their fears of data loss or contamination, some users rely on external hard drives or disk storage. But that means they have to remember to perform the backup, and these options do not provide protection against a fire or other emergencies that destroy that hard drive along with the computer.

Online backups involve backing up the data on remote servers. This provides a more secure, less user-dependent alternative. Carbonite was one of the first entrants into this market. It provides simple, affordable, unlimited online backup for individual home users as well as small and medium businesses. With these target markets, Carbonite has kept its service, price, and customer support well within the reach of users. The basic yearly rate for a home customer is $59 per computer; a business pays $269 a year to cover all company computers.

Carbonite software runs invisibly on both Macs and PCs, performing backups automatically. With customers in more than 100 countries, the company has backed up more than 100 billion files and recovered nearly 10 billion of them in the past few years. For portable digital access, the company offers free mobile applications for BlackBerry, iPad, iPhone, and Android devices. In addition, it has expanded its capabilities as it has grown, such that it now helps clients in medical professions ensure the security of patients' information, in line with existing privacy regulations (e.g., the Health Insurance Portability and Accountability Act [HIPAA]).

To live up to its promise of hassle-free service, the company also offers free support by telephone, e-mail, and online live chat. It answers customer inquiries on its Twitter and Facebook sites, which then provide transparent proof of its handling of customer complaints. As for security, Carbonite's system is comparable to the safeguards used by major banks, credit card companies, and online retailers. All files are encrypted with two layers of technology, stored on

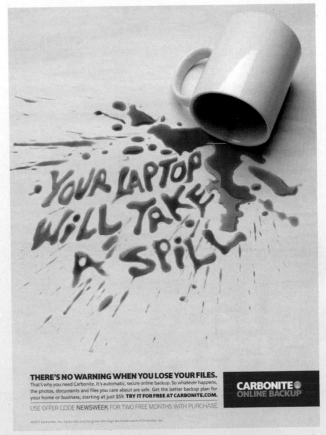

Carbonite backs up computer data on remote servers.
Courtesy Carbonite, Inc.

enterprise-grade servers to protect against mechanical disk failure, and kept in state-of-the-art data centers guarded 24 hours a day, 365 days a year. Personnel must pass through biometric scans and electronic pin coding to enter.

Carbonite thus has firmly established its market position by delivering a reliable, secure, easy-to-use service, combined with reasonable pricing and easily accessible technical support. As the shift to cloud computing intensifies, the company's main advantage may be its focus on staying abreast of user needs and expectations so it can keep all its customers happy.

---

can't be recalled; by the time the firm recognizes a problem, the damage has been done.

Marketers also can use the variable nature of services to their advantage. A micromarketing segmentation strategy can customize a service to meet customers' needs exactly (see Chapter 9). Exercise facilities might generally provide the same weights, machines, and mats, but at Planet Fitness, customers know that the gym explicitly seeks to offer a laidback, less intense setting. Planet Fitness actively avoids targeting hardcore gym rats with its service offering. Instead, local storefronts offer pizza nights and bowls of free Tootsie Rolls, varying the details to match the needs and preferences of their local

members. Thus each gym seeks to live up to the chain's overall promise to make going to exercise a pleasant experience rather than an intimidation festival.[6]

In an alternative approach, some service providers tackle the variability issue by replacing people with machines. For simple transactions such as getting cash, using an automated teller machine (ATM) is usually quicker and more convenient—and less variable—than waiting in line for a bank teller. Many retailers have installed kiosks in their stores. In addition to offering customers the opportunity to order merchandise not available in the store, kiosks can provide routine customer service, freeing employees to deal with more

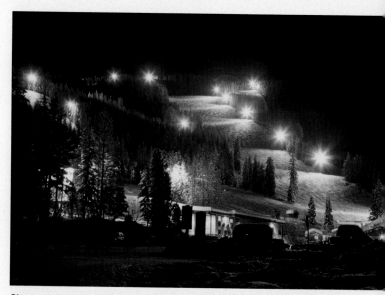

Since services are perishable, service providers like ski areas offer less expensive tickets at night to stimulate demand.
© Buddy Mays/Corbis

Planet Fitness' service offerings are customized to their customers' needs.
© Hand-out/PLANET FITNESS/Newscom

demanding customer requests and problems and reducing service variability. Kiosks can also be used to automate existing store services, such as gift registry management, rain checks, film drop-off, credit applications, and preordering service for bakeries and delicatessens.

Perishable

Services are **perishable** in that they cannot be stored for use in the future. You can't stockpile your membership at Planet Fitness like you could a six-pack of V8 juice, for instance. The perishability of services provides both challenges and opportunities to marketers in terms of the critical task of matching demand and supply. As long as the demand for and supply of the service match closely, there is no problem, but unfortunately, this perfect matching rarely occurs. A ski area, for instance, can be open as long as there is snow, even at night, but demand peaks on weekends and holidays, so ski areas often offer less expensive tickets during off-peak periods to stimulate demand. Airlines, cruise ships, movie theaters, and restaurants confront similar challenges and attack them in similar ways.

Certainly, providing great service is not easy, and it requires a diligent effort to analyze the service process piece by piece. In the next section, we examine what is known as the Gaps Model, which is designed to highlight those areas where customers believe they are getting less or poorer service than they should (the gaps) and how these gaps can be closed.

 check yourself

1. What are the four marketing elements that distinguish services from products?
2. Why can't we separate firms into just service or just product sellers?

LO 13-2 Discuss the four gaps in the Service Gaps Model.

PROVIDING GREAT SERVICE: THE GAPS MODEL

Customers have certain expectations about how a service should be delivered. When the delivery of that service fails to meet those expectations, a **service gap** results. The Service Gaps Model (Exhibit 13.3) is designed to encourage the systematic examination of all aspects of the service delivery process and prescribes the steps needed to develop an optimal service strategy.[7]

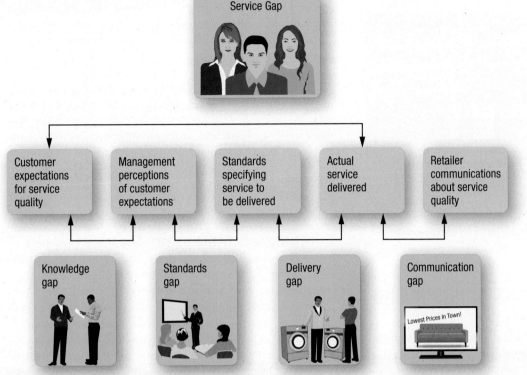

▼ EXHIBIT 13.3 Gaps Model for Improving Retail Service Quality

Service Gap

Customer expectations for service quality

Management perceptions of customer expectations

Standards specifying service to be delivered

Actual service delivered

Retailer communications about service quality

Knowledge gap

Standards gap

Delivery gap

Communication gap

Lowest Prices In Town!

Sources: Adapted from Valarie Zeithaml, A. Parasuraman, and Leonard Berry, *Delivering Quality Customer Service* (New York: The Free Press, 1990); and Valarie Zeithaml, Leonard Berry, and A. Parasuraman, "Communication and Control Processes in the Delivery of Service Quality," *Journal of Marketing* 52, no. 2 (April 1988), pp. 35–48.

knowledge gap A type of *service gap;* reflects the difference between customers' *expectations* and the firm's perception of those expectations.

standards gap A type of *service gap;* pertains to the difference between the firm's perceptions of customers' expectations and the service standards it sets.

delivery gap A type of *service gap;* the difference between the firm's service standards and the actual service it provides to customers.

communication gap A type of *service gap;* refers to the difference between the actual service provided to customers and the service that the firm's promotion program promises.

As Exhibit 13.3 shows, there are four service gaps:

1. The **knowledge gap** reflects the difference between customers' expectations and the firm's perception of those customer expectations. Firms can close this gap by determining what customers really want by doing research using marketing metrics such as service quality and the zone of tolerance (discussed later).

2. The **standards gap** pertains to the difference between the firm's perceptions of customers' expectations and the service standards it sets. By setting appropriate service standards, training employees to meet and exceed those standards, and measuring service performance, firms can attempt to close this gap.

3. The **delivery gap** is the difference between the firm's service standards and the actual service it provides to customers. This gap can be closed by getting employees to meet or exceed service standards when the service is being delivered by empowering service providers, providing support and incentives, and using technology where appropriate.[8]

4. The **communication gap** refers to the difference between the actual service provided to customers and the service that the firm's promotion program promises. If firms are more realistic about the services they can provide and at the same time manage customer expectations effectively, they generally can close this gap.

As we discuss the four gaps subsequently, we will apply them to the experience that Marcia Kessler had with a motel in Maine. She saw an ad for a package weekend that quoted a very reasonable daily rate and listed the free amenities available at Green Valley Motel: free babysitting services, a piano bar with a nightly singer, a free continental breakfast, a heated swimming pool, and newly decorated rooms. When she booked the room, Marcia discovered that the price advertised was not available during the weekend, and a three-day minimum stay was required. Because of the nice amenities, however, she went ahead. After checking in with a very unpleasant person at the front desk, Marcia and her husband found that their room appeared circa-1950 and had not been cleaned. When she complained, all she got was attitude from the assistant manager. Resigned to the fact that they were slated to spend the weekend, she decided to go for a swim. Unfortunately, the water was heated by Booth Bay and stood at around 50 degrees. No one was using the babysitting services because there were few young children at the resort. It turns out the piano bar singer was the second cousin of the owner, and he couldn't carry a tune, let alone play the piano very well. The continental breakfast must have come all the way from the Continent, because everything was stale and tasteless. Marcia couldn't wait to get home.

the service quality
Customers' perceptions of how well a service meets or exceeds their expectations.

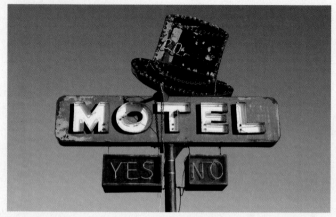

What service gaps did Marcia experience while on vacation at the motel in Maine?
© Sascha Burkard/Getty Images

The Knowledge Gap: Understanding Customer Expectations

An important early step in providing good service is knowing what the customer wants. It doesn't pay to invest in services that don't improve customer satisfaction. To reduce the

name, be aware of her dietary preferences, and to have placed fresh fruit of her choice and fresh-cut flowers in her room before she arrived. At the Green Valley Motel, she expected easy check-in/checkout, easy access to a major highway, a clean room with a comfortable bed, and a TV, at a bare minimum.

People's expectations also vary depending on the situation. If she had been traveling on business, the Green Valley Motel might have been fine (had the room at least been clean and modern), but if she were celebrating her 10th wedding anniversary, she probably would prefer the Ritz. Thus, the service provider needs to know and understand the expectations of the customers in its target market.

LO 13-3 | Examine the five service quality dimensions.

Evaluating Service Quality Using Well-Established Marketing Metrics To meet or exceed customers' expectations, marketers must determine what those expectations are. Yet because of their intangibility, **the service quality**, or customers' perceptions of how well a service meets or exceeds their expectations, is often difficult for customers to evaluate.[10] Customers generally use five distinct service dimensions to determine overall service quality: reliability, responsiveness, assurance, empathy, and tangibles (see Exhibit 13.4).

> ❝ It doesn't pay to invest in services that don't improve customer satisfaction. ❞

knowledge gap, firms must understand customers' expectations. To understand those expectations, firms undertake customer research and increase the interaction and communication between managers and employees.

Customers' expectations are based on their knowledge and experiences.[9] Marcia's expectations were that her room at the motel in Maine would be ready when she got there, the swimming pool would be heated, the singer would be able to sing, and the breakfast would be fresh. Not a lot to expect, but in this extreme example, the Green Valley Motel was suffering a severe knowledge gap, perhaps based on its assumption that being on the ocean in Maine was enough. If the resort never understood her expectations, it is unlikely it would ever be able to meet them.

Expectations vary according to the type of service. Marcia's expectations might have been higher, for instance, if she were staying at a Ritz-Carlton rather than the Green Valley Motel. At the Ritz, she might have expected employees to know her by

▼ **EXHIBIT 13.4** Building Blocks of Service Quality

5 Reliability:
The ability to perform the service dependably and accurately.

4 Responsiveness:
The willingness to help customers and provide prompt service.

3 Assurance:
The knowledge of and courtesy by employees and their ability to convey trust and confidence.

2 Empathy:
The caring, individualized attention provided to customers.

1 Tangibles:
The appearance of physical facilities, equipment, personnel, and communication materials.

Adding Value 13.2 describes how the Broadmoor Hotel maintains its five-star rating by focusing on these five service characteristics.

If you were to apply the five service dimensions to your own decision-making process, for instance, when you selected a college—which provides you the service of education—you might find results like those in Exhibit 13.5.

If your expectations include an individualized experience at a state-of-the-art institution, perhaps University B is a better alternative for you. But if you are relying heavily on academic performance and career placement from your university experience, then University A might be a better choice in terms of the five service dimensions. If a strong culture and tradition are important to you, University A offers this type of environment. What your expectations are has a lot to do with your perception of how your university falls within these service dimensions.

Marketing research (see Chapter 10) provides a means to better understand consumers' service expectations and their perceptions of service quality. In Marketing Analytics 13.1, we describe how Kroger uses data to learn about customers' expectations. This research can be extensive and expensive, or it can be integrated into a firm's everyday interactions with customers. Today, most service firms have developed voice-of-customer programs and employ ongoing marketing research to assess how well they are meeting their customers' expectations. A systematic

Adding Value 13.2

The Broadmoor Manages Service Quality for a Five-Star Rating[ii]

Established in 1891 as a gambling casino and transformed into a grand resort in 1918, the Broadmoor, in Colorado Springs, Colorado, is one of the world's premier resorts. It has received a record 50 consecutive years of five-star ratings from the *Forbes Travel Guide*. Perry Goodbar, former vice president of sales and marketing for the Broadmoor, emphasizes, "It's the people who truly make this place special. Exceptional service quality begins with exceptional people." Some aspects of its service quality are as follows:

Reliability Every new Broadmoor employee, before ever encountering a customer, attends a two-and-a-half-day orientation session and receives an employee handbook. Making and keeping promises to customers is a central part of this orientation. Employees are trained always to give an estimated time for service, whether it be room service, laundry service, or simply how long it will take to be seated at one of the resort's restaurants. When an employee makes a promise, he or she keeps that promise. Employees are trained to never guess if they don't know the answer to a question. Inaccurate information only frustrates customers. When an employee is unable to answer a question accurately, he or she immediately contacts someone who can.

Assurance The Broadmoor conveys trust by empowering its employees. An example of an employee empowerment policy is the service recovery program. If a guest problem arises, employees are given discretionary resources to rectify the problem or present the customer with something special to help mollify them. For example, if a meal is delivered and there's a mistake in the order or how it was prepared, a server can offer the guest a free item such as a dessert or, if the service was well below expectations, simply take care of the bill. Managers then review each situation to understand the nature of the problem and help prevent it from occurring again.

Tangibles One of the greatest challenges for the Broadmoor in recent years has been updating rooms built in the early part of the 20th century to meet the needs of 21st-century visitors. To accomplish this, it spent millions in improvements, renovating rooms, and adding a new outdoor pool complex.

Empathy One approach used to demonstrate empathy is personalizing communications. Employees are instructed to always address a guest by name, if possible. To accomplish this, employees are trained to listen and observe carefully to determine a guest's name. Subtle sources for this information include convention name tags, luggage ID tags, credit cards, or checks. In addition, all phones within the Broadmoor display a guest's room number and name on a screen.

Responsiveness Every employee is instructed to follow the HEART model of taking care of problems. First, employees must "Hear what a guest has to say." Second, they must "Empathize with them" and then "Apologize for the situation." Fourth, they must "Respond to the guest's needs" by "Taking action and following up."

The Broadmoor in Colorado Springs, Colorado, is known for exceptional service quality.
Courtesy The Broadmoor

voice-of-customer (VOC) program
An ongoing marketing research system that collects customer inputs and integrates them into managerial decisions.

zone of tolerance
The area between customers' expectations regarding their desired service and the minimum level of acceptable service—that is, the difference between what the customer really wants and what he or she will accept before going elsewhere.

voice-of-customer (VOC) program collects customer inputs and integrates them into managerial decisions.

| LO 13-4 | Explain the zone of tolerance. |

An important marketing metric to evaluate how well firms perform on the five service quality dimensions (again see Exhibit 13.4) is the **zone of tolerance**, which refers to the area between customers' expectations regarding their desired service and the minimum level of acceptable service—that is,

▼ **EXHIBIT 13.5** Collegiate Service Dimensions

	University A	University B
Reliability	Offers sound curriculum with extensive placement services and internships.	Curriculum covers all the basics but important courses are not always available. Career placement is haphazard at best.
Responsiveness	Slow to respond to application. Very structured visitation policy. Rather inflexible with regard to personal inquiries or additional meetings.	Quick response during application process. Open visitation policy. Offers variety of campus resources to help with decision making.
Assurance	Staff seems very confident in reputation and services.	Informal staff who convey enthusiasm for institution.
Empathy	Seems to process student body as a whole rather than according to individual needs or concerns.	Very interested in providing a unique experience for each student.
Tangibles	Very traditional campus with old-world look and feel. Facilities are manicured. Dorm rooms are large, but bathrooms are a little old.	New campus with modern architecture. Campus is less manicured. Dorm rooms are spacious with newer bathrooms.

Marketing Analytics 13.1

Using Analytics to Reduce Wait Time at Kroger[iii]

Shopping for groceries is rarely considered a pleasant task. But what makes the experience so odious? As Kroger found out when it asked customers, the answer is often the long checkout lines. To help alleviate the problem, it began analyzing customer data to find an answer to a simple question: What would happen if it could open up a lane exactly when needed? The answer was that it could significantly improve customer satisfaction. So Kroger developed QueVision.

QueVision combines infrared sensors over store doors and cash registers, predictive analytics, and real-time data feeds from point-of-sale systems to calculate how many registers are needed and what the actual wait times are, all in real time. Wait times appear on a screen at the front of the store. The overall goal of the combined system is to ensure there is never more than one person ahead of any shopper in the checkout line.

This technology has been so successful that it has cut the average wait time for customers from more than 4 minutes to less than 30 seconds. QueVision also has had some unexpected positive consequences, in the form of happier employees. Friendly associates are really important for defining customer-oriented metrics. Although the math might not have predicted it, the cashier friendliness metric, as measured by customer surveys, has improved throughout the company by approximately 24 percent. Shorter lines makes

customers happy, and when employees encounter happy customers, they're happier too. Kroger also uses its QueVision data in more detailed simulations. It has correlated enough data to keep people moving in the front of stores, including checkout lines, even in stores with unusual layouts. QueVision data also have helped Kroger evaluate new shopping systems, such as self-checkout.

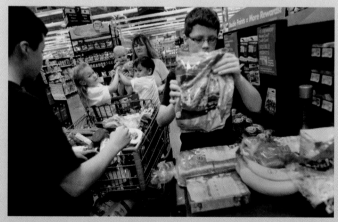

Grocery shoppers really hate long checkout lines. So Kroger developed a system to calculate how many registers are needed and what the actual wait times are, all in real time.
© ZUMA Press, Inc/Alamy

the difference between what the customer really wants and what he or she will accept before going elsewhere. To define the zone of tolerance, firms ask a series of questions about each service quality dimension that relate to

- The desired and expected level of service for each dimension, from low to high.

- Customers' perceptions of how well the focal service performs and how well a competitive service performs, from low to high.

- The importance of each service quality dimension.

Exhibit 13.6 illustrates the results of such an analysis for Lou's Local Diner, a family-owned restaurant. The rankings on the left are based on a nine-point scale, on which 1 is low and 9 is high. The length of each box illustrates the zone of tolerance for each service quality dimension. For instance, according to the short length of the reliability box, customers expect a fairly high level of reliability (top of the box) and will accept only a fairly high level of reliability (bottom of the box). On the other end of the scale, customers expect a high level of assurance (top of the box) but will also accept a fairly low level (bottom of the box). This difference is to be expected because the customers also were asked to assign

Lou's Local Diner always rates higher than its primary competitor, Well-Known National Chain, on each service quality dimension.
© McGraw-Hill Education/Gideon Kindall, photographer

an important score to the five service quality dimensions so that the total equals 100 percent (see bottom of Exhibit 13.6). Looking at the average importance score, we conclude that reliability is relatively important to these customers but assurance is not. So customers have a fairly narrow zone of tolerance for service dimensions that are fairly important to them and a wider range of tolerance for those service dimensions that are less important. Also note that Lou's Local Diner always rates higher than its primary competitor, Well-Known National Chain, on each dimension.

Further note that Well-Known National Chain scores below the zone of tolerance on the tangibles dimension, meaning that customers are not willing to accept the way the restaurant looks and smells. Lou's Local Diner, in contrast, performs above the zone of tolerance on the responsiveness dimension—maybe even too well. Lou's may wish to conduct further research to verify which responsiveness aspects it is performing so well, and then consider toning those aspects down. For example, being responsive to customers' desires to have a diner that serves breakfast 24 hours a day can be expensive and may not add any further value to Lou's Diner, because customers would accept more limited times.

A very straightforward and inexpensive method of collecting consumers' perceptions of service quality is to gather them at the time of the sale.

▼ **EXHIBIT 13.6** Customers' Evaluation of Service Quality

■ Lou's Local Diner

▲ Competitor: Well-Known National Chain

■ Customers' zone of tolerance

Importance scores	40 points	25 points	20 points	10 points	5 points	Total = 100 points

Dimensions of service quality

Note: The scale ranges from a 9 indicating very high service quality on a given service quality dimension, to a 1 indicating very low service quality.

" A VERY STRAIGHTFORWARD AND INEXPENSIVE METHOD OF COLLECTING CONSUMERS' PERCEPTIONS OF SERVICE QUALITY IS TO GATHER THEM AT THE TIME OF THE SALE. "

Service providers can ask customers how they liked the service—though customers often are reticent to provide negative feedback directly to the person who provided the service—or distribute a simple questionnaire. Regardless of how information is collected, companies must take care not to lose it, which can happen if there is no effective mechanism for filtering it up to the key decision makers. Furthermore, in some cases, customers cannot effectively evaluate the service until several days or weeks later. Automobile dealers, for instance, often call their customers a week after they perform a service such as an oil change to assess their service quality.

Another excellent method for assessing customers' expectations is making effective use of customer complaint behavior. Even if complaints are handled effectively to solve customers' problems, the essence of the complaint is too often lost on managers. For instance, an airline established a policy that customer service reps could not discuss any issues involving fees to travel agents with customers. So when a customer calls to complain about these fees, the representative just changes the subject, and management therefore never finds out about the complaint.[11]

Even firms with the best formal research mechanisms in place must put managers on the frontlines occasionally to interact directly with the customers. The late Sam Walton, founder of Walmart, participated in and advocated this strategy, which is known as "management by walking around."[12] Unless the managers who make the service quality decisions know what their service providers are facing on a day-to-day basis, and unless they can talk directly to the customers with whom those service providers interact, any customer service program they create will not be as good as it could be.

Service providers, like this room service delivery person at a hotel, generally want to do a good job, but they need to be trained to know what exactly a good job entails.
© Chris Ryan/OJO Images/Getty Images RF

The Standards Gap: Setting Service Standards

Getting back to the Green Valley Motel in Maine for a moment, suppose because of a number of complaints or because business was falling off, it set out to determine customers' service expectations and gained a pretty good idea of them. The next step would be to set its service standards accordingly and develop systems to meet the customers' service expectations. How, for instance, can it make sure that every room is cleaned and ready by an optimum time of day in the eyes of the customers, or that the breakfast is checked for freshness and quality every day? To consistently deliver service that meets customers' expectations, firms must set specific, measurable goals. For instance, for the Green Valley Motel, the most efficient process might have been to start cleaning rooms at 8:00 a.m. and finish by 5:00 p.m. But many guests want to sleep late, and new arrivals want to get into their room as soon as they arrive, often before 5:00. So a customer-oriented standard would mandate that the rooms get cleaned between 10:00 a.m. and 2:00 p.m.

> " Service providers generally want to do a good job as long as they know what is expected of them. "

Service providers generally want to do a good job as long as they know what is expected of them. Motel employees should be shown, for instance, exactly how managers expect them to clean a room and what specific tasks they are responsible for performing. In general, more employees will buy into a quality-oriented process if they are involved in setting the goals. For instance, suppose an important employee of the motel objects to disposable plastic cups and suggests actual drinking glasses in the rooms would be classier as well as more ecological. There might be a cost–benefit trade-off to consider here, but if management listens to her and makes the change in this case, it should likely make the employee all the more committed to other tasks involved in cleaning and preparing rooms.

The employees must be thoroughly trained not only to complete their specific tasks but also how to treat guests, and the manager needs to set an example of high service standards, which will permeate throughout the organization. The kind of attitude Marcia got, for instance, when she registered a complaint with the assistant manager at the Green Valley is not a recipe for generating repeat customers and should not be tolerated. For frontline service employees under stress, however, pleasant interactions with customers do not always come naturally. Although people can be taught specific tasks related to their jobs, this is not easily extended to interpersonal relations. But it is simply not enough to tell employees to be nice or do what customers want. A quality goal should be specific, such as: Greet every customer/guest you encounter with "Good morning/afternoon/evening, Sir or Ma'am." Try to greet customers by name.

The Delivery Gap: Delivering Service Quality

The delivery gap is where the rubber meets the road, where the customer directly interacts with the service provider. Even if there are adequate standards in place, the employees are well trained, and management is committed to meeting or exceeding customers' service expectations, there can still be delivery gaps. It could very well have been that Marcia experienced several delivery gaps at the Green Valley Motel. It could have been that the unclean room, the assistant manager's attitude, the unheated swimming pool, the poor piano bar singer, or the stale food resulted from unforeseen or unusual circumstances. Although some of these issues such as an unclean room or the attitude Marcia encountered should have been avoided, it is possible that the motel had a power outage resulting in the unheated swimming pool, the regular piano bar singer was ill, and the breakfast was stale because of a missed delivery. The maid could not vacuum the room because of the lack of power, and the assistant manager felt assaulted on all sides by these problems. But the result was a lost customer. Even if there are no other gaps, a delivery gap always results in a service failure.

Delivery gaps can be reduced when employees are empowered to spontaneously act in the customers' and the firm's best interests when problems or crises are experienced. Such empowerment might have saved the day for Marcia and the Green Valley Motel. Empowerment means employees are supported in their efforts to do their jobs effectively.[13]

Empowering Service Providers

In the service context, **empowerment** means allowing employees to make decisions about how service is provided to customers. When frontline employees are authorized to make decisions to help their customers, service quality generally improves. Empowerment becomes more important when the service is more individualized. Nordstrom provides an overall objective—satisfy customer needs—and then encourages employees to do whatever is necessary to achieve the objective. For example, a Nordstrom shoe sales associate decided to break up two pairs of shoes, one a size 10 and the other a size 10½, to sell a hard-to-fit customer. Although the other two shoes were unsalable and therefore it made for an unprofitable sale, the customer purchased five other pairs that day and became a loyal Nordstrom customer as a result. Empowering service providers with only a rule like "Use your best judgment" (as Nordstrom does) might cause chaos. At Nordstrom, department managers avoid abuses by coaching and training salespeople to understand what "Use your best judgment" specifically means.

Support and Incentives for Employees

To ensure that service is delivered properly, management needs to support the service providers in several ways and give them incentives. This is basic. A service provider's job can often be difficult, especially when customers are unpleasant or less than reasonable. But the service provider cannot be rude or offensive just because the customer is. The old cliché "Service with a smile" remains the best approach, but for this to work, employees must feel supported.

First, managers and coworkers should provide **emotional support** to service providers by demonstrating a concern for their well-being and standing behind their decisions. Because it can be very disconcerting when a server is abused by a customer who believes her food was improperly prepared, for instance, restaurant managers must be supportive and help the employee get through his or her emotional reaction to the berating experienced.[14] Such support can extend to empowering the server to rectify the situation by giving the customer new food and a free dessert, in which case the manager must understand the server's decision, not punish him for giving away too much.

Second, service providers require **instrumental support**— the systems and equipment to deliver the service properly. Many retailers provide state-of-the-art instrumental support for their service providers. In-store kiosks help sales associates provide more detailed and complete product information and enable them to make sales of merchandise that is either not carried in the store or is temporarily out of stock.

Third, the support that managers provide must be consistent and coherent throughout the organization. Patients expect physicians to provide great patient care using state-of-the-art procedures and medications, but because they are tied to managed-care systems (health maintenance organizations [HMOs]), many doctors must squeeze more people into their office hours and prescribe less optimal, less expensive courses of treatment. These conflicting goals can be very frustrating to patients.

Finally, a key part of any customer service program is providing rewards to employees for their excellent service. Numerous firms have developed a service reputation by ensuring that their employees are themselves recognized for recognizing the

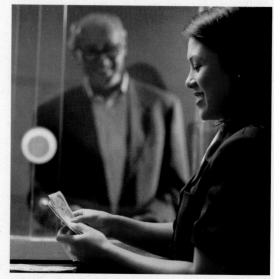

Which bank has better customer service: the one with self-checkout (left), or the bank offering a face-to-face interaction with the customer? It depends on whom you ask.

(Left): © Picturenet/Blend Images/Getty Images RF, (Right): © Keith Brofsky/Photodisc/Getty Images RF

value the firm places on customer service. Travelocity, for example, features employees who champion the customer service experience in a weekly e-mail. Believing that engaged employees are the key to customer satisfaction, it works to create an atmosphere that reinforces the commitment to customers by encouraging employees to nominate colleagues who exemplify its commitment to customers. Through constant feedback about who is serving the customer best, as well as smaller events such as monthly lunches with the CEO for selected employees, Travelocity creates a business environment that recognizes and rewards customer service.[15] The results for Travelocity have been a wealth of awards, such as a top ranking on the Customer Online Respect Survey and a designation as the World's Leading Travel Internet Site for several consecutive years.[16]

Use of Technology As our chapter opener confirmed, technology can be employed to reduce delivery gaps. Technology has become an increasingly important facilitator of the delivery of services. Using technology to facilitate service delivery can provide many benefits, such as access to a wider variety of services, a greater degree of control by the customer over the services, and the ability to obtain information. Social and Mobile Marketing 13.1 describes one such option. The use of technology also improves the service provider's efficiency and reduces servicing costs; in some cases, it can lead to a competitive advantage over less service-oriented competitors.[17]

Technological advances that help close the delivery gap are expanding. Salons and cosmetics counters use kiosks to show customers how they would look with different beauty products and various hair colors. Stores enable customers to scan price tags and then have a kiosk recommend complementary items. Touchscreen terminals at tables in restaurants, from Uno Chicago Grill to Applebee's to Chili's, let customers order food and play games from the comfort of their own table.[18] The technological delivery of services can cause problems though. Some customers either do not embrace the idea of replacing a human with a machine for business interactions or have problems using the technology. In other cases, the technology may not perform adequately, such as ATMs that run out of money or are out of order. Supermarket self-checkout devices are too challenging for some customers.

The Communications Gap: Communicating the Service Promise

Poor communication between marketers and their customers can result in a mismatch between an ad campaign's or a salesperson's promises and the service the firm can actually offer. Although firms have difficulty controlling service quality because it can vary from day to day and provider to provider, they have nearly constant control over how they communicate their service package to their customers. This control involves a significant responsibility, as Ethical and Societal Dilemma 13.1 notes.

> "Although firms have difficulty controlling service quality because it can vary from day to day and provider to provider, they have nearly constant control over how they communicate their service package to their customers."

Social & Mobile Marketing 13.1
Linking American Express Members to Purchases[iv]

Even when online retailers offer great merchandise, the customer service they offer can be a deciding factor in their success. But relating to customers also can be highly variable. How do you mobilize an entire company to speak with one voice and meet various customers' needs, so that the service provision consistently meets, or exceeds, customers' service standards?

For American Express, the solution is to make it easy for its members to connect with the offers they want most from a wide variety of merchants. To start, American Express made it possible for cardholders to load special offers from various sellers onto their credit card accounts by using specific hashtags when they link with American Express's Twitter account. For example, if someone was looking for a new Sony television, she could visit American Express, post "#sony," and gain access to any special deals the company might have on offer for cardholders that week.

Then American Express expanded these delivery options, such that with the specific, special hashtags it had provided to cardholders, customers could make purchases from partners such as Amazon and Microsoft.

Beyond just product purchases, in a partnership with the travel website TripAdvisor, American Express enabled its members to link their credit cards to their travel profiles. Once they booked a trip, members received special offers for local hotels, car rental agencies, and so on. Of course, they could purchase these add-on options readily because their credit card already was linked to the site.

American Express facilitates a conversation between its members and its merchants by providing special offers on Twitter.
Courtesy American Express

> ## A RELATIVELY EASY WAY TO MANAGE CUSTOMER EXPECTATIONS IS TO COORDINATE HOW THE EXPECTATION IS CREATED AND THE WAY THE SERVICE IS PROVIDED.

If a firm promises more than it can deliver, customers' expectations won't be met. An advertisement may lure a customer into a service situation once, but if the service doesn't deliver on the promise, the customer will never return. Dissatisfied customers also are likely to tell others about the underperforming service, using word of mouth or, increasingly, the Internet, which has become an important channel for dissatisfied customers to vent their frustrations.

The communications gap can be reduced by managing customer expectations and by promising only what you can deliver, or possibly even a little less.[19] Suppose you need an operation, and the surgeon explains, "You'll be out of the hospital in five days and back to your normal routine in a month." You have the surgery and feel well enough to leave the hospital three days later. Two weeks after that, you're playing tennis again. Clearly, you will tend to think your surgeon is a genius. However, regardless of the operation's success, if you had to stay in the hospital for 10 days and it took you two months to recover, you would undoubtedly be upset.

A relatively easy way to manage customer expectations is to coordinate how the expectation is created and the way the service is provided. Expectations typically are created through promotions, advertising, or personal selling. Delivery is

Fake Reviews[v]

Yelp, TripAdvisor, and Amazon have all made user ratings and reviews a familiar—and even essential—part of the online toolbox for shoppers and other consumers. From the consumer's perspective, what better preparation could there be for a major purchase than to see what other, objective customers have to say about the product or service under consideration?

For retailers and service professionals, online reviews offer a huge benefit too. For some companies, especially small service providers that cannot afford much marketing, online reviews function as a low-cost form of advertising. A business seeking to meet or exceed customer expectations receives valuable, candid feedback from customers, which it can use to measure how well it is meeting customer expectations. Some firms even use this feedback in their formal marketing research process to improve company operations.

From this straightforward perspective, honest reviews are the most valuable resource that exists in review sites. But such straightforwardness is not enough for companies that provide poor service and attract reviews befitting their abilities. Rather than improving their service, many of these companies engage in the unethical practice of writing fake reviews themselves, hiring dedicated companies to flood sites with positive fake reviews, or bribing customers to pad their comments with positive assertions. Considering this unethical practice just another example—though in a modern form—of false advertising, state and federal regulators are taking action to ensure that such deceptive advertising does not pay. Moreover, as customers get wise to these moves, companies that fake their reviews often get caught.

VIP Deals, an online retailer that sells leather cases for digital tablets on Amazon,

Online reviews like this one from Yelp benefit consumers, retailers, and service providers as long as the reviews are written by unbiased customers.
© Yelp.com

invited its customers to post reviews—and promised that if those reviews were positive, the customer would receive a complete refund. Within weeks, nearly all of the company's 355 online reviews gave the VIP Deals leather case four or five stars. But Amazon guidelines prohibit compensation for customer reviews, and the VIP Deals page soon disappeared.

A leather case for your iPad is one thing. Accurate, truthful information takes on paramount importance for a service like plastic surgery. But Lifestyle Lift seemed to disregard customers' expectations that they could receive truthful information. When unhappy customers started posting too many negative comments on its website, the company launched a coverup rather than investigating the complaints to help its physicians and staff address the problems.

On bogus websites, fictitious posters gave high praise to the company while also asserting that previously posted complaints had been phony. The state of New York soon filed suit and prompted a $300,000 settlement from Lifestyle Lift. New York's attorney general also has announced that his office will be pursuing such false advertisers more actively in the future, doling out stringent penalties as it finds them.

Crowd-sourced online opinions of consumers have become a major source of information about products and services (recall our discussion of crowd-sourcing in Chapter 11). When that information is authentic, it serves consumers and companies both. But when companies manipulate online reviews, it seems as if all of society is harmed. What—if anything—should be done about it?

another function altogether. If a salesperson promises a client that an order can be delivered in one day, and that delivery actually takes a week, the client will be disappointed. However, if the salesperson coordinates the order with those responsible for the service delivery, the client's expectations likely will be met.

Customer expectations can be managed when the service is delivered. Recorded messages tell customers who have phoned a company with a query how many minutes they will have to wait before the next operator is available. Sellers automatically inform online customers of any items that are out of stock. Whether online or in a store, retailers can warn their customers to shop early during a sale because supplies of the sale item are limited. People are generally reasonable when they are warned that some aspect of the service may be below their expectations. They just don't like surprises!

Service Quality and Customer Satisfaction and Loyalty

Good service quality leads to satisfied and loyal customers. As we discussed in Chapter 6, customers inevitably wind up their purchase decision process by undertaking a postpurchase evaluation. This evaluation after the purchase may produce three outcomes: satisfaction, dissonance, and loyalty (see again Exhibit 6.3 in Chapter 6). Dissonance may just be a passing emotion that is overcome; we will discuss recovery from an actual service failure in the next section. Satisfaction, on the other hand, often leads to loyalty.

Assuming that none of the service gaps that we have discussed occur, or at least are not too wide, customers should be more or less satisfied. Surveys of customers that ask them to identify the retailer that provides the best customer service thus often show some consistency. A service provider that does a good job one year is likely to keep customers satisfied the next year too. Some of the best service providers year after year include Amazon, Zappos, L.L.Bean, and Nordstrom.

If a firm not only minimizes but also eliminates any service gaps, customers are likely to exhibit significant loyalty to it.

Customers want to continue receiving such superior service and have no desire to go elsewhere for the offerings it provides them.

check yourself

1. Explain the four service gaps identified by the Service Gaps Model.
2. List at least two ways to overcome each of the four service gaps.

LO 13-5 Identify three service recovery strategies.

SERVICE RECOVERY

Despite a firm's best efforts, sometimes service providers fail to meet customer expectations. When this happens, the best course of action is to attempt to make amends with the customer and learn from the experience. Of course, it is best to avoid a service failure altogether, but when a failure does occur, the firm has a unique opportunity to demonstrate its customer

> "Of course, it is best to avoid a service failure altogether, but when a failure does occur, the firm has a unique opportunity to demonstrate its customer commitment."

Nordstrom consistently is ranked at the top of customer satisfaction surveys.
© Greg Smith/Corbis

commitment. Effective service recovery efforts can significantly increase customer satisfaction, purchase intentions, and positive word of mouth, though customers' postrecovery satisfaction levels usually fall lower than their satisfaction level prior to the service failure.

Remember the Green Valley Motel in Maine? It could have made amends with Marcia Kessler after its service failures if it had taken some relatively simple, immediate steps: The assistant manager could have apologized for his bad behavior and quickly upgraded her to a suite and/or given her a free night's lodging for a future stay. The motel could also have given her a free lunch or dinner to make up for the bad breakfast. Alternatively, the assistant manager could have asked Marcia how he could resolve the situation and worked with her to come up with an equitable solution. None of these actions would have cost the motel much money.

Had it used the customer lifetime value approach we described in Chapter 10, the motel would have realized that by not taking action, it lost Marcia as a customer forever. Over the next few years, she could have been responsible for several thousand dollars in sales. Instead, Marcia is now likely to spread negative word of mouth about the motel to her friends, family, and through online review sites, such as Yelp.com, because of its failure to recover. Effective service recovery thus demands (1) listening to the customers and involving them in the service recovery, (2) providing a fair solution, and (3) resolving the problem quickly.[20]

Listening to the Customers and Involving Them in the Service Recovery

Firms often don't find out about service failures until a customer complains. Whether the firm has a formal complaint department or the complaint is offered directly to the service provider, the customer must have the opportunity to air the complaint completely, and the firm must listen carefully to what he or she is saying.

Customers can become very emotional about a service failure, whether the failure is serious (a botched surgical operation) or minor (the wrong change at a restaurant). In many cases, the customer may just want to be heard, and the service provider should give the customer all the time he or she needs to get it out. The very process of describing a perceived wrong to a sympathetic listener or the Twitterverse is therapeutic in and of itself. Service providers therefore should welcome the opportunity to be that sympathetic ear, listen carefully, and appear (and actually be) eager to rectify the situation to ensure it doesn't happen again.[21]

When the company and the customer work together, the outcome is often better than either could achieve on their own. This co-creation logic applies especially well to service recovery. A service failure is a negative experience, but when customers participate in its resolution, it results in a more positive outcome than simply listening to their complaint and providing a preapproved set of potential solutions that may satisfy them.

Suppose, for instance, that when you arrived at the airport in San Francisco, your flight had been overbooked and you were bumped. Of course, good customer service required the ticket agent to listen to your frustration and help provide a fair solution. But the most obvious potential solution from the airline's perspective might not have been the best solution for you. It might have been inclined to put you on the next available flight, which would be a red-eye that left at midnight and got you to New York at 6:30 a.m. But if you don't sleep well on planes and

you have an important business meeting the next afternoon, the best solution from your perspective would be to have the airline put you up in an airport hotel so you can get a good night's sleep and then put you on an early morning flight that would get you to New York in time for your meeting, well-rested and ready to go. Thus, by working closely with you to understand your needs, the ticket agent would be able to co-create a great solution to the service failure.

Finding a Fair Solution

Most people realize that mistakes happen. But when they happen, customers want to be treated fairly, whether that means *distributive* or *procedural* fairness.[22] Their perception of what "fair" means is based on their previous experience with other firms, how they have seen other customers treated, material they have read, and stories recounted by their friends.

Distributive Fairness **Distributive fairness** pertains to a customer's perception of the benefits he or she received compared with the costs (inconvenience or loss). Customers want to be compensated a fair amount for a perceived loss that resulted from a service failure. If, for instance, a person arrives at the airport gate and finds her flight is overbooked, she may believe that taking the next flight that day and receiving a travel voucher is adequate compensation for the inconvenience. But if no flights are available until the next day, the traveler may require additional compensation, such as overnight accommodations, meals, and a round-trip ticket to be used at a later date.[23]

The key to distributive fairness, of course, is listening carefully to the customer. One customer, traveling on vacation, may be satisfied with a travel voucher, whereas another may need to get to the destination on time because of a business appointment. Regardless of how the problem is solved, customers typically want tangible restitution—in this case, to get to their destination—not just an apology. If providing tangible restitution isn't possible, the next best thing is to assure the customer that steps are being taken to prevent the failure from recurring.

> Regardless of how the problem is solved, customers typically want tangible restitution—not just an apology.

Procedural Fairness With regard to complaints, **procedural fairness** refers to the perceived fairness of the process used to resolve them. Customers want efficient complaint procedures over whose outcomes they have some influence. Customers tend to believe they have been treated fairly if the service providers follow specific company guidelines. Nevertheless, rigid adherence to rules can have deleterious effects. Have you ever returned an item to a store, even a very inexpensive item, and been told that the return needed a manager's approval? The process likely took several minutes and irritated everyone in the checkout line. Furthermore, most managers' cursory inspection of the item or the situation would not catch a fraudulent return. In a case like this, the procedure the company uses to handle a return probably overshadows any potential positive outcomes. Therefore, as we noted previously, service providers should be empowered with some procedural flexibility to solve customer complaints.

A no-questions-asked return policy has been offered as a customer service by many retailers such as L.L.Bean. But because of its high cost as a result of customers abusing the policy, many retailers such as Bean's competitor, REI, have modified their return policies.[24] Some large retailers now limit their returns to 90 days, considered a reasonable amount of time for customers to return an item. Others will only grant a store credit based on the lowest selling price for the item if the customer doesn't have a receipt. In addition, for some consumer electronics products that have been opened, customers must pay a 15 percent restocking fee.

Resolving Problems Quickly

The longer it takes to resolve a service failure, the more irritated the customer will become and the more people he or she is likely to tell about the problem. To resolve service failures quickly, firms need clear policies, adequate training for their employees, and empowered employees. Health insurance companies, for instance, have made a concerted effort in recent years to avoid service failures that occur because customers' insurance claims have not been handled quickly or to the customers' satisfaction. ■

check yourself

1. Why is service recovery so important to companies?
2. What can companies do to recover from a service failure?

CONNECT Increase your engagement and learning with Connect Marketing.

These Connect activities, available only through your Connect course, have been designed to make the following concepts more meaningful and applicable:

▶ Employee and Customer Services: Wegmans Case Analysis

▶ Services Marketing versus Product Marketing: Click and Drag Activity

▶ Service Excellence: Netflix Video Case

▶ Service Quality: iSeeit! Video

SMARTBOOK™   iSeeit!

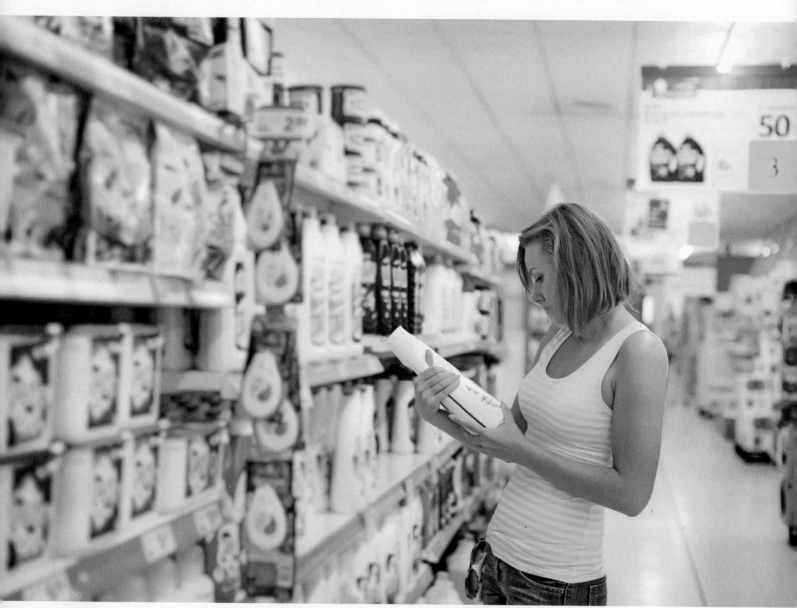

Chapter fourteen

pricing concepts for establishing value

P ricing is a key part of the value proposition for any purchase. After all, among the other definitions we have used in this book, value reflects the relationship between benefits and costs. When the economy sours, and consumer income drops, no sticker prices can escape sharp scrutiny, especially in the supermarket. For example, shoppers on tight budgets still need to buy cleaning supplies, but when they do so, they tend to be much more sensitive to the prices for the various detergents their household needs.

In such price-sensitive and highly competitive markets, companies must be creative in finding ways to balance profits and consumers. Procter & Gamble (P&G) had long floated high above its competitors in the sea of laundry detergents, with its Tide brand enjoying a 38 percent share of the laundry soap market in North America.[1] However, a wave of lower-priced competitors crashed onto P&G when consumers began looking more actively for better deals. Thrifty shoppers began turning from their trusty Tide brand

LEARNING OBJECTIVES

After reading this chapter, you should be able to:

LO 14-1 List the four pricing orientations.

LO 14-2 Explain the relationship between price and quantity sold.

LO 14-3 Explain price elasticity.

LO 14-4 Describe how to calculate a product's break-even point.

LO 14-5 Indicate the four types of price competitive levels.

LO 14-6 Describe the difference between an everyday low price strategy (EDLP) and a high/low price strategy.

LO 14-7 Describe the pricing strategies used when introducing a new product.

LO 14-8 List the pricing practices that are illegal or unethical.

continued on p. 284

continued from p. 283

to cheaper alternatives, such as Arm & Hammer detergent, made by Church & Dwight, Co.

Not a company to rest on its laurels, P&G pursued several strategic responses to the challenge. For consumers interested in convenience, it introduced, developed, and expanded on the concept of laundry detergent pods—single-use packs that eliminate the mess and the need for measuring associated with liquids or powders. Although this option has expanded the breadth of Tide's product lines and established an approximately $1 billion market for P&G, the pods create higher per-wash costs for consumers.[2]

Therefore, for consumers determined to use cheaper detergents, it also has developed and introduced Tide Simply Clean & Fresh, a liquid detergent that retails for about 35 percent less than the $12 price of a 100-ounce bottle of regular Tide.[3] In an effort to reduce the risk of sales cannibalization of its premium, higher-priced products, P&G makes sure that Simply Clean never appears for sale alongside other Tide brands, nor does it sport the easily recognizable orange Tide-branded container. In stores, Simply Clean is placed alongside its competitor brand on store shelves. The primary target markets are consumers from hardworking households, many of whom work in tough, odor-generating jobs and environments. With this approach, P&G can ensure that it never turns its back on its flagship brand.

However, to offset the lower profit margins earned on Tide Simply Clean, P&G also needs to increase margins on premium Tide

P&G uses multiple strategies, including offering different products to compete in the hyper-price-sensitive detergent market.
© McGraw-Hill Education

detergents, including Tide Plus, which contain extra ingredients (e.g., color-safe bleach). In the consumer-goods industry a popular pricing method allows brands to raise their prices in a way that remains largely hidden to consumers, unless they do a lot of extra research. Specifically, the brand increases wholesale prices while also reducing the size of the containers; what was formerly a 100-ounce bottle of detergent becomes a 92-ounce bottle, and what was previously a 50-ounce bottle contains only 46 ounces. The retail price remains the same; the package looks practically identical. Few consumers check the actual volume of such commonly purchased products, so they likely never realize that their detergent is costing them more per ounce.

Less for More

Procter & Gamble is cutting the number of loads but not the price on some of its premium Tide detergents, compensating for its new low-cost version.

Note: Pricing is determined by individual retailers. Each 100 oz. bottle recently cost $11.99 at a New York City Target store.

OLD **100 oz.**   **NEW** 92 oz.

TIDE PLUS FEBREZE

LOADS   PRICE PER LOAD:

60 | 48 | ▲ **25%**

TIDE PLUS BLEACH ALTERNATIVE

52 | 48 | ▲ **9%**

TIDE PLUS DOWNY

48 | 48 | **Unchanged**

Source: analyst reports, company documents
The Wall Street Journal

Source: Serena Ng, "At P&G, New Tide Comes In, Old Price Goes Up," *The Wall Street Journal,* February 10, 2014, http://wsj.online.com.

Although P&G's product portfolio is broad, including various detergent brands such as Gain, Era, and Cheer, it has chosen to focus where consumers are most invested, namely, in its Tide products. In trying to ensure Tide's market share advantage, P&G has shown its willingness to adjust its regular pricing strategies, develop new products with varying profit margins, and reduce bottle sizes while maintaining the same retail price. In essence, Procter & Gamble is keeping an eye on the way the tides are turning in the laundry detergent market. ∎

Although knowing how consumers arrive at their perceptions of value is critical to developing successful pricing strategies, sellers also must consider other factors—which is why developing a good pricing strategy is such a formidable challenge to all firms. Do it right, and the rewards to the firm will be substantial. Do it wrong, and failure will be swift and severe. But even if a pricing strategy is implemented well, consumers, economic conditions, markets, competitors, government regulations, and even a firm's own products change constantly—and that means that a good pricing strategy today may not remain an effective pricing strategy tomorrow.

Imagine that a consumer realizes that to save money on a particular item, she will have to drive an additional 20 miles. She may determine that her time and travel costs are not worth the savings, so even though the price tag is higher at a nearby store, she judges the overall cost of buying the product there to be lower. To include aspects of price such as this, we may define **price** as the overall sacrifice a consumer is willing to make to acquire a specific product or service. This sacrifice necessarily includes the

Knowing that price is so critical to success, why don't managers put greater emphasis on it as a strategic decision variable? Price is the most challenging of the four Ps to manage, partly because it is often the least understood. Historically, managers have treated price as an afterthought to their marketing strategy, setting prices according to what competitors were charging or, worse yet, adding up their costs and tacking a desired profit on to set the sales price. Prices rarely changed except in response to radical shifts in market conditions. Even today pricing decisions are often relegated to standard rules of thumb that fail to reflect our current understanding of the role of price in the marketing mix.

In summary, marketers should view pricing decisions as a strategic opportunity to create value rather than as an afterthought to the rest of the marketing mix. Let us now turn to the five basic components of pricing strategies.

> **price** The overall sacrifice a consumer is willing to make—money, time, energy—to acquire a specific product or service.

THE FIVE Cs OF PRICING

Successful pricing strategies are built around the five critical components (the five Cs) of pricing found in Exhibit 14.1. We examine these components in some detail because each makes a significant contribution to formulating good pricing policies.[6] To start, the first step is to develop the company's pricing objectives.

Company Objectives

By now, you know that different firms embrace very different goals. These goals should spill down to the pricing strategy,

> " A good pricing strategy today may not remain an effective pricing strategy tomorrow. "

money that must be paid to the seller to acquire the item, but it also may involve other sacrifices. These sacrifices may be nonmonetary, like the value of the time necessary to acquire the product or service, or monetary, like travel costs, taxes, shipping costs, and so forth, all of which the buyer must give up to take possession of the product.[4] It's useful to think of overall price like this to see how the narrower sense of purchase price fits in.

Because price is the only element of the marketing mix that does not generate costs but instead generates revenue, it is important in its own right. Every other element in the marketing mix may be perfect, but with the wrong price, sales and thus revenue will not accrue. Research has consistently shown that consumers usually rank price as one of the most important factors in their purchase decisions.[5]

▼ **EXHIBIT 14.1** The Five Cs of Pricing

Competition
Costs
Company objectives
Value
Customers
Channel members

such that the pricing of a company's products and services should support and allow the firm to reach its overall goals. For example, a firm with a primary goal of very high sales growth will likely have a different pricing strategy than a firm with the goal of being a quality leader.

Each firm then embraces objectives that seem to fit with where management thinks the firm needs to go to be successful, in whatever way it defines success. These specific objectives usually reflect how the firm intends to grow. Do managers want it to grow by increasing profits, increasing sales, decreasing competition, or building customer satisfaction?

Company objectives are not as simple as they might first appear. They often can be expressed in slightly different forms that mean very different things. Exhibit 14.2 introduces some common company objectives and corresponding examples of their implications for pricing strategies. These objectives are not always mutually exclusive, because a firm may embrace two or more noncompeting objectives.

| LO 14-1 | List the four pricing orientations. |

Profit Orientation
Even though all company methods and objectives may ultimately be oriented toward making a profit, firms implement a **profit orientation** specifically by focusing on target profit pricing, maximizing profits, or target return pricing.

- Firms usually implement **target profit pricing** when they have a particular profit goal as their overriding concern. To meet this targeted profit objective, firms use price to stimulate a certain level of sales at a certain profit per unit.

- The **maximizing profits** strategy relies primarily on economic theory. If a firm can accurately specify a mathematical model that captures all the factors required to explain and predict sales and profits, it should be able to identify the price at which its profits are maximized. Of course, the problem with this approach is that actually gathering the data on all these relevant factors and somehow coming up with an accurate mathematical model is an extremely difficult undertaking.

- Other firms are less concerned with the absolute level of profits and more interested in the rate at which their profits are generated relative to their investments. These firms typically turn to **target return pricing** and employ pricing strategies designed to produce a specific return on their investment, usually expressed as a percentage of sales.

Sales Orientation
Firms using a **sales orientation** to set prices believe that increasing sales will help the firm more

▼ **EXHIBIT 14.2** Company Objectives and Pricing Strategy Implications

Company Objective	Example of Pricing Strategy Implications
Profit oriented	Institute a companywide policy that all products must provide for at least an 18 percent profit margin to reach a particular profit goal for the firm.
Sales oriented	Set prices very low to generate new sales and take sales away from competitors, even if profits suffer.
Competitor oriented	To discourage more competitors from entering the market, set prices very low.
Customer oriented	Target a market segment of consumers who highly value a particular product benefit and set prices relatively high (referred to as premium pricing).

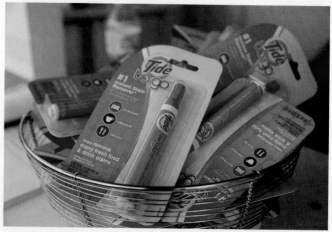

P&G increases sales by introducing new Tide products.
© Rob Kim/Getty Images

than will increasing profits. Tide might adopt such an orientation selectively when it introduces new products that it wants to establish in the market. A new health club might focus on unit sales, dollar sales, or market share and therefore be willing to set a lower membership fee and accept less profit at first to focus on and generate more unit sales. In contrast, a high-end jewelry store might focus on dollar sales and maintain higher prices. The jewelry store relies on its prestige image, as well as the image of its suppliers, to provoke sales. Even though it sells fewer units, it can still generate high dollar sales levels.

Some firms may be more concerned about their overall market share than about dollar sales per se (though these often go hand in hand) because they believe that market share better reflects their success relative to the market conditions than do sales alone. A firm may set low prices to discourage new firms from entering the market, encourage current firms to leave the market, and/or take market share away from competitors—all to gain overall market share.

Yet adopting a market share objective does not always imply setting low prices. Rarely is the lowest-price offering the dominant brand in a given market. Heinz ketchup, Philadelphia cream cheese, Crest toothpaste, and Nike athletic shoes have all dominated their markets, yet all are premium-priced brands. On the services side, IBM claims market dominance in human resource outsourcing, but again, it is certainly not the lowest-price competitor.[7] **Premium pricing** means the firm deliberately prices a product above the prices set for competing products to capture those customers who always shop for the best or for whom price does not matter. Thus, companies can gain market share by offering a high-quality product at a price that is perceived to be fair by its target market as long as they use effective communication and distribution methods to generate high value perceptions among consumers. Although the concept of value is not overtly expressed in sales-oriented strategies, it is at least implicit because, for sales to increase, consumers must see greater value.

Competitor Orientation

When firms take a **competitor orientation**, they strategize according to the premise that they should measure themselves primarily against their competition. Some firms focus on **competitive parity**, which means they set prices that are similar to those of their major competitors. Another competitor-oriented strategy, **status quo pricing**, changes prices only to meet those of the competition. For example, when Delta increases its average fares, American Airlines and United often follow with similar increases; if Delta rescinds that increase, its competitors tend to drop their fares too.[8] Value is only implicitly considered in competitor-oriented strategies in the sense that competitors may be using value as part of their pricing strategies, and therefore copying competitors' strategies might provide value.

Customer Orientation

A **customer orientation** is when a firm sets its pricing strategy based on how it can add value to its products or services. When CarMax promises a "no-haggle" pricing structure, it exhibits a customer orientation because it

Philadelphia brand cream cheese dominates its market and is a premium-priced brand.
© Michael J. Hruby

"SOME FIRMS MAY BE MORE CONCERNED ABOUT THEIR OVERALL MARKET SHARE THAN ABOUT DOLLAR SALES PER SE (THOUGH THESE OFTEN GO HAND IN HAND) BECAUSE THEY BELIEVE THAT MARKET SHARE BETTER REFLECTS THEIR SUCCESS."

Can you tell the difference between the $8,998 and the $299 speakers?
Courtesy Paradigm Electronics, Inc.

provides additional value to potential used car buyers by making the process simple and easy.[9]

Firms may offer very high-priced, "state-of-the-art" products or services in full anticipation of limited sales. These offerings are designed to enhance the company's reputation and image and thereby increase the company's value in the minds of consumers. Paradigm, a Canadian speaker manufacturer, produces what many audiophiles consider a high-value product, yet offers speakers priced as low as $299 per pair. However, Paradigm also offers a very high-end speaker for $8,998[10] per pair. Although few people will spend nearly $9,000 on a pair of speakers, this "statement" speaker communicates what the company is capable of and can increase the image of the firm and the rest of its products—even that $299 pair of speakers. Setting prices with a close eye to how consumers develop their perceptions of value can often be the most effective pricing strategy, especially if it is supported by consistent advertising and distribution strategies.

After a company has a good grasp on its overall objectives, it must implement pricing strategies that enable it to achieve those objectives. Apple has varying objectives for each of its innovations, and thus varying ways to price them, as Adding Value 14.1 notes. As the second step in this process, the firm should look toward consumer demand to lay the foundation for its pricing strategy.

Adding Value   14.1

Using Price to Position the Apple Watch[i]

Apple first entered the market as a computer manufacturer, and it made a name for itself there with its reliable offerings, which were generally less susceptible to viruses than PCs. Although Apple still enjoys tremendous success with its desktop and laptop models, computers are not its biggest success story. Nor is the iPod, one of the first truly innovative products released by Apple. Rather, arguably its greatest innovation has been the way it changed the landscapes and habits of consumers everywhere with—can you guess it?—the iPhone. Now positioned as an everyday essential, iPhones sparked the huge market for smartphones in general: More than 180 million Americans own smartphones. Despite this long and successful history of innovating by creating previously unknown items that become utterly essential, Apple's newest product, the Apple Watch, seemingly reflects a different category, as its strategic pricing demonstrates.

The Apple Watch does not offer any new "It" apps, nor is its greater utility, compared with the iPhone, particularly evident. So how is Apple planning to market the watch? The price points announced prior to its release signaled that it would be appearing as a luxury item. The average Apple Watch will cost users more than $500; even the "value-priced" Apple Watch Sport version will set a buyer back $300 or so. But on the other end of the spectrum, Apple also will be opening the field with a solid gold watch, priced at $10,000, in an effort to create luxury cachet for the Apple Watch franchise.

Is Apple Watch priced right to meet its objectives and customers' expectations?
© Stefanie Loos/Reuters/Landov

In the world of luxury items, pricing is critical. It does not cost Rolex thousands of dollars—or even $1,000—to make one of its famous watches. So why do many Rolexes cost upward of $7,000? The carefully calculated prices for luxury items seek to reflect the value of the brand. For luxury customers, brand value stems from quality and the brand's pedigree, but also from the exclusivity of the product. Pricing in the luxury market is even more important than in most markets because if an item is priced too low, luxury customers will not buy it, whereas other customers will. In that case, the image of the brand suffers often irreparable harm. But luxury items also might suffer if they are priced too high in relation to the perceived quality they offer: Affluent shoppers will draw the line and refuse to pay significantly more for a product that is perceived to be essentially equivalent to a more conventional option.

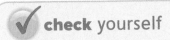

check yourself

1. What are the five Cs of pricing?
2. Identify the four types of company objectives.

Customers

When firms have developed their company objectives, they turn to understanding consumers' reactions to different prices. The second C of the five Cs of pricing focuses on the customers. Customers want value, and as you likely recall, price is half of the value equation.

To determine how firms account for consumers' preferences when they develop pricing strategies, we must first lay a foundation of traditional economic theory that helps explain how prices are related to demand (consumers' desire for products) and how managers can incorporate this knowledge into their pricing strategies.[11]

> **LO 14-2** Explain the relationship between price and quantity sold.

Demand Curves and Pricing A **demand curve** shows how many units of a product or service consumers will demand during a specific period of time at different prices. Although we call them "curves," demand curves can be either straight or curved, as Exhibit 14.3 shows. Of course, any demand curve relating demand to price assumes that everything

▼ **EXHIBIT 14.3** Demand Curve for Teeth Whitening Kits

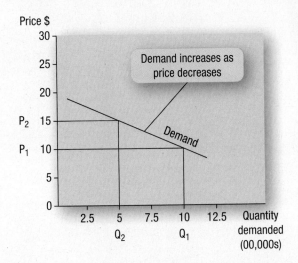

else remains unchanged. For the sake of expediency, marketers creating a demand curve assume that the firm will not increase its expenditures on advertising and that the economy will not change in any significant way.

Exhibit 14.3 illustrates a classic downward-sloping demand curve for teeth whitening kits. As price increases, demand for the product or service decreases. In this case, consumers will buy more as the price decreases. We can expect a demand curve similar to this one for many, if not most, products and services.

The horizontal axis in Exhibit 14.3 measures the quantity demanded for the teeth whitening kits in units and plots it against the various price possibilities indicated on the vertical axis. Each point on the demand curve then represents the quantity demanded at a specific price. So, in this instance, if the price of a kit is $10 per unit ($P_1$), the demand is 1,000,000 units (Q_1), but if the price were set at $15 ($P_2$), the demand would be only 500,000 units (Q_2). The firm will sell far more teeth whitening kits at $10 each than at $15 each. Why? Because of the greater value this price point offers.

Knowing the demand curve for a product or service enables a firm to examine different prices in terms of the resulting demand and relative to its overall objective. In our preceding example, the retailer will generate a total of $10,000,000 in sales at the $10 price ($10 × 1,000,000 units) and $7,500,000 in sales at the $15 price ($15 × 500,000 units). In this case, given only the two choices of $10 or $15, the $10 price is preferable as long as the firm wants to maximize its sales in terms of dollars and units. But what about a firm that is more interested in profit? To calculate profit, it must consider its costs, which we cover in the next section.

But not all products or services follow the downward-sloping demand curve for all levels of price depicted in Exhibit 14.3. Consider **prestige products or services**, which consumers purchase for their status rather than their functionality. The higher the price, the greater the status associated with it and the greater the exclusivity because fewer people can afford to purchase it. German automaker Porsche is known for making fabulous and fast sports cars. Its entry-level car, the Boxster, was introduced in 1997 with a starting price of about $40,000.[12] In 2013, the starting price of the newly designed Boxster was over $51,000.[13] But with options, the sportier Boxster S could run over $100,000.[14] Remember, this is the entry-level model!

demand curve
Shows how many units of a product or service consumers will demand during a specific period at different prices.

prestige products or services Those that consumers purchase for status rather than functionality.

> " The firm will sell far more teeth whitening kits at $10 each than at $15 each. Why? Because of the greater value this price point offers. "

However, prestige products can also run into pricing difficulties. The Fender Telecaster and Stratocaster guitars are absolute necessities for any self-respecting guitar hero, but for students just learning or hobbyists, the price of owning a Fender "axe" was simply too much. In response, Fender introduced a separate, budget-priced line of similar guitars under a different brand name so as not to dilute the prestige of the Fender name. The Squier line, made in Japan with automated manufacturing and less expensive parts, offers a look similar to the famous Fender guitars and performance just a notch below the originals. Today, an American-made Vintage Hot Rod '57 Fender Stratocaster lists for $1,700, more than 14 times as much as a Squier Bullet Strat model that retails for around $120.[15]

Based on Exhibit 14.3, what is the best price for WhiteLight?
© Miami Herald/McClatchy-Tribune/Getty Images

With prestige products or services, a higher price may lead to a greater quantity sold, but only up to a certain point. The price demonstrates just how rare, exclusive, and prestigious the product is. When customers value the increase in prestige more than the price differential between the prestige product and other products, the prestige product attains the greater value overall.

Have you ever wanted a Porsche? You can have the entry-level Boxster without options for only $51,000.
© Ed Aldridge/ZUMA Press/Newscom

Singer Avril Lavigne uses a Fender guitar.
© George Pimentel/Contributor/WireImage/Getty Images

price elasticity of demand Measures how changes in a price affect the quantity of the product demanded; specifically, the ratio of the percentage change in quantity demanded to the percentage change in price.

elastic Refers to a market for a product or service that is price sensitive; that is, relatively small changes in price will generate fairly large changes in the quantity demanded.

the percentage change in price. We can calculate it with the following formula:

$$\text{Price elasticity of demand} = \frac{\% \text{ Change in quantity demanded}}{\% \text{ Change in price}}$$

The demand curve provides the information we need to calculate the price elasticity of demand. For instance, what is the price elasticity of demand if we increase the price of our teeth whitening kit from $10 to $15?

$$\text{\% Change in quantity demanded} = \frac{(1,000,000 - 500,000)}{1,000,000} = 50\%, \text{ and}$$

$$\text{\% Change in price} = \frac{(\$10 - \$15)}{10} = -50\%, \text{ so}$$

$$\text{Price elasticity of demand} = \frac{50\%}{-50\%} = -1.$$

Thus, the price elasticity of demand for our teeth whitening kit is −1.

In general, the market for a product or service is price sensitive (or **elastic**) when the price elasticity is less than −1, that is, when a 1 percent decrease in price produces more than a

Exhibit 14.4 illustrates a demand curve for a hypothetical prestige service, a Caribbean cruise. As the graph indicates, when the price increases from $1,000 ($P_1$) to $5,000 ($P_2$), the quantity demanded actually increases from 200,000 (Q_1) to 500,000 (Q_2) units. However, when the price increases to $8,000 ($P_3$), the demand then decreases to 300,000 (Q_3) units.

Although the firm likely will earn more profit selling 300,000 cruises at $8,000 each than 500,000 cruises at $5,000 each, we do not know for sure until we bring costs into the picture. However, we do know that more consumers are willing to book the cruise as the price increases initially from $1,000 to $5,000 and that more consumers will choose an alternative vacation as the price increases further from $5,000 to $8,000.

We must consider this notion of consumers' sensitivity to price changes in greater depth.

| LO 14-3 | Explain price elasticity. |

Price Elasticity of Demand

Although we now know something about how consumers react to different price levels, we still need to determine how consumers respond to actual changes in price. These responses vary depending on the product or service. For example, consumers are generally less sensitive to price increases for necessary items, like milk, because they have to purchase the items even if the price climbs. When the price of milk goes up, demand does not fall significantly because people still need to buy milk. However, if the price of T-bone steaks rises beyond a certain point, people will buy less because they can turn to the many substitutes for this cut of meat. Marketers need to know how consumers will respond to a price increase (or decrease) for a specific product or brand so they can determine whether it makes sense for them to raise or lower prices.

Price elasticity of demand measures how changes in a price affect the quantity of the product demanded. Specifically, it is the ratio of the percentage change in quantity demanded to

Consumers are less sensitive to the price of milk than to that of steak. When the price of milk goes up, demand does not fall significantly because people still need to buy milk. However, if the price of steak rises beyond a certain point, people will buy less because they can turn to many substitutes for steak.
Left: © McGraw-Hill Education/Bob Coyle, photographer;
Right: © FoodCollection/StockFood RF

1 percent increase in the quantity sold. In an elastic scenario, relatively small changes in price will generate fairly large changes in the quantity demanded, so if a firm is trying to increase its sales, it can do so by lowering prices. However, raising prices can be problematic in this context because doing so will lower sales. To refer back to our grocery examples, a retailer can significantly increase its sales of filet mignon by lowering its price, because filets are elastic.

The market for a product is generally viewed as price insensitive (or **inelastic**) when its price elasticity is greater than −1, that is, when a 1 percent decrease in price results in less than a 1 percent increase in quantity sold. Generally, if a firm must raise prices, it is helpful to do so with inelastic products or services because in such a market, fewer customers will stop buying or reduce their purchases. However, if the products are inelastic, lowering prices will not appreciably increase demand; customers just don't notice or care about the lower price.

Consumers are generally more sensitive to price increases than to price decreases.[16] That is, it is easier to lose current customers with a price increase than it is to gain new customers with a price decrease. Also, the price elasticity of demand usually changes at different points in the demand curve unless the curve is actually a straight line, as in Exhibit 14.3. For instance, a prestige product or service, like our Caribbean cruise example in Exhibit 14.4, enjoys a highly inelastic demand curve up to a certain point, so price increases do not affect sales significantly. But when the price reaches that certain point, consumers start turning to other alternatives, because the value of the cruise has finally been reduced by the extremely high price.

Ideally, firms could maximize their profits if they charged each customer as much as the customer was willing to pay. The travel industry and airlines in particular realize this benefit particularly well, as Marketing Analytics 14.1 explains. For instance, if a wealthy, price-insensitive customer wants to buy a new car, a Ford dealer would like to price a particular car at $40,000, but then price the same car at $35,000 to a more price-sensitive customer. Such a practice is legal when retailers sell to consumers such as in an eBay auction, but is permitted only under certain circumstances in B2B settings.[17]

Although charging different prices to different customers is legal and widely used in some retail sectors such as

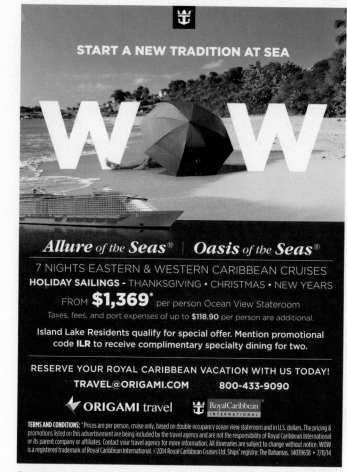

Based on Exhibit 14.4, price increases on a Caribbean cruise do not affect sales significantly up to a certain point. But after that point, sales decrease because consumers believe it is no longer a good value.
Used with permission of Royal Caribbean Cruises Ltd

> **In an elastic scenario, relatively small changes in price will generate fairly large changes in the quantity demanded, so if a firm is trying to increase its sales, it can do so by lowering prices.**

automobile and antique dealers, it has not been very practical in most retail stores until recently. Retailers have increased their use of dynamic pricing techniques due to the information that is available from point-of-sale data collected on Internet purchases and in stores. **Dynamic pricing**, also known as **individualized pricing**, refers to the process of charging different prices for goods or services based on the type of customer, time of the day, week, or even season, and level of demand. Retailers may also charge customers different prices based on their loyalty status derived from their CRM systems (e.g., platinum customers receive lower prices than silver ones). Early adopters of dynamic pricing techniques were service retailers such as airlines, hotels, cruises lines, and so on. It is quite common for passengers on the same plane to have paid different fares depending on when they bought their ticket. The ease of using dynamic pricing when selling merchandise on the Internet is much greater than in a store because only one person sees the price.

Factors Influencing Price Elasticity of Demand

We have illustrated how price elasticity of demand varies across different products and at different points along a demand curve, as well as how it can change over time. What causes these differences in the price elasticity of demand? We discuss a few of the more important factors next.

Income Effect The **income effect** refers to the change in the quantity of a product demanded by consumers due to a change in their income. Generally, as people's income increases, their spending behavior changes: They tend to shift their demand from lower-priced products to higher-priced alternatives. That is, consumers buy hamburger when they're stretching their money but steak when they're flush. Similarly, they may increase the quantity they purchase and splurge on a five-star hotel during their six-day Las Vegas trip rather than three-star

lodging over a weekend visit. Conversely, when incomes drop, consumers turn to less expensive alternatives or purchase less.

Substitution Effect The **substitution effect** refers to consumers' ability to substitute other products for the focal brand. The greater the availability of substitute products, the higher the price elasticity of demand for any given product will be. For example, there are many close substitutes in the laundry detergent category. If Tide raises its prices, many consumers will turn to competing brands (e.g., Arm & Hammer Detergent) because they are more sensitive to price increases when they can easily find lower-priced substitutes. Extremely brand-loyal consumers, however, are willing to pay a higher price, up to a point, because in their minds, Tide still offers a better value than the competing brands, and they believe the other brands are not adequate substitutes.

income effect Refers to the change in the quantity of a product demanded by consumers due to a change in their income.

substitution effect Refers to consumers' ability to substitute other products for the focal brand, thus increasing the price elasticity of demand for the focal brand.

Marketing Analytics

14.1

Airlines Offer Ticket Prices Based on Customers' Willingness to Pay[ii]

The airline industry has been using analytics to influence pricing for decades. Early implementers of data-based pricing strategies, such as American Airlines, enjoyed a significant advantage over their competitors that maintained a single, flat rate for all tickets. By predicting demand for each particular flight, American Airlines could price different tickets at different rates and ensure that it sold as many tickets as possible. For example, when its analytics system identified which tickets might not sell, American Airlines began offering those seats at a significant discount, but it increased the rates for seats that were very likely to be purchased.

American Airlines' pricing strategy grew so effective that every other airline faced an obvious choice: adopt it or go out of business. Some of the popularity of data-based pricing results from a key feature that it provides, in that it allows customers the freedom to determine the price they will pay. Travelers well know that they will find vast discrepancies in flight prices, depending on when they travel (spring break or the off-season?), when they book (Tuesday nights or Saturday mornings?), and where they want to sit (pay a lot extra for first class, a little extra for the exit row, or just the base fare for a middle seat?). Customers can weight the value of the convenience of these various factors for themselves, then select the flight that best fits their own individual needs.

Despite the great deals offered and the resultant benefits for both firms and customers, the use of strategic pricing analytics can require time-consuming hunts for the best deal. To combat the hassle of searching for airline deals, many service providers introduced travel booking sites. Some

American Airlines pioneered marketing analytics in pricing by setting its prices based on demand.
© NetPhotos3/Alamy

are specific to a particular airline; others compile pricing information about various flights between two locations to make the price comparison evident and convenient for the customer. Kayak.com has taken it a step further and begun implementing predictive pricing analytics of its own in the form of its price forecast feature. Kayak takes information from the billions of requests for travel information that it processes each day, then predicts whether the price for a given destination on a particular date is likely to go up or down over the next seven days. It computes the accuracy of its predictions daily in an effort to perfect its use of these analytics.

cross-price elasticity The percentage change in demand for product A that occurs in response to a percentage change in price of product B; see also *complementary products.*

complementary products Products whose demand curves are positively related, such that they rise or fall together; a percentage increase in demand for one results in a percentage increase in demand for the other.

substitute products Products for which changes in demand are negatively related; that is, a percentage increase in the quantity demanded for product A results in a percentage decrease in the quantity demanded for product B.

example, Polo/Ralph Lauren sells millions of its classic polo shirts at $85, while shirts of equal quality but without the polo player logo sell for much less. Getting consumers to believe that a particular brand is unique, different, or extraordinary in some way makes other brands seem less substitutable, which in turn increases brand loyalty and decreases the price elasticity of demand.

Keep in mind that marketing plays a critical role in making consumers brand loyal. And because of this brand loyalty and the lack of what consumers judge to be adequate substitutes, the price elasticity of demand for some brands is very low. For

Cross-Price Elasticity **Cross-price elasticity** is the percentage change in the quantity of Product A demanded compared with the percentage change in price in Product B. If

> ## If Product A's price increased, Product B could either increase or decrease, depending on the situation and whether the products are complementary or substitutes.

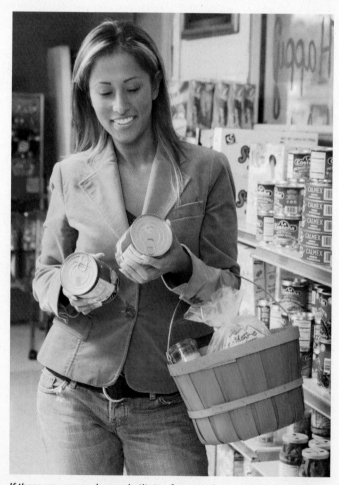

If there are many close substitutes for a product, customers will be sensitive to small price changes, and the product will be highly elastic. If, for instance, Hunt's raises its price, many customers will switch to another brand.

© Photodisc/Getty Images RF

Product A's price increased, Product B could either increase or decrease, depending on the situation and whether the products are complementary or substitutes. We refer to products like Blu-ray discs and Blu-ray players as **complementary products,** which are products whose demands are positively related, such that they rise or fall together. In other words, a percentage increase in the quantity demanded for Product A results in a percentage increase in the quantity demanded for Product B.[18] However, when the price for Blu-ray players dropped, the demand for DVD players went down, so DVD players and Blu-ray players are **substitute products** because changes in their demand are negatively related. That is, a percentage increase in the quantity demanded for Product A results in a percentage decrease in the quantity demanded for Product B.[19] Shopping bots like TheFind.com and Bizrate.com have made it much easier for people to shop for substitutable products like consumer electronics, which likely has affected the price elasticity of demand for such products.[20]

Clearly, knowing how prices affect sales is important, but it cannot give us the whole picture. To know how profitable a pricing strategy will be, we must also consider the third C, costs.

 check yourself

1. What is the difference between elastic demand and inelastic demand?
2. What are the factors influencing price elasticity?

Costs

To make effective pricing decisions, firms must understand their cost structures so they can determine the degree to which their products or services will be profitable at different prices.

In general, prices should *not* be based on costs, because consumers make purchase decisions based on their perceived value; they care little about the firm's costs to produce and sell a product or deliver a service. Although companies incur many different types of costs as a natural part of doing business, there are two primary cost categories: variable and fixed.

Variable Costs

Variable costs are those costs, primarily labor and materials, that vary with production volume. As a firm produces more or less of a good or service, the total variable costs increase or decrease at the same time. Because each unit of the product produced incurs the same cost, marketers generally express variable costs on a per-unit basis. Consider a bakery like Entenmann's: The majority of the variable costs are the cost of the ingredients, primarily flour. Each

always the case, variable costs per unit may go up or down (for all units) with significant changes in volume.

Fixed Costs

Fixed costs are those costs that remain essentially at the same level, regardless of any changes in the volume of production. Typically, these costs include items such as rent, utilities, insurance, administrative salaries (for executives and higher-level managers), and the depreciation of the physical plant and equipment. Across reasonable fluctuations in production volume, these costs remain stable; whether Entenmann's makes 100,000 loaves or a million, the rent it pays for the bakery remains unchanged.

Total Cost

Finally, the **total cost** is simply the sum of the variable and fixed costs. For example, in one year, our

> " WHETHER ENTENMANN'S MAKES 100,000 LOAVES OR A MILLION, THE RENT IT PAYS FOR THE BAKERY REMAINS UNCHANGED. "

time Entenmann's makes a loaf of bread, it incurs the cost of the ingredients.

In the service industry, variable costs are far more complex. A hotel, for instance, incurs certain variable costs each time it rents a room, including the costs associated with the labor and supplies necessary to clean and restock the room. Note that the hotel does not incur these costs if the room is not booked. Suppose that a particular hotel calculates its total variable costs to be $10 per room; each time it rents a room, it incurs another $10 in variable costs. If the hotel rents out 100 rooms on a given night, the total variable cost is $1,000 ($10 per room × 100 rooms).

In either case, however, variable costs tend to change depending on the quantity produced. If Entenmann's makes 100,000 loaves of bread in a month, it would have to pay a higher price for ingredients on a per pound basis than if it were producing a million loaves. Similarly, a very large hotel will be able to get a lower per unit price on most, if not all, the supplies it needs to service the room because it purchases such a large volume. However, as the hotel company continues to grow, it may be forced to add more benefits for its employees or increase wages to attract and keep long-term employees. Such changes will increase its overall variable labor costs and affect the total variable cost of cleaning a room. Thus, though not

hypothetical hotel incurred $100,000 in fixed costs. We also know that, because the hotel booked 10,000 room nights, its total variable cost is $100,000 (10,000 room nights × $10 per room). Thus, its total cost is $200,000.

Next, we illustrate how to use these costs in simple analyses that can inform managerial decision making about setting prices.

| LO 14-4 | Describe how to calculate a product's break-even point. |

Break-Even Analysis and Decision Making

A useful technique that enables managers to examine the relationships among cost, price, revenue, and profit over different levels of production and sales is called **break-even analysis**. Central to this analysis is the determination of the **break-even point**, or the point at which the number of units sold generates just enough revenue to equal the total costs. At this point, profits are zero. Although profit, which represents the difference between the total cost and the total revenue (Total revenue or sales = Selling price of each unit sold × Number of units sold), can indicate how much money the firm is making or losing at a single period of time, it cannot tell managers how many units a firm must produce and sell before it stops losing money and at least breaks even, which is what the break-even point does.

How do we determine the break-even point? Exhibit 14.5 presents the various cost and revenue information we have discussed in a graphic format. The graph contains three curves (recall that even though they are straight, we still call them curves): fixed costs, total costs, and total revenue. The vertical axis measures the revenue or costs in dollars, and the horizontal axis measures the quantity of units sold. The fixed cost curve will always appear as a horizontal line straight across the graph, because fixed costs do not change over different levels of volume.

The total cost curve starts where the fixed cost curve intersects the vertical axis at $100,000. When volume is equal to zero (no units are produced or sold), the fixed costs of operating the business remain and cannot be avoided. Thus, the lowest point the total costs can ever reach is equal to the total fixed costs. Beyond that point, the total cost curve increases by the amount of variable costs for each additional unit, which we calculate by multiplying the variable cost per unit by the number of units, or quantity.

Finally, the total revenue curve increases by the price of each additional unit sold. To calculate it, we multiply the price per unit by the number of units sold. The formulas for these calculations are as follows:

$$\text{Total variable costs} = \text{Variable cost per unit} \times \text{Quantity}$$
$$\text{Total costs} = \text{Fixed costs} + \text{Total variable costs}$$
$$\text{Total revenue} = \text{Price} \times \text{Quantity}$$

We again use the hotel example to illustrate these relationships. Recall that the fixed costs are $100,000 and the variable costs are $10 per room rented. If the rooms rent for $50 per night, how many rooms must the hotel rent over the course of a year to break even? If we study the graph carefully, we find the break-even point at 2,500, which means that the hotel must rent 2,500

rooms before its revenues equal its costs. If it rents fewer rooms, it loses money (the pink area); if it rents more, it makes a profit (the gold area). To determine the break-even point in units mathematically, we must introduce one more variable, the **contribution per unit**, which is the price less the variable cost per unit.

In this case,

$$\text{Contribution per unit} = \$50 - \$10 = \$40$$

Therefore, the break-even point becomes

$$\text{Break-even point (units)} = \frac{\text{Fixed costs}}{\text{Contributions per unit}}$$

That is,

$$\text{Break-even point (units)} = \frac{\$100,000}{\$40} = 2,500 \text{ room nights}$$

When the hotel has crossed the break-even point of 2,500 rooms, it will start earning profit at the same rate of the contribution per unit. So if the hotel rents 4,000 rooms—1,500 rooms more than the break-even point—its profit will be $60,000 (1,500 rooms × $40 contribution per unit).

$$\text{Profit} = (\text{Contribution per unit} \times \text{Quantity}) - \text{Fixed costs}$$
$$\text{Profit} = (\$40 \times 4,000) - \$100,000 = \$60,000$$

Or an alternative formula would be:

$$\text{Profit} = (\text{Price} \times \text{Quantity}) - (\text{Fixed costs} + (\text{Variable costs} \times \text{Quantity}))$$
$$\text{Profit} = (\$50 \times 4,000) - (\$100,000 + (\$10 \times 4,000))$$
$$\text{Profit} = \$200,000 - (\$100,000 + \$40,000) = \$60,000$$

Let's extend this simple break-even analysis to show how many units a firm must produce and sell to achieve a target profit. Say the hotel wanted to make $200,000 in profit each year. How many rooms would it have to rent at the current price? In this instance, we need only add the targeted profit to the fixed costs to determine that number:

$$\text{Break-even point (units)} = \frac{(\text{Fixed costs} + \text{Target profit})}{\text{Contributions per unit}}$$

or

$$7,500 \text{ rooms} = \frac{(\$100,000 + \$200,000)}{\$40}$$

Although a break-even analysis cannot actually help managers set prices, it does help them assess their pricing strategies, because it clarifies the conditions in which different prices may make a product or service profitable. It becomes an even more powerful tool when performed on a range of possible prices for comparative purposes. For example, the hotel management could analyze various prices, not just $50, to determine how many hotel rooms it would have to rent at what price to make a $200,000 profit.

Naturally, however, there are limitations to a break-even analysis. First, it is unlikely that a hotel has one specific price that it charges for each and every room, so the price it would use in its

▼ **EXHIBIT 14.5** Break-Even Analysis

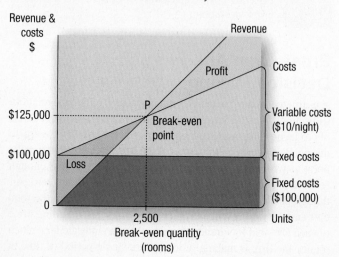

Break-even quantity (rooms)

break-even analysis probably represents an "average" price that attempts to account for these variances. Second, prices often get reduced as quantity increases, because the costs decrease, so firms must perform several break-even analyses at different quantities. Third, a break-even analysis cannot indicate for sure how many rooms will be rented or, in the case of products, how many units will sell at a given price. It only tells the firm what its costs, revenues, and profitability will be given a set price and an assumed quantity. To determine how many units the firm actually will sell, it must bring in the demand estimates we discussed previously.

Markup and Target Return Pricing

In many situations, the manufacturer may want to achieve a standard markup—let's say 10 percent of cost. In our example of the teeth whitening kit, let's assume:

Variable costs per unit are:	$8.00
Fixed costs are:	$1,000,000.00
Expected sales are:	1,000,000 units

In a hotel, the cost of the physical structure, including the lobby, is fixed—it is incurred even if no rooms are rented. The costs of washing the towels and sheets are variable—the more rooms that are rented, the more the costs.

Top: © Erik Isakson/Blend Images/Getty Images RF; Bottom: © Eric Audras/Onoky/SuperStock RF

The teeth whitening kit manufacturer would like to calculate the price at which it would make a 10 percent markup.

The formula for calculating a target return price based on a markup on cost is:

$$\text{Target return price} = (\text{Variable costs} + (\text{Fixed costs} \div \text{Expected Unit sales})) \times (1 + \text{Target return \% [expressed as a decimal]})$$

In this example, this would result in the firm charging $9.90.

$$\text{Target return price} = (\$8.00 + (\$1,000,000.00 \div 1,000,000.00)) \times (1 + 0.10)$$

$$\text{Target return price} = \$9.00 \times 1.1 = \$9.90$$

 check yourself

1. What is the difference between fixed costs and variable costs?
2. How does one calculate the break-even point in units?

LO 14-5 Indicate the four types of price competitive levels.

Competition

Because the fourth C, competition, has a profound impact on pricing strategies, we use this section to focus on its effect, as well as on how competitors react to certain pricing strategies. There are four levels of competition—monopoly, oligopolistic competition, monopolistic competition, and pure competition—and each has its own set of pricing challenges and opportunities (see Exhibit 14.6).

In a **monopoly**, one firm provides the product or service in a particular industry, which results in less price competition. For example, there is often only one provider of power in each region of the country: Florida Power and Light in most of Florida, NStar in most of Massachusetts, and so forth. Power companies operate more efficiently when there is one service provider, so the government regulates the pricing of utility monopolies to prevent them from raising prices uncontrollably. A monopoly that restricts competition by controlling an industry can be deemed illegal and broken apart by the government.

When a market is characterized by **oligopolistic competition**, only a few firms dominate. Firms typically change their prices in reaction to competition to avoid upsetting an otherwise stable competitive environment. Examples of oligopolistic markets include the soft drink market and commercial airline travel. Sometimes reactions to prices in oligopolistic markets can result in a **price war**, which occurs

predatory pricing A firm's practice of setting a very low price for one or more of its products with the intent to drive its competition out of business; illegal under both the Sherman Antitrust Act and the Federal Trade Commission Act.

monopolistic competition Occurs when there are many firms that sell closely related but not homogeneous products; these products may be viewed as substitutes but are not perfect substitutes.

pure competition Occurs when different companies sell commodity products that consumers perceive as substitutable; price usually is set according to the laws of supply and demand.

when two or more firms compete primarily by lowering their prices. Firm A lowers its prices; Firm B responds by meeting or beating Firm A's new price. Firm A then responds with another new price, and so on. In some cases though, these tactics result in **predatory pricing**, when a firm sets a very low price for one or more of its products with the intent to drive its competition out of business. Predatory pricing is illegal in the United States.

Monopolistic competition occurs when there are many firms competing for customers in a given market but their products are differentiated. When so many firms compete, product differentiation rather than strict price competition tends to appeal to consumers. This is the most common form of competition. Hundreds of firms make wristwatches, thus the market is highly differentiated. Timex sells a durable watch that tells time and has a stopwatch and a sporty design. Swatch watches have more style than Timex watches, but if you are looking for style, fashion designers such as Armani have their own wristwatches. Timepiece aficionados may opt for high-quality watches such as Patek Philippe or Vacheron Constantin. Depending on the features, style, and quality, companies compete for very different market segments. By differentiating their products using various attributes, prices, and brands, they

> "When so many firms compete, product differentiation rather than strict price competition tends to appeal to consumers."

▼ **EXHIBIT 14.6** Four Levels of Competition: Can you match each photo to its respective type of competition?

Less price competition | More price competition

Monopoly One firm controls the market

Oligopoly A handful of firms control the market — Fewer firms

Monopolistic competition Many firms selling differentiated products at different prices

Pure competition Many firms selling commodities for the same prices — Many firms

First: © Steve Cole/Getty Images RF; Second: © Corbis RF; Third: © Ingram Publishing/SuperStock RF; Fourth: © Brand X Pictures/PunchStock RF

create unique value propositions in the minds of their customers.

With **pure competition**, a large number of sellers offer standardized products or commodities that consumers perceive as substitutable, such as grains, gold, meat, spices, or minerals. In such markets, price usually is set according to the laws of supply and demand. For example, wheat is wheat, so it does not matter to a commercial bakery whose wheat it buys. However, the secret to pricing success in a pure competition market is not necessarily to offer the lowest price, because doing so might create a price war and erode profits. Instead, some firms have brilliantly decommoditized their products. For example, most people feel that all chickens purchased in a grocery are the same. But companies like Tyson have branded their chickens to move into a monopolistically competitive market.

When a commodity can be differentiated somehow, even if simply by a sticker or logo, there is an opportunity for consumers to identify it as distinct from the rest, and in this case, firms can at least partially extricate their product from a pure competitive market.

check yourself

1. What are the four different types of competitive environments?

Channel Members

Channel members—manufacturers, wholesalers, and retailers—have different perspectives when it comes to pricing strategies. Consider a manufacturer that is focused on increasing the image and reputation of its brand but working with a retailer that is primarily concerned with increasing its sales. The manufacturer may desire to keep prices higher to convey a better image, whereas the retailer wants lower prices and will accept lower profits to move the product, regardless of consumers' impressions of the brand. Unless channel members carefully communicate their pricing goals and select channel partners that agree with them, conflict will surely arise.

Channels can be very difficult to manage, and distribution outside normal channels does occur. A **gray market** employs irregular but not necessarily illegal methods; generally, it legally circumvents authorized channels of distribution to sell goods at prices lower than those intended by the manufacturer.[21] Many manufacturers of consumer electronics therefore require retailers to sign an agreement that demands certain activities (and prohibits others) before they may become authorized dealers. But if a retailer has too many high-definition televisions in stock, it may sell them at just above its own cost to an unauthorized discount dealer. This move places the merchandise in the market at prices far below what authorized dealers can charge, and in the long term, it may tarnish the image of the manufacturer if the discount dealer fails to provide sufficient return policies, support, service, and so forth.

To discourage this type of gray market distribution, many manufacturers have resorted to large disclaimers on their websites, packaging, and other communications to warn consumers that the manufacturer's product warranty becomes null and void unless the item has been purchased from an authorized dealer. In some cases, these authorized dealers also purposefully seek to sell at the lowest prices, as we discuss in the next section.

PRICING STRATEGIES

In this section, we discuss a number of commonly used price strategies: everyday low pricing, high/low pricing, and new product strategies.[22]

| LO 14-6 | Describe the difference between an everyday low price strategy (EDLP) and a high/low price strategy. |

Everyday Low Pricing (EDLP)

With an **everyday low pricing (EDLP)** strategy, companies stress the continuity of their retail prices at a level somewhere between the regular, nonsale price and the deep-discount sale prices their competitors may offer.[23] By reducing consumers' search costs, EDLP adds value; consumers can spend less of their valuable time comparing prices, including sale prices, at different stores. With its EDLP strategy, Walmart communicates to consumers that, for any given group of often-purchased items, its prices will tend to be lower than those of any other company in that market. This claim does not necessarily mean that every item that consumers may purchase will be priced lower at Walmart than anywhere else—in fact, some competitive retailers will offer lower prices on some items. However, for an average purchase, Walmart's prices tend to be lower overall.

High/Low Pricing

An alternative to EDLP is a **high/low pricing** strategy, which relies on the promotion of sales, during which prices are temporarily reduced to encourage purchases. A high/low strategy is appealing because it attracts two distinct market segments: those who are not price sensitive and are willing to pay the "high" price and more price sensitive customers who wait for the "low" sale price. High/low sellers can also create excitement and attract customers through the "get them while they last" atmosphere that occurs during a sale.

A high/low pricing strategy relies on the promotion of sales, during which prices are temporarily reduced to encourage purchases.
© Jeff Greenberg/PhotoEdit

gray market Employs irregular but not necessarily illegal methods; generally, it legally circumvents authorized channels of distribution to sell goods at prices lower than those intended by the manufacturer.

everyday low pricing (EDLP) A strategy companies use to emphasize the continuity of their retail prices at a level somewhere between the regular, nonsale price and the deep-discount sale prices their competitors may offer.

high/low pricing A *pricing* strategy that relies on the promotion of sales, during which prices are temporarily reduced to encourage purchases.

Sellers using a high/low pricing strategy often communicate their strategy through the creative use of a **reference price**, which is the price against which buyers compare the actual selling price of the product and that facilitates their evaluation process. The seller labels the reference price as the "regular price" or an "original price." When consumers view the "sale price" and compare it with the provided reference price, their perceptions of the value of the deal will likely increase.[24]

In the advertisement on this page, Sears has provided a reference price, in smaller print and labeled "Reg.," to indicate that $24.99 is the regular price of Lee jeans. In addition, the advertisement highlights the current "sale" price of $21.99. Thus, the reference price suggests to consumers that they are getting a good deal and will save money. However, as Ethical and Societal Dilemma 14.1 notes, sometimes the veracity of such a reference price is open to challenge.

> **WHEN THE NEW PRODUCT IS TRULY INNOVATIVE, OR WHAT WE CALL "NEW TO THE WORLD," DETERMINING CONSUMERS' PERCEPTIONS OF ITS VALUE AND PRICING IT ACCORDINGLY BECOME FAR MORE DIFFICULT.**

The reference price for each pair of pants is $24.99. It provides potential customers with an idea of the "regular price" before it was put on sale.
Courtesy Sears, Roebuck and Co.

LO 14-7	Describe the pricing strategies used when introducing a new product.

New Product Pricing Strategies

Developing pricing strategies for new products is one of the most challenging tasks a manager can undertake. When the new product is similar to what already appears on the market, this job is somewhat easier, because the product's approximate value has already been established and the value-based methods described earlier in this chapter can be employed. But when the new product is truly innovative, or what we call "new to the world," determining consumers' perceptions of its value and pricing it accordingly become far more difficult.

Two distinct new product pricing strategies are discussed next: market penetration pricing and price skimming.

Market Penetration Pricing Firms using a **market penetration strategy** set the initial price low for the introduction of the new product or service. Their objective is to build sales, market share, and profits quickly. The low market penetration price is an incentive to purchase the product immediately. Firms using a market penetration strategy expect the unit cost to drop significantly as the accumulated volume sold increases, an effect known as the **experience curve effect**. With this effect, as sales continue to grow, the costs continue to drop.

In addition to offering the potential to build sales, market share, and profits, penetration pricing discourages competitors from entering the market because the profit margin is relatively

ethical&societal dilemma

14.1

Is It Really 45 Percent Off?[iii]

For the truly fashionable—or at least those who consider themselves as members of that group—the trade-off between luxury and affordability can be a tricky one. You want the newest, hottest fashion, but trying to keep up can be exhausting on your wallet. What's a maven to do?

Private sale online sites such as Gilt, RueLaLa, and HauteLook promise a solution. They host limited-time sales of products from high-end fashion brands. A sale starts at a specified time and lasts for 48 hours or until the sale is sold out. So, if you must have the Nova Armored Baby Beaton handbag from Burberry, you can have it for 45 percent off the list price, or $877 instead of $1,595, as long as you are on Hautelook.com when the sale starts. Brick-and-mortar retailers are following suit with "flash sales," such as when Banana Republic offers 40 percent off its full-priced sweaters but only between 11:00 a.m. and 2:00 p.m. on specific days.

But is it really 40 or 45 percent off, and 45 percent off what? A reference price like $1,595 gives consumers a cue as to what that specific handbag should be worth. Research shows that the greater the difference between a suggested retail and a sale price, the greater the perceived value. When customers see Sears offering a refrigerator for $1,300 off its original price, that huge number is nearly impossible to ignore. The better the deal, the more consumers will be attracted to buy. But if the retailer inflates the suggested or original price, the percentage discount and dollars off seem much better than they actually are.

When the private sale sites have been caught inflating the suggested retail prices to show a greater percentage discount, they generally claim that the original prices they list are

accurate and come from the manufacturer. Any errors, they argue, are because the manufacturer gave them the wrong price, or else it might be due to employee error. For example, if the suggested retail price of the Burberry bag was actually only $1,100 instead of $1,595, then the bag was discounted only 20 percent. A customer in the heat of the moment may buy the bag because it is reported to be 45 percent off; were it only 20 percent off, she might not have purchased.

In some cases, the complicated coupon, discount, and flash pricing offers make it nearly impossible to determine the extent of the deal without a calculator. Because consumers rarely have the time or energy to calculate exactly what kind of discount they are getting, retailers can play on their excitement when it seems like a great deal.

Should private sale sites and in-store retailers be required to substantiate their reference prices? Which price should they use as the reference price? Is it their responsibility if the manufacturer gives them the wrong pricing information? Do you think they are intentionally misleading their customers?

What does a 45 percent off sale on private online sales sites like HauteLook really mean? Is it as good a deal as it appears?
© HauteLook

low. Furthermore, if the costs to produce the product drop because of the accumulated volume, competitors that enter the market later will face higher unit costs, at least until their volume catches up with the early entrant.

A penetration strategy has its drawbacks. First, the firm must have the capacity to satisfy a rapid rise in demand—or

at least be able to add that capacity quickly. Second, low price does not signal high quality. Of course, a price below their expectations decreases the risk for consumers to purchase the product and test its quality for themselves. Third, firms should avoid a penetration pricing strategy if some segments of the market are willing to pay more for the

CHAPTER 14 | Pricing Concepts for Establishing Value **301**

price skimming A strategy of selling a new product or service at a high price that *innovators* and *early adopters* are willing to pay in order to obtain it; after the high-price market segment becomes saturated and sales begin to slow down, the firm generally lowers the price to capture (or skim) the next most price-sensitive segment.

product; otherwise, the firm is just "leaving money on the table."

Price Skimming In many markets, and particularly for new and innovative products or services, innovators and early adopters (see Chapter 12) are willing to pay a higher price to obtain the new product or service. This strategy, known as **price skimming**, appeals to these segments of consumers who are willing to pay the premium price to have the innovation first. This tactic is particularly common in technology markets, where sellers know that customers of the hottest and coolest products will wait in line for hours, desperate to be the first to own the newest version. These innovators are willing to pay the very highest prices to obtain brand-new examples of technology advances, with exciting product enhancements. However, after this high-price market segment becomes saturated and sales begin to slow down, companies generally lower the price to capture (or skim) the next most price-sensitive market segment, which is willing to pay a somewhat lower price. For most companies, the price dropping process can continue until the demand for the product has been satisfied, even at the lowest price points.

The spread of new media for movies illustrates a price skimming strategy. As with VCRs in the 1970s and DVD players

> " For price skimming to work, the product or service must be perceived as breaking new ground in some way, offering consumers new benefits currently unavailable in alternative products. "

in the 1990s, consumers were slow to embrace the new, more expensive Blu-ray discs. But enough early adopters purchased the Blu-ray discs that manufacturers continued to refine Blu-ray players to penetrate wider target markets. Consumers are buying the devices at a faster pace than the earlier movie-playing devices. One obvious reason for this sales growth is that prices for high-quality Blu-ray players have dropped below $80,[25] a steep drop from the $300-plus that retailers charged for debut models.[26]

For price skimming to work, the product or service must be perceived as breaking new ground in some way, offering consumers new benefits currently unavailable in alternative products. When they believe it will work, firms use skimming strategies for a variety of reasons. Some may start by pricing relatively high to signal high quality to the market. Others may decide to price high at first to limit demand, which gives them time to build their production capacities. Similarly, some firms employ a skimming strategy to try to quickly earn back some of the high research and development investments they made for the new product. Finally, firms employ skimming strategies to test consumers' price sensitivity. A firm that prices too high can always lower the price, but if the price is initially set too low, it is almost impossible to raise it without significant consumer resistance.

Furthermore, for a skimming pricing strategy to be successful, competitors cannot be able to enter the market easily; otherwise, price competition will likely force lower prices and undermine the whole strategy. Competitors might be prevented from entering the market through patent protections, their inability to copy the innovation (because it is complex to manufacture, its raw materials are hard to get, or the product relies on proprietary technology), or the high costs of entry.

Skimming strategies also face a significant potential drawback in the relatively high unit costs associated with producing small volumes of products. Therefore, firms must consider the trade-off between earning a higher price and suffering higher production costs. Finally, firms using a skimming strategy for new products must face the consequences of ultimately having to lower the price as demand wanes. Margins suffer, and customers who purchased the product or service at the higher initial price may become irritated when the price falls.

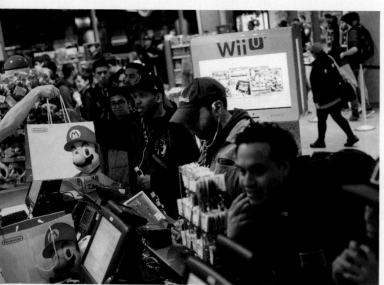

Price skimming is often used for high-demand video games like Mario Kart *because fans will pay a higher price to be one of the first to own the newest version.*

© Michael Nagle/Bloomberg via Getty Images

 check yourself

1. Explain the difference between EDLP and high/low pricing.

2. What pricing strategies should be considered when introducing a new product?

LEGAL AND ETHICAL ASPECTS OF PRICING

With so many different pricing strategies and tactics, it is no wonder that unscrupulous firms find ample opportunity to engage in pricing practices that can hurt consumers. We now take a look at some of the legal and ethical implications of pricing.

Prices tend to fluctuate naturally and respond to varying market conditions. Thus, though we rarely see firms attempting to control the market in terms of product quality or advertising, they often engage in pricing practices that can unfairly reduce competition or harm consumers directly through fraud and deception. A host of laws and regulations at both the federal and state levels attempt to prevent unfair pricing practices, but some are poorly enforced, and others are difficult to prove.

Deceptive or Illegal Price Advertising

Although it is always illegal and unethical to lie in advertising, a certain amount of "puffery" is typically allowed (see Chapter 18).[27] But price advertisements should never deceive consumers to the point of causing harm. For example, a local car dealer's advertising that it had the "best deals in town" would likely be considered puffery. In contrast, advertising "the lowest prices, guaranteed" makes a very specific claim and, if not true, can be considered deceptive.

Deceptive Reference Prices Previously, we introduced reference prices, which create reference points for the buyer against which to compare the selling price. If the reference price is bona fide, the advertisement is informative. If the reference price has been inflated or is just plain fictitious, however, the advertisement is deceptive and may cause harm to consumers. But it is not easy to determine whether a reference price is bona fide. What standard should be used? If an advertisement specifies a "regular price," just what qualifies as regular? How many units must the store sell at this price for it to be a bona fide regular price—half the stock? A few? Just one? Finally, what if the store offers the item for sale at the regular price but customers do not buy any? Can it still be considered a regular price? In general, if a seller is going to label a price as a regular price, the Better Business Bureau suggests that at least 50 percent of the sales have occurred at that price.[28]

Loss Leader Pricing As we discussed previously, leader pricing is a legitimate attempt to build store traffic by pricing a regularly purchased item aggressively but still above the

> ## A host of laws and regulations at both the federal and state levels attempt to prevent unfair pricing practices, but some are poorly enforced, and others are difficult to prove.

UK-based Tesco wasn't allowed to make the claim that it is "Britain's Biggest Discounter" because it was considered misleading. Such a claim would probably be considered puffery in the United States, and therefore allowed.
© Alex Segre/Alamy

Is this a legitimate sale, or is the retailer using deceptive reference prices?
© Jeff Greenberg/PhotoEdit

loss leader pricing
Loss leader pricing takes the tactic of *leader pricing* one step further by lowering the price below the store's cost.

bait and switch A deceptive practice of luring customers into the store with a very low advertised price on an item (the bait), only to aggressively pressure them into purchasing a higher-priced model (the switch) by disparaging the low-priced item, comparing it unfavorably with the higher-priced model, or professing an inadequate supply of the lower-priced item.

predatory pricing A firm's practice of setting a very low price for one or more of its products with the intent to drive its competition out of business; illegal under both the Sherman Antitrust Act and the Federal Trade Commission Act.

price discrimination The practice of selling the same product to different resellers (wholesalers, distributors, or retailers) or to the ultimate consumer at different prices; some, but not all, forms of price discrimination are illegal.

price fixing The practice of colluding with other firms to control prices.

store's cost. **Loss leader pricing** takes this tactic one step further by lowering the price *below* the store's cost. No doubt you have seen "buy one, get one free" offers at grocery and discount stores. Unless the markup for the item is 100 percent of the cost, these sales obviously do not generate enough revenue from the sale of one unit to cover the store's cost for both units, which means it has essentially priced the total for both items below cost, unless the manufacturer is absorbing the cost of the promotion to generate volume. In some states, this form of pricing is illegal.

Bait and Switch Another form of deceptive price advertising occurs when sellers advertise items for a very low price without the intent to really sell any. This **bait-and-switch** tactic is a deceptive practice because the store lures customers in with a very low price on an item (the bait), only to aggressively pressure these customers into purchasing a higher-priced model (the switch) by disparaging the low-priced item, comparing it unfavorably with the higher-priced model, or professing an inadequate supply of the lower-priced item. Again, the laws against bait-and-switch practices are difficult to enforce because salespeople, simply as a function of their jobs, are always trying to get customers to trade up to a higher-priced model without necessarily deliberately baiting them. The key to proving deception centers on the intent of the seller, which is also difficult to prove.

Predatory Pricing

When a firm sets a very low price for one or more of its products with the intent to drive its competition out of business, it is using **predatory pricing**. Predatory pricing is illegal under both the Sherman Antitrust Act and the Federal Trade Commission Act because it constrains free trade and represents a form of unfair competition. It also tends to promote a concentrated market with a few dominant firms (an oligopoly).

But again, predation is difficult to prove. First, one must demonstrate intent; that is, that the firm intended to drive out its competition or prevent competitors from entering the market.

Second, the complainant must prove that the firm charged prices lower than its average cost, an equally difficult task.

The issue of predatory pricing has arisen because of Google's dominance in the search engine market. Advertisers on Google bid on specific keywords; if they win the auction, their product appears first in the paid results section on the search engine. However, Google also includes a "quality handicap" and charges poor-quality advertisers more. It claims this tactic ensures that users are more likely to find high-quality results from their searches. The algorithm it uses to define quality is confidential, but some experts allege that Google has manipulated the paid search results in such a way that it undermines competitors' offerings while promoting its own. It appears these claims may be true; in 2012 the Federal Trade Commission (FTC) found enough evidence for search results manipulation that it recommended the government sue Google, and in 2013 a European Commission came to similar conclusions.[29] The unresolved question is: because of Google's dominance in the search engine market, with its resulting ability to control prices, would its practice of charging more for its "quality handicap" be predatory?

Price Discrimination

There are many forms of price discrimination, but only some of them are considered illegal under the Clayton Act and the Robinson-Patman Act. When firms sell the same product to different resellers (wholesalers, distributors, or retailers) at different prices, it can be considered **price discrimination**; usually, larger firms receive lower prices.

We have already discussed the use of quantity discounts, which is a legitimate method of charging different prices to different customers on the basis of the quantity they purchase. The legality of this tactic stems from the assumption that it costs less to sell and service 1,000 units to one customer than 100 units to 10 customers. But quantity discounts must be available to all customers and not be structured in such a way that they consistently and obviously favor one or a few buyers over others.

The Robinson-Patman Act does not apply to sales to end consumers, at which point many forms of price discrimination occur. For example, students and seniors often receive discounts on food and movie tickets, which is perfectly acceptable under federal law. Those engaged in online auctions like eBay are also practicing a legal form of price discrimination because sellers are selling the same item to different buyers at various prices. In addition, to deal ethically with the rising costs of health care, some hospitals offer a "sliding scale" based on income, such that lower-income patients receive discounts or even free medical care, especially for children.[30]

Price Fixing

Price fixing is the practice of colluding with other firms to control prices. Price fixing might be either horizontal or vertical. Whereas horizontal price fixing is clearly illegal under the Sherman Antitrust Act, vertical price fixing falls into a gray area.[31]

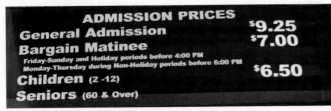

Is this price discrimination illegal?
© Tom Prettyman/PhotoEdit

Horizontal price fixing occurs when competitors that produce and sell competing products or services collude, or work together, to control prices, effectively taking price out of the decision process for consumers. This practice clearly reduces competition and is illegal. Six South African airlines were accused of colluding to hike the price of fares for flights within the country during the World Cup.[32] The major tobacco companies also have been accused of colluding to fix the prices of cigarettes worldwide.[33] As a general rule of thumb, competing firms should refrain from discussing prices or terms and conditions of sale with competitors. If firms want to know competitors' prices, they can look at a competitor's advertisements, its websites, or its stores.

Vertical price fixing occurs when parties at different levels of the same marketing channel (e.g., manufacturers and retailers) agree to control the prices passed on to consumers. Manufacturers often encourage retailers to sell their merchandise at a specific price, known as the **manufacturer's suggested retail price (MSRP)**. Manufacturers set MSRPs to reduce retail price competition among retailers, stimulate retailers to provide complementary services, and support the manufacturer's merchandise. Manufacturers enforce MSRPs by withholding benefits such as cooperative advertising or even refusing to deliver merchandise to noncomplying retailers. The Supreme Court has ruled that the ability of a manufacturer to require retailers to sell merchandise at MSRP should be decided on a case-by-case basis, depending on the individual circumstances.[34]

As these legal issues clearly demonstrate, pricing decisions involve many ethical considerations. In determining both their pricing strategies and their pricing tactics, marketers must always balance their goal of inducing customers, through price, to find value and the need to deal honestly and fairly with those same customers. Whether they are another business or individual consumers, buyers can be influenced by a variety of pricing methods. It is up to marketers to determine which of these methods works best for the seller, the buyer, and the community. ■

horizontal price fixing Occurs when competitors that produce and sell competing products collude, or work together, to control prices, effectively taking price out of the decision process for consumers.

vertical price fixing Occurs when parties at different levels of the same marketing channel (e.g., manufacturers and retailers) collude to control the prices passed on to consumers.

manufacturer's suggested retail price (MSRP) The price that manufacturers suggest retailers use to sell their merchandise.

 check yourself

1. What common pricing practices are considered to be illegal or unethical?

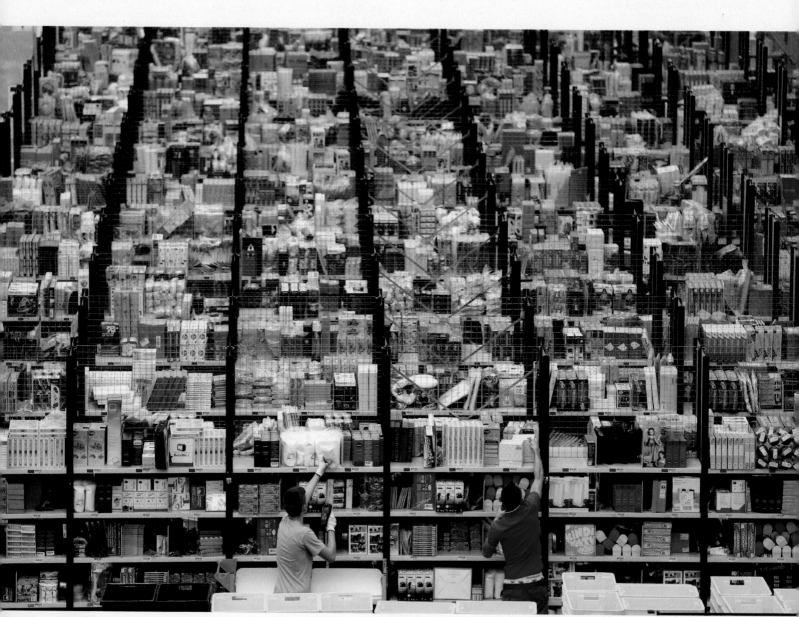

Chapter fifteen

supply chain and channel management

Already well established as an efficient shipper of orders, Amazon continues to seek to do even better. Currently, Amazon receives an order, labels and packages it, loads it onto a delivery truck (run by UPS or the U.S. Postal Service, depending on the day and delivery details), and waits for confirmation that this third-party logistics provider has delivered the product directly to the customer's door. In this traditional process, the online retail giant seeks to improve by adding more warehouses that can provide more customers with overnight or same-day delivery.

But two more striking innovations instead aim to reinvent the supply chain completely, to benefit both customers and itself. First, Amazon recently applied for and received a patent for its "anticipatory shipping" system, which starts readying packages for delivery before the customer even adds the item to his or her virtual cart.[1] With anticipatory shipping, Amazon boxes and ships out products that it expects customers will want, according to their previous purchases, in the belief that they are likely to order

LEARNING OBJECTIVES

After reading this chapter, you should be able to:

LO 15-1   Understand the importance of marketing channels and supply chain management.

LO 15-2   Understand the difference between direct and indirect marketing channels.

LO 15-3   Describe how marketing channels are managed.

LO 15-4   Describe the flow of information and merchandise in the marketing channel.

them soon. To determine what to ship, Amazon uses information from customers' previous orders, product searches, shopping cart contents, and previous returns.

This innovation promises to be particularly beneficial for popular books, movies, and games, which people clearly have

continued on p. 308

marketing channel management Also called supply chain management; refers to a set of approaches and techniques firms employ to efficiently and effectively integrate their suppliers.

supply chain management Refers to a set of approaches and techniques firms employ to efficiently and effectively integrate their suppliers, manufacturers, warehouses, stores, and transportation intermediaries into a seamless value chain in which merchandise is produced and distributed in the right quantities, to the right locations, and at the right time, as well as to minimize systemwide costs while satisfying the service levels their customers require.

continued from p. 307

announced their desire to have in hand the very day they are released. If Amazon can get it to their homes on that same day, it might discourage customers from visiting physical retail locations, because their wait times would be even lower than brick-and-mortar stores can offer. In this sense, Amazon is using Big Data to predict demand and thus edge out its rivals. However, critics caution that when Amazon's algorithms are incorrect, the necessary returns could grow rapidly to become quite costly. In response, Amazon has suggested that it might simply convert any unwanted deliveries into gifts, thus building goodwill among customers who receive a desirable new order for no cost.

Second, Amazon has not limited its streamlining efforts to the retailer–customer link. Instead, it has created its Vendor Flex program, which seeks to lower overall transportation costs. Among the first

Always on the forefront of retail innovation, Amazon is experimenting with "anticipatory shipping," which ships out products that it <u>expects</u> customers will want before they order them. It is also lowering its transportation costs by engaging its largest suppliers to operate Amazon fulfillment centers within the suppliers' warehouses, thus eliminating the cost of getting merchandise to Amazon's fulfillment centers.
© Bloomberg/Getty Images

Target reacted by moving all P&G products from prominent end-cap positions in its stores to less prestigious and less visible locations. Target also stopped using P&G as its primary source of advice for planning merchandising strategies within each category. ■

In this chapter, we discuss the third P, *place,* which includes all activities required to get the right product to the right customer when that customer wants it.[2] Specifically, as we noted in Chapter 1, **marketing channel management**, which also has been called **supply chain management**, refers to a set of

> ## "Students of marketing often overlook or underestimate the importance of place in the marketing mix, simply because it happens behind the scenes."

partners in Amazon's Vendor Flex program is Procter & Gamble (P&G), which agreed to allow Amazon to build fulfillment centers within P&G's own warehouses. The cost savings accrue because the new system eliminates the costs of transporting P&G's products to Amazon's fulfillment centers.

Not everyone is excited about this innovative new partnership, though. Companies such as Target, which have enjoyed long-term relationships with P&G, are taking notice and taking action. After learning of the Vendor Flex program between Amazon and P&G,

approaches and techniques firms employ to efficiently and effectively integrate their suppliers, manufacturers, warehouses, stores, and transportation intermediaries into a seamless operation in which merchandise is produced and distributed in the right quantities, to the right locations, and at the right time, as well as to minimize systemwide costs while satisfying the service levels their customers require.[3] Students of marketing often overlook or underestimate the importance of place in the marketing mix, simply because it happens behind the scenes. Yet marketing channel management adds value, say for Amazon's customers, because it gets the products to them efficiently, quickly, and at low cost.

LO 15-1 | Understand the importance of marketing channels and supply chain management.

THE IMPORTANCE OF MARKETING CHANNEL/ SUPPLY CHAIN MANAGEMENT

So far in this book we have reviewed the methods companies use to conduct in-depth market research, gain insights into consumer and business behaviors, segment markets, select the best target markets, develop new products and services, and set prices that provide good value. But even if firms execute these activities flawlessly, unless they can secure the placement of products in appropriate outlets in sufficient quantities exactly when customers want them, they are likely to fail. Adding Value 15.1 examines how Goya Foods recognized it needed to do a better job at getting products into stores to satisfy customers' demands and what it did about it.

Convincing wholesalers and retailers to carry new products can be more difficult than you might think. **Wholesalers** are firms that buy products from manufacturers and resell them to retailers; retailers sell products directly to consumers. For example, PenAgain, a small California-based manufacturer of ergonomic pens and other writing instruments, wanted to put its offerings in Walmart stores, but first it had to get Walmart to buy what it was selling.[4] After a tough selling session, Walmart agreed to give PenAgain a one-month trial in 500 stores, but only if it lowered its costs. PenAgain thus moved production overseas. Walmart provided no marketing support though, and PenAgain was too small to afford traditional print or television advertising, so it developed a viral marketing program and produced displays to use in the stores. A **viral marketing program** is one that encourages people to pass along a marketing message to

wholesaler Firm engaged in buying, taking title to, often storing, and physically handling goods in large quantities, then reselling the goods (usually in smaller quantities) to retailers or industrial or business users.

viral marketing program A promotional strategy that encourages people to pass along a marketing message to other potential consumers.

Adding Value 15.1

The Beans May Be Slow Cooked, but the Delivery Is Quick[i]

As Goya Foods celebrated its 75th year in business, its top managers were dealing with some very serious growing pains. Selling a wide variety of Hispanic and Latin foods, the company had achieved a dominant market share, was the largest Hispanic-owned company in the United States, and had annual sales of around $1 billion. In specific local and regional markets, demand for its products was substantial—a great success that also came with a notable challenge.

That is, many of the markets that loved Goya products had slightly different preferences, reflecting the diversity of Hispanic consumers in the United States. People of Cuban heritage wanted items made somewhat differently than did consumers whose families originated in Mexico, and so on. Thus, the number of unique inventory items or stock-keeping units (SKUs) that Goya provided reached over 1,600. The supply chain network grew more complex. And in all the confusion, service levels, as measured by its in-stock availability, dropped. Quite simply, with all the complexity, buyers were spending too much time manually calculating and determining shipments and inventory levels, leaving them insufficient time or energy to think strategically. Making decisions without sophisticated analytics was not something that Goya could sustain anymore.

To satisfy its diverse market of Hispanic consumers, Goya expanded the number of unique inventory items it carried to 1,600. To keep service levels high, Goya implemented an automated transportation and inventory planning system.
© Goya Foods Inc

For Goya, the solution was to automate the transportation and inventory planning processes, using software that enabled it to keep track of demand, order fulfillment, and replenishment with minimal effort. By automating its ordering processes, Goya's buyers could work smarter. For example, making sure delivery trucks were more efficiently used resulted in millions of dollars in transportation savings. The new system also improved its in-stock availability to 98 percent, which resulted in a proportional increase in sales.

other potential consumers. To keep track of sales, it relied on Walmart's Internet-based Retail Link system, though it also hired a firm that sends representatives into stores to check out display placement and customer traffic. Finally, PenAgain agreed to adhere to strict packaging, labeling, and shipping requirements. And remember, for all this effort, its entry in stores was only a test, and a very expensive gamble! But if it could succeed in Walmart stores, PenAgain would be well on its way to prosperity.

In the simplified supply chain in Exhibit 15.1, manufacturers make products and sell them to retailers or wholesalers. The exhibit would be much more complicated if we had included the suppliers of materials to manufacturers and all the manufacturers, wholesalers, and stores in a typical marketing channel.

Exhibit 15.1 represents a typical flow of manufactured goods: Manufacturers ship to a wholesaler or to a retailer's distribution center (e.g., Manufacturer 1 and Manufacturer 3) or directly to stores (Manufacturer 2). In addition, many variations on this supply chain exist. Some retail chains, such as Home Depot or Costco, function as both

> *Some retail chains, such as Home Depot or Costco, function as both retailers and wholesalers.*

retailers and wholesalers. They act as retailers when they sell to consumers directly and as wholesalers when they sell to other businesses such as building contractors or restaurant owners. When manufacturers such as Avon sell directly to consumers, they perform both production and retailing activities. When Dell sells computers to a university or business, it engages in a business-to-business (B2B) transaction, but when it sells to students or employees individually, it is a B2C (business-to-consumer) operation.

Marketing Channels Add Value

Why do manufacturers use wholesalers or retailers? Don't these added channel members just cut into their profits? Wouldn't it be cheaper for consumers to buy directly from manufacturers? In a simple agrarian economy, the best supply chain likely does follow a direct route from manufacturer to consumer: The consumer goes to the farm and buys food directly from the farmer. Modern eat-local environmental campaigns suggest just such a process. But before the consumer can eat a fresh steak procured from a local farm, she needs to cook it. Assuming the

▼ **EXHIBIT 15.1** Simplified Supply Chain

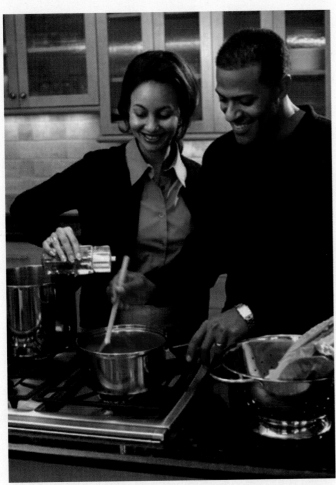

How many companies are involved in making and getting a stove to your kitchen?
© Thinkstock/Alamy RF

and materials. The stove maker turns the components into the stove. The transportation company gets the stove to the retailer. The retailer stores the stove until the customer wants it, educates the customer about product features, and delivers and installs the stove. At each step, the stove becomes more costly but also more valuable to the consumer.

Marketing Channel Management Affects Other Aspects of Marketing

Every marketing decision is affected by and has an effect on marketing channels. When products are designed and manufactured, how and when the critical components reach the factory must be coordinated with production. The sales department must coordinate its delivery promises with the factory or distribution or fulfillment centers. A **distribution center**, a facility for the receipt, storage, and redistribution of goods to company stores, may be operated by retailers, manufacturers, or distribution specialists.[6] Similar to a distribution center, instead of shipping to stores, **fulfillment centers** are used to ship directly to customers. Furthermore, advertising and promotion must be coordinated with those departments that control inventory and transportation. There is no faster way to lose credibility with customers than to promise deliveries or run a promotion and then not have the merchandise when the customer expects it.

> THERE IS NO FASTER WAY TO LOSE CREDIBILITY WITH CUSTOMERS THAN TO PROMISE DELIVERIES OR RUN A PROMOTION AND THEN NOT HAVE THE MERCHANDISE WHEN THE CUSTOMER EXPECTS IT.

consumer doesn't know how to make a stove and lacks the materials to do so, she must rely on a stove maker. The stove maker, which has the necessary knowledge, must buy raw materials and components from various suppliers, make the stove, and then make it available to the consumer. If the stove maker isn't located near the consumer, the stove must be transported to where the consumer has access to it. To make matters even more complicated, the consumer may want to view a choice of stoves, hear about all their features, and have the stove delivered and installed.

Each participant in the channel adds value.[5] The components manufacturer helps the stove manufacturer by supplying parts

| LO 15-2 | Understand the difference between direct and indirect marketing channels. |

DESIGNING MARKETING CHANNELS

When a firm is just starting out or entering a new market, it doesn't typically have the option of designing the best marketing channel structure—that is, choosing from whom it buys or to whom it sells. A new sporting goods retailer may not have

direct marketing channel The manufacturer sells directly to the buyer.

indirect marketing channel When one or more intermediaries work with manufacturers to provide goods and services to customers.

the option of carrying all the manufacturer lines it wants because other competing retailers in its market area might carry the same products. On the other side, a small specialty sporting goods apparel manufacturer may not be able to place its products in major stores like Sports Authority because its line is unproven, and the products might duplicate lines that the retailer already carries. Chapter 16 discusses how manufacturers choose their retailer partners in more depth.

Although there are thus various constraints on marketing channel partners with regard to the design of the best channel structure, all marketing channels take the form of a direct channel, an indirect channel, or some combination thereof.

Direct Marketing Channel

As shown on the left side of Exhibit 15.2, there are no intermediaries between the buyer and seller in a **direct marketing channel**. Typically, the seller is a manufacturer, such as when

a carpentry business sells bookcases through its own store and online to individual consumers. The seller also can be an individual, such as when a knitter sells blankets and scarves at craft fairs, on Etsy, and through eBay. (Recall our discussion of consumer-to-consumer [C2C] transactions in Chapter 1.) When the buyer is another business, such as when Boeing sells planes to JetBlue, the marketing channel still is direct, but in this case, the transaction is a business-to-business one (see Chapter 7).

Indirect Marketing Channel

In **indirect marketing channels**, one or more intermediaries work with manufacturers to provide goods and services to customers. In some cases, only one intermediary might be involved. Automobile manufacturers such as Ford and General Motors often use indirect distribution, such that dealers act as retailers, as shown in the middle of Exhibit 15.2. The right side of Exhibit 15.2 reveals how wholesalers are more common when the company does not buy in sufficient quantities to make it cost effective for the manufacturer to deal directly with them—independent book sellers, wine merchants, or independent drug stores, for example. Wholesalers are also prevalent in less developed economies, in which large retailers are rare.

LO 15-3 | Describe how marketing channels are managed.

MANAGING THE MARKETING CHANNEL AND SUPPLY CHAIN

Marketing channels and supply chains comprise various buying entities such as retailers and wholesalers, sellers such as manufacturers or wholesalers, and facilitators of the exchange such as transportation companies. Similar to interpersonal interactions, their relationships can range from close working partnerships to one-time arrangements. In almost all cases, though, interactions occur because the parties want something from each other: Home Depot wants hammers from Stanley Tool Company; Stanley wants an opportunity to sell its tools to the general public; both companies want UPS to deliver the merchandise.

Each member of the marketing channel also performs a specialized role. If one member believes that another has failed to do its job correctly or efficiently, it can replace that member. So, if Stanley isn't getting good service from UPS, it can switch to FedEx. If Home Depot believes its customers do not perceive Stanley tools as a good value, it may buy from another tool company. Home Depot even could decide to make its own tools or use its own trucks to pick up tools from Stanley. However, anytime a marketing channel member is replaced, the function it has performed remains, so someone needs to complete it.[7]

If a marketing channel is to run efficiently, the participating members must cooperate. Often, however, supply chain members

▼ **EXHIBIT 15.2** Direct and Indirect Channel Strategies

Direct channel

Direct channel
One intermediary

Direct channel
Two intermediaries

Manufacturer

Manufacturer

Manufacturer

Wholesaler

Retailer

Retailer

Customer

Customer

Customer

▼ EXHIBIT 15.3 Vertical versus Horizontal Channel Conflict

vertical channel conflict A type of channel conflict in which members of the same marketing channel, for example, manufacturers, wholesalers, and retailers, are in disagreement or discord.

horizontal channel conflict A type of channel conflict in which members at the same level of a marketing channel, for example, two competing retailers or two competing manufacturers, are in disagreement or discord, such as when they are in a price war.

have conflicting goals, and this may result in channel conflict (Exhibit 15.3). For instance, Stanley wants Home Depot to carry all its tools but not those of its competitors so that Stanley can maximize its sales. But Home Depot carries a mix of tool brands so it can maximize the sales in its tool category. When supply chain members that buy and sell to one another are not in agreement about their goals, roles, or rewards, **vertical channel conflict** or discord results.

Horizontal channel conflict can also occur when there is disagreement or discord among members at the same level in a marketing channel, such as two competing retailers or two competing manufacturers. As we mentioned in the opening vignette, Target experiences a conflict with Amazon because of its Vendor Flex program with Procter & Gamble (P&G). Amazon benefits from the program, which lowers its transportation costs, but Target believes that it gives its competitor an unfair advantage.

Avoiding vertical channel conflicts demands open, honest communication. Buyers and vendors all must understand what

drives the other party's business, their roles in the relationship, each firm's strategies, and any problems that might arise over the course of the relationship. Amazon and P&G recognize that it is in their common interest to remain profitable business partners. Amazon's customers demand and expect to find P&G products on its website; P&G needs the sales generated through Amazon. Amazon cannot demand prices so low that P&G cannot make money, and P&G must be flexible enough to accommodate the needs of this important customer. With a common goal, both firms have the incentive to cooperate because they know that by doing so, each will boost its sales.

Common goals also help sustain the relationship when expected benefits fail to arise. If one P&G shipment fails to reach the Amazon section of one of its fulfilment centers due to an uncontrollable event such as a demand forecasting miscalculation, Amazon does not suddenly call off the whole arrangement. Instead, it recognizes the incident as a simple, isolated mistake and maintains the good working relationship, because Amazon knows that both it and P&G are committed to the same goals in the long run.

> " With a common goal, both firms have the incentive to cooperate because they know that by doing so, each will boost its sales. "

The Home Depot and Stanley Tool Company have a mutually beneficial partnership. Home Depot buys tools from Stanley because its customers find value in Stanley products. Stanley sells tools to Home Depot because it has established an excellent market for its products.
Courtesy The Stanley Works

independent (conventional) marketing channel A marketing channel in which several independent members—a manufacturer, a wholesaler, and a retailer—each attempts to satisfy its own objectives and maximize its profits, often at the expense of the other members.

vertical marketing system A supply chain in which the members act as a unified system; there are three types: *administered, contractual,* and *corporate*.

administered vertical marketing system A *supply chain* system in which there is no common ownership and no contractual relationships, but the dominant channel member controls the channel relationship.

power A situation that occurs in a marketing channel in which one member has the means or ability to have control over the actions of another member in a channel at a different level of distribution, such as if a retailer has power or control over a supplier.

reward power A type of marketing channel power that occurs when the channel member exerting the power offers rewards to gain power, often a monetary incentive, for getting another channel member to do what it wants it to do.

In this sense, their partnership exhibits both of the non–mutually exclusive ways that exist to manage a marketing channel or supply chain: Coordinate the channel using a vertical marketing system and develop strong relationships with marketing channel partners—topics we now examine.

Managing the Marketing Channel and Supply Chain through Vertical Marketing Systems

Although conflict is likely in any marketing channel, it is generally more pronounced when the channel members are independent entities. Marketing channels that are more closely aligned, whether by contract or ownership, share common goals and therefore are less prone to conflict.

In an **independent** or **conventional marketing channel**, several independent members—a manufacturer, a wholesaler, and a retailer—attempt to satisfy their own objectives and

▼ **EXHIBIT 15.4** Independent versus Vertical Marketing Channels

Independent marketing channel

Vertical marketing channel

> ❝ THE MORE FORMAL THE VERTICAL MARKETING SYSTEM, THE LESS LIKELY CONFLICT IS TO ENSUE. ❞

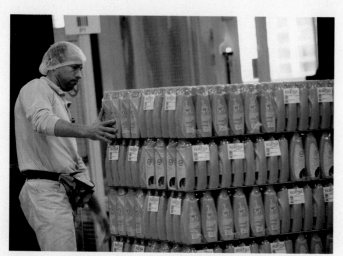

Amazon and Procter & Gamble recognize that it is in their common interest to remain profitable business partners.
© Daniel Mihailescu/AFP/Getty Images

maximize their profits, often at the expense of the other members, as we portray in Exhibit 15.4 (left). None of the participants have any control over the others. Using our previous example, the first time Walmart purchases pens from PenAgain, both parties likely try to extract as much profit from the deal as possible. After the deal is consummated, neither party feels any responsibility to the other.

Over time, though, Walmart and PenAgain might develop a relationship marked by routinized, automatic transactions, such that Walmart's customers come to expect PenAgain products in stores, and PenAgain depends on Walmart to buy a good portion of its output. This scenario represents the first phase of a **vertical marketing system**, a marketing channel in which the members act as a unified system, as in Exhibit 15.4 (right). Three types of vertical marketing systems—administered, contractual, and corporate—reflect increasing phases of formalization and control. The more formal the vertical marketing system, the less likely conflict is to ensue.

coercive power
Threatening or punishing the other channel member for not undertaking certain tasks. Delaying payment for late delivery would be an example.

referent power
A type of marketing channel power that occurs if one channel member wants to be associated with another channel member. The channel member with whom the others wish to be associated has the power and can get them to do what they want.

expertise power
When a channel member uses its expertise as leverage to influence the actions of another channel member.

information power
A type of marketing channel power within an administered vertical marketing system in which one party (e.g., the manufacturer) provides or withholds important information to influence the actions of another party (e.g., the retailer).

legitimate power
A type of marketing channel power that occurs if the channel member exerting the power has a contractual agreement with the other channel member that requires the other channel member to behave in a certain way. This type of power occurs in an administered vertical marketing system.

Administered Vertical Marketing System The Walmart–PenAgain marketing channel relationship offers an example of an **administered vertical marketing system**: There is no common ownership or contractual relationships, but the dominant channel member controls or holds the balance of power. Because of its size and relative power, Walmart imposes controls on PenAgain. **Power** in a marketing channel exists when one firm has the means or ability to dictate the actions of another member at a different level of distribution (Exhibit 15.5). A retailer like Walmart exercises its power over suppliers in several ways. With its **reward power**, Walmart offers rewards, often a monetary incentive, if PenAgain will do what Walmart wants it to do. **Coercive power** arises when Walmart threatens to punish or punishes the other channel member for not undertaking certain tasks, such as if it were to delay payment to PenAgain for a late delivery. Walmart may also have **referent power** over PenAgain if the supplier desperately wants to be associated with Walmart, because being known as an important Walmart supplier enables PenAgain to attract other retailers' business. If Walmart exerts **expertise power** over PenAgain, it relies on its expertise with marketing pens. Because Walmart has vast information about the office supply and back-to-school markets, it can exert **information power** over PenAgain by providing or withholding such important market information. Finally, **legitimate power** is based on getting a channel member such as PenAgain to behave in a certain way because of a contractual agreement between the two firms. As Walmart deals with PenAgain and its other suppliers, it likely exerts multiple types of power to influence their behaviors. If either party dislikes the way the relationship is going though, it can simply walk away.

Contractual Vertical Marketing System Over time, Walmart and PenAgain may formalize their relationship by entering into contracts that dictate various terms, such as how much Walmart will buy each month and at what price, as well as the penalties for late deliveries. In **contractual vertical marketing systems** like this, independent firms at different levels of the marketing channel join through contracts to obtain economies of scale and coordination and to reduce conflict.[8]

Franchising is the most common type of contractual vertical marketing system. **Franchising** is a contractual agreement

contractual vertical marketing system A system in which independent firms at different levels of the supply chain join together through contracts to obtain economies of scale and coordination and to reduce conflict.

franchising A contractual agreement between a *franchisor* and a *franchisee* that allows the franchisee to operate a business using a name and format developed and supported by the franchisor.

Anytime Fitness was ranked the number one franchise by Entrepreneur *magazine in 2014.*
© Bryan Mitchell/AP Photo

▼ **EXHIBIT 15.5** Bases of Power

POWER

Reward | Coercive | Referent | Expertise | Information | Legitimate

corporate vertical marketing system

A system in which the parent company has complete control and can dictate the priorities and objectives of the supply chain; it may own facilities such as manufacturing plants, warehouse facilities, retail outlets, and design studios.

between a franchisor and a franchisee that allows the franchisee to operate a retail outlet using a name and format developed and supported by the franchisor. Exhibit 15.6 lists the United States' top franchise opportunities. These rankings, determined by *Entrepreneur* magazine, are created using a number of objective measures such as financial strength, stability, growth rate, and size of the franchise system.[9]

In a franchise contract, the franchisee pays a lump sum plus a royalty on all sales in return for the right to operate a business in a specific location. The franchisee also agrees to operate the outlet in accordance with the procedures prescribed by the franchisor. The franchisor typically provides assistance in locating and building the business, developing the products or services sold, management training, and advertising. To maintain the franchisee's reputation, the franchisor also makes sure that all outlets provide the same quality of services and products.

> " A franchise system combines the entrepreneurial advantages of owning a business with the efficiencies of vertical marketing systems that function under single ownership. "

A franchise system combines the entrepreneurial advantages of owning a business with the efficiencies of vertical marketing systems that function under single ownership (i.e., a corporate system, as we discuss next). Franchisees are motivated to make their stores successful because they receive the profits after they pay the royalty to the franchisor. The franchisor is motivated to develop new products, services, and systems and to promote the franchise because it receives royalties on all sales. Advertising, product development, and system development are all done efficiently by the franchisor, with costs shared by all franchisees.

Corporate Vertical Marketing System

In a **corporate vertical marketing system**, the parent company has complete control and can dictate the priorities and objectives of the marketing channel because it owns multiple segments of the channel, such as manufacturing plants, warehouse facilities, and retail outlets. By virtue of its ownership and resulting control, potential conflict among segments of the channel is lessened.

American Apparel, a clothing manufacturer based in Los Angeles, California, represents a corporate vertical marketing system because it manufactures its own products rather than having contractual relationships with other firms, and it operates its own retail stores selling T-shirts and other men's and women's sportswear. With this corporate ownership structure, it is able to bring fashion-sensitive items from the idea stage to market in a very short time.

Managing Marketing Channels and Supply Chains through Strategic Relationships

There is more to managing marketing channels and supply chains than simply exercising power over other members in an administered system or establishing a contractual or corporate vertical marketing system. There is also a human side.

In a conventional marketing channel, relationships between members reflect their arguments over the split of the profit pie: If one party gets ahead, the other party falls behind. Sometimes this type of transaction is acceptable if the parties have no interest in a long-term relationship. If Walmart believes that PenAgain's ergonomic pens are just a short-term fad, it may only be interested in purchasing once. In that case, it might seek to get the best one-time price it can, even if doing so means that PenAgain will make very little money and therefore might not want to sell to Walmart again.

▼ **EXHIBIT 15.6** Top 10 Franchises for 2014

Rank	Franchise Name	Number of U.S. Outlets	Start-Up Costs
1	**Anytime Fitness** Fitness center	2,425	$56.3K–353.9K
2	**Hampton Hotels** Midprice hotels	1,942	$3.7M–13.52M
3	**Subway** Subs, salads	41,121	$85.69K–262.85K
4	**Supercuts** Hair salon	2,324	$108.75K–203.6K
5	**Jimmy John's Gourmet Sandwiches** Gourmet sandwiches	1,872	$300.5K–489.5K
6	**7-Eleven Inc.** Convenience stores	50,944	$30.79K–1.63M
7	**Servpro** Insurance/disaster restoration and cleaning	1,614	$134.8K–183.44K
8	**Denny's Inc.** Family restaurant	1,697	$1.17M–2.4M
9	**Pizza Hut Inc.** Pizza, pasta, wings	14,357	$297K–2.1M
10	**Dunkin' Donuts** Coffee shop	10,862	$294K–1.51M

Source: *Entrepreneur's* 2014 Franchise 500, http://www.entrepreneur.com.

American Apparel represents a corporate vertical marketing system because it manufactures its own products and operates its own retail stores.
© Justin Kase zsixz/Alamy

strategic (partnering) relationship A supply chain relationship that the members are committed to maintaining long term, investing in opportunities that are mutually beneficial; requires mutual trust, open communication, common goals, and credible commitments.

relationships, monitoring supply chain members becomes particularly pertinent when suppliers are located in less developed countries, where issues such as the use of child labor, poor working conditions, and below-subsistence wages have become a shared responsibility. Ethical and Societal Dilemma 15.1 highlights how Apple has both stumbled in this responsibility and changed its practices to improve its dedication to ethical choices.

Open Communication
To share information, develop sales forecasts together, and coordinate deliveries, Walmart and its suppliers maintain open and honest communication. This maintenance may sound easy in principle, but some businesses don't tend to share information with their business partners. But open, honest communication is a key to developing successful relationships because supply chain members need to understand what is driving each other's business, their roles in the relationship, each firm's strategies, and any problems that arise over the course of the relationship.

Common Goals
Supply chain members must have common goals for a successful relationship to develop. Shared goals give both members of the relationship an incentive to pool their strengths and abilities and exploit potential opportunities together. Such commonality also offers an assurance that the other partner won't do anything to hinder the achievement of those goals within the relationship.

Walmart and its suppliers recognize that it is in their common interest to be strategic partners. Walmart needs its suppliers to satisfy its customers, and those manufacturers recognize that if they can keep Walmart happy, they will have more than enough business for years to come. With common goals, both firms have an incentive to cooperate, because they know that by doing so, both can boost sales. If Walmart needs a special production run of pens to meet demand for back-to-school buyers, PenAgain will work to meet the challenge. If PenAgain has difficulty financing its inventory, it is in Walmart's best interest to help it, because they are committed to the same goals in the long run.

Interdependence
When supply chain members view their goals and ultimate success as intricately linked, they develop deeper long-term relationships. Interdependence between supply chain members that is based on mutual benefits is key to developing and sustaining the relationship.[10] Walmart's suppliers recognize that without Walmart, their sales would be significantly less. Although certainly the more powerful member of the supply chain, Walmart also recognizes that it can depend on these suppliers to be a dependable source of supply, thus enabling it to have a very efficient marketing channel.

More frequently, firms seek a **strategic relationship**, also called a **partnering relationship**, in which the marketing channel members are committed to maintaining the relationship over the long term and investing in opportunities that are mutually beneficial. In a conventional or administered marketing channel, there are significant incentives to establish a strategic relationship, even without contracts or ownership relationships. Both parties benefit because the size of the profit pie has increased, so both the buyer and the seller increase their sales and profits. These strategic relationships are created explicitly to uncover and exploit joint opportunities, so members depend on and trust each other heavily; share goals and agree on how to accomplish those goals; and are willing to take risks, share confidential information, and make significant investments for the sake of the relationship. Successful strategic relationships require mutual trust, open communication, common goals, interdependence, and credible commitments.

Mutual Trust
Mutual trust holds a strategic relationship together. Trust is the belief that a partner is honest (i.e., reliable, stands by its word, sincere, fulfills obligations) and benevolent (i.e., concerned about the other party's welfare). When vendors and buyers trust each other, they are more willing to share relevant ideas, clarify goals and problems, and communicate efficiently. Information shared between the parties, such as inventory positions in stores, thus becomes increasingly comprehensive, accurate, and timely.

With trust, there's also less need for the supply chain members to constantly monitor and check up on each other's actions, because each believes the other won't take advantage, even if given the opportunity. Although it is important in all

ethical&societal dilemma

15.1

Do Customers Care More about the Newest iPhone or about Working Conditions in China?[ii]

An iPad user reading a recent issue of *The New York Times* on his or her tablet might have suffered a strange sense of guilt. The newspaper published reports of labor abuses that seemingly run rampant in the Chinese factories responsible for producing Apple's most popular products. These in-depth reports cataloged a long list of failures: the presence of child workers, more than 12-hour shifts, regular workweeks of longer than 60 hours, workers housed in tiny dormitories with approximately 20 people limited to three rooms, allegations of suicides, and lax safety standards that have led to fatal explosions.

The reports focus mostly on a Foxconn factory in Chengdu, in southwestern China, that manufactures iPhones and iPads. An explosion caused by insufficient ventilation of aluminum dust (created when the cases for the gadgets are polished) in May 2011 killed four workers. A similar explosion followed six months later at another factory. The ensuing investigations by *The New York Times* revealed multiple other violations of the code of conduct that Apple has established for its suppliers.

With this code of conduct, as well as the frequent audits it performs, Apple asserts that it is doing the best that it can to ensure its suppliers live up to reasonable standards and fair labor practices. An anonymous former Apple executive asserts, "There is a genuine, companywide commitment to the code of conduct." Yet abuses continue, as Apple's own corporate responsibility reports reveal. Audits show that several supply companies continue to engage in labor practices that violate the code, with few punishments or changes to the supply chain.

Although Apple attempts to monitor its channel partners' behavior with regard to labor issues, sometimes abuses fall through the cracks.
© Kin Cheung/AP Photo

Part of the reason stems from Apple's need for secrecy—once it finds a supply partner that can manufacturer its high-tech gadgets, it wants to maintain that relationship to avoid any leakage of innovation information. So even if a supplier violates the code again and again, Apple is unlikely to switch.

Furthermore, Apple's focus on innovation means that it must work constantly to come up with new ideas and products, which it needs to produce quickly and in sufficient quantities to keep customers happy. This demanding supply chain leaves little room for flexibility. When Apple says it needs 1 million products, then its supplier is going to do whatever it takes to get those products ready in time. The code of conduct might ask that factory workers be limited to 60-hour workweeks, but in truth, Apple is asking the factories to keep running all day, every day, to make the order. In fact, an investigation by the Fair Labor Association in late 2013 found that while working conditions are improving, Foxconn facilities continue to require their workers to exceed the legal limits for overtime hours.

To keep its costs low, Apple also offers very slim profit margins to suppliers. In turn, these factories aim to reduce their own costs. Another Apple supplier thus began using a toxic chemical instead of rubbing alcohol to polish the screens of iPhones, because the chemical dries faster. But it exposes workers to the threat of paralysis and nerve damage.

The primary reason for these labor abuses may come only at the end of the supply chain—the consumer. A survey of Apple consumers showed that only 2 percent of them recognized labor issues as a concern. In a remarkably succinct summary of the challenge, another anonymous Apple executive asserted, "You can either manufacture in comfortable, worker-friendly factories, or you can reinvent the product every year, and make it better and faster and cheaper, which requires factories that seem harsh by American standards. And right now, customers care more about a new iPhone than working conditions in China."

318 SECTION 6 | Value Delivery: Designing the Channel and Supply Chain

Credible Commitments Successful relationships develop because both parties make credible commitments to, or tangible investments in, the relationship. These commitments go beyond just making the hollow statement, "I want to be your partner"; they involve spending money to improve the products or services provided to the customer and on information technology to improve supply chain efficiency.[11] As our chapter opener described, Amazon and P&G have worked closely to set up their Vendor Flex program, enabling Amazon to operate fulfillment centers within P&G's own warehouses and thereby lower transportation expenses.

Similar to many other elements of marketing, managing the marketing channel can seem like an easy task at first glance: Put the right merchandise in the right place at the right time. But the various elements and actors involved in a marketing channel create its unique and compelling complexities and require firms to work carefully to ensure they are achieving the most efficient and effective chain possible. We now turn our attention to how information and merchandise flow through marketing channels.

check yourself

1. What is the difference between an indirect and a direct marketing channel?

2. What are the differences among the three types of vertical marketing systems?

3. How do firms develop strong strategic partnerships with their marketing channel partners?

LO 15-4 Describe the flow of information and merchandise in the marketing channel.

MAKING INFORMATION FLOW THROUGH MARKETING CHANNELS

Information flows from the customer to stores, to and from distribution centers, possibly to and from wholesalers, to and from product manufacturers, and then on to the producers of any components and the suppliers of raw materials. To simplify our discussion—and because information flows are similar in other

marketing channel links and B2B channels—we shorten the supply chain in this section to exclude wholesalers as well as the link from suppliers to manufacturers. Exhibit 15.7 illustrates the flow of information that starts when a customer buys a Sony HDTV at Best Buy. The flow follows these steps:

Flow 1 (Customer to Store): The sales associate at Best Buy scans the **Universal Product Code (UPC)** tag on the HDTV packaging, and the customer receives a receipt. The UPC tag is the black-and-white bar code found on most merchandise. It contains a 13-digit code that indicates the manufacturer of the item, a description of the item, information about special packaging, and special promotions.[12] In the future, RFID tags, discussed later in this chapter, may replace UPC tags.

Flow 2 (Store to Buyer): The point-of-sale (POS) terminal records the purchase information and electronically sends it to the buyer at Best Buy's corporate office. The sales information is incorporated into an inventory management system and used to monitor and analyze sales and decide to reorder more HDTVs, change a price, or plan a promotion. Buyers also send information to stores about overall sales for the chain, ways to display the merchandise, upcoming promotions, and so on.

▼ **EXHIBIT 15.7** Information Flows

Customer

Buyer

Stores

Manufacturers

Distribution center

> "Information flows from the customer to stores, to and from distribution centers, possibly to and from wholesalers, to and from product manufacturers, and then on to the producers of any components and the suppliers of raw materials."

Flow 3 (Buyer to Manufacturer): The purchase information from each Best Buy store is typically aggregated by the retailer as a whole, which creates an order for new merchandise and sends it to Sony. The buyer at Best Buy may also communicate directly with Sony to get information and negotiate prices, shipping dates, promotional events, or other merchandise-related issues.

Flow 4 (Store to Manufacturer): In some situations, the sales transaction data are sent directly from the store to the manufacturer, and the manufacturer decides when to ship more merchandise to the distribution centers and the stores. In other situations, especially when merchandise is reordered frequently, the ordering process is done automatically, bypassing the buyers. By working together, the retailer and manufacturer can better satisfy customer needs.

Flow 5 (Store to Distribution Center): Stores also communicate with the Best Buy distribution center to coordinate deliveries and check inventory status. When the store inventory drops to a specified level, more HDTVs are shipped to the store, and the shipment information is sent to the Best Buy computer system.

Flow 6 (Manufacturer to Distribution Center and Buyer): When the manufacturer ships the HDTVs to the Best Buy distribution center, it sends an advanced shipping notice to the distribution centers. An **advanced shipping notice (ASN)** is an electronic document that the supplier sends the retailer in advance of a shipment to tell the retailer exactly what to expect in the shipment. The center then makes appointments for trucks to make the delivery at a specific time, date, and loading dock. When the shipment is received at the distribution center, the buyer is notified and authorizes payment to the vendor.

Data Warehouse

Purchase data collected at the point of sale (information flow 2 in Exhibit 15.7) goes into a huge database known as a data warehouse, similar to those described in Chapter 10. Using the data warehouse, the CEO not only can learn how the corporation is generally doing but also can look at the data aggregated by quarter for a merchandise division, a region of the country, or the total corporation. A buyer may be more interested in a particular manufacturer in a certain store on a particular day. Analysts from various levels of the retail operation extract information from the data warehouse to make a plethora of marketing decisions about developing and replenishing merchandise assortments.

In some cases, manufacturers also have access to this data warehouse. They communicate with retailers by using electronic data interchange (EDI) and supply chain systems known as vendor-managed inventory.

In information flows 3, 4, and 6 in Exhibit 15.7, the retailer and manufacturer exchange business documents through EDI. **Electronic data interchange (EDI)** is the computer-to-computer exchange of business documents from a retailer to a vendor and back. In addition to sales data, purchase orders, invoices, and data about returned merchandise can be transmitted back and forth. With EDI, vendors can transmit information about on-hand inventory status, vendor promotions, and cost changes to the retailer, as well as information about purchase order changes, order status, retail prices, and transportation routings. Thus EDI enables channel members to communicate more quickly and with fewer errors than in the past, ensuring that merchandise moves from vendors to retailers more quickly.

Vendor-managed inventory (VMI) is an approach for improving marketing channel efficiency in which the manufacturer is responsible for maintaining the retailer's inventory levels in each of its stores.[13] By sharing the data in the retailer's data warehouse and communicating that information via EDI, the manufacturer automatically sends merchandise to the retailer's store or distribution or fulfillment center when the inventory at the store reaches a prespecified level.[14]

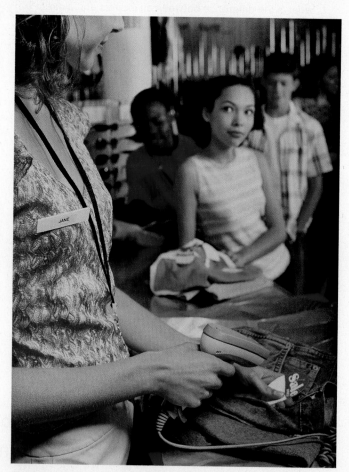

The flow of information starts when the UPC tag is scanned at the point of purchase.

© Digital Vision/Getty Images RF

In ideal conditions, the manufacturer replenishes inventories in quantities that meet the retailer's immediate demand, reducing stockouts with minimal inventory. In addition to providing a better match between retail demand and supply, VMI can reduce the vendor's and the retailer's costs. Manufacturer salespeople no longer need to spend time generating orders on items that are already in the stores, and their role shifts to selling new items and maintaining relationships. Retail buyers and planners no longer need to monitor inventory levels and place orders.

 check yourself

1. What are the marketing channel links associated with each information flow?

2. How do marketing channel members use data warehouses to make decisions?

3. What is EDI and how is it used?

4. Why do some marketing channels use VMI, while others do not?

MAKING MERCHANDISE FLOW THROUGH MARKETING CHANNELS

Exhibit 15.8 illustrates different types of merchandise flows:

1. Sony to Best Buy's distribution centers, or

2. Sony directly to stores.

3. If the merchandise goes through distribution centers, it is then shipped to stores,

4. and then to the customer.

▼ **EXHIBIT 15.8** Merchandise Flows

Making merchandise flow involves first deciding whether the merchandise will go from the manufacturer to a retailer's distribution center or directly on to stores. Once in a distribution center, multiple activities take place before it is shipped on to a store.

Distribution Centers versus Direct Store Delivery

As indicated in Exhibit 15.8, manufacturers can ship merchandise directly to a retailer's stores—direct store delivery (flow 2)—or to their distribution centers (flow 1). Although manufacturers and retailers may collaborate, the ultimate decision is usually up to the retailer and depends on the characteristics of the merchandise and the nature of demand. To determine which distribution system—distribution centers or direct store delivery—is better, retailers consider the total cost associated with each alternative and the customer service criterion of having the right merchandise at the store when the customer wants to buy it.

There are several advantages to using a distribution center:

- More accurate sales forecasts are possible when retailers combine forecasts for many stores serviced by one distribution center rather than doing a forecast for each store. Consider a set of 50 Target stores, serviced by a single distribution center that each carries Michael Graves toasters. Each store normally stocks 5 units for a total of 250 units in the system. By carrying the item at each store, the retailer must develop individual forecasts, each with the possibility of errors that could result in either too much or too little merchandise. Alternatively, by delivering most of the inventory to a distribution center and feeding the stores merchandise as they need it, the effects of forecast errors for the individual stores are minimized, and less backup inventory is needed to prevent stockouts.

- Distribution centers enable the retailer to carry less merchandise in the individual stores, which results in lower inventory investments systemwide. If the stores get frequent deliveries from the distribution center, they need to carry relatively less extra merchandise as backup stock.

- It is easier to avoid running out of stock or having too much stock in any particular store because merchandise is ordered from the distribution center as needed.

- Retail store space is typically much more expensive than space at a distribution center, and distribution centers are better equipped than stores to prepare merchandise for sale. As a result, many retailers find it cost effective to store merchandise and get it ready for sale at a distribution center rather than in individual stores.

But distribution centers aren't appropriate for all retailers. If a retailer has only a few outlets, the expense of a distribution center is probably unwarranted. Also, if many outlets are concentrated in metropolitan areas, merchandise can be consolidated and delivered by the vendor directly to all the stores in one area

planner In a retailing context, an employee who is responsible for the financial planning and analysis of merchandise, and its allocation to stores.

dispatcher The person who coordinates deliveries to distribution centers.

receiving The process of recording the receipt of merchandise as it arrives at a distribution center or store.

checking The process of going through the goods upon receipt to ensure they arrived undamaged and that the merchandise ordered was the merchandise received.

radio frequency identification (RFID) tag Tiny computer chip that automatically transmits to a special scanner all the information about a container's contents or individual products.

economically. Direct store delivery gets merchandise to the stores faster and thus is used for perishable goods (meat and produce), items that help create the retailer's image of being the first to sell the latest product (e.g., video games), or fads. Finally, some manufacturers provide direct store delivery for retailers to ensure that their products are on the store's shelves, properly displayed, and fresh. For example, employees delivering Frito-Lay snacks directly to supermarkets replace products that have been on the shelf too long and are stale, replenish products that have been sold, and arrange products so they are neatly displayed.

The Distribution (or Fulfillment) Center

The distribution center performs the following activities: managing inbound transportation; receiving and checking; storing and cross-docking; getting merchandise floor-ready; ticketing and marking; preparing to ship merchandise to stores; and shipping merchandise to stores. Fulfillment centers perform the same functions, but because they deliver directly to customers rather than to stores, they do not have to

center on Monday between 1:00 and 3:00 p.m. The buyer also specifies how the merchandise should be placed on pallets for easy unloading.

The truck must arrive within the specified time because the distribution center has all of its 100 receiving docks allocated throughout the day, and much of the merchandise on this particular truck is going to be shipped to stores that evening. Unfortunately, the truck was delayed in a snowstorm. The **dispatcher**—the person who coordinates deliveries to the distribution center—reassigns the truck delivering the HDTVs to a Wednesday morning delivery slot and charges the firm several hundred dollars for missing its delivery time. Although many manufacturers pay transportation expenses, some retailers negotiate with their vendors to absorb this expense. These retailers believe they can lower their net merchandise cost and better control merchandise flow if they negotiate directly with trucking companies and consolidate shipments from many vendors.

Receiving and Checking Using UPC or RFID

Receiving is the process of recording the receipt of merchandise as it arrives at a distribution center. **Checking** is the

> FULFILLMENT CENTERS PERFORM THE SAME FUNCTIONS AS DISTRIBUTION CENTERS, BUT BECAUSE THEY DELIVER DIRECTLY TO CUSTOMERS RATHER THAN TO STORES, THEY DO NOT HAVE TO GET MERCHANDISE FLOOR READY.

get merchandise floor ready. To illustrate these activities being undertaken in a distribution center, we'll continue our example of Sony HDTVs being shipped to a Best Buy distribution center.

Managing Inbound Transportation
Traditionally, buyers focused their efforts, when working with vendors, on developing merchandise assortments, negotiating prices, and arranging joint promotions. Now, buyers and planners are much more involved in coordinating the physical flow of merchandise to stores. **Planners** are employees responsible for the financial planning and analysis of merchandise and its allocation to stores. The TV buyer has arranged for a truckload of HDTVs to be delivered to its Houston, Texas, distribution

process of going through the goods upon receipt to make sure they arrived undamaged and that the merchandise ordered was the merchandise received.

In the past, checking merchandise was a very labor-intensive and time-consuming process. Today, however, many distribution systems using EDI are designed to minimize, if not eliminate, these processes. The advance shipping notice (ASN) tells the distribution center what should be in each carton. A UPC label or radio frequency identification (RFID) tag on the shipping carton that identifies the carton's contents is scanned and automatically counted as it is being received and checked. **Radio frequency identification (RFID) tags** are tiny computer chips that automatically transmit to a special scanner all the information about a container's contents or individual

Walmart speeds merchandise from its distribution centers to stores.
Courtesy Wal-Mart Stores, Inc.

Merchandise sales rate and degree of perishability or fashionability typically determine whether cartons are cross-docked or stored. For instance, because Sony's HDTVs sell so quickly, it is in Best Buy's interest not to store them in a distribution center. Similarly, cross-docking is preferable for fashion apparel or perishable meat or produce.

Getting Merchandise Floor-Ready
For some merchandise, additional tasks are undertaken in the distribution center to make the merchandise floor-ready. **Floor-ready merchandise** is merchandise that is ready to be placed on the selling floor. Getting merchandise floor-ready entails ticketing, marking, and, in the case of some apparel, placing garments on hangers (or maybe attaching RFID chips). For the UK-based grocery chain Tesco, it is essential that products ship in ready-to-sell units so that it has little manipulation or sorting to do at the distribution center or in the stores. To move the store-ready merchandise it receives from suppliers quickly into the store, Tesco demands that products sit on roll cages rather than pallets. Then, store employees can easily wheel them onto the retail floor. The stores' backrooms only have two or three days' worth of backup inventory, and it is important to keep inventory levels low and receive lots of small, accurate deliveries from its suppliers—which also helps cut costs.[15]

products. Approximately as large as a pinhead, these RFID tags consist of an antenna and a chip that contains an electronic product code that stores far more information about a product than bar (UPC) codes can. The tags also act as passive tracking devices, signaling their presence over a radio frequency when they pass within a few yards of a special scanner. The tags have long been used in high-cost applications such as automated highway toll systems and security identification badges. As the cost of the tags and implementation technology has decreased, their uses have become more prevalent in retail supply chain applications.

Storing and Cross-Docking
After the merchandise is received and checked, it is either stored or cross-docked. When merchandise is stored, the cartons are transported by a conveyor system and forklift trucks to racks that go from the distribution center's floor to its ceiling. Then, when the merchandise is needed in the stores, a forklift driver or a robot goes to the rack, picks up the carton, and places it on a conveyor system that routes the carton to the loading dock of a truck going to the store.

Using a **cross-docking distribution center**, merchandise cartons are prepackaged by the vendor for a specific store. The UPC or RFID labels on the carton indicate the store to which it is to be sent. The vendor also may affix price tags to each item in the carton. Because the merchandise is ready for sale, it is placed on a conveyor system that routes it from the unloading dock at which it was received to the loading dock for the truck going to the specific store—hence the name *cross-docked*. The cartons are routed on the conveyor system automatically by sensors that read the UPC or RFID label on the cartons. Cross-docked merchandise is in the distribution center only for a few hours before it is shipped to the stores.

> "Approximately as large as a pinhead, RFID tags consist of an antenna and a chip that contains an electronic product code that stores far more information about a product than bar (UPC) codes can."

Ticketing and Marking
Ticketing and marking refers to affixing price and identification labels to the merchandise. It is more efficient for a retailer to perform these activities at a distribution center than in its stores. In a distribution center, an area can be set aside and a process implemented to efficiently add labels and put apparel on hangers. Conversely, getting merchandise floor-ready in stores can block aisles and divert sales people's attention from their customers. An even better approach from the retailer's perspective is to get vendors to ship floor-ready merchandise, thus totally eliminating the expensive, time-consuming ticketing and marking process.

Preparing to Ship Merchandise to a Store

At the beginning of the day, the computer system in the distribution center generates a list of items to be shipped to each store on that day. For each item, a pick ticket and shipping label is generated. The **pick ticket** is a document or display on a screen in a forklift truck indicating how much of each item to get from specific storage areas. The forklift driver goes to the storage area, picks up the number of cartons indicated on the pick ticket, places UPC shipping labels on the cartons that indicate the stores to which the items are to be shipped, and puts the cartons on the conveyor system, where they are automatically routed to the loading dock for the truck going to the stores. In some distribution and fulfillment centers, these functions are performed by robots.

Shipping Merchandise to Stores

Shipping merchandise to stores from a distribution center has become increasingly complex. Most distribution centers run 50 to 100 outbound truck routes in one day. To handle this complex transportation problem, the centers use sophisticated routing and scheduling computer systems that consider the locations of the stores, road conditions, and transportation operating constraints to develop the most efficient routes possible. As a result, stores are provided with an accurate estimated time of arrival, and vehicle usage is maximized.

Inventory Management through Just-in-Time Inventory Systems

Marketing channel management offers the 21st century's answer to a host of distribution problems faced by firms. As recently as the early 1990s, even the most innovative firms needed 15 to 30 days—or even more—to fulfill an order from

Robots are often used to help prepare merchandise to be shipped to stores.
© Quiet Logistics

the warehouse to the customer. The typical order-to-delivery process had several steps: order creation, usually using a telephone, fax, or mail; order processing, using a manual system for credit authorization and assignment to a warehouse; and physical delivery. Things could, and often did, go wrong. Ordered goods were not available. Orders were lost or misplaced. Shipments were misdirected. These mistakes lengthened the time it took to get merchandise to customers and potentially made the entire process more expensive.

Faced with such predicaments, firms began stockpiling inventory at each level of the supply chain (retailers, wholesalers, and manufacturers), but keeping inventory where it is not needed becomes a huge and wasteful expense. If a manufacturer has a huge stock of items stuck in a warehouse, it not only is not earning profits by selling those items but also must pay to maintain and guard that warehouse.

Therefore, many firms, such as American Apparel, Zara, Mango, and Forever 21, have adopted a practice developed by Toyota in the 1950s. **Just-in-time (JIT) inventory systems**, also known as **quick response (QR) inventory systems** in retailing, are inventory management systems that deliver less merchandise on a more frequent basis than traditional inventory systems. The firm gets the merchandise just in time for it to be used in the manufacture of another product or for sale when the customer wants it. The benefits of a JIT system include reduced **lead time** (the amount of time between the recognition that an order needs to be placed and the arrival of the needed merchandise at the seller's store and is available for sale), increased product availability, and lower inventory investment.[16]

> ## Most distribution centers run 50 to 100 outbound truck routes in one day.

To reduce lead time, UPS works with adidas by providing it with special labeling, garments on hangers, and advanced shipping notices.
© Brian Kersey/UPI/Newscom

Reduced Lead Time By eliminating the need for paper transactions, the EDI in the JIT systems reduces lead time. Even better, the shorter lead times further reduce the need for inventory, because the shorter the lead time, the easier it is for the retailer to forecast its demand.

Increased Product Availability and Lower Inventory Investment In general, as a firm's ability to satisfy customer demand by having stock on hand increases, so does its inventory investment; that is, it needs to keep more backup inventory in stock. But with JIT, the ability to satisfy demand can actually increase while inventory decreases. Because a firm like American Apparel can make purchase

commitments or produce merchandise closer to the time of sale, its own inventory investment is reduced. American Apparel needs less inventory because it's getting less merchandise in each order but receiving those shipments more often. Because firms using JIT order merchandise to cover shorter-term demand, their inventory is reduced even further.

The ability to satisfy customer demand by keeping merchandise in stock also increases in JIT systems as a result of the more frequent shipments. For instance, if an American Apparel store runs low on a medium-sized, red T-shirt, its JIT system ensures a shorter lead time than those of more traditional retailers. As a result, it is less likely that the American Apparel store will be out of stock for its customers before the next T-shirt shipment arrives.

Costs of a JIT System Although firms achieve great benefits from a JIT system, it is not without its costs. The distribution function becomes much more complicated with more frequent deliveries. With greater order frequency also come smaller orders, which are more expensive to transport and more difficult to coordinate. Therefore, JIT systems require a strong commitment by the firm and its vendors to cooperate, share data, and develop systems. ■

 check yourself

1. How does merchandise flow through a typical marketing channel?

2. Why have just-in-time inventory systems become so popular?

 connect Increase your engagement and learning with Connect Marketing.

These Connect activities, available only through your Connect course, have been designed to make the following concepts more meaningful and applicable:

▶ Supply Chain Information Communication Timeline

▶ Pioneering Supply Chain Management: Walmart Case Analysis

▶ Supply Chain Icebreaker Video Case

▶ Supply Chain: iSeeit! Video

 SMARTBOOK™   iSeeit!

Chapter sixteen

retailing and omnichannel marketing

When H&M opened its flagship Times Square store, it aimed to create not just the most exciting store in the fashionable chain's range of locations but also perhaps the most cutting-edge example of retail in the world. Consider some of the innovations and offerings the store provides to customers.

Before they even walk through the doors, customers can enjoy the display created by massive 30 × 200-foot LED screens over the entrance and morphing onto the sides of the building. For those who happen to be just passing by, the interactive window displays are nearly impossible to ignore, drawing attention and foot traffic. During the Super Bowl, for example, people could vote for which version of an underwear ad would appear on these screens: one with David Beckham fully clothed or one in which he appeared in only his eponymous brand of underwear.

Inside, the space is remarkably massive, even for Times Square, at approximately 42,000 square feet. Rents in this area of town average around $2,000 per square

LEARNING OBJECTIVES

After reading this chapter, you should be able to:

LO 16-1 Discuss the four factors manufacturers should consider as they develop their strategies for working with retailers.

LO 16-2 Outline the considerations associated with choosing retail partners.

LO 16-3 List the three levels of distribution intensity.

LO 16-4 Describe the various types of retailers.

LO 16-5 Describe the components of a retail strategy.

LO 16-6 Identify the benefits of stores.

LO 16-7 Identify the benefits of omnichannel retailing.

LO 16-8 Detail the challenges of omnichannel retailing.

foot, so H&M needs to make a lot of sales. To cover all this ground, the retailer has more than 300 sales clerks on staff, and it

continued on p. 328

retailing The set of business activities that add value to products and services sold to consumers for their personal or family use; includes products bought at stores, through catalogs, and over the Internet, as well as services like fast-food restaurants, airlines, and hotels.

continued from p. 327

stays open 16 hours per day (closing only between 1:00 and 9:00 a.m.), seven days a week. It also keeps 24 cash registers ringing, though there's no need for every customer to visit a cash register. The 44 dressing rooms also are equipped with iPads and individual checkout stations for people to "try and buy." At the very moment a customer tries on an outfit and realizes it works, he or she can also go ahead and buy it, without having to wait in line.

Then again, waiting in line might be fun because the store features a wealth of entertaining distractions. On opening day, Lady Gaga offered a command performance. More regularly, light boxes display messages summarizing temporary deals or upcoming events. From the third-floor ceiling, trusses support mannequins, making it appear as if well-dressed bodies are flying above the shop floor. A glitter wall dresses the background behind the checkout stations, and a DJ booth keeps the music playing constantly and interactively.

Because H&M appeals largely to a youthful, technologically savvy target market that is eternally ready to share through social media, shoppers can show off their clothing options on an LED-recorded runway. The captured video is available to send to their personal e-mail address, upload to a social media site (with the hash tag "hmtimessquare"), and be broadcast throughout the store on the same day. Thus if a shopper is convinced that the latest offerings from Dividend, a trendy flannel and fatigue clothing line, look utterly fabulous on her, she can make sure all her friends, as well as hundreds of the other shoppers in the store, see her in them.[1] ∎

Retailing sits at the end of the supply chain, where marketing meets the consumer. But there is far more to retailing than just manufacturing a product and making it available to customers. It is primarily the retailer's responsibility to make sure that these customers' expectations are fulfilled.

What technological innovations are available to customers at the H&M store in Times Square, New York?
© D Dipasupil/Getty Images for Extra

Retailing is defined as the set of business activities that add value to products and services sold to consumers for their personal or family use. Our definition includes products bought at stores, through catalogs, and over the Internet, as well as services such as fast-food restaurants, airlines, and hotels. Some retailers claim they sell at wholesale prices, but if they sell to customers for their personal use, they are still retailers, regardless of their prices. Wholesalers (see Chapter 15) buy products from manufacturers and resell them to retailers or industrial or business users.

Retailing today is changing, both in the United States and around the world. Manufacturers no longer rule many supply chains, as they once did. Retailers such as Walmart (U.S. food retailer), Tesco (UK-based food retailer), Costco (U.S. warehouse club), Carrefour (French hypermarket), Kroger (U.S. grocery chain), Schwarz (German conglomerate), Metro (German retail conglomerate), Home Depot (U.S. home improvement), Aldi Enkauf (German discount food retailer), Target (U.S. food retailer), and Walgreens (U.S. drugstore)[2]—the largest retailers in the world—dictate to their suppliers what should be made, how it should be configured, when it should be delivered, and, to some extent, what it should cost. These retailers are clearly in the driver's seat.

LO 16-1	Discuss the four factors manufacturers should consider as they develop their strategies for working with retailers.

This chapter extends Chapter 15's discussion of supply chain management by examining why and how manufacturers use retailers. The manufacturer's strategy depends on its overall

> ❝ **IT IS PRIMARILY THE RETAILER'S RESPONSIBILITY TO MAKE SURE THAT THESE CUSTOMERS' EXPECTATIONS ARE FULFILLED.** ❞

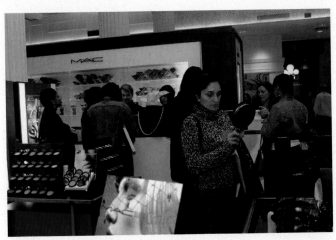

M-A-C will use different criteria than will either Coach for Men or Eva's green cosmetics for placing products in retail stores.
© Linda Matlow/Alamy

they want to place their products. The overall size and level of sophistication of the manufacturer will determine how many of the marketing channel functions it performs and how many it will hand off to other channel members. Finally, the type and availability of the product and the image the manufacturer wishes to portray will determine how many retailers within a geographic region will carry the products.

For the second factor, manufacturers identify the types of retailers that would be appropriate to carry their products. Although the choice is often obvious—such as a supermarket for fresh produce—manufacturers may have a choice of retailer types for some products.

As we discussed in Chapter 15, a hallmark of a strong marketing channel is one in which manufacturers and retailers coordinate their efforts. In the third factor, manufacturers

omnichannel (multichannel) strategy Selling in more than one channel (e.g., stores, Internet, catalog).

> "The overall size and level of sophistication of the manufacturer will determine how many of the marketing channel functions it performs and how many it will hand off to other channel members."

market power and how consistent a new product or product line is with current offerings. Consider the following scenarios:

- Scenario 1: Cosmetics conglomerate Estée Lauder's subsidiary brand M-A-C is introducing a new line of mascara.

- Scenario 2: Coach, well known for its women's handbags, has introduced a line of men's leather goods, apparel, gifts, shoes, and other accessories—products not previously in its assortment.

- Scenario 3: Eva, a young entrepreneur, is launching a new line of environmentally friendly (green) cosmetics.

Each of these scenarios is different and requires the manufacturer to consider alternatives for reaching its target markets through retailers.

Exhibit 16.1 illustrates four factors manufacturers consider to establish their strategies for working with retailers.[3] In choosing retail partners, the first factor, manufacturers assess how likely it is for certain retailers to carry their products. Manufacturers also consider where their target customers expect to find the products, because those are exactly the stores in which

and retailers therefore develop their strategy by implementing the four Ps.

Finally, many retailers and some manufacturers use an **omnichannel** or **multichannel strategy**, which involves selling in more than one channel (e.g., store, catalog, and Internet). The fourth factor therefore consists of examining the circumstances in which sellers may prefer to adopt a particular strategy. Although these factors are listed consecutively, manufacturers may consider them all simultaneously or in a different order.

| LO 16-2 | Outline the considerations associated with choosing retail partners. |

CHOOSING RETAILING PARTNERS

Imagine, as a consumer, trying to buy a new leather jacket without being able to visit a retailer or buy online. You would have to figure out exactly what size, color, and style of jacket you wanted. Then you would need to contact various manufacturers, whether in person, by phone, or over the Internet, and order the jacket. If the jacket fit you reasonably well but not perfectly, you still

▼ **EXHIBIT 16.1** Factors for Establishing a Relationship with Retailers

1. Choosing retailing partners → 2. Identifying types of retailers → 3. Developing a retail strategy → 4. Managing an omnichannel strategy

> ## "BECAUSE M-A-C IS MADE BY ESTÉE LAUDER AND OPERATES ITS OWN STORES, WHEN THE NEW MASCARA LINE IS INTRODUCED, THE STORES RECEIVE THE NEW LINE AUTOMATICALLY WITH NO DECISION ON THE PART OF THE RETAILER."

Coach partners with retailers to help conveniently deliver its products to satisfied customers.
© Peter Horree/Alamy

might need to take it to a tailor to have the sleeves shortened. You wouldn't find this approach to shopping very convenient.

Manufacturers like Coach use retailers such as Macy's to undertake partnerships that create value by pulling together all the actions necessary for the greatest possible customer convenience and satisfaction. The store offers a broad selection of purses, leather jackets, scarves, and other accessories that its buyers have carefully chosen in advance. Customers can see, touch, feel, and try on any item while in the store. They can buy one scarf or leather jacket at a time or buy an outfit that works together. Finally, the store provides a salesperson to help customers coordinate their outfits and a tailor to make the whole thing fit perfectly.

When choosing retail partners, manufacturers look at the basic channel structure, where their target customers expect to find the products, channel member characteristics, and distribution intensity.

Channel Structure

The level of difficulty a manufacturer experiences in getting retailers to purchase its products is determined by the degree to which the channel is vertically integrated, as described in

Chapter 15; the degree to which the manufacturer has a strong brand or is otherwise desirable in the market; and the relative power of the manufacturer and retailer.

Scenario 1 represents a corporate vertical marketing system. Because M-A-C is made by Estée Lauder and operates its own stores, when the new mascara line is introduced, the stores receive the new line automatically with no decision on the part of the retailer. In contrast, Revlon would have a much more difficult time getting CVS to buy a new mascara line because these supply chain partners are not vertically integrated.

When an established firm such as Coach enters a new market with men's leather goods, apparel, gifts, shoes, and other accessories, as is the case in Scenario 2. It must determine where its customers would expect to find these products and then use its established relationships with women's handbag buyers, the power of its brand, and its overall reputation to leverage its position in this new product area.

Eva (Scenario 3) would have an even more difficult time convincing a retailer to buy and sell her green cosmetics line because she lacks power in the marketplace—she is small, and her brand is unknown. She would have trouble getting buyers to see her, let alone consider her line. She might face relatively high slotting allowances just to get space on retailers' shelves. But like Coach in Scenario 2, Eva should consider where the end customer expects to find her products, as well as some important retailer characteristics.

Customer Expectations

Retailers should also know customer preferences regarding manufacturers. Manufacturers, in contrast, need to know where their target market customers expect to find their products and those of their competitors. As we see in the hypothetical example in Exhibit 16.2, Coach currently sells handbags at stores such as Dillard's, Neiman Marcus, and Marshalls as well as in its own stores (red arrows). Its competitor Cole Haan sells at Dillard's and Neiman Marcus (teal arrows). A survey of male Coach customers shows that they would expect to find its products at Saks Fifth Avenue, Dillard's, Neiman Marcus, and its own Coach stores (all of the stores in the light blue box). On the basis of this information, Coach decides to try selling at Saks Fifth Avenue but to stop selling at Marshalls to better meet customers' expectations.

Customers generally expect to find certain products at some stores but not at others. For example, Estée Lauder

▼ EXHIBIT 16.2 Coach and Cole Haan Distribution

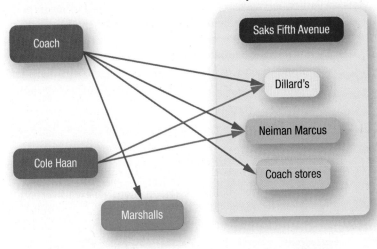

Customer expectations of where they would find the product

[Coach] → [Saks Fifth Avenue, Dillard's, Neiman Marcus, Coach stores]
[Cole Haan] → [Dillard's, Neiman Marcus, Marshalls]

in the industry. In the same way, an independent grocery store might buy merchandise from a wholesaler, but Walmart, the world's largest grocer, only buys directly from the manufacturer. Larger firms often find that by performing the channel functions themselves, they can gain more control, be more efficient, and save money.

Distribution Intensity

When setting up distribution for the first time, as is the case with Eva's green cosmetics (Scenario 3), or introducing a new product line, as is the case with Coach for men (Scenario 2), firms decide the appropriate level of **distribution intensity**—the number of channel members to use at each level of the marketing channel. Distribution intensity commonly is divided into three levels: intensive, exclusive, and selective.

Intensive Distribution An **intensive distribution** strategy is designed to place products in as many outlets as possible. Most consumer packaged-goods companies, such as

would not choose to sell to CVS or Dollar General because its customers would not expect to shop at those stores for high-end cosmetics such as Estée Lauder's. Instead, CVS might carry less expensive cosmetic brands, such as Revlon and Maybelline, and bargain closeouts probably appear at Dollar General. But male Coach customers definitely expect to find the brand's clothing offerings at major department stores and at Coach stores.

Channel Member Characteristics

Several factors pertaining to the channel members themselves help determine the channel structure. Generally, the larger and more sophisticated the channel member, the less likely that it will use supply chain intermediaries. Eva will probably use a group of independent salespeople to help sell her line of green cosmetics, whereas a large manufacturer such as Estée Lauder will use its own sales force that already has existing relationships

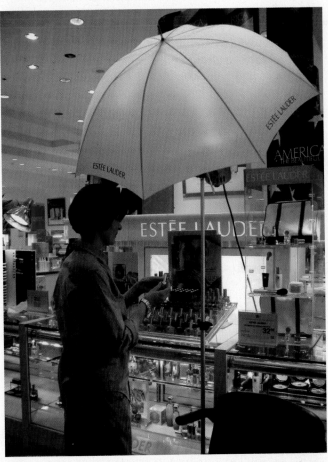

Most consumer packaged-goods companies, such as Pepsi (left), strive for intensive distribution—they want to be everywhere. But cosmetics firms such as Estée Lauder (right) use an exclusive distribution strategy by limiting their distribution to a few select higher-end retailers in each region.
Left: © Jeff Greenberg/PhotoEdit; Right: © Susan Van Etten/PhotoEdit

exclusive distribution
Strategy in which only
selected retailers can
sell a manufacturer's
brand.

selective distribution
Lies between the intensive
and exclusive distribution
strategies; uses a few
selected customers in a
territory.

Pepsi, Procter & Gamble, Kraft, and other nationally branded products found in grocery and discount stores, strive for and often achieve intensive distribution. Pepsi wants its product available everywhere—grocery stores, convenience stores, restaurants, and vending machines. The more exposure the products get, the more they sell.

LO 16-3 | List the three levels of distribution intensity.

Exclusive Distribution
Manufacturers also might use an **exclusive distribution** policy by granting exclusive geographic territories to one or very few retail customers so no other retailers in the territory can sell a particular brand. Exclusive distribution can benefit manufacturers by assuring them that the most appropriate retailers represent their products. Luxury goods firms such as Coach limit distribution to a few select, higher-end retailers in each region. The company believes that selling its products to full-line discount stores or off-price retailers would weaken its image.

When supply is limited or a firm is just starting out, providing an exclusive territory to one retailer or retail chain helps ensure enough inventory to provide the buying public an adequate selection. By granting exclusive territories, Eva guarantees her retailers will have an adequate supply of her green cosmetics. This guarantee gives these retailers a strong incentive to market her products. The retailers that Eva uses know there will be no competing retailers to cut prices, so their profit margins are protected. This knowledge gives them an incentive to carry more inventory and use extra advertising, personal selling, and sales promotions.

Selective Distribution
Between the intensive and exclusive distribution strategies lies **selective distribution**, which relies on a few selected retail customers in a territory to sell products. Like exclusive distribution, selective distribution helps a seller maintain a particular image and control the flow of merchandise into an area. These advantages make this approach attractive to many shopping goods manufacturers. Recall that shopping goods are those products for which consumers are willing to spend time comparing alternatives, such as most apparel items, home items like branded pots and pans or sheets and towels, branded hardware and tools, and consumer electronics. Retailers still have a strong incentive to sell the products but not to the same extent as if they had an exclusive territory.

> Like exclusive distribution, selective distribution helps a seller maintain a particular image and control the flow of merchandise into an area.

As we noted in Chapter 15, like any large complicated system, a marketing channel is difficult to manage. Whether the balance of power rests with large retailers such as Walmart or with large manufacturers such as Procter & Gamble, channel members benefit by working together to develop and implement their channel strategy. In the next section, we explore the different types of retailers with an eye toward which would be most appropriate for each of our scenarios: M-A-C Cosmetics, Coach's products for men, and Eva's new line of environmentally friendly cosmetics.

 check yourself

1. What issues should manufacturers consider when choosing retail partners?
2. What are the differences among intensive, exclusive, and selective levels of distribution intensity?

LO 16-4 | Describe the various types of retailers.

IDENTIFY TYPES OF RETAILERS

At first glance, identifying the types of retailers that Coach and Eva may wish to pursue when attempting to place their new lines seems straightforward. But the choice is not always easy. Manufacturers need to understand the general characteristics of different types of retailers to determine the best channels for their product. The characteristics of a retailer that are important to a food manufacturer may be quite different from those considered valuable by a cosmetics manufacturer. In the next few sections, we examine the various types of retailers, identify some major players, and discuss some of the issues facing each type (Exhibit 16.3).

Food Retailers
The food retailing landscape is changing dramatically. Twenty years ago, consumers purchased food primarily at conventional supermarkets. Now conventional supermarkets account for only slightly more than 60 percent of food sales (not including restaurants).[4] Not only do full-line discount stores like Walmart and Target now offer a full assortment of grocery items in their superstores, but traditional supermarkets also are carrying more nonfood items. Many supermarkets offer pharmacies, health care clinics, banks, and cafés.

The world's largest food retailer, Walmart, attains more than $443 billion in sales of supermarket-type merchandise. On this measure, it is followed by Carrefour (France), Tesco (United Kingdom), Metro

Group (Germany), Schwartz Group (Germany), and Kroger (United States).[5] In North America specifically, the largest supermarket chains in order are Walmart, Kroger, Costco, Target, Safeway, Supervalu, Loblaw, Publix, and Ahold US.[6]

Supermarkets

A **conventional supermarket** is a large, self-service retail food store offering groceries, meat, and produce, as well as some nonfood items such as health and beauty aids and general merchandise.[7] Perishables including meat, produce, baked goods, and dairy products account for 30 percent of supermarket sales and typically have higher margins than packaged goods.[8]

Whereas conventional supermarkets carry about 30,000 SKUs, **limited-assortment supermarkets**, or **extreme-value food retailers**, stock only about 1,500 SKUs.[9] The two largest limited-assortment supermarket chains in the United States are Save-A-Lot and ALDI. Rather than carrying 20 brands of laundry detergent, limited-assortment supermarkets offer one or two brands and sizes, one of which is a store brand. By trimming costs, limited-assortment supermarkets can offer merchandise at prices 40 percent lower than those at conventional supermarkets.[10]

Although conventional supermarkets still sell the majority of food merchandise, they are under substantial competitive pressure on multiple sides: from supercenters, warehouse clubs, extreme-value retailers, convenience stores, and even drug stores.[11] All these types of retailers have increased the amount of space they devote to consumables.

To compete successfully against intrusions by other food retailing formats, conventional supermarkets are differentiating their offerings by (1) emphasizing fresh perishables, (2) targeting green and ethnic consumers, (3) providing better value with private-label merchandise, and (4) providing a better shopping experience. One excellent example of these efforts comes in the form of a stellar grocer, Trader Joe's, as Adding Value 16.1 explains.

Supercenters
Supercenters are large stores (185,000 square feet) that combine a supermarket with a full-line discount store. Walmart operates more than 3,000 supercenters in the United States,[12] accounting for the vast majority of total supercenter sales—far outpacing its competitors Meijer, SuperTarget (Target), Fred Meyer (Kroger Co.), and Super Kmart Center (Sears Holding). By offering broad assortments of grocery and general merchandise products under one roof, supercenters provide a one-stop shopping convenience to customers.

Warehouse Clubs
Warehouse clubs are large retailers (100,000 to 150,000 square feet) that offer a limited and irregular

---

conventional supermarket Type of retailer that offers groceries, meat, and produce with limited sales of nonfood items, such as health and beauty aids and general merchandise, in a self-service format.

limited-assortment supermarkets Retailers that offer only one or two brands or sizes of most products (usually including a store brand) and attempt to achieve great efficiency to lower costs and prices.

extreme-value food retailer See *limited-assortment supermarkets*.

supercenter Large stores combining full-line discount stores with supermarkets in one place.

warehouse clubs Large retailers with an irregular assortment, low service levels, and low prices that often require membership for shoppers.

▼ **EXHIBIT 16.3** Types of Retailers

Food	General merchandise		Service
Supermarket	Full-line discount	Specialty	Auto rental
Supercenter	Category specialist	Department	Health spa
Convenience	Drug	Off-price	Vision center
Warehouse club	Extreme value		Bank

" Although conventional supermarkets still sell the majority of food merchandise, they are under substantial competitive pressure on multiple sides: from supercenters, warehouse clubs, extreme-value retailers, convenience stores, and even drug stores. "

Adding Value 16.1

Meet the Captain and Visit the Island[i]

The employees are wearing tropical shirts, the product labels feature puns and silly rhymes, and the manager goes by "Captain." But dismissing Trader Joe's as a joke is a bad idea, especially if you're another grocery store chain that wants to appeal to discerning shoppers. Just ask Whole Foods. The roots of its success are as diverse as the customers Trader Joe's attracts. For example, its product lines offer organic, gourmet, and multicultural options (and sometimes combinations of all three), rather than focusing on any one type of product appeal. Furthermore, those options rarely are available anywhere else, because 80 percent of Trader Joe's product assortment consists of its own private labels. The plentiful, unique options also tend to be relatively low priced—likely an artifact of Trader Joe's ownership by the same family that runs the low-priced ALDI chain.

With these product and price offerings, rather than being all things to everyone, Trader Joe's is a little something for anyone. Full, stock-up shopping trips still require another grocer, but for a little something special and tasty, Trader Joe's provides a compelling alternative. Accordingly, it attracts a diverse fan base, approximately equally split between households that earn more than $100,000 annually and those that average closer to $25,000. Still, many of the customers at Trader Joe's exhibit some appealing similarities for retailers, including high levels of education, a health emphasis, and a high level of comfort with technological innovations.

If you don't think shopping for groceries is fun, try Trader Joe's.
© ZUMA Press, Inc/Alamy

In these traits, Trader Joe's customers are remarkably similar to those who shop at Whole Foods, despite the vast differences in the price positions the two chains take. Whole Foods' CEO even has admitted that the company views Trader Joe's as its primary competitor and that its own "365" private label represents a direct response to the offerings on hand at Trader Joe's. Yet its unique positioning sets Trader Joe's apart from other grocers in consumers' minds; it also helps it stand alone when it comes to some pertinent measures of success. Namely, in the grocery industry, the average rate of sales per square foot is $521. Whole Foods, with its high-end, pricey, trendy image, nearly doubles that rate, with sales per square foot of $973. And Trader Joe's, with its small, island-themed stores? It achieves an utterly astounding $1,723 per square foot on average.

---

assortment of food and general merchandise, little service, and low prices to the general public and small businesses. The largest warehouse club chains are Costco, Sam's Club (Walmart), and BJ's Wholesale Club (operating only on the U.S. East Coast). Customers are attracted to these stores because they can stock up on large packs of basics like paper towels, mega-sized packaged groceries such as a quart of ketchup, best-selling books and CDs, fresh meat and produce, and an unpredictable assortment of

upscale merchandise and services (e.g., jewelry, electronics, and home decor) at lower prices than are available at other retail stores. Typically, members pay an annual fee of around $50, which amounts to significant additional income for the chains.

Although both Coach for Men and Eva's products could be sold in warehouse clubs, these retailers probably are not the best choices. Both product lines will have an upscale image,

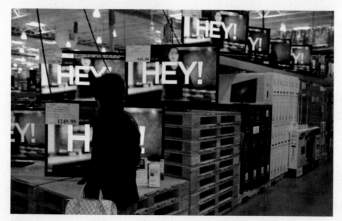

Warehouse clubs have expanded their assortment of the electronics category, and are known for great prices.
© Bloomberg/Contributor/Getty Images

In addition to convenience, 7-Eleven is a trendy place for young consumers in Indonesia to hang out.
© Francis Dean/Corbis

which is inconsistent with any warehouse club. If, however, either firm has overstock merchandise as a result of overestimating demand or underestimating returned merchandise from retailers, warehouse clubs are a potential outlet.

Convenience Stores

Convenience stores provide a limited variety and assortment of merchandise at a convenient location in 3,000- to 5,000-square-foot stores with speedy checkout. They are the modern version of the neighborhood mom-and-pop grocery or general store. Convenience stores enable consumers to make purchases quickly without having to search through a large store and wait in a lengthy checkout line. Convenience store assortments are limited in

To compete and gain better traction among younger consumers, who generally favor smaller specialty stores,[14] many department stores are increasing the amount of exclusive and private-label merchandise they sell. For example, Jennifer Lopez has a clothing line at Kohl's, and Ralph Lauren has a line of casual apparel exclusively at JCPenney called American Living. Customers looking for exclusive dinnerware

> "IN RESPONSE TO COMPETITIVE PRESSURES, CONVENIENCE STORES ARE TAKING STEPS TO DECREASE THEIR DEPENDENCY ON GASOLINE SALES BY OFFERING FRESH FOOD AND HEALTHY FAST FOOD, TAILORING ASSORTMENTS TO LOCAL MARKETS, AND MAKING THEIR STORES EVEN MORE CONVENIENT TO SHOP."

terms of depth and breadth, and they charge higher prices than supermarkets. Milk, eggs, and bread once represented the majority of their sales, but now most sales come from gasoline and cigarettes.

Convenience stores also face increased competition from other retail formats. In response to these competitive pressures, convenience stores are taking steps to decrease their dependency on gasoline sales by offering fresh food and healthy fast food, tailoring assortments to local markets, and making their stores even more convenient to shop. Finally, convenience stores are adding new services, such as financial service kiosks that give customers the opportunity to cash checks, pay bills, and buy prepaid telephone minutes, theater tickets, and gift cards.

General Merchandise Retailers

The major types of general merchandise retailers are department stores, full-line discount stores, specialty stores, category specialists, home improvement centers, off-price retailers, and extreme-value retailers.

Department Stores

Department stores are retailers that carry a broad variety and deep assortment of merchandise, offer customer services, and organize their stores into distinct departments for displaying merchandise. The largest department store chains in the United States include Sears, Macy's, Kohl's, JCPenney, and Nordstrom.[13] Department stores would be an excellent retail channel for Coach for Men and Eva's new lines.

Department stores like Macy's carry a broad variety and deep assortment of merchandise, offer customer services, and organize their stores into distinct departments for displaying merchandise.
© Daniel Acker/Bloomberg via Getty Images

collections can go to Macy's and get the Rachel Bilson line, or else find the Kardashian Kollection at Sears.[15] Macy's has also developed its own brands available exclusively at its stores, including Alfani (women's fashion) and the Hotel Collection (luxury fabrics).

Full-Line Discount Stores

Full-line discount stores are retailers that offer a broad variety of merchandise, limited service, and low prices. The largest full-line discount store chains are Walmart, Target, and Kmart (Sears Holding).

Although full-line discount stores typically might carry men's leather goods, accessories, and cosmetics, they are not good options for Coach for Men or Eva's new green cosmetics line. Customers do not expect higher-end products in full-line discount stores. Rather, they are looking for value prices and are willing to compromise on quality or cachet.

Walmart accounts for approximately two-thirds of full-line discount store retail sales in the United States.[16] Target has experienced considerable growth because its stores offer fashionable merchandise at low prices in a pleasant shopping environment. The retailer has developed an image of cheap chic by offering limited-edition exclusive apparel and cosmetic lines.

Specialty Stores

Specialty stores concentrate on a limited number of complementary merchandise categories targeted toward very specific market segments by offering deep but narrow assortments and sales associate expertise. Although such shops are familiar in brick-and-mortar forms, more retailers also are expanding their online specialty profile as well.

Estée Lauder's M-A-C line of cosmetics sells in the company's own retail specialty stores as well as in some department stores. Certain specialty stores would be excellent outlets for the new lines by Coach for Men and Eva. Customers likely expect to find Coach for Men leather goods and accessories in men's apparel or leather stores. Eva's line of green cosmetics would fit nicely in a cosmetics specialty store such as Sephora.

Drugstores

Drugstores are specialty stores that concentrate on pharmaceuticals and health and personal grooming merchandise. Prescription pharmaceuticals represent almost

Estée Lauder's M-A-C cosmetic lines sell in specialty stores such as Sephora.
© Rachel Murray/WireImage/Getty Images

70 percent of drugstore sales. The largest drugstore chains in the United States are CVS, Walgreens, and Rite Aid.[17]

Drugstores face competition from pharmacies in discount stores and from pressure to reduce health care costs. In response, the major drugstore chains are offering a wider assortment of merchandise such as frequently purchased food items as well as new services such as convenient drive-through windows for picking up prescriptions, in-store medical clinics, and even makeovers and spa treatments.[18]

Although Estée Lauder's new line would not be consistent with the merchandise found in drugstores, Eva's green cosmetics may be a welcome addition. Some drugstores have recognized consumer demand for green products, even though Eva's cosmetics may be priced higher than its competitors. Eva must decide whether her high-end products will suffer a tarnished image if she sells them in drugstores or whether drugstores could be a good channel for increasing her brand awareness.

Category Specialists

Category specialists are **big-box retailers** or **category killers** that offer a narrow but deep assortment of merchandise. Most category specialists use a predominantly self-service approach, but they offer assistance to customers in some areas of the stores. For example, the office supply store Staples has a warehouse atmosphere with cartons of copy paper stacked on pallets, plus equipment in boxes on

> "Target has experienced considerable growth because its stores offer fashionable merchandise at low prices in a pleasant shopping environment."

shelves. But in some departments, such as computers, electronics, and other high-tech products, salespeople staff the display area to answer questions and make suggestions.

By offering a complete assortment in a category at somewhat lower prices than their competition, category specialists can kill a category of merchandise for other retailers, which is why they are frequently called category killers. Using their category dominance, these retailers exploit their buying power to negotiate low prices.

Extreme-Value Retailers

Extreme-value retailers are small, full-line discount stores that offer a limited merchandise assortment at very low prices. The largest extreme-value retailers are Dollar General and Family Dollar Stores.

Like limited assortment food retailers, extreme-value retailers reduce costs and maintain low prices by buying opportunistically from manufacturers with excess merchandise, offering a limited assortment, and operating in low-rent locations. They offer a broad but shallow assortment of household goods, health and beauty aids, and groceries.

Many value retailers target low-income consumers, whose shopping behavior differs from that of typical discount store or warehouse club customers. Although these consumers might demand well-known national brands, they often cannot

Off-price retailers like Big Lots offer an inconsistent assortment of brand name merchandise at a significant discount from the manufacturer's suggested retail price (MSRP).
© Chris Lee/MCT/Newscom

afford to buy large-sized packages. So vendors such as Procter & Gamble often create special, smaller packages for extreme-value retailers, often using the reverse innovation approaches we discussed in Chapter 8. Also, higher-income consumers are increasingly patronizing these stores for the thrill of the hunt. Some shoppers regard the extreme-value retailers as an opportunity to find some hidden treasure among the household staples.

Extreme-value retailers would not be an obvious consumer choice for Coach for Men or Eva's new lines, because these stores are not consistent with the brands' image. But if these manufacturers find themselves in an overstock situation, they could use these retailers to reduce inventory. For the same reason, they might use off-price retailers.

Off-Price Retailers

Off-price retailers offer an inconsistent assortment of brand name merchandise at a significant discount from the manufacturer's suggested retail price (MSRP). In today's market, these off-price retailers may be brick-and-mortar stores, online outlets, or a combination of both. America's largest off-price retail chains are TJX Companies (which operates TJMaxx, Marshalls, Winners [Canada], HomeGoods, AJWright, and HomeSense [Canada]), Ross

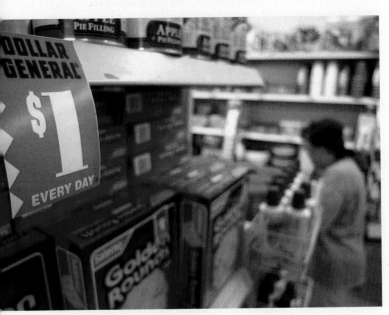

Dollar General is one of the United States' largest extreme-value retailers. It has small full-line discount stores that offer a limited assortment at very low prices.
© Mark Humphrey/AP Photo

> "Many value retailers target low-income consumers, whose shopping behavior differs from that of typical discount store or warehouse club customers."

Stores, Burlington Coat Factory, Big Lots Inc., Overstock.com, and Bluefly.com.

To be able to sell at prices 20 to 60 percent lower than the MSRP,[19] most merchandise is bought opportunistically from manufacturers or other retailers with excess inventory at the end of the season. Therefore, customers cannot be confident that the same merchandise or even type of merchandise will be available each time they visit a store or website. The discounts off-price retailers receive from manufacturers reflect what they do not do as well: They do not ask suppliers to help them pay for advertising, make them take back unsold merchandise, charge them for markdowns, or ask them to delay payments.

Service Retailers

The retail firms discussed in the previous sections sell products to consumers.[20] However, **service retailers**, or firms that primarily sell services rather than merchandise, are a large and growing part of the retail industry. Consider a typical Saturday: After a bagel and cup of coffee at a nearby Peet's Coffee and Tea, you go to the Laundromat to wash and dry your clothes, drop off a suit at a dry cleaner, have a prescription filled at a CVS drugstore, and make your way to Jiffy Lube to have your car's oil changed. In a hurry, you drive through a Burger King so you can eat lunch quickly and be on time for your haircut at Supercuts. By midafternoon, you're ready for a workout at your health club. After stopping at home for a change of clothes, you're off to dinner, a movie, and dancing with a friend. Finally, you end your day with a café latte at Starbucks, having interacted with 10 service retailers during the day.

There are a wide variety of service retailers, along with some national companies that provide these services. These companies are retailers because they sell goods and services to consumers. However, some are not just retailers. For example, airlines, banks, hotels, and insurance and express mail companies sell their services to businesses as well as consumers.

Organizations such as banks, hospitals, health spas, legal clinics, entertainment firms, and universities that offer services to consumers traditionally have not considered themselves retailers. Yet due to increased competition, these organizations are adopting retailing principles to attract customers and satisfy their needs.

Several trends suggest considerable future growth in services retailing. For example, the aging population will increase demand for health care services. Younger people are also spending more time and money on health and fitness. Busy parents in two-income families are willing to pay to have their homes cleaned, lawns maintained, clothes washed and pressed, and meals prepared so they can spend more time with their families.

Now that we've explored the types of stores, we can examine how manufacturers and retailers coordinate their retail strategy using the four Ps.

Service retailers, like this night club, sell services rather than merchandise.
© Lane Oatey/Blue Jean Images/Getty Images RF

 check yourself

1. What strategies distinguish the different types of food retailers?
2. What strategies distinguish the different types of general merchandise retailers?
3. Are organizations that provide services to consumers retailers?

LO 16-5 | Describe the components of a retail strategy.

DEVELOPING A RETAIL STRATEGY USING THE FOUR PS

Like other marketers, retailers perform important functions that increase the value of the products and services they sell to consumers. We now examine these functions, classified into the four Ps: product, price, promotion, and place.

Product

A typical grocery store carries 30,000 to 40,000 items; a regional department store might carry as many as 100,000. Providing the right mix of merchandise and services that satisfies the needs of the target market is one of retailers' most fundamental activities. Offering assortments gives customers a choice. To reduce transportation costs and handling, manufacturers typically ship cases of merchandise, such as cartons of mascara or boxes of leather jackets, to retailers. Because customers generally do not want or need to buy more than one of the same item, retailers break up the cases and sell customers the smaller quantities they desire. Adding Value 16.2 highlights how Home Depot is providing customers better access to more products both in the store and online.

Manufacturers don't like to store inventory because their factories and warehouses are typically not available or attractive shopping venues. Consumers don't want to purchase more than they need because storage consumes space. Neither group likes keeping inventory that isn't being used because doing so ties up money that could be used for something else. Retailers thus provide, in addition to other values to both manufacturers and customers, a storage function, though many retailers are beginning to push their suppliers to hold the inventory until they need it. (Recall our discussion of JIT inventory systems in Chapter 15.)

Material Girl is a Macy's exclusive brand developed by Madonna and her daughter Lourdes Leon.
© Tina Paul/Camera Press/Redux Pictures

> "NEITHER MANUFACTURERS NOR RETAILERS LIKE KEEPING INVENTORY THAT ISN'T BEING USED BECAUSE DOING SO TIES UP MONEY THAT COULD BE USED FOR SOMETHING ELSE. RETAILERS THUS PROVIDE, IN ADDITION TO OTHER VALUES TO BOTH MANUFACTURERS AND CUSTOMERS, A STORAGE FUNCTION."

Adding Value 16.2

Home Depot—Providing Customers Better Access to Products[ii]

By paying attention to what shoppers actually are buying in their stores, many big-box retailers that previously sought to stock a focused product assortment are shifting their inventories to feature more seemingly mismatched items. Shoppers at Home Depot wanted charcoal to go along with the new grills they had just bought, and laundry detergent to use with their new washer–dryer combos, so the home improvement store has expanded its offerings of such consumer goods. Other examples may seem even less convergent though. Staples now stocks coffee pods, because office employees and home-based workers rely on their single-serving machines for a caffeine boost. But it also provides personal deodorant and shaving cream. By stocking such items, Staples hopes that people popping in for toner will also appreciate the convenience of purchasing some basic necessities in the same store rather than visiting another retailer to gather such items.

Additionally, as customers continue to grow more comfortable with online buying, Home Depot is increasing its investment in its e-commerce operations. This provides customers access to more than 600,000 items, whereas the largest store can carry only 35,000 products. It also allows customers to enjoy in-home delivery of bulky products such as sinks or

Why does Home Depot's Internet site carry more than 600,000 items, while its largest stores carry only 35,000?
© Scott Olson/Getty Images

patio sets, rather than having to find a way to lug the heavy items home on their own. It also has set predictions for what it believes will be the fastest movers online: quick purchases such as lightbulbs and extension cords, combined with big, heavy items such as appliances.

With its online efforts, Home Depot also hopes to appeal to its business customers. Online ordering would enable a contractor to put together an e-commerce order for the project it has scheduled for the next day, then stop by the store to pick up the entire supply on the way to the project site.

It is difficult for retailers to distinguish themselves from their competitors through the merchandise they carry because competitors can purchase and sell many of the same popular brands. Thus, many retailers have developed **private-label brands** (also called **store brands**), which are products developed and marketed by a retailer and available only from that retailer. For example, if you want a Giani Bernini leather handbag, you have to go to Macy's.

Retailers often work together with their suppliers to develop an exclusive brand. An **exclusive brand** is a brand that is developed by a national brand vendor, often in conjunction with a retailer, and is sold exclusively by the retailer. So, for example, cosmetics powerhouse Estée Lauder sells two brands of cosmetics and skin care products—American Beauty and Flirt—exclusively at Kohl's. The products are priced between mass-market brands such as CoverGirl or Maybelline (sold mainly in drugstores, discount stores, and supermarkets) and Lauder's higher-end brands (sold primarily in more fashion-forward department stores such as Macy's and Dillard's).

Exclusive brands offer a double benefit: They are available at only one retailer, and they provide name recognition similar to that of a national brand. The disadvantage of exclusive brands, from the manufacturer's perspective, is that they can be sold by only one retailer, and therefore, the manufacturer's market is limited. From the retailer's perspective, the disadvantage is that it has to share its profits with the national brand manufacturer, whereas with a private-label brand, it does not.

Given the price of a Coach bag, would you expect to find it in Saks Fifth Avenue or JCPenney?
© Peter Horree/Alamy

Price

Price helps define the value of both the merchandise and the service, and the general price range of a particular store helps define its image. Although both Saks Fifth Avenue and JCPenney are department stores, their images could not be more different. Thus, when Coach considers which of these firms is most appropriate for its new line for men, it must keep in mind customers' perceived images of these retailers' price–quality relationship. The company does not, for instance, want to attempt to sell its new line at JCPenney if it is positioning the line with a relatively high price.

Price must always be aligned with the other elements of a retailer's strategy: product, promotion, and place. A customer would not expect to pay $600 for a Coach for Men briefcase at a JCPenney store, but she might question the briefcase's quality if its price is significantly less than $600 at Neiman Marcus. As we discovered in Chapter 14, there is much more to pricing

> "Price must always be aligned with the other elements of a retailer's strategy: product, promotion, and place."

than simply adding a markup onto a product's cost. Manufacturers must consider at what price they will sell the product to retailers so that both the manufacturer and the retailer can make a reasonable profit. At the same time, both the manufacturer and the retailer are concerned about what the customer is willing and expecting to pay.

Promotion

Retailers and manufacturers know that good promotion, both within the retail environments and in the media, can mean the difference between flat sales and a growing consumer base. Advertising in traditional media such as newspapers, magazines, and television continues to be important to get customers into stores. Increasingly, electronic communications are being used for promotions as well. Some traditional approaches, such as direct mail, are being reevaluated by retailers, but many are still finding value in sending catalogs to customers and selected mailing lists. Companies also offer real-time promotions on their websites. For example, CVS.com contains in-store and online coupons that customers can use immediately on the website or print to use in the store. Coupons.com offers coupons that customers can use immediately for many grocery store items. Customers can follow this vendor on Twitter @Coupons to find even more savings opportunities.

Technology is thus expanding the ways in which retailers can reach customers with their promotional message. For example, customers can access a retailer's Internet site using a variety of devices, ranging from a computer to a mobile phone. Due to the rapid growth of domestic and international broadband access through mobile devices, retailers are investing in **mobile commerce (M-commerce)**—product and service purchases through mobile devices. However, the typical retailer's website is not designed to accommodate a mobile device's small screen and slower download speeds. Various firms, including Sephora, therefore have developed special sites for users to access through mobile devices. In addition, Sephora and other retailers have created specialized applications that enable mobile device users to shop or obtain more merchandise information.

A coordinated effort between the manufacturer and retailer helps guarantee that the customer receives a cohesive message and that both entities maintain their image. For example, Coach

Consumers can access retailers' coupons from their mobile devices.
© iPhone/Alamy

mobile commerce (M-commerce) Communicating with or selling to consumers through wireless handheld devices such as cellular phones.

cooperative (co-op) advertising An agreement between a manufacturer and retailer in which the manufacturer agrees to defray some advertising costs.

In addition to traditional forms of promotion, many retailers are devoting more resources to their overall retail environment as a means to promote and showcase what the store has to offer. These promotions may take the form of recognizable approaches, such as in-store and window displays, or they may be entirely new experiences designed to help retailers draw customers and add value to the shopping experience. Bass Pro Shops Outdoor World in Lawrenceville, Georgia, offers a 30,000-gallon aquarium stocked with fish for casting demonstrations, an indoor archery range, and a 43-foot climbing wall. These features enhance customers' visual experiences, provide them with educational information, and enhance the store's sales potential by enabling customers to try before they buy. In addition to adding fun to the shopping experience, these activities help offset the current drop in brick-and-mortar customers engendered by online shopping.

A variety of factors influence whether customers will actually buy once they are in the store. Some of these factors are quite subtle. Consumers' perceptions of value and their subsequent patronage are heavily influenced by their perceptions of the store's look and feel. Music, color, scent, aisle size, lighting,

> ## Store credit cards and gift cards are subtler forms of promotion that also facilitate shopping.

for Men might work with its most important retailers to develop advertising and point-of-sale signs. It may even help defray the costs of advertising by paying all or a portion of the advertising's production and media costs, an agreement called **cooperative (co-op) advertising**.

Store credit cards and gift cards are subtler forms of promotion that also facilitate shopping. Retailers might offer pricing promotions—such as coupons, rebates, and in-store or online discounts, or perhaps buy-one-get-one-free offers—to attract consumers and stimulate sales. These promotions play a very important role in driving traffic to retail locations, increasing average purchase size, and creating opportunities for repeat purchases. But retail promotions also are valuable to customers; they inform customers about what is new and available and how much it costs.

Another type of promotion occurs inside the store, where retailers use displays and signs placed at the point of purchase (POP) or in strategic areas such as the end of aisles to inform customers and stimulate purchases of the featured products.

The customer experience is enhanced at C. Wonder by displaying merchandise in a variety of nooks with different personalities, having electronically enhanced fitting rooms, and using microchips embedded in the sales tags so customers can check out anywhere in the store.
© C. Wonder

the availability of seating, and crowding can also significantly affect the overall shopping experience.[21] Therefore, the extent to which stores offer a more pleasant shopping experience fosters a better mood, resulting in greater spending.

Consider the funky C. Wonder emporium for example. This 7,000-square-foot store is divided into various nooks, each with its own personality or feel, including English Town House, Vail Cabin, Palm Springs Modern, and Hollywood Regency. The separate sectors help customers navigate through the vast amount of merchandise available. To grant them control over their experience, C. Wonder's fitting rooms also come equipped with control panels, such that people trying on items can adjust the type and volume of music played, as well as the lighting, to suit their preferences.[22]

Personal selling and customer service representatives are also part of the overall promotional package. Retailers must provide services that make it easier to buy and use products, and retail associates—whether in the store, on the phone, or on the Internet—provide customers with information about product characteristics and availability. These individuals can also facilitate the sale of products or services that consumers perceive as complicated, risky, or expensive, such as an air conditioning unit, a computer, or a diamond ring. Manufacturers can play an important role in preparing retail sales and service associates to sell their products. Eva thus could conduct seminars or webinars about how to use and sell her new

management (CRM). Using this information, retailers may modify product, price, and/or promotion to attempt to increase their **share of wallet**—the percentage of the customer's purchases made from that particular retailer. For instance, omnichannel retailers use consumer information collected from the customers' Internet browsing and buying behavior to send dedicated e-mails to customers promoting specific products or services. Retailers also may offer special discounts to good customers to help them become even more loyal.

Place

Retailers already have realized that convenience is a key ingredient to success, and an important aspect of this success is convenient locations.[24] As the old cliché claims, the three most important things in retailing are location, location, location. Many customers choose stores on the basis of where they are located, which makes great locations a competitive advantage that few rivals can duplicate. For instance, once Starbucks saturates a market by opening in the best locations, Peet's will have difficulty breaking into that same market—where would it put its stores?

In pursuit of better and better locations, retailers are experimenting with different options to reach their target markets. Walgreens has free-standing stores, unconnected to other retailers, so the stores can offer a drive-up window for customers to pick up their prescriptions. Walmart, Staples, and others are opening smaller stores in urban locations to serve those markets better.

THE MOST SUCCESSFUL RETAILERS CONCENTRATE ON PROVIDING MORE VALUE TO THEIR BEST CUSTOMERS.

line of green cosmetics and supply printed educational materials to sales associates. Last but not least, sales reps handle the sales transactions.

In some retail firms, salesperson and customer service functions are being augmented, or even replaced, by technology in the form of in-store kiosks, the Internet, or self-checkout lanes. At C. Wonder, microchips embedded in the sales tags of every item help the sales staff keep track of where the merchandise is in the store. They also can check out customers anywhere in the store using handheld registers, which eliminates the need for customers to head to the checkout counter before they leave.[23]

Traditionally, retailers treated all their customers the same. Today, the most successful retailers concentrate on providing more value to their best customers. The knowledge retailers gain from their store personnel, the Internet browsing and buying activities of customers, and the data they collect on customer shopping habits can be used in customer relationship

To make their locations more convenient, Walgreens has some freestanding stores not connected to other retailers so the stores can offer a drive-up window for customers to pick up their prescriptions.
© McGraw-Hill Education/Andrew Resek, photographer

BENEFITS OF STORES FOR CONSUMERS

In this section, we explore the relative advantages of the most traditional retail channels, the brick-and-mortar stores, from consumers' perspective. In the following section, we examine how the addition of the Internet channel has added value to retailers' ability to satisfy their customers' needs.

Browsing Shoppers often have only a general sense of what they want (e.g., a sweater, something for dinner, a gift) but don't know the specific item they want. They go to a store to see what is available before making their final decision about what to buy. Although some consumers surf the web and look through catalogs for ideas, many still prefer browsing in stores, a trend that IKEA discovered by analyzing its data, as we report in Marketing Analytics 16.1. Some also employ both approaches, getting a sense of what's available through catalogs or the Internet and then going to the store to try on apparel or view the actual object.

Touching and Feeling Products Perhaps the greatest benefit offered by stores is the opportunity for customers

At LegoLand in Minneapolis' Mall of America, customers can browse, touch, and feel the product, enjoy personal service, be entertained, and interact with others.
Courtesy Mall of America.

Marketing Analytics   16.1

In-Store and Online Analytics at IKEA[iii]

IKEA's affordable, ready-to-assemble product line has made it the go-to place for furnishing a new home, apartment, or room. Much of its success stems from its unique store layouts, which force shoppers to walk past virtually every product offered, as displayed in sample rooms that have been designed to inspire their design ideas. The layout also helps IKEA recognize which sorts of displays of what types of products invoke purchases—a sort of elemental analytics that benefits its strategy. Thus, when IKEA first decided to launch its website, it already recognized the importance of analytics as vital information that would enable it to serve its customers better.

Initially, IKEA's analytics-oriented focus was on website development. With its massive product range, the retailer had to find ways to discover pertinent patterns in consumers' product navigation and selection approaches. As it gathered such information, IKEA could begin to revise its site and successfully design a web page that encouraged customers to slow down during their online browsing, enabling them to be inspired by new products, design ideas, and other services the company offers, but without ever sacrificing the convenience they demanded.

Having achieved that goal, IKEA turned its focus to increasing its online presence. For this feat, it needed to do more than analyze data that it had

IKEA's analytics are used for website development and to improve its social media presence.
© Sergio Dionisio/Bloomberg/Getty Images

gathered from its own site. It needed data from social networking sites. These social media-derived insights suggest channels and routes for improving consumers' perceptions of the brand. The influences of these analytics on many of IKEA's online actions are evident. For example, when "The Dress" became a vastly and inexplicably trending topic (is it white and gold or black and blue? And why could no one agree?), IKEA rapidly leveraged the social media sensation to plug its products by using a #TheDress hashtag.

online chat Instant messaging or voice conversation with an online sales representative.

to use all five of their senses—touch, smell, taste, vision, and hearing—to examine products.

Personal Service Sales associates have the capability to provide meaningful, personalized information. Salespeople can be particularly helpful when purchasing a complicated product, like consumer electronics, or something the customer doesn't know much about, like raw Japanese selvedge denim jeans.

Cash and Credit Payment Stores are the only channel that accepts cash payments. Some customers prefer to pay with cash because it is easy, resolves the transaction immediately, and does not result in potential interest payments. And, of course, some people don't have a credit card. Some customers also prefer to use their credit card or debit card in person rather than send the payment information electronically via the Internet.

First, the addition of an Internet channel has the potential to offer a greater selection of products. Second, an Internet channel enables retailers to provide customers with more personalized information about products and services. Third, it offers sellers the unique opportunity to collect information about consumer shopping behavior—information that they can use to improve the shopping experience across all channels. Fourth, the Internet channel allows sellers to enter new markets economically.

Deeper and Broader Selection

One benefit of adding the Internet channel is the vast number of alternatives retailers can make available to consumers without crowding their aisles or increasing their square footage. Stores and catalogs are limited by their size. By shopping on the Internet, consumers can easily visit and select merchandise from a

> "Stores are the only channel that accepts cash payments. Some customers prefer to pay with cash because it is easy, resolves the transaction immediately, and does not result in potential interest payments."

Entertainment and Social Experience In-store shopping can be a stimulating experience for some people, providing a break in their daily routine and enabling them to interact with friends.

Immediate Gratification Stores have the advantage of allowing customers to get the merchandise immediately after paying for it.

Risk Reduction When customers purchase merchandise in stores, the physical presence of the store reduces their perceived risk of buying and increases their confidence that any problems with the merchandise will be corrected.

LO 16-7 | Identify the benefits of omnichannel retailing.

BENEFITS OF THE INTERNET AND OMNICHANNEL RETAILING

In the previous section, we detailed the relative benefits of stores from the consumers' perspective. In this section, we examine how the addition of the Internet channel to traditional store-based retailers has improved their ability to serve their customers and build a competitive advantage in several ways.

broader array of retailers. Individual retailers' websites typically offer deeper assortments of merchandise (more colors, brands, and sizes) than are available in stores or catalogs. This expanded offering enables them to satisfy consumer demand for less popular styles, colors, or sizes. Many retailers also offer a broader assortment (more categories) on their websites. Staples.com, for instance, offers soft drinks and cleaning supplies, which are not available in stores, so that its business customers will view it as a one-stop shop.

Personalization

Another benefit of adding the Internet channel is the ability to personalize promotions and services economically, including heightened service or individualized offerings.

Personalized Customer Service Traditional Internet channel approaches for responding to customer questions—such as FAQ (frequently asked question) pages and offering an 800 number or e-mail address to ask questions—often do not provide the timely information customers are seeking. To improve customer service from an electronic channel, many firms offer live **online chats**, so that customers can click a button at any time and participate in an instant messaging conversation with a customer service representative. This technology also enables firms to send a proactive chat invitation at specific times to visitors to the site. Virgin Airlines programs its chat windows to appear at the moment a customer chooses a flight, because its goal is to upsell these willing buyers to a more expensive fare.[25] Other online retailers use metrics such as the amount of time spent on the site or number of repeat visits to determine which customers will receive an invitation to chat.

Personalized Offering The interactive nature of the Internet also provides an opportunity for retailers to personalize their offerings for each of their customers, based on customers' behavior. Just as a well-trained salesperson would make recommendations to customers prior to checkout, an interactive web page can make suggestions to the shopper about items that he or she might like to see based on previous purchases, what other customers who purchased the same item purchased, or common web viewing behavior.

Some omnichannel retailers are able to personalize promotions and Internet home pages on the basis of several attributes tied to the shopper's current or previous web sessions, such as the time of day, time zone as determined by a computer's Internet address, and assumed gender.[26] However, some consumers worry about this ability to collect information about purchase histories, personal information, and search behavior on the Internet. How will this information be used in the future? Will it be sold to other firms, or will the consumer receive unwanted promotional materials online or in the mail?

Expanded Market Presence

The market for customers who shop in stores is typically limited to consumers living in proximity to those stores. The market for catalogs is limited by the high cost of printing and mailing them and increasing consumer interest in environmentally friendly practices. By adding the Internet channel, retailers can expand their market without having to build new stores or incur the high cost of additional catalogs. Adding an Internet channel is particularly attractive to retailers with strong brand names but limited locations and distribution. For example, retailers such as Nordstrom, REI, IKEA, and L.L.Bean are widely known for offering unique, high-quality merchandise. If these retailers only had a store, customers would have to travel vast distances to buy the merchandise they carry.

EFFECTIVE OMNICHANNEL RETAILING

Consumers desire a seamless experience when interacting with omnichannel retailers. They want to be recognized by a retailer, whether they interact with a sales associate, the retailer's website, or the retailer's call center by telephone. Customers want to buy a product through the retailer's Internet or catalog channels and pick it up or return it to a local store; find out if a product offered on the Internet channel is available at a local store; and, when unable to find a product in a

> ## "BECAUSE EACH OF THE CHANNELS IS SOMEWHAT DIFFERENT, A CRITICAL DECISION FACING OMNICHANNEL RETAILERS IS THE DEGREE TO WHICH THEY SHOULD OR ARE ABLE TO INTEGRATE THE OPERATIONS OF THE CHANNELS."

store, determine if it is available for home delivery through the retailer's Internet channel.

However, providing this seamless experience for customers is not easy for retailers. Because each of the channels is somewhat different, a critical decision facing omnichannel retailers is the degree to which they should or are able to integrate the operations of the channels.[27] To determine how much integration is best, each retailer must address issues such as integrated CRM, brand image, pricing, and the supply chain.

Integrated CRM

Effective omnichannel operations require an integrated CRM (customer relationship management) system with a centralized customer data warehouse that houses a complete history of each customer's interaction with the retailer, regardless of whether the sale occurred in a store, on the Internet, or on the telephone.[28] This information storehouse allows retailers to efficiently handle complaints, expedite returns, target future promotions, and provide a seamless experience for customers when they interact with the retailer through multiple channels.

Brand Image

Retailers need to provide a consistent brand image across all channels. For example, Patagonia reinforces its image of selling high-quality, environmentally friendly sports equipment in its stores, catalogs, and website. Each of these channels emphasizes function, not fashion, in the descriptions of Patagonia's products. Patagonia's position about taking care of the environment is communicated by carefully lighting its stores and using recycled polyester and organic rather than pesticide-intensive cotton in many of its clothes.

Pricing

Pricing represents another difficult decision for an omnichannel retailer. Customers expect pricing consistency for the same SKU across channels (excluding shipping charges and sales tax). However, in some cases, retailers need to adjust their pricing strategy because of the competition they face in different channels. For example, Barnes & Noble offers lower prices through its Internet channel (www.bn.com) than in its stores to compete effectively against Amazon.com.

Retailers with stores in multiple markets often set different prices for the same merchandise to compete better with local stores. Customers generally are not aware of these price differences because they are only exposed to the prices in their local markets. However, omnichannel retailers may have difficulties sustaining these regional price differences when customers can easily check prices on the Internet.

Supply Chain

Omnichannel retailers struggle to provide an integrated shopping experience across all their channels because unique skills and resources are needed to manage each channel.[29] For example, store-based retail chains operate and manage many stores, each requiring the management of inventory and people. With Internet and catalog operations, inventory and telephone salespeople instead are typically centralized in one or two locations. Also, retail distribution centers (DCs) supporting a store channel are designed to ship many cartons of merchandise to stores. In contrast, the DCs supporting a catalog and Internet channel are designed to ship a few items at a time to many individual customers. The

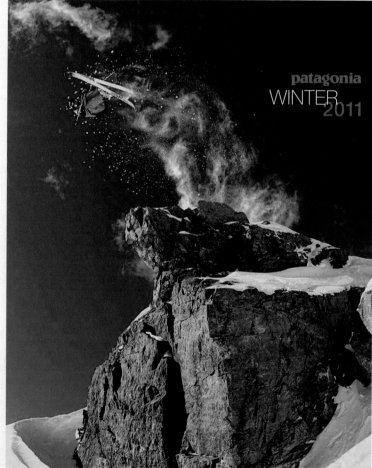

Multichannel retailers like Patagonia sell on the Internet (upper left), in catalogs (right), and in stores (lower left).
Courtesy Patagonia, Inc.

difference in shipping orientation for the two types of operations requires a completely different type of distribution center.

Due to these operational differences, many store-based retailers have a separate organization to manage their Internet and catalog operations. But as the omnichannel operation matures, retailers tend to integrate all operations under one organization. Both Walmart and JCPenney initially had separate organizations for their Internet channel but subsequently integrated them with stores and catalogs. ∎

 check yourself

1. What are the components of a retail strategy?
2. What are the advantages of traditional stores versus Internet-only stores?
3. What challenges do retailers face when marketing their products through multiple channels?

  Increase your engagement and learning with Connect Marketing.

<u>These Connect activities, available only through your Connect course, have been designed to make the following concepts more meaningful and applicable:</u>

▶ Supply Chain Information Communication Timeline

▶ Pioneering Supply Chain Management: Walmart Case Analysis

▶ Supply Chain Icebreaker Video Case

▶ Supply Chain: iSeeit! Video

SMARTBOOK™   **iSeeit!**

Chapter seventeen

The incredible expansion of the Internet and online tools has radically changed the manner in which marketers communicate with customers. More and more, companies spread their messages over all sorts of media—television, print, radio, e-mail, Internet, and so on. To really stand out then, a company may need to go further than ever.

To achieve success in a market, companies invariably must communicate the value of their offerings in diverse, well-rounded ways. When companies promote their brands through multiple channels, they stand a better chance of reaching their customers. Coordination across these platforms is the key to effective omnichannel (or multichannel) marketing communications. But it is difficult to ensure brand consistency when radio, television, online, and print ads each require different types of elements, unique voices, and varying styles. In addition, firms need to integrate their marketing communications even further by incorporating new opportunities to reach

integrated marketing **communications**

LEARNING OBJECTIVES

After reading this chapter, you should be able to:

LO 17-1 Identify the components of the communication process.

LO 17-2 Explain the four steps in the AIDA model.

LO 17-3 Describe the various integrative communication channels.

LO 17-4 Explain the methods used to allocate the integrated marketing communications (IMC) budget.

LO 17-5 Identify marketing metrics used to measure IMC success.

customers through social media sites such as Facebook and Twitter.

Even well-known brands need to consider these issues. It might seem, for example, that Coca-Cola is such a well-defined

continued on p. 350

continued from p. 349

brand that its communications would be automatically consistent across marketing channels. But as sales of its iconic Coke and Diet Coke brands have suffered some stagnation in recent years—likely attributable to increasing emphases on healthy lifestyles and concerns about artificial sweeteners and too much sugar in our diets[1]—this assumption has required some rethinking. The amount of sugar in one 12-ounce can of Coke exceeds the total recommended daily amount for an adult consumer,[2] which suggests that Coca-Cola needs to find a new way to appeal to buyers. In particular, for Millennials—young consumers who "expect unlimited choice, personalized and delivered through multiple channels at maximum speed"—Coca-Cola has adopted a multipronged communication strategy.[3]

For example, the very shape of a Coke bottle represents a form of communication, leading Coca-Cola to enhance its reliance on packaging as a means to appeal to consumers. The "Share a Coke" campaign enables customers to order personalized bottles of Coke at the shareacoke.com Internet site. For five dollars a bottle plus shipping, Coke prints names and messages on the bottle. The messages include everything from nicknames to marriage proposals.[4]

Along with these packaging innovations, Coca-Cola is experimenting with new product innovations, which it markets in various ways. To encourage expanded uses of its Freestyle machines, for example (see Social and Mobile Marketing 17.1 later in the chapter), it has developed an app that saves users' preferences and favored soda blends. Thus it emphasizes its personalization ability through mobile communications as well.

Along with these personalized forms of communication, Coca-Cola aims for a consistent message that it can specify as needed. A recent example, "Live Positively," provides Coca-Cola with a framework for discussing all its brands, including those that refer to non-carbonated beverages such as Powerade, Minute Maid juices, and Dasani water. In this framework, the company seeks to establish that Coke, Diet Coke, and other beverages are all elements of a healthy lifestyle, such that none of them requires complete abstinence, nor should any of them be the only thing a person drinks all day. This healthy lifestyle approach also is evident in Coca-Cola's consistent

Coca-Cola has adopted a multi-pronged communications approach to appeal to Millennials.
© Jonathan Leibson/Getty Images

sponsorships of sports events, such as the FIFA World Cup. For this event, it has developed an integrated campaign titled "The World's Cup" that includes several short documentary films under the heading "Where Will Happiness Strike Next?"; an official anthem; a massive photomosaic of fans' pictures and messages combined in the "Happiness Flag"; and a digital film for release on television titled "One World, One Game."[5]

Even as it reportedly mulls new acquisitions of tea, coffee, and other beverage brands, Coca-Cola promises to focus most of its advertising communications on its flagship Coke brand, including an increase of $1 billion in its global advertising budget in coming years.[6] As the boundaries of advertising shift to include digital and social media, the integration of multiple marketing channels is crucial for catching customers wherever they are: through apps on their mobile devices, in front of the television, typing on their home computer, or on the go. The challenge persists, even for a marketing giant like Coca-Cola. ■

As this description of Coca-Cola's marketing campaigns attests, each element of an integrated marketing communications (IMC) strategy must have a well-defined purpose and support and extend the message delivered by all the other elements.

Throughout this book, we have focused our attention on how firms create value by developing products and services. However, consumers are not likely to come flocking to new products and services unless they are aware of them. Therefore, marketers must consider how to communicate the value of a product and/or service—or more specifically, the value proposition—to the target market. A firm must develop a communication strategy to demonstrate the value of its product. We begin our discussion by examining what IMC is, how it has developed, and how it contributes to value creation.

Integrated marketing communications (IMC) represents the promotion P of the four Ps. It encompasses a variety of communication disciplines—advertising, personal selling, sales promotion, public relations, direct marketing, and online marketing including social media—in combination to provide clarity, consistency, and maximum communicative impact.[7] Instead of consisting of separated marketing communications elements with no unified control, IMC programs regard each of the firm's marketing communications elements as part of a whole, each of which offers a different means to connect with the target audience. This integration of elements provides the firm with the best means to reach the target audience with the desired message, and it enhances the value story by offering a clear and consistent message.

There are three elements in any IMC strategy: the consumer, the channels through which the message is communicated, and the evaluation of the results of the communication. This chapter is organized around these three elements. In the first section, the focus is on consumers, so we examine how consumers receive communications, whether via media or other methods, as well as how the delivery of that communication affects a message's form and contents. The second section examines the various communication channels that make up the components of IMC and how each is used in an overall IMC strategy. The third section considers how the level of complexity in IMC strategies leads marketers to design new ways to measure the results of IMC campaigns.

> **Consumers are not likely to come flocking to new products and services unless they are aware of them.**

integrated marketing communications (IMC) Represents the promotion dimension of the four Ps; encompasses a variety of communication disciplines—general advertising, personal selling, sales promotion, public relations, direct marketing, and electronic media—in combination to provide clarity, consistency, and maximum communicative impact.

LO 17-1 | Identify the components of the communication process.

COMMUNICATING WITH CONSUMERS

As the number of communication media has increased, the task of understanding how best to reach target consumers has become far more complex. In this section, we examine a model that describes how communications go from the firm to the consumer and the factors that affect the way the consumer perceives the message. Then we look at how marketing communications influence consumers—from making them aware that a product or service exists to moving them to buy.

The Communication Process

Exhibit 17.1 illustrates the communication process. Let's first define each component and then discuss how they interact.

▼ **EXHIBIT 17.1** The Communication Process

Noise from the environment

Sender (Firm) → Transmitter encodes message → Communications channel (Media) → Receiver (Consumer) decodes message

Feedback

sender The firm from which an IMC message originates; the sender must be clearly identified to the intended audience.

transmitter An agent or intermediary with which the sender works to develop the marketing communications; for example, a firm's creative department or an advertising agency.

encoding The process of converting the sender's ideas into a message, which could be verbal, visual, or both.

communication channel The medium—print, broadcast, the Internet—that carries the message.

receiver The person who reads, hears, or sees and processes the information contained in the message or advertisement.

To make customers aware of Coke's Freestyle vending machines, it works with retailers such as Dairy Queen to send messages about its new machines.
© ZUMA Press, Inc/Alamy

The Sender
The message originates from the **sender**, who must be clearly identified to the intended audience. As our opening vignette revealed, Coca-Cola has introduced new options in its packaging and products, which it must communicate to consumers.

For its Freestyle vending machines, for example, Coca-Cola works with retailers and other outlets that host Freestyle, such as Dairy Queen, Burger King, Kroger, Five Guys Burgers, or Kmart, to send messages about its new machines. To highlight the free song downloads, it partners with Sony. In other cases, Coca-Cola works independently to send out various types of messages through different channels that highlight its familiar red-and-white color scheme, images of happy consumers, or its iconic bottle shape.

The Transmitter
The sender works with a creative department, whether in-house or from a marketing (or advertising) agency, to develop marketing communications to highlight the new beverage. With the assistance of its marketing department, Coca-Cola and its partners might develop its websites, mobile apps, flyers, in-store displays, and televised commercials. The marketing department or external agency receives the information and transforms it for use in its role as the **transmitter**.

Encoding
Encoding means converting the sender's ideas into a message, which could be verbal, visual, or both. A television commercial could show consumers drinking a Coca-Cola. Billboards showcasing the well-designed machines might highlight their pictures with a message asking, "Have You Tried It

> "Although a picture can be worth a thousand words, the most important facet of encoding is not what is sent but rather what is received."

To appeal to a broad audience, Coca-Cola has successfully placed its products on American Idol, featuring judges Keith Urban, Jennifer Lopez, and Harry Connick Jr.
© FOX/Contributor/Getty Images

Yet?" Although a picture can be worth a thousand words, the most important facet of encoding is not what is sent but rather what is received. Consumers must receive information that makes them want to try the new machine and to continue to buy from it for the innovation to be successful.

The Communication Channel
The **communication channel** is the medium—print, broadcast, the Internet, and so forth—that carries the message. Coca-Cola could transmit through television, radio, and various print advertisements, but it also realizes that the media chosen must be appropriate to connect itself (the sender) with its desired recipients. If the company believes its target market is broad, Coca-Cola might advertise or place its products on popular television shows such as *The Big Bang Theory* and *American Idol*.

The Receiver
The **receiver** is the person who reads, hears, or sees and processes the information contained in the message

and/or advertisement. The sender, of course, hopes that the person receiving it will be the one for whom it was originally intended. Coca-Cola wants its message received and decoded properly by a broad population, including teens, young adults, and families. **Decoding** refers to the process by which the receiver interprets the sender's message.

Noise **Noise** is any interference that stems from competing messages, a lack of clarity in the message, or a flaw in the medium. It poses a problem for all communication channels. Coca-Cola may choose to advertise in newspapers that its target market doesn't read, which means the rate at which the message is received by those to whom it has relevance has been slowed considerably. As we have already defined, encoding is what the sender intends to say, and decoding is what the receiver hears. If there is a difference between them, it is probably due to noise.

Feedback Loop The **feedback loop** allows the receiver to communicate with the sender and thereby informs the sender whether the message was received and decoded properly. Feedback can take many forms: a customer's purchase of the item, a complaint or compliment, the redemption of a coupon or rebate, a tweet about the product on Twitter, and so forth.

How Consumers Perceive Communication

The actual communication process is not as simple as the model in Exhibit 17.1 implies. Each receiver may interpret the sender's message differently, and senders often adjust their message according to the medium used and the receivers' level of knowledge about the product or service.

Receivers Decode Messages Differently Each receiver decodes a message in his or her own way, which is not necessarily the way the sender intended. Different people shown the same message will often take radically different meanings from it. For example, what does the image on this page convey to you?

If you are a user of this brand, it may convey satisfaction. If you recently went on a diet and gave up your soda, it may convey dismay or a sense of loss. If you have chosen to be a nonuser, it may convey some disgust. If you are a recently terminated employee, it may convey anger. The sender has little, if any, control over what meaning any individual receiver will take from the message.

Senders Adjust Messages according to the Medium and Receivers' Traits Different media communicate in varied ways, so marketers make adjustments to their messages and media depending on whether they want to communicate with suppliers, shareholders, customers, or the general public, as well as the specific segments of those groups.[8]

For example, the high-technology firm Analtech sells thin layer chromatography plates to companies that need equipment to determine the ingredients of samples of virtually anything. It is not a particularly easy product to explain and sell to laypeople, particularly since some purchasers might not have a science degree. Therefore, in addition to traditional marketing through trade shows and scientific conferences, Analtech developed a Monty Python–inspired YouTube video (http://www.ichromatography .com/adventuresofana.html) that features a witch that overcomes threats to drown her by proving that the ink in the king's decree is actually from the sheriff's pen. It

decoding The process by which the receiver interprets the sender's message.

noise Any interference that stems from competing messages, a lack of clarity in the message, or a flaw in the medium; a problem for all communication channels.

feedback loop Allows the receiver to communicate with the sender and thereby informs the sender whether the message was received and decoded properly.

Consumers will perceive this giant billboard differently depending on their level of knowledge and attitude toward the brand.

© imago stock&people/Newscom

AIDA model A common model of the series of mental stages through which consumers move as a result of marketing communications: *A*wareness leads to *I*nterests, which lead to *D*esire, which leads to *A*ction.

brand awareness Measures how many consumers in a market are familiar with the brand and what it stands for; created through repeated exposures of the various brand elements (brand name, logo, symbol, character, packaging, or slogan) in the firm's communications to consumers.

aided recall Occurs when consumers recognize a name (e.g., of a brand) that has been presented to them.

top-of-mind awareness A prominent place in people's memories that triggers a response without them having to put any thought into it.

also highlights points in *CSI* episodes when the television detectives rely on its products. With these more broadly popular appeals, Analtech ensures its messages reach and can be received accurately by a wider audience, with less noise than might occur through more scientific appeals.

| LO 17-2 | Explain the four steps in the AIDA model. |

The AIDA Model

Clearly, IMC is not a straightforward process. After being exposed to marketing communications, consumers go through several steps before actually buying or taking some other action. There is not always a direct link between a particular form of marketing communications and a consumer's purchase.

To create effective IMC programs, marketers must understand how marketing communications work. Generally, marketing communications move consumers stepwise through a series of mental stages, for which there are several models. The most common is the **AIDA model** (Exhibit 17.2),[9] which suggests that **A**wareness leads to **I**nterest, which leads to **D**esire, which leads to **A**ction. At each stage, the consumer makes judgments about whether to take the next step in the process. Customers actually have three types of responses, so the AIDA model is also known as the think, feel, do model. In making a purchase decision, consumers go through each of the AIDA steps to some degree, but the steps may not always follow the AIDA order. For instance, during an impulse purchase, a consumer may feel and do before he or she thinks.

Awareness Even the best marketing communications can be wasted if the sender doesn't gain the attention of the consumer first. **Brand awareness** refers to a potential customer's ability to recognize or recall that the brand name is a particular type of retailer or product/service. Thus, brand awareness is the strength of the link between the brand name and the type of merchandise or service in the minds of customers.

Coca-Cola already has excellent brand awareness and thus might not have to focus as much effort on this step when it wants to introduce a new flavor or its Freestyle machines. Social and Mobile Marketing 17.1 highlights how Google used these Freestyle machines to allow customers to send a Coke across the world.

> IN MAKING A PURCHASE DECISION, CONSUMERS GO THROUGH EACH OF THE AIDA STEPS TO SOME DEGREE, BUT THE STEPS MAY NOT ALWAYS FOLLOW THE AIDA ORDER.

▼ **EXHIBIT 17.2** The AIDA Model

There are several awareness metrics, including aided recall and top-of-mind awareness. **Aided recall** is when consumers indicate they know the brand when the name is presented to them. **Top-of-mind awareness**, the highest level of awareness, occurs when consumers mention a specific brand name first when they are asked about a product or service. For example, Harley-Davidson has top-of-mind awareness if a consumer responds "Harley" when asked about American-made motorcycles. High top-of-mind awareness means that the brand probably enters the evoked set of brands (see Chapter 6) when customers decide to shop for that particular product or service. Manufacturers, retailers, and service providers build top-of-mind awareness by having memorable names; repeatedly exposing their name to customers through advertising, locations, and sponsorships; and using memorable symbols.

As an excellent example of the last method, imagine two smaller circles, sitting on opposite sides atop a larger circle. Did you see Mickey Mouse ears? Did you think of Disney? In

Social & Mobile Marketing
Making the Old New by Turning a Classic Campaign into a Mobile Event[i]

In 1971, Coca-Cola premiered a powerful ad campaign in which hundreds of people sang on top of a mountain about teaching the world to sing and buying the world a Coke. This enduring familiarity reflects the success of the original ad campaign, which is a significant part of the reason that Google is remixing the notion, both literally and figuratively, in its latest marketing communications.

The utopian ideal behind the Hilltop advertisement and song was that everyone across the world could get along, if only given the chance to share a Coke. Google's advertising seeks to put that theory to the test by establishing a mobile app that allows people to buy a drink for someone on the other side of the Earth. A user in New York purchases the Coke, and then a specially designed vending machine in Buenos Aires, Argentina, or Cape Town, South Africa, distributes the can to a surprised buyer. In addition, the machine records the recipient's reaction and allows him or her to send a thank-you note, if he or she chooses. After receiving the video of the reaction, the Coke-sender

has an option to post it to social media sites to demonstrate the connection made.

Although the program might seem to be advertising for Coca-Cola (and certainly it creates communication about Coke), it is actually a campaign by and for Google, "to show what our technology was capable of, not talk about it," as Google's product marketing manager put it.

The campaign, which Google calls Project Re:Brief, also is not limited to Coke. Google also has put a modern spin on Alka-Seltzer's classic 1972 "I can't believe I ate the whole thing" advertisement as well as two ads from the 1960s: Volvo's "Drive it like you hate it" and Avis car rental's "We try harder." In the revised Volvo commercial, Google links the car's driver to Google Maps, showing where he has gone as his car approaches 3 million miles on its odometer. The Alka-Seltzer update shows videos of the overeater throughout the day, using links to Google's YouTube service.

The Re:Brief ads thus marry nostalgia with modern conveniences—a combination that Google would love to exploit in all its communications.

Google's Project Re:Brief campaign marries classic advertising from companies like Coca-Cola, Volvo, Alka-Seltzer, and Avis, with Google's state-of-the-art technology.

© Google Inc.

addition, the company has moved on to images brighter than circles to ensure that its name comes easily to the front of young consumers' minds. Whether individual acts such as Austin Mahone, Selena Gomez, or Demi Lovato or groups such as the R5, Lemonade Mouth, and Allstar Weekend, Disney starts off its stars with Disney Channel shows, records them on

the Disney-owned Hollywood Record label, plays the songs in heavy rotation on Radio Disney and Disney movie soundtracks, organizes concert tours with Disney-owned Buena Vista Concerts, and sells tie-in merchandise throughout Disney stores. Each of these marketing elements reminds the various segments of the target market about both the brand (e.g., One Direction)

lagged effect A delayed response to a marketing communication campaign.

and its owner, Disney. With this omnichannel approach, Disney gets the same product into more markets than would be possible with a more conservative approach—further building top-of-mind awareness for both Disney and its stars.[10]

Interest Once the consumer is aware that the company or product exists, communication must work to increase his or her interest level. It isn't enough to let people know that the product exists; consumers must be persuaded that it is a product worth investigating. Because Stouffer's was suffering from a reputation of offering poor-quality meal options, it reoriented its marketing campaigns to focus on its "real food" ingredients that led to meals good enough to make even a teenager put down her phone to join her family at dinnertime.[11] Thus, the ads' messages include attributes that are of interest to the target audience—in this case, parents who want to sit down to a nice dinner with their children. Disney increases interest in an upcoming tour or record by including a mention, whether casual or not, in the stars' television shows. Because the primary target market for the tour is also probably watching the show, the message is received by the correct recipient.

Desire After the firm has piqued the interest of its target market, the goal of subsequent IMC messages should move the consumer from "I like it" to "I want it." If Lucy Hale appears on *Good Morning America* (on ABC, which is owned by Disney) and talks about her upcoming album and how great it is going to be, the viewing audience is all the more likely to demand access—in this case, probably parents who hope to score points with their adolescent children by buying the latest single or reserving seats to an upcoming tour. Stouffer's aims to enhance consumers' desire through its food truck initiatives, which offer free samples of various frozen entrees, dressed up with extra ingredients to show families how delicious a frozen dinner can be with just a few extra steps.[12]

Action The ultimate goal of any form of marketing communications is to drive the receiver to action. Thus Stouffer's likely hands out coupons for its products from its food trucks, to help push customers to make the purchase during their next trip to the grocery store. As long as the message has caught consumers' attention and made them interested enough to consider the product as a means to satisfy a specific desire of theirs, they likely will act on that interest by either searching for the product or making a purchase. If young consumers watch the Disney Channel's show *Shake It Up* or visit Disney's Fashion Studio website to see what the stars are wearing, they might in turn beg their parents to make an actual purchase of Bella Thorne and Zendaya's most recent "Shake It Up" album.

> It isn't enough to let people know that the product exists; consumers must be persuaded that it is a product worth investigating.

When Zendaya (left) and Bella Thorne (right) appear on Shake It Up, demand for their albums increases.
© Jen Lowery/Splash News/Newscom

The Lagged Effect Sometimes consumers don't act immediately after receiving a form of marketing communications because of the **lagged effect**—a delayed response to a marketing communications campaign. It generally takes several exposures to an ad before a consumer fully processes its message.[13] In turn, measuring the effect of a current campaign becomes more difficult because of the possible lagged response to a previous one. For example, Toyota's "Prius Goes Plural" campaign promotes its addition of a family-sized (Prius v) and urban version (Prius c) of its popular hybrid car model. The campaign demands consumer participation by challenging the viewing public to come up with a plural form of the word *Prius* (e.g., Prii, Prien, Priuses), as touted in online banner and television ads, virtual polling booths, and videos. But the Prius v was not slated for release until six months after the campaign started, and the lag time for the Prius c was even longer. Thus the company might never know for sure whether exposure to this form of marketing communications actually led consumers to check out or purchase the new vehicles.[14]

prius goes plural

Toyota's Prius Goes Plural campaign promotes its addition of a family-sized (Prius v) and urban version (Prius c) to its popular hybrid car model.
© Bloomberg/Getty Images

Now that we've examined various aspects of the communication process, let's look at how specific media are used in an IMC program.

 check yourself

1. What are the different steps in the communication process?

2. What is the AIDA model?

ELEMENTS OF AN INTEGRATED MARKETING COMMUNICATIONS STRATEGY

For any communications campaign to succeed, the firm must deliver the right message to the right audience through the right media, with the ultimate goal of profiting from long-term customer relationships rather than just short-term transactions. Reaching the right audience is becoming more difficult, however, as the media environment grows more complicated.

No single channel is necessarily better than another channel; the goal of IMC is to use them in conjunction so that the sum exceeds the total of the individual channels. However, advances in technology have led to a variety of new and traditional media options for consumers, all of which vie for consumers' attention. Print media have also grown and become more specialized. This proliferation of media has led many firms to shift their promotional dollars from advertising to direct marketing, website development, product placements, and other forms of promotion in search of the best way to deliver messages to their target audiences.

LO 17-3 Describe the various integrative communication channels.

We now examine the individual elements of IMC and the way each contributes to a successful IMC campaign (see Exhibit 17.3). The elements can be viewed on two axes: passive and interactive (from the consumer's perspective) and offline and online. Some elements (e.g., advertising, sales promotion, public relations, personal selling, direct and online marketing) are discussed in far more detail in subsequent chapters, so we discuss them only briefly here.

Note that as the marketer's repertoire of IMC elements has expanded, so too have the ways in which marketers can communicate with their customers. So, for instance, direct marketing appears in all four boxes. Firms have expanded their use of these traditional media (e.g., advertising, public relations, and sales promotions) from pure offline approaches to a combination of offline and online.

Advertising

Perhaps the most visible of the IMC components, **advertising** entails the placement of announcements and persuasive messages in time or space purchased in any of the mass media by business firms, nonprofit organizations, government agencies, and individuals who seek to inform and/or persuade members of a particular target market or audience about their products,

▼ **EXHIBIT 17.3** Elements of an IMC Strategy

public relations (PR)
The organizational function that manages the firm's communications to achieve a variety of objectives, including building and maintaining a positive image, handling or heading off unfavorable stories or events, and maintaining positive relationships with the media.

services, organizations, or ideas.[15] In Chapter 18, we discuss the purpose of advertising and its various types, but for now, we note that advertising is extremely effective for creating awareness of a product or service and generating interest. Mass advertising can entice consumers into a conversation with marketers, though it does not necessarily require much action by consumers, which places it on the passive end of the spectrum. Traditionally, advertising has been passive and offline (e.g., television, magazines, newspapers; see Exhibit 17.3), though

recently there has been a growth in online advertising and interactive features. Advertising thus must break through the clutter of other messages to reach its intended audience. To do so, many advertisers rely on certain images; Ethical and Societal Dilemma 17.1 notes the conflict when advertisers use underweight models in ads they aim at teenaged consumers.

Public Relations

Public relations (PR) is the organizational function that manages the firm's communications to achieve a variety of objectives, including building and maintaining a positive image, handling or heading off unfavorable stories or events, and maintaining positive relationships with the media. Like advertising, this tactic is relatively passive in that customers do not

ethical&societal dilemma 17.1

Too Skinny[ii]

The objective of an integrated marketing communications (IMC) campaign is to build profits by encouraging consumers to purchase more products. But what happens if the campaign leads to harmful behaviors? Companies could claim that shoppers have a choice about the goods they purchase or assert that marketing only influences brand decisions. But sometimes marketing directed at younger consumers complicates that reasoning, because few children or teens can separate unhealthy body images from the popular fashion looks that surround them.

Advertising models have always tended to be thin, but they have become increasingly so in the past decade. The tragic deaths of Ana Carolina Reston and Isabelle Caro—two very thin models suffering from anorexia—led some fashion industry leaders to call for a change. That was nearly a decade ago, and still underage and dangerously thin young girls continue to find work as fashion advertising models. The designers and clothing companies continue to hire girls as young as 14 years of age to walk the runway—a clear child-labor law violation according to critics. Even worse, it continues to reinforce the notion that to be beautiful, women and girls need to starve themselves.

These concerns apply not only to the teenaged girls targeted by such ads but also to the models themselves—young girls who are working long hours, subjected to harsh criticisms and widespread rejection. Most child

development research suggests that children younger than 16 years are ill-prepared to deal with such scenarios.

In the United Kingdom, the Advertising Standards Authority (ASA) has banned some ads outright for being "socially irresponsible." An ad run by Drop Dead, a British clothing line, prompted the watchdog agency to condemn the brand's image: a shockingly thin model who sends dangerously inappropriate style signals to teenaged girls. In its statement, the ASA complained that the young model's "hip, rib and collar bones were highly visible" and noted that she had visible (and unnatural) "hollows in her thighs." Under such pressures, some UK companies have begun to respond. The fashion brand Topshop removed an ad from its website after advocates complained that the featured model was dangerously gaunt and thus a negative influence on young shoppers.

In the United States, the Council of Fashion Designers of America (CFDA) also has denounced the hiring of underage models, yet violations continue. Recently, it called on designers and modeling agencies to require identification from models, showing that they were at least 16 years old. It also began educating industry members to recognize early signs of eating disorders, called for the provision of healthy snacks backstage, and banned the use of models under 18 years at fittings or photo shows held after midnight. Despite widespread skepticism that the industry can regulate itself, the National Eating Disorders Association has applauded the CFDA guidelines.

Promoting products using ultra-thin models sends dangerously inappropriate style signals to teenaged girls.
© Fernanda Calfat/Getty Images

Change appears to be coming, but slowly still. Designers such as Tommy Hilfiger and Tory Burch complain that the models who apply with them continue to appear young and thin. "I still see some girls coming in who are really emaciated," Burch said. "It's still a problem." Those concerned about the ultra-thin style promoted by fashion advertising for young girls will be watching, but changing the tone of this communication is more challenging than just checking IDs and offering up a snack.

have to take any action to receive it. Public relations activities support the other promotional efforts by the firm by generating free media attention, as we discuss further in Chapter 18.

Sales Promotions

Sales promotions are special incentives or excitement-building programs that encourage the purchase of a product or service, such as coupons, rebates, contests, free samples, and point-of-purchase (POP) displays. Marketers typically design these incentives for use in conjunction with other advertising or personal selling programs. Many sales promotions, such as free samples or POP displays, are designed to build short-term sales. Others, such as contests and sweepstakes, have become integral components of firms' CRM programs as a means to build customer loyalty. We discuss such sales promotions in more detail in Chapter 18.

Personal Selling

Personal selling is the two-way flow of communication between a buyer and a seller that is designed to influence the buyer's purchase decision. Personal selling can take place in various settings: face-to-face, video teleconferencing, on the

sales promotions Special incentives or excitement-building programs that encourage the purchase of a product or service, such as coupons, rebates, contests, free samples, and point-of-purchase displays.

personal selling The two-way flow of communication between a buyer and a seller that is designed to influence the buyer's purchase decision.

direct marketing Sales and promotional techniques that deliver promotional materials individually.

variety of traditional and new forms of marketing communications initiatives. Traditional direct marketing includes mail and catalogs sent through the mail; direct marketing also includes e-mail and mobile marketing.

Internet-based technologies have had a profound effect on direct marketing initiatives. E-mail, for instance, can be directed to a specific consumer. Firms use e-mail to inform customers of new merchandise and special promotions, confirm the receipt of an order, and indicate when an order has been shipped. Currently available technologies also mean handheld devices can function as a payment medium: Just tap your cell phone, and the transaction occurs in much the same way it occurs with a credit card.[17]

The increased use of customer databases has enabled marketers to identify and track consumers over time and across purchase situations, which has contributed to the rapid growth of direct marketing. Marketers have been able to build these

> ## Many sales promotions, such as free samples or POP displays, are designed to build short-term sales.

telephone, or over the Internet. Although consumers don't often interact with professional sales people, personal selling represents an important component of many IMC programs, especially in business-to-business (B2B) settings.

The cost of communicating directly with a potential customer is quite high compared with other forms of promotion, but it is simply the best and most efficient way to sell certain products and services. Customers can buy many products and services without the help of a salesperson, but salespeople simplify the buying process by providing information and services that save customers time and effort. In many cases, sales representatives add significant value, which makes the added expense of employing them worthwhile. We devote Chapter 19 to personal selling and sales management.

Direct Marketing

The component of IMC that has received the greatest increase in aggregate spending recently is **direct marketing,** or marketing that communicates directly with target customers to generate a response or transaction.[16] Direct marketing contains a

databases, thanks to consumers' increased use of credit and debit cards, store-specific credit and loyalty cards, and online shopping, all of which require the buyer to give the seller personal information that becomes part of its database. Because firms understand customers' purchases better when they possess such information, they can more easily focus their direct marketing efforts appropriately. Ethical and Societal Dilemma 17.2 details how companies are targeting consumers with promotions based on their purchasing behavior and how the government has reacted to curb potential abuse.

Direct marketing retailers try to target their customers carefully so they will be more receptive to their messages. Omaha Steaks, for example, sends e-mail coupons for items that customers have purchased previously, mails slick pictures of gourmet steaks and meal packages to addresses that have received orders in the past, and calls customers personally during likely gift-giving occasions, such as the holidays, to offer to repeat a previous gift order. These different forms of direct marketing demonstrate how this IMC format can vary on both the interactivity and online–offline dimensions of the matrix.

Mobile marketing is marketing through wireless handheld devices, such as cellular telephones.[18] Smartphones have become far more than tools to place calls; they offer a kind of mobile computer with the ability to obtain sports scores, weather, music, videos, and text messages as well as purchase merchandise. Marketing success rests on integrating marketing communications with fun, useful apps that are consistent with these consumer attitudes toward mobile devices. In response, firms are steadily improving customers' potential experience with their mobile interface. Exhibit 17.4 highlights five successful mobile marketing campaigns.

Online Marketing

We now examine several electronic media vehicles: websites, blogs, and social media.

Websites Firms have increased their emphasis on communicating with customers through their websites. They use their websites to build their brand image and educate customers about their products or services as well as where they can be purchased. Retailers and some manufacturers sell merchandise directly to consumers over the Internet. For example, in addition to selling merchandise, Office Depot's website hosts a Business Resource Center for its business customers that provides advice, product knowledge, and connections to networking contacts in other businesses. It also provides forms that businesses can use to comply with Occupational Safety and Health Act (OSHA) requirements, check job applicant records, estimate cash flow, and develop a sexual harassment policy; posts workshops for running a business; and summarizes local and national business news. By providing this information, Office Depot reinforces its image as an

> IN ADDITION TO SELLING MERCHANDISE, OFFICE DEPOT'S WEBSITE HOSTS A BUSINESS RESOURCE CENTER FOR ITS BUSINESS CUSTOMERS THAT PROVIDES ADVICE, PRODUCT KNOWLEDGE, AND CONNECTIONS TO NETWORKING CONTACTS IN OTHER BUSINESSES.

ethical&societal dilemma 17.2

The Consumer Privacy Bill of Rights[iii]

Whereas once companies bought ads on websites related to the product being promoted (e.g., a healthy drink on the GNC website), more targeted advertising now pursues a particular customer rather than all visitors to a particular site. Based on web browsing activity and past purchases, a firm such as Target can, for instance, determine with some degree of accuracy who among its customers is pregnant. It can then entice those women or their husbands to visit Target or Target.com and buy baby-related products, using promotions and coupons geared directly to them. But how would these customers react if they were to receive these promotions knowing that Target should have no idea that they were pregnant? Even

worse, what would be the reaction if a targeted promotion was sent to the home of an unwed teenaged mother whose father was unaware of the pregnancy?

Because of the changing ways in which firms are using data collected from their customers, the Consumer Privacy Bill of Rights was passed so that consumers can more easily choose not to be tracked. In particular, consumers now have the following rights:

- **Individual Control** Consumers can control what personal data companies collect and how it is used.

- **Transparency** Consumers should be able to easily find and understand the privacy practices of companies.

- **Context** Companies that collect and use personal data will do so in ways consistent with how consumers provided the data.

- **Security** The use of personal data will not put consumers at risk.

- **Access and Accuracy** Companies should make efforts to make sure that personal data is accurate and provide access to consumers to correct data that is inaccurate.

- **Focused Collection** The collection of consumers' personal data will be limited and restricted by the context of how it was supplied in the first place.

- **Accountability** Companies are responsible to establish systems, train employees, and limit the access of third parties to consumers' personal data. They are responsible both to consumers and enforcement authorities to ensure that this takes place.

Are consumers' personal privacy rights being unjustly invaded by firms that provide them with targeted promotions based on their browsing habits? Or are the marketing firms engaged in these activities just providing them with helpful information that may make their buying decisions more pleasant and efficient?

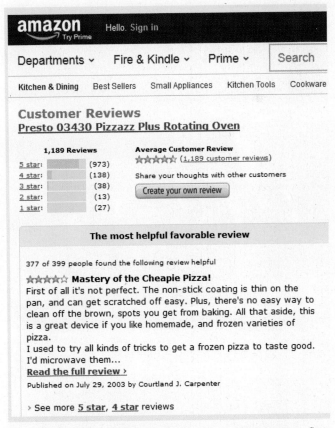

▼ EXHIBIT 17.4 Illustrative Mobile Marketing Campaigns

Company	Campaign
Fiat 2014 500L launch campaign	To celebrate the launch of the four-door Fiat 500L, the company created dynamic ads that included photo galleries and 360-degree views of the car. Once the customer engages the ad (by swiping a car across the screen), she can change the color of the car, watch videos, and find a local dealer. Fiat reports an 80 percent engagement rate with the campaign.
Ford "Are You Human?"	Ford recognized that most people hate CAPTCHA verifications. To make a fun alternative and drive brand awareness, Ford created a human verification task that requires a person to drag a Ford Fiesta across a map of the United States along a dotted line. The system was used by more than 3,200 websites.
JetBlue Voice-activated ads	Although most mobile campaigns emphasize touch and rich media, such as videos, JetBlue decided to get consumers' attention in another way—voice. Customers had the opportunity to play a "Learn to Speak Pigeon" game by speaking into the microphone of the phone.
McDonald's Social mobile ads	After embedding ads for McDonald's in social media apps such as Twitter and Facebook, the company created a campaign in which its new "McDonald's Mighty Wings" were stolen. Customers could look at the seven potential culprits, including NFL quarterbacks Joe Flacco and Colin Kaepernick, via the mobile ads. The ad then directed customers to the nearest McDonald's to try the Mighty Wings.
Pinkberry "How Close Are You?"	Pinkberry created a mobile campaign that used customers' GPS to identify the nearest store and included it in ads within the Pandora music app. Customers were told Pinkberry is only X miles away, and when they clicked on the ad they were given a $1 off coupon.

Source: Adapted from Lauren Johnson, "Top 10 Mobile Advertising Campaigns of 2013," *Mobile Marketer*, December 24, 2013, http://www.mobilemarketer.com.

essential source of products, services, and information for small businesses.

Many firms operate websites devoted to community building. These sites offer an opportunity for customers with similar interests to learn about products and services that support their hobbies and share information with others. Visitors can also post questions seeking information and/or comments about issues, products, and services. Many firms, especially retailers (e.g., Amazon), encourage customers to post reviews of products they have bought or used and even have visitors to their websites rate the quality of the reviews. Research has shown that these online product reviews increase customer loyalty and provide a competitive advantage for sites that offer them.[19]

Blogs A **blog (weblog)** contains periodic posts on a common web page. A well-received blog can communicate trends, announce special events, create positive word of mouth, connect customers by forming a community, allow the company to respond directly to customers' comments, and develop a

long-term relationship with the company. By its very nature, a blog is supposed to be transparent and contain authors' honest observations, which can help customers determine their trust and loyalty levels. Nowadays, blogs are becoming more interactive as the communication between bloggers and customers has increased. In addition, blogs can be linked to other social media such as microblog Twitter. See Chapter 3 for greater discussion.

Social Media The term **social media** refers to media content distributed through social interactions (see Chapter 3). The three most popular facilitators of social media are YouTube, Facebook, and Twitter. In these online sites, consumers review, communicate about, and aggregate information about products, prices, and promotions. These social media also allow users to interact among themselves (e.g., form a community) as well as provide other like-minded consumers (i.e., members of their community) and marketers their thoughts and evaluations about a firm's products or services. Thus, social media help facilitate the consumer decision process

> **blog (weblog)** A web page that contains periodic posts; corporate blogs are a new form of marketing communications.
>
> **social media** Media content used for social interactions such as YouTube, Facebook, and Twitter.

To increase customer loyalty and provide a competitive advantage, firms like Amazon encourage customers to post reviews of products or services they have bought or used.

© Amazon.com, Inc.

(Chapter 6) by encouraging need recognition, information search, alternative evaluation, purchase, and postpurchase reviews.

 check yourself

1. What are the different elements of an IMC program?

PLANNING FOR AND MEASURING IMC SUCCESS

We begin by examining how marketers set strategic goals before implementing any IMC campaign. After they have established those goals, marketers can set the budget for the campaign and choose the marketing metrics they will use to evaluate whether it has achieved its strategic objectives.

Goals

As with any strategic undertaking, firms need to understand the outcome they hope to achieve before they begin.

These goals can be short term, such as generating inquiries, increasing awareness, and prompting trial. Or they can be long term in nature, such as increasing sales, market share, and customer loyalty. Some other goals are outlined in Exhibit 17.5.

Such goals, both short and long term, should be explicitly defined and measured. They also might change over time, as Adding Value 17.1 describes. Regardless of their measure or changes, though, goals constitute part of the overall promotional plan, which is usually a subsection of the firm's marketing plan. Another part of the promotional plan is the budget.

| LO 17-4 | Explain the methods used to allocate the integrated marketing communications (IMC) budget. |

Setting and Allocating the IMC Budget

Firms use a variety of methods to plan their marketing communications budgets. Because all the methods of setting a promotional budget have both advantages and disadvantages, no one method should be used in isolation.[20]

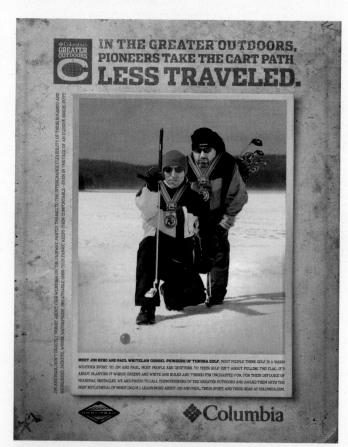

Southwest Airlines' "Grab Your Bag. It's On!" campaign's goal is to encourage travelers to fly despite tough economic conditions.
Courtesy Southwest Airlines; Photographer: Irwin Thompson.

Columbia Sportswear Company's Greater Outdoors campaign's goal is to showcase Columbia's technical innovation ability and overcome perceptions of inferior products.
Courtesy Columbia Sportswear Company

Company and Campaign	Goal	Target Market	Media Used	Outcome
ASICS "Sound Mind, Sound Body"	Branch out beyond serious runner market segment and target casual runners.	Even split males and females, aged 30–49	Television and print ads, online advertising	12% increase in market share
Columbia Sportswear Company "Greater Outdoors"	Showcase Columbia's technical innovation ability and overcome perceptions of inferior products.	60% males, aged 20–59	Print ads, mobile media, social media, videos, online advertising	1% increase in sales, and +2-point brand awareness increase compared with previous year
GAP "Ready for Holiday Cheer"	Capture consumers' attention and get them to shop in the store during the holiday season.	Even split males and females, aged 20–39	Print inserts, television ads, special website, social media, customizable videos	Kelly Awards Best Inset Winner, sales turned from a 12% decline in the previous year to a 1% increase
Southwest Airlines "Grab Your Bag. It's On!"	Encourage travelers to fly despite tough economic conditions.	Even split males and females, all ages	Television, radio, print, and in-airport ads	Contributed $99 million in profits
BMW "Diesel Reinvented"	Overcome the negative image of diesel that most consumers have.	Three segments: idea class, enthusiasts, and environmentally conscious	Print ads, videos	+1,463% year-to-year sales increase

Source Adapted from: http://www.magazine.org/advertising/case_studies/.

Adding Value 17.1

Changing Priceline by Killing Captain Kirk—and Then Bringing Him Back[iv]

When Priceline, the online travel service, started offering a new fixed-price discount, in addition to its longstanding "name your own price" discounts, the company basically had to change the subject. That meant killing the messenger: the over-the-top actor William Shatner. His mouthy, dramatic "The Negotiator" character had personified Priceline's negotiated discount approach for more than a decade.

As a global leader in online travel services, Priceline offers online reservations for airline tickets, hotel rooms, rental cars, vacation packages, and cruises. It serves consumers in more than 140 countries, with services available in 41 languages. The company has long offered travelers a way to negotiate low-price discounts, but it also needed to expand its offer and redefine its goals to become known for offering fixed-price options for same-day reservations.

Although it was rapidly becoming the fastest-growing part of its hotel business, Priceline also wanted to alert more customers to its new fixed-price Tonight-Only Deals service. To get that new message through, Priceline decided it needed a new approach, especially in its television advertising. According to Priceline's chief marketing officer, Shatner's bawdy parody of a tough guy "negotiator" had so dominated the company's commercial image that it might make it tough for viewers to pick up on Priceline's new, same-day fixed-pricing. "One of the challenges we face is that Bill is so awesome and so closely associated with Priceline that we needed to grab back consumers' attention," he said.

So Priceline had Shatner rush travelers off a bus as it hit a bend in the road, then teetered at the edge of a cliff. Without their vehicle, these riders would need a place to stay the night, so Shatner hands them his mobile phone—just as the bus pitches over into the abyss and crashes in flames. ("It's what he would have wanted," protests one survivor who has taken the time to book a room rather than mourn the lost Negotiator.)

To make its fixed-price discount deals even more accessible to its highly mobile customer base, Priceline developed free apps for Apple's iPad, iPhone, and iPod Touch, as well as for Android devices. A Tonight-Only Deals

To appeal to a younger audience, Priceline replaced longtime tough guy "negotiator" William Shatner with Kaley Cuoco of The Big Bang Theory.
© priceline.com

app is part of its free Hotel Negotiator application. Noting the easier, faster, hipper approach to booking rooms, Priceline then bridged the generational gap in 2013 by hiring actress Kaley Cuoco of *The Big Bang Theory* to play the Negotiator's daughter, schooled in the art of modern negotiation and never without her mobile phone.

objective-and-task method An IMC budgeting method that determines the cost required to undertake specific tasks to accomplish communication objectives; process entails setting objectives, choosing media, and determining costs.

rule-of-thumb methods Budgeting methods that base the IMC budget on either the firm's share of the market in relation to competition, a fixed percentage of forecasted sales, or what is left after other operating costs and forecasted sales have been budgeted.

The **objective-and-task method** determines the budget required to undertake specific tasks to accomplish communication objectives. To use this method, marketers first establish a set of communication objectives, then determine which media best reach the target market and how much it will cost to run the number and types of communications necessary to achieve the objectives. This process—set objectives, choose media, and determine costs—must be repeated for each product or service. The sum of all the individual communication plan budgets becomes the firm's total marketing communications budget. In addition to the objective-and-task method, various **rule-of-thumb methods** can be used to set budgets (see Exhibit 17.6).

These rule-of-thumb methods use prior sales and communication activities to determine the present communication budget. Although they are easy to implement, they have various limitations, as noted in Exhibit 17.6. Clearly, budgeting—not a simple process—may take several rounds of negotiations among the various managers, who are each competing for resources for their own areas of responsibility, to devise a final IMC budget.

▼ **EXHIBIT 17.6** Rule-of-Thumb Methods

Method	Definition	Limitations
Competitive parity	The communication budget is set so that the firm's share of communication expenses equals its share of the market.	Does not allow firms to exploit the unique opportunities or problems they confront in a market. If all competitors use this method to set communication budgets, their market shares will stay approximately the same over time.
Percentage-of-sales	The communication budget is a fixed percentage of forecasted sales.	Assumes the same percentage used in the past, or by competitors, is still appropriate for the firm. Does not take into account new plans (e.g., to introduce a new line of products in the current year).
Available budget	Marketers forecast their sales and expenses, excluding communication, during the budgeting period. The difference between the forecast sales and expenses plus desired profit is reserved for the communication budget. That is, the communication budget is the money available after operating costs and profits have been budgeted.	Assumes communication expenses do not stimulate sales and profit.

LO 17-5	Identify marketing metrics used to measure IMC success.

Measuring Success Using Marketing Metrics

Once a firm has decided how to set its budget for marketing communications and its campaigns have been developed and implemented, it reaches the point that it must measure the success of the campaigns, using various marketing metrics.[21] Each step in the IMC process can be measured to determine how effective it has been in motivating consumers to move to the next step in the buying process. However, recall that the lagged effect influences and complicates marketers' evaluations of a promotion's effectiveness as well as the best way to allocate marketing communications budgets. Because of the cumulative effect of marketing communications, it may take several exposures before consumers are moved to buy, so firms cannot expect too much too soon. They must invest in the marketing communications campaign with the idea that it may not reach its full potential for some time. In the same way, if firms cut marketing communications expenditures, it may take time before they experience a decrease in sales.

Traditional Media When measuring IMC success, the firm should examine when and how often consumers have been exposed to various marketing communications. Specifically, the

> "Clearly, budgeting—not a simple process—may take several rounds of negotiations among the various managers, who are each competing for resources for their own areas of responsibility."

When calculating the gross rating points (GRP) of *America's Next Top Model, the advertiser would multiply the reach times the frequency.*

© Nicole Weingart/Redux Pictures

of the same campaign, run during the program *America's Next Top Model,* which has a rating (reach) of 9.2. The total GRP generated by these 15 advertisements is 138 (9.2 × 15 = 138). However, advertisements typically appear in more than one television program. So, if Kenneth Cole also advertises 12 times during *The Voice,* which earns a rating of 1.8, its GRP would be 1.8 × 12 = 21.6, and the total GRP for both programs would be 138 + 21.6 = 159.6.

Web-Based Media

Taken together, firms are spending over $130 billion annually on online advertising, which includes paid search, display ads, e-mail, and sponsorships.[23] As shown in Exhibit 17.7, while the percentage

frequency Measure of how often the audience is exposed to a communication within a specified period of time.

reach Measure of consumers' exposure to marketing communications; the percentage of the target population exposed to a specific marketing communication, such as an advertisement, at least once.

gross rating points (GRP) Measure used for various media advertising—print, radio, or television; *GRP = Reach × Frequency.*

firm uses measures of frequency and reach to gauge consumers' exposure to marketing communications. For most products and situations, a single exposure to a communication is hardly enough to generate the desired response. Therefore, marketers measure the **frequency** of exposure—how often the audience is exposed to a communication within a specified period of time. The other measure used to measure consumers' exposure to marketing communications is **reach**, which describes the percentage of the target population exposed to a specific marketing communication, such as an advertisement, at least once.[22] Marketing communications managers usually state their media objectives in terms of **gross rating points (GRP)**, which represent reach multiplied by frequency (GRP = Reach × Frequency).

This GRP measure can refer to print, radio, or television, but any comparisons require a single medium. Suppose that Kenneth Cole places seven advertisements in *Vogue* magazine, which reaches 50 percent of the fashion-forward target segment. The total GRP generated by these seven magazine advertisements is 50 reach × 7 advertisements = 350 GRP. Now suppose Kenneth Cole includes 15 television ads as part

▼ **EXHIBIT 17.7** Digital Ad Spending Worldwide, 2010–2016
(billions, % change and % of total media ad spending)

Note: Includes advertising that appears on desktop and laptop computers as well as mobile phones and tablets, and includes all the various formats of advertising on those platforms; excludes SMS, MMS, and P2P messaging-based advertising.

Source: eMarketer.com, December 2012.

> " TAKEN TOGETHER, FIRMS ARE SPENDING OVER $130 BILLION ANNUALLY ON ONLINE ADVERTISING, WHICH INCLUDES PAID SEARCH, DISPLAY ADS, E-MAIL, AND SPONSORSHIPS. "

**web tracking
software** Used to
assess how much time
viewers spend on particular
web pages and the number
of pages they view.

increase of digital ad spending to total spending is slowing somewhat (yellow line), the absolute level of spending (bar chart) and relative share of digital ad spending to total spending continues to increase (red line). Although GRP is an adequate measure for television and radio advertisements, assessing the effectiveness of any web-based communication efforts in an IMC campaign generally requires **web tracking software**, which measures how much time viewers spend on particular web pages, the number of pages they view, how many times users click banner ads, which website they came from, and so on. All these performance metrics can be easily measured and assessed using a variety of software, including Google Analytics. Marketing Analytics 17.1 describes how Puma makes use of Google Analytics.

Facebook also helps companies see who has been visiting their fan pages, what those people are doing on the fan pages, and who is clicking their advertisements.[24] By keeping track of who is visiting their fan pages, marketers can better customize the material on their pages by getting to know the people visiting.

Planning, Implementing, and Evaluating IMC Programs—an Illustration of Google Advertising

Imagine a hypothetical upscale sneaker store in New York City, called Transit, that is modeled after vintage New York City subway trains. Transit's target market is young, well-educated, hip men and women aged 17 to 34 years. The owner's experience indicates the importance of personal selling for this market because these consumers (1) make large purchases and (2) seek considerable information before making a decision. Thus, Jay Oliver, the owner, spends part of his communication budget on training his sales associates. Oliver has realized his communication budget is considerably less than that of other sneaker stores in the area. He has therefore decided to concentrate his limited budget on a specific segment and use electronic media exclusively in his IMC program.

The IMC program Oliver has developed emphasizes his store's distinctive image and uses his website, social shopping, and some interesting community building techniques.

Marketing Analytics

17.1

Puma's Use of Google Analytics[v]

The international sports brand Puma offers clothing and accessories alongside its iconic shoes. It enjoys continued success mainly because it has turned to analytics to define its integrated marketing strategies and develop its advertising. When Puma first partnered with Google Analytics, its primary goals were to showcase the breadth of its products online and centralize its online presence. But to compete in the modern age among customers who are accustomed to shopping anywhere at any time, it needed to do more than update its website. Thus, Puma integrated its advertising with its online marketing strategy to devise an overall branded content online strategy.

The insights gained from Google Analytics drive these new advertising and online strategies. For example, Puma recently launched a new photo-driven site with multiple profiles of famous athletes such as Olympian Usain Bolt and soccer star Mario Balotelli. Instead of traditional web formats, the site weaves the featured apparel together with buy buttons that appear interspersed throughout the content. The new site also was integrated with the brand's new "Forever Faster" campaign—a campaign that also featured the same athletes in television commercials and social media campaigns. Although Puma.com is still a relatively small player in the online world, it saw a significant increase in the number of site visits and engagement as a result of these efforts.

Google Analytics also helped Puma develop another aspect of its marketing strategy: By analyzing each product line individually, Puma came to recognize exactly which products and lines were most popular. This analysis

The insights gained from Google Analytics were used to launch a photo-driven site with profiles of famous athletes such as Olympian Usain Bolt, and introduce the brand's "Forever Faster" campaign used in television commercials and social media campaigns.
© Jamie McCarthy/Getty Images

in turn revealed the need to improve the visibility of its women's lines. To address this need, Puma decided to add inspirational women to its list of celebrity endorsements, alongside the mostly male athletes it had been featuring. In the hope of reaching more young female customers for example, Puma named Rihanna as a brand ambassador and creative director of its women's line.

Advertisers pay Google to show up in the Sponsored Links section in the right-hand column of this screen grab based on the keywords customers use in their searches.

© Google, Inc.

Social shopping is the use of the Internet to communicate about product preferences with other shoppers. For instance, he has an extensive customer database as part of his CRM system from which he draws information for matching new merchandise with his customers' past purchase behaviors and little personal nuggets of information that he or other sales associates have collected on the customers. He then e-mails specific customers information about new products that he believes they will be interested in. He also encourages customers to use blogs hosted on his website. Customers chat about the hot new sneakers, club events, and races. He does everything with a strong sense of style.

To reach new customers, he is using **search engine marketing (SEM)**. In particular, he is using Google AdWords, a search engine marketing tool offered by Google that allows advertisers to show up in the Sponsored Links section of the search results page based on the keywords potential customers use (see the sponsored link section in the right-hand column of the nearby Google screen grab). He likes this option because of Google's efforts to rank pages fairly.

Oliver must determine the best keywords to use for his sponsored link advertising program. Some potential customers might search using the keywords "sneakers," "sneakers in New York City," "athletic shoes," or other such versions. Using Google AdWords, Oliver can assess the effectiveness of his advertising expenditures by measuring the reach, relevance, and return on investment for each of the keywords that potential customers used during their Internet searches.

To estimate reach, Oliver uses the number of **impressions** (the number of times the ad appears in front of the user) and the **click-through rate (CTR)**. To calculate CTR, he divides the number of times a user clicks an ad by the number of impressions.[25] For example, if a sponsored link was delivered 100 times and 10 people clicked on it, then the number of impressions is 100, the number of clicks is 10, and the CTR would be 10 percent.

The **relevance** of the ad describes how useful an ad message is to the consumer doing the search. Google provides a measure of relevance through its AdWords system using a quality score. The quality score looks at a variety of factors to measure how relevant a keyword is to an ad's text and to a user's search query. In general, a high-quality score means that a keyword will trigger ads in a higher position and at a lower cost-per-click.[26] In a search for "sneaker store," the Transit ad showed up fourth, suggesting high relevance.

Using the following formula, Oliver also can determine an ad's **return on marketing investment (ROMI)**:

$$ROMI = \frac{\text{Gross Margin} - \text{Marketing Expenditure}}{\text{Marketing Expenditure}} \times 100$$

> "Google AdWords allows advertisers to show up in the Sponsored Links section of the search results page based on the keywords potential customers use."

(1) Keyword	(2) Clicks	(3) Marketing Expenditure	(4) Sales	(5) Gross Margin = Sales × Gross Margin% = Sales × 50%	(6) Gross Margin ($) (Col. 5) — Marketing Expenditure (Col. 3)	(7) ROMI = (Col. 6/Col. 3) × 100
Sneaker store	110	$10/day	$70/day	$35/day	$25	250%
New York City sneakers	40	$25/day	$80/day	$40/day	$15	60%

The cost of the sneakers is 50 percent of the sale price.

▼ **EXHIBIT 17.9** Program Effectiveness Results

Communication Objective	Question	Before Campaign	Six Months After	One Year After
Awareness (% mentioning store)	What stores sell sneakers?	38%	46%	52%
Knowledge (% giving outstanding rating for sales assistance)	Which stores would you rate outstanding on the following characteristics?	9	17	24
Attitude (% first choice)	On your next shopping trip for sneakers, which store would you visit first?	13	15	19
Visit (% visited store)	Which of the following stores have you been to?	8	15	19

For the two keyword searches in Exhibit 17.8, Oliver finds how much the advertising cost him (Column 3), the sales produced as a result (Column 4), the gross margin in dollars (Column 5), and the ROMI (Column 7). For "sneaker store," the Transit website had a lot more clicks (110) than the clicks received from "New York City sneakers" (40) (see Column 2, Exhibit 17.8). Even though the sales were lower for the keywords "sneaker store" at $35/day, versus $40/day for the keywords "New York City sneakers," the ROMI was much greater for the "sneaker store" keyword combination. In the future, Oliver should continue this keyword combination, in addition to producing others that are similar to it, in the hope that he will attain an even greater return on investment.

To evaluate his IMC program, Oliver compares the results of the program with his objectives (Exhibit 17.9). To measure his program's effectiveness, he conducted an inexpensive online survey using the questions in Exhibit 17.9, which shows the survey results for one year.

The results show a steady increase in awareness, knowledge of the store, and choice of the store as a primary source of sneakers. This research provides evidence that the IMC program was conveying the intended message to the target audience.

 check yourself

1. Why is the objective-and-task method of setting an IMC budget better than the rule-of-thumb methods?

2. How do firms use GRP to evaluate the effectiveness of traditional media?

3. How would a firm evaluate the effectiveness of its Google advertising?

Increase your engagement and learning with Connect Marketing.

These Connect activities, available only through your Connect course, have been designed to make the following concepts more meaningful and applicable:

- The Communication Process Timeline Activity
- Integrated Marketing Communication: Frito-Lay Video Case
- Creating an IMC Campaign: Jay-Z and Microsoft Case Analysis
- B2C versus B2B Strategies: iSeeit! Video

 SMARTBOOK™   **iSeeit!**

© Joe Raedle/Getty Images

advertising, public relations, and sales promotions

When it comes down to it, what is the point of advertising? Generally we think that its goal is to get someone—normally, the person receiving the ad—to do something, and that "something" is nearly always a purchase. But as advertising grows more creative, innovative, and varied, the action induced by such communications might remain several steps away from purchasing.

Consider the advertising plan exhibited by the fast-food chain Chipotle Mexican Grill. Once McDonald's held a large ownership share of the company, but Chipotle has been on its own for nearly a decade—a status many consumers have not realized.[1] The quickly growing chain distinguishes itself with its mission statement, "Food with Integrity," which it interprets as "our commitment to finding the very best ingredients, raised with respect for the animals, the environment, and the farmers."[2] Thus it seeks to get across a message about its own identity, but also about the importance of sustainable farming and foods produced

LEARNING OBJECTIVES

After reading this chapter, you should be able to:

LO 18-1 Describe the steps in designing and executing an advertising campaign.

LO 18-2 Identify three objectives of advertising.

LO 18-3 Describe the different ways that advertisers appeal to consumers.

LO 18-4 Identify the various types of media.

LO 18-5 Identify agencies that regulate advertising.

LO 18-6 Describe the elements of a public relations toolkit.

LO 18-7 Identify the various types of sales promotions.

continued on p. 372

advertising A paid form of communication from an identifiable source, delivered through a communication channel, and designed to persuade the receiver to take some action, now or in the future.

continued from p. 371

more naturally. To do so, Chipotle has adopted a marketing plan that spans a range of media. In animated YouTube films, two artful spots feature characters that reject a factory model of food production by embracing farm-fresh vegetables and meats. Only at the very end of each spot does the name Chipotle even appear. The focus is more on the message than on the brand, which may be why consumers are so willing to interact with and share that message. The spots both feature music by popular musicians, namely, Fiona Apple and Willie Nelson (covering a Coldplay track). The animation is sophisticated and of high quality. And in each case, the protagonist—a farmer or a scarecrow—rejects a model in which pigs, cows, and chickens are artificially fattened by chemicals and kept in cages, in preference for a free-range approach.[3] Expanding on this idea, Chipotle proposed and produced a series of 30-minute films for Hulu titled *Farmed and Dangerous*. These scripted, live-action comedies mention Chipotle only once and are presented alongside every other series offered by Hulu, with no signal that they are advertising. Ads for various products instead appear within the shows themselves. In the satiric show content, the horrors of industrial agriculture are the focus, including the dastardly deeds of an evil scientist seeking to develop eight-winged chickens.[4]

Such fearful depictions of inhumane treatment and unnatural food production lead viewers readily to value-based judgments—namely, that it would be better to eat food produced ethically. From this broad perception, Chipotle hopes that ultimately consumers will more readily include it in their consideration set as a company that reflects such values.

Once they do, Chipotle reinforces its status as something more than just a burrito outlet. In its "Cultivating Thought" initiative, Chipotle agreed to inscribe its disposable cups with "Two-Minute Thoughts" written by renowned authors and public figures. The

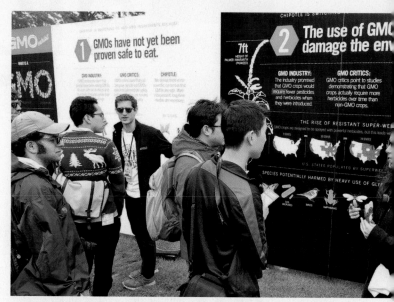

Chipotle Mexican Grill "lives" its mission statement, "Food with Integrity," by sponsoring Cultivate San Francisco at Golden Gate Park. Note the name Chipotle does not appear on the billboards. Chipotle hopes this subtle messaging will strengthen its relationship with its customers through shared values.
© Steve Jennings/Stringer/Getty Image

writers range from the comedians Bill Hader and Sarah Silverman to the Nobel Laureate Toni Morrison to the social scientists Steven Pinker and Malcolm Gladwell. By providing these short texts on its cups, Chipotle guarantees that lone diners have somewhere to put their eyes while they eat; it also gives consumers access to some deep thoughts written by some very smart people.[5]

As these elements of Chipotle's advertising strategy reveal, advertising does far more than encourage consumers to buy stuff. It can make them laugh, prompt them to think about their consumption, encourage them to embrace a particular set of values, and lead them to read challenging texts. And if all that communication comes together just right, it also can sell quite a lot of guacamole. ■

Advertising is a paid form of communication delivered through media from an identifiable source about an organization, product, service, or idea designed to persuade the receiver to take some action now or in the future.[6] This definition provides some important distinctions between

> "Advertising represents a persuasive form of communication, designed to get the consumer to take some action."

Step 1 Identify target audience → Step 2 Set advertising objectives → Step 3 Determine the advertising budget → Step 4 Convey the message → Step 5 Evaluate and select media → Step 6 Create advertisements → Step 7 Assess impact

" FIRMS MUST KEEP IN MIND THAT THEIR TARGET AUDIENCE MAY OR MAY NOT BE THE SAME AS CURRENT USERS OF THE PRODUCT. "

advertising and other forms of promotion, which we discussed in the previous chapter. First, advertising is not free; someone has paid, with money, trade, or other means, to get the message shown. Second, advertising must be carried by some medium—television, radio, print, the web, T-shirts, sidewalks, and so on. Third, legally, the source of the message must be known or knowable. Fourth, advertising represents a persuasive form of communication, designed to get the consumer to take some action. That desired action can range from "free-range chickens are better" to "buy a Chipotle burrito."

Advertising encompasses an enormous industry and clearly is the most visible form of marketing communications—so much so that many people think of marketing and advertising as synonymous. Global advertising expenditures are almost $500 billion, and almost half that amount is spent in the United States. Although expenditures dropped somewhat during the global downturn, advertising remains virtually everywhere, and predictions are that it will continue to grow.[7]

Yet how many of the advertisements you were exposed to yesterday do you remember today? Probably not more than three or four. As you learned in Chapter 6, perception is a highly selective process. Consumers simply screen out messages that are not relevant to them. When you notice an advertisement, you may not react to it. Even if you react to it, you may not remember it later. Even if you remember the ad, you may not remember the brand or sponsor—or worse yet from the advertiser's point of view, you may remember it as an advertisement for another brand.[8]

To get you to remember their ad and the brand, advertisers must first get your attention. As we discussed in Chapter 17, the increasing number of communication channels and changes in consumers' media usage have made the job of advertisers far more difficult.[9] As our opening example about Chipotle's varied and innovative ads demonstrated, advertisers continually

endeavor to use creativity and various media to reach their target markets.

As a consumer, you are exposed only to the end product—the finished advertisement. But many actions must take place before you actually get to see an ad, as the Toolkit available online for this chapter will show you. In this chapter, we examine the ingredients of a successful advertising campaign from identifying a target audience to creating the actual ad to assessing performance. Although our discussion is generally confined to advertising, much of the process for developing an advertising campaign is applicable to the IMC media vehicles discussed in Chapter 17. We conclude with some regulatory and ethical issues for advertising, then move on to public relations and sales promotions and their use.

Designing and carrying out a successful advertising program requires much planning and effort. Exhibit 18.1 shows the key steps in the process, each of which helps ensure that the intended message reaches the right audience and has the desired effect. We examine these steps in the sections that follow.

| LO 18-1 | Describe the steps in designing and executing an advertising campaign. |

STEP 1: IDENTIFY TARGET AUDIENCE

The success of an advertising program depends on how well the advertiser can identify its target audience. Firms conduct research to identify their target audience, then use the information they gain to set the tone for the advertising program and help them select the media they will use to deliver the message to that audience.

During this research, firms must keep in mind that their target audience may or may not be the same as current users of the

advertising plan
A section of the firm's overall marketing plan that explicitly outlines the objectives of the advertising campaign, how the campaign might accomplish those objectives, and how the firm can determine whether the campaign was successful.

push strategy
Designed to increase demand by motivating sellers—wholesalers, distributors, or salespeople—to highlight the product, rather than the products of competitors, and thereby push the product onto consumers.

pull strategy A strategy in which the goal is to get consumers to pull the product through the marketing channel by demanding it.

STEP 2: SET ADVERTISING OBJECTIVES

Advertising campaign objectives are derived from the overall objectives of the marketing program and clarify the specific goals that the ads are designed to accomplish. Generally, these objectives appear in the **advertising plan**, a subsection of the firm's overall marketing plan that explicitly analyzes the marketing and advertising situation, identifies the objectives of the advertising campaign, clarifies a specific strategy for accomplishing those objectives, and indicates how the firm can determine whether the campaign was successful.[12] An advertising plan is crucial because it will later serve as the yardstick against which advertising success or failure is measured.

Generally, in advertising to consumers, the objective is a **pull strategy** in which the goal is to get consumers to pull the product into the marketing channel by demanding it. **Push strategies** also exist and are designed to increase demand by focusing on wholesalers, retailers, or salespeople. These

product. For example, adidas knows that FIFA fans likely are at least familiar with its offerings, even if they do not currently purchase sports gear from adidas. Thus some advertisements feature the international football (or soccer) stars Jozy Altidore and Lionel Messi to encourage them to buy more of the brand's products.[10] But teenaged pop music fans might be less likely to pay attention to sporting goods. So adidas also brought in Selena Gomez to put her name on its Neo line and appear in related advertising.[11]

adidas uses different ads to appeal to different target markets. Jozy Altidore (left) appeals to soccer fans, while Selena Gomez (right) attracts teenaged pop music fans.
© Adidas

campaigns attempt to motivate the seller to highlight the product, rather than the products of competitors, and thereby push the product to consumers. In this chapter, we focus on pull strategies. Push strategies are examined in Chapters 15, 16, and 19.

All advertising campaigns aim to achieve certain objectives: to inform, persuade, and remind customers. Another way of looking at advertising objectives is to examine an ad's focus. Is the ad designed to stimulate demand for a particular product or service or more broadly for the institution in general? Also, ads can be used to stimulate demand for a product category or an entire industry or for a

informative advertising Communication used to create and build brand awareness, with the ultimate goal of moving the consumer through the buying cycle to a purchase.

persuasive advertising Communication used to motivate consumers to take action.

reminder advertising Communication used to remind consumers of a product or to prompt repurchases, especially for products that have gained market acceptance and are in the maturity stage of their life cycle.

Reminder Advertising

Finally, **reminder advertising** is a communication used to remind or prompt repurchases, especially for products that have gained market acceptance and are in the maturity

> ## If you decide to buy facial tissue, do you carefully consider all the options, comparing their sizes, prices, and performance, or do you just grab the first thing you see on the shelf?

specific brand, firm, or item. We first look at the broad overall objectives: to inform, persuade, and remind. Then we examine advertising objectives based on the focus of the ad: product versus institutional.

| LO 18-2 | Identify three objectives of advertising. |

Informative Advertising

Informative advertising is a communication used to create and build brand awareness, with the ultimate goal of moving the consumer through the buying cycle to a purchase. Such advertising helps determine some important early stages of a product's life cycle (see Chapter 12), particularly when consumers have little information about the specific product or type of product. Retailers often use informative advertising to tell their customers about an upcoming sales event or the arrival of new merchandise.

Persuasive Advertising

When a product has gained a certain level of brand awareness, firms use **persuasive advertising** to motivate consumers to take action. Persuasive advertising generally occurs in the growth and early maturity stages of the product life cycle, when competition is most intense, and attempts to accelerate the market's acceptance of the product. In later stages of the product life cycle, persuasive advertising may be used to reposition an established brand by persuading consumers to change their existing perceptions of the advertised product. Firms such as Lancôme often use persuasive advertising to convince consumers to take action—switch brands,[13] try a new product, or even continue to buy the advertised product.

Lancôme's persuasive ads attempt to motivate consumers to take action: try the product, switch brands, or continue to buy the product.
© Bill Aron/PhotoEdit

stage of their life cycle. Such advertising certainly appears in traditional media, such as television or print commercials, but it also encompasses other forms of advertising. For example, if you decide to buy facial tissue, do you carefully consider all the options, comparing their sizes, prices, and performance, or do you just grab the first thing you see on the shelf? When your grocery store places a display of Kleenex facial tissues on the end of the paper products aisle, it relies on your top-of-the-mind awareness of the Kleenex brand, which the manufacturer has achieved through advertising. That is, Kleenex tissue maintains a prominent place in people's memories and triggers their response without them having to put any thought into it. The advertising and the end

cap display thus prompt you and many other consumers to respond by buying a package, just the response Kleenex hoped to attain.

Focus of Advertisements

An ad campaign's objectives determine each specific ad's focus. The ad can be product focused, might have an institutional focus, or could have a public service focus. **Product-focused advertisements** inform, persuade, or remind consumers about a specific product or service. The Pepsi Max ad shown here is designed to generate sales for Pepsi Max.

Institutional advertisements inform, persuade, or remind consumers about issues related to places, politics, or an industry. Perhaps the best-known institutional advertising campaign is the long-running "Got Milk?" campaign to encourage milk consumption by appealing to consumers' needs to affiliate with the milk-mustached celebrities shown in the ads.[14] The ads highlight the beneficial properties of milk for building strong bones, which involves a more informative appeal, combined with a mild emotional fear appeal in its

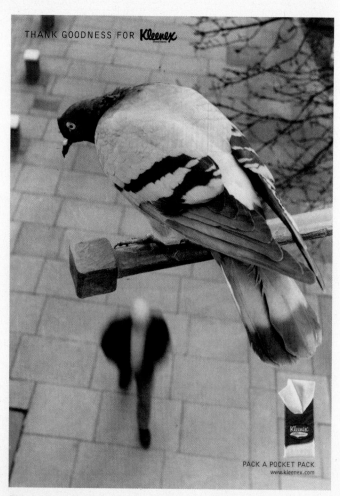

This ad is designed to remind consumers that when you need tissues, don't think too hard. Just pick up a box of Kleenex.
Image Courtesy of The Advertising Archives

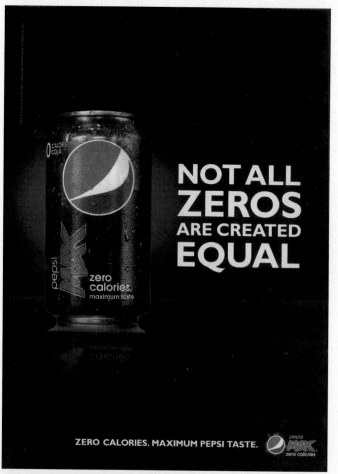

Is this product-focused advertisement designed to inform, persuade, or remind consumers about Pepsi Max?
Courtesy Pepsi-Cola Company

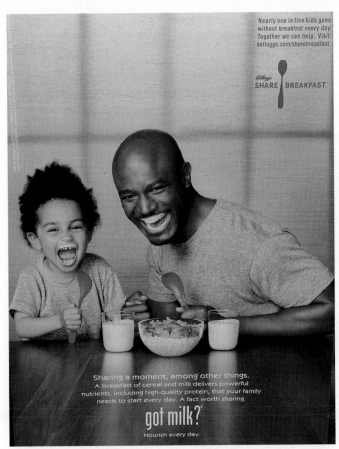

The Got Milk institutional advertising campaign is used to encourage milk consumption by appealing to consumers' needs to affiliate with milk-mustached celebrities like actor Taye Diggs.
© WENN Ltd/Alamy

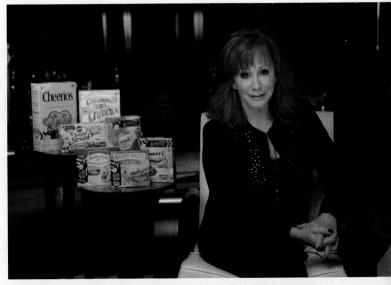

Entertainer Reba McEntire is the spokesperson for a PSA called Outnumber Hunger, designed to raise awareness of the hunger problem in America.
© Rick Diamond/Wirelmag/Getty Images

public service advertising (PSA)
Advertising that focuses on public welfare and generally is sponsored by nonprofit institutions, civic groups, religious organizations, trade associations, or political groups; a form of *social marketing*.

social marketing
The application of marketing principles to a social issue to bring about attitudinal and behavioral change among the general public or a specific population segment.

assertion that failing to drink milk can lead to medical problems. Its Spanish-language ad campaign, "Toma Leche," similarly touts milk as a wonder tonic that fights cavities, sleeplessness, and bone loss. A recent campaign featuring Rebecca Romjin and her babies even promises that drinking milk helps families stay together.[15]

A specific category of institutional advertising is **public service advertising (PSA)**. PSAs focus on public welfare; generally they are sponsored by nonprofit institutions, civic groups, religious organizations, trade associations, or political groups.[16] Like product and institutionally focused advertising, PSAs also inform, persuade, or remind consumers, but the focus is for the betterment of society. As such, PSAs represent a form of **social marketing**, defined as the application of marketing principles to a social issue to bring about attitudinal and behavioral change among the general public or a specific population segment.

> "Like product and institutionally focused advertising, PSAs also inform, persuade, or remind consumers, but the focus is for the betterment of society."

Entertainer Reba McEntire is the spokesperson for a PSA for Outnumber Hunger, designed to raise awareness of the hunger problem in America. Sponsored by General Mills, Big Machine Label Group and Feeding America, Reba has appeared in special concert events and has been featured on more than 60 million General Mills packages, including Cheerios. For each General Mills product code entered by its customers at OutnumberHunger.com, five meals are acquired for their local Feeding America food banks.[17]

Because PSAs are a special class of advertising, under Federal Communications Commission (FCC) rules, broadcasters must devote a specific amount of free airtime to them. Also, since they often are designed by top advertising agencies for nonprofit clients, PSAs usually are quite creative and stylistically appealing. For example, what is your reaction to the "truth" public service antismoking campaign summarized in Ethical and Societal Dilemma 18.1?

ethical&societal dilemma

Getting to the Truth[i]

Smoking is the single biggest preventable cause of death in the world; someone dies from tobacco use every eight seconds. Smoking causes cancers of the lung, throat, and mouth; it also leads to high blood pressure, heart problems, and lung diseases other than cancer. Yet worldwide, one in five teens between the ages of 13 and 15 years smokes, and many of those smokers will reach for their cigarettes for another 15 to 20 years. What can marketers do to help people avoid or quit this hazardous habit?

As part of the historic tobacco settlement between various states' attorneys general and the tobacco industry, the American Legacy Foundation receives over a billion dollars to educate the public about the dangers of smoking. The foundation uses this money to fund the "truth" campaign, the largest national young antismoking campaign and the only campaign not controlled by the tobacco industry. The campaign's goal is to tell the truth about the tobacco industry, including health effects, marketing strategies, and manufacturing practices. Focused primarily on youths between the ages of 12 and 17 years, the campaign presents facts and allows teens to make their own decisions rather than telling them what they should or should not do.

The campaign had a direct impact on smoking, accelerating the decline in teen smoking during its first two years. Seven years after "truth" was launched, research showed that teens exposed to the campaign had a more accurate perception of the

The American Legacy Foundation produces antismoking ads like this one designed to tell the truth about the tobacco industry, including health effects, marketing strategies, and manufacturing practices.
© Legacy for Health

number of their peers who smoke. Considering how much most teens want to fit in with their peers, changing perceptions can help reduce the number of young people who pick up cigarettes.

To reach them, "truth" uses videos online and in cinemas as well as social media, website games, television integration, radio advertising, and live tours. It has employed scare tactics, such as a pile of body bags piled up in front of Philip Morris headquarters. But it also relies on humor, animation, murals at the SXSW music festival, and Broadway-style song and dance routines to communicate the message.

But is humor the right way to communicate about a subject that kills millions of people each year? Is a pile of body bags an effective way to reach young smokers, who don't believe nicotine-related diseases will happen to them? Is this kind of messaging, which tobacco companies claim is abusive to them and their employees, appropriate or fair? How would you feel if you worked for a tobacco company? How would you feel about tobacco advertising if someone in your family had emphysema from smoking?

Regardless of whether the advertising campaign's objective is to inform, persuade, or remind, with a focus on a particular product or the institution in general, each campaign's objectives must be specific and measurable. For a brand awareness campaign, for example, the objective might be to increase brand awareness among the target market by 50 percent within six months. Another campaign's goal may be to persuade 10 percent of a competitor's customers to switch to the advertised brand. Once the advertising campaign's objectives are set, the firm sets the advertising budget.

STEP 3: DETERMINE THE ADVERTISING BUDGET

The various budgeting methods for marketing communications (Chapter 17) also apply to budgeting for advertising. First, firms must consider the role that advertising plays in their attempt to meet their overall promotional objectives. Second, advertising expenditures vary over the course of the product life cycle. Third, the nature of the market and the product influence the size of advertising budgets. The nature of the market also determines the amount of money spent on advertising. For instance, less money is spent on advertising in B2B (business-to-business) marketing contexts than in B2C (business-to-consumer) markets. Personal selling, as we discuss in Chapter 19, likely is more important in B2B markets.

> LESS MONEY IS SPENT ON ADVERTISING IN B2B (BUSINESS-TO-BUSINESS) MARKETING CONTEXTS THAN IN B2C (BUSINESS-TO-CONSUMER) MARKETS.

STEP 4: CONVEY THE MESSAGE

In this step, marketers determine what they want to convey about the product or service. First, the firm determines the key message it wants to communicate to the target audience. Second, the firm decides what appeal would most effectively convey the message. We present these decisions sequentially, but in reality they must be considered simultaneously.

The Message

The message provides the target audience with reasons to respond in the desired way. A logical starting point for deciding on the advertising message is to tout the key benefits of the product or service. The message should communicate its problem-solving ability clearly and in a compelling fashion. In this context, advertisers must remember that products and services solve problems, whether real or perceived. That is, people are not looking for 1/4-inch drill bits; they are looking for 1/4-inch holes to hang a picture on the wall.[18] Because there are many ways to make a 1/4-inch hole, a firm like Black & Decker must convey to consumers that its drill bit is the best way to get that hole.

Another common strategy differentiates a product by establishing its unique benefits. This distinction forms the basis for the **unique selling proposition (USP)** or the value proposition (as discussed in Chapter 9), which is often the common theme or slogan in an advertising campaign. A good USP communicates the unique attributes of the product and thereby becomes a snapshot of the entire campaign. Some of the most famous USPs include the following:

Red Bull . . . Gives You Wings

Ford . . . Built Tough

Oreo . . . Milk's Favorite Cookie

TNT . . . We Know Drama

Kellogg's Corn Flakes Is The Original and Best Cereal

The New York Times . . . All The News That's Fit to Print

Trek . . . We Believe in Bikes

Vail . . . Like Nothing On Earth

YouTube . . . Broadcast Yourself

Wrangler . . . Long Live Cowboys

The selling proposition communicated by the advertising must be not only unique to the brand but also meaningful to the consumer. It furthermore must be sustainable over time, even with repetition.

| LO 18-3 | Describe the different ways that advertisers appeal to consumers. |

The Appeal

Advertisers use different appeals to portray their products or services and persuade consumers to purchase them, though advertising tends to combine the types of appeals into two categories: informational and emotional.

Informational Appeals **Informational appeals** help consumers make purchase decisions by offering factual

emotional appeal
Aims to satisfy consumers' emotional desires rather than their utilitarian needs.

USPs like these by YouTube and Wrangler send powerful messages about the benefits of their offerings.

Top: © Realimage/Alamy; Bottom: © Tom DonoghueTom Donoghue/Polaris/Newscom

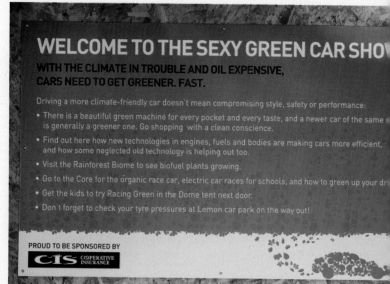

Ads for the Sexy Green Car Show in Cornwall, UK, espouse multiple ways in which consumers can educate themselves and act in a more environmentally conscious manner when it comes to their automobiles.
© Global Warming Images/Alamy

comes to their automobiles. This appeal is well suited to this type of product: By informing consumers about a potential source of its competitive advantage, including tangible features and images of science, the advertising copy directly delivers an informational, persuasive message.

Emotional Appeals

An **emotional appeal** aims to satisfy consumers' emotional desires rather than their utilitarian needs. These appeals therefore focus on feelings about the self.[20] The key to a successful emotional

> ## The key to a successful emotional appeal is the use of emotion to create a bond between the consumer and the brand.

information that encourages consumers to evaluate the brand favorably on the basis of the key benefits it provides.[19] Thus, ads for the Sexy Green Car Show in Cornwall, UK, espouse multiple ways in which consumers can educate themselves and act in a more environmentally conscious manner when it

appeal is the use of emotion to create a bond between the consumer and the brand. Exhibit 18.2 shows firms and examples of the most common types of emotional appeals: fear, safety, humor, happiness, love (or sex),[21] comfort, and nostalgia.[22]

▼ EXHIBIT 18.2 Emotional Appeals in Advertising

Emotional Appeal	Company	Example
Fear/safety	Wandsworth	"Partied too hard? Do you know who you're leaving with?"
Humor	Ocean Spray	"10 hours of cleansing and purifying . . . in one glass."
Happiness	Tropicana	"Awake to Alive"
Love/sex	Axe Body Spray	"Unleash the Chaos"
Comfort	Kleenex	"Softness Worth Sharing"
Nostalgia	Chevrolet	"Find New Roads"

media planning The process of evaluating and selecting the *media mix* that will deliver a clear, consistent, compelling message to the intended audience.

media mix The combination of the media used and the frequency of advertising in each medium.

media buy The actual purchase of airtime or print pages.

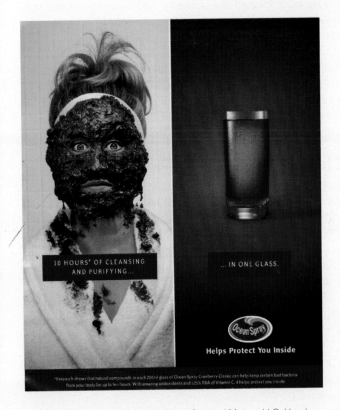

Which emotional appeals are these ads using?
Left: Image Courtesy of The Advertising Archives; Right: Image Courtesy of The Advertising Archives; Top Right: General Motors LLC. Used with permission, GM Media Archives.

STEP 5: EVALUATE AND SELECT MEDIA

The content of an advertisement is tied closely to the characteristics of the media that firms select to carry the message, and vice versa. **Media planning** refers to the process of evaluating and selecting the **media mix**—the combination of the media used and the frequency of advertising in each medium—that will deliver a clear, consistent, compelling message to the intended audience.[23] For example, Macy's may determine that a heavy dose of television, radio, print, and billboards is appropriate for the holiday selling season between Thanksgiving and the end of the year.

Because the **media buy**, the actual purchase of airtime or print pages, is generally the largest expense in the advertising budget, marketers must make their decisions carefully. Television advertising is by far the most expensive. To characterize these various types of media, we use a dichotomy: mass and niche media.

mass media
Channels that are ideal for reaching large numbers of anonymous audience members; include national newspapers, magazines, radio, and television.

niche media Channels that are focused and generally used to reach narrow segments, often with unique demographic characteristics or interests.

advertising schedule The specification of the timing and duration of advertising.

continuous advertising schedule Runs steadily throughout the year and therefore is suited to products and services that are consumed continually at relatively steady rates and that require a steady level of persuasive or reminder advertising.

flighting (advertising schedule) An advertising schedule implemented in spurts, with periods of heavy advertising followed by periods of no advertising.

LO 18-4 | Identify the various types of media.

Mass and Niche Media

Mass media channels include outdoor/billboards, newspapers, magazines, radio, and television and are ideal for reaching large numbers of anonymous audience members. **Niche media** channels are more focused and generally used to reach narrower segments, often with unique demographic characteristics or interests. Specialty television channels (e.g., Home and Garden TV) and specialty magazines such as *Skateboarder* or *Cosmo Girl* all provide examples of niche media. The Internet provides an opportunity to appeal to the masses through ads on the home page of Internet sites such as www.comcast.net or www.yahoo.com or more niched opportunities such as an American Express business card on the *Wall Street Journal* site (wsjonline.com).

Choosing the Right Medium

For each class of media, each alternative has specific characteristics that make it suitable for meeting specific objectives (see Exhibit 18.3).[24] For example, consumers use different media for different purposes, to which advertisers should match their messages. Television is used primarily for escapism and entertainment, so most television advertising relies on a mix of visual and auditory techniques.

Communication media also vary in their ability to reach the desired audience. For instance, radio is a good medium for products such as grocery purchases or fast food because many consumers decide what to purchase either on the way to the store or while in the store. Because many people listen to the radio in their cars, it becomes a highly effective means to reach consumers at a crucial point in their decision process. Twitter offers several options for advertisers to enhance their reach, as Social and Mobile Marketing 18.1 explains. As we discussed in Chapter 17, each medium also varies in its reach and frequency. Advertisers can determine how effective their media mix has been in reaching their target audience by calculating the total GRP (Reach × Frequency) of the advertising schedule, which we discuss next.

Determining the Advertising Schedule

Another important decision for the media planner is the **advertising schedule**, which specifies the timing and duration of advertising. There are three types of schedules:

- A **continuous schedule** runs steadily throughout the year and therefore is suited to products and services that are consumed continually at relatively steady rates and that require a steady level of persuasive and/or reminder advertising. For example, Procter & Gamble advertises its Tide brand of laundry detergent continuously.

- **Flighting** refers to an advertising schedule implemented in spurts, with periods of heavy advertising followed by periods of no advertising. This pattern generally functions for products whose demand fluctuates, such as suntan lotion, which manufacturers may advertise heavily in the months leading up to and during the summer.

▼ **EXHIBIT 18.3** Types of Media Available for Advertising

Medium	Advantages	Disadvantages
Television	Wide reach; incorporates sound and video.	High cost; several channel and program options; may increase awareness of competitors' products.
Radio	Relatively inexpensive; can be selectively targeted; wide reach.	No video, which limits presentation; consumers give less focused attention than TV; exposure periods are short.
Magazines	Very targeted; subscribers pass along to others.	Relatively inflexible; takes some time for the magazine to be available.
Newspapers	Flexible; timely; able to localize.	Can be expensive in some markets; advertisements have short life span.
Internet/mobile	Can be linked to detailed content; highly flexible and interactive; allows for specific targeting.	Becoming cluttered; the ad may be blocked by software on the computer.
Outdoor/billboard	Relatively inexpensive; offers opportunities for repeat exposure.	Is not easily targeted; has placement problems in some markets; exposure time is very short.
Direct marketing	Is highly targeted; allows for personalization.	Cost can vary depending on type of direct marketing used; traditional media, like mail, will be more expensive than newer media.

- **Pulsing** combines the continuous and flighting schedules by maintaining a base level of advertising but increasing advertising intensity during certain periods. For example, airlines, hotels, and car rental companies might continuously advertise to ensure brand awareness but might increase the advertising in spikes during certain low-demand periods.

STEP 6: CREATE ADVERTISEMENTS

After the advertiser has decided on the message, type of ad, and appeal, its attention shifts to the actual creation of the advertisement. During this step, the message and appeal are translated creatively into words, pictures, colors, and/or music. Often, the execution style for the ad will dictate the type of medium used to deliver the message. To demonstrate an image, advertisers can use television and magazines. To promote price, they can use newspapers and radio. To appeal to specific target markets, they can use some of the electronic media vehicles described in Chapter 17. When using multiple media to deliver the same message, however, they must maintain consistency across the execution styles—that is, integrated marketing—so that the different executions deliver a consistent and compelling message to the target audience.

How do advertisers go about creating advertisements? They simultaneously consider the objectives of the ad, the targeted customer segment(s), the product or service's value proposition or the unique selling proposition, and how the ad will be coordinated with other IMC elements.

They then go about creating an ad or the ad campaign. Using the print ad for the Ila Dusk Personal Alarm shown on the next page as an example, the first component that the reader generally notices is the visual, and as such it should be eye-catching. The picture of the personal alarm on a chain

pulsing (advertising schedule) Combines the continuous and flighting schedules by maintaining a base level of advertising but increasing advertising intensity during certain periods.

> " TO DEMONSTRATE AN IMAGE, ADVERTISERS CAN USE TELEVISION AND MAGAZINES. TO PROMOTE PRICE, THEY CAN USE NEWSPAPERS AND RADIO. "

Social & Mobile Marketing   18.1
Simplicity as a Strength and as a Weakness: Twitter's Advertising Formats and Future Plans[ii]

The overall strategy embraced by Twitter seems to follow the KISS principle: Keep it simple, stupid! The microblogging service provider is defined by the simplicity of the communication it enables, and its advertising strategy has matched that simplicity—at least thus far.

Twitter sells advertising in three formats, and three formats only. Unlike popular social media competitors such as Facebook, it does not collect detailed demographic information, so it lacks the ability to target advertising on an individual level. Instead, Twitter allows advertisers to

1. Pay to appear at the top of a list of suggested accounts that users can follow.

2. Buy a "trending" ranking, such that the firm's name or product appears to be particularly popular among users. This option is clearly labeled as advertising, but it also exploits Twitter's popular "trending topics" summary of the top 10 newsworthy events or celebrities or topics that users are searching Twitter to find at that very moment.

3. Insert a promoted tweet. These tweets appear in the user's feed alongside tweets by others whom the user expressly seeks to follow. They also can be personalized to some extent, in that they reflect search terms entered by the user (e.g., a search for "cool tech" returns, before any other content, an advertisement from Verizon Wireless touting its latest smartphone deal).

Twitter is preparing for its initial public offering. In this process, it is taking a few steps that suggest it might be adding a bit more complexity to its advertising strategy. Twitter recently purchased MoPub, a company that specializes in inserting marketing messages into mobile applications through an auction mechanism. Other predictions indicate that Twitter will seek to diversify its market by building a global presence.

headline In an advertisement, large type designed to draw attention.

subhead An additional smaller headline in an ad that provides a great deal of information through the use of short and simple words.

body copy The main text portion of an ad.

brand elements Characteristics that identify the sponsor of a specific ad.

Image Courtesy of The Advertising Archives

"screams for your safety." Headlines and subheads should be short and use simple words and include the primary product or service benefits, the name of the brand, and an interest-provoking idea. They should ideally contain an action verb and give enough information for learning even if only the headline is read.

The **body copy** represents the main text portion of the ad. It is used to build on the interest generated by the visual and headlines, explains in more depth what the headline and subheads introduced, arouses desire for the product, and provides enough information to move the target consumer to action. In this case, the body copy, "Protect yourself this party season with the ila DUSK personal alarm. As well as looking pretty, it emits a high decibel human scream for help. The only fashion accessory you need to be seen out with this Christmas," tells the story of this product and its use. This particular body copy is necessarily longer than for other products because it requires some explanation—the other ad elements are insufficient to explain and sell the product.

Finally, the ad typically has a number of **brand elements** that identify the sponsor of the ad, typically through a logo (M&S, which is the logo for Marks & Spencer department store in the UK) and a unique selling proposition (not found in this ad). The advertiser must convey its message using compelling visuals, headlines, body copy, and identifying brand elements.

Although creativity plays a major role in the execution stage, advertisers must remain careful not to let their

> Although creativity plays a major role in the execution stage, advertisers must remain careful not to let their creativity overshadow the message.

is attractive and feminine. Although it is not always possible to meet all possible objectives with the visual, other important purposes are to identify the subject of the ad, show the product being used and its unique features, create a favorable impression of the product or advertiser, and arouse the readers' interest in the headline, which is generally noticed second.[25]

The **headline** is the large type in an ad that is designed to draw attention. In the Ila DUSK Personal Alarm ad, the headline "ILA PERSONAL ALARM" simply identifies the product. But the **subhead**, a smaller headline, provides more information about the alarm it is selling; specifically, it

creativity overshadow the message. Whatever the execution style, the advertisement must be able to attract the audience's attention, provide a reason for the audience to spend its time viewing the advertisement, and accomplish what it set out to do. In the end, the execution style must match the medium and objectives.

Automobile manufacturers and dealers are among the most active advertisers and use very different messages in their advertising campaigns. Consider, for instance, two well-known car companies that recently introduced new four-door sedan models, each with very different advertising campaigns.

Although the Chevy Malibu offers a fuel-efficient hybrid model, it is positioned as a family sedan.
© General Motors

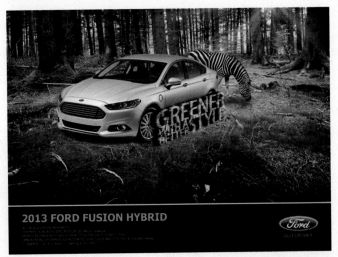

Ads for the new Ford Fusion emphasize fuel economy as well as interesting technology that it hopes will appeal to young consumers.

- **Chevrolet Malibu.** Another entry into the hybrid market, the Malibu employs a battery pack and offers good gas mileage. It is also positioned as a family sedan, though the most recent revamping reduced the size of the backseat. Likely advertising outlets include family-oriented magazines and television spots.

- **Ford Fusion.** With a focus on fuel economy, ads for the new Fusion promise its availability with both a hybrid and a conventional engine. Furthermore, it emphasizes Ford's SYNC technology which uses voice recognition to make phone calls, find and play music, and get directions. With these appeals, Ford is focusing largely on social media to get young consumers, who tend to care about technology and environmental concerns, attached to the new model.[26]

At times, though, even when advertisers think they have done their best to appeal to consumers, their actions can backfire, as Ethical and Societal Dilemma 18.2 describes.

ethical&societal dilemma 18.2

When Makeup Companies Really Do Make Up Models' Faces[iii]

Is Julia Roberts really that good looking? Of course, she's beautiful, but the portrayal of her face in advertising has, more likely than not, been given a Photoshop fix. Airbrushing may be as old as advertising, but improved technology makes the changes nearly imperceptible—it is difficult to tell the difference between the normal thickness of an eyelash and the version that Taylor Swift sported in a CoverGirl Nature-Leuxe Mousse Mascara ad. Ultimately, the National Advertising Division of the Council of Better Business Bureaus ruled the ad was misleading, prompting the brand to pull the ad.

But in other cases, cosmetics and fashion companies claim that fixing elements of appearance is both ubiquitous and expected by consumers. They assert they are not misleading anyone but rather creating a perfect image for their brand. So is it wrong for cosmetic companies to retouch ads, brushing away wrinkles and skin imperfections digitally?

The UK Advertising Standards Agency considers touching up photos in ads to be wrong. That oversight agency banned two ads by L'Oréal recently, charging that they were misleading. One ad featured Julia Roberts promoting Teint Miracle, a new Lancôme skin product that, according to the company, provides "luminosity to the skin." The other featured model Christy Turlington, promoting a cosmetic concealer called Eraser that promises to hide wrinkles and skin discoloration. Although the company protested that the ads did not exaggerate their product effectiveness, the UK Advertising Standards Agency was not convinced.

When selling cosmetics, is it ethical to touch up photos of models and celebrities like Julia Roberts to make them even more beautiful?
© Gregg DeGuire/FilmMagic/Getty Images

Do consumers want realistic images and measured promises, or do they accept and even prefer exaggerated claims and unrealistic images of beauty?

STEP 7: ASSESS IMPACT USING MARKETING METRICS

The effectiveness of an advertising campaign must be assessed before, during, and after the campaign has run. **Pretesting** refers to assessments performed before an ad campaign is implemented to ensure that the various elements are working in an integrated fashion and doing what they are intended to do.[27] **Tracking** includes monitoring key indicators such as daily or weekly sales volume while the advertisement is running to shed light on any problems with the message or the medium. **Posttesting** is the evaluation of the campaign's impact after it is has been implemented. At this last stage, advertisers assess the sales and/or communication impact of the advertisement or campaign.

Measuring sales impact can be especially challenging because of the many influences other than advertising on consumers' choices, purchase behavior, and attitudes. These influences include the level of competitors' advertising, economic conditions in the target market, sociocultural changes, in-store merchandise availability and even the weather, all of which can influence consumer purchasing behavior. For instance, the sales resulting from even the best ads can be foiled by a lack of

Sales volume is a good indicator of advertising effectiveness for frequently purchased consumer goods in the maturity stage of the product life cycle, such as Red Bull energy drink.
© McGraw-Hill Education/ Jill Braaten, photographer

merchandise in the stores or a blizzard. Advertisers must try to identify these influences and isolate those of the particular advertising campaign.

For frequently purchased consumer goods in the maturity stage of the product life cycle, such as soda, sales volume offers a good indicator of advertising effectiveness. Because their sales are relatively stable, and if we assume that the other elements of the marketing mix and the environment have not changed, we can attribute changes in sales volume to changes in advertising. Exhibit 18.4 illustrates a hypothetical sales history for Red Bull in a grocery store chain. Using a statistical technique called time-series analysis, sales data from the past is used to forecast the future. The data in Exhibit 18.4 can be decomposed into its basic trend (green), the seasonal influences (red), and the **lift** or additional sales caused by the advertising (yellow). In this case, the lift caused by the advertising campaign is substantial.

For other types of goods in other stages of the product life cycle, sales data offer but one of the many indicators that marketers need to examine to determine advertising effectiveness. For instance, in high-growth markets, sales growth alone can be misleading because the market as a whole is growing. In such a situation, marketers measure sales relative to those of competitors to determine their relative market share. Firms find creative ways to identify advertising effectiveness. For example, digital cable allows them to present a specific advertisement to certain neighborhoods and then track sales by local or regional retailers.

▼ **EXHIBIT 18.4** Hypothetical Sales History for Red Bull in a Grocery Store Chain

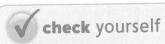
puffery The legal exaggeration of praise, stopping just short of deception, lavished on a product.

LO 18-5   Identify agencies that regulate advertising.

REGULATORY AND ETHICAL ISSUES IN ADVERTISING

In the United States, the regulation of advertising involves a complex mix of formal laws and informal restrictions designed to protect consumers from deceptive practices.[28] Many federal and state laws, as well as a wide range of self-regulatory agencies and agreements, affect advertising (Exhibit 18.5). The primary federal agencies that regulate advertising activities are the Federal Trade Commission (FTC), Federal Communications Commission (FCC), and Food and Drug Administration (FDA). In addition to these agencies, others such as the Bureau of Alcohol, Tobacco, Firearms, and Explosives and the U.S. Postal Service regulate advertising to some degree.

The FTC is the primary enforcement agency for most mass media advertising, although occasionally it cooperates with other agencies to investigate and enforce regulations on particular advertising practices. In one recent case, the FTC charged Pure Green Coffee, a Florida company, with false advertising and misrepresentation in its efforts to sell green coffee beans as a weight-loss aid. The company not only promised more benefits of the coffee beans than have been proven but also created fake websites designed to look like news outlets, and used logos from *The Dr. Oz Show* to imply that the popular television personality endorsed the product.[29]

Many product categories fall under self-regulatory restrictions or guidelines. For example, advertising to children is regulated primarily through self-regulatory mechanisms designed by the National Association of Broadcasters and the Better Business Bureau's Children's Advertising Review Unit. The only formal regulation of children's advertising appears in the Children's Television Act of 1990, which limits the amount of advertising broadcast during children's viewing hours.[30]

Recently, to make matters even more complicated for advertisers, state attorney general offices have begun to inquire into various advertising practices and assert their authority to regulate advertising in their states. The European Union also has increased its regulation of advertising for member nations. Many of these state and European regulations are more restrictive than existing U.S. federal requirements.

The line between what is legal and illegal is more difficult to discern when it comes to **puffery**, which is the legal

> THE ONLY FORMAL REGULATION OF CHILDREN'S ADVERTISING APPEARS IN THE CHILDREN'S TELEVISION ACT OF 1990, WHICH LIMITS THE AMOUNT OF ADVERTISING BROADCAST DURING CHILDREN'S VIEWING HOURS.

▼ **EXHIBIT 18.5** Federal Agencies That Regulate Advertising

Federal Agency	General Purpose	Specific Jurisdiction
Federal Trade Commission (FTC) (1914)	Enforces federal consumer protection laws.	Enforces truth in advertising laws; defines deceptive and unfair advertising practices.
Federal Communications Commission (FCC) (1934)	Regulates interstate and international communications by radio, television, wire, satellite, and cable.	Enforces restrictions on broadcasting material that promotes lotteries (with some exceptions); cigarettes, little cigars, or smokeless tobacco products; or that perpetuates a fraud. Also enforces laws that prohibit or limit obscene, indecent, or profane language.
Food and Drug Administration (1930)	Regulates food, dietary supplements, drugs, cosmetics, medical devices (including radiation-emitting devices such as cell phones), biologics (biological issues), and blood products.	Regulates package labeling and inserts, definition of terms such as *light* and *organic,* and required disclosure statements (warning labels, dosage requirements, etc.).

exaggeration of praise, stopping just short of deception, lavished on a product. When Match.com claims that it leads to "better first dates," it's puffery because *better* is a subjective measure. But if it claims it produces "more second dates," it must be able to back up its numerical, quantitative assertion. Even cartoon bears must follow the rules: Charmin's animated spokescharacters need to be drawn with a few pieces of toilet paper on their rears, instead of none, to ensure that Charmin's claims extend only to leaving less toilet paper behind than other brands (puffery), not eliminating the problem altogether (deception).[31]

How do the courts determine what makes an ad deceptive rather than simply puffery? The FTC's position is that it "will not pursue cases involving obviously exaggerated or puffing representations, i.e., those that ordinary consumers do not take seriously."[32] In general, the less specific the claim, the less likely it is considered to be deceptive. In the end, puffery is acceptable as long as consumers know that the firm is stretching the truth through exaggeration.[33]

PUBLIC RELATIONS

As you may recall from Chapter 17, **public relations (PR)** involves managing communications and relationships to achieve various objectives such as building and maintaining a positive image of the firm, handling or heading off unfavorable stories or events, and maintaining positive relationships with the media. In many cases, public relations activities support other promotional efforts by generating free media attention and general goodwill.

Designers, for example, vie to have celebrities, especially those nominated for awards, wear their fashions on the red carpet. Their brands offer intangible benefits, not just functional benefits. Events such as the Oscars, with its 35 million annual viewers, provide an unparalleled opportunity to showcase the emotional benefits of the brand and make others want to be a part of it. Thus, the celebrities whom designers pursue and offer their items to are those who will sell the most or provide the best iconic images. Lupita Nyong'o's great popularity during the recent awards season meant that she could wear Ralph Lauren to the Golden Globes, then switch to Prada for the Academy Awards, and garner press for both design firms.[34] The placement of designer apparel at media events benefits both the designer and the celebrity. And neither happens by accident. Public relations people on both sides help orchestrate the events to get the maximum benefit for both parties.

Is this ad an example of puffery or deception?
Image Courtesy of The Advertising Archives

Prada garnered positive public relations when Lupita Nyong'o wore its gown to the Academy Awards.
© Jason LaVeris/Getty Images

Chili's restaurants partners with St. Jude's Children's Research Hospital in a cause-related marketing campaign. Among other Chili's-related fund-raising initiatives, customers can make a digital pepper and give a donation, and then share the pepper with friends via Facebook, Twitter, or Instagram.
© Brinker International

Good PR has always been an important success factor. Yet in recent years, the importance of PR has grown as the costs of other forms of marketing communications have increased. At the same time, the influence of PR has become more powerful as consumers have become increasingly skeptical of marketing claims made in other media.[35] In many instances, consumers view media coverage generated through PR as more credible and objective than any other aspects of an IMC program because the firm does not buy the space in print media or time on radio or television.

Certainly the Chili's restaurant chain conducts plenty of media buys in traditional advertising spaces. But it also has partnered with St. Jude's Children's Research Hospital in one of the most successful examples of **cause-related marketing** (i.e., commercial activity in which businesses and charities form a partnership to market an image, product, or service for their mutual benefit)[36] in history. For several years, the restaurant has offered customers the opportunity to purchase a paper icon—in the shape of a chili pepper, natch—that they may color and hang on restaurant walls. The cause marketing campaign runs in September, which is also National Childhood Cancer Awareness Month. On the last Monday of the month, the restaurant puts its money where its mouth is and donates all its profits on sales during the day to St. Jude. In addition to the relatively common Create-a-Chili paper icons, employees of the restaurants make and sell customized T-shirts and wristbands. Making peppers out of paper is not the only way people can donate to St. Jude. Chili's now has a website, http://morehope.chilis.com, that allows customers to make a digital pepper (and give a donation) and then share the pepper with friends via Facebook, Twitter, or Instagram.

Civic-minded consumers can also buy St. Jude–branded Chili's gift cards on this site.[37]

Another very popular PR tool is event sponsorship. **Event sponsorship** occurs when corporations support various activities (financially or otherwise), usually in the cultural or sports and entertainment sectors. Red Bull is a frequent sponsor of various kinds of sports events, such as Red Bull Air Race and numerous extreme sports events (e.g., cliff diving). Some of them are big-name events; the titles of most college football playoff games now include the name of their sponsors (e.g., the Allstate Sugar Bowl). Others are slightly less famous; for

Part of Red Bull's PR toolkit is its event sponsorship of a cliff-diving event.
© James Davies/Alamy

sales promotions Special incentives or excitement-building programs that encourage the purchase of a product or service, such as coupons, rebates, contests, free samples, and point-of-purchase displays.

coupon Provides a stated discount to consumers on the final selling price of a specific item; the retailer handles the discount.

▼ **EXHIBIT 18.6** Elements of a Public Relations Toolkit

PR Element	Function
Publications: Brochures, special-purpose single-issue publications such as books	Inform various constituencies about the activities of the organization and highlight specific areas of expertise.
Video and audio: Programs, public service announcements	Highlight the organization or support cause-related marketing efforts.
Annual reports	Give required financial performance data and inform investors and others about the unique activities of the organization.
Media relations: Press kits, news releases, speeches, event sponsorships	Generate news coverage of the organization's activities or products/services.
Electronic media: Websites, e-mail campaigns	Websites can contain all the previously mentioned toolbox elements while e-mail directs PR efforts to specific target groups.

example, Rollerblade USA, the maker of Rollerblade in-line skates, sponsors Skate-In-School, a program it developed with the National Association for Sport and Physical Education (NASPE) to promote the inclusion of rollerblading in physical education curricula.

Firms often distribute a PR toolkit to communicate with various audiences. Some toolkit elements are designed to inform specific groups directly, whereas others are created to generate media attention and disseminate information. We describe the various elements of a PR toolkit in Exhibit 18.6.

LO 18-6 Describe the elements of a public relations toolkit.

 check yourself

1. Why do companies use public relations as part of their IMC strategy?
2. What are the elements of a public relations toolkit?

LO 18-7 Identify the various types of sales promotions.

SALES PROMOTION

Advertising rarely provides the only means to communicate with target customers. As we discussed in Chapter 17, a natural link appears between advertising and sales promotion. **Sales promotions** are special incentives or excitement-building programs that encourage consumers to purchase a particular product or service, typically used in conjunction with other advertising or personal selling programs. Many sales promotions, like free samples or point-of-purchase (POP) displays, attempt to build short-term sales, whereas others, such as loyalty programs, contests, and sweepstakes, have become integral components of firms' long-term customer relationship management (CRM) programs, which they use to build customer loyalty.

We present these sales promotion tools next. The tools of any sales promotion can be focused on any channel member—wholesalers, retailers, or end-user consumers. Just as we delineated for advertising, when sales promotions are targeted at channel members, the marketer is employing a push strategy; when it targets consumers themselves, it is using a pull strategy. Some sales promotion tools can be used with either a push or pull strategy. We now consider each of the tools and how they are used.

Types of Sales Promotion

Coupons **Coupons** offer a discount on the price of specific items when they're purchased. Coupons are issued by manufacturers and retailers in newspapers, on products, on the shelf, at the cash register, over the Internet, and through the mail to stimulate demand. Some retailers have linked their coupons directly to their loyalty programs. As Marketing Analytics 18.1 describes, the drugstore chain CVS tracks customers' purchases when they use their ExtraCare loyalty card and gives them coupons that are tailored just for them and their unique needs.[38] If a customer typically spends a small amount during each shopping trip, he or she might receive coupons to encourage larger purchases, such as buy one, get one free.

Internet sites also provide customers with instant coupons of their choosing. Imagine a customer who visits her local

> " When sales promotions are targeted at channel members, the marketer is employing a push strategy; when it targets consumers themselves, it is using a pull strategy. "

Marketing Analytics

How CVS Uses Loyalty Data to Define Coupons[iv]

In general, loyalty programs offer an effective means to provide more value to customers. In particular, the CVS ExtraCare program represents a flagship loyalty program, as one of the oldest and largest in the United States. The program has been running for nearly 20 years; one in every three people in the United States has an ExtraCare card. Thus, more than 90 million households use it in a typical year.

The primary focus of the ExtraCare program has been to provide personalized offers that are relevant to and appreciated by customers, while also encouraging their consistent shopping behavior. In recent developments, the program has spread across multiple channels, allowing customers to connect with offers in print, online, or through a mobile app. For example, customers can access the newly launched, omnichannel MyWeeklyAd program online or from a mobile device, or they can visit coupon kiosks in stores to scan their loyalty program cards and print coupons on the spot.

To support a unique, relevant, and well-appreciated shopping experience that encourages these customers to interact with the program and undertake additional sales, CVS relies heavily on customer data analytics. It collects vast amounts of data on the purchases that each ExtraCare member makes, and then it analyzes those data to uncover interesting or unexpected relationships among the items purchased. For example, customers who buy skin and hair products also purchase cosmetics, though not always at CVS. Furthermore, CVS discovered notable and helpful purchase timing patterns, such as its recognition that people typically buy toothpaste every five weeks.

By using the established relationships among the items that appear together in market baskets, CVS can obtain valuable insights, which in turn inform the personalized offers it sends to customers in an effort to adjust their behaviors. Thus, if an ExtraCare member buys face wash or conditioner, she might receive a coupon for lipstick. If another customer hasn't bought toothpaste in four and a half weeks, he will receive a coupon that provides him with a special incentive to purchase a high-end brand of toothpaste. CVS also uses these analytics to encourage customers to buy more each trip, such that a customer who typically spends $20 may receive

Marketing analytics are used to analyze data on the purchases of each ExtraCare customer, uncover interesting or unexpected relationships among items purchased, and use the information to provide personalized offers that are relevant to and appreciated by customers.
© McGraw-Hill Education/Mark Dierker, photographer

a special offer if she spends $30 the next time she shops. Finally, the data analytics give CVS important insights into which types of loyalty program offers are most successful—as well as which ones are not. For example, it determined that brand-specific coupons (e.g., for Pantene shampoo) were less effective than promotions geared toward the whole category (i.e., shampoos of various brands).

Walmart and finds a Hot Wheels video game for $29.99. By scanning the bar code using her cell phone, she connects to ShopSavvy.com and finds that the same item at a Target store a mile away is only $19.99. Another scan and a connection to MyCoupons.com provides her with a $10 coupon—which means she's saved $20 in a matter of minutes and just a few clicks.

Some coupons, whether printed from the Internet or sent to mobile phones, also contain information about the customer who uses it.[39] The bar code may identify the customer,

his or her Internet address, Facebook page information, and even the search terms the customer used to find the coupon in the first place. These new breeds of coupons may look standard, but they offer up a startling amount of data, which promises benefits for advertisers who want to target their marketing more closely. Traditionally, coupons had low redemption rates and were therefore a relatively inexpensive sales promotion tool, but using customer data to create more targeted promotions has resulted in higher redemption rates, increasing their expense.

deal A type of short-term price reduction that can take several forms, such as a "featured price," a price lower than the regular price; a "buy one, get one free" offer; or a certain percentage "more free" offer contained in larger packaging; can involve a special financing arrangement, such as reduced percentage interest rates or extended repayment terms.

premium An item offered for free or at a bargain price to reward some type of behavior, such as buying, sampling, or testing.

contest A brand-sponsored competition that requires some form of skill or effort.

sweepstakes A form of sales promotion that offers prizes based on a chance drawing of entrants' names.

sampling Offers potential customers the opportunity to try a product or service before they make a buying decision.

BUY ONE GET ONE 1/2 OFF EVERYTHING

Buy 1, get 2nd item of equal or lesser value for 1/2 off the Payless ShoeSource® marked price! Entire stock included.

BO GO

SECOND PAIR PRICE 17.49
REG 34.99
TAUPE FLAT SLOUCH BOOT

SECOND ITEM PRICE 8.99
REG 17.99
STUDDED WHIPSTITCH HOBO

Payless SHOESOURCE®

©2006 PSSW Styles vary by store. While supplies last. Sale runs August 17 through September 5, 2006.

Payless ShoeSource®
www.payless.com

This sales promotion deal for Payless ShoeSource is a short-term price promotion that encourages customers to buy a second pair of shoes at one-half off.

Courtesy Payless Shoe Source, Inc.

Deals A **deal** refers generally to a type of short-term price reduction that can take several forms, such as a featured price, a price lower than the regular price; a certain percentage more free offer contained in larger packaging; or a buy one, get one half off offer as shown in the Payless ad above. Another form of a deal involves a special financing arrangement such as reduced percentage interest rates or extended repayment terms. Deals encourage customers to try a product because they lower the risk for consumers by reducing the cost of the good.

But deals can also alter perceptions of value—a short-term price reduction may signal a different price–quality relationship than would be ideal from the manufacturer's perspective. In addition, as Old Spice learned, offering too many deals can offset likely gains. Its popular Old Spice Guy campaign attracted consumer attention through funny television commercials and interactive online campaigns, and sales of Old Spice jumped. But the company offered so many buy one, get one free deals at the same time that the potential profit impact of the great ads was essentially eliminated by the costs of the deals.[40]

Premiums A **premium** offers an item for free or at a bargain price to reward some type of behavior, such as buying, sampling, or testing. These rewards build goodwill among consumers, who often perceive high value in them. Premiums can be distributed in a variety of ways: They can be included in the product packaging, such as the toys inside cereal boxes; placed visibly on the package, such as a coupon for free milk on a box of Cheerios; handed out in the store; or delivered in the mail, such as the free perfume offers Victoria's Secret mails to customers. Furthermore, premiums can be very effective if they are consistent with the brand's message and image and highly desirable to the target market. However, finding a premium that meets these criteria at a reasonable cost can be a serious challenge.

Contests A **contest** refers to a brand-sponsored competition that requires some form of skill or effort. ESPN's website hosts a page devoted just to sports-related contests: Get Me to the World Cup sponsored by Sony or Player of the Month presented by Kia.[41] For the Get Me to the World Cup contest, each participant must create and upload a short video demonstrating why he or she should be the one picked to attend the international event. For those who need some help sparking their creativity, ESPN provides some sample videos—including one by Kobe Bryant.

Sweepstakes A form of sales promotion that offers prizes based on a chance drawing of entrants' names, **sweepstakes** do not require the entrant to complete a task other than buying a ticket or filling out a form. Often the key benefit of sweepstakes is that they encourage current consumers to consume more if the sweepstakes form appears inside the packaging or with the product. Many states, however, specify that no purchase can be required to enter sweepstakes.

Samples

Sampling offers potential customers the opportunity to try a product or service before they make a buying decision. Distributing samples is one of the most costly sales promotion tools but also one of the most effective. Quick-service restaurants and grocery stores frequently use sampling. For instance, Starbucks provides samples of new products to customers. Costco uses so many samples that customers can have an entire meal. Sometimes trial-sized samples come in the mail or are distributed in stores.

Loyalty Programs

As part of a sales promotion program, **loyalty programs** are specifically designed to retain customers by offering premiums or other incentives to customers who make multiple purchases over time. Well-designed loyalty programs encourage consumers to increase their engagement and purchases from a given firm. Such sales promotions are growing increasingly popular and are tied to long-term CRM systems. (Loyalty programs are examined in Chapters 2 and 3.) These programs need to be carefully managed because they can be quite costly.

Point-of-Purchase Displays

Point-of-purchase (POP) displays are merchandise displays located at the point of purchase, such as at the checkout counter in a supermarket. Retailers have long recognized that the most valuable real estate in the store is at the POP since they increase product visibility and encourage trial. Customers see products such as a

the added exposure when they appear on consumer websites like PriceGrabber.com and Nextag.com, where products are sorted by the price, with links to the retailer's website. The firms garner considerable value from rebates because they attract consumers and therefore stimulate sales, but they may not have to pay off all the rebates offered.

Product Placement

When marketers use **product placement**, they pay to have their product included in nontraditional situations, such as in a scene in a movie or television program.[42] By doing so, they increase the visibility of their products. Product placement may be subtle, such as when American Idol judges are seen drinking Coca-Cola. On CBS's *The Big Bang Theory,* not only do scenes regularly show the characters working and eating there, but Sheldon also asserts his need to get "access to the Cheesecake Factory walk-in freezer." Although many firms would embrace product placement in hit shows and movies and are willing to pay for it, for Apple, the

> ## STARBUCKS PROVIDES SAMPLES OF NEW PRODUCTS TO CUSTOMERS. COSTCO USES SO MANY SAMPLES THAT CUSTOMERS CAN HAVE AN ENTIRE MEAL.

magazine or a candy bar while they are waiting to pay for their purchases and impulsively purchase them. In the Internet version of a POP display, shoppers are stimulated by special merchandise, price reductions, or complementary products that Internet retailers feature on the checkout screen.

Rebates

Rebates are a particular type of price reduction in which a portion of the purchase price is returned by the seller to the buyer in the form of cash. Many products, such as consumer electronics, offer significant mail-in rebates that may lower the price of the item significantly. Some companies enjoy

challenge is a little less stringent. U.S. film and television directors seem to love its sleek white laptops, ear-budded iPods, and ubiquitous iPhones. Thus more than one-third of all top-grossing films at the U.S. box office—129 of 374 movies—have included Apple-branded products in the past decade. Recent appearances include both popular offerings and critically acclaimed broadcasts, from Phil's desperate efforts to score an iPad on *Modern Family* to more nefarious uses depicted in *House of Cards*.[43] Apple is also unique in that it claims it does not pay for product placement, nor does it comment on film appearances. An analytics firm that estimates the dollar value of product placements has reported that Apple's five-minute screen time in *Mission Impossible* alone was worth more than $23 million.[44] Apple seemingly can earn those returns without paying for the placements, but not all companies are so lucky.

Using Sales Promotion Tools

Marketers must be careful in their use of sales promotions, especially those that focus on lowering prices. Depending on the item, consumers may stock up when items are offered at a lower price, which simply shifts sales from the future to now

consumers. J.Crew has teamed up with several famous brands, including Havaianas, Barbour, Timex, New Balance, Ray-Ban and Speedo, to offer well-known brands in the J.Crew stores and website.[45]

The goal of any sales promotion is to create value for both the consumers and the firm. By understanding the needs of its customers, as well as how best to entice them to purchase or consume a particular product or service, a firm can develop promotional messages and events that are of interest to and achieve the desired response from those customers. Traditionally, the role of sales promotion has been to generate short-term results, whereas the goal of advertising was to generate long-term results. As this chapter demonstrates, though, both

> "Consumers may stock up when items are offered at a lower price, which simply shifts sales from the future to now and thereby leads to short-run benefits at the expense of long-term sales stability."

and thereby leads to short-run benefits at the expense of long-term sales stability. For instance, using sales promotions such as coupons to stimulate sales of household cleaning supplies may cause consumers to stockpile the products and decrease demand for those products in the future. But a similar promotion used with a perishable product such as Dannon yogurt should increase its demand at the expense of competitors like Yoplait.

Many firms are also realizing the value of **cross-promoting**, when two or more firms join to reach a specific target market. To achieve a successful cross-promotion, the two products must appeal to the same target market and together create value for

sales promotion and advertising can generate both long- and short-term effects. The effective combination of both types of activities leads to impressive results for the firm and the consumers. ■

 check yourself

1. What are various forms of sales promotions?
2. What factors should a firm consider when evaluating a sales promotion?

Increase your engagement and learning with Connect Marketing.

These Connect activities, available only through your Connect course, have been designed to make the following concepts more meaningful and applicable:

- Planning an Ad Campaign Timeline Activity
- Types of Sales Promotion Click and Drag Activity
- Ford Advertising Video Case
- Differentiating between Advertising, PR, and Sales Promotion: iSeeit! Video

 SMARTBOOK™   iSeeit!

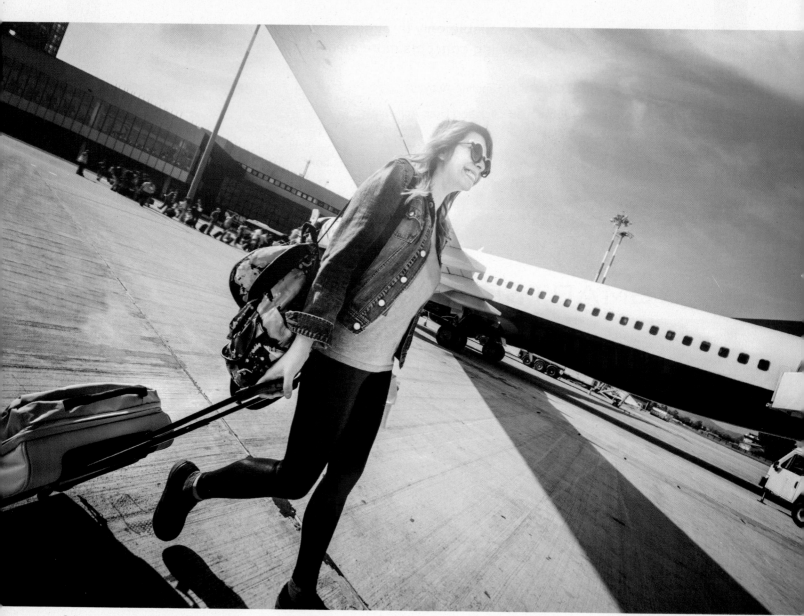

nineteen

T he Boeing Company is one of the largest manufacturers of airplanes in the world;[1] following an industry consolidation in the mid-1990s, it is actually one of two members of an industrywide duopoly (Airbus is the other).[2] The long production and R&D lead times in this sector, combined with very high prices per unit, have led to a fierce rivalry between Boeing and Airbus.

For many years, Boeing ranked second in terms of market share, leading to some challenging managerial and strategic concerns during the 2000s. A series of CEOs were dismissed for various reasons, leaving Boeing's reputation in question. Although strong in the defense sector, Boeing continued to cede market share to Airbus in the commercial airline segment, largely due to the introduction of the innovative, exciting Airbus 330. Finally, Boeing was in the midst of divesting a large percentage of its manufacturing facilities in an attempt to move to an outsourcing model.[3]

The competitive landscape thus forced Boeing to make a strategic move if it hoped to survive. Headed by Michael Bair and

personal selling and sales management

LEARNING OBJECTIVES

After reading this chapter, you should be able to:

LO 19-1 Describe the value added of personal selling.

LO 19-2 Define the steps in the personal selling process.

LO 19-3 Describe the key functions involved in managing a sales force.

LO 19-4 Describe the ethical and legal issues in personal selling.

three other top Boeing executives, the firm decided to develop a new line of jet planes, designated 787 "Dreamliners." The 787 could fly internationally but would carry fewer passengers than traditional international airplanes. With this innovation, Boeing positioned itself to capture a "blue ocean" market, in which it could potentially

continued on p. 398

continued from p. 397

personal selling
The two-way flow of communication between a buyer and a seller that is designed to influence the buyer's purchase decision.

support around 400 new international routes that attracted too little demand for larger planes but might be profitable for airlines that flew the new 787. Furthermore, because cost savings represented a key deciding factor for its business customers (i.e., the airlines), Boeing designed the plane with new composite materials that reduced fuel costs by 20 percent.[4]

To meet the related design requirements, not only was the cutting-edge plane model made almost entirely of composite parts but these parts also allowed each plane to be "snapped together" in as little as three days. But the complexity of the design forced Boeing to outsource more than 70 percent of its production, using an unprecedented "global systems integrator" strategy in this business-to-business market. Whereas once Boeing controlled the majority of production, now it was trusting the manufacturing quality of its expensive, complex products to partners in the supply chain.

Unfortunately, its trust was misplaced. The new manufacturing approach saved time and money, but the Dreamliner has continued to be awash in production and design issues. In 2013, fires caused by short circuits in the new lithium ion batteries that Boeing included in its planes caused the entire global fleet of 787s to be grounded for three months. Despite clearance to fly again, the U.S. National Transportation Safety Board continued to express concern about the safety of the 140 Dreamliners currently in flight worldwide.[5]

How does a company that sells jets for prices ranging from $76 million to $360 million respond to a crisis like this?[6] Boeing relied on its world-class salespeople such as John Wojick. Empowered by Boeing, Wojick offered greater flexibility in delivery times as well as heavy discounts to his business customers. He also noted the need to engage in tough conversations with his customers, during which he was required to communicate truthfully about what Boeing knows and does not know about the failures.[7]

The personal selling approach adopted by Wojick and his colleagues has helped stem the damage for Boeing. Within four months of taking over as global head of sales, Wojick landed a contract for 150 planes (at a value of nearly $15 billion). As a result, Boeing was able to overtake Airbus as the top ranking airline manufacturer, in terms of orders and deliveries.[8] ■

Despite manufacturing setbacks on Boeing's 787 Dreamliner, a strong and professional personal selling approach enabled it to overcome an initial poor market response and overtake Airbus as the top-ranking airline manufacturer.
© Richard Baker Farnborough/Alamy

Just like advertising, which we discussed in Chapter 18, personal selling is so important to integrated marketing communications that it deserves its own chapter. Almost everyone is engaged in some form of selling. On a personal level, you sell your ideas or opinions to your friends, family, employers, and professors. Even if you have no interest in personal selling as a career, a strong grounding in the topic will help you in numerous career choices. Consider, for instance, Harry Turk, a very successful labor attorney. He worked his way through college selling sweaters to fraternities across the country. Although he loved his part-time job, Harry decided to become an attorney. When asked whether he misses selling, he said, "I use my selling skills every day. I have to sell new clients on the idea that I'm the best attorney for the job. I have to sell my partners on my legal point of view. I even use selling skills when I'm talking to a judge or jury."

LO 19-1 Describe the value added of personal selling.

THE SCOPE AND NATURE OF PERSONAL SELLING

Personal selling is the two-way flow of communication between a buyer or buyers and a seller, designed to influence the buyer's purchase decision. Personal selling can take place in various situations: face-to-face, via video teleconferencing, on the telephone, or over the Internet, for example. More than 14 million people are employed in sales positions in the United States,[9] including those involved in business-to-business (B2B) transactions—like manufacturer's representatives selling to retailers or other businesses—and those completing business-to-consumer (B2C) transactions, such as retail salespeople, real estate agents, and insurance agents. Salespeople are referred to in many ways: sales representatives or reps, account executives, agents. And as Harry Turk found, most professions rely on personal selling to some degree.

Salespeople don't always get the best coverage in popular media. In Arthur Miller's famous play *Death of a Salesman,* the main character Willie Loman leads a pathetic existence and suffers from the loneliness inherent in being a traveling salesman.[10] The characters in David Mamet's play *Glengarry Glen Ross* portray salespeople as crude, ruthless, and of questionable character. Unfortunately, these powerful Pulitzer Prize–winning pieces of literature weigh heavily on our collective consciousness and often overshadow the millions of hardworking professional salespeople who have fulfilling and rewarding careers and who add value to their firm and provide value for their customers.

Personal Selling as a Career

Personal or professional selling can be a satisfying career for several reasons. First, many people love the lifestyle. Salespeople are typically out on their own. Although they occasionally work with their managers and other colleagues, salespeople tend to be responsible for planning their own days. This flexibility translates into an easier balance between work and family than many office-bound jobs can offer. Many salespeople now can rely on virtual offices, which enable them to communicate from anywhere and at any time with their colleagues and customers. Because salespeople are evaluated primarily on the results they produce, as long as they meet and exceed their goals, they experience little day-to-day supervision. You might find a salesperson at the gym in the middle of the day, when few other people are there, because no one keeps track of the length of his or her lunch break.

Second, the variety of the job often attracts people to sales. Every day is different, bringing different clients and customers, often in a variety of places. Their issues and problems and the solutions to those problems all differ and require creativity.[11] Third, professional selling and sales management can be a very lucrative career. Sales is among the highest-paying careers for college graduates, and compensation often includes perks such as the use of a company car or bonuses for high performance. A top performer can have a total compensation package of over $150,000; even starting salespeople can make well over $50,000. Although the monetary compensation can be significant, the satisfaction of being involved in interesting, challenging, and creative work is rewarding in and of itself.

Fourth, because salespeople are the frontline emissaries for their firms, they are very visible to management. Furthermore,

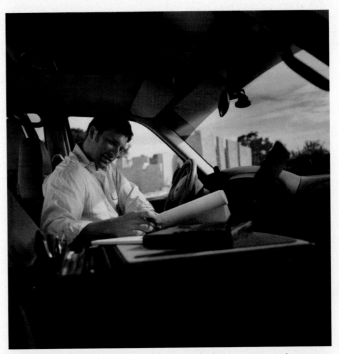

Many salespeople now can rely on virtual offices, which enable them to communicate via the Internet with colleagues and customers.
© Stanley Fellerman/Corbis RF

their performance is fairly straightforward to measure, which means that high-performing salespeople who aspire to management positions are in a good position to be promoted.

The Value Added by Personal Selling

The benefits for salespeople mean that they are expensive for firms. Experts estimate that the average cost of a single B2B sales call is about $600.[12] So why include them in the marketing channel at all? In response to this question, some firms have turned to the Internet and technology to lower the costs of personal selling (see Social and Mobile Marketing 19.1). Other firms, especially retailers, have made the decision not to use a sales force and thus require customers to perform the sales function on their own. But the firms that continue to use personal selling as part of their integrated marketing communications program recognize the value that it adds to their product or service mix. That is, personal selling is worth more than it costs. Personal selling adds value by educating customers and providing advice, saving the customer time, making things easier for customers, and building long-term strategic relationships with customers.[13]

> " **A top performer can have a total compensation package of over $150,000; even starting salespeople can make well over $50,000.** "

Social & Mobile Marketing
Personal Selling Goes Virtual[i]

Rising fuel costs, increasing staff productivity, cutbacks in airline service, minimizing carbon footprints, reducing corporate expenditure—these are just some of the reasons for meetings to go virtual. Foremost among them is that the technology has matured to the point that conversing in cyberspace frequently makes more sense than meeting in the same room. Accordingly, sales personnel infrequently need to meet potential customers face-to-face, because they instead rely on GoToMeeting, WebEx, or Skype to get to know their clients. Such telepresence technologies strongly influence firms' bottom lines by enabling them to transition from expensive field sales staff to less costly inside sales representatives.

In its most advanced forms, telepresence goes far beyond Skype though. It relies on three screens that display life-sized images of conference attendees, plus an additional screen for shared work. Resolution on the screens exceeds that of high-definition televisions. Images can be magnified, allowing attendees to view minute product details from across the globe. These systems, which also feature custom lighting and acoustics, cost as much as $350,000. For corporations such as Cisco, which has more than 200 telepresence rooms, the investment still represents a savings over travel costs. It isn't alone: The management consulting and technology service firm Accenture estimates its teleconferencing rooms save millions of dollars each year, as well as saving its staff the wear and tear of travel.

Other collaborative technologies involve less financial outlay. Web-meeting services, for example, allow companies to conduct online training, edit documents collaboratively, demonstrate applications, give training or sales presentations, poll attendees, chat online, conduct question-and-answer sessions, and provide technical support. As long as participants have a computer with a web browser and an Internet connection, they can use collaborative tools such as wikis or voice-over-Internet protocol (VoIP) technology.

Such technologies also help small companies go global. Lisa Kirschner, president of a Chicago-based marketing and graphic design firm, had a hot lead in Italy. But she lacked the resources to meet in person and felt brainstorming via e-mail would be too cumbersome. Taking the risk of investing in web conferencing, which was unheard of in her industry, she ultimately secured clients in Italy, Japan, and Britain. The technology has earned her $100,000—one-eighth of her total annual revenue.

In parallel, new technologies that enable virtual conferences have led to reductions in business travel and slumps in the conference business. For example, Expos2 digitizes conferences, such that attendees begin with a screen showing the convention center layout. From there they can follow links to exhibits, programs, and live presentations with interactive functionality. Digital meeting technology aims not simply to replace face-to-face meetings or travel but rather to provide an alternative for companies that must optimize their travel budgets. Still, closing a deal is more likely during an in-person meeting, and business travel to other countries provides important insights into communities and cultures. All transactions benefit from a personal touch. But web-based and videoconferencing technology appear likely to keep influencing the ways companies do business.

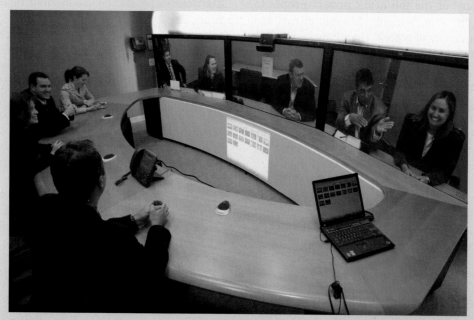

Salespeople no longer have to meet face to face with their customers to make the sale.

© Hiroko Masuike/The New York Times/Redux Pictures

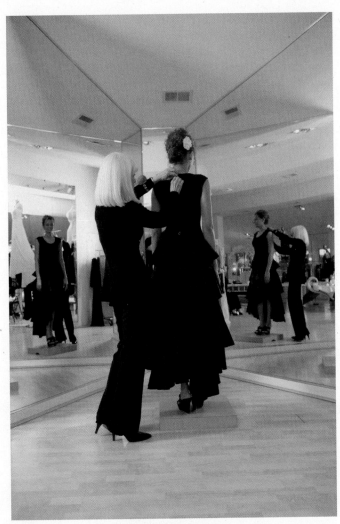
Salespeople Provide Information and Advice

Imagine how difficult it would be to buy a custom suit, a house, or a car without the help of a salesperson. UPS wouldn't dream of investing in a new fleet of airplanes without the benefit of Boeing's selling team. Boeing's sales team can provide UPS with the technical aspects of the aircraft as well as the economic justification for the purchase. If you need formalwear for your friend's upcoming wedding or a school dance, you might find it helpful to solicit the input of a retail sales associate who can tell you what colors are hot this season, how to tie a bowtie, how each garment tends to fit, what the latest fashions are in formalwear, and how long your dress should be for a function that starts at 6:00 p.m. Certainly you could figure out most of this information on your own, but most customers find value in and are willing to pay for the education and advice that salespeople provide.

Salespeople Save Time and Simplify Buying

Time is money! Customers perceive value in time and labor

savings. In many grocery and drugstore chains, salespeople employed by the vendor that supplies the merchandise straighten stock, set up displays, assess inventory levels, and write orders. In some cases, such as bakeries or soft drink sales, salespeople and truck drivers even bring in the merchandise and stock the shelves. These are all tasks that retail employees would otherwise have to do. To appeal to end customers, manufacturers might send salespeople into stores to provide cooking demonstrations or free samples in the case of grocery stores, or trunk or made-to-measure shows in the case of apparel or shoe retailers. In this case, the vendor increases convenience for both its immediate customer (the retailer) and the end consumer.

relationship selling
A sales philosophy and process that emphasizes a commitment to maintaining the relationship over the long term and investing in opportunities that are mutually beneficial to all parties.

Salespeople Build Relationships As we discussed in Chapter 15, building strong marketing channel relationships is a critical success factor. Who in the organization is better equipped to manage this relationship than the salesperson, the frontline emissary for the firm? The most successful salespeople are those who build strong relationships with their customers—a rule that holds across all sorts of sales. That is, whether you are selling yourself as a job candidate, a product produced by your company, or a concept to a client, your sale is not successful if it leads to just a one-time transaction. Instead, good salespeople of all stripes consistently take a long-term perspective.

Building on the relationship concept introduced in Chapter 15, **relationship selling** refers to a sales philosophy

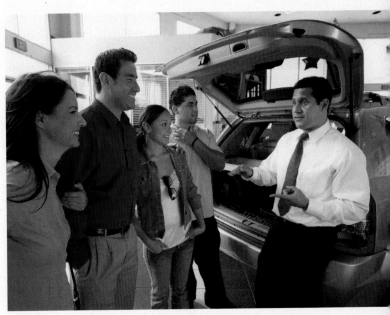

A salesperson's product knowledge and ability to facilitate the sale can make buying a car easy and possibly even enjoyable.
© Barry Austin Photography/Photodisc/Getty Images RF

leads A list of potential customers.

qualify The process of assessing the potential of sales leads.

inbound marketing Marketing activities that draw the attention of customers through blogs, Twitter, LinkedIn, and other online sources, rather than using more traditional activities that require having to go out to get customers' attention, such as making a sales call.

trade shows Major events attended by buyers who choose to be exposed to products and services offered by potential suppliers in an industry.

and process that emphasizes a commitment to maintaining the relationship over the long term and investing in opportunities that are mutually beneficial to all parties.[14] Relationship-oriented salespeople work with their customers to find mutually beneficial solutions to their wants and needs. As we described in Chapter 7, colleges often negotiate long-term agreements with apparel companies to supply their sports teams. Similarly, a Lenovo sales team might be working with your university to provide you with the computer support and security you need during the years you spend working on the school's network.

LO 19-2 | Define the steps in the personal selling process.

THE PERSONAL SELLING PROCESS

Although selling may appear a rather straightforward process, successful salespeople must follow several steps. Depending on the sales situation and the buyer's readiness to purchase, the salesperson may not use every step, and the time required for each step varies with the situation. For example, if a customer goes into The Gap already prepared to purchase some chinos, the selling process will be fairly quick. But if Lenovo is attempting to sell personal computers for the first time to your university, the process may take several months. With this in mind, let's examine each step of the selling process (Exhibit 19.1).

Step 1: Generate and Qualify Leads

The first step in the selling process is to generate a list of potential customers (**leads**) and assess their potential (**qualify**). Salespeople who already have an established relationship with a customer will skip this step, and it is not used extensively in retail settings. In B2B situations, however, it is important to work continually to find new and potentially profitable customers.

Salespeople can generate and qualify leads in a variety of ways.[15] They might discover potential leads by talking to current customers, doing research on the Internet, or networking at events such as trade shows, industry conferences, or chamber of commerce meetings. Salespeople can also generate leads through cold calls and social media.

The Internet, and sites like LinkedIn and Twitter in particular, have been a boon for generating and qualifying leads. Prior

to the explosion of Internet use, it was cumbersome to perform research on products, customers, or competitors. Salespeople would rely on a research staff for this information, and it could take weeks for the research to be completed and sent through the mail. Today, salespeople connect with potential customers through Twitter and LinkedIn. Salespeople curate blogs to draw in customers and generate leads, a process known as **inbound marketing**. While these are all important tools, they are unlikely to replace cold calling anytime soon as many customers still cannot be reached via social media.[16]

Trade shows also offer an excellent forum for finding leads. These major events are attended by buyers who choose to be exposed to products and services offered by potential suppliers in an industry. Consumer electronics buyers always make sure that they attend the annual International Consumer Electronics Show (CES) in Las Vegas, the world's largest trade show for consumer technology (http://www.cesweb.org). The most recent show was attended by 155,000 people (including more than 34,000 international attendees) such as vendors, developers, and suppliers of consumer-technology hardware, content, technology delivery systems, and related products and services.[17] Nearly 3,100 vendor exhibits took up 1.861 million net square feet of exhibit space, showcasing the very latest products and services. Vendors often use CES to introduce new

▼ **EXHIBIT 19.1** The Personal Selling Process

Generate and qualify leads

↓

Preapproach

↓

Sales presentation and overcoming reservations

↓

Closing the sale

↓

Follow-up

Trade shows, like the International Consumer Electronics Show in Las Vegas, are an excellent way to generate and qualify leads.
© Paul Sakuma/AP Photos

cold calls A method of prospecting in which salespeople telephone or go to see potential customers without appointments.

telemarketing A method of prospecting in which salespeople telephone potential customers.

products, including the first camcorder (1981), high-definition television (HDTV, 1998), and Internet protocol television (IP TV, 2005). At the 2014 CES conference more than 3,000 exhibitors showed off tens of thousands of new products.[18] In addition to providing an opportunity for retail buyers to see the latest products, the CES conference program features prominent speakers from the technology sector.[19]

Cold calls are a method of prospecting in which salespeople telephone or go to see potential customers without appointments.[20] **Telemarketing** is similar to a cold call, but it always occurs over the telephone. Sometimes professional telemarketing firms rather than the firm's salespeople make such calls. Adding Value 19.1 examines how colleges use it to boost attendance at sports events.

However, cold calls and telemarketing have become less popular over time, primarily because their success rate is

> **COLD CALLS AND TELEMARKETING HAVE BECOME LESS POPULAR OVER TIME, PRIMARILY BECAUSE THEIR SUCCESS RATE IS FAIRLY LOW.**

Adding Value 19.1

College Athletics Turn to the Pros for Sales Help[ii]

Not that long ago, a few billboards and word of mouth were enough to sell out tickets for a college game. Demand for tickets to college basketball and football games was so high that many schools added seats as fast as they could and still had to turn fans away. But a dip in the economy, increased demands on leisure time, rising gas prices, and better television technology have combined to diminish ticket sales, leaving colleges with empty seats and a diminishing revenue stream, even as they face other budget constraints. In response, some athletic programs are outsourcing ticket sales to commission-driven experts in the hopes of bringing fans back to the bleachers.

Ticket marketing companies catering to colleges use the model adopted by professional sports organizations: Sales staff work for commissions and make as many as 100 calls a day to students, alumni, faculty, and anyone else connected to the university. As these callers chat about the team, the school, or college athletics, they listen for clues to customers' personalities and needs, then adjust their sales strategy accordingly. The commission structure ensures the strong motivation of the sales force, which benefits the schools because every ticket sold promises

additional potential income in the form of concessions. Furthermore, filled stadiums significantly improve the public perception of the team, team spirit, and the likelihood of national publicity.

Some ticketing companies also provide related services to help generate revenue. Callers versed in the specifics of the college's athletics program might request donations for athletic scholarships or sport-related programming. Sport marketers with contacts in the world of professional athletics can help schools pull together appropriate fundraising events. They provide research and insights, coordinate print production for programs and signage, assist with challenging media situations, help build sales of apparel and merchandise, and even rent seat cushions for homecoming games. Sophisticated software programs link ticketing, fundraising, and marketing functions to help track interactions, increase ticket sales, and improve the college's brand.

Other athletic departments prefer to hire and manage their own ticket sales staff. This approach gives the school greater control over its brand. It also avoids privacy concerns about sharing university databases with an external seller, which may be too aggressive for the school's educational environment, or running afoul of complex NCAA rules. However, internal sales might not be as effective, considering the competing priorities that confront the athletic department, the limited experience of the sales staff, the prohibitions on commission-based incentives for university employees, and ineffective channels of communication.

fairly low. During cold calls, the salesperson is not able to establish the potential customer's specific needs because the receiver of the call is not expecting it and therefore may not be willing to participate in it. Accordingly, these methods can be very expensive. Second, both federal and state governments are regulating the activities of telemarketers. Federal rules prohibit telemarketing to consumers whose names appear on the national Do-Not-Call list, which is maintained by the Federal Trade Commission. Even for those consumers whose names are not on the list, the rules prohibit calling before 8:00 a.m. or after 9:00 p.m. (in the consumer's time zone) or after the consumer has told the telemarketer not to call. Federal rules also prohibit unsolicited fax messages, calls, or messages to cell phones.

After salespeople generate leads, they must qualify those leads by determining whether it is worthwhile to pursue them and attempt to turn them into customers. In B2B settings, the costs of preparing and making a presentation are so substantial that the seller must assess a lead's potential. Salespeople consider, for example, whether the potential customer's needs pertain to a product or a service. They should assess whether the lead has the financial resources to pay for the product or service.[21] Clients looking to sell multimillion-dollar properties want real estate agents to qualify potential buyers first. Therefore, the sales agents might create a password-protected website that features floor plans and inside views for the shopping convenience of interested buyers. But to obtain the password, the customer must be prequalified as someone who could actually afford to buy the property. Such qualifications save both the agent and the seller the trouble of showing properties to curious people who could never actually afford to buy.

In a retail setting, though, qualifying potential customers is both dangerous and potentially illegal. Retail salespeople should never judge a book by its cover and assume that a person in the store doesn't fit the store's image or cannot afford to purchase there. Such actions can quickly rise to the level of unethical and illegal discrimination, as recently alleged by several African American shoppers against such well-known retail names as Macy's and Barneys.[22] Although not illegal, imagine the frustration you might feel if you visit an upscale jewelry store to purchase an engagement ring, only to be snubbed because you are dressed in your everyday, casual school clothes.

Step 2: Preapproach and the Use of CRM Systems

The **preapproach** occurs prior to meeting the customer for the first time and extends the qualification of leads procedure described in Step 1. Although the salesperson has learned about the customer during the qualification stage, in this step he or she must conduct additional research and develop plans

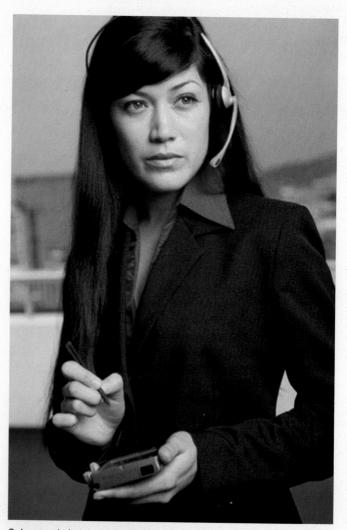

Salespeople input customer information into their tablets to develop a customer database for CRM systems.
© Alex Maloney/Zefa/Corbis RF

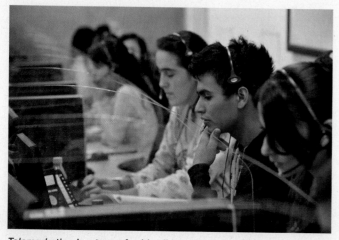

Telemarketing is a type of cold call in which salespeople generate or qualify leads on the telephone.
© Guillermo Legaria/Getty Images

for meeting with the customer. Suppose, for example, a management consulting firm wants to sell a bank a new system for finding checking account errors. The consulting firm's salesperson should first find out everything possible about the bank: How many checks does it process? What system is the bank using now? What are the benefits of the consultant's proposed system compared with the competition? The answers to these questions provide the basis for establishing value for the customer.

In the past, this customer information, if it was available at all, was typically included in a manual system that each individual salesperson kept, using a notebook or a series of cards. Today, salespeople often can access all this information immediately and conveniently from their firm's customer relationship management (CRM) system.

In most cases, these CRM systems have several components. There is a customer database or data warehouse. Whether the salesperson is working for a retail store or manages a selling team for an aerospace contractor, he or she can record transaction information, customer contact information, customer preferences, and market segment information about the customer. Once the data have been analyzed and CRM programs developed, salespeople can help implement the programs. Adding Value 19.2 describes the success of the most popular CRM system today, Salesforce.com.

Having done the additional research, the salesperson establishes goals for meeting with the customer. It is important that he or she knows ahead of time exactly what should be accomplished. For instance, the consulting firm's salesperson cannot expect to get a purchase commitment from the bank after just the first visit. But a demonstration of the system and a short presentation about how the system would benefit the customer would be appropriate. It is often a good idea to practice the presentation prior to the meeting, using a technique known as **role playing**, in which the salesperson acts out a simulated buying situation while a colleague or manager acts as the buyer. Afterward, the practice sales presentation can be critiqued and adjustments can be made.

> **role playing** A good technique for practicing the sales presentation prior to meeting with a customer; the salesperson acts out a simulated buying situation while a colleague or manager acts as the buyer.

Adding Value
19.2
Selling in the Cloud: The Growth and Success of Salesforce.com[iii]

At one time, CRM systems were the exclusive domain of wealthy companies. With costs running into hundreds of thousands of dollars, CRM systems represented a massive investment in both money and the time required to establish them. Each system needed its own servers and support from vendors to ensure its maintenance and consistent functioning.

This scenario clearly represented an opportunity for a company that could offer easier, less expensive, leaner services. Enter Salesforce.com. Instead of complete, onsite CRM solutions, it promised to host all computing and data storage on its own servers, in the cloud. Clients did not need to find massive funds to purchase the system, because Salesforce.com initiated the first CRM-related software-as-a-service (SaaS) model. That is, client firms did not buy any software but instead paid Salesforce.com a subscription fee that varied according to the number of licenses they needed. Each user license cost approximately $65 a month, representing a substantial cost savings compared with full CRM systems. Moreover, because the software was in the cloud, salespeople could access their customer data anywhere, through their smartphones or tablets, rather than having to return to the office to link into an in-house system.

And Salesforce.com didn't stop there. To build the most comprehensive service possible, the company created an entire section on its website that enabled clients to build and trade apps that would integrate with and extend the functionality of its system. To add value to its platform, it also has acquired dozens of firms that have developed innovative CRM technology. In recognition of its innovative, aggressive efforts, *Forbes* named Salesforce.com as one of the most innovative companies in practice today.

The move to a SaaS, cloud-based CRM model in turn opened doors for vast segments of companies that never would have been able to purchase a full system. For several years, Salesforce.com thus has enjoyed a leading position in the CRM service market in terms of total revenue, revenue growth, and market share growth, including revenues that surpassed $20 billion and a 13.7 percent adjusted gross revenue. As Salesforce.com's president and vice chair Keith Block asserts, "Salesforce.com's CRM market share leadership is a reflection of the consistent innovation we deliver to our customers."

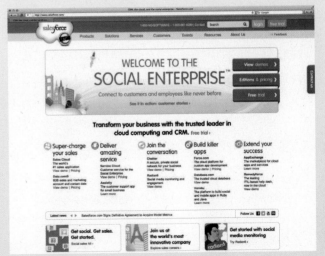

Salesforce.com offers its clients CRM solutions at a price most businesses can afford.

© Studio 101/Alamy

Step 3: Sales Presentation and Overcoming Reservations

The Presentation Once all the background information has been obtained and the objectives for the meeting are set, the salesperson is ready for a person-to-person meeting. Let's continue with our bank example. During the first part of the meeting, the salesperson needs to get to know the customer, get his or her attention, and create interest in the presentation to follow. The beginning of the presentation may be the most important part of the entire selling process, because it is when the salesperson establishes exactly where the customer is in his or her

▼ **EXHIBIT 19.2** Aligning the Personal Selling Process with the B2B Buying Process

buying process (Exhibit 19.2). (For a refresher on the B2B buying process, see Chapter 7.)

Suppose, for instance, that the bank is in the first stage of the buying process: need recognition. It would not be prudent for the salesperson to discuss the pros and cons of different potential suppliers, because doing so would assume that the customer already had reached Step 4 (of the B2B buying process), proposal analysis and customer selection. By asking a series of questions though, the salesperson can assess the bank's need for the product or service and adapt or customize the presentation to match the customer's need and stage in the decision process.[23]

Asking questions is only half the battle; carefully listening to the answers is equally important. Some salespeople, particularly inexperienced ones, believe that to be in control, they must do all the talking. Yet it is impossible to really understand where the customer stands without listening carefully. What if the chief operating officer (COO) says, "It seems kind of expensive"? If the salesperson isn't listening carefully, he or she won't pick up on the subtle nuances of what the customer is really thinking. In this case, it probably means the COO doesn't see the value in the offering.

When the salesperson has gotten a good feel for where the customer stands, he or she can apply that knowledge to help the customer solve its problem or satisfy its need. The salesperson might begin by explaining the features or characteristics of the system that will reduce checking account errors. It may not be obvious, solely on the basis of these features, that the system adds value beyond the bank's current practices. Using the answers to some of the questions the salesperson posed earlier in the meeting, he or she can clarify the product's advantages over current or past practices, as well as the overall benefits of adopting the new system. The salesperson might explain, for instance, that the bank can expect a 20 percent improvement in checking account errors and

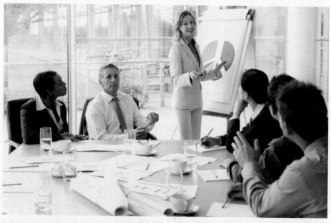

It is important to ask questions at the beginning of a sales presentation to establish where the customer is in his or her buying process.
© Chris Ryan/OJO Images/AGE Fotostock RF

closing the sale
Obtaining a commitment
from the customer to make
a purchase.

that, because of the size of the bank and number of checks it processes per year, this improvement would represent $2 million in annual savings. Because the system costs $150,000 per year and will take only three weeks to integrate into the current system, it will add significant and almost immediate value.

As this hypothetical example hints, personal selling often relies on an old-fashioned skill: storytelling. Even if they use advanced technologies and Internet-based communication media, salespeople must communicate their messages and sales pitches in ways that resonate with their audience of potential customers. As research in neuroscience continues to affirm, virtually everyone uses at least some level of emotional reaction in determining their choices. To appeal to customers, salespeople thus need to tell a story that engages people's imaginations.[24]

Handling Reservations An integral part of the sales presentation is handling reservations or objections that the buyer might have about the product or service. Although reservations can arise during each stage of the selling process, they are very likely to occur during the sales presentation. Customers may raise reservations pertaining to a variety of issues, but they usually relate in some way to value, such as that the price is too high for the level of quality or service.

Good salespeople know the types of reservations buyers are likely to raise. They may know, for instance, that their service is slower than competitors' or that their selection is limited. Although not all reservations can be forestalled, effective salespeople can anticipate and handle some. For example, when the bank COO said the check service seemed expensive, the salesperson was ready with information about how quickly the investment would be recouped.

As in other aspects of the selling process, the best way to handle reservations is to relax and listen, then ask questions to clarify any reservations.[25] For example, the salesperson could respond to the COO's reservation by asking, "How much do you think the bank is losing through checking account errors?" Her answer might open up a conversation about the positive trends in a cost–benefit analysis. Such questions are usually more effective than trying to prove the customer's reservation is not valid, because the latter approach implies the salesperson isn't really listening and could lead to an argument—the last thing a customer usually wants.

Step 4: Closing the Sale

Closing the sale means obtaining a commitment from the customer to make a purchase. Without a successful close, the salesperson goes away emptyhanded, so many salespeople find this part of the sales process very stressful. Although losing a sale is never pleasant, salespeople who are involved in a relationship with their customers must view any specific sales presentation as part of the progression toward ultimately making the sale or building the relationship. An unsuccessful close on one day may just be a means of laying the groundwork for a successful close during the next meeting.

Although we have presented the selling process as a series of steps, closing the sale rarely follows so neatly. However, good salespeople listen carefully to what potential customers say and pay attention to their body language. By reading these signals, they can achieve an earlier close. Suppose that our hypothetical bank, instead of being in the first step of the buying process, were in the final step of negotiation and selection. An astute salesperson would pick up on these signals and ask for the sale.

Step 5: Follow-Up

> "It ain't over till it's over."
> —Yogi Berra[26]

A postsale follow-up letter, call, or e-mail is the first step in initiating a new order and sustaining the relationship.
© Susan Van Etten/PhotoEdit

With relationship selling, it is never really over, even after the sale is closed. The attitudes customers develop after the sale become the basis for how they purchase in the future. The follow-up therefore offers a prime opportunity for a salesperson to solidify the customer relationship through great service quality. Let's

> " CUSTOMERS MAY RAISE RESERVATIONS PERTAINING TO A VARIETY OF ISSUES, BUT THEY USUALLY RELATE IN SOME WAY TO VALUE, SUCH AS THAT THE PRICE IS TOO HIGH FOR THE LEVEL OF QUALITY OR SERVICE. "

apply the five service quality dimensions we discussed in Chapter 13 to understand the follow-up:[27]

- **Reliability.** The salesperson and the supporting organization must deliver the right product or service on time.

- **Responsiveness.** The salesperson and support group must be ready to deal quickly with any issue, question, or problem that may arise.

- **Assurance.** Customers must be assured through adequate guarantees that their purchase will perform as expected.

- **Empathy.** The salesperson and support group must have a good understanding of the problems and issues faced by their customers. Otherwise, they cannot give them what they want.

- **Tangibles.** Because tangibles reflect the physical characteristics of the seller's business, such as its website, marketing communications, and delivery materials, their influence is subtler than that of the other four service quality dimensions. That doesn't mean it is any less important. Retail customers are generally more pleased with a purchase if it is carefully wrapped in nice paper instead of being haphazardly thrown into a crumpled plastic bag. The tangibles offer a signal that the product is of high quality, even though the packaging has nothing to do with the product's actual performance.

When customers' expectations are not met, they often complain—about deliveries, the billing amount or process, the product's performance, or after-sale services such as installation or training (recall the Gaps Model from Chapter 13). Effectively handling complaints is critical to the future of the relationship. As we noted in Chapter 13, the best way to handle complaints is to listen to the customer, provide a fair solution to the problem, and resolve the problem quickly.

The best way to nip a postsale problem in the bud is to check with the customer right after he or she takes possession of the product or immediately after the service has been completed. This speed demonstrates responsiveness and empathy. It also shows the customer that the salesperson and the firm care about customer satisfaction. Finally, a postsale follow-up call, e-mail, or letter takes the salesperson back to the first step in the sales process for initiating a new order and sustaining the relationship.

 check yourself

1. Why is personal selling important to an IMC strategy?
2. What are the steps in the personal selling process?

LO 19-3 Describe the key functions involved in managing a sales force.

MANAGING THE SALES FORCE

Like any business activity involving people, the sales force requires management. **Sales management** involves the planning, direction, and control of personal selling activities, including recruiting, selecting, training, motivating, compensating, and evaluating, as they apply to the sales force.

Managing a sales force is a rewarding yet complicated undertaking. In this section, we examine how sales forces can be structured, some of the most important issues in recruiting and selecting salespeople, sales training issues, ways to compensate salespeople, and finally how to supervise and evaluate salespeople.

Sales Force Structure

Imagine the daunting task of putting together a sales force from scratch. Will you hire your own salespeople, or should they be manufacturer's representatives? What will each salesperson's primary duties be: order takers, order getters, sales support? Finally, will they work together in teams? In this section, we examine each of these issues.

Company Sales Force or Manufacturer's Representative A **company sales force** comprises people who are employees of the selling company. **Independent agents**, also known as **manufacturer's representatives**, or **reps**, are salespeople who sell a manufacturer's products on an extended contract basis but are not employees of the

> "Retail customers are generally more pleased with a purchase if it is carefully wrapped in nice paper instead of being haphazardly thrown into a crumpled plastic bag."

manufacturer. They are compensated by commissions and do not take ownership or physical possession of the merchandise.

Manufacturer's representatives are useful for smaller firms or firms expanding into new markets, because such companies can achieve instant and extensive sales coverage without having to pay full-time personnel. Good sales representatives have many established contacts and can sell multiple products from noncompeting manufacturers during the same sales call. Also, the use of manufacturer's reps facilitates flexibility; it is much easier to replace a rep than an employee and much easier to expand or contract coverage in a market with a sales rep than with a company sales force.

Company sales forces are more typically used for established product lines. Because the salespeople are company employees, the manufacturer has more control over what they do. If, for example, the manufacturer's strategy is to provide extensive customer service, the sales manager can specify exactly what actions a company sales force must take. In contrast, because manufacturer's reps are paid on a commission basis, it is difficult to persuade them to take any action that doesn't directly lead to sales.

Salesperson Duties
Although the life of a professional salesperson is highly varied, salespeople generally play three important roles: order getting, order taking, and sales support.

Order Getting An **order getter** is a salesperson whose primary responsibilities are identifying potential customers and engaging those customers in discussions to attempt to make a sale. An order getter is also responsible for following up to ensure that the customer is satisfied and to build the relationship. In B2B settings, order getters are primarily involved in new buy and modified rebuy situations (see Chapter 7). As a result, they require extensive sales and product knowledge training. The Coca-Cola salesperson who goes to Safeway's headquarters to sell a special promotion of Vanilla Coke is an order getter.

Order Taking An **order taker** is a salesperson whose primary responsibility is to process routine orders, reorders, or rebuys for products. Colgate employs order takers around the globe who go into stores and distribution centers that already carry Colgate products to check inventory, set up displays, write new orders, and make sure everything is going smoothly.

Sales Support **Sales support personnel** enhance and help with the overall selling effort. For example, if a Best Buy customer begins to experience computer problems, the company has a Geek Squad door-to-door service as well as support in the store. Those employees who respond to the customer's technical

order getter A salesperson whose primary responsibilities are identifying potential customers and engaging those customers in discussions to attempt to make a sale.

order taker A salesperson whose primary responsibility is to process routine orders or reorders or rebuys for products.

sales support personnel Employees who enhance and help with a firm's overall selling effort, such as by responding to the customer's technical questions or facilitating repairs.

selling teams Combinations of sales specialists whose primary duties are order getting, order taking, or sales support but who work together to service important accounts.

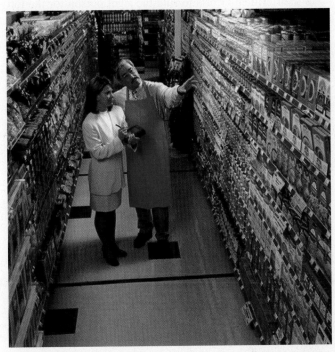

Order takers process routine orders, reorders, or rebuys for products.
© Mark Tuschman Photography

questions and repair the computer serve to support the overall sales process.

Combination Duties Although some salespeople's primary function may be order getting, order taking, or sales support, others fill a combination of roles. For instance, a computer salesperson at Staples may spend an hour with a customer educating him or her about the pros and cons of various systems and then make the sale. The next customer might simply need a specific printer cartridge. A third customer might bring in a computer and seek advice about an operating system problem. The salesperson was first an order getter, next an order taker, and finally a sales support person.

Some firms use **selling teams** that combine sales specialists whose primary duties are order getting, order taking, or sales support but who work together to service important accounts. As companies become larger and products more complicated, it is nearly impossible for one person to perform all the necessary sales functions.

Recruiting and Selecting Salespeople
When the firm has determined how the sales force will be structured, it must find and hire salespeople. Although superficially

this task may sound as easy as posting the job opening on the Internet or running an ad in a newspaper, it must be performed carefully, because firms don't want to hire the wrong person. Salespeople are very expensive to train. Among other creative hiring tactics, Zappo's famously considers finding the right people so important that it will pay them to leave after a few weeks if they are not a good fit.[28]

In their critical efforts to find the right person for the job though, companies must take care to avoid biased practices, such that they would hire on the basis of stereotypes instead of qualifications. For most people, the picture of someone selling Avon products likely involves a middle-aged woman, namely, the "Avon Lady." But sales revenues for these products continue to provide salespeople a successful living, prompting plenty of women and men to try their hand at selling Avon.[29] Hiring based on misplaced assumptions about gender or other categories can be damaging to the company, as well as discriminatory.

The most important activity in the recruiting process is to determine exactly what the salesperson will be doing and what

- *Optimism.* Good salespeople tend to look at the bright side of things. Optimism also may help them be resilient—the third trait.

- *Resilience.* Good salespeople don't easily take no for an answer. They keep coming back until they get a yes.

- *Self-motivation.* As we have already mentioned, salespeople have lots of freedom to spend their days the way they believe will be most productive. But if the salespeople are not self-motivated to get the job done, it probably won't get done.

- *Empathy.* Empathy is one of the five dimensions of service quality discussed previously in this chapter and in Chapter 13. Good salespeople must care about their customers, their issues, and their problems.

Sales Training

Even people who possess all these personal traits need training. All salespeople benefit from training about selling and negotiation techniques, product and service knowledge, technologies

HIRING BASED ON MISPLACED ASSUMPTIONS ABOUT GENDER OR OTHER CATEGORIES CAN BE DAMAGING TO THE COMPANY, AS WELL AS DISCRIMINATORY.

personal traits and abilities a person should have to do the job well. For instance, the Coca-Cola order getter who goes to Safeway to pitch a new product will typically need significant sales experience, coupled with great communication and analytical skills. Coke's order takers need to be reliable and able to get along with lots of different types of people in the stores, from managers to customers.

Many firms give candidates personality tests, but they stress different personality attributes, depending on the requisite traits for the position and the personality characteristics of their most successful salespeople.[30] For instance, impatience is often a positive characteristic for sales because it creates a sense of urgency to close the sale. But for very large, complicated sales targeting large institutions, like the bank in our previous example, an impatient salesperson may irritate the decision makers and kill the deal.

When recruiting salespeople, it helps to possess certain personal traits. What are those personal traits? Managers and sales experts generally agree on the following:[31]

- *Personality.* Good salespeople are friendly, sociable, and, in general, like being around people. Customers won't buy from someone they don't like.

used in the selling process, time and territory management, and company policies and procedures.

Firms use varied delivery methods to train their salespeople, depending on the topic of the training, what type of salesperson is being trained, and the cost versus the value of the training. For instance, an on-the-job training program is excellent for communicating selling and negotiation skills, because managers can observe the sales trainees in real selling situations and provide instant feedback. They can also engage in role-playing exercises in which the salesperson acts out a simulated buying situation and the manager critiques the salesperson's performance.

A much less expensive, but for some purposes equally valuable, training method is the Internet. Online training programs have revolutionized the way training happens in many firms. Firms can provide new product and service knowledge, spread the word about changes in company policies and procedures, and share selling tips in a user-friendly environment that salespeople can access anytime and anywhere. Distance learning sales training programs through teleconferencing enable a group of salespeople to participate with their instructor or manager in a virtual classroom. And testing can occur online as

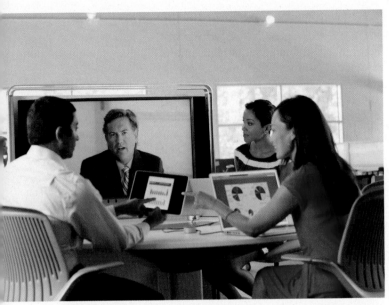

Technology has changed the lives of salespeople and the delivery methods of sales training. Companies can conduct distance learning and training through videoconferencing.
© Blend Images/Ariel Skelley/Getty Images RF

well. Online sales training may never replace the one-on-one interaction of on-the-job training for advanced selling skills, but it is quite effective and efficient for many other aspects of the sales training task.[32]

Motivating and Compensating Salespeople

An important goal for any effective sales manager is to get to know his or her salespeople and determine what motivates them to be effective. Some salespeople prize their freedom and like to be left alone; others want attention and are more productive when they receive accolades for a job well done. Still others are motivated primarily by monetary compensation. Great sales managers determine how best to motivate each of their salespeople according to what is most important to each individual. Although sales managers can emphasize different motivating factors, except in the smallest companies, the methods used to compensate salespeople must be fairly standardized and can be divided into two categories: financial and nonfinancial.

Financial Rewards Salespeople's compensation usually has several components. Most salespeople receive at least part of their compensation as a **salary**, a fixed sum of money paid at regular intervals. Another common financial incentive is a **commission**, which is money paid as a percentage of the sales volume or profitability. A **bonus** is a payment made at management's discretion when the salesperson attains certain goals. Bonuses usually are given only periodically, such as at the end of the year. A **sales contest** is a short-term incentive designed to elicit a specific response from the sales force. Prizes might be cash or other types of financial incentives. For instance, Volkswagen may give a free trip to Germany for the salesperson who sells the most Touaregs.

The bulk of any compensation package is made up of salary, commission, or a combination of the two. The advantage of a salary plan is that salespeople know exactly what they will be paid, and sales managers have more control. Salaried salespeople can be directed to spend a certain percentage of their time handling customer service issues. Under a commission system, however, salespeople have only one objective—make the sale! Thus, a commission system provides the most incentive for the sales force to sell.

salary Compensation in the form of a fixed sum of money paid at regular intervals.

commission Compensation or financial incentive for salespeople based on a fixed percentage of their sales.

bonus A payment made at management's discretion when the salesperson attains certain goals; usually given only periodically, such as at the end of the year.

sales contest A short-term incentive designed to elicit a specific response from the sales force.

Volkswagen may give a free trip to Germany for the salesperson who sells the most Touaregs.
© STOCK4B-RF/Getty Images

Mary Kay gives high-performing salespeople an award that has both high symbolic value and material value—a pink Cadillac.
Courtesy Mary Kay, Inc.

Evaluating Salespeople by Using Marketing Metrics

Salespeople's evaluation process must be tied to their reward structure. If salespeople do well, they should receive their rewards in the same way that if you do well on your exams and assignments in a class, you should earn a good grade. However, salespeople should be evaluated and rewarded for only those activities and outcomes that fall under their control. If Macy's makes a unilateral decision to put Diesel jeans in all its stores after a negotiation with Diesel's corporate headquarters in Italy, the Diesel sales representatives responsible for individual Macy's stores should not receive credit for making the sale, nor should they get all the windfall commission that would ensue from the added sales.

Considering this guiding principle—evaluate and reward salespeople for what they do and not for what they don't do—how should sales managers evaluate salespeople? The answer is never easy because measures must be tied to performance, and there are many ways to measure performance in a complex job such as selling. For example, evaluating performance on the basis of monthly sales alone fails to consider how profitable the sales were, whether any progress was made to build new business that will be realized sometime in the future, or the level of customer service the salesperson provided. Because the sales job is multifaceted with many contributing success factors, sales managers should use multiple measures.[35]

In business practice, salesperson evaluation measures can be objective or subjective. Sales, profits, and the number of orders represent examples of objective measures. Although each is somewhat useful to managers, such measures do not provide an adequate perspective for a thorough evaluation, because there is no means of comparison with other salespeople. For instance,

Nonfinancial Rewards

As we have noted, good salespeople are self-motivated. They want to do a good job and make the sale because it makes them feel good. But this good feeling also can be accentuated by recognition from peers and management. For instance, the internal monthly magazine at the cosmetics firm Mary Kay provides an outlet for not only selling advice but also companywide recognition of individual salespeople's accomplishments.[33]

Nonfinancial rewards should have high symbolic value, as plaques, pens, or rings do. Free trips or days off are also effective rewards. More important than what the reward is, however,

> ## "If salespeople do well, they should receive their rewards in the same way that if you do well on your exams and assignments in a class, you should earn a good grade."

is the way it is operationalized. For instance, an award should be given at a sales meeting and publicized in the company newsletter. It should also be done in good taste, because if the award is perceived as tacky, no one will take it seriously.[34] Mary Kay recognizes salespeople's success with unusually large rewards that have both high symbolic and high material value. More than 100,000 independent beauty consultants and sales directors have earned the use of one of the famous pink Cadillacs, but it is also possible to gain rewards and recognition such as a set of faux pearl earrings within the first week of becoming a consultant.

suppose salesperson A generated $1 million last year, but salesperson B generated $1.5 million. Should salesperson B automatically receive a significantly higher evaluation? Now consider that salesperson B's territory has twice as much potential as salesperson A's. Knowing this, we might suppose that salesperson A has actually done a better job. For this reason, firms use ratios such as profit per customer, orders per call, sales per hour, or expenses compared to sales as their objective measures.

Whereas objective measures are quantitative, subjective measures seek to assess salespeople's behavior: what they do

> SOMETIMES SALESPEOPLE FACE A CONFLICT BETWEEN WHAT THEY BELIEVE REPRESENTS ETHICAL SELLING AND WHAT THEIR COMPANY ASKS THEM TO DO TO MAKE A SALE.

and how well they do it. By their very nature, subjective measures reflect one person's opinion about another's performance. Thus, subjective evaluations can be biased and should be used cautiously and only in conjunction with multiple objective measures.

 check yourself

1. What do sales managers need to do to manage their sales force successfully?
2. What is the difference between monetary and nonmonetary incentives?

LO 19-4 Describe the ethical and legal issues in personal selling.

ETHICAL AND LEGAL ISSUES IN PERSONAL SELLING

Although ethical and legal issues permeate all aspects of marketing, they are particularly important for personal selling. Unlike advertising and other communications with customers, which are planned and executed on a corporate level, personal selling involves a one-to-one, and often face-to-face, encounter with the customer. Therefore, sellers' actions are not only highly visible to customers but also to other stakeholders, such as the communities in which they work.

Ethical and legal issues arise in three main areas. First, there is the relationship between the sales manager and the sales force. Second, in some situations, an inconsistency might exist between corporate policy and the salesperson's ethical comfort zone. Third, both ethical and legal issues can arise when the salesperson interacts with the customer, especially if that salesperson or the selling firm collects significant information about the customer. To maintain trustworthy customer relationships, companies must take care that they respect customer privacy and respect the information comfort zone—that is, the amount of information a customer feels comfortable providing.[36]

The Sales Manager and the Sales Force

Like any manager, a sales manager must treat people fairly and equally in everything he or she does. With regard to the sales force, this fairness must include hiring, promotion, supervision, training, assigning duties and quotas, compensation and incentives, and firing.[37] Federal laws cover many of these issues. For instance, equal employment opportunity laws make it unlawful to discriminate against a person in hiring, promotion, or firing because of race, religion, nationality, sex, or age.

The Sales Force and Corporate Policy

Sometimes salespeople face a conflict between what they believe represents ethical selling and what their company asks them to do to make a sale. Suppose an insurance agent whose compensation is based on commission sells a homeowner's policy to a family that has just moved to New Orleans, an area prone to flooding as a result of hurricanes. Even though the policy covers hurricane damage, it does not cover water damage from hurricanes. If the salesperson discloses the inadequate coverage, the sale might be lost because additional flood insurance is very expensive. What should the salesperson do? Salespeople must live within their own ethical comfort zone. If this or any other situation is morally

Salespeople must live within their own ethical comfort zone. Should insurance salespeople disclose inadequate hurricane coverage and risk not making the sale?
© Charlie Riedel/AP Photo

ethical&societal dilemma

When Realtors Become Reality Stars[iv]

Reality television has spread to nearly every facet of life, and real estate is no exception. On shows such as *Million Dollar Listing, House Hunters, Property Virgins, Selling New York,* and *Designed to Sell,* viewers can watch as homeowners try to sell their properties and potential buyers search for their perfect home. Helping them every step of the way are real estate professionals, some of whom have gained notoriety as reality television stars themselves.

The *Million Dollar Listing* series, with versions in New York and Los Angeles, has made household names out of agents such as Ryan Serhant and Josh Altman. The handsome young realtors not only broker massive real estate deals but also share stories about their personal lives and even allow cameras to catch them in the shower, in at least one memorable episode. As Altman recognized, "Nobody wants to see the guy who just sells houses every week. They want to see that drama between the realtors." As a result, some of the featured realtors have developed such

an extensive fan base that they have hired publicists, managers, and drivers, as well as assistants whose sole job is to respond to contacts from fans.

The depictions of real estate transactions clearly make for great television. Consumers enjoy the voyeuristic glimpse into other people's financial affairs and living conditions, especially when those conditions include multimillion-dollar homes. The *Million Dollar Listing* episodes each average around 1.25 million viewers, leading networks such as Bravo and HGTV to keep adding new versions and twists to their lineups of real estate reality television shows.

But according to some observers, the shows create a destructive and potentially dangerous impression of what real estate transactions involve and what the responsibilities of professional realtors are. The agents often are presented in a less than flattering light, which could be damaging for their reputation. For example, one cast member on *The Real Housewives of Orange County* who was a real estate agent left the show mainly because she believed that participating in bickering and being subjected to wine thrown on her ultimately would be too professionally embarrassing to be healthy for her business.

Agencies that prohibit their brokers from appearing on such shows also note that discretion and clients' privacy are central goals for realtors—aspects that rarely are prioritized on reality television. Furthermore, if the agent becomes the star, the broker might come to overshadow the agency's brand as well as the sale itself.

The shows also present a condensed, highly edited version of the real estate process, naturally. Sales of big properties (and even smaller ones) take months to complete, and much of the activity involves paperwork, e-mailing, and research. None of these elements are particularly compelling in video, so the shows tend to exclude them and focus more on loud negotiations, flashy open houses, or snarky interactions.

Yet for many of the star realtors, these potentially negative effects fade away in the face of the massive marketing bump they receive from their notoriety. Bravo asserts that every broker who has appeared on one of its shows has enjoyed increased business through the association. The well-known agents agree: One indicated that his business had jumped by 20 percent, and another noted that he moved from selling midrange condos to dealing in luxury estates, which earned him $200 million in commissions in a single recent year.

---

repugnant to the salesperson, he or she must question the choice to be associated with such a company.[38]

Salespeople also can be held accountable for illegal actions sanctioned by the employer. If the homeowner asks if the home is above the floodplain or whether water damage from flooding is covered by the policy, and it is company policy to intentionally mislead potential customers, both the salesperson and the insurance dealership could be susceptible to legal action.

The Salesperson and the Customer

As the frontline emissaries for a firm, salespeople have a duty to be ethically and legally correct in all their dealings with their customers. Not only is it the right thing to do, it simply means good business. Long-term relationships can deteriorate quickly if customers believe that they have not been treated in an ethically proper manner. Unfortunately, salespeople

sometimes get mixed signals from their managers or simply do not know when their behaviors might be considered unethical or illegal. Formal guidelines can help, but it is also important to integrate these guidelines into training programs in which salespeople can discuss various issues that arise in the field with their peers and managers.[39] Most important, however, is for sales managers to lead by example. If managers are known to cut ethical corners in their dealings with customers, it shouldn't surprise them when their salespeople do the same. Ethical and Societal Dilemma 19.1 considers the ethical issues that realtors face. ■

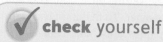

check yourself

1. What are three areas of personal selling in which ethical and legal issues are more likely to arise?

Increase your engagement and learning with Connect Marketing.

These Connect activities, available only through your Connect course, have been designed to make the following concepts more meaningful and applicable:

▶ The Personal Selling Process Timeline Activity

▶ Textbook Selling and Technology: Case Analysis

▶ Personal Selling: GPI Video Case

▶ Personal Selling: Sweetwater Video Case

ⅠSMARTBOOK™ **ⅠiSeeit!**

endnotes

CHAPTER 1

1. Stephanie Strom, "Starbucks Plans to Move Beyond Beans," *The New York Times*, October 8, 2013.

2. Starbucks, "Starbucks Company Profile," http://globalassets .starbucks.com/assets/4286be0614af48b6bf2e17ffcede5ab7 .pdf.

3. Alvin Chang and Matt Carroll, "Split Country: Dunkin' vs. Starbucks," *Boston Globe/Boston.com* (n.d.).

4. Alexandra Wolfe, "Howard Schultz: What Next, Starbucks?," *The Wall Street Journal*, September 27, 2013; Susan Berfield, "Starbucks Starts Throwing a Very Big Tea Party," *Bloomberg Businessweek*, October 25, 2013.

5. Stephanie Strom, "Want a Yogurt with That Vente Latte? Starbucks and Danone to Join Forces," *The New York Times*, July 23, 2013.

6. The American Marketing Association, http://www.marketingpower .com. We added the word in italics. Discussions of the latest revision of the AMA's marketing definition are widespread. See Gregory T. Gundlach and William L. Wilkie, "AMA's New Definition of Marketing: Perspective and Commentary on the 2007 Revision," *Journal of Public Policy & Marketing* 28, no. 2 (2008), pp. 259–64; see also the fall 2007 issue of the *Journal of Public Policy & Marketing* 26, no. 2, which contains eight different perspectives on the new definition.

7. Mike Esterl, "Coke Tailors Its Soda Sizes," *The Wall Street Journal*, September 19, 2011, http://online.wsj.com; Natalie Zmuda, "Diet Coke Blasts Past Pepsi," *Advertising Age*, March 17, 2011, http://adage.com; Natalie Zmuda, "Can Pepsi's Big Marketing Shake-Up Bring Back Fizz to Its Beverage Brands?," *Advertising Age*, June 20, 2011.

8. http://www.lexus.com.

9. The idea of the four Ps was conceptualized by E. Jerome McCarthy, *Basic Marketing: A Managerial Approach* (Homewood, IL: Richard D. Irwin, 1960).

10. Raphael Thomadsen, "Seeking an Expanding Competitor: How Product Line Expansion Can Increase All Firms' Profits," *Journal of Marketing Research* 49 (June 2012), pp. 349–60.

11. Wolfgang Ulaga and Werner Reinartz, "Hybrid Offerings: How Manufacturing Firms Combine Goods and Services Successfully," *Journal of Marketing* 75 (November 2011), pp. 5–23.

12. Anja Lambrecht and Catherine Tucker, "Paying with Money or Effort: Pricing When Customers Anticipate Hassle," *Journal of Marketing Research* 49 (February 2012), pp. 66–82.

13. Stuart Elliot, "A New Coronation for the King of Elephants," *The New York Times*, November 13, 2012.

14. Personal communication, Trang Connelly, TJX Companies, Inc., September 2013.

15. Peter C. Verhoef et al., "A Cross-National Investigation into the Marketing Department's Influence within the Firm: Toward Initial Empirical Generalizations," *Journal of International Marketing* 19 (September 2011), pp. 59–86.

16. George S. Day, "Aligning the Organization with the Market," *Marketing Science Institute* 5, no. 3 (2005), pp. 3–20.

17. Kimmy Wa Chan, Chi Kin (Bennett) Yim, and Simon S. K. Lam, "Is Customer Participation in Value Creation a Double-Edged Sword? Evidence from Professional Financial Services across Cultures," *Journal of Marketing* 74, no. 3 (May 2010); Dhruv Grewal, Kent B. Monroe, and R. Krishnan, "The Effects of Price Comparison Advertising on Buyers' Perceptions of Acquisition Value and Transaction Value," *Journal of Marketing* 62 (April 1998), pp. 46–60.

18. Anne L. Roggeveen, Michael Tsiros, and Dhruv Grewal, "Understanding the Co-Creation Effect: When Does Collaborating with Customers Provide a Lift to Service Recovery?," *Journal of the Academy of Marketing Science* 40, no. 6 (2012), pp. 771–90; Sigurd Troye and Magne Supphellen, "Consumer Participation in Coproduction: 'I Made It Myself' Effects on Consumers' Sensory Perceptions and Evaluations of Outcome and Input Product," *Journal of Marketing* 76 (March 2012), pp. 33–46.

19. Anita Luo and V. Kumar, "Recovering Hidden Buyer-Seller Relationship States to Measure the Return on Marketing Investment in Business-to-Business Markets," *Journal of Marketing Research* 50, no. 1 (2013), pp. 143–60; V. Kumar and Denish Shah, "Can Marketing Lift Stock Prices?," *Sloan Management Review* 52, no. 4 (2011), pp. 24–26; V. Kumar et al., "Is Market Orientation a Source of Sustainable Competitive Advantage or Simply the Cost of Competing?," *Journal of Marketing* 75 (January 2011), pp. 16–30; Stephen A. Samaha, Robert W. Palmatier, and Rajiv P. Dant, "Poisoning Relationships: Perceived Unfairness in Channels of Distribution," *Journal of Marketing* 75 (May 2011), pp. 99–117.

20. Luo and Kumar, "Recovering Hidden Buyer-Seller Relationship States"; V. Kumar, Denish Shah, and Rajkumar Venkatesan, "Managing Retailer Profitability—One Customer at a Time!," *Journal of Retailing* 82, no. 4 (2006), pp. 277–94.

21. Belle Beth Cooper, "10 Surprising Social Media Statistics That Will Make You Rethink Your Social Strategy," *Fast Company*, http://www.fastcompany.com.

22. Harsh Ajmera, "Social Media Facts, Figures, and Statistics 2013," *Digital Insights*, http://blog.digitalinsights.in.

23. http://thenextweb.com.

24. "World Internet Penetration Rates," *Internet World Stats*, http:// www.internetworldstats.com.

25. U.S. Travel Association, "Travel Facts and Statistics," http://www .ustravel.org.

26. "5 Apps for Searching Nearby Restaurants," *The RecApp*, April 23, 2012, http://www.therecapp.com.

27. Ibid.

i. Andrew Adam Newman, "Snacks for Soccer Stars, and Their Fans," *The New York Times*, October 8, 2013; Warc, "Mondelez in Twitter Tie-Up," *Warc.com*, September 13, 2013, http://www .warc.com; Angela Watercutter, "How Oreo Won the Marketing Super Bowl with a Timely Blackout Ad on Twitter," *Wired*, February 4, 2013, http://www.wired.com.

ii. Alvaris Falcon, "20 Gadgets That Make Your Smartphone Even Smarter," *Hongkiat.com*, http://www.hongkiat.com/; David Pogue, "2 Wristbands Keep Tabs on Fitness," *The New York Times*, November 14, 2012, http://www.nytimes.com; Clare Cain Miller, "New Apps Arrive on Google Glass," *The New York Times*, May 16, 2013, http://bits.blogs.nytimes.com; Daniel J. Simons and Christopher F. Chabris, "Is Google Glass Dangerous?," *The New York Times*, May 24, 2013, http://www.nytimes.com.

iii. Barbara Thau, "How Big Data Helps Chains Like Starbucks Pick Store Locations—An (Unsung) Key to Retail Success," *Forbes*, April 24, 2014, http://www.forbes.com; Malcolm Wheatley, "Data-Driven Location Choices Drive Latest Starbucks Surge," *Data Informed*, January 10, 2013, http://data-informed.com/data-driven-location-choices-drive-latest-starbucks-surge/.

iv. Matthew Panzarino, "The Open Secret of iBeacon: Apple Could Have 250M Potential Units in the Wild by 2014," *TechCrunch*, December 7, 2013, http://techcrunch.com; Zach Miners, "Apple Tracks Shoppers in Iits Stores with Nationwide iBeacon Rollout," *InfoWorld*, December 9, 2013, http://www.infoworld.com.

CHAPTER 2

1. "About Nike Inc.," http://www.nike.com/us/en_us/.

2. Kurt Badenhausen, "LeBron James Leads the NBA's Endorsement All-Stars 2015," *Forbes*, February 13, 2015, http://www.forbes.com.

3. "Nike+ iPod," http://www.apple.com.

4. Austin Carr, "Nike: The Number 1 Most Innovative Company of 2013," *Fast Company*, February 11, 2013.

5. Don Blair, "Case Study: Nike CFO Don Blair Reveals Strategy for Profit Growth," *CFOGlobalHQ*, October 30, 2013, http://www.cfoglobalhq.com.

6. Nike, "Nike.inc Unveils ColorDry Technology and High-Tech Facility to Eliminate Water and Chemicals in Dyeing," December 2, 2013, http://nikeinc.com.

7. Ibid.

8. Trefis Team, "Why Nike Will Outpace the Sports Apparel Market's Growth," *Forbes.com*, May 13, 2013, http://www.forbes.com.

9. Michael Treacy and Fred Wiersema, *The Disciplines of Market Leaders* (Reading, MA: Addison-Wesley, 1995). Treacy and Wiersema suggest the first three strategies. We suggest the fourth—locational excellence.

10. V. Kumar et al., "Establishing Profitable Customer Loyalty for Multinational Companies in the Emerging Economies: A Conceptual Framework," *Journal of International Marketing* 21 (March 2013), pp. 57–80; Yuping Liu-Thompkins and Leona Tam, "Not All Repeat Customers Are the Same: Designing Effective Cross-Selling Promotion on the Basis of Attitudinal Loyalty and Habit," *Journal of Marketing* 77 (September 2013), pp. 21–36.

11. Melea Press and Eric J. Arnould, "How Does Organizational Identification Form? A Consumer Behavior Perspective," *Journal of Consumer Research* 38 (December 2011), pp. 650–66.

12. Tanzina Vega, "Self Magazine Refocuses for a Younger Audience," *The New York Times*, February 10, 2013.

13. Valarie A. Zeithaml, Mary Jo Bitner, and Dwayne D. Gremler, *Services Marketing: Integrating Customer Focus across the Firm*, 5th ed. (Burr Ridge, IL: McGraw-Irwin, 2009).

14. Brooks Barnes, "At Disney Parks, a Bracelet Meant to Build Loyalty (and Sales)," *The New York Times*, January 7, 2013.

15. Carmine Gallo, "Customer Service the Disney Way," *Forbes*, April 14, 2011.

16. Diane M. Martin and John W. Schouten, "Consumption-Driven Market Emergence," *Journal of Consumer Research* 40 (February 2014), pp. 855–70. Also see articles in special issue edited by John T. Mentzer and Greg Gundlach, "Exploring the Relationship between Marketing and Supply Chain Management: Introduction to the Special Issue," *Journal of the Academy of Marketing Science* 38, no. 1 (2010), pp. 1–4.

17. Hilary Stout, "In War for Same-Day Delivery, Racing Madly to Go Last Mile," *The New York Times*, November 23, 2013, http://www.nytimes.com.

18. http://www.interbrand.com.

19. "Marketing Plan," *American Marketing Association Dictionary*, http://www.marketingpower.com.

20. Donald Lehman and Russell Winer, *Analysis for Marketing Planning*, 7th ed. (Burr Ridge, IL: McGraw-Hill/Irwin, 2008).

21. Nancy J. Sirianni et al., "Branded Service Encounters: Strategically Aligning Employee Behavior with the Brand Positioning," *Journal of Marketing* 77 (November 2013), pp. 108–23; Andrew Campbell, "Mission Statements," *Long Range Planning* 30 (1997), pp. 931–33.

22. Gene R. Laczniak and Patrick E. Murphy, "Stakeholder Theory and Marketing: Moving from a Firm-Centric to a Societal Perspective," *Journal of Public Policy & Marketing* 31 (Fall 2012), pp. 284–92; Alfred Rappaport, *Creating Shareholder Value: The New Standard for Business Performance* (New York: Wiley, 1988).

23. http://help-us.nike.com.

24. "Corporate Mission Statement," *adidas Group*, http://adidas-group.corporate-publications.com.

25. "About Us," Movember.com, http://us.movember.com/about/vision-goals

26. Pink Ribbon International, http://www.pinkribbon.org.

27. Matt Townsend, "As Nike Scoffs, Toning Shoes Gain Traction," *Bloomberg Businessweek*, June 7–13, 2010, pp. 22–24.

28. Sebastian Joseph, "Nike Exploits Winter Olympics Interest with 'Play Russian' Campaign," *Marketing Week*, November 29, 2013, http://www.marketingweek.co.uk.

29. Nike, 10-K report, July 20, 2010.

30. Russel Parsons, "Nike Beating Official Sponsor adidas in World Cup Stakes," *Marketing Week*, June 24, 2010, p. 7.

31. Eric Siemans, "New Balance TV Spots Target Nike," *Portland Business Journal*, March 7, 2011, http://www.bizjournals.com.

32. Nike, 10-K report, July 19, 2013.

33. https://www.hertz.com/rentacar/productsandservices/productsandservicesRegions.do.

34. https://images.hertz.com/pdfs/VMVWeb.pdf; http://www.adweek.com/aw/content_display/creative/new-campaigns/e3i21cea1586dd4edf5d50f9a17e7f18bf3.

35. Terence A. Shimp, *Advertising Promotion and Other Aspects of Integrated Marketing Communication*, 8th ed. (Mason, OH: South-Western, 2008); T. Duncan and C. Caywood, "The Concept, Process, and Evolution of Integrated Marketing Communication," in *Integrated Communication: Synergy of Persuasive Voices*, ed. E. Thorson and J. Moore (Mahwah, NJ: Erlbaum, 1996); see also various issues of the *Journal of Integrated Marketing Communications*, http://jimc.medill.northwestern.edu.

36. Annie Gasparro, "In the Low-Carb Age, Does Cereal Have a Future?," *The Wall Street Journal*, September 19, 2013.

37. Ofer Mintz and Imran S. Currim "What Drives Managerial Use of Marketing and Financial Metrics and Does Metric Use Affect Performance of Marketing-Mix Activities?," *Journal of Marketing* 77 (March 2013), pp. 17–40.

38. Kirsten Acuna, "Google Says It Can Predict Which Films Will Be Huge Box Office Hits," *Business Insider*, June 6, 2013.

39. Goodyear, 10-K, February 12, 2013.

40. This discussion is adapted from Roger A. Kerin, Steven W. Hartley, and William Rudelius, *Marketing,* 10th ed. (Burr Ridge, IL: McGraw-Hill/Irwin, 2011).

41. P. Farris et al., *Marketing Metrics: 50+ Metrics Every Executive Should Master* (Upper Saddle River, NJ: Pearson, 2006), p. 17.

42. Relative market share = Brand's market share ÷ Largest competitor's market share. If, for instance, there are only two products in a market, A and B, and product B has 90 percent market share, then A's relative market share is 10 ÷ 90 = 11.1 percent. If, on the other hand, B only has 50 percent market share, then A's relative market share is 10 ÷ 50 = 20 percent. Ibid., p. 19.

43. Apple Inc., "Form 10-K 2011 Annual Report," October 30, 2013.

44. Sherilynn Macale, "Apple Has Sold 300M iPods, Currently Holds 78% of the Music Player Market," *The Next Web,* October 4, 2011, http://thenextweb.com; Chris Smith, "iPad Tablet Market Share Down to 57 Percent," *Techradar.com,* February 16, 2012, http://www.techradar.com; Ken Yeung, "Apple Sold 4.6M Macs and 3.49M iPods in Q4 FY2013," *The Next Web,* October 28, 2013, http://thenextweb.com.

45. Roger Kerin, Vijay Mahajan, and P. Rajan Varadarajan, *Contemporary Perspectives on Strategic Market Planning* (Boston: Allyn & Bacon, 1991), Chapter 6; Susan Mudambi, "A Topology of Strategic Choice in Marketing," *International Journal of Market & Distribution Management* (1994), pp. 22–25.

46. http://www.gamestop.com/xbox-360/movies-tv/yoostar-on-mtv/91616.

47. http://www.mtv.com/shows/teen_mom/season_3/series.jhtml.

48. http://www.stayteen.org/; http://www.mtv.com/mobile/.

49. A. A. Thompson et al., *Crafting and Executing Strategy,* 18th ed. (New York: McGraw-Hill/Irwin, 2012).

50. http://www.mtv.com/shows/made/series.jhtml; Tim Arango, "Make Room, Cynics; MTV Wants to Do Some Good," *The New York Times,* April 18, 2009; Robert Seidman, "MTV Continues to Diversify Slate with New Scripted Comedies 'The Hard Times of RJ Berger' and 'Warren the Ape,'" *tvbythenumbers. com,* January 15, 2010.

i. Peter Johnston, "Share of the Mobile Pie," *Stores,* October 2011; Brad Tuttle, "Hungry and Lazy Customers Rejoice! It's Getting Even Easier to Order Food," *Time,* April 25, 2013.

ii. Ibid.; Tesco, "Tesco HomePlus Expands Number of Virtual Stores," news release, February 7, 2012, http://www.tescoplc .com; Andy Potts, "The Emporium Strikes Back," *The Economist,* July 13, 2013, http://www.economist.com.

iii. Angela Doland, "How Volkswagen Overcame a Crisis in China, in Three Lessons," *Advertising Age,* August 14, 2014, http:// adage.com.

iv. Aaron M. Kessler and B. X. Chen, "Google and Apple Fight for the Car Dashboard," *The New York Times*, February 22, 2015, http://www.nytimes.com; Tim Stevens, "2014's Battle for Dashboard Supremacy: Apple's CarPlay vs. Google's OAA vs. MirrorLink," *CNET,* March 4, 2014, http://www.cnet.com/ news/2014s-battle-for-dashboard-supremacy-apples-carplay-vs-googles-oaa-vs-mirrorlink/.

CHAPTER 3

1. Adam Ostrow, "Inside Gatorade's Social Media Control Center," *Mashable.com,* June 15, 2010, http://mashable.com.

2. PepsiCo, "Gatorade Mission Control," YouTube, https://www .youtube.com.

3. Ekaterina Walter, "How Top Brands Like Gatorade and the Super Bowl Use Social-Media Command Centers," *Fast Company,* June 22, 2012.

4. Sarah McNew, "Social Media Breakdown: A Look at Gatorade's Social Media Marketing Efforts," *Social Toaster,* May 6, 2013, http://www.socialtoaster.com/blog-entry/social-media-break-down-look-gatorades-social-media-marketing-efforts.

5. "Gatorade's Social Media Command Center?," *Hive Health Media,* May 17, 2013, http://www.hivehealthmedia.com/ gatorades-social-media-command-center/.

6. Mike Gingerich, "4 Ways to Boost Your Facebook Engagement with Promotions," *Social Media Examiner,* January 8, 2013, http://www.socialmediaexaminer.com/boost-your-facebook-engagement-with-promotions/.

7. Nikon, press release, August 22, 2007, http://press.nikonusa .com/post/2007/08/22/nikons-new-digital-learning-center-on-flickr-provides-a-first-of-its-kind-interactive-experience-that-assists-everyday-people-in-taking-better-photos/.

8. Chris Barry et al., "Putting Social Media to Work," 2011, Bain & Co., http://www.bain.com/Images/BAIN_BRIEF_Putting_social_ media_to_work.pdf.

9. Tim Nudd, "American Apparel, Gap Blasted for Hurricane Sandy Ad Fails," *Adweek,* October 30, 2012.

10. Coca-Cola Retailing Research Council and the Integer Group, "Social Networking Personas: A Look at Consumer and Shopper Mind Sets," in *Untangling the Social Web: Insights for Users, Brands, and Retailers,* March 2012, http://www.cokesolutions .com/BusinessSolutions/Studies/Untangling%20the%20 Social%20Web_Part%203.pdf.

11. We Are Social, and IAB Singapore, "Leading Social Networks Worldwide as of March 2015, Ranked by Number of Active Users (in Millions)," *Statista—The Statistics Portal,* http://www .statista.com/statistics/272014/global-social-networks-ranked-by-number-of-users/ (accessed March 19, 2015).

12. Forever 21 Facebook Fan Page, http://www.facebook.com/#!/ Forever21?ref=ts.

13. We Are Social, and IAB Singapore, "Leading Social Networks Worldwide as of March 2015, Ranked by Number of Active Users (in Millions)," *Statista,* Accessed 19 March 2015, http://www .statista.com/statistics/272014/global-social-networks-ranked-by-number-of-users/.

14. Experian, "Most Popular Social Media Websites in the United States in December 2014, Based on Share of Visits," *Statista— The Statistics Portal,* http://www.statista.com/statistics/265773/ market-share-of-the-most-popular-social-media-websites-in-the-us/ (accessed March 19, 2015).

15. Dorie Clark, "Why You Should Be on Google Plus (Even Though No One Else Is)," *Forbes,* January 14, 2013.

16. Ross Blum, "Where Have All the Customers Gone?," p. 8.

17. "In The Know," YouTube, Fall 2009, http://www.gstatic.com/ youtube/engagement/platform/autoplay/advertise/downloads/ YouTube_InTheKnow.pdf.

18. "Brand Channels," YouTube, http://www.gstatic.com/youtube/ engagement/platform/autoplay/advertise/downloads/YouTube_ BrandChannels.pdf.

19. We Are Social, and IAB Singapore, "Leading Social Networks Worldwide as of March 2015, Ranked by Number of Active Users (in Millions)," *Statista,* Accessed 19 March 2015, http://www .statista.com/statistics/272014/global-social-networks-ranked-by-number-of-users/.

20. Somini Sengupta, Nicole Perlroth, and Jenna Wortham, "Behind Instagram's Success, Networking the Old Way," *The New York Times,* April 13, 2012, http://www.nytimes.com/2012/04/14/technology/instagram-founders-were-helped-by-bay-area-connections.html?pagewanted=all&_r=2&.

21. Shayndi Raice and Spencer E. Ante, "Insta-Rich: $1 Billion for Instagram," *The Wall Street Journal,* April 10, 2012, http://online.wsj.com/article/SB10001424052702303815404577333840377381670.html.

22. Finlo Rohrer, "Vine: Six Things People Have Learned about Six-Second Video in a Week," *BBC News Magazine,* January 31, 2013, http://www.bbc.co.uk/news/magazine-21267741.

23. "Brands on Flickr," *Supercollider,* July 12, 2008, http://geoffnorthcott.com/blog/2008/07/brands-on-flickr/.

24. Mark W. Schaefer, "The 10 Best Corporate Blogs in the World," *BusinessGrow.com,* January 1, 2011, http://www.businessesgrow.com/2011/01/05/the-10-best-corporate-blogs-in-the-world/.

25. Elizabeth Holmes, "Tweeting without Fear," *The Wall Street Journal,* December 9, 2011.

26. David H Deans, "184 Million People in America Own a Smartphone," *Social Media Today,* March 15, 2015, http://www.socialmediatoday.com/technology-data/2015-03-15/184-million-people-america-own-smartphone.

27. Bill Siwicki, "On Smartphones, More Older Folks Make Purchases Than Youngsters," *Internet Retailer,* April 17, 2014, https://www.internetretailer.com/2014/04/17/smartphones-more-older-folks-make-purchases-youngsters.

28. Gartner, "Number of Mobile App Downloads Worldwide from 2009 to 2017 (in Millions)," *Statista—The Statistics Portal,* http://www.statista.com/statistics/266488/forecast-of-mobile-app-downloads/ (accessed March 19, 2015).

29. Gartner, "Number of Free Mobile App Downloads Worldwide from 2012 to 2017 (in Billions)," *Statista—The Statistics Portal,* http://www.statista.com/statistics/241587/number-of-free-mobile-app-downloads-worldwide/ (accessed March 19, 2015).

30. Gartner, "Number of Mobile App Downloads Worldwide from 2009 to 2017 (in Millions)," *Statista,* March 19 2015, http://www.statista.com/statistics/266488/forecast-of-mobile-app-downloads/.

31. David Barboza, "A Popular Chinese Social Networking App Blazes Its Own Path," *The New York Times,* January 20, 2014.

32. "Vision Statement: How People Really Use Mobile."

33. Ibid.

34. Ashley Feinberg, "I Just Spent $236 on Candy Crush, Help," *Gizmodo,* August 7, 2013, http://www.gizmodo.com.

35. Stuart Dredge, "Candy Crush Saga: '70% of People on the Last Level Haven't Paid Anything,'" *The Guardian,* September 10, 2013, http://www.theguardian.com; "Candy Crush Saga Most Popular Game App on the Planet," *Metro,* January 30, 2014, http://www.metro.co.uk.

36. Josh Wolonick, "Here's How Big the In-App Purchases Market Is for Apple and Google," *Minyanville,* January 16, 2014, http://www.minyanville.com.

37. Katie Van Domelin, "Social Media Monitoring Tools—How to Pick the Right One," July 7, 2010, http://www.convinceandconvert.com/social-media-monitoring/social-media-monitoring-tools-how-to-pick-the-right-one/.

38. "New Salesforce.com Features Help to Scale 'Social' across the Enterprise," Salesforce.com website, November 12, 2011, http://www.Salesforce.com.com.

39. Salesforce.com website, http://www.Salesforce.com.com.

40. Let's Get Ready website, http://www.letsgetready.org.

41. Laura S. Quinn and Kyle Andrei, "A Few Good Web Analytics Tools," *TechSoup,* May 19, 2011, http://www.techsoup.org.

42. Christina Warren, "How to Measure Social Media ROI," *Mashable,* October 27, 2009, http://mashable.com/2009/10/27/social-media-roi/.

43. "iNoobs: What Is Google Analytics?," http://inspiredm.com; http://www.google.com/analytics/features/index.html; http://www.advanced-web-metrics.com; Kevin Ryan, "What Can the Average Marketer Learn from Google Creative Lab?," *Advertising Age,* April 19, 2013.

44. Amy Porterfield, "3 Steps to an Effective Social Media Strategy," *Social Media Examiner,* March 1, 2012, http://www.socialmediaexaminer.com.

45. "Lay's Brand Names Cheesy Garlic Bread Flavored Potato Chips as 'Do Us a Flavor' Contest Winner; Creator Receives $1 Million or More in Grand Prize Winnings," *Pepsico,* May 7, 2013, http://www.pepsico.com; http://www.fritolays.com/lays/; Jenna Mullins, "The Submissions for New Lay's Chip Flavors Are Getting Out of Control (but We Love It)," *E! Online,* http://www.eonline.com/.

46. Andy Shaw, "How to Create a Facebook Ad Campaign," *Social Media Tips,* September 23, 2011, http://exploringsocialmedia.com/how-to-create-a-facebook-ad-campaign/.

i. Stuart Elliot, "Live Commercials Coming to 'Late Night,'" *The New York Times,* September 18, 2013; Jeanine Poggi, "Lexus to Air Live Ads, Fueled by Social Suggestions, during NBC's 'Late Night,'" *Advertising Age,* September 18, 2013; Chris Perry, "How Social Media Propelled Fallon's Tonight Show Takeover," *Forbes,* April 6, 2013; YouTube, "Late Night with Jimmy Fallon," http://www.youtube.com/user/latenight.

ii. http://www.hubspot.com/customers/hy-line-cruises.

iii. Ann-Christine Diaz, "Facebook 101: Is Your Brand Worth a Like?," *Ad Age Digital,* January 30, 2012; Facebook. "Number of Monthly Active Facebook Users Worldwide as of 2nd Quarter 2015 (in Millions)." *Statista—The Statistics Portal. Statista.* August 28, 2015. http://www.statista.com/statistics/264810/number-of-monthly-active-facebook-users-worldwide/. Pam Dyer, "Facebook Advertising Case Study: Clorox Green Works," http://www.pamorama.net/2011/02/26/facebook-advertising-case-study-clorox-green-works/.

iv. Kate Kaye, "eHarmony's Love for Data Goes Beyond Dating: It's Good for Marketing Too," *Advertising Age,* February 18, 2015, http://adage.com; Samuel Greengard, "eHarmony Enhances Its Relationship with Big Data," *Baseline,* February 2, 2015, http://www.baseline.com; "IBM Big Data & Analytics Helps eHarmony Identify More Compatible Matches in Real Time," *IBM Big Data & Analytics Hub,* September 8, 2014, http://www.ibmbigdatahub.com.

CHAPTER 4

1. James Glanz, Jeff Larson, and Andrew W. Lehren, "Spy Agencies Tap Data Streaming from Phone Apps," *The New York Times,* January 27, 2014.

2. John Bussey, "Taming the Spies of Web Advertising," *The Wall Street Journal,* August 8, 2013.

3. Claire Cain Miller and Somini Sengupta, "Selling Secrets of Phone Users to Advertisers," *The New York Times,* October 5, 2013.

4. Theodore Levitt, *Marketing Imagination* (Detroit, MI: Free Press, 1983).

5. Amy Harmon and Andrew Pollack, "Battle Brewing over Labeling of Genetically Modified Food," *The New York Times,* May 24, 2012.

6. Laura Parker, "The GMO Labeling Battle Is Heating Up—Here's Why," *National Geographic,* January 11, 2014; Stefanie Strom, "Major Grocer to Label Foods with Gene-Modified Content," *The New York Times,* March 8, 2013.

7. For a detailed compilation of articles that are involved with ethical and societal issues, see Gregory T. Gundlach, Lauren G. Block, and William W. Wilkie, *Explorations of Marketing in Society* (Mason, OH: Thompson Higher Education, 2007); G. Svensson and G. Wood, "A Model of Business Ethics," *Journal of Business Ethics* 77, no. 3 (2007), pp. 303–22.

8. http://www.cmomagazine.com. This survey was conducted in 2006; more recent reports suggest that 49 percent of respondents to a 2009 survey reported having seen ethical misconduct overall. See Ethics Resource Center, "2009 National Business Ethics Survey," http://www.ethics.org.

9. American Marketing Association, "Statement of Ethics," April 8, 2014, https://www.ama.org/AboutAMA/Pages/Statement-of-Ethics.aspx.

10. Alexander Dahlsrud Lists 37 Definitions! See "How Corporate Social Responsibility Is Defined," *Corporate Social Responsibility and Environmental Management* 15, no. 1 (January/February 2008), pp. 1–13.

11. "Social Responsibility," *AMA Dictionary of Marketing Terms,* http://www.marketingpower.com/_layouts/Dictionary.aspx?dLetter=S.

12. Christopher Marquis et al., "The Dannon Company: Marketing and Corporate Social Responsibility," *Harvard Business School Case 9-410-121,* April 1, 2010.

13. Rick Ungar, "Walmart Store Holding Thanksgiving Charity Food Drive—for Its Own Employees!" *Forbes,* November 18, 2013; http://foundation.walmart.com.

14. Michael Connor, "Survey: U.S. Consumers Willing to Pay for Corporate Responsibility," *Business Ethics,* March 29, 2010, http://business-ethics.com.

15. Richard Stengel, "Doing Well by Doing Good," *Time magazine,* September 10, 2009, http://www.time.com.

16. "2011 World's Most Ethical Companies," *Ethisphere,* http://ethisphere.com/2011-worlds-most-ethical-companies.

17. http://www.burtsbees.com.

18. General Electric, "Sustainable Growth: GE 2010 Citizenship Report," http://www.gecitizenship.com; General Electric, "The Spirit and the Letter," http://integrity.ge.com.

19. Interviews with Nell Newman and Peter Meehan, cofounders of Newman's Own Organic, 2007; http://www.newmansown.com/charity/.

20. Ross Wilson, "The Best and Worst of Facebook 2012," *Ignite Social Media,* December 13, 2012, http://www.ignitesocialmedia.com.

21. Andrew J. Blumberg and Peter Eckerdsly, "On Locational Privacy, and How to Avoid Losing It Forever," *Electronic Frontier Foundation White Paper,* August 2009, http://www.eff.org.

22. Elizabeth A. Harris, Nicole Perlroth, and Nathaniel Popper, "Neiman Marcus Data Breach Worse Than First Said," *The New York Times,* January 23, 2014.

23. http://about.van.fedex.com/.

24. The most famous proponent of this view was Milton Friedman. See, for example, *Capitalism and Freedom* (Chicago: University of Chicago Press, 2002); or *Free to Choose: A Personal Statement* (Orlando, FL: Harcourt, 1990).

25. Dan Amos, "Aflac's Ethics in Action: Pay for Performance—Keep Stakeholders Informed," January 12, 2009, http://ethisphere.com.

26. https://thewaltdisneycompany.com/blog/infographic-disneys-charitable-giving-reaches-370-million-2013; http://disneyparks.disney.go.com/blog/galleries/2014/01/disney-cast-members-create-an-extreme-village-makeover-for-give-kids-the-world/#photo-5.

27. http://www.ge.com/news/our_viewpoints/energy_and_climate.html; "GE Launches New Ecomagination Healthcare Products, Opens Renewable Energy HQ," February 2, 2010, http://www.greenbiz.com.

28. D. B. Bielak, S. Bonini, and J. M. Oppenheim, "CEOs on Strategy and Social Issues," *McKinsey Quarterly,* 2007, http://www.mckinseyquarterly.com.

29. United Press International, "Diet Soda Sales: Flat Would Be Better," December 9, 2013, http://www.upi.com.

30. U.S. Environmental Protection Agency, "What Is Sustainability?," http://www.epa.gov/sustainability/basicinfo.htm.

i. Hannah Tregear, "Case Study/Kellogg's: Kellogg's Boosts Social Media Campaign ROI," *Brandwatch,* November 23, 2013, http://www.brandwatch.com/wp-content/uploads/2013/11/Brandwatch_CS_Kelloggs.pdf; Jennifer Rooney, "Kellogg's Completes Major Brand Overhaul," *Forbes,* May 10, 2012, http://www.forbes.com/; E.J. Schultz, "Media Maven Bob Arnold Leads Kellogg Into Digital-Buying Frontier," *Advertising Age,* September 23, 2013, http://adage.com/; Larisa Bedgood, "5 Compelling Reasons to Ramp Up Your Digital Marketing Strategy," *SmartData Collective,* March 18, 2015, http://smartdatacollective.com/lbedgood/305186/5-compelling-reasons-ramp-your-digital-marketing-strategy.

ii. http://www.toms.com/our-movement; http://www.toms.com/corporate-info/; http://www.insightargentina.org; Andrew Adam Newman, "'Buy One, Give One' Spirit Imbues an Online Store," *Los Angeles Times,* November 4, 2013; George Anderson, "Toms Offers a Different Way to Shop," *Retail Wire,* November 6, 2013; Christina Binkley, "Charity Gives Shoe Brand Extra Shine," *The Wall Street Journal,* April 1, 2010, http://online.wsj.com.

iii. "Market for Selling Fake Social Media Clicks Has Big Following," *Los Angeles Times,* January 6, 2014; Suzanne Vranica, "Tweeting to Sell Cars," *The Wall Street Journal,* November 14, 2010; http://business.ftc.gov; Gary Hoffman, "Selling Cars on Twitter," *AOL Autos,* August 10, 2010.

iv. "Walmart Energy Efficiency Program Achieves Energy Savings of 20% across 210 Supplier Factories in China," *PR Newswire,* April 22, 2013; Jessica Wohl, "Walmart Announces $50 Billion Buy American Campaign," *The Huffington Post,* January 15, 2013; "Walmart Launches Major Initiative to Make Food Healthier and Healthier Food More Affordable," http://walmartstores.com; Stephanie Rosenbloom, "At Walmart, Labeling to Reflect Green Intent," *The New York Times,* July 16, 2009; Stephanie Rosenbloom, "Wal-Mart to Toughen Standards," *The New York Times,* October 22, 2008; Adam Aston, "Walmart: Making Its Suppliers Go Green," *BusinessWeek,* May 18, 2009.

CHAPTER 5

1. Stephanie Rosenbloom, "Now Checking In: Pampered Pets," *The New York Times,* September 18, 2013, http://www.nytimes.com.

2. Peter F. Drucker, *The Essential Drucker* (New York: HarperCollins, 2001).

3. "Corning Announces Third-Quarter Results," *Corning News Release,* October 24, 2012, http://www.corning.com.

4. Linda Doell, "In Razor vs. Razor, neither Gillette nor Schick Gains Edge with Ad Watchdog," March 17, 2011, http://www.dailyfinance.com.

5. http://www.nau.com; Chris Dannen, "Wanted: The Light, Recycled Trench," *Fast Company*, November 19, 2010, http://www.fastcompany.com; Polly Labarre, "Leap of Faith," *Fast Company*, June 2007.

6. Del I. Hawkins and David L. Mothersbaugh, *Consumer Behavior: Building Marketing Strategy*, 11th ed. (Burr Ridge, IL: McGraw-Hill/Irwin, 2009); Philip Cateora and John Graham, *International Marketing*, 16th ed. (Burr Ridge, IL: McGraw-Hill/Irwin, 2012).

7. http://popvssoda.com/.

8. http://www.drpepper.com.

9. "Corporate Responsibility," http://info.cvscaremark.com.

10. Geoffrey E. Meredith, Charles D. Schewe, and Janice Karlovich, *Defining Markets, Defining Moments: America's 7 Generational Cohorts, Their Shared Experiences, and Why Businesses Should Care* (New York: Wiley, 2002).

11. "Consumers of Tomorrow: Insights and Observations about Generation Z," Grail Research, June 2010.

12. Suzy Menkes, "Marketing to the Millennials," *The New York Times*, March 2, 2010; Pamela Paul, "Getting Inside Gen Y," *American Demographics* 23, no. 9; Sharon Jayson, "A Detailed Look at the Millennials," *USA Today*, February 23, 2010.

13. http://www.familiesusa.org; http://www.bls.gov; U.S. Bureau of the Census, "Income, Poverty, and Health Insurance Coverage in the United States, 2010," http://www.census.gov.

14. Dave Gilson and Carolyn Perot, "It's the Inequality, Stupid," *Mother Jones* (March/April 2011), http://motherjones.com; Organisation for Economic Co-operation and Development, "Growing Unequal? Income Distribution and Poverty in OECD Countries," 2008, http://www.oecd.org.

15. http://www.Hammacher.com.

16. http://www.census.gov; http://www.infoplease.com.

17. http://www.familiesusa.org; http://www.bls.gov; U.S. Bureau of the Census, "Income, Poverty, and Health Insurance Coverage in the United States, 2010," http://www.census.gov.

18. Richard Thaler, "Breadwinning Wives and Nervous Husbands," *The New York Times*, June 1, 2013, http://www.nytimes.com.

19. Tom Pirovano, "U.S. Demographics Are Changing . . . Are Your Marketing Plans Ready?," *NielsenWire*, March 10, 2010, http://blog.nielsen.com; "Cents and Sensibility: Why Marketing to Multicultural Consumers Requires a Subtle Touch," *Knowledge@Wharton*, March 10, 2010, http://www.wharton.universia.net; "Ethnic Consumers Hold $282 Billion in Purchasing Power," February 24, 2009, http://news.newamericamedia.org.

20. Jeffrey S. Passel and D'Vera Cohn, "U.S. Population Projections: 2005–2050," Pew Research Center, http://pewhispanic.org.

21. Joel Kotkin, "The Changing Demographics of America," *Smithsonian* magazine (August 2010), http://www.smithsonianmag.com.

22. Julie Jargon, "Pizza Chain Seeks Slice of Bicultural Pie," *The Wall Street Journal*, December 30, 2010, http://online.wsj.com.

23. Todd Wasserman, "Report: Shifting African American Population," *Adweek*, January 12, 2010, http://www.adweek.com; U.S. Bureau of the Census, "Annual Social and Economic Supplement to the Current Population Survey," http://www.census.gov.

24. Nielsen, "The State of the African-American Consumer," September 2011, p. 5.

25. Centers for Disease Control and Prevention, "National Diabetes Fact Sheet, 2011," http://www.cdc.gov.

26. "Guidelines for Marketing Food to Kids Proposed," CSPI, press release, January 5, 2005.

27. Yoga Buzz, "Yoga Biz Thrives Despite Economy," October 24, 2011, http://blogs.yogajournal.com.

28. Catherine Clifford, "Yoga: The Booming Business of Zen," *CNNMoney*, October 18, 2011, http://money.cnn.com.

29. This definition of green marketing draws on work by Jacquelyn A. Ottman, *Green Marketing: Opportunity for Innovation* (Chicago: NTC Publishing, 1997).

30. "SunChips Marketing Campaign Brings Light to Its Solar Energy Efforts," PR Newswire, April 3, 2008, http://www.prnewswire.com/news-releases/sunchips-marketing-campaign-brings-light-to-its-solar-energy-efforts-57042102.html.

31. Elizabeth A. Harris et al., "A Sneaky Path into Target Customers' Wallets," *The New York Times*, January 17, 2014, http://www.nytimes.com.

32. John Bussey, "Taming the Spies of Web Advertising," *The Wall Street Journal*, August 8, 2013.

33. http://www.irs.gov/.

34. Brendan Greeley, "Providing Internet Access to the Poor," *Bloomberg Businessweek*, November 17, 2011, http://www.businessweek.com.

i. Bonnie Fuller, "Baby-Boomer Marketers Are Misreading Millennials' Media Behavior," *Advertising Age*, May 13, 2013; Chingching Chang, "Dual System Model Comparisons of Print Advertisements and e-Store Product Pages: The Influence of Dominant Pictures on Decision Making," working paper (under review at *Journal of Advertising*).

ii. Image source, http://www.iprospect.com/digital-affluent-male; text sources, Natasha Singer, "E-Tailer Customization: Convenient or Creepy?," *The New York Times*, June 23, 2012; "Who Makes the Call at the Mall, Men or Women?," *The Wall Street Journal*, April 23, 2011; Tom Ryan, "'His' and 'Her' Grocery Aisles," *Retail Wire*, June 6, 2011; Susan Reda, "Guess What? Men Shop, Too!" *Stores*, April 2010; Miguel Bustillo and Mary Ellen Lloyd, "Best Buy Tests New Appeals to Women," *The Wall Street Journal*, June 16, 2010.

iii. E. J. Schultz, "The Next Big Weapon for Supermarkets—the Dietician," *Advertising Age*, April 15, 2013, http://www.adage.com.

iv. Emily Steel, "Nestlé Takes a Beating on Social-Media Sites," *The Wall Street Journal*, March 29, 2010, http://online.wsj.com; Jerry Lynch, "Achieving a Sustainable Palm Oil Commitment," *Taste of General Mills*, December 7, 2012, http://www.blog.generalmills.com; "Haagen-Dazs and General Mills to Help Smallholder Vanilla Farmers Increase Yields and Improve Sustainability Practices in Madagascar," *MarketWatch*, press release, February 20, 2013; "General Mills Joins U.S. Food Waste Challenge as Founding Partner," *The Wall Street Journal*, June 4, 2013, http://online.wsj.com; "General Mills Reports Progress on Global Responsibility Efforts," *The New York Times*, April 30, 2013, http://markets.on.nytimes.com.

v. Scott M. Fulton III, "Netflix Has an Exchange So Complex that It Has Triggered a Scientific Renaissance," *The New Stack*, February 24, 2015, http://thenewstack.io/netflix-exchange-complex-triggered-scientific-renaissance/; Ben Kunz, "Why Netflix Walked Away from Personalization," *ThoughtGadgets*, January 4, 2014, http://www.thoughtgadgets.com/why-netflix-walked-away-from-personalization/; Amol Sharma, "Amazon Mines Its Data Trove to Bet on TV's Next Hit," *The Wall Street Journal*, November 1, 2013, http://www.wsj.com/; Derrick Harris, "Netflix Analyzes a lot of Data about Your Viewing Habits," *Gigaom*, June 14, 2012, https://gigaom.com/2012/06/14/

netflix-analyzes-a-lot-of-data-about-your-viewing-habits/; Phil Simon, "Big Data Lessons from Netflix," *Wired*, March 11, 2014, http://www.wired.com/; Marianne Zumberge, "'House of Cards' Sees Unusual Social-Media Spike Ahead of Season 3," *Boston Herald*, February 27, 2015, http://www.bostonherald.com/.

vi. Jeanine Poggi, "The Top Three Trends at CES This Year, according to LiquidThread's Brent Poer," *Advertising Age,* January 8, 2014; Jeanine Poggi, "The Top CES Trends—as Seen by Tech Geek and GroupM Chairman-CEO Irwin Gotleib," *Advertising Age,* January 10, 2014.

CHAPTER 6

1. David Pogue, "2 Wristbands Keep Tabs on Fitness," *The New York Times,* November 14, 2012, http://www.nytimes.com.

2. Clare Cain Miller, "New Apps Arrive on Google Glass," *The New York Times,* May 16, 2013, http://bits.blogs.nytimes.com/2013/05/16/new-apps-arrive-on-google-glass/; Daniel J. Simons and Christopher F. Chabris, "Is Google Glass Dangerous?" *The New York Times,* May 24, 2013, http://www.nytimes.com.

3. American Marketing Association, "Consumer Behavior," http://www.marketingpower.com/_layouts/Dictionary.aspx.

4. Bill Wasik, "Why Wearable Tech Will Be as Big as the Smartphone," *Wired,* December 17, 2013, http://www.wired.com.

5. Ewan Spence, "2014 Will Be the Year of Wearable Technology," *Forbes,* November 2, 2013, http://www.forbes.com.

6. Claire Cain Miller, "Google Glass to Be Covered by Vision Care Insurer VSP," *The New York Times,* January 28, 2014, http://www.nytimes.com.

7. http://www.statisticbrain.com/corrective-lenses-statistics/.

8. Hayley Tsukayama, "Google's Smart Contact Lens: What It Does and How It Works," *The Washington Post,* January 17, 2014, http://www.washingtonpost.com.

9. For example, when trying on a dress, Katie might be influenced by the way that same dress looks on a salesperson in the store. See Darren W. Dahl, Jennifer J. Argo, and Andrea C. Morales, "Social Information in the Retail Environment: The Importance of Consumption Alignment, Referent Identity, and Self-Esteem," *Journal of Consumer Research* 38, no. 5 (February 2012), pp. 860–71.

10. For a detailed discussion of customer behavior, see Michael R. Solomon, *Consumer Behavior: Buying, Having, and Being,* 11th ed. (Upper Saddle River, NJ: Pearson Prentice Hall, 2014).

11. Martin R. Lautman and Koen Pauwels, "Metrics That Matter: Identifying the Importance of Consumer Wants and Needs," *Journal of Advertising Research* 49, no. 3 (2009), 339–59.

12. Liz C. Wang et al., "Can a Retail Web Site Be Social?" *Journal of Marketing* 71, no. 3 (2007), pp. 143–57; Barry Babin, William Darden, and Mitch Griffin, "Work and/or Fun: Measuring Hedonic and Utilitarian Shopping Value," *Journal of Consumer Research* 20 (March 1994), pp. 644–56.

13. Jing Xu and Norbert Schwarz, "Do We Really Need a Reason to Indulge?" *Journal of Marketing Research* 46, no. 1 (February 2009), pp. 25–36.

14. "Lana Marks Cleopatra Bag," *Lord Glamour,* February 8, 2014, http://www.lordglamour.com/; Lopa Mohanty, "10 Most Expensive Handbag Brands in the World," *Fashion Lady,* May 31, 2013, http://www.fashionlady.in/; "Celebrities," *Lana Marks,* http://www.lanamarks.com/.

15. Peng Huang, Nicholas H. Lurie, and Sabyasachi Mitra, "Searching for Experience on the Web: An Empirical Examination of Consumer Behavior for Search and Experience Goods," *Journal of Marketing* 73, no. 2 (March 2009), pp. 55–69.

16. http://www.nordstrom.com; http://www.baronidesigns.com.

17. http://www.truefit.com.

18. Lan Luo, Brian T. Ratchford, and Botao Yang, "Why We Do What We Do: A Model of Activity Consumption," *Journal of Marketing Research* 50 (February 2013), pp. 24–43.

19. Ying Zhang et al., "Been There, Done That: The Impact of Effort Investment on Goal Value and Consumer Motivation," *Journal of Consumer Research* 38, no. 1 (June 2011), pp. 78–93.

20. Debabrata Talukdar, "Cost of Being Poor: Retail Price and Consumer Price Search Differences across Inner-City and Suburban Neighborhoods," *Journal of Consumer Research* 35, no. 3 (October 2008), pp. 457–71.

21. David Dubois, Derek D. Rucker, and Adam D. Galinsky, "Super Size Me: Product Size as a Signal of Status," *Journal of Consumer Research* 38, no. 6 (April 2012), pp. 1047–62.

22. Benjamin Scheibehenne, Rainer Greifeneder, and Peter M. Todd, "Can There Ever Be Too Many Options? A Meta-Analytic Review of Choice Overload," *Journal of Consumer Research* 37, no. 3 (October 2010), pp. 409–45.

23. The term *determinance* was first coined by James Myers and Mark Alpert nearly three decades ago; http://www.sawtoothsoftware.com.

24. http://www.sawtoothsoftware.com.

25. Julie R. Irwin and Rebecca Walker Naylor, "Ethical Decisions and Response Mode Compatibility: Weighting of Ethical Attributes in Consideration Sets Formed by Excluding versus Including Product Alternatives," *Journal of Marketing Research* 46, no. 2 (April 2009), pp. 234–46; Richard Lutz, "Changing Brand Attitudes through Modification of Cognitive Structure," *Journal of Consumer Research* 1, no. 1 (1975), pp. 125–36.

26. Caroline Goukens, Siegfried Dewitte, and Luk Warlop, "Me, Myself, and My Choices: The Influence of Private Self-Awareness on Choice," *Journal of Marketing Research* 46, no. 5 (October 2009), pp. 682–92.

27. "30 Under 30 2011: Where Are They Now?" http://www.inc.com; http://www.renttherunway.com.

28. "Beware of Dissatisfied Consumers: They Like to Blab," *Knowledge@Wharton,* March, 8, 2006, based on the "Retail Customer Dissatisfaction Study 2006" conducted by the Jay H. Baker Retailing Initiative at Wharton and The Verde Group.

29. Goutam Challagalla, R. Venkatesh, and Ajay K. Kohli, "Proactive Postsales Service: When and Why Does It Pay Off?" *Journal of Marketing* 73, no. 2 (March 2009), pp. 70–87.

30. Randall Stross, "Consumer Complaints Made Easy. Maybe Too Easy," *The New York Times,* May 28, 2011, http://www.nytimes.com.

31. For a more extensive discussion on these factors, see Banwari Mittal, *Consumer Behavior* (Cincinnati, OH: Open Mentis, 2008); Peter and Olson, *Consumer Behavior and Marketing Strategy.*

32. A. H. Maslow, *Motivation and Personality* (New York: Harper & Row, 1970).

33. Kelly D. Martin and Ronald Paul Hill, "Life Satisfaction, Self-Determination, and Consumption Adequacy at the Bottom of the Pyramid," *Journal of Consumer Research* 38, no. 6 (April 2012), pp. 1155–68; Hazel Rose Markus and Barry Schwartz, "Does Choice Mean Freedom and Well-Being?" *Journal of Consumer Research* 37, no. 2 (August 2010), pp. 344–55.

34. Stacy Wood, "The Comfort Food Fallacy: Avoiding Old Favorites in Times of Change," *Journal of Consumer Research* 36, no. 6 (April 2010), pp. 950–63; Stacey Finkelstein and Ayelet Fishbach, "When Healthy Food Makes You Hungry," *Journal of Consumer Research* 37, no. 3 (October 2010), pp. 357–67.

35. For recent research on the link between emotions and consumer behavior, see the "Emotions and Consumer Behavior" special issue of *Journal of Consumer Research* 40 (February 2014).

36. Leonard Lee, On Amir, and Dan Ariely, "In Search of Homo Economicus: Cognitive Noise and the Role of Emotion in Preference Consistency," *Journal of Consumer Research* 36, no. 2 (2009), pp. 173–87; Anish Nagpal and Parthasarathy Krishnamurthy, "Attribute Conflict in Consumer Decision Making: The Role of Task Compatibility," *Journal of Consumer Research* 34, no. 5 (February 2008), pp. 696–705.

37. http://www.bostonbackbay.com/.

38. For more discussion on these factors, see Mittal, *Consumer Behavior;* Peter and Olson, *Consumer Behavior and Marketing Strategy;* Michael Levy, Barton A. Weitz, and Dhruv Grewal, *Retailing Management,* 9th ed. (Burr Ridge, IL: Irwin/McGraw-Hill, 2013), Chapter 4; and the "Social Influence and Consumer Behavior" special issue of *Journal of Consumer Research* 40 (August 2013).

39. Juliano Laran, "Goal Management in Sequential Choices: Consumer Choices for Others Are More Indulgent than Personal Choices," *Journal of Consumer Research* 37, no. 2 (August 2010), pp. 304–14.

40. "Teenage Consumer Spending Statistics," *Statisticsbrain.com,* September 8, 2012, http://www.statisticsbrain.com; "Retailers Must Understand Modern Family Buying Decisions."

41. Glenn Ruffenach, "How Much Are Your Grandkids Really Costing You?" *The Wall Street Journal,* August 1, 2011, http://online.wsj.com.

42. Todd Hale, "Mining the U.S. Generation Gaps," *Nielsen Wire,* March 4, 2010, http://blog.nielsen.com.

43. Gokcen Coskuner-Balli and Craig J. Thompson, "The Status Costs of Subordinate Cultural Capital: At-Home Fathers' Collective Pursuit of Cultural Legitimacy through Capitalizing Consumption Practices," *Journal of Consumer Research* 40 (June 2013), pp. 19–41.

44. Morgan K. Ward and Susan Bronziarczyk, "It's Not Me, It's You: How Gift Giving Creates Giver Identity Threat as a Function of Social Closeness," *Journal of Consumer Research* 38, no. 1 (June 2011), pp. 164–81.

45. Carol Bryant, "The Truth about Paid Product Reviews and Disclosure," *Blog Paws,* September 5, 2013, http://www.blogpaws.com; see sites that recruit bloggers to do paid reviews: http://www.sponsoredreviews.com, http://www.payperpost.com, http://www.reviewme.com.

46. For an expanded discussion on these factors, see Mittal, *Consumer Behavior;* Peter and Olson, *Consumer Behavior and Marketing Strategy.* For some interesting experiments involving consumers' physical positioning and its effects on behavior, see Jeffrey S. Larson and Darron M. Billeter, "Consumer Behavior in 'Equilibrium': How Experiencing Physical Balance Increases Compromise Choice," *Journal of Marketing Research* 50 (August 2013), pp. 535–47.

47. Tracey S. Dagger and Peter J. Danaher, "Comparing the Effect of Store Remodeling on New and Existing Customers," *Journal of Marketing* (forthcoming). doi: http://dx.doi.org/10.1509/jm.13.0272.

48. The concept of atmospherics was introduced by Philip Kotler, "Atmosphere as a Marketing Tool," *Journal of Retailing 49* (Winter 1973), pp. 48–64.

49. Sylvie Morin, Laurette Dubé, and Jean-Charles Chebat, "The Role of Pleasant Music in Servicescapes: A Test of the Dual onmental Perception," *Journal of Retailing 83,* no. 1 (2007), pp. 115–30.

50. http://www.wegmans.com; http://wholefoodsmarket.com/stores/cooking-classes/; Tracy Turner, "New Hangout Supermarket," *Columbus Dispatch,* March 20, 2011.

51. Tim Bajarin, "6 Reasons Apple Is So Successful," *Time,* May 7, 2012, http://techland.time.com.

52. Carmine Gallo, "Apple's Secret Employee Training Manual Reinvents Customer Service in Seven Ways," *Forbes,* August 30, 2012.

53. Ahreum Maeng, Robin J. Tanner, and Dilip Soman, "Conservative When Crowded: Social Crowding and Consumer Choice," *Journal of Marketing Research* 50 (December 2013), pp. 739–52; Alexander Chernev and Ryan Hamilton, "Assortment Size and Option Attractiveness in Consumer Choice among Retailers," *Journal of Marketing Research* 46, no. 3 (June 2009), pp. 410–20; Marc-Andre Kamel, Nick Greenspan, and Rudolf Pritzl, "Standardization Is Efficient but Localization Helps Shops to Stand Out," *The Wall Street Journal,* January 21, 2009.

54. Jeffrey Trachtenberg, "Publishers Bundle E-Books to Boost Sales, Promote Authors," *The Wall Street Journal,* February 11, 2011.

55. Pierre Chandon et al., "Does In-Store Marketing Work? Effects of the Number and Position of Shelf Facings on Brand Attention and Evaluation at the Point of Purchase," *Journal of Marketing* 73, no. 6 (November 2009), pp. 1–17.

56. Kirk Henderson and Kusum Ailawadi, "Shopper Marketing: Six Lessons for Retail from Six Years of Mobile Eye Tracking Research," *Review of Marketing Research* 12 (2014).

57. Christine Birkner, "Thinking Outside of the Box," *Marketing News,* March 30, 2011.

58. Dan King and Chris Janiszewski, "Affect-Gating," *Journal of Consumer Research* 38, no. 4 (December 2011), pp. 697–711.

59. Mittal, *Consumer Behavior;* Peter and Olson, *Consumer Behavior and Marketing Strategy.*

60. Yuping Liu-Thompkins and Leona Tam, "Not All Repeat Customers Are the Same: Designing Effective Cross-Selling Promotion on the Basis of Attitudinal Loyalty and Habit," *Journal of Marketing* 77 (September 2013), pp. 21–36; Karen M. Stilley, J. Jeffrey Inman, and Kirk L. Wakefield, "Planning to Make Unplanned Purchases? The Role of In-Store Slack in Budget Deviation," *Journal of Consumer Research* 37, no. 2 (2010), pp. 264–78; doi: 10.1086/651567.

i. Kathy Collins, "Here's How to Use Analytics to Tell a Brand Story," *Forbes*, April 4, 2014, http://www.forbes.com/sites/onmarketing/2014/04/07/heres-how-to-use-analytics-to-tell-a-brand-story/; Ashley Rodriguez, "H&R Block Ushers in 'Refund Season' with Slew of New Ads," *Advertising Age,* January 9, 2015, http://adage.com; "H&R Block Turns to Domo to Make Data Avalanche Less Taxing," June 25, 2013, http://www.domo.com/news/press/hr-block-turns-to-domo-to-make-data-avalanche-less-taxing.

ii. Bianca Banova, "The Future of Mobile Technology in Medicine: Innovative Medical Apps," *MedCity News,* April 24, 2013, http://medcitynews.com; William Cook, "Is That Little Mole a Big

Problem?" *Daily Mail*, October 3, 2012, http://www.dailymail .co.uk; "mySugr App, Award-Winning iPhone App That Gamifies Blood Sugar Monitoring for People with Diabetes, Launches in US," *The Wall Street Journal*, June 6, 2013, press release, http://online.wsj.com; Mike H, "'Diabetes Monster' App Actually Motivates!" *Diabetes Mine*, June 19, 2013, http://www .diabetesmine.com.

iii. Ronnie Cummins, "ORCA to Attack 'Natural' Products Labeling Fraud," *Organic Consumers Association*, March 7, 2013, http:// www.organicconsumers.org; Ashby Jones, "Is Your Dinner 'All Natural'?" *The Wall Street Journal*, September 20, 2011; "Diet and Nutrition Report," *Consumer Reports*, February 2009, http:// www.consumerreports.org; Rachel Gross, "Farmers Seek to Raise Standards for Berries," *The New York Times*, September 23, 2011, http://www.nytimes.com; Mayo Clinic Staff, "Organic Foods: Are They Safer? More Nutritious?" http://www.mayoclinic .com; Natural and Organic Foods Backgrounder, Food Marketing Institute, http://www.fmi.org; Stacey R. Finkelstein and Ayelet Fishbach, "When Healthy Food Makes You Hungry," *Journal of Consumer Research* 37, no. 3 (October 2010), pp. 357–67.

iv. John Schwartz, "Chicago and 2 California Counties Sue Over Marketing of Painkillers," *The New York Times*, August 24, 2014, http://www.nytimes.com.

v. Roger Dooley, "The Smartest Supermarket You Never Heard Of," *Forbes*, January 28, 2014, http://www.forbes.com.

vi. Lauren Johnson, "Sephora Magnifies Mobile Ambitions via In-Store Signage, Updated App," *Mobile Commerce Daily*, August 23, 2013.

CHAPTER 7

1. "GE Is So Stoked about 3D Printing, They're Using It to Make Parts for Jet Engines," *The Economist*, November 24, 2013.

2. Beth McKenna, "3D Printing in the Aerospace Industry: How General Electric and United Technologies Are Using This Technology," *The Motley Fool*, February 28, 2014, http://www .fool.com.

3. "GE Says 3D Printing Will 'Touch' 50% of Manufacturing," *Investors Business Daily*, October 7, 2013.

4. Clint Boultin, "Printing Out Barbies and Ford Cylinders," *The Wall Street Journal*, June 5, 2013, http://online.wsj.com.

5. Tim Catts, "GE Turns to 3D Printers for Plane Parts," *Bloomberg Businessweek*, November 27, 2013, http://www.businessweek .com.

6. Samuel Gibs, "Battle for the Car: Will Google, Apple, or Microsoft Dominate?" *The Guardian*, March 6, 2014, http:// www.theguardian.com.

7. Corey Eridon, "The Average Large Company Has 178 Social Media Accounts," *Hub Spot*, January 10, 2012, http://blog.hubspot.com.

8. http://www.constantcontact.com.

9. http://www.volkswagenag.com.

10. http://www.vwgroupsupply.com.

11. "Budget of the United States Government: Fiscal Year 2014," Executive Office of the United States: Office of Management and Budget.

12. Ibid.

13. http://www.guru.com.

14. These definitions are provided by http://www.marketingpower .com (the American Marketing Association's website). We have bolded the key terms.

15. E. J. Schultz, "GE Tells the Secret of Making Geeky Cool," *Advertising Age*, October 5, 2013, http://adage.com.

16. http://www.goer.state.ny.us.

17. Philip Letts, "Why Do B2B Firms Still Not 'Get' the Internet?," *Real Business*, March 13, 2014, http://realbusiness.co.uk; Amber Mac, "5 (Relatively Simple) Steps to B2B Social Media Success," *Fast Company*, February 14, 2014, http://www.fastcompany.com.

18. http://www.hootsuite.com.

19. Tracey Peden, "The Use of White Papers in Today's B2B Market," *Marketing Resources Blog*, May 28, 2013, http://blog .ubmcanon.com/bid/285080/.

20. Michael Krause, "How Does Oregon Football Keep Winning? Is It the Uniforms?," *Grantland*, August 30, 2011, http://www .grantland.com.

21. Fabiana Ferreira et al., "The Transition from Products to Solutions: External Business Model Fit and Dynamics," *Industrial Marketing Management* 42, no. 7 (2013), pp. 1093–1101; Mark W. Johnston and Greg W. Marshall, *Contemporary Selling: Building Relationships, Creating Value* (New York: Routledge, 2013); Barton A. Weitz, Stephen B. Castleberry, and John F. Tanner, *Selling Building Partnerships*, 6th ed. (Burr Ridge, IL: McGraw-Hill/Irwin, 2005), p. 93.

22. Maggie Hira, "How Does a Fashion Buyer Spend a Workday?" http://www.ehow.com; U.S. Department of Labor, http://www .bls.gov.

i. Quentin Harvey, "IBM Plans Big Spending for the Cloud," *The New York Times*, January 17, 2014, http://www.nytimes.com; Alex Barinka, "IBM's Watson to Help Rich DBS Clients with 'Jeopardy' Smarts," *Bloomberg Technology*, January 8, 2014, http://www.bloomberg.com/.

ii. Stephanie Reitz, "Many US Schools Adding iPads, Trimming Textbooks," *Yahoo Finance*, September 3, 2011, http://finance .yahoo.com; "Do iPads in Schools Change Behavior?" February 22, 2011, http://www.ipadinschools.com; Nick Wingfield, "Once Wary, Apple Warms Up to Business Market," *The New York Times*, November 15, 2011, http://www.nytimes.com; Rachel King, "Apple Woos Businesses Despite Security Worries," *Bloomberg Businessweek*, July 7, 2010, http://www.msnbc.msn .com; Dawn Kawamoto, "iPad 2 Launch Adds Muscle to Apple's Invasion of Corporate America," *Daily Finance*, March 10, 2011, http://www.dailyfinance.com; Leander Kahney, "iPad May Replace Computers and Textbooks in Schools, Experts Predict," *Cult of Mac*, http://www.cultofmac.com.

iii. Sean Silverthorne, "Business Ethics: Pay the Bribe?" *CBS Money Watch*, http://www.cbsnews.com; Stephen H. Unger, "Ethical Aspects of Bribing People in Other Countries," http://www1.cs .columbia.edu; Transparency International, "Bribe Payers Index 2011," http://bpi.transparency.org/; "International Back Scratching," *The Economist*, November 2, 2011, http://www .economist.com; Julia Kollewe, "GlaxoSmithKline's Boss's 2013 Bonus Doubled, Despite Scandal in China," *The Guardian*, February 27, 2014, http://www.theguardian.com; Ernst and Young, "European Fraud Survey 2011: Recovery, Regulation and Integrity," http://www.ey.com.

iv. LinkedIn Press Center, "About Us," http://press.linkedin.com; Heidi Cohen, "5 LinkedIn Business Goals," March 25, 2011, http://heidicohen.com; Maria Tabaka, "How to Launch a Linked-In Company Page," *Inc.*, April 17, 2011, http://www.inc.com.

v. http://www.hubspot.com; http://www.hubspot.com/customer-case-studies/; "Should Your Startup Be Hubspotting?" *Tech Cocktail*, May 6, 2013, http://www.tech.co; "2013 State of Inbound Marketing," *HubSpot*, May 2013, http://www .stateofinboundmarketing.com.

CHAPTER 8

1. Coca-Cola India, "Company History," http://www.coca-colaindia .com.

2. Ratna Bhushan, "Coca-Cola Plans Aggressive Ad Campaign in 2014 to Be India's Favourite Soft Drink," *Economic Times,* January 1, 2014, http://articles.economictimes.indiatimes.com.

3. Nikhil Gulati and Rumman Ahmed, "India Has 1.2 Billion People, but Not Enough Drink Coke," *The Wall Street Journal,* July 13, 2012, http://online.wsj.com.

4. Ibid.

5. Pierre-Richard Agenor, *Does Globalization Hurt the Poor?* (Washington, DC: World Bank, 2002); "Globalization: Threat or Opportunity," International Monetary Fund, http://www.imf.org.

6. For example, the deficit for the month of December 2013 was $57.6 million. See http://www.census.gov.

7. http://www.acdi-cida.gc.ca.

8. http://siteresources.worldbank.org/DATASTATISTICS/Resources/ GNIPC.pdf; Arthur O'Sullivan, Steven Sheffrin, and Steve Perez, *Macroeconomics: Principles and Tools,* 8th ed. (Upper Saddle River, NJ: Prentice Hall, 2013).

9. *The Economist,* "The Big Mac Index," January 23, 2014, http:// www.economist.com/content/big-mac-index.

10. Justin Dove, "Taking Advantage of Dollar Weakness," *Investor U,* July 28, 2011, http://www.investmentu.com.

11. Jack Neff, "Emerging-Market Growth War Pits Global Brand Giants against Scrappy Local Rivals," *Advertising Age,* June 13, 2011, http://adage.com.

12. "Coca-Cola Tackles Rural Indian Market" (video), *The Wall Street Journal,* May 3, 2010.

13. Melissa Ip, "Bottom of the Pyramid—a Decade of Observations," *Social Enterprise Buzz,* January 21, 2013, http://www .socialenterprisebuzz.com.

14. Kate O'Keeffe, "The Cheapest, Richest Casino in Macau," *The Wall Street Journal,* February 5, 2014.

15. Neff, "Emerging-Market Growth War."

16. Wayne Ma, "China Levies 6.5% Tariff on U.S. on U.S. Solar-Panel Materials," *The Wall Street Journal,* September 18, 2013, http:// www.online.wsj.com.

17. Leslie Josephs, "U.S. Increases Sugar Quota for Second Time," *The Wall Street Journal,* June 23, 2011, http://online.wsj.com.

18. Leslie Josephs, "U.S. Unlikely to Raise Sugar-Import Quota," *The Wall Street Journal,* February 19, 2013, http://online .wsj.com.

19. "Exchange Rate," http://en.wikipedia.org/wiki/Exchange_rate.

20. http://ucatlas.ucsc.edu.

21. http://www.unescap.org.

22. Johny Johansson, *Global Marketing,* 5th ed. (New York: McGraw-Hill/Irwin, 2008).

23. Philip R. Cateora, Mary C. Gilly, and John L. Graham, *International Marketing,* 15th ed. (New York: McGraw-Hill, 2011); Danielle Medina Walker and Thomas Walker, *Doing Business Internationally: The Guide to Cross-Cultural Success,* 2nd ed. (Princeton, NJ: Trade Management Corporation, 2003).

24. Nicola Clark, "French Signal Flexibility on Sunday Closings," *The New York Times,* September 30, 2013, http://www.nytimes.com; 2014 IKEA French Store Hours, such as: http://www.ikeafans .com/directory/ikea-rennes-pac-153.html; Devorah Lauter, "IKEA Fined for Sunday Opening in France," *Forbes,* April 6, 2008.

25. Peter Siegenthaler, "Store Opening Hours: A Regular Vote Topic," *Swissinfo.ch,* June 18, 2012, http://www.swissinfo.ch/.

26. For a website dedicated to Hofstede's research, see http:// www.geert-hofstede.com/.

27. Rosalie L. Tung and Alain Verbeke, eds., "Beyond Hofstede and GLOBE: Improving the Quality of Cross-Cultural Research," *Journal of International Business Studies* 41 (Special Issue, 2010).

28. Note that the time orientation and indulgence dimensions are relatively more recent additions to the categorization. See Geert Hofstede, "Dimensions of National Cultures," http://www .geerthofstede.eu/dimensions-of-national-cultures.

29. http://geert-hofstede.com/countries.html.

30. James W. Carey, *Communication as Culture,* rev. ed. (New York: Routledge, 2009).

31. *The Economist,* "Why Is South Africa Included in the BRICS?" March 29, 2013, http://www.economist.com/blogs/ economist-explains/.

32. "Brazil," U.S. Department of State, http://www.state.gov; CIA, *The CIA World Factbook,* https://www.cia.gov/library/publications/ the-world-factbook/.

33. "Russia," U.S. Department of State, http://www.state.gov; CIA, *The CIA World Factbook,* https://www.cia.gov.

34. Robin Wauters, "Already Europe's Largest Internet Market and Still Growing Astoundingly Fast: Russia by the Numbers," *The Next Web,* April 20, 2012, http://www.thenextweb.com.

35. "India," U.S. Department of State, http://www.state.gov; CIA, *The CIA World Factbook,* https://www.cia.gov.

36. Megha Bahree, "India Unlocks Door for Global Retailers," *The Wall Street Journal,* November 25, 2011.

37. "China," U.S. Department of State, http://www.state.gov; CIA, *The CIA World Factbook* https://www.cia.gov.

38. Lance Eliot Brouthers et al., "Key Factors for Successful Export Performance for Small Firms," *Journal of International Marketing* 17, no. 3 (2009), pp. 21–38; "Selling Overseas," November 12, 2009, http://www.entrepreneur.com.

39. Juro Osawa and Lorraine Luk, "How Lenovo Built a Tech Giant," *The Wall Street Journal,* January 30, 2014, http://online.wsj.com; Juro Osawa and Yun-Hee Kim, "PC Firm Lenovo Hunts for Brazil Acquisitions," *The Wall Street Journal,* May 28, 2012, http:// online.wsj.com.

40. Philip R. Cateora, Mary C. Gilly, and John L. Graham, *International Marketing,* 14th ed. (New York: McGraw-Hill, 2009).

41. Jack Neff, "Yahoo Ramps Up Global Study of Moms and Technology," *Advertising Age,* November 17, 2011, http://adage .com.

42. http://www.pgeverydaysolutions.ca/thankyoumom/helping-moms .jsp.

43. Natalie Zmuda, "P&G, Levi's, GE Innovate by Thinking in Reverse," *Advertising Age,* June 13, 2011, http://adage.com.

44. Julie Jargon, "Can M'm, M'm Good Translate?" *The Wall Street Journal,* July 9, 2007, p. A16; Brad Dorfman and Martinne Geller, "Campbell Soup in Joint Venture to Expand in China," *Reuters,* January 12, 2011, http://www.reuters.com; Julie Jargon, "Campbell Soup to Exit Russia," *The Wall Street Journal,* June 29, 2011, http://online.wsj.com.

45. http://www.pringles.it/.

46. Bill Johnson, "The CEO of Heinz on Powering Growth in Emerging Markets," *Harvard Business Review,* October 2011.

47. Silvia Fabiana et al., eds., *Pricing Decisions in the Euro Era: How Firms Set Prices and Why* (Oxford: Oxford University Press, 2007); Cateora et al., *International Marketing*.

48. Fabiana et al., *Pricing Decisions;* Amanda J. Broderick, Gordon E. Greenley, and Rene Dentiste Mueller, "The Behavioural Homogeneity Evaluation Framework: Multi-Level Evaluations of Consumer Involvement in International Segmentation," *Journal of International Business Studies* 38 (2007), pp. 746–63; Terry Clark, Masaaki Kotabe, and Dan Rajaratnam, "Exchange Rate Pass-Through and International Pricing Strategy: A Conceptual Framework and Research Propositions," *Journal of International Business Studies* 30, no. 2 (1999), pp. 249–68.

49. Sarah Morris, "How Zara Clothes Turned Galacia into a Retail Hotspot," *Reuters,* October 31, 2011, http://www.reuters.com.

50. "India: Creating Rural Entrepreneurs," http://www.unilever.com.

51. CIA, *The CIA World Factbook,* https://www.cia.gov/library/publications/the-world-factbook/fields/2103.html.

52. Jess Halliday, "Industry Prepares to Fight Junk Food Ad Watershed," *Food and Drink Europe.com,* January 3, 2008, http://www.foodanddrinkeurope.com.

53. Michael Wines, "Picking Brand Names in Asia Is a Business Itself," *Advertising Age,* November 11, 2011, http://www.nytimes.com; Brand Channel, http://www.brandchannel.com.

54. Rachel Lamb, "Cartier, Ferragamo Ramp Up Global Marketing through New York Times China," *Luxury Daily,* June 29, 2012, http://www.luxurydaily.com/.

55. Joan Voight, "How to Customize Your U.S. Branding Effort to Work around the World," *Adweek,* September 3, 2008.

i. Rose Yu and Colum Murphy, "In China, Air Pollution Rules Spur Big Car Purchases," *The Wall Street Journal,* August 7, 2013, http://online.wsj.com.

ii. Jason Kincaid, "Mark Zuckerberg on Facebook's Strategy for China (and His Wardrobe)," *Tech Crunch,* October 16, 2010, http://techcrunch.com; Loretta Chao, "Brazil: The Social Media Capital of the Universe," *The Wall Street Journal,* February 4, 2013, http://online.wsj.com; Normandy Madden, "What Will Facebook Find If It Ventures into China?" *Advertising Age Global,* June 13, 2011, http://adage.com; Chloe Albanesius, "Human Rights Group Slams Facebook over China Strategy," *PCMag.com,* June 3, 2011, http://www.pcmag.com.

iii. Anil Urs and K. Giriprakash, "Tata Starbucks CEO: Our Business in India Continues to Exceed Expectations," *Hindu Business Line,* November 27, 2013, http://www.thehindubusinessline.com; Starbucks, "Starbucks Celebrates Its First Year in India with Launch of India Estates Blend," October 21, 2013, http://news.starbucks.com.

iv. Mike Ramsay, "Ford to Take Mustang Sports Car Global," *The New York Times,* December 4, 2013; "With 2015 Mustang, Ford Puts American Icon on Global Path," *Advertising Age,* December 5, 2013.

CHAPTER 9

1. David Carr, "Giving Viewers What They Want," *The New York Times,* February 24, 2013, http://www.nytimes.com.

2. "Dreamworks Animation to Create Netflix's First Original Kids' Show," *Advertising Age,* February 12, 2013.

3. James Agarwal, Naresh K. Malhotra, and Ruth N. Bolton, "A Cross-National and Cross-Cultural Approach to Global Market Segmentation: An Application Using Consumers' Perceived Service Quality," *Journal of International Marketing* 18, no. 3 (September 2010), pp. 18–40.

4. Bill Carter, "ABC Viewers Tilt Female for a Network Light on Sports," *The New York Times,* December 17, 2013, http://www.nytimes.com; Alex Sood, "The Lost Boys Found: Marketing to Men through Games," *Fast Company,* March 10, 2011, http://www.fastcompany.com; Jeanine Poggi, "Men's Shopping Shrines," *Forbes,* September 30, 2008, http://www.forbes.com.

5. Michael R. Solomon, *Consumer Behavior,* 10th ed. (Upper Saddle River, NJ: Prentice Hall, 2012).

6. Rosellina Ferraro, Amna Kirmani, and Ted Matherly, "Look at Me! Look at Me! Conspicuous Brand Usage, Self-Brand Connection, and Dilution," *Journal of Marketing Research* 50, no. 4 (2013), pp. 477–88; Keith Wilcox and Andrew T. Stephen, "Are Close Friends the Enemy? Online Social Networks, Self-Esteem, and Self-Control," *Journal of Consumer Research* 40, no. 1 (2013), pp. 90–103.

7. Eric Wilson, "Less Ab, More Flab," *The New York Times,* May 22, 2013.

8. Michael R. Solomon, *Consumer Behavior: Buying, Having, and Being,* 10th ed. (Upper Saddle River, NJ: Prentice Hall, 2012).

9. James M. Hagerty, "Harley, with Macho Intact, Tries to Court More Women," *The Wall Street Journal,* October 31, 2011, http://online.wsj.com; Harley-Davidson, "Global Customer Focus," http://investor.harley-davidson.com.

10. Harley-Davidson, "Women Riders," http://www.harley-davidson.com.

11. http://www.strategicbusinessinsights.com/vals/store/USconsumers/intro.shtml.

12. http://www.strategicbusinessinsights.com/vals/applications/apps-pos.shtml.

13. "Segmentation and Targeting," http://www.kellogg.northwestern.edu; Carson J. Sandy, Samuel D. Gosling, and John Durant, "Predicting Consumer Behavior and Media Preferences: The Comparative Validity of Personality Traits and Demographic Variables," *Psychology & Marketing* 30, no. 11 (2013), pp. 937–49.

14. For an interesting take on this issue, see Joseph Jaffe, *Flip the Funnel* (Hoboken, NJ: Wiley, 2010).

15. V. Kumar, Ilaria Dalla Pozza, and Jaishankar Ganesh, "Revisiting the Satisfaction–Loyalty Relationship: Empirical Generalizations and Directions for Future Research," *Journal of Retailing* 89, no. 3 (2013), pp. 246–62; Irit Nitzan and Barak Libai, "Social Effects on Customer Retention," *Journal of Marketing* 75, no. 6 (November 2011), pp. 24–38.

16. ESRI, "Tapestry Segmentation Reference Guide" and "Tapestry Segmentation: The Fabric of America's Neighborhood," www.esri.com.

17. ESRI, "Lifestyles-Esri Tapestry Segmentation," http://www.esri.com/data/esri_data/tapestry

18. Thorsten Blecker, *Mass Customization: Challenges and Solutions* (New York: Springer, 2006).

19. Jessica Guynn, "Social Networks Showing Users More Targeted Ads," *Los Angeles Times,* December 10, 2013, http://www.latimes.com.

20. C. Page Moreau, Leff Bonney, and Kelly B. Herd, "It's the Thought (and the Effort) That Counts: How Customizing for Others Differs from Customizing for Oneself," *Journal of Marketing* 75, no. 5 (September 2011), pp. 120–33.

21. This circular depiction of the value proposition is based on work by John Bers (Vanderbilt University) and adaptation and development of circles of success by Ronald Goodstein (Georgetown University).

22. http://www.gatorade.com/frequently_asked_questions/default.aspx.

23. http://www.drpeppersnapplegroup.com/brands/7up/.

24. Kyle Stock, "Louis Vuitton Shops for Even Richer Customers," *Bloomberg Businessweek,* September 25, 2013, http://www.businessweek.com.

i. Chris Matyszczyk, "For Teens, Facebook Is 'Dead and Buried,'" *CNET,* December 27, 2013, http://news.cnet.com.

ii. Sarah Halzack, "Starbucks Has Managed to Get You Addicted to Its Coffee—And Its App," *Washington Post,* January 23, 2015, http://www.washingtonpost.com; Kate Kaye, "At Starbucks, Data Pours In. But What to Do With It?" *Advertising Age,* March 22, 2013, http://adage.com; WBAL NewsRadio 1090, "Why Consumers Are Addicted to Starbucks App," *WBAL News,* February 19, 2015, http://www.wbal.com/article/113508/21/why-consumers-are-addicted-to-starbucks-app.

iii. Kate Kaye, "Rockefeller to Marketing Data Giants: You're on Notice," *Advertising Age,* December 18, 2013; Kate Kaye, "7 Reasons This Senior Senator Hates Your Loyalty Program," *Advertising Age,* December 20, 2013.

iv. Joe Flint, "Why TV Hit 'Longmire' Got Cancelled: Fans Too Old," *The Wall Street Journal,* September 11, 2014, http://online.wsj.com.

CHAPTER 10

1. Brooks Barnes, "At Disney Parks, a Bracelet Meant to Build Loyalty (and Sales)," *The New York Times,* January 7, 2013, http://www.nytimes.com.

2. Christopher Palmeri, "Disney Bets $1 Billion on Technology to Track Theme-Park Visitors," *Bloomberg Businessweek,* March 7, 2014, http://www.businessweek.com.

3. Jack Honomichl, "The 2013 Honomichl Global Top 25 Report," August 25, 2013.

4. Detailed illustrations of scales are provided in two books: Gordon C. Bruner, *Marketing Scales Handbook: A Compilation of Multi-Item Measures,* vol. 7 (Carbondale, IL: GCBII Productions, Fort Worth, TX: 2013); William O. Bearden, Richard G. Netemeyer, and Kelly L. Haws, *Handbook of Marketing Scales: Multi-Item Measures for Marketing and Consumer Behavior Research* (Thousand Oaks, CA: Sage, 2011).

5. For a more thorough discussion of effective written reports, see A. Parasuraman, Dhruv Grewal, and R. Krishnan, *Marketing Research,* 2nd ed. (Boston: Houghton Mifflin, 2007), Ch. 16.

6. John Cloud, "McDonald's Chef: The Most Influential Cook in America?" *Time,* February 22, 2010, http://www.time.com.

7. Jeff Kelly, "Big Data: Hadoop, Business, Analytics, and Beyond," *Wikibon,* February 5, 2014, http://wikibon.org.

8. Rachel Wolfson, "Retailers Using Big Data: The Secret Behind Amazon and Nordstrom's Success," *Big Data News,* December 11, 2014, http://www.bigdatanews.com.

9. "How Amazon Is Leveraging Big Data," *BigData Startups,* http://www.bigdata-startups.com/BigData-startup/amazon-leveraging-big-data/.

10. Amazon, http://www.amazon.com.

11. Wolfson, "Retailers Using Big Data."

12. "Tesco Doubles Customer Rewards in Further Boost to Clubcard," press release, August 14, 2009.

13. Jenny Davey, "Every Little Bit of Data Helps Tesco Rule Retail," *TimesOnline.com,* October 4, 2009.

14. Quentin Hardy, "Big Data Picks Up the Pace," *The New York Times,* March 5, 2014, http://bits.blogs.nytimes.com.

15. Google, "Analytic Guide," http://www.google.com.

16. Google, "Puma Kicks Up Order Rate 7% with Insights from Google Analytics and Viget," case study, 2013.

17. "In Retail Stores, Research Tool Uses Kinect to Track Shoppers' Behavior," *Retail,* December 29, 2011, http://www.springwise.com.

18. Jennifer Reingold, "Can P&G Make Money in a Place Where People Earn $2 Per Day?" *CNN Money,* January 6, 2011, http://features.blogs.fortune.cnn.com.

19. http://www.thetruthaboutcars.com/.

20. "Client Story: Kraft," http://www.communispace.com.

21. Rachael King, "Sentiment Analysis Gives Companies Insight into Consumer Opinion," *Bloomberg Businessweek,* March 1, 2011, http://www.businessweek.com.

22. Richard A. Krueger and Mary Anne Casey, *Focus Groups: A Practical Guide for Applied Research* (Thousand Oaks, CA: Sage, 2009).

23. http://www.campbellsoup.com.

24. Adapted from Parasuraman et al., *Marketing Research,* Ch. 10.

25. Floyd J. Fowler, *Survey Research Methods* (Thousand Oaks, CA: Sage, 2009); Don A. Dillman et al., "Response Rate and Measurement Differences in Mixed-Mode Surveys Using Mail, Telephone, Interactive Voice Response (IVR) and the Internet," *Social Science Research* 38 (March 2009), pp. 1–18.

26. https://pulse.asda.com; "Asda Wins Vision Critical's European Insight Community Award," press release, *Research,* September 30, 2013, http://www.research-live.com/news/.

27. Facebook, "State Bicycle Co.: Building a Strong Customer Base," case study, https://www.facebook.com/advertising/success-stories/state-bicycle.

28. Facebook, https://www.facebook.com/business/a/online-sales.

29. http://www.marketingpower.com/AboutAMA/Pages/Statement%20of%20Ethics.aspx; http://www.helleniccomserve.com.

30. Federal Trade Commission, "Widespread Data Breaches Uncovered by FTC Probe: FTC Warns of Improper Release of Sensitive Consumer Data on P2P File-Sharing Networks," February 22, 2010, http://www.ftc.gov.

31. Roger Dooley, "Neuromarketing: for Coke, It's the Real Thing," *Forbes,* March 7, 2013, http://www.forbes.com.

32. Natasha Singer, "Face Recognition Makes the Leap from Sci-Fi," *The New York Times,* November 12, 2011.

33. Cecilia Kang, "Library of Congress Plan for Twitter: A Big, Permanent Retweet," *The Washington Post,* April 16, 2010; http://www.cdt.org; Mark Penn, "Did Google Violate Privacy Laws?" http://www.politicallyillustrated.com, April 2, 2010; Lona M. Farr, "Whose Files Are They Anyway? Privacy Issues for the Fundraising Profession," *International Journal of Nonprofit and Voluntary Sector Marketing* 7, no. 4 (November 2002), p. 361.

34. Somini Sengupta, "No U.S. Action, So States Move on Privacy Law," *The New York Times,* October 30, 2013, http://www.nytimes.com.

35. MP Mueller, "The Secret of Neuromarketing: Go for the Pain," *The New York Times,* August 7, 2012, http://www.nytimes.com.

36. Ilan Brat, "The Emotional Quotient of Soup Shopping," *The Wall Street Journal,* February 17, 2010, http://online.wsj.com.

i. Ashley Lutz, "McDonald's Comes Even Closer to Offering a 24-Hour Breakfast," *Business Insider,* June 6, 2013; Robert Lara, "The True Steamy Story of the Egg McMuffin Hockey Puck Breakfast Turns 40," Adweek.com, August 9, 2013.

ii. Amol Sharma and Suzanne Vranica, "Nielsen to Add Data for Mobile TV Viewing," *The Wall Street Journal,* September 19, 2013.

iii. Kirsten Acuna, "Google Says It Can Predict Which Films Will Be Huge Box Office Hits," *Business Insider,* June 6, 2013.

iv. Andrew Roberts, "In Some Stores, the Mannequins Are Watching You," *Bloomberg Businessweek,* December 6, 2012, http://www.businessweek.com; Amar Toor, "EyeSee Mannequin Silently Collects Customer Data for Overzealous Retailers," *The Verge,* November 20, 2012, http://www.theverge.com; Joanna Stern, "Department Store Mannequins Are Watching You. No, Really," *ABC News,* November 26, 2012, http://abcnews.go.com.

CHAPTER 11

1. John Tierney, "24 Miles, 4 Minutes, and 834 M.P.H., All in One Jump," *The New York Times,* October 14, 2012, http://www.nytimes.com.

2. http://www.trekbikes.com.

3. Sharon Ng, "Cultural Orientation and Brand Dilution: Impact of Motivation Level and Extension Typicality," *Journal of Marketing Research* 47, no. 1 (February 2010), pp. 186–98.

4. Sam Byford, "Sony Quits the PC Business to Focus on Mobile," *The Verge,* February 6, 2014, http://www.theverge.com.

5. Michael A. Wiles, Neil A. Morgan, and Lopo L. Rego, "The Effect of Brand Acquisition and Disposal on Stock Returns," *Journal of Marketing* 76, no. 1 (2012), pp. 38–58.

6. Austin Carr, "Deep Inside Taco Bell's Doritos Locos Tacos," *Fast Company,* May 1, 2013, http://www.fastcompany.com.

7. Ellen Byron, "Tide Turns 'Basic' for P&G in Slump," *The Wall Street Journal,* August 6, 2009; Barry Silverstein, "P&G Scrubs Out Tide Basic," *BrandChannel,* June 6, 2010, http://www.brandchannel.com.

8. Natalie Zmuda, "Under Armour Unveils Anthem to Kick Off Its Biggest Global Ad Push," *Advertising Age,* February 12, 2013.

9. Kevin Lane Keller, *Strategic Brand Management: Building, Measuring, and Managing Brand Equity,* 4th ed. (Upper Saddle River, NJ: Prentice Hall, 2012); David A. Aaker, *Building Strong Brands* (New York: Simon & Schuster, 2012).

10. This discussion of the advantages of strong brands is adapted from Keller, *Strategic Brand Management.*

11. Kevin Lane Keller and Donald R. Lehmann, "Assessing Long-Term Brand Potential," *Journal of Brand Management* 17 (2009), pp. 6–17.

12. Evan Carmichael, "Obsess over Your Customers—Jeff Bezos," http://www.youngentrepreneur.com, April 7, 2009; http://www.amazon.com/New-Rules-Marketing-PR-Podcasting/dp/0470113456.

13. http://www.interbrand.com. The net present value of the earnings over the next 12 months is used to calculate the value.

14. David Aaker, *Brand Portfolio Strategy: Creating Relevance, Differentiation, Energy, Leverage, and Clarity* (New York: Free Press, 2004); David A. Aaker, *Managing Brand Equity* (New York: Free Press, 1991).

15. Rong Huang and Emine Sarigöllü, "How Brand Awareness Relates to Market Outcome, Brand Equity, and the Marketing Mix," *Journal of Business Research* 65, no. 1 (2012), pp. 92–99; Lopo L. Rego, Matthew T. Billett, and Neil A. Morgan, "Consumer-Based Brand Equity and Firm Risk," *Harvard Business Review* 73, no. 6 (November 2009), pp. 47–60; Natalie Mizik and Robert Jacobson, "Valuing Branded Businesses," *Harvard Business Review* 73, no. 6 (November 2009), pp. 137–53.

16. David Kiefaber, "Activia Shows That Inside Shakira's Famous Stomach Are . . . More Shakiras!," *Adweek,* March 18, 2014, http://www.adweek.com.

17. Tim Nudd, "Zoinks! State Farm Saves Scooby-Doo and the Gang in Groovy Animated Spot," *Adweek,* October 29, 2013, http://www.adweek.com.

18. Katherine Rosman, "Grumpy Cat Has an Agent, and Now a Movie Deal," *The New York Times,* May 31, 2013, http://www.nytimes.com.

19. http://www.marketingpower.com/_layouts/Dictionary.aspx?dLetter=B.

20. Lien Lamey el al., "How Business Cycles Contribute to Private-Label Success: Evidence from the United States and Europe," *Journal of Marketing* 71 (January 2007), pp. 1–15; PLMA (2009), http://www.plmainternational.com.

21. Stephanie Strom, "Groceries Are Cleaning Up in Store Brand Aisles," *The New York Times,* October 2, 2013, http://www.nytimes.com.

22. "Kellogg's 2010 Annual Report," http://annualreport2010.kelloggcompany.com.

23. The distinction between brand and line extensions is clarified in Barry Silverstein, "Brand Extensions: Risks and Rewards," Brandchannel.com, January 5, 2009.

24. See Alokparna Basu Monga and Deborah Roedder John, "What Makes Brands Elastic? The Influence of Brand Concept and Styles of Thinking on Brand Extension Evaluation," *Journal of Marketing* 74, no. 3 (May 2010), pp. 80–92; Thorsen Hennig-Thurau, Mark B. Houson, and Torsten Heitjans, "Conceptualizing and Measuring the Monetary Value of Brand Extensions: The Case of Motion Pictures," *Journal of Marketing* 73, no. 6 (November 2009), pp. 167–83; Rajeev Batra, Peter Lenk, and Michel Wedel, "Brand Extension Strategy Planning: Empirical Estimation of Brand–Category Personality Fit and Atypicality," *Journal of Marketing Research* 47, no. 2 (April 2010), pp. 335–47.

25. David Aaker, *Aaker on Branding: 20 Principles That Drive Success* (Morgan James, 2014); Aaker, *Building Strong Brands.*

26. http://www.neutrogena.com; Vanitha Swaminathan, Richard J. Fox, and Srinivas K. Reddy, "The Impact of Brand Extension Introduction on Choice," *Journal of Marketing* 65, no. 3 (2001), pp. 1–15.

27. Rosellina Ferraro, Amna Kirmani, and Ted Matherly, "Look at Me! Look at Me! Conspicuous Brand Usage, Self-Brand Connection, and Dilution," *Journal of Marketing Research* 50, no. 4 (August 2013), pp. 477–88; Sanjay Sood and Kevin Lane Keller, "The Effects of Brand Name Structure on Brand Extension Evaluations and Parent Brand Dilution," *Journal of Marketing Research* 49, no. 3 (June 2012), pp. 373–82.

28. Ferraro et al. "Look at Me!"; Sharon Ng, "Cultural Orientation and Brand Dilution: Impact of Motivation Level and Extension Typicality," *Journal of Marketing Research* 47, no. 1 (February 2010), pp. 186–98.

29. Mario Marsicano, "Cheetos Lip Balm & More Bizarre Brand Extensions," *The Wall Street Journal,* July 15, 2009.

30. Susan Spiggle, Hang T. Nguyen, and Mary Caravella. "More Than Fit: Brand Extension Authenticity," *Journal of Marketing Research* 49, no. 6 (2012), pp. 967–83; Franziska Völckner et al., "The Role of Parent Brand Quality for Service Brand Extension Success," *Journal of Service Research* 13, no. 4 (2010), pp. 379–96.

31. Guoqun Fu, Jiali Ding, and Riliang Qu, "Ownership Effects in Consumers' Brand Extension Evaluations," *Journal of Brand Management* 16 (2009), pp. 221–33; Christoph Burmann, Sabrina Zeplin, and Nicola Riley, "Key Determinants of Internal Brand Management Success: An Exploratory Empirical Analysis," *Journal of Brand Management* 16 (2009), pp. 264–84.

32. Robert Klara, "The Best (and Worst) Brand Extensions" Ad Week, February 4, 2013.

33. http://www.marriott.com/corporateinfo/glance.mi.

34. Aaker, *Building Strong Brands*.

35. Keller, *Strategic Brand Management*.

36. Ibid.

37. Mukesh Kumar Mishra and Dibyendu Choudhury, "The Effect of Repositioning on Brand Personality: An Empirical Study on BlackBerry Mobile Phones," *IUP Journal of Brand Management* 10, no. 2 (2013); Pascale G. Quester and Nathalie Fleck, "Club Med: Coping with Corporate Brand Evolution," *Journal of Product & Brand Management* 19, no. 2 (2010), pp. 94–102.

38. Maureen Morrison and Natalie Zmuda, "When Good Logos Go Bad," *Advertising Age,* March 17, 2014, http://adage.com.

39. "Morton Salt Girl Birthday Brings Brand Refresh," *Packaging World,* March 12, 2014, http://www.packworld.com.

40. "Daisy Updates Cottage Cheese Pack," *Packaging World,* March 13, 2014, http://www.packworld.com.

41. "Microsoft, Waste Management, The Coca-Cola Company and More at Sustainability in Packaging 2014," *Sustainability in Packaging,* January 6, 2014.

42. Kate Little, "Chobani Yogurt Is Latest Victim in Shrinking Grocery Case," CNBC, January 4, 2014, http://www.cnbc.com.

i. Mark van Rijmenam, "Macy's Is Changing the Shopping Experience with Big Data Analytics," *DataFloq,* March 14, 2014, https://datafloq.com/read/macys-changing-shopping-experience-big-data-analyt/286; Nicole Marie Melton, "Macy's Boosts Web Sales, Email Marketing with Predictive Analytics," *FierceRetailT,* May 14, 2014, http://www.fierceretail.com/retailit/story/macys-boosts-web-sales-email-marketing-predictive-analytics/2014-05-14; Joe Keenan, "Customer Retention: Macy's Uses Predictive Analytics to Grow Customer Spend," *Retail Online Integration,* August 2014, http://www.retailonlineintegration.com/article/macys-uses-predictive-analytics-grow-customer-spend/1.

ii. http://www.axeanarchy.axe.us/novel; Andrew Adam Newman, "Axe Adds Fragrance for Women to Its Lineup," *The New York Times,* January 8, 2012, http://www.nytimes.com; Dianna Dilworth, "Axe Campaign Has Fans Collaboratively Write Graphic Novel Online," *Direct Marketing News,* January 10, 2012, http://www.dmnews.com; Todd Wasserman, "Axe Launches Fragrance with a Graphic Novel on YouTube," *Mashable Business,* January 10, 2012, http://mashable.com.

iii. Tiffany Hsu, "Coca-Cola Anti-Obesity Promises Include No Advertising to Kids," *Los Angeles Times,* May 8, 2013, http://articles.latimes.com; Mike Esterl and Paul Ziobro, "Coke to Limit Ads to Kids, Push Diet Drinks," *The Wall Street Journal,* http://online.wsj.com.

iv. Mark Wilson, "American Airlines Rebrands Itself, and America Along with It," *Fast Company,* January 22, 2012.

v. U.S. Government Accounting Office, "Bottled Water: FDA Safety and Consumer Protections Are Often Less Stringent Than Comparable EPA Protections for Tap Water," July 8, 2009; Associated Press, "Stricter Labeling Urged for Bottled Water," *The Wall Street Journal,* July 8, 2008.

CHAPTER 12

1. Steven Kurutz, "Taking Fashion to a New Dimension: With 3-D Printing, Clothing That Leaves Out the Sewing Machine," *The New York Times,* December 13, 2013, http://www.nytimes.com.

2. Beth McKenna, "3D Printing in the Aerospace Industry: How General Electric and United Technologies Are Using This Technology," *The Motley Fool,* February 28, 2014, http://www.fool.com.

3. Tim Laseter and Jeremy Hutchison-Krupat, "A Skeptic's Guide to 3D Printing," *strategy + business,* November 26, 2013, http://www.strategy-business.com.

4. Phyllis Korkki, "Beyond 3-D Printers' Magic, Possible Legal Wrangling," *The New York Times,* November 23, 2013, http://www.nytimes.com.

5. A. J. Jacobs, "Dinner Is Printed," *The New York Times,* September 21, 2013, http://www.nytimes.com.

6. Tess Stynes, "Hershey Envisions a 3-D Printer for Chocolate," *The Wall Street Journal,* January 16, 2014, http://online.wsj.com.

7. "Doing the Right Thing," http://www.frogbox.com/therightthing.php.

8. Andrew Adam Newman, "Making the Diaper Change Easier for the Changer," *The New York Times,* July 28, 2011, http://www.nytimes.com; "The Huggies Brand Encourages Parents to Showcase Their Active Babies," *The New York Times,* January 19, 2012, http://markets.on.nytimes.com.

9. Koen Pauwels, et al., "New Products, Sales Promotions, and Firm Value: The Case of the Automobile Industry," *Journal of Marketing* 68, no. 4 (2008), p. 142.

10. Elaine Watson, "What's the Size of the US Gluten-Free Prize? $490m, $5bn, or $10bn?" *Food Navigator USA,* February 17, 2014, http://www.foodnavigator-usa.com.

11. http://www.bettycrocker.com/products/gluten-free-products; Keith O'Brien, "Should We All Go Gluten-Free?" *The New York Times,* November 25, 2011, http://www.nytimes.com.

12. Kalpesh Kaushik Desai and Kevin Lane Keller, "The Effects of Ingredient Branding Strategies on Host Brand Extendibility," *Journal of Marketing* 66, no. 1 (2002), pp. 73–93.

13. Erik Kain, "'Madden NFL 25' Sales Down over Last Year, First Week Still Tops 1M Units," *Forbes,* September 5, 2013, http://www.forbes.com.

14. http://www.ideo.com/work/featured/kraft.

15. http://www.marketingpower.com/_layouts/Dictionary.aspx?dLetter=D.

16. Michael J. Barone and Robert D. Jewell, "The Innovator's License: A Latitude to Deviate from Category Norms," *Journal of Marketing* 77 (January 2013), pp. 120–34; Barak Libai, Eitan Muller, and Renana Peres, "The Diffusion of Services," *Journal of Marketing Research* 46 (April 2009), pp. 163–75; Yvonne van Everdingen, Dennis Fok, and Stefan Stremersch, "Modeling Global Spillover of New Product Takeoff," *Journal of Marketing Research* 46 (October 2009), pp. 637–52.

17. Stanley F. Slater, Jakki J Mohr, and Sanjit Sengupta, "Radical Product Innovation Capability: Literature Review, Synthesis, and Illustrative Research Propositions," *Journal of Product Innovation Management* 31, no. 3 (May 2014), pp. 552–566. Rosabeth Moss Kanter, *SuperCorp: How Vanguard Companies Create Innovation, Profits, Growth, and Social Good* (New York: Crown Business, 2009); Rajesh K. Chandy, Jaideep C. Prabhu, and Kersi D. Antia, "What Will the Future Bring? Dominance,

Technology Expectations, and Radical Innovation," *Journal of Marketing* 67, no. 3 (2003), pp. 1–18; Harald J. van Heerde, Carl F. Mela, and Puneet Manchanda, "The Dynamic Effect of Innovation on Market Structure," *Journal of Marketing Research* 41, no. 2 (2004), pp. 166–83.

18. http://www.apple.com; Clayton M. Christensen and Michael E. Raynor, *The Innovator's Solution* (Boston: Harvard Business School Press, 2003).

19. Rajan Varadarajan, Manjit S. Yadav, and Venkatesh Shankar, "First-Mover Advantage in the Internet-Enabled Market Environment," in *Handbook of Strategic e-Business Management* (Heidelberg: Springer, 2014), pp. 157–85; James L. Oakley et al., "Order of Entry and the Moderating Role of Comparison Brands in Brand Extension Evaluation," *Journal of Consumer Research* 34, no. 5 (2008), pp. 706–12; Fernando F. Suarez and Gianvito Lanzolla, "Considerations for a Stronger First Mover Advantage Theory," *Academy of Management Review* 33, no. 1 (2008), pp. 269–70; Ralitza Nikolaeva, "The Dynamic Nature of Survival Determinants in E-commerce," *Journal of the Academy of Marketing Science* 35, no. 4 (2007), pp. 560–71.

20. "Top 10 Reasons for New Product Failure," *The Marketing Fray*, January 7, 2010, http://www.marketingfray.com.

21. http://smashinghub.com/10-coolest-upcoming-gadgets-of-2011.htm.

22. Barak Libai, Eitan Muller, and Renana Peres, "Decomposing the Value of Word-of-Mouth Seeding Programs: Acceleration versus Expansion," *Journal of Marketing Research* 50, no. 2 (2013), pp. 161–76; Jacob Goldenberg, et al., "The Role of Hubs in the Adoption Process," *Journal of Marketing* 73 (March 2009), pp. 1–13.

23. Chris Gaylord, "Future Is Fuzzy for 4K, Ultra-High-Definition TVs," *The Christian Science Monitor*, February 26, 2014, http://www.csmonitor.com.

24. Ellen Byron, "The Cleanest House of All," *The Wall Street Journal*, March 20, 2013, http://online.wsj.com.

25. Carol Matlack, "Electrolux's Holy Trinity for Hit Products," *Bloomberg Businessweek*, October 31, 2013, http://www.businessweek.com.

26. Gabriel Beltrone, "Most Inclusive Ad Ever? Swiffer Spot Stars Interracial Family, and Dad's an Amputee," *Adweek*, January 21, 2014, http://www.adweek.com.

27. Matlack, "Electrolux's Holy Trinity for Hit Products."

28. https://www.youtube.com/user/Blendtec.

29. Natalie Zmuda, "P&G, Levi's, GE Innovate by Thinking in Reverse," *Advertising Age,* June 13, 2011, http://adage.com; "Minute Maid Pulpy Joins Growing List of Billion Dollar Brands for the Coca-Cola Company," press release, February 1, 2011, http://www.thecoca-colacompany.com.

30. Rajani Baburajan, "U.S. Cable Industry Launches CableLabs—Energy Lab within Its R&D Consortium," *Green Technology World,* November 21, 2011, http://green.tmcnet.com.

31. Stefan Stremersch and Walter Van Dyck, "Marketing of the Life Sciences: A New Framework and Research Agenda for a Nascent Field," *Journal of Marketing* 73 (July 2009), pp. 4–30; Brady Huggett, John Hodgson, and Riku Lähteenmäki, "Public Biotech 2010—The Numbers," *Nature Biotechnology* 29 (2011), pp. 585–91, http://www.nature.com.

32. "Pilates Allegra 2 Reformer for Balanced Body," IDEO Case Study, 2011.

33. Dominik Mahr, Annouk Lievens, and Vera Blazevic, "The Value of Customer Cocreated Knowledge during the Innovation Process," *Journal of Product Innovation Management* (2013); Pilar Carbonell, Ana I. Rodríguez-Escudero, and Devashish Pujari, "Customer Involvement in New Service Development: An Examination of Antecedents and Outcomes," *Journal of Product Innovation Management* 26 (September 2009), pp. 536–50; Glen L. Urban and John R. Hauser, "'Listening In' to Find and Explore New Combinations of Customer Needs," *Journal of Marketing* 68, no. 2 (2004), p. 72.

34. Jeff Bellairs, "Innovation and Collaboration Swiftly Launch Green Giant Snack Chips," *Taste of General Mills*, June 19, 2013, http://www.blog.generalmills.com.

35. Josephy Flaherty, "How Home Depot Copied Apple to Build an Ingenious New Bucket," *Wired*, December 31, 2013, http://www.wired.com.

36. Michael Nir, *Agile Project Management* (New York: CreateSpace, 2013); Jim Highsmith, *Agile Product Management: Creating Innovative Products* (Boston, Addison-Wesley, 2009); http://www.betterproductdesign.net; Eric von Hippel, *The Sources of Innovation* (New York: Oxford University Press, 1988); Eric von Hippel, "Successful Industrial Products from Consumers' Ideas," *Journal of Marketing* 42, no. 1 (1978), pp. 39–49.

37. Karl T. Ulrich and Steven D. Eppinger, *Product Design and Development,* 5th ed. (Boston: Irwin/McGraw-Hill, 2011).

38. http://www.marketingpower.com.

39. Ulrich and Eppinger, *Product Design and Development*.

40. Min Zhao, Steven Hoeffler, and Darren W. Dahl, "The Role of Imagination-Focused Visualization on New Product Evaluation," *Journal of Marketing Research* 46 (February 2009), pp. 46–55; http://www.marketingpower.com.

41. Ulrich and Eppinger, *Product Design and Development*.

42. Frederic Lardinois, "YouEye Raises $3M for Its Webcam-Based Usability Testing Service with Emotion Recognition," *Tech Crunch,* May 7, 2013, http://www.techcrunch.com.

43. http://en-us.nielsen.com/tab/product_families/nielsen_bases.

44. Gernot H. Gessinger, *Materials and Innovative Product Development: From Concept to Market* (Oxford: Elsevier, 2009).

45. Michael Cieply, "New Challenge for Filmmakers: Adding Dimension to 3-D Movies," *The New York Times*, August 11, 2013, http://www.nytimes.com.

46. Product Development Management Association, *The PDMA Handbook of New Product Development,* 3rd ed., Kenneth K. Kahn, ed. (New York: Wiley, 2012).

47. Jan Hendrik Fisch and Jan-Michael Ross, "Timing Product Replacements under Uncertainty—the Importance of Material–Price Fluctuations for the Success of Products That Are Based on New Materials," *Journal of Product Innovation Management* (2014); Yuhong Wu, Sridhar Balasubramanian, and Vijay Mahajan, "When Is a Preannounced New Product Likely to Be Delayed?" *Journal of Marketing* 68, no. 2 (2004), p. 101.

48. http://www.walletpop.com/specials/top-25-biggest-product-flops-of-all-time.

49. http://www.pdma.org/.

50. Theodore Levitt, *Marketing Imagination* (New York: Free Press, 1986).

51. Donald R. Lehmann and Russell S. Winer, *Analysis for Marketing Planning,* 7th ed. (Burr Ridge IL: McGraw-Hill/Irwin, 2008).

52. Ibid.; Glen L. Urban and John R. Hauser, *Design and Marketing of New Products,* 2nd ed. (Upper Saddle River, NJ: Prentice Hall, 1993), pp. 120–21.

53. http://www.organicearthday.org/DelMonteFoods.htm; http://www.delmonte.com/Products/.

54. Euromonitor International, "A Revival in Hair Care Innovation," August 12, 2013, http://blog.euromonitor.com.

55. "Winning in Emerging Markets to Drive Growth in the Life Sciences Industry," *Accenture*, 2013, http://www.accenture.com; Eric D. Beinhocker, Diana Farrell, and Adil S. Zainulbhai, "Tracking the Growth of India's Middle Class," *McKinsey Quarterly* (August 2007).

56. Wallace Witkowski, "iPhones and Other Portables Suffering from 'Device Exhaustion,' Analyst Says," *The Wall Street Journal*, August 20, 2013, http://blogs.marketwatch.com.

57. Natalie Zmuda and Jennifer Rooney, "Hallmark Breaks Out of Special Occasion Mold," *Advertising Age*, July 6, 2011, http://adage.com.

58. Alan Kozzin, "Weaned on CDs, They're Reaching for Vinyl," *The New York Times*, June 9, 2013, http://www.nytimes.com; Ed Christman, "Digital Music Sales Decrease for First Time in 2013," *BillboardBiz*, January 3, 2014, http://www.billboard.com.

59. Yvonne Zipp, "As Vinyl Records Get Back in the Groove, Kalamazoo Record Stores See Sales Climb," *MLive*, January 15, 2012, http://www.mlive.com.

60. Steven Levenstein, "Sony's New USB Turntable Sparks Vinyl Revival," March 14, 2008, http://www.inventospot.com; http://www.electronichouse.com; Roy Bragg, "LP Vinyl Records Are Making a Comeback in Audiophile Circles," *Knight Ridder Tribune Business News*, January 3, 2004 (ProQuest Document ID: 521358371); Susan Adams, "You, the Record Mogul," *Forbes*, October 27, 2003, p. 256ff.

61. Goutam Challagalla, R. Venkatesh, and Ajay Kohli, "Proactive Postsales Service: When and Why Does It Pay Off?," *Journal of Marketing* 73 (March 2009), pp. 70–87; Kevin J. Clancy and Peter C. Krieg, "Product Life Cycle: A Dangerous Idea," *Brandweek*, March 1, 2004, p. 26; Nariman K. Dhalla and Sonia Yuseph, "Forget the Product Life-Cycle Concept," *Harvard Business Review* (January/February 1976), p. 102ff.

62. Jan R. Landwehr, Daniel Wentzel, and Andreas Herrmann, "Product Design for the Long Run: Consumer Responses to Typical and Atypical Designs at Different Stages of Exposure," *Journal of Marketing* 77, no. 5 (2013), pp. 92–107; Peter Golder and Gerard Tellis, "Cascades, Diffusion, and Turning Points in the Product Life Cycle," MSI Report No. 03-120, 2003.

i. Phil Patton, "Out of the Melting Pot and into a Global Market," *The New York Times*, January 13, 2012, http://www.nytimes.com; Paul Stenquist, "A Buffet of Canny Tweaks in Hot Pursuit of Mileage," *The New York Times*, January 13, 2012, http://www.nytimes.com; "Ford to Take Mustang Sports Car Global," *The New York Times*, December 4, 2013, http://www.nytimes.com; "With 2015 Mustang, Ford Puts American Icon on Global Path," *Advertising Age*, December 5, 2013, http://adage.com.

ii. Chris Murphy, "GM's Data Strategy Pushed to Center Stage," Information Week, March 27, 2014, http://www.informationweek.com/; Mark van Rijmenam, "Three Use Cases of How General Motors Applies Big Data to Become Profitable Again," DataFloq, Aug. 25, 2014, https://datafloq.com/; Jonathan H. Owen, David J. VanderVeen, and Lerinda L. Frost, "General Motors: Using O.R. to Meet Auto Industry Challenges and Provide Value to Customers and the Company," Informs Online, December 2013, http://www.orms-today.org.

iii. Jack Adams, "US Search Engine Market Share Figures Steady in February," *Clickthrough*, March 21, 2014, http://www.clickthrough-marketing.com; Steve Lohr, "Can Microsoft Make You 'Bing'?" *The New York Times*, July 30, 2011, http://www.nytimes.com; Renay San Miguel, "Bing's New Bells and Whistles Could Leave Searchers' Heads Ringing," *TechNewsWorld*, March 29, 2010; Jared Newman, "How Microsoft Plans to Beat Google with Bing," *PCWorld*, August 1, 2011, http://www.pcworld.com.

iv. The Humane Society, "Cosmetic and Product Testing," http://www.humanesociety.org; The Body Shop, "Saying No to Animal Testing," http://www.thebodyshop.com; Procter & Gamble, "Animal Welfare and Alternatives," http://www.pg.com; http://www.peta.org; http://ec.europa.eu/consumers/sectors/cosmetics/animal-testing/index_en.htm.

CHAPTER 13

1. Stu Woo, "Amazon 'Primes' Pump for Loyalty," *The Wall Street Journal*, November 14, 2011, http://online.wsj.com; Stu Woo and John Letzing, "Amazon's Spending Habit Hurts Profit," *The Wall Street Journal*, February 1, 2012, http://online.wsj.com; David Streitfield, "Complaints as Amazon Raises the Cost of Prime," *The New York Times*, March 13, 2014, http://www.nytimes.com.

2. Valarie A. Zeithaml, Mary Jo Bitner, and Dwayne D. Gremler, *Services Marketing: Integrating Customer Focus across the Firm*, 6th ed. (Burr Ridge, IL: McGraw-Hill/Irwin, 2012).

3. Bureau of Economic Analysis, news release, January 27, 2012, http://www.bea.gov; "Fortune 500," *CNNMoney*, May 23, 2011, http://money.cnn.com.

4. Zeithaml et al., *Services Marketing*.

5. Choice Hotels, "Special Guest Policies," http://www.choicehotels.com.

6. Andrew Adam Newman, "A Gym for People Who Don't Like Gyms," *The New York Times*, January 2, 2013, http://www.nytimes.com.

7. The discussion of the Gaps Model and its implications draws heavily from Michael Levy, Barton A. Weitz, and Dhruv Grewal, *Retailing Management*, 9th ed. (Burr Ridge, IL: Irwin/McGraw-Hill, 2013); it is also based on the classic work of Zeithaml, Parasuraman, and Berry, *Delivering Quality Service*; Valerie Zeithaml, Leonard Berry, and A. Parasuraman, "Communication and Control Processes in the Delivery of Service Quality," *Journal of Marketing* 52, no. 2 (April 1988), pp. 35–48.

8. Zhen Zhu, et al., "Fix It or Leave It? Customer Recovery from Self-Service Technology Failures," *Journal of Retailing* 89, no. 1 (2013), pp. 15–29.

9. Velitchka D. Kaltcheva, Robert D. Winsor, and A. Parasuraman, "Do Customer Relationships Mitigate or Amplify Failure Responses?" *Journal of Business Research* 66, no. 4 (2013), pp. 525–32; Ruth N. Bolton, et al., "Small Details That Make Big Differences: A Radical Approach to Consumption Experience as a Firm's Differentiating Strategy," *Journal of Service Management* 25, no. 2 (2014), pp. 253–74; Lance A. Bettencourt, Stephen W. Brown, and Nancy J. Sirianni, "The Secret to True Service Innovation," *Business Horizons* 56, no. 1 (2013), pp. 13–22.

10. Zeithaml et al., *Services Marketing*.

11. Janelle Barlow, "A Complaint Is a Gift Corner," http://www.tmius.com.

12. Michael Bergdahl, *The Retail Revolution: How Wal-Mart Created a Brave New World of Business* (New York: Metropolitan Books, 2009); Michael Bergdahl, *The 10 Rules of Sam Walton: Success Secrets for Remarkable Results* (Hoboken, NJ: Wiley, 2006).

13. Steven W. Rayburn, "Improving Service Employee Work Affect: The Transformative Potential of Work Design," *Journal of Services Marketing* 28, no. 1 (2014), pp. 71–81; Zhu et al., "Fix It or Leave It?"; Ying Hong, et al., "Missing Link in the Service Profit Chain: A Meta-Analytic Review of the Antecedents, Consequences, and Moderators of Service Climate," *Journal of Applied Psychology* 98, no. 2 (2013), p. 237.

14. Jason Colquitt, Jeffery LePine, and Michael Wesson, *Organizational Behavior: Improving Performance and Commitment in the Workplace,* 3rd ed. (Burr Ridge, IL: McGraw-Hill, 2012); Felicitas M. Morhart, Walter Herzog, and Torsten Tomczak, "Brand-Specific Leadership: Turning Employees into Brand Champions," *Journal of Marketing* 73 (September 2009), pp. 122–42.

15. Daisy Wademan Dowling, "The Best Advice I Ever Got: Michelle Peluso, President and Chief Executive Officer, Travelocity," *The Harvard Business Review,* October 2008, https://hbr.org.

16. "Travelocity," http://www.sabre-holdings.com/ourBrands/travelocity.html; "Awards," http://svc.travelocity.com.

17. Suzanne C. Makarem, Susan M. Mudambi, and Jeffrey S. Podoshen, "Satisfaction in Technology-Enabled Service Encounters," *Journal of Services Marketing* 23, no. 1 (2009).

18. Sarah Nassauer, "Chili's to Install Tabletop Computer Screens," *The Wall Street Journal,* September 15, 2013, http://online.wsj.com; Alicia Kelso, "Uno Chicago Grill Engages Customers with Tabletop Technology," *Pizza Marketplace,* October 29, 2013, http://www.pizzamarketplace.com; Jeff Morganteen, "CEO: 100,000 Tablets Coming to Applebee's in 2014," *CNBC,* December 10, 2013, http://www.cnbc.com.

19. Anita Whiting and Naveen Donthu, "Closing the Gap between Perceived and Actual Waiting Times in a Call Center: Results from a Field Study," *Journal of Services Marketing* 23, no. 5 (2009), pp. 279–328.

20. Zhu et al., "Fix It or Leave It?"; María Leticia Santos-Vijande, et al., "An Integrated Service Recovery System (ISRS): Influence on Knowledge-Intensive Business Services Performance," *European Journal of Marketing* 47, no. 5/6 (2013), pp. 934–63.

21. Christian Grönroos and Päivi Voima, "Critical Service Logic: Making Sense of Value Creation and Co-creation," *Journal of the Academy of Marketing Science* 41, no. 2 (2013), pp. 133–50; Anne L. Roggeveen, Michael Tsiros, and Dhruv Grewal, "Understanding the Co-Creation Effect: When Does Collaborating with Customers Provide a Lift to Service Recovery?" *Journal of the Academy of Marketing Science* 40, no. 6 (2012), pp. 771–90.

22. Kaltcheva et al., "Do Customer Relationships Mitigate or Amplify Failure Responses?"; Yany Grégoire, Thomas M. Tripp, and Renaud Legoux, "When Customer Love Turns into Lasting Hate: The Effects of Relationship Strength and Time on Customer Revenge and Avoidance," *Journal of Marketing* 73 (November 2009), pp. 18–32.

23. Roggeveen, et al., "Understanding the Co-Creation Effect."

24. Amy Martinez, "REI Now Limiting Returns to One Year," *Seattle Times,* June 3, 2013.

i. Ramon Ray, "Carbonite Offers Data Peace of Mind: A Solid Solution for Small Biz," *Business Insider,* January 24, 2012, http://www.businessinsider.com; David Huber, "Carbonite Inc. (CARB) Online Backup Service," IRA.com, January 26, 2011, http://www.ira.com; "Carbonite Gains from HIPAA Regulations," *Zacks,* March 24, 2014, http://www.zacks.com; "Pricing," http://www.carbonite.com; Eric A. Taub, "Storing Your Files inside the Cloud," *The New York Times,* March 2, 2011, http://www.nytimes.com.

ii. http://www.forbestravelguide.com/five-star-spas.htm; Allison Scott, "New Renovations Add to the Guest and Meeting Experience," http://www.release-news.com; http://www.broadmoor.com.

iii. "About Kroger," http://www.thekrogerco.com/about-kroger; Laurianne McLaughlin, "Kroger Solves Top Customer Issue: Long Lines," *InformationWeek,* April 2, 2014, http://www.informationweek.com/strategic-cio/executive-insights-and-innovation/kroger-solves-top-customer-issue-long-lines/d/d-id/1141541?page_number=1.

iv. Chanelle Bessette, "Social Media Superstars 2014," *CNN,* January 16, 2014, http://money.cnn.com.

v. David Streitfeld, "For $2 a Star, an Online Retailer Gets 5-Star Product Reviews," *The New York Times,* January 26, 2012, http://www.nytimes.com; David Streitfeld, "Faking It to Make It: A Beautiful Try," *The New York Times,* January 27, 2012, http://bits.blogs.nytimes.com; David Streitfeld, "Give Yourself 5 Stars? Online, It Might Cost You," *The New York Times,* September 22, 2013, http://www.nytimes.com.

CHAPTER 14

1. Serena Ng, "At P&G, New Tide Comes In, Old Price Goes Up," *The Wall Street Journal,* February 10, 2014, http://wsj.online.com.

2. Dale Buss, "P&G Looks to Wring More Value out of Tide Brand with Lower-Priced Detergent," *BrandChannel,* September 4, 2013, http://www.brandchannel.com.

3. Ng, "At P&G, New Tide Comes In."

4. R. Suri and M. V. Thakor, "'Made in Country' versus 'Made in County': Effects of Local Manufacturing Origins on Price Perceptions," *Psychology & Marketing* 30, no. 2 (2013), pp. 121–32; R. Suri, K. B. Monroe, and U. Koc, "Math Anxiety and Its Effects on Consumers' Preference for Price Promotion Formats," *Journal of the Academy of Marketing Science* 41, no. 3 (2013), pp. 271–82; Kent B. Monroe, *Pricing: Making Profitable Decisions,* 3rd ed. (New York: McGraw-Hill, 2003); Dhruv Grewal, Kent B. Monroe, and R. Krishnan, "The Effects of Price Comparison Advertising on Buyers' Perceptions of Acquisition Value and Transaction Value," *Journal of Marketing* 62 (April 1998), pp. 46–60.

5. Jennifer Frighetto, "U.S. Consumers Place More Importance on Price and Value," ACNielsen, October 28, 2008.

6. Dhruv Grewal et al., "Evolving Pricing Practices: The Role of New Business Models," *Journal of Product & Brand Management* 20, no. 7 (2011), pp. 510–13; Bang-Ning Hwang et al., "An Effective Pricing Framework in a Competitive Industry: Management Processes and Implementation Guidelines," *Journal of Revenue and Pricing Management* (November 2009); Robert J. Dolan, "Note on Marketing Strategy," Harvard Business School Background Note (November 2000), pp. 1–17.

7. "IBM Market Share Leader in Human Resources (HR) Business Transformation Outsourcing, Enterprise Sector," press release.

8. Rebecca Heslin, "Virgin America Joins Airline Fare Sale Stampede," *USA Today,* January 6, 2010; "Delta Rescinds Fare Increase on Some of Its U.S. Routes," *Salt Lake City News,* September 11, 2007.

9. http://www.carmax.com/enus/car-dealer/default.html.

10. http://www.paradigm.com/products-current/

11. Nick Wingfield, "Apple's Lower Prices Are All Part of the Plan," *The New York Times,* October 24, 2011, http://www.nytimes.com.

12. http://auto.howstuffworks.com/porsche-boxster-history.htm.

13. http://www.motortrend.com/new_cars/12/porsche/sports_car/pricing/.

14. http://jalopnik.com/2013-porsche-boxster-s-the-jalopnik-review-558339290.

15. Fender Electric Guitars, http://www.fender.com.

16. Monroe, *Pricing: Making Profitable Decisions.*

17. This type of B2B price discrimination is illegal under the Robinson-Patman Act of 1936. B2B sellers are allowed to charge different prices for merchandise of the same "grade and quality" if (1) the price difference is justified by different costs in manufacture, sale, or delivery (e.g., volume discounts); or (2) the price concession was given in good faith to meet a competitor's price. See http://www.ftc.gov/tips-advice/competition-guidance/guide-antitrust-laws/price-discrimination-robinson-patman.

18. http://www.marketingpower.com/_layouts/Dictionary.aspx?dLetter=C.

19. http://www.marketingpower.com/_layouts/Dictionary.aspx?dLetter=S.

20. Joan Lindsey-Mullikin and Dhruv Grewal, "Market Price Variation: The Availability of Internet Market Information," *Journal of the Academy of Marketing Science* 34, no. 2 (2006), pp. 236–43.

21. *Merriam-Webster's Dictionary of Law,* 1996.

22. R. Hamilton and A. Chernev, "Low Prices Are Just the Beginning: Price Image in Retail Management," *Journal of Marketing* 77, no. 6 (2013), pp. 1–20; Dinesh K. Gauri, Minakshi Trivedi, and Dhruv Grewal, "Understanding the Determinants of Retail Strategy: An Empirical Analysis," *Journal of Retailing* 84, no. 3 (2008), pp. 256–67.

23. Michael Levy, Barton A. Weitz, and Dhruv Grewal, *Retailing Management,* 9th ed. (Burr Ridge, IL: Irwin/McGraw-Hill, 2014).

24. Abhijit Biswas et al., "Consumer Evaluations of Sale Prices: Role of the Subtraction Principle," *Journal of Marketing* 77, no. 4 (2013), pp. 49–66.

25. http://www.amazon.com.

26. Eric A. Staub, "As Prices Fall, Blu-Ray Players Are Invited Home," *The New York Times,* December 13, 2009.

27. Alison Jing Xu and Robert S. Wyer Jr., "Puffery in Advertisements: The Effects of Media Context, Communication Norms and Consumer Knowledge," *Journal of Consumer Research,* August 2010.

28. J. Lindsey-Mullikin and R. D. Petty, "Marketing Tactics Discouraging Price Search: Deception and Competition," *Journal of Business Research* 64, no. 1 (2011), pp. 67–73. doi: 10.1016/j.jbusres.2009.10.003.

29. Steve Lohr, "Drafting Antitrust Case, F.T.C. Raises Pressure on Google," *The New York Times,* October 12, 2012, http://www.nytimes.com; Claire Cain Miller, "Europeans Reach Deal with Google on Searches," *The New York Times,* April 14, 2013, http://www.nytimes.com.

30. Uwe E. Reinhardt, "Ending Hospital Price Discrimination against the Uninsured," *The New York Times,* January 8, 2010.

31. Daniel M. Garrett, Michelle Burtis, and Vandy Howell, "Economics of Antitrust: An Economic Analysis of Resale Price Maintenance," http://www.GlobalCompetitionReview.com, 2008; Stephen Labaton, "Century-Old Ban Lifted on Minimum Retail Pricing," *The New York Times,* June 29, 2007.

32. "South African Airlines to Be Investigated for Alleged World Cup Price-Fixing, Report DialAFlight," *Business Wire,* February 1, 2010.

33. Tom Bawden, "Bloody Nose for OFT in Row over Tobacco Price-Fixing," *The Independent (London),* December 13, 2011, http:// www.independent.co.uk; "The Marlboro Cartel," http://www.smokingate.com.

34. Garrett et al., "Economics of Antitrust"; Labaton, "Century-Old Ban Lifted."

i. Trefis Team, "Why Apple's Solid-Gold Watch Represents Good Strategy," *Forbes,* March 19, 2015, http://www.forbes.com; Jonathan S. Geller, "No One Understands the Apple Watch Strategy, and It's Totally a Winner," *BRG,* September 8, 2014, http://bgr.com; Rohit Arora, "8 P's of Luxury Brand Marketing," *Luxury Daily,* May 8, 2013, http://www.luxurydaily.com

ii. "A Look Back: How Predictive Analytics Transformed the Airline Industry," *Cusotra,* https://www.custora.com/university/for-marketers/predictive-analytics/basic/predictive-analytics-and-the-airline-industry; "Price Trends & Tips Explanation," *Kayak,* 2015, http://www.kayak.com.

iii. Carl Bialik, Elizabeth Holmes, and Ray A. Smith, "Many Discounts, Few Deals," *The Wall Street Journal,* December 15, 2010, http://online.wsj.com; Vanessa O'Connell, "It's 50% Off . . . Well, Maybe 35%. How Good Are Deals on Members-Only Web Sites?" *The Wall Street Journal,* January 16, 2010; http://www.hautelook.com; http://www.gilt.com.

CHAPTER 15

1. Greg Besinger, "Amazon Wants to Ship Your Package Before You Buy It," *The Wall Street Journal,* January 17, 2014, http://wsjonline.com.

2. This chapter draws from Michael Levy, Barton A. Weitz, and Dhruv Grewal, *Retailing Management,* 9th ed. (Burr Ridge, IL: McGraw-Hill/Irwin, 2012).

3. Ibid.

4. Based on Barton A. Weitz, "PenAgain Sells to Walmart," in Michael Levy and Barton A. Weitz, *Retailing Management,* 8th ed. (Burr Ridge, IL: McGraw-Hill/Irwin, 2012), pp. 564–65; http://www.Penagain.com; Gwendolyn Bounds, "The Long Road to Walmart," *The Wall Street Journal,* September 19, 2005, p. R1; Gwendolyn Bounds, "One Mount to Make It," *The Wall Street Journal,* May 30, 2006, p. B1.

5. Terry L. Esper et al., "Demand and Supply Integration: A Conceptual Framework of Value Creation through Knowledge Management," *Journal of the Academy of Marketing Science* 38, no. 1 (2010), pp. 5–18.

6. See http://www.marketingpower.com/_layouts/Dictionary.aspx.

7. George E. Stigler, "The Division of Labor Is Limited by the Extent of the Market," *Journal of Political Economy* 59, no. 3 (1951), pp. 185–93.

8. http://www.marketingpower.com/live/mg-dictionary.

9. "Entrepreneur's 2014 Franchise 500," http://www.entrepreneur.com.

10. Lisa Scheer, Fred Miao, and Jason Garrett, "The Effects of Supplier Capabilities on Industrial Customers' Loyalty: The Role of Dependence," *Journal of the Academy of Marketing Science* 38, no. 1 (2010), pp. 90–104; Robert W. Palmatier, Rajiv Dant, and Dhruv Grewal, "A Longitudinal Analysis of Theoretical Perspectives of Interorganizational Relationship Performance," *Journal of Marketing* 71 (October 2007), pp. 172–94; Robert W. Palmatier et al., "A Meta-Analysis on the Antecedents and Consequences of Relationship Marketing Mediators: Insight into Key Moderators," *Journal of Marketing* 70 (October 2006), pp. 136–53.

11. Donna Davis and Susan Golicic, "Gaining Comparative Advantage in Supply Chain Relationships: The Mediating Role

of Market-Oriented IT Competence," *Journal of the Academy of Marketing Science* 38, no. 1 (2010), pp. 56–70; Beth Davis-Sramek, Richard Germain, and Karthik Iyer, "Supply Chain Technology: The Role of Environment in Predicting Performance," *Journal of the Academy of Marketing Science* 38, no. 1 (2010), pp. 42–55; Erin Anderson and Barton Weitz, "The Use of Pledges to Build and Sustain Commitment in Distribution Channels," *Journal of Marketing Research* 29 (February 1992), pp. 18–34.

12. http://www.marketingpower.com/_layouts/Dictionary.aspx.

13. http://www.vendormanagedinventory.com.

14. G. P. Kiesmüller and R. A. C. M. Broekmeulen, "The Benefit of VMI Strategies in a Stochastic Multi-Product Serial Two Echelon System," *Computers and Operations Research* 37, no. 2 (2010), pp. 406–16; Dong-Ping Song and John Dinwoodie, "Quantifying the Effectiveness of VMI and Integrated Inventory Management in a Supply Chain with Uncertain Lead-Times and Uncertain Demands," *Production Planning & Control* 19, no. 6 (2008), pp. 590–600; S. P. Nachiappan, A. Gunasekaran, and N. Jawahar, "Knowledge Management System for Operating Parameters in Two-Echelon VMI Supply Chains," *International Journal of Production Research* 45, no. 11 (2007), pp. 2479–505; Andres Angulo, Heather Nachtmann, and Matthew A. Waller, "Supply Chain Information Sharing in a Vendor Managed Inventory Partnership," *Journal of Business Logistics* 25 (2004), pp. 101–20.

15. Kevin Scarpati, "Tesco Big Price Drop Helped by Supply Chain Management," *Supply Chain Digital,* September 23, 2011, http://www.supplychaindigital.com; Michael Garry, "Supply Chain Systems Seen Boosting Tesco's U.S. Stores," *Supermarket News* 55, no. 43 (2007).

16. André Luís Shiguemoto and Vinícius Amaral Armentano, "A Tabu Search Procedure for Coordinating Production, Inventory and Distribution Routing Problems," *International Transactions in Operational Research* 17, no. 2 (2009), pp. 179–95; Ayse Akbalik et al., "Exact Methods and a Heuristic for the Optimization of an Integrated Replenishment-Storage Planning Problem," *International Transactions in Operational Research* 15, no. 2 (March 2008), pp. 195–214.

i. SCDigest, "Supply Chain News: Goya Foods Shows Path to Success for Mid-Market Companies from New Supply Chain Planning Tools," July 13, 2011, http://www.scdigest.com.

ii. Connie Guglielmo, "Apple's Supplier Labor Practices in China Scrutinized after Foxconn, Pegatron Reviews," *Forbes,* December 12, 2013, http://www.forbes.com; "Apple's Chinese Factories Improved Working Conditions," Associated Press, December 12, 2013; Charles Duhigg and David Barboza, "In China, Human Costs Are Built into an iPad," *The New York Times,* January 25, 2012, http://www.nytimes.com/; Melissa J. Anderson, "The Supply Chain Enters the Spotlight," *Evolved Employer,* February 14, 2012, http://www.evolvedemployer.com/.

CHAPTER 16

1. Susannah Edelbaum, "LED Screens, Interactive Windows, a High-Tech H&M, Oh My!!" *The High Low,* November 12, 2013, http://thehighlow.com; Sharon Edelson, "H&M Opening High-Tech Flagship in Times Square," *Women's Wear Daily,* November 12, 2013; Ruth La Ferla, "Lady Gaga Drops In at H&M and the Crowd Goes . . . Well, You Know," *The New York Times,* November 15, 2013, http://www.nytimes.com; Joel Landau, "David Beckham Appears at H&M Store in Times Square," *New York Daily News,* February 1, 2014, http://www.nydailynews.com/.

2. "2011 Global 250 Retailers," *Stores Magazine,* January 2012, http://www.stores.org/STORES%20Magazine%20January%20 2014/global-powers-retailing-top-250.

3. This chapter draws heavily from Michael Levy, Barton A. Weitz, and Dhruv Grewal, *Retailing Management,* 9th ed. (Burr Ridge, IL: McGraw-Hill/Irwin, 2015).

4. "Sales of Food at Home by Type of Outlet Table," *USDA Economic Research Service,* 2010, http://www.ers.usda.gov/datafiles/Food_Expenditures/Food_Expenditures/2010table14_percent.xls.

5. "Top 25 Global Food Retailers 2012," *Supermarket News,* 2012, http://supermarketnews.com/top-25-global-food-retailers-2012/.

6. "Top 75 Retailers & Wholesalers 2012," *Supermarket News,* 2012, http://supermarketnews.com/top-75-retailers-wholesalers-2012.

7. "Conventional Supermarket," *TermWiki,* http://en.termwiki.com/EN:conventional_supermarket (accessed September 6, 2012).

8. "The Fresh Perspective Industry Newsletter," *Perishables Group,* December 2011, http://www.perishablesgroup.com/dnn/LinkClick.aspx?fileticket=CZXbD9yso5g%3D&tabid=4162.

9. "Low-End Grocery Stores Carve Out Niche," *Contact Center Solutions Industry News,* October 13, 2007, http://www.tmcnet.com/usubmit/2007/10/13/3012485.htm.

10. Ibid.

11. Emily Bryson York, "Stuck in the Middle, Big Grocers Make Changes," *Chicago Tribune,* January 6, 2011.

12. "Walmart Supercenters," http://walmartstores.com.

13. https://www.deloitte.com/assets/Dcom-Global/Local%20 Assets/Documents/Consumer%20Business/dtt_CBT_GPRetailing2012.pdf.

14. Karen Talley, "Department Stores Are in Good Position after 1Q Resurgence," *Dow Jones Newswires,* May 16, 2011.

15. Stephanie Clifford, "To Stand Out, Retailers Flock to Exclusive Lines," *The New York Times,* February 14, 2011; Amy Verner, "How Department Stores Can Stay Relevant (and Chic)," *Globe and Mail* (Toronto), April 21, 2012.

16. "Walmart Annual Report," http://walmartstores.com; Sandra M. Jones, "Wal-Mart Making Little Plans," *Chicago Tribune,* May 14, 2011.

17. Russell Redman, "Industry Outlook: Drug Chains Lifted by Improved Economy," *Chain Drug Review,* May 2, 2011, http://www.chaindrugreview.com.

18. Katherine Rosman, "Aspirin, Q-Tips and a New You," *The Wall Street Journal,* March 25, 2010; Sandra M. Jones, "Walgreens Plans Makeover in More Stores," *Chicago Tribune,* March 24, 2010.

19. http://www.wikinvest.com/industry/Off-price_Retail.

20. This section draws from Levy et al., *Retailing Management,* Chapter 2.

21. Nancy M. Pucinelli et al., "The Value of Knowing What Customers Really Want: Interpersonal Accuracy as an Environmental Cue," working paper (2012); Nancy Puccinelli et al., "Customer Experience Management in Retailing: Understanding the Buying Process," *Journal of Retailing* 85 (2009), pp. 15–30.

22. Patricia Marx, "C. Wonder," *The New Yorker,* November 21, 2011, p. 34.

23. Ibid.

24. Kathleen Seiders et al., "SERVCON: A Multidimensional Scale for Measuring Perceptions of Service Convenience," *Journal of the Academy of Marketing Science* 35, no. 1 (2007), pp. 144–56; Leonard Berry, Kathleen Seiders, and Dhruv Grewal, "Understanding Service Convenience," *Journal of Marketing* 66, no. 3 (July 2002).

25. Sherice Jacobs, "3 Ways Live Chat Software Can Improve Your Conversion Rates," *The Daily Egg*, July 23, 2013, http://blog .crazyegg.com.

26. "Sponsored Supplement: Expanding the Reach of Personalization," *Internet Retailer*, March 2010.

27. Christian Homburg, Josef Vollmayr, and Alexander Hahn, "Firm Value Creation through Major Channel Expansions: Evidence from an Event Study in the United States, Germany, and China," *Journal of Marketing*, 2014, http://dx.doi.org/10.1509/jm.12.0179.

28. Hongshuang (Alice) Li and P. K. Kannan, "Attributing Conversions in a Multichannel Online Marketing Environment: An Empirical Model and a Field Experiment," *Journal of Marketing Research* 51 (February 2014), pp. 40–56.

29. Jie Zhang et al., "Crafting Integrated Multichannel Retailing Strategies," *Journal of Interactive Marketing*, 2010.

i. Elaine Watson, "Quirky, Cult-Like, Aspirational, but Affordable: The Rise and Rise of Trader Joe's," *The Packaged Facts*, April 15, 2014.

ii. Shelly Banjo and Serena Ng, "Home Depot: The Place to Go for Toilet Paper?" *The Wall Street Journal*, June 6, 2014; Shelly Banjo, "Home Depot Lumbers into E-Commerce," *The Wall Street Journal*, April 16, 2014.

iii. Huge Inc., "Master Plan: IKEA," *Huge Inc.*, 2012, http://hbs.hugeinc .com/casestudies/ikea; Case Studies, "IKEA and Brandwatch: Embedding Social across the Enterprise," *PerformanceIN*, March 9, 2015, http://performancein.com/news/2015/03/09/ikea-and-brandwatch-embedding-social-across-enterprise/; "IKEA: A Data Matching Love Story," *Cream Global*, 2012, https://www .creamglobal.com/case-studies/latest/17798/33834/ikea-a-data-matching-love-story/; Matt Kwong, "Building Your Career in Hashtags," *Toronto Star*, March 16, 2015, http://www.thestar.com/; James Ainsworth, "IKEA Speaks the Language of Emoticons," *SmartData Collective*, February 12, 2015, http://smartdatacollective .com/mike-longfellow/298876/ikea-speaks-language-emoticons-flat-packswords-mobile.

CHAPTER 17

1. Mike Esterl, "Coke Sticks to Its Strategy While Soda Sales Slide," *The Wall Street Journal*, April 9, 2014, http://online.wsj.com.

2. Ibid.

3. Avi Dan, "Just How Does Coca-Cola Reinvent Itself in a Changed World?" *Forbes*, October 7, 2013, http://www.forbes.com.

4. Jay Moye, "Special Delivery: Inside the 'Share a Coke' e-Commerce Operation," *Coca-Cola Journey: Innovation*, August 10, 2015, http://www.coca-colacompany.com/innovation/special-delivery-inside-the-share-a-coke-e-commerce-operation#TCCC.

5. Coca-Cola, "2014 FIFA World Cup," http://www.coca-colacompany .com/fifa-world-cup/; Lara O'Reilly, "Coke Holds Back Marketing Spend as It Prepares for World Cup Splurge," *Marketing Week*, April 15, 2014, http://www.marketingweek.co.uk.

6. Esterl, "Coke Sticks to Its Strategy."

7. Terence Shimp and J. Craig Andrews, *Advertising Promotion and Other Aspects of Integrated Marketing Communications* (Boston: Cengage Learning, 2013).

8. Ibid.

9. E. K. Strong, *The Psychology of Selling* (New York: McGraw-Hill, 1925).

10. Disney, "Music," http://music.disney.com; Phil Gallo, "Disney Music Tops Interscope in Album Market Share, Enters the EDM Fray," *Billboard*, May 10, 2014, http://www.billboard.com.

11. Andrew Adam Newman, "Trying to Bolster the Image of Frozen Meals as Sales Lag," *The New York Times*, April 23, 2014, http://www.nytimes.com.

12. Ibid.

13. John Philip Jones, "What Makes Advertising Work?" *The Economic Times*, July 24, 2002.

14. http://popsop.com/wp-content/uploads/toyota_prius_plural_02 .jpg; http://www.youtube.com/watch?v=nUor4gdFoyg&feature5_ player_embedded#!; http://www.saatchi.com/news/archive/ prius_goes_plural_through_new_integrated_campaign.

15. American Marketing Association, "Advertising," *Dictionary of Marketing Terms*, https://www.ama.org/resources/Pages/Dictionary.

16. Teri Evans, "Firms Hold Fast to Snail Mail Marketing," *The Wall Street Journal*, January 12, 2010, http://online.wsj.com; George E. Belch and Michael A. Belch, *Advertising and Promotion: An Integrated Marketing Communications Perspective* (New York: McGraw-Hill, 2007).

17. Rebecca Lieb, "Q&A: Cindy Krum Cuts through the Mobile Marketing Alphabet Soup of NFC and RFID," http://econsultancy .com, March 16, 2010.

18. Akihisa Fujita, "Mobile Marketing in Japan: The Acceleration of Integrated Marketing Communications," *Journal of Integrated Marketing Communications* (2008), pp. 41–46; Mobile update, http://www.businessinsider.com; http://www.informationweek .com; http://www.nearbynow.com (accessed May 26, 2010).

19. Yubo Chen, Scott Fay, and Qi Wang, "The Role of Marketing in Social Media: How Online Consumer Reviews Evolve," *Journal of Interactive Marketing* 25, no. 2 (May 2011), pp. 85–94.

20. This section draws from Michael Levy, Barton A. Weitz, and Dhruv Grewal, *Retailing Management*, 9th ed. (Burr Ridge, IL: McGraw-Hill /Irwin, 2015).

21. Megan Halscheid, Micheline Sabatté, and Sejal Sura, "Beyond the Last Click: Measuring ROI and Consumer Engagement with Clickstream Analysis," *Journal of Integrated Marketing Communications*, 2009, pp. 43–50; Vikram Mahidhar and Christine Cutten, "Navigating the Marketing Measurement Maze," *Journal of Integrated Marketing Communications*, 2007, pp. 41–46.

22. http://www.riger.com.

23. Robert Hof, "Digital Ad Spending Tops $100 Billion in 2012," *Forbes*, January 9, 2013, http://www.forbes.com.

24. "Facebook Pages: Insights for Your Facebook Page," http:// www.facebook.com.

25. "Marketing and Advertising Using Google," Google 2007.

26. http://publishing2.com.

i. Todd Wasserman, "How Coke Spread Happiness (and Cokes) via Mobile," *Mashable.com*, August 7, 2012, http://mashable .com; Stuart Elliot, "Google Remixes Old Campaigns, Adding Dash of Digital Tools," *The New York Times*, March 8, 2012, http://www.nytimes.com.

ii. Eric Wilson, "Checking Models' IDs at the Door," *The New York Times*, February 8, 2012, http://www.nytimes.com; David Gianastasio, "Fashion Site Nixes Photo of Freakishly Thin-Looking Model," *Adweek*, July 13, 2011, http://www.adweek .com; Ellie Krupnick, "Drop Dead Ads Banned by ASA for

Too-Skinny Model," *The Huffington Post,* November 10, 2011, http://www.huffingtonpost.com.

iii. Emily Steel, "How Marketers Hone Their Aim Online," *The Wall Street Journal,* June 19, 2007; Charles Duhigg, "How Companies Learn Your Secrets," *The New York Times,* February 16, 2012; George Anderson, "White House, Web Giants Address Consumer Privacy Online," *Retail Wire,* February 24, 2012.

iv. David Vinjamuri, "Priceline Just Killed William Shatner—or Did They?" *Forbes,* February 3, 2012, http://www.forbes.com; Dennis Schaal, "Priceline Unveils New Ad Campaign with Shatner and Kareem," *tnooz,* February 14, 2011, http://www.tnooz.com; Rich Tomaselli, "Priceline Kills the Messenger Because Ads Worked Too Well," *Advertising Age,* January 30, 2010, http://adage.com; "Priceline.com to Webcast 4th Quarter 2011 Financial Results on February 27th," *The New York Times,* January 30, 2012, http://markets.on.nytimes.com; "Priceline Shocker: The Negotiator's Secret Daughter Revealed!" YouTube, January 8, 2013, http://www.youtube.com/watch?v=EDSnjfxu_Ig; Lynn Elber, "Kaley Cuoco Joins Shatner in Priceline Ad Campaign," Associated Press, January 9, 2013, http://bigstory.ap.com.

v. Google Analytics, "Case Study: Puma Kicks Up Order Rate 7% with Insights from Google Analytics and Viget," *Google,* 2013, https://static.googleusercontent.com/media/www.google.com/en/us/analytics/customers/pdfs/puma.pdf; Caitlin Carter, "Rihanna Signs On as Puma's New Creative Director," *Music Times,* December 16, 2014, http://www.musictimes.com/articles/20450/20141216/rihanna-pumas-new-creative-director-new-album-global-ambassador-fashion-icon.htm; Puma, "Rihanna: Gamechanger," Puma.com, http://us.puma.com/en_US/sports/ambassadors/rihanna; Lucia Moses, "Inside Puma's Branded Content Strategy," *Digiday,* December 15, 2014, http://digiday.com/brands/nielsenes-puma-branded-content/; Aaron Ricadela, "Puma's Marketing Strategy Is a Whole New Ball Game," *Business World,* September 19, 2014, http://www.independent.ie/business/world/pumas-marketing-strategy-is-a-whole-new-ball-game-30598229.html; Larissa Faw, "Puma Adds New Channels To Its 'Forever Faster' Campaign," *Media Post,* August 26, 2014, http://www.mediapost.com/publications/article/232889/puma-adds-new-channels-to-its-forever-faster-cam.html.

CHAPTER 18

1. Noam Cohen, "Chipotle Blurs Lines with Satirical Series about Industrial Farming," *The New York Times,* January 27, 2014, http://www.nytimes.com.

2. Chipotle, "What Is Food with Integrity?" http://www.chipotle.com/en-us/fwi/fwi.aspx.

3. Stuart Elliot, "Chipotle Returns to Animation to Support Sustainable Farming," *The New York Times,* September 16, 2013.

4. Cohen, "Chipotle Blurs Lines."

5. Kristina Monllos, "Eating Alone? Chipotle Cups Now Come with Original Writing from Literary Giants," *Adweek,* May 15, 2014, http://www.adweek.com.

6. George E. Belch and Michael A. Belch, *Advertising and Promotion: An Integrated Marketing Communications Perspective* (New York: McGraw-Hill, 2007); Jef I. Richards and Catherine M. Curran, "Oracles on 'Advertising': Searching for a Definition," *Journal of Advertising* 31, no. 2 (Summer 2002), pp. 63–77.

7. Alexandra Bruell, "ZenithOptimedia Forecasts Slow, Steady Growth in Global Ad Spend," *Advertising Age,* March 12, 2012, http://www.adage.com.

8. Dan Zigmond et al., "Measuring Advertising Quality on Television: Deriving Meaningful Metrics from Audience Retention Data," *Journal of Advertising Research* 49, no. 4 (December 2009), pp. 419–28; Robert G. Heath, Agnes C. Nairn, and Paul A. Bottomley, "How Effective Is Creativity? Emotive Content in TV Advertising Does Not Increase Attention," *Journal of Advertising Research* 49, no. 4 (December 2009), pp. 450–63; Raymond R. Burke and Thomas K. Srull, "Competitive Interference and Consumer Memory for Advertising," *Journal of Consumer Research* 15 (June 1988), pp. 55–68; Kevin Lane Keller, "Memory Factors in Advertising: The Effect of Advertising Retrieval Cues on Brand Evaluation," *Journal of Consumer Research* 14 (December 1987), pp. 316–33.

9. Markus Pfeiffer and Markus Zinnbauer, "Can Old Media Enhance New Media? How Traditional Advertising Pays Off for an Online Social Network," *Journal of Advertising Research* 50, no. 1 (2010), pp. 42–49; Terry Daugherty, Matthew Eastin, and Laura Bright, "Exploring Consumer Motivations for Creating User-Generated Content," *Journal of Interactive Advertising* 8, no. 2 (2008); Anthony Bianco, "The Vanishing Mass Market," *BusinessWeek,* July 12, 2004, pp. 61–68.

10. Brendan Greeley, "World Cup Shootout: Can Nike Beat adidas at Soccer?" *Bloomberg Businessweek,* May 15, 2014, http://www.businessweek.com.

11. adidas, "Neo," http://www.adidas.com/us/content/selenagomez.

12. William F. Arens, Michael F. Weigold, and Christian Arens, *Contemporary Advertising,* 12th ed. (New York: McGraw-Hill, 2008).

13. Tulin Erdem, Michael Keane, and Baohong Sun, "The Impact of Advertising on Consumer Price Sensitivity in Experience Goods Markets," *Quantitative Marketing and Economics* 6 (June 2008), pp. 139–76; Xiaojing Yang and Robert E. Smith, "Beyond Attention Effects: Modeling the Persuasive and Emotional Effects of Advertising Creativity," *Marketing Science* 28 (September/October 2009), pp. 935–49; Matthew Shum, "Does Advertising Overcome Brand Loyalty? Evidence from the Breakfast Cereal Market," *Journal of Economics and Management Strategy* 13, no. 2 (2004), pp. 77–85.

14. "Got Milk?" http://www.gotmilk.com.

15. Elaine Wong, "Rebecca Romjin Makes Milk Run," *Brandweek,* January 13, 2010.

16. http://www.marketingpower.com/_layouts/Dictionary.aspx?dLetter=P.

17. https://www.outnumberhunger.com/

18. Theodore Levitt, *The Marketing Imagination* (New York: Free Press, 1986).

19. Belch and Belch, *Advertising and Promotion.*

20. Katherine White and John Peloza, "Self-Benefit versus Other-Benefit Marketing Appeals: Their Effectiveness in Generating Charitable Support," *Journal of Marketing* 73 (July 2009), pp. 109–24.

21. Darren W. Dahl, Jaideep Sengupta, and Kathleen D. Vohs, "Sex in Advertising: Gender Differences and the Role of Relationship Commitment," *Journal of Consumer Research* 36, no. 2 (2009), pp. 215–31; Jaideep Sengupta and Darren W. Dahl, "Gender-Related Reactions to Gratuitous Sex Appeals in Advertising," *Journal of Consumer Psychology* 18, no. 1 (2008), pp. 62–78.

22. Jack Loftus, "ADT Ad Campaign Scares Homeowners into Buying ADT Security," *Gizmodo,* http://gizmodo.com; Jack Neff, "What the Stylish Garbage Can Is Wearing," *Advertising Age,* November 3, 2011, http://adage.com; Natalie Zmuda, "Best Buy Ups Holiday Spending, Introduces 'Game On, Santa' Campaign," *Advertising Age,* November 17, 2011, http://adage.com; Andrew

Adam Newman, "Axe Adds Fragrance for Women to Its Lineup," *The New York Times,* January 8, 2012, http://www.nytimes.com.

23. *AMA Dictionary,* http://www.marketingpower.com/_layouts/Dictionary.aspx?dLetter=M.

24. Some illustrative articles look at the effectiveness of given media: H. Risselada, P. C. Verhoef, and T. H. Bijmolt, "Dynamic Effects of Social Influence and Direct Marketing on the Adoption of High-Technology Products," *Journal of Marketing* 78, no. 4 (2014); Robert Heath, "Emotional Engagement: How Television Builds Big Brands at Low Attention," *Journal of Advertising Research* 49, no. 1 (March 2009), pp. 62–73; Lex van Meurs and Mandy Aristoff, "Split-Second Recognition: What Makes Outdoor Advertising Work?" *Journal of Advertising Research* 49, no. 1 (March 2009), pp. 82–92.

25. William F. Arens, David H. Schaefer, and Michael F. Weigold, *Advertising, M-Series* (Burr Ridge: Irwin/McGraw-Hill, 2012).

26. Stephen Williams, "New Sedans Aim to Break Out of the Pack," *Advertising Age,* February 20, 2012, http://adage.com.

27. Dean M. Krugman et al., *Advertising: Its Role in Modern Marketing* (New York: Dryden Press, 1994), pp. 221–26.

28. Herbert Jack Rotfeld and Charles R. Taylor, "The Need for Interdisciplinary Research of Advertising Regulation: A Roadmap for Avoiding Confusion and Errors," *Journal of Advertising,* Winter 2009.

29. "FTC Charges Green Coffee Bean Sellers with Deceiving Consumers through Fake News Sites and Bogus Weight Loss Claims," May 19, 2014, http://www.ftc.gov/news-events/press-releases.

30. Debra Harker, Michael Harker, and Robert Burns, "Tackling Obesity: Developing a Research Agenda for Advertising Researchers," *Journal of Current Issues & Research in Advertising* 29, no. 2 (2007), pp. 39–51; N. Kapoor and D. P. S. Verma, "Children's Understanding of TV Advertisements: Influence of Age, Sex and Parents," *Vision* 9, no. 1 (2005), pp. 21–36; Catharine M. Curran and Jef I. Richards, "The Regulation of Children's Advertising in the U.S.," *International Journal of Advertising and Marketing to Children* 2, no. 2 (2002).

31. Irina Slutsky, "Nine Things You Can't Do in Advertising If You Want to Stay on the Right Side of the Law," *Advertising Age,* March 7, 2011, http://adage.com.

32. Bob Hunt, "Truth in Your Advertising: Avoid Puffery?" *Realty Times,* June 20, 2007.

33. Ibid.

34. Blue Carreon, "The 2014 Oscars Best Dressed List," *Forbes,* March 2, 2014, http://www.forbes.com.

35. Diego Rinallo and Suman Basuroy, "Does Advertising Spending Influence Media Coverage of the Advertiser?" *Journal of Marketing* 73 (November 2009), pp. 33–46; Carl Obermiller and Eric R. Spangenberg, "On the Origin and Distinctness of Skepticism toward Advertising," *Marketing Letters* 11, no. 4 (2000), p. 311.

36. Jackie Huba, "A Just Cause Creating Emotional Connections with Customers," http://www.inc.com.

37. http://morehope.chilis.com; http://causerelatedmarketing.blogspot.com/2008/03/how-chilis-used-cause-related-marketing.html.

38. Personal communication with Rob Price, VP of Retail Marketing, CVS, June 16, 2009; Carol Angrisani, "CVS Moves to Personalization," *SN: Supermarket News* 56, no. 2 (March 24, 2008), p. 29.

39. Stephanie Clifford, "Web Coupons Know Lots about You, and They Tell," *The New York Times,* April 16, 2010.

40. Jack Neff, "Old Spice Is Killing It on YouTube Again, but Sales Are Down Double-Digits," *Advertising Age,* August 4, 2011, http://adage.com.

41. http://sports.espn.go.com/espn/contests/index.

42. Eva A. van Reijmersdal, Peter C. Neijens, and Edith G. Smit, "A New Branch of Advertising: Reviewing Factors That Influence Reactions to Product Placement," *Journal of Advertising Research* 49, no. 4 (December 2009), pp. 429–49; Pamela Mills Homer, "Product Placement: The Impact of Placement Type and Repetition on Attitude," *Journal of Advertising,* Fall 2009.

43. Abe Sauer, "Beats and Apple: A Match Made in Product Placement Heaven," *Brandchannel.com,* May 28, 2014, http://www.brandchannel.com; Abe Sauer, "The Envelope, Please: The 2014 Brandcameo Product Placement Awards," *Brandchannel.com,* February 27, 2014, http://www.brandchannel.com; Abe Sauer, "Announcing the 2012 Brandcameo Product Placement Award Winners," *Brandchannel.com,* February 13, 2012, http://www.brandchannel.com.

44. Abe Sauer, "The Envelope, Please."

45. http://www.jcrew.com.

i. truth, "Facts," http://www.thetruth.com/facts/; Alina Tugend, "Cigarette Makers Take Anti-Smoking Ads Personally," *The New York Times,* October 27, 2002.

ii. Vindu Goel, "For Twitter, Key to Revenue Is No Longer Ad Simplicity," *The New York Times,* September 16, 2013, http://www.nytimes.com.

iii. David Kiefaber, "Taylor Swift's CoverGirl Ad Is Pulled over Bogus Eyelashes," *Adweek,* December 23, 2011, http://www.adweek.com; David Gianastasio, "Turlington Ads: So Photoshopped They're Misleading?" *Adweek,* July 28, 2011, http://www.adweek.com; Tanzina Vega, "British Authority Bans Two Ads by L'Oréal," *The New York Times,* July 27, 2011, http://mediadecoder.blogs.nytimes.com.

iv. Elyse Dupré, "CVS/Pharmacy Devotes Extracare to Its Loyalty Program," *DM News* 36, no. 8 (2014), pp. 19–22; Stephanie Clifford, "Using Data to Stage-Manage Paths to the Prescription Counter," *The New York Times,* June 19, 2013, http://bits.blogs.nytimes.com.

CHAPTER 19

1. Sam Howe, "The Tale of Boeing's High-Risk Flight into the Jet Age," *Seattle Times,* October 2, 2010.

2. "Airlines Industry Profile: United States," *Datamonitor,* October 2010, pp. 13–14.

3. Suresh Kotha et al., "Boeing 787: The Dreamliner," *Harvard Business School Case #9-305-101,* June 21, 2005.

4. Ibid.

5. Clive Irving, "NTSB Doesn't Think the Boeing 787 Dreamliner Is Safe Enough to Fly," *The Daily Beast,* May 28, 2014.

6. http://www.boeing.com/boeing/commercial/prices/.

7. Jon Ostrower, "Boeing's Top Salesman Works to Rebuild Customer Trust, Fend Off Airbus," *The Wall Street Journal,* October 8, 2013, http://online.wsj.com.

8. Ibid.

9. Bureau of Labor Statistics, http://www.bls.gov.

10. This section draws from Mark W. Johnston and Greg W. Marshall, *Relationship Selling,* 3rd ed. (Burr Ridge, IL: Irwin/McGraw-Hill, 2009); Mark W. Johnston and Greg W. Marshall, *Relationship Selling and Sales Management,* 2nd ed. (Burr Ridge, IL: Irwin/McGraw-Hill, 2007).

11. Geoffrey James, "Selling Gets Complex," *Strategy+Business,* August 27, 2009; Dale Carnegie, *How to Win Friends and Influence People* (New York: Pocket, 1990); Neil Rackham, *SPIN Selling* (New York: McGraw-Hill, 1988).

12. http://4dsales.com/the-cost-of-a-sales-call/.

13. Bill Stinnett, *Think Like Your Customer* (Burr Ridge, IL: McGraw-Hill, 2004).

14. Pam Baker, "Best Sales Practices: Build Lasting Relationships," *CRM Buyer,* January 27, 2009.

15. Mark W. Johnston and Greg W. Marshall, *Relationship Selling,* 2nd ed. (Burr Ridge, IL: Irwin/McGraw-Hill, 2008).

16. S. Anthony Iannarino, "The Last Word on Cold Calling versus Social Media," *The Sales Blog,* April 21, 2014, http://www.thesalesblog.com; Justin Fishaw, "Has LinkedIn Replaced Cold Calling?" *SocialMediaToday,* August 21, 2013, http://www.socialmediatoday.com; Ken Krogue, "Cold Calling Is Dead, Thanks to LinkedIn," *Forbes,* August 9, 2013, http://www.forbes.com.

17. Mark Ward, "CES 2014: What Does the Show Mean to Las Vegas?" *BBC News,* January 9, 2014, http://www.bbc.com.

18. Pete Pachal, "Mashable's Best Tech of CES 2014," *Mashable,* January 7, 2014, http://www.mashable.com.

19. "2012 CES Grows, Excites, and Catalyzes," January 13, 2012, http://www.cesweb.org.

20. Christine Comaford, "Sales Stuck? Try Sticking to a Script," *BusinessWeek,* April 4, 2008.

21. Christine Comaford-Lynch, "A Bad Lead Is Worse Than No Lead at All," *BusinessWeek,* March 26, 2008.

22. J. David Goodman, "Profiling Complaints by Black Shoppers Followed Changes to Stores' Security Policies," *The New York Times,* October 29, 2013, http://www.nytimes.com.

23. Barton A. Weitz, Harish Sujan, and Mita Sujan, "Knowledge, Motivation, and Adaptive Behavior: A Framework for Improving Selling Effectiveness," *Journal of Marketing,* October 1986, pp. 174–91.

24. Dennis Nishi, "To Persuade People, Tell Them a Story," *The Wall Street Journal,* November 9, 2013, http://online.wsj.com.

25. Robert Keller, "Handling Objections in Today's Tough Environment," *SMM,* March 30, 2009.

26. http://www.quotedb.com/quotes/1303.

27. Mark W. Johnston and Greg W. Marshall, *Churchill/Ford/Walker's Sales Force Management,* 9th ed. (Burr Ridge, IL: McGraw-Hill/Irwin, 2009).

28. Adam Auriemma, "Zappos Zaps Its Job Postings," *The Wall Street Journal,* May 26, 2014, http://online.wsj.com.

29. Lynn Huber, "Can Men Sell Avon?" *Online Beauty Biz,* May 25, 2014, http://www.onlinebeautybiz.com; Sadie Whitelocks, "I'm an Avon Laddie! Salesman, 21, Is Part of the New Breed of Men Muscling in on Door-to-Door Trade," *DailyMail,* December 14, 2011, http://www.dailymail.co.uk.

30. Susan Greco, "Personality Testing for Sales Recruits," *INC.,* March 1, 2009.

31. Ned Smith, "10 Traits of Successful Salespeople," *Business News Daily,* March 20, 2013, http://www.businessnewsdaily .com; Steven W. Martin, "Seven Personality Traits of Top Salespeople," *Harvard Business Review,* June 27, 2011, http://blogs.hbr.org; Julie Chang, "Born to Sell?" *Sales and Marketing Management,* July 2003, p. 36.

32. Felicia G. Lassk et al., "The Future of Sales Training: Challenges and Related Research Questions," *Journal of Personal Selling and Sales Management* 32, no 1 (2012), pp. 141–54.

33. "Mary Kay: Where's the Money?" http://www.marykay.com; http://www.Marykay.com/lsoulier; "Mary Kay Museum," http://www.addisontexas.net.

34. Johnston and Marshall, *Relationship Selling and Sales Management.*

35. For a discussion of common measures used to evaluate salespeople, see Johnston and Marshall, *Churchill/Ford/Walker's Sales Force Management.*

36. David H. Holtzman, "Big Business Knows Us Too Well," *BusinessWeek,* June 22, 2007.

37. Johnston and Marshall, *Churchill/Ford/Walker's Sales Force Management.*

38. Nicolas McClaren, "The Personal Selling and Sales Management Ethics Research: Managerial Implications and Research Directions from a Comprehensive Review of the Empirical Literature," *Journal of Business Ethics* 112, no. 1 (January 2013), pp. 101–25; Sean R. Valentine and Connie R. Bateman, "The Impact of Ethical Ideologies, Moral Intensity, and Social Context on Sales-Based Ethical Reasoning," *Journal of Business Ethics* 102, no. 1 (August 2011), pp. 155–68.

39. Casey Donoho and Timothy Heinze, "The Personal Selling Ethics Scale: Revisions and Expansions for Teaching Sales Ethics," *Journal of Marketing Education* 33, no. 1 (April 2011), pp. 107–22.

i. Jeff Green, "Sales Moves Beyond Face-to-Face Deals, onto the Web," *Bloomberg Businessweek,* January 10, 2013, http://www.businessweek.com; Al Jury, "The Golden Ratio of Virtual Meetings to Face-to-Face," June 19, 2011, http://virtualteamsblog.com; Joe Sharkey, "On the Road—New Meetings Industry Arises after Boom and Bust," *The New York Times,* February 1, 2010; Brad Grimes, "Have Web, Don't Travel," http://pcworld.about.com; "Brainstorming Online," *BusinessWeek,* Fall 2005, http://www.businessweek.com.

ii. Steve Berkowitz, "Marketers Reshape How College Teams Sell Tickets," *USA Today,* August 5, 2011, http://www.usatoday.com; "Accelerating the Trend toward Outsourcing Athletic Event Ticket Sales, Two More Universities Partner with IMG College," press release, May 31, 2011, http://www.imgworld.com; IMG College, http://www.imgcollege.com.

iii. "Salesforce.com Named #1 CRM Software Provider in Gartner's Worldwide CRM Market Share Report for Second Consecutive Year," *The Wall Street Journal,* April 29, 2014, http://online.wsj.com; Victoria Barret, "Why Salesforce.com Ranks #1 on Forbes' Most Innovative List," *Forbes,* September 5, 2012, http://www.forbes.com; Mi Ji et al., "Salesforce.com: Creating a Blue Ocean in the B2B Space," *INSEAD Case# INS255,* 2013.

iv. Candace Jackson, "A Real Estate Star Is Born," *The Wall Street Journal,* August 1, 2013.

name index

A

Aaker, David A., 429, 430
Abanesius, Chloe, 427
Acuna, Kirsten, 418, 428
Adams, Amy, 177
Adams, Jack, 432
Adams, Susan, 432
Agarwal, James, 427
Agenor, Pierre-Richard, 426
Ahmed, Rumman, 426
Ainsworth, James, 435, 436
Ajmera, Harsh, 417
Akbalik, Ayse, 435
Allawadi, Kusum, 424
Allstar Weekend, 355
Alpert, Mark, 423
Altidore, Jozy, 374
Altman, Josh, 414
Amir, On, 424
Amos, Dan, 421
Anderson, Erin, 435
Anderson, George, 421, 437
Anderson, Melissa J., 435
Andrei, Kyle, 420
Andrews, J. Craig, 436
Angulo, Andres, 435
Ante, Spencer E., 420
Anthony, Carmelo, 21
Antia, Kersi D., 430
Apple, Fiona, 372
Arango, Tim, 419
Arens, Christian, 437
Arens, William F., 437, 438
Argo, Jennifer J., 423
Ariely, Dan, 424
Aristoff, Mandy, 438
Armentano, Vinicius
          Amaral, 435
Armstrong, Neil, 51
Arnould, Eric J., 418
Arora, Rohit, 434
Aston, Adam, 421
Auriemma, Adam, 439

B

Babin, Barry, 423
Baburajan, Rajani, 431
Bahree, Megha, 426
Bair, Michael, 397
Bajarin, Tim, 424
Baker, Pam, 439
Balasubramanian,
          Sridhar, 431
Balotelli, Mario, 51
Banjo, Shelly, 436
Banner, David, 48
Bannova, Bianca, 424
Barboza, David, 420, 435
Barinka, Alex, 425

Barker, Barry, 156
Barlow, Janelle, 432
Barnes, Brooks, 418, 428
Barone, Michael J., 430
Barret, Victoria, 439
Barry, Chris, 419
Basuroy, Suman, 438
Bateman, Connie R., 439
Batra, Rajeev, 429
Baumgartner, Felix, 217, 218
Bawden, Tom, 434
Bearden, William O., 428
Beckham, David, 327
Bedgood, Larisa, 421
Beinhocker, Eric D., 432
Belch, George E., 436, 437
Belch, Michael A., 436, 437
Bell, Alexander Graham, 257
Bellairs, Jeff, 431
Beltrone, Gabriel, 431
Berfield, Susan, 417
Bergdahl, Michael, 432
Berkowitz, Steve, 439
Berra, Yogi, 407
Berry, Leonard, 269, 432, 436
Bers, John, 427
Besinger, Greg, 434
Bessette, Chanelle, 433
Bettencourt, Lance A., 432
Bhushan, Ratna, 426
Bialik, Carl, 434
Bianco, Anthony, 437
Bieber, Justin, 51, 55, 247
Bielak, D. B., 421
Bijmoit, T. H., 438
Billeter, Darron M., 424
Billett, Matthew T., 429
Binkley, Christina, 421
Birkner, Christine, 424
Biswas, Abhijit, 434
Bitner, Mary Jo, 418, 432
Blair, Don, 418
Blazevic, Vera, 431
Blecker, Thorsten, 427
Block, Keith, 405
Block, Lauren G., 421
Blum, Ross, 419
Blumberg, Andrew J., 421
Bolt, Usain, 366
Bolton, Ruth N., 427, 432
Bonini, S., 421
Bonney, Leff, 427
Bottomley, Paul A., 437
Boultin, Clint, 425
Bounds, Gwendolyn, 434
Bragg, Roy, 432
Brat, Ilan, 428
Bright, Laura, 437
Broderick, Amanda J., 427
Broekmeulen, R. A. C. M., 435
Bronziarczyk, Susan, 424
Brothers, Lance Eliot, 426

Brown, Stephen W., 432
Bruell, Alexandra, 437
Bruner, Gordon C., 428
Bryant, Carol, 424
Bryant, Kobe, 392
Burke, Raymond R., 437
Burmann, Christoph, 429
Burns, Robert, 151, 438
Burtis, Michelle, 434
Buss, Dale, 433
Bussey, John, 420, 422
Bustillo, Miguel, 422
Butch, Tory, 358
Buzz, Yoga, 422
Byford, Sam, 429
Byron, Ellen, 429, 431

C

Campbell, Andrew, 418
Caravella, Mary, 429
Carboneli, Pilar, 431
Carey, James W., 426
Carmichael, Evan, 429
Carnegie, Dale, 439
Caro, Isabelle, 358
Carr, Austin, 418, 429
Carr, David, 427
Carreon, Blue, 438
Carroll, Matt, 417
Carter, Bill, 427
Carter, Caitlin, 437
Casey, Mary Anne, 428
Castleberry, Stephen B., 425
Cateora, Philip R., 422, 426
Catts, Tim, 425
Caywood, C., 418
Chabris, Christopher F., 417, 423
Challagalla, Goutam, 423, 432
Chan, Kimmy Wa, 417
Chandon, Pierre, 424
Chandy, Rajesh K., 430
Chang, Alvin, 417
Chang, Chingching, 422
Chang, Julie, 439
Chebat, Jean-Charles, 424
Chen, B. X., 419
Chen, Yubo, 436
Chernev, Alexander,
          424, 434
Choudhury, Dibyendu, 430
Chrishnan, Ed, 432
Christensen, Clayton M., 431
Cieply, Michael, 431
Clancy, Kevin J., 432
Clark, Dorie, 419
Clark, Nicola, 426
Clark, Terry, 427
Clifford, Catherine, 422
Clifford, Stephanie, 435, 438
Cloud, John, 428

Cohen, Kobi, 154
Cohen, Noam, 437
Cohn, D'Vera, 422
Cole, Kenneth, 365
Collins, Kathy, 424
Colquitt, Jason, 433
Comaford-Lynch, Christine, 439
Connelly, Trang, 417
Connick, Harry, Jr., 352
Connor, Michael, 421
Cooper, Belle Beth, 417
Coskuner-Balli, Gokcen, 424
Cummins, Ronnie, 425
Cuoco-Sweeting, Kaley, 363
Curran, Catherine M., 437, 438
Currim, Imran S., 418
Cutten, Christine, 436

D

Dagger, Tracey S., 424
Dahl, Darren W., 423, 431,
          437, 438
Dahlsrud, Alexander, 421
Dan, Avi, 436
Danaher, Peter J., 424
Dannen, Chris, 422
Dant, Rajiv P., 417, 434
Darden, William, 423
Daugherty, Terry, 437
Davey, Jenny, 428
Davis, Donna, 434
Davis-Sramek, Beth, 434
Day, George S., 417
Deans, David H., 420
Defensor, Naomi, 44
Dekel, Noa, 154
Dempsey, Clint, 11
DeWitte, Siegfried, 423
Dhalla, Nariman K., 432
Diaz, Ann-Christine, 420
Dillman, Don A., 428
Dilworth, Dianna, 430
Ding, Jiali, 429
Dinwoodie, John, 435
Doell, Linda, 422
Dolan, Robert J., 433
Doland, Angela, 419
Donoho, Casey, 439
Donthu, Naveen, 433
Dooley, Roger, 425, 428
Dorfman, Brad, 426
Dove, Justin, 426
Dowling, Daisy Wademan, 433
Downey, Robert, Jr., 116
Dredge, Stuart, 420
Drucker, Peter F., 422
Dubé, Laurette, 424
Dubois, David, 423
Duhigg, Charles, 435, 437
Duncan, T., 418

Dupré, Elyse, 438
Durant, John, 427
Dyer, Pam, 420

E

Eastin, Matthew, 437
Eastwood, Clint, 177
Eckerdsly, Peter, 421
Edison, Thomas, 85
Elber, Lynn, 437
Elliot, Stuart, 417, 420, 436, 437
Eppinger, Steven D., 431
Erdem, Tulin, 437
Eridon, Corey, 425
Esper, Terry L., 434
Esterl, Mike, 417, 430, 436
Evans, Tom, 436

F

Fabiana, Silvia, 427
Falcon, Alvaris, 417
Fallon, Jimmy, 49, 50, 184
Farr, Lona M., 428
Farrell, Diana, 432
Farris, P., 419
Faw, Larissa, 437
Fay, Scott, 436
Feinberg, Ashley, 420
Ferraro, Rosellina, 427, 429
Ferreira, Fabiana, 425
Fincher, David, 169
Finkelstein, Stacey R., 424, 425
Fisch, Jan Hendrik, 431
Fishaw, Justin, 439
Fishbach, Ayelet, 424, 425
Flaherty, Josephy, 431
Fleck, Nathalie, 430
Flint, Joe, 428
Fok, Dennis, 430
Ford, Henry, 12
Fowler, Floyd J., 428
Fox, Richard J., 429
Freedman, David H., 420
Friedman, Milton, 421
Frighetto, Jennifer, 433
Frost, Lerinda, 432
Fu, Guoqun, 429
Fujita, Akihisa, 436
Fuller, Bonnie, 422
Fulton, Scott M., III, 422

G

Galinsky, Adam D., 423
Gallo, Carmine, 418, 424
Gandhi, Mahatma, 75
Ganesh, Jaishankar, 427
Garrett, Daniel M., 434
Garrett, Jason, 434
Garry, Michael, 435
Gasparro, Annie, 418
Gates, Bill, 251

Gauri, Dinesh K., 434
Gaylord, Chris, 431
Geller, Jonathan S., 434
Geller, Martinne, 426
Germain, Richard, 434
Gessinger, Gernot H., 431
Gianastasio, David, 437, 438
Gibs, Samuel, 425
Gilly, Mary C., 426
Gilson, Dave, 422
Gingerich, Mike, 419
Giriprakash, K., 427
Gladwell, Malcolm, 372
Glanz, James, 420
Goel, Vindu, 438
Goldenberg, Jacob, 431
Golder, Peter, 432
Golicic, Susan, 434
Gomez, Selena, 355, 374
Gonzalez, Omar, 11
Goodbar, Perry, 271
Goodman, J. David, 439
Goodstein, Ronald, 427
Gosling, Samuel D., 427
Goukens, Caroline, 423
Graham, John L., 422, 426
Greco, Susan, 439
Greeley, Brendan, 422, 437
Green, Jeff, 439
Greengard, Samuel, 420
Greenley, Gordon E., 427
Greenspan, Nick, 424
Grégoire, Yany, 433
Greifeneder, Rainer, 423
Gremler, Dwayne D., 418, 432
Grewal, Dhruv, 417, 424, 428, 432, 433, 434, 435, 436
Griffin, Mitch, 423
Grimes, Brad, 439
Grönroos, Christian, 433
Gross, Rachel, 425
Guglielmo, Connie, 435
Gulati, Nikhil, 426
Gunasekaran, A., 435
Gundlach, Gregory T., 417, 418, 421
Guynn, Jessica, 427

H

Hader, Bill, 372
Hagerty, James M., 427
Hahn, Alexander, 436
Hale, Lucy, 356
Hale, Todd, 424
Halliday, Jess, 427
Halscheid, Megan, 436
Halzack, Sarah, 428
Hamilton, Ryan, 424, 434
Hardy, Quentin, 428
Harker, Debra, 438
Harker, Michael, 438
Harmon, Amy, 421
Harris, Derrick, 423
Harris, Elizabeth A., 421, 422

Hartley, Steven W., 419
Harvey, Quentin, 425
Harvey, Steve, 92
Hauser, John R., 431
Hawk, Tony, 55
Hawkins, Del I., 422
Haws, Kelly L., 428
Heath, Robert G., 437, 438
Heinze, Timothy, 439
Heitjans, Torsten, 429
Hemel, Elad, 154
Henderson, Kirk, 424
Hennig-Thurau, Thorsen, 429
Herd, Kelly B., 427
Herrimann, Andreas, 432
Herzog, Walter, 433
Heslin, Rebecca, 433
Highsmith, Jim, 431
Hilfiger, Tommy, 358
Hill, Ronald Paul, 423
Hira, Maggie, 425
Hodgson, John, 431
Hoeffler, Steven, 431
Hof, Robert, 436
Hoffman, Gary, 421
Hofstede, Geert, 153, 154, 155, 426
Holmes, Elizabeth, 420, 434
Holtzman, David H., 439
Homburg, Christian, 436
Homer, Pamela Mills, 438
Honomichi, Jack, 428
Hopper, Dennis, 175
Horton, Tony, 410
Houson, Mark B., 429
Howe, Sam, 438
Howell, Vandy, 434
Hsu, Tiffany, 430
Huang, Peng, 423
Huang, Rong, 429
Huba, Jackie, 438
Huber, Lynn, 439
Huggett, Brady, 431
Hunt, Bob, 438
Hwang, Bang-Ning, 433

I

Iannarino, S. Anthony, 439
Inman, J. Jeffrey, 424
Ip, Melissa, 426
Irving, Clive, 438
Irving, Kyrie, 21
Irwin, Julie R., 423
Iyer, Karthik, 434

J

Jackson, Candace, 439
Jacobs, A. J., 430
Jacobs, Sherice, 436
Jacobson, Robert, 429
Jaffe, Joseph, 427
James, Geoffrey, 439
James, LeBron, 21
Janiszewski, Chris, 424

Jargon, Julie, 422, 426
Jawahar, N., 435
Jayson, Sharon, 422
Jepson, Carly Rae, 50
Jewell, Robert D., 430
Jie Zhang, 436
Jing Xu, 423
Johansson, Johny, 426
John, Deborah Roedder, 429
Johnson, Bill, 426
Johnson, Lauren, 361, 425
Johnston, Mark W., 425, 439
Johnston, Peter, 419
Jones, Ashby, 425
Jones, John Philip, 436
Jones, Sandra M., 435
Jordan, Michael, 21
Joseph, Sebastian, 418
Josephs, Leslie, 426
Joyner, Tom, 92
Jury, Al, 439

K

Kahney, Leander, 425
Kain, Erik, 430
Kalpesh, Kraushik Desai, 430
Kaltcheva, Velitchka, 432, 433
Kamel, Marc-Andre, 424
Kang, Cecilia, 428
Kannan, P. K., 436
Kanter, Rosebeth Moss, 430
Kapoor, N., 438
Kardashian, Kim, 55
Karlovich, Janice, 422
Kawamoto, Dawn, 425
Kaye, Kate, 420, 428
Keane, Michael, 437
Keenan, Joe, 430
Keller, Kevin Lane, 224, 429, 430, 437
Keller, Robert, 439
Kelly, Jeff, 428
Kelso, Alicia, 433
Kerin, Roger A, 419
Kessler, Aaron M., 419
Kessler, Marcia, 269, 279
Kiara, Robert, 430
Kiefaber, David, 429, 438
Kim, Yun-Hee, 426
Kincaid, Jason, 427
King, Dan, 424
King, Rachael, 428
Kirmani, Amna, 427, 429
Kirschner, Lisa, 400
Koc, U., 433
Kohli, Ajay K., 423, 432
Kollewe, Julia, 425
Korkki, Phyllis, 430
Kotabe, Masaaki, 427
Kotha, Suresh, 438
Kotkin, Joel, 422
Kozzin, Alan, 432
Krause, Michael, 425
Kresmüller, G. P., 435

Krieg, Peter C., 432
Krishnan, R., 417, 428, 433
Krogue, Ken, 439
Krueger, Richard A., 428
Krugman, Dean M., 438
Krupnick, Ellie, 437
Kumar, V., 417, 418, 427
Kunz, Ben, 422S
Kurutz, Steven, 430
Kwong, Matt, 435, 436

L

Labarre, Polly, 422
Labaton, Stephen, 434
Laczniak, Gene R., 418
Lady Gaga, 328
Lahteenmaki, Riku, 431
Lam, Simon S. K., 417
Lamb, Rachel, 427
Lambrecht, Anja, 417
Lamey, Lien, 429
Landwehr, Jan R., 432
Lanzolla, Gianvito, 431
Lara, Robert, 428
Laran, Juliano, 424
Lardinois, Frederic, 431
Larson, Jeffrey S., 420, 424
Lassk, Felicia G., 439
Laurman, Martin R., 423
Lauter, Devorah, 426
Lavigne, Avril, 290
Lee, Leonard, 424
Legoux, Renaud, 433
Lehmann, Donald R., 418, 429, 431
Lehren, Andrew W., 420
Lemonade Mouth, 355
Lenk, Peter, 429
Leon, Lourdes, 339
LePine, Jeffery, 433
Letts, Philip, 425
Letzing, John, 432
Levenstein, Steven, 432
Levitt, Theodore, 421, 431, 437
Levy, Michael, 424, 432, 434, 435, 436
Li, Bingbing, 104
Li, Hongshuang (Alice), 436
Libai, Barak, 427, 430, 431
Lieb, Rebecca, 436
Lievens, Annouk, 431
Lindsey-Mullikin, Joan, 434
Little, Kate, 430
Liu-Thompkins, Yuping, 418
Lloyd, Mary Ellen, 422
Loftus, Jack, 438
Lohr, Steve, 434
Longoria, Eva, 63, 64
Lopez, Jennifer, 335, 352
Lovato, Demi, 355
Luk, Lorraine, 426
Luo, Anita, 417
Luo, Lan, 423
Lurie, Nicholas H., 423

Lutz, Ashley, 428
Lutz, Richard, 423
Lynch, Jerry, 422

M

Ma, Wayne, 426
Mac, Amber, 425
Macale, Sherilynn, 419
Madden, Normandy, 427
Madonna, 339
Maeng, Ahreum, 424
Mahajan, Vijay, 419, 431
Mahidhar, Vikram, 436
Maht, Dominik, 431
Makarem, Suzanne C., 433
Malhotra, Naresh K., 427
Malone, Austin, 355
Mamet, David, 399
Manchanda, Puneet, 430
Marquis, Christopher, 421
Mars, Bruno, 9
Marshall, Greg W., 425, 439
Marsicano, Mario, 429
Marter, Heather, 44
Martin, Diane M., 418
Martin, Kelly D., 423
Martin, Steven W., 439
Martinez, Amy, 433
Marx, Patricia, 435
Maslow, Abraham H., 114, 116, 423
Matherly, Ted, 427, 429
Matlack, Carol, 431
Matyszczyk, Chris, 428
McCarthy, E. Jerome, 417
McCarthy, Melissa, 177
McClaren, Nicolas, 439
McEntire, Reba, 377
McKenna, Beth, 425, 430
McLaughlin, Laurianne, 433
McNew, Sarah, 419
Meehan, Peter, 421
Melton, Nicole Marie, 430
Menkes, Suzy, 422
Mentzer, John T., 418
Meredith, Geoffrey E., 422
Messi, Lionel, 374
Meta, Carl F., 430
Miao, Fred, 434
Miller, Arthur, 399
Miller, Claire Cain, 417, 421, 423, 434
Miners, Zach, 418
Minkov, Michael, 155
Mintz, Ofer, 418
Min Zhao, 431
Mirren, Helen, 104
Mischka, Badgley, 111
Mishra, Mukesh Kumar, 430
Mitra, Sabyasachi, 423
Mittal, Banwari, 423, 424
Mizik, Natalie, 429
Mohanty, Lopa, 423

Mohr, Jakki J., 430
Monga, Atokparma Basu, 429
Monllos, Kristina, 437
Monroe, Kent B., 417, 433, 434
Moore, J., 418
Morales, Andrea C., 423
Moreau, C. Page, 427
Morgan, Alex, 11
Morgan, Neil A., 429
Morganteen, Jeff, 433
Morhart, Felicitas M., 433
Morin, Sylvie, 424
Morris, Sarah, 427
Morrison, Maureen, 430
Morrison, Toni, 372
Moses, Lucia, 437
Mothersbaugh, David L., 422
Moye, Jay, 436
Mudambi, Susan M., 419, 433
Mueller, M. P., 420, 428
Mueller, Rene Debtiste, 427
Muhammad, 158
Muller, Eitan, 430, 431
Mullins, Jenna, 420
Murphy, Colum, 427
Murphy, Patrick E., 418
Mycoskie, Blake, 73
Myers, James, 423

N

Nachiappan, S. P., 435
Nachtmann, Heather, 435
Nadal, Rafael, 8, 9
Nagpal, Anish, 424
Nairn, Agnes C., 437
Nassauer, Sarah, 433
Naylor, Rebecca Walker, 423
Neff, Jack, 426, 438
Neijens, Peter C., 438
Nelson, Willie, 372
Netemeyer, Richard D., 428
Newman, Andrew Adam, 417, 421, 430, 432, 436, 438
Newman, Jared, 432
Newman, Nell, 421
Newman, Paul, 76
Ng, Serena, 433, 436
Ng, Sharon, 429
Nguyen, Hang T., 429
Nikolaeva, Ralitza, 431
Nishi, Dennis, 439
Nit, Michael, 431
Nitzen, Irit, 427
Nudd, Tim, 419, 429
Nyong'o, Lupita, 388

O

Oakley, James L., 431
Obama, Barack, 50
Obermiller, Carl, 438
O'Brien, Keith, 430
O'Connell, Vanessa, 434
O'Hagan, Patrick, 16

O'Keeffe, Kate, 426
Olson, Jerry C., 424
Oppenheim, J. M., 421
O'Reilly, Lara, 436
Orner, Daphne, 154
Osawa, Juro, 426
Ostrow, Adam, 419
Ostrower, Jon, 439
O'Sullivan, Arthur, 426
Ottman, Jacqueline A., 422
Ovechkin, Alexander, 30
Owen, Jonathan H., 432

P

Pachal, Pete, 439
Palmatier, Robert W., 417, 434
Palmer, Keke, 30
Palmeri, Christopher, 428
Panzarino, Matthew, 418
Parasuraman, A., 269, 428, 432
Parker, Laura, 421
Parsons, Russel, 418
Passel, Jeffrey S., 422
Patton, Phil, 432
Paul, Pamela, 422
Pauwels, Koen, 423, 430
Peden, Tracey, 425
Peloza, John, 437
Penn, Mark, 428
Peres, Renana, 430, 431
Perez, Steve, 426
Perlroth, Nicole, 421
Perot, Carolyn, 422
Perry, Chris, 420
Perry, Katy, 7
Pesso, Mor, 154
Peter, J. Paul, 424
Petty, R. D, 434
Pfeiffer, Markus, 437
Pinker, Steven, 372
Pirovano, Tom, 422
Podoshen, Jeffrey S., 433
Poggi, Jeanine, 420, 423, 427
Pogue, David, 417, 423
Pollack, Andrew, 421
Popper, Nathaniel, 421
Porterfield, Amy, 420
Potts, Andy, 419
Pozza, Ilaria Della, 427
Prabhu, Jaideep C., 430
Press, Melea, 418
Price, Rob, 438
Pritzl, Rudolf, 424
Protalinski, Emil, 420
Pucinelli, Nancy M., 435
Pujari, Devashish, 431

Q

Qu, Riliang, 429
Quester, Pascale G., 430
Quinn, Laura S., 420

R

Rabinovich, Nataly, 154
Rackham, Neil, 439
Raice, Shayndi, 420
Rajaratnam, Dan, 427
Ramsay, Mike, 427
Rappaport, Alfred, 418
Ratchford, Brian T., 423
Ray, Ramon, 433
Raynor, Michael E., 431
Raynurn, Steven W., 432
Reda, Susan, 422
Reddy, Srinivas K., 429
Redman, Russell, 435
Regev, Idan, 154
Rego, Lopo L., 429
Reinartz, Werner, 417
Reingold, Jennifer, 428
Reinhardt, Uwe E., 434
Reitz, Stephanie, 425
Reston, Ana Carolina, 358
Reynaud, Jasmine, 44
R5, 355
Ricadela, Aaron, 437
Richards, Jef I., 437, 438
Riley, Nicola, 429
Rinallo, Diego, 438
Risselada, H., 438
Riven, Tal, 154
Roberts, Andrew, 429
Roberts, Julia, 385
Rockefeller, John, 180
Rodgers, Everett M., 244
Rodriguez, Ashley, 424
Rodriguez-Escudero, Ana I., 431
Roggeveen, Anne L., 417, 433
Rohrer, Finlo, 420
Romjin, Rebecca, 377
Rooney, Jennifer, 421, 432
Roosevelt, Theodore, 78
Rosenbloom, Stephanie, 421
Rosman, Katherine, 429, 435
Ross, Jan-Michael, 431
Roteld, Herbert Jack, 438
Rucker, Derek D., 423
Rudelius, William, 419
Ruffenach, Glenn, 424
Ryan, Kevin, 420
Ryan, Tom, 422

S

Sabatté, Micheline, 436
Samaha, Stephen A., 417
Sandler, Adam, 177
Sandy, Carson J., 427
San Miguel, Renay, 432
Santos-Vijande, Maria Leticia, 433
Sarigöllü, Emine, 429
Sauer, Abe, 438
Scarpati, Kevin, 435
Schaal, Dennis, 437
Schaefer, David H., 438
Schaefer, Mark W., 420

Scheer, Lisa, 434
Scheibehenne, Benjamin, 423
Schewem, Charles, 422
Schoger, Christel, 60
Schouten, John W., 418
Schultz, E. J., 421, 422, 425
Schultz, Howard, 3
Schwartz, Barry, 424
Schwartz, John, 425
Schwarz, Norbert, 423
Scott, Allison, 433
Seiders, Kathleen, 436
Seidman, Robert, 419
Sengupta, Jaideep, 437, 438
Sengupta, Sanjit, 430
Sengupta, Somini, 420, 421, 428
Serhant, Ryan, 414
Shah, Denish, 417
Shakira, 227
Shankar, Venkatesh, 431
Sharkey, Joe, 439
Sharma, Amol, 423, 428
Shatner, William, 363
Shaw, Andy, 420
Sheffrin, Steven, 426
Shiguemoto, André Luis, 435
Shimp, Terence A., 418, 436
Shum, Matthew, 437
Siegenthaler, Peter, 426
Siemans, Eric, 418
Silverman, Sarah, 372
Silverstein, Barry, 429
Silverthorne, Sean, 425
Simon, Phil, 423
Simons, Daniel J., 417, 423
Sinclair, Upton, 78
Singer, Natasha, 422, 428
Sirianni, Nancy J., 418, 432
Siwicki, Bill, 420
Slater, Stanley F., 430
Slutsky, Irina, 438
Smit, Edith G., 438
Smith, Chris, 419
Smith, Ned, 439
Smith, Robert E., 437
Smith, Roy A., 434
Snowden, Edward, 67
Solomon, Michael R., 423, 427
Soman, Dilip, 424
Song, Dong-Ping, 435
Sood, Alex, 427
Sood, Sanjay, 429
Sotnikova, Adelina, 30
Spacey, Kevin, 169, 170
Spade, Kate, 111
Spangenbeg, Eric R., 438
Spence, Ewan, 423
Spiggle, Susan, 429
Srull, Thomas K., 437
Staub, Eric A., 434
Steel, Emily, 422, 437
Stengel, Richard, 421
Stenquist, Paul, 432
Stephen, Andrew T., 427
Stern, Joanna, 429

Stevens, Tim, 419
Stigler, George E., 434
Stilley, Karen M., 424
Stinnett, Bill, 439
Stock, Kyle, 427
Stout, Hilary, 418
Streitfield, David, 432, 433
Stremersch, Stefan, 430, 431
Strom, Stephanie, 417, 421, 429
Strong, E. K., 436
Stross, Randall, 423
Stynes, Tess, 430
Suarez, Fernando F., 431
Sujan, Harish, 439
Sujan, Mita, 439
Sun, Baohong, 437
Supphelien, Magne, 417
Sura, Sejal, 436
Suri, R., 433
Svensson, G., 421
Swaminathan, Vanitha, 429
Swift, Taylor, 385
Symon, Michael, 56

T

Tabaka, Maria, 425
Talley, Karen, 435
Talukdar, Debabrata, 423
Tam, Leona, 418, 424
Tanner, John F., 425
Tanner, Robin J., 424
Taub, Eric A., 433
Taylor, Charles R., 438
Team, Trefis, 418, 434
Tellis, Gerard, 432
Thakor, M. V., 433
Thaler, Richard, 422
Thau, Barbara, 418
Theron, Charlize, 104
Thomadsen, Raphael, 417
Thompson, A. A., 419
Thompson, Craig J., 424
Thompson, Don, 197
Thorne, Bella, 356
Thorne, Zendaya, 356
Thorson, E., 418
Tierney, John, 429
Timberlake, Justin, 177
Todd, Peter M., 423
Tomaselli, Rich, 437
Tomczak, Torsten, 433
Toor, Amar, 429
Townsend, Matt, 418
Trachtenberg, Jeffrey, 424
Treacy, Michael, 418
Tregear, Hannah, 421
Tripp, Thomas M., 433
Trivedi, Minakshi, 434
Troye, Sigurd, 417
Tsiros, Michael, 417, 433
Tsukayama, Hayley, 423
Tucker, Catherine, 417
Tugend, Alina, 438

Tung, Rosalie L., 426
Turk, Harry, 398, 399
Turlington, Christy, 385
Turner, Tracy, 424
Tuttle, Brad, 419

U

Ulaga, Wolfgang, 417
Ulrich, Karl T., 431
Ungar, Rick, 421
Unger, Stephen H., 425
Urban, Glen L., 431
Urban, Keith, 352
Urs, Anil, 427

V

Valentine, Sean R., 439
VanderVeen, David J., 432
Van Domelin, Katie, 420
Van Everdingen, Yvonne, 430
Van Heerde, Harald J., 430
Van Meurs, Lex, 438
Van Reijmersdal, Eva A., 438
Van Rijmenam, Mark, 430, 432
Varadarajan, P. Rajan, 419, 431
Vega, Tanzina, 418, 438
Venkatesan, Rajkumar, 417
Venkatesh, R., 423, 432
Verbeke, Alain, 426
Verhoef, Peter C., 417
Verma, D. P. S., 438
Verner, Amy, 435
Vinjamuri, David, 437
Vohs, Kathleen D., 437
Voight, Joan, 427
Voima, Päivi, 433
Volckner, Franziska, 429
Vollmayr, Josef, 436
Von Hippel, Eric, 431
Vranica, Suzanne, 421, 428

W

Wakefield, Kirk L., 424
Walker, Danielle Medina, 426
Walker, Thomas, 426
Waller, Matthew A., 435
Walter, Ekaterina, 419
Walton, Sam, 274
Wang, Liz C., 423
Wang, Qi, 436
Wang, Vera, 111
Ward, Mark, 439
Ward, Morgan K., 424
Warlop, Luk, 423
Warren, Christine, 420
Wasik, Bill, 423
Wasserman, Todd, 422, 430, 436
Watercutter, Angela, 417

Watson, Elaine, 430, 436
Wauters, Robin, 426
Weber-Mendham, Karen, 63
Wedel, Michael, 429
Weigold, Michael F., 437, 438
Weitz, Barton A., 424, 425,
    432, 434, 435,
    436, 439
Wentzel, Daniel, 432
Wesson, Michael, 433
Wheatley, Malcolm, 418
White, Katherine, 437
Whitelocks, Sadie, 439
Whiting, Anita, 433
Wiersema, Fred, 418
Wilcox, Keith, 427
Wiles, Michael A., 429
Wilkie, William W., 417, 421
Williams, Stephen, 438
Wilson, Eric, 427, 437

Wilson, Mark, 430
Wilson, Ross, 421
Winer, Russell S., 418, 431
Wines, Michael, 427
Winfrey, Oprah, 218
Wingfield, Nick, 425, 433
Winsor, Robert D., 432
Witherspoon, Reese, 106
Witkowski, Wallace, 432
Wohl, Jessica, 421
Wojick, John, 398
Wolfe, Alexandra, 417
Wolfson, Rachel, 428
Wolonick, Josh, 420
Wong, Elaine, 437
Woo, Stu, 432
Wood, G., 421
Wood, Stacy, 424
Wright, Robin, 169
Wu, Jason, 228

Wu, Yuhong, 431
Wyer, Robert S., Jr., 434

X

Xiaojing Yang, 437
Xu, Alison Jing, 434

Y

Yadav, Manjit, 431
Yang, Botao, 423
Yehezkelli, Shai, 154
Yeung, Ken, 419
Ying Hong, 432
Ying Zhang, 423
York, Emily Bryson, 435
Yu, Rose, 427

Yuping, Liu-Thompkins, 424
Yuseph, Sonia, 432

Z

Zainulbhai, Adil S., 432
Zatlawi, Racheli, 154
Zeithaml, Valerie A., 269, 418, 432
Zeplin, Sabrina, 429
Zhen Zhu, 432, 433
Zidane, Zinedine, 374
Zigmond, Dan, 437
Ziobro, Paul, 430
Zipp, Yvonne, 432
Zito, Dustin, 44
Zmuda, Natalie, 417, 426, 429, 430,
    431, 432, 438
Zuckerberg, Mark, 158
Zumberge, Marianne, 423

company/product index

A

A&E channel, 182
A&W, 231
ABC network, 356
Abercrombie & Fitch, 208
Accenture, 127, 160, 165, 400
Activia, 227
Acxion, 180
adidas, 28, 30, 39, 146, 374
Adobe SiteCatalyst, 63
Adomic, 63
ad:tech, 63
Aflac, 79
Ahold U.S., 333
Airbus, 397
Air Jordan, 21
AJWright, 337
Albertson's, 122
Aldi, 333
Alfani, 336
Alka-Seltzer, 355
All-Bran, 172
Almax, 214
Alterna, 258
Altuzarra, 228
Amazon, 15, 33, 58, 63, 78,
    185, 204, 225, 278,
    279, 307–308, 313,
    314, 346, 361
Amazon Mechanical Turk
    Site, 211
Amazon Prime, 25, 263–264
Amazon Vendor Flex program,
    308, 313, 319
American Airlines, 185, 233,
    287, 293
American Airlines/U.S. Airways, 187
American Apparel, 52, 316, 317,
    324, 325
American Beauty, 340
American Express, 204, 277, 382
American Giving, 61
American Legacy Foundation, 378
American Living, 335
Analtech, 353
Android, 33, 267
Android Auto, 39
Android Auto System, 39
Android bootcamp, 39
Angry Birds, 67, 68
Animals, 242
Anytime Fitness, 315, 316
AppClix, 63
Apple App Store, 60
Applebee's, 276
Apple CarPlay, 127–129
Apple Inc., 5, 7, 15, 16, 18, 21–24,
    25, 26, 39, 41, 132, 224,
    226, 243, 257, 258, 259,
    288, 318, 363, 393, 394

Apple Newton, 244
Apple's App Store, 60
Apple self-driving
    car, 97
Apple's Safari, 68
Apple Stores, 69, 121
Apple Watch, 42, 288
Aquafina, 6
Arcade Fire, 212
ArdGIS, 16
Arm & Hammer detergent,
    284, 293
Armani, 298
Asda, 211
ASICS, 60, 363
AT&T, 68, 98
Audi, 97, 129, 130, 151, 181
Audi Quattro, 188
Avaya, 165
Aveda, 234
Avon Products, 313, 410
Axe, 222
Axe Anarchy, 223

B

Babar, 10
Balanced Body, 250
Banana Republic, 102, 109, 301
Band-Aid, 227
Bango, 63
Barbour, 394
Barnes & Noble, 346
Barneys, 404
Baroni, 106
Baroni Expressive Pendant, 106
Bass Pro Shops Outdoor
    World, 341
Beautyrest, 115
Bed, Bath, & Beyond, 33, 248
Bell Labs, 165, 257
Ben & Jerry's, 253
Benetton, 174
Bentley, 130
Best Buy, 57, 91, 319, 320, 322,
    323, 409
BestBuyDeals, 57
BestBuyNews, 57
Bic disposable underwear, 231
Bic Underwear, 244
Big Gripper bucket, 252
Big Knit charity promotion, 56
Big Lots Inc., 337, 338
Big Machine Label Group, 377
Bing, 106, 251
Bing Maps, 251
Birkenstock sandals, 119
Birkin bag, 188
Bizrate.com, 294
BJ's Wholesale Club, 334
Black & Decker, 248, 379

Blackberry, 244, 267
Blendtec, 247
Bloomingdale's, 166
Bluefly.com, 338
Blu-Ray, 257, 260
BMW, 78, 181, 220–221, 363
BMW K1600 motorcycle,
    103, 104
Body Shop, 254
Boeing Company, 56, 312,
    397–398, 401
Boeing 787 Dreamliner, 398
Booth Bay, 269
Boston Consulting Group,
    40–42
Bottled Water for Pets,
    244, 256
Bravo, 416
Broadmoor Hotel, 271
Buena Vista Concerts, 355
Buffalo Wild Wings, 17–18
Bugaboo Inc., 90
Bugatti, 130
Buick Encore, 241
Build-A-Bear, 185, 186
Burger King, 92, 231, 338, 352
Burlington Coat Factory, 338
BurnMed, 107
Burton snowboards, 54
Burt's Bees, 76
Business Calendar, 58
Buy Plus, 77

C

C. Wonder, 341–342
CabeLabs-Energy Lab
    consortium, 250
Cadbury candies, 11
Cadbury International, 150
Cadillac, 32, 181, 230
Cadillac ATS, 241
Call of Duty Advanced
    Warfare, 242
Camaro, 32
Campbell Soup Company,
    163–164, 209, 214–215
Candy Crush Saga, 57, 69
Capri Sun, 239, 242
CarMax, 287
CarPlay, 127–129
Carrefour, 328
Cartier, 166
CBS, 88
CCTV (China's television
    agency), 38
Center for Democracy &
    Technology, 213
Chanel, 188
Charmin, 388
Cheer, 285

Cheerios, 37, 69, 111, 377, 392
Cheesecake Factory, 105, 120,
    121, 393
Cheetos Lip Balm, 231
Cheez-Its, 230
Chef Jet, 238
Cherry Coke, 32
Chevrolet, 32, 230, 381
Chevrolet Concept Code
    130R, 241
Chevrolet Malibu, 385
Chevrolet Sonic, 241
Chevrolet Tru 140S, 241
Chevy Camaro, 163
Chevy Cobalt, 249
Chevy Volt, 241
Chex cereals, 241
Chili's restaurants, 276, 389
Chipotle Mexican Grill,
    371–372, 373
Chips Ahoy, 11
Chips Deluxe, 242
Chobani, 235
Choice Hotels, 266
Christian Louboutin, 109
Chrysler Corporation, 241
Church & Dwight Company, 284
Cisco Systems Inc., 160, 400
Clairol, 244
Clarion Motels, 266
Cleopatra clutch purse, 104
Clickstream, 63
ClickTale, 63
Clorox, 54, 227
Coach, 329, 330, 331, 332, 340
Coach for Men, 329, 334, 335,
    336, 337, 340, 341
Coborn's, 93
Coca Cola Company, 25, 26, 32,
    39, 78, 145–146, 150, 171,
    208, 213, 225, 226, 227,
    229, 234, 244, 249,
    349–351, 352, 353,
    354, 393, 409, 410
Cocoa Krispies, 172
Coco Pops, 172
Coke, 6, 32, 87, 88, 120, 144, 219,
    348, 350
Coke II, 32
Coke Zero, 32, 171
Coldplay, 372
Cole Haan, 24, 184, 330, 331
Colgate, 149, 230, 409
Colgate Kitchen Entrees,
    231, 244
Columbia Sportswear Company,
    362, 363
Comfort Inn, 224, 266
Comfort Suites, 266
Communispace, 208
Condé Nast, 183, 184
Corning, 85

Corvette, 32
Costco, 230, 233, 310, 328, 333, 334
Coupons.com, 341
CoverGirl, 340, 385
Crate & Barrell, 120
Crest toothpaste, 230, 287
Crispy Beef, 244
CVS, 15, 330, 331, 336, 340–341, 390, 391

D

Daimler, 132
Dairy Brand, 234
Dairy Milk Shots, 150
Dairy Queen, 352
Dannon yogurt, 71, 394
Danone, 3
Dasani, 6
DBS Group Holdings, 131
DejaBlue, 234
Dell Inc., 184–185, 255, 310
Del Monte, 258
Delta Air Lines, 287
Denizen brand, 249
Denny's Inc., 316
Diet Coke, 6, 32, 125, 202, 227, 350
Diet Pepsi, 6, 114, 202
Dillard's, 330, 331, 340
Disney Channel, 356
Disney's Fashion Studio, 356
Distimo, 59
Doctor Mole, 107
Dodge Charger, 163
Dollar General, 331, 337
Domino's Pizza, 160
Doritos Locos, 222
Doublemint Gum, 122
Drawbridge, 68
Dreamworks, 170
Driscoll Strawberry Associates, 110
Drop Dead clothing line, 358
Dr Pepper, 88, 124
Dunkin' Donuts, 3, 8, 224, 316
Dyson, 33–34, 36, 248
Dyson Ball Vacuum, 247

E

E. L. Fudge, 242
eBay, 10, 292, 312
eBay Now, 25, 26
ecomagination, 80
Edition hotels, 231
Eggo Syrup, 230
eHarmony, 61, 62
ElbowMed screws, 136
Electrolux, 247
Electronic Privacy Information Center, 214
Energizer Bunny, 224
Energizer USA, 85

Enkauf, 328
Entenmann's, 295
Epsilon, 180
Era, 285
Eraser, 385
ESPN, 392
ESRI, 179
Esri's Geographic Information System, 16
Estée Lauder, 329, 330, 331, 336, 340
Etsy, 312
Eva, 328, 331, 332, 334, 335, 336, 337, 342
Evolution Fresh, 3
Expedia, 17
Experian, 180
Expos2, 400
EyeSee mannequins, 214

F

Facebook, 5, 7, 16–17, 48, 49, 50, 53, 54, 55, 58, 60, 61, 63, 64, 65, 77, 88, 96, 113, 141, 158, 173, 205, 208, 211, 214, 218, 223, 239, 257, 267, 349, 361, 366, 383, 389, 391
Facebook analytics, 212
Facebook Insights, 63
Famous Amos, 230
FedEx, 78, 312
Feeding America, 12, 71
Fender Telecaster, 290
Ferragamo, 166
Ferrari, 129
Fiat, 241, 361
Fitbit, 58
Five Guys Burgers, 352
Flickr, 52, 55, 56, 77
Flipboard, 58–59
Flirt, 340
Florida Power & Light, 297
Flurry, 63
Flyknit, 29
Foodspotting, 17
Foot Locker, 23
Ford Anglia, 241
Ford Cargo Van, 32
Ford Explorer, 32
Ford Fiesta, 77, 241
Ford Focus, 77
Ford Fusion, 32, 116, 241, 385
Ford Fusion Energi, 241
Ford Motor Company, 12, 77, 127, 163, 208, 292, 312, 361, 379
Ford Mustang, 163
Forever 21, 53, 324
Forrester Research, 88
4G, 95
Four Young Guys, 50
Foxconn, 318
Fox network, 106

Frappuccino, 8
Fred Meyer, 333
Friskies cat food, 228
Frito-Lay, 177, 231, 322
Frito-Lay Lemonade, 244
Frito-Lay SunChips, 94
Frogbox, 239, 240
Froot Loops, 172, 230
Fruitopia, 32
FuelBand, 21–24, 29
Fujitsu, 249
Fusion ProGlide Razor, 86
Futurebrand, 233

G

Gain, 285
Gap, Inc., 52, 109, 232, 363, 402
Gap.com, 52
Garage Parties, 174
Gatorade, 47–48, 188, 189–191
Geek Squad, 409
General Electric, 25, 26, 56, 61, 76, 78, 80, 112, 127–128, 138, 163, 226
General Mills, 37, 69, 94, 241, 251, 377
General Motors, 97, 129, 181, 230, 241, 248, 249, 312
Gerber Baby, 189
Giani Bernini, 340
Gillette Company, 85–86
Gillette Fusion Proglide, 245
Gilt, 301
Give Kids, 79
GlaxoSmithKline, 137
GMC brand, 230
GNC, 360
GoodData, 204
Goodyear, 40
Google+, 49, 51, 55, 77
Google AdWords, 205, 367
Google Analytics, 63, 205, 366–367
Google Calendar, 58
Google Glass, 14, 101, 102, 246
Google Inc., 25, 26, 37, 39, 63, 78, 88, 102, 106, 129, 204, 205, 226, 227, 251, 304, 354
Google Maps, 355
Google Open Automotive Alliance, 129
Google self-driving car, 97
Google's Play App Store, 69
Google Wallet, 95
Gorilla Glass, 85
GoToMeeting, 400
Goya Foods, 309
Green Giant, 251
Green Valley Motel, 269, 270, 274–275, 279
Green Works products, 54
Grey Poupon, 77
Grilled Chicken, 244

Gripz, 242
Groupon, 36
GrubHub, 69
Gucci, 13, 14
Guru.com, 134

H

H. J. Heinz Company, 164
Häagen-Dazs, 94, 231
Haier, 150
Hallmark, 259
Hammacher Schlemmer, 90
Hampton Hotels, 316
H&M, 254, 326–328
H&R Block, 104, 105
HappyCow, 17
Harley-Davidson, 175, 354
Harley-Davidson Perfume, 244, 256
HauteLook, 301
Havaianas, 394
HeatMax Hot Hands Hand Warmers, 220
H-E-B Supermarkets, 121
Heinz Ketchup, 287
Hermès, 188
Hertz, 31–32
Hewlett-Packard, 231
HGTV, 416
Hole in the Wall Gang camps, 76
Holiday Inn, 160
Home and Garden TV, 382
Home Depot, 52, 92, 252, 310, 312–313, 328, 339
Home Goods, 337
HomePlus Virtual Stores, 35
Home Sense, 337
Home Shopping Network, 55
Honda, 97, 129
Hone, 14
HootSuite, 63, 139
Hotel Collection, 336
Hot Wheels video game, 391
Hovercraft, 90
HubSpot, 51, 141
Huggies, 240
Hugo Boss, 254
Hulu, 372
Hunt's, 294
Hydro razor, 85–86
Hy-Line Cruises, 51
Hyundai, 97, 129
Hy Vee, 93

I

iBeacon, 18
IBM, 25, 26, 63, 127, 130, 131, 160, 161, 226, 248, 287
IBM SurfAid, 63
IDEO, 250
iHealth Wireless Scales, 58

IKEA, 15, 153, 343, 345
iMac, 42
iMac Desktop, 41
Imgur, 56
Ina Dusk Personal Alarm, 383, 384
Ina Personal Alarm, 384
Infiniti, 32
Innocent, 56
In-N-Out Burger, 125
Instagram, 55–56, 77, 389
InstagramEngine, 77
Intel Corporation, 25, 26, 224, 226
iPad, 5, 18, 22, 33, 41, 42, 95, 132, 170, 239, 243, 244, 247, 257, 258, 259, 267, 278, 328, 363, 393
iPhone, 18, 22, 33, 41, 239, 243, 246, 258, 259, 267, 288, 318, 363, 393
iPod, 41, 243, 259, 288, 363, 393
IRI, 88, 201, 202
Isis Mobile Wallet, 95
iTunes, 5, 7, 52, 257
iTunes Store, 7

J

J. Crew, 394
J. D. Power & Associates, 201
Jawbone, 14
Jawbone UP, 58
JCPenney, 335, 340, 347
JetBlue Airways, 312, 361
Jiffy Lube, 338
Jimmy John's Gourmet, 316
Jolly Green Giant, 189

K

Kardashian Kollection, 336
Kashi, 69, 111
Kayak, 17
Kayak.com, 293
K-Cup Packs, 243
K-Cups, 4
Keebler, 230, 242
Kellogg's, 69, 172, 202, 225, 229, 230
Kellogg's Breakfast Mates, 244
Kellogg's Corn Flakes, 379
Kentucky Fried Chicken, 160, 231
KeyMetric, 63
Kia, 392
Kindle, 225
KitchenAid, 113, 229
Kleenex, 227, 376
Kmart, 119, 336, 352
Kodak, 61, 255
Kohl's, 228, 335, 340
Kraft cheese, 8
Kraft Foods, 202, 207, 208, 239, 242, 332

Kraft Macaroni & Cheese, 122
Krave, 69
Kroger, 15, 172, 204, 229, 271, 272, 328, 333

L

L. L. Bean, 279, 281, 345
Lacoste, 225
Lamborghini, 130
Lana Marks, 104–105, 120
Lancôme, 375
Land Rover, 77
Lands' End, 184
Latitude, 63
Lay's, 63, 64
Lee jeans, 300
L'eggs, 234
Lego, 146, 147, 238
LegoLand, 343
Lenovo, 161, 402
Let's Get Ready, 61
Levi's, 128, 157, 249
Lexus, 6, 50, 77, 97, 181
Lifesavers Soda, 231
Lifestyle Lift, 278
Lilly Pulitzer, 228
Li Ning, 30
LinkedIn, 53, 54–55, 139, 141, 402
Little Movers Slip-Ons, 240
Liz Claiborne, 254
Loblaw, 333
Localytics, 63
Longines, 166
Long John Silver's, 231
Louis Vuitton, 188
Lowe's, 204
LSTN, 73
LTE, 95
Lucent Technologies, 165

M

Ma Bell, 98
Macbook, 18
M-A-C Cosmetics, 329, 330, 332, 336
Mac Desktop, 42
Mack Weldon brand, 174
Macy's, Inc., 102, 109, 112, 118, 119, 124, 181, 185, 204, 221, 330, 335, 336, 340, 381, 404
MADD, 218
Madone 7 Series bicycles, 219, 220
Magic Band, 25
Magic Kingdom, 25
Magnet Theater Touring Company, 50
M&Ms, 218, 219
M&Ms Chocolate Candies, 185
Mango, 324

Mario Kart, 302
Marks & Spencer, 384
Marriott Hotels, 115, 231
Mars Chocolate North America, 185
Marshall's, 12, 337
Mars Inc., 218
Marvel films, 116
MasterCard's Easy Pay, 95
Match.com, 388
Material Girl brand, 339
Maybelline, 331, 340
Maytag, 113
MB's Dream, 50
McCafés, 3
McDonald's, 3, 8, 25, 26, 78, 148, 155, 160, 189, 196–200, 211, 212, 224, 226, 361, 371
McKinsey & Company, 80
MediaCloud, 63
Medialets, 63
Mediamark Research Inc., 201
MediaMelon, 63
Meijer, 333
Men's Wearhouse, 177
Mercedes-Benz, 14, 129, 132, 151, 166
Mercedes-Benz St. 550, 241
Merck, 248
Metro Group, 328, 332–333
Metronome, 63
Michael Graves toasters, 321
Microsoft Corporation, 25, 26, 33, 61, 160, 226, 234, 251
Microsoft Kinect, 206–207
Mind Controlled UFO, 90
Mini, 220–221
Minnesota Timberwolves, 49
Minute Maid, 227, 350
Minute Maid Pulpy, 249
Mobile Hotspots, 95
Mondelez International, 11
MoPub, 383
Morningstar Farms, 230
Morton Salt, 233
Motorola, 161
Motorrad, 220
Movember, 28, 29
Mozilla's Firefox, 68
MSN, 133
Mtracking, 63
MTV, 43–45
Music Connection, 260
MyCoupons.com, 391
MyFitnessPal, 58
My Magic wristband, 25, 193
My Starbucks, 5
mySugr app, 107

N

National Basketball Association, 232
National Football League, 60, 61, 232

National Hockey League, 232
National Purchase Dairy Panel, 198, 201
Nau, 86
NBC, 182
Neiman Marcus, 330, 331, 340
Neo, 374
Nestlé, 94
Netflix, 15, 57, 95, 96, 111, 169–170, 204, 246
Netscape, 257
NeuroFocus, 215
Neutragena Wave, 230
New Balance, 30, 140, 141, 394
New Coke, 244
Newman's Own, 76
Newman's Own Organic, 76
Newton Running, 184
New York Times, 379
Nextag PriceGrabber, 393
Nickelodeon, 30
Nielsen BASES, 255
Nielsen Company, 195, 198, 201, 202
Nike, 8, 9, 14, 21–24, 26, 28, 29, 30, 39, 45, 86, 140, 157, 166, 172, 176, 184, 189, 224, 229, 287
Nike Fit band, 101
Nike ID brand, 8
Nike+iPod, 29
Nikon Digital Learning Center, 52
Nokia, 160
NOP World, 201
Nordstrom, 204, 275, 279, 335, 345
North Face, 118
Nova Armored Baby Beaton handbag, 301
NStar, 297

O

Office Depot, 360
Old Spice, 392
Olive Garden, 232
Omaha Steaks, 359
OnStar, 249
Opioid painkillers, 117
Oracle Corporation, 127
Orbitz, 17
Oreo, 11, 379
Outback Steakhouse, 120
Outlook Calendar, 58
Outnumber Hunger, 377
Overstock.com, 338

P

Palm Pilot, 244
Paradigm, 288
Passion Pit, 212
Patagonia, 86, 346
Patek Philippe, 188, 298

Payless ShoeSource, 392
Pebble, 257
Peet's Coffee and Tea, 338, 342
PenAgain, 309–310, 314–317
Pepsi, 6, 87, 120, 190, 224, 331, 332
PepsiCo, 8, 39, 47, 61, 145, 202, 208, 225
Pepsi Max, 376
Pfizer, 248
Philadelphia cream cheese, 287
Philips Electronics, 74
Photobucket, 56
Photoshop, 385
Pilates, 250
Pinkberry, 361
Pink Ribbon, 28, 29
Pinterest, 55
Pizza Hut Inc., 32–33, 160, 231, 316
Planet Fitness, 267, 268
P90X, 410
Polo/Ralph Lauren, 294
Porsche, 14, 181
Porsche Boxter, 289, 290
Post cereals, 111
Powerade, 189–191, 350
Prada, 388
PR & Communications, 38
Premier Crue Music, 260
Priceline, 17, 363
PricewaterhouseCoopers, 63
Pringles, 122, 164
Proactiv, 172
Procter & Gamble, 78, 149, 150, 162, 207, 222, 254, 283–285, 286, 308, 313, 314, 319, 332, 337, 382
Propel Fitness Water, 190
Publix, 333
Puma, 205, 366
PUMA Golf, 205
Pure Green Coffee, 387

Q

Quality Motels, 266
Qualtrics, 211

R

Rachel Bilson, 336
Radio Disney, 355
Radio Shack, 226
Ralph Lauren, 12, 189, 335, 388
Ray-Ban, 394
Recon ski goggles, 102
Red Box, 246
Red Bull, 216–218, 379, 386, 389
Reebok, 140
REI, 281, 345
Renaissance Hotels, 231
Rent the Runway, 111
Research and Markets, 201

Revlon, 330, 331
Rice Krispies, 224, 225, 230
Rite Aid, 336
Ritz-Carlton, 83, 231, 270
Rolex, 159, 288
Rollerblade, 390
Rolls-Royce, 220–221
Rolls-Royce Ghost, 221
Rolls-Royce Phantom, 221
Rolls-Royce Wraith, 221
Roost, 51
Roper Center for Public Opinion Research, 201
Ross Stores, 337–338
RueLaLa, 301

S

Saddleback Leather, 189
Safeway, 93, 172, 333, 409
St. Jude's Children's Research Hospital, 389
Saks Fifth Avenue, 330, 331, 340
Salesforce.com, 61, 113, 404
Sam's Club, 334
Samsung 4K televisions, 245
Samsung Electronics, 25, 26, 226, 264, 388
Samsung's Galaxy Gear, 102
Samsung smartwatch, 102
Sandies, 242
SAP, 204
SAS, 63
Save-A-Lot, 333
Schedulicity, 51
Schick, 85–86
Schwarz Group, 328, 333
Sears, 300, 301, 335, 336
Sears Holdings, 333, 336
Seat, 130
Self magazine, 24
Sephora, 122, 123, 341
Servpro, 316
7-Eleven Inc., 316, 331
7 for All Mankind, 106
7Up, 188
Sexy Green Car Show, 380
Shearer's Chips, 251
ShopSavvy, 391
Siemens, 128
Siemens Energy, 132
Simmons Market Research Bureau, 201
Singapore Airlines, 26
Sirius XM Satellite Radio, 7
Six Flags theme parks, 218, 265, 266
Skoda, 130
Skype, 400
Sleep Inn Hotel, 266
Snapchat, 173
Snapple, 110, 224
Snickers, 218
Snoobi, 63

SoftLayer, 131
Sony Betamax, 244
Sony Corporation, 221, 229, 257, 276, 319, 322, 323, 392
Sony PlayStation 3, 225
Sour Patch Kids Stride gum, 11
Sour Patch Kids T-shirt, 11
South Beach product line, 207, 208
Southwest Airlines, 26, 78, 187, 208, 362, 363
Spartan, 83
Special K, 172, 230
Speedo, 394
Splunk, 204
Sports Authority, 312
Sprite, 32
Squier Bullet Strat guitar, 290
Stanley Tool Company, 312–313
Staples, 50, 185, 336, 342, 409
Staples.com, 344
Starbucks, 2–5, 9, 15, 16, 78, 160, 161, 178, 231, 338, 393
State Bicycle Company, 212
State Farm Insurance, 224, 228
Stelmatzky, 154
Stone + Cloth, 73
Stone Cold Fox, 50
Stop & Shop, 230
Stouffer's, 356
Strategic Business Insights, 175, 176
Stratocaster guitars, 290
Subaru, 189, 348
Subway, 92, 316, 410
Supercuts, 316, 338
Super Kmart Center, 333
Super Target, 333
Supervalu, 333
Survey-Monkey, 211
Swatch, 298
Sweet Tomatoes, 105
SymphonyIRI Group, 88
Sysco, 142

T

Taco Bell, 115, 222, 231
Tangy Fish, 244
Target.com, 360
Target stores, 95, 119, 146, 228, 249, 308, 313, 321, 328, 333, 336, 360
Tata Consultancy Services, 160
Tata Group, 161
Tata Starbucks, 161
Tax Institute, H&R Block, 105
Teavana, 3
Teint Miracle, 385
Temptalia, 52
Tesco, 35, 203, 204, 303, 323, 328
Texaco, 189
TheFind.com, 294
Thirsty Cat, 244

3M Corporation, 242
Thums Up, 146
Tide, 8, 222, 283–284, 293, 382
Tide Basic, 222
Tide Plus, 284
Tide Simply Clean & Fresh, 284
Tie-a-Tie, 52
Tiffany & Company, 120, 122
Timex, 298
TJMaxx, 12, 337
TJX Companies, Inc., 12, 337
TNT, 379
TOMS Marketplace website, 73
Toms Shoes, 73
TomTom, 255
Tony the Tiger, 189
Toolkit, 373
Tootsie Rolls, 268
Touch of Yogurt Shampoo, 244
Toyota, 97, 224, 226, 227
Toyota Prius, 32, 228, 241, 356–357
Toyota Rav 4, 32
Toys "R" Us, 147
Trader Joe's, 230, 334
Travelocity, 17, 276
Trek, 219, 220, 379
TripAdvisor, 276, 278
Tropicana, 224, 232
TrueFit.com, 106
Tumblr, 50, 51
TweetDeck, 63
TwinPic, 56
Twitter, 5, 11, 48, 50, 51, 52, 55, 58, 60, 61, 63, 77, 96, 113, 139, 141, 158, 185, 202, 205, 208, 223, 265, 267, 277, 349, 353, 361, 382, 383, 389, 402
Twitter@Coupons, 341
Twitter Web Analytics, 63

U

Under Armour, 224
Unilever, 165, 223
United Airlines, 9, 287
United Parcel Service, 127, 307, 312, 325, 401
United States Postal Service, 307
Uno Chicago Grill, 276
UP brand, 14
Urban Outfitters, 91
U.S. Airways, 187
U.S. Foods, 142

V

Vacheron Constantin, 298
Vail, 379
Vanilla Coke, 409
Vanilla Wafers, 242
vCath, 107

Vegin'sOut, 17
V8 juice, 268
Verizon, 68
Victoria's Secret, 181, 392
Victoria's Secret Fashion Show,
    237, 238
Vienna Fingers, 242
Vine, 55
Vintage Hot Rod, 290
VIP Deals, 278
Virgin Airlines, 344
VisiStat, 63
Volkswagen, 37, 38, 411
Volkswagen Commercial
    Vehicles, 130
Volkswagen Group, 129–130
Volkswagen Group China, 38
VoluntEAR program, Disney, 79
Volvo, 129, 355
VSP, 102
VWSupplyGroup.com, 130

W

Walgreen's, 95, 328, 336, 342
Walkman, 226, 257
Walmart, 72, 80, 90, 119, 120,
    136, 157, 164, 204, 211,
    274, 299, 309–310,
    314–317, 323, 328, 331,
    332, 333, 334, 336,
    342, 347, 391
Walt Disney Company, 25,
    26, 79, 87, 170, 193–195,
    354–356
Waste Management, 234
Watson computer, 131
Webtrends, 63
Wegmans, 56, 93, 120
Weixin, 58
Wells Fargo Bank, 132
Wendy's, 125, 198, 199, 200

WhatsApp, 173
Wheat Thins, 11
Whirlpool, 113
WhiteLight, 290
Whole Foods, 69, 119,
    120, 334
Wi-Fi, 95
Wii consoles, 170
Windows Model 7, 33
Winners, 337
WordPress, 51
WornOnTv.net, 106
Wrangler, 378, 380
WRU Welsh Rugby
    Team, 224

X

Xbox 360, 33, 43
Xerox Corporation, 130

Y

Yahoo!, 133, 162
Yankelovich, 201
Yelp, 17, 278
Yoostar, 43
Yoplait, 394
YouTube, 48, 51, 52, 55, 56,
    77, 158, 205, 223, 247,
    353, 355, 361, 372,
    379, 380
Yum! Brands, 231

Z

Zappo's, 234, 410
Zara, 165, 324
Zippo, 231
Zoomerang, 211

subject index

A page number with an e indicates an exhibit.

A

Absolute budget, 364
Academy Awards, 388
Achievers, 176e
Acquisitions
  by General Electric, 127–128
  by Starbucks, 3–4
Action, 356
  in ethical decision-making, 74–75
Action plan, 199–200
Actual product, 219
Adding value
  at American Airlines, 233
  Apple Watch, 288
  automobile innovations, 241
  Baby Boomers and TV, 182
  Broadmoor resort, 271
  college sports tickets, 403
  digital devices, 14
  Ford Motor Company, 163
  gender and buying patterns, 91
  grocery stores as health providers, 93
  H-E-B Supermarkets, 121
  Home Depot, 339
  Hy-Line Cruises, 51
  inbound marketing, 141
  marketing channels, 310–312
  McDonald's, 197
  online backups, 267
  personal selling, 399–402
  Priceline, 363
  quick delivery, 309
  Salesforce.com, 405
  Tata Starbucks, 161
  Trader Joe's, 334
  virtual stores, 35
Administered vertical marketing system, 314
Ad-supported app, 59
Advanced shipping notice, 320, 323
Advertising, 357, 372
  body copy, 384
  and brand association, 228
  brand elements, 384
  budget, 378–379
  Chipotle Mexican Grill, 371–372
  cooperative, 341
  creation of, 383–385
  deceptive, 70
  deceptive and illegal, 303–304
  frequency, 365
  and generation gap, 88
  gross rating points, 365
  by H&R Block, 105

headlines, 384
and health concerns, 92
impact assessment, 386
innovations on social media, 50
institutional, 376–377
in IMC, 357–358
and language differences, 165–166
legislation on, 98
and marketing channels, 312
media evaluation and selection, 381–383
media for, 373
message conveyance
  emotional appeals, 380
  informational appeals, 379–380
objectives
  focus, 376–378
  informative, 375
  persuasive, 375
  pull and push strategies, 374–375
  reminder, 375–376
  versus other promotions, 372–373
paid for, 373
persuasive, 373
pretesting, 386
product-focused, 376
public service announcements, 377
puffery, 387–388
reach, 365
regulatory and ethical issues, 387–388
relevance of ads, 367
sales impact, 386
scheduling, 382–383
  continuous, 382
  flighting, 382
  pulsing, 383
shifting boundaries of, 350
subheads, 384
target audience identification, 373
targeted, 68
tracking, 386
in traditional media, 340
websites for, 340–341
Advertising campaign
  Babar books, 10
  cultural differences, 166–167
  dairy industry, 12
  Got Milk, 377
  objectives, 374–378
  against smoking, 378
Advertising expenditures
  digital spending, 365e
  global, 373
Advertising plan, 374
Advertising schedule, 382

Advertising Standards Authority (UK), 358
Affective component, 116
African American consumers, 90–92
Aggressive marketing tactics, 117
AIDA model, 354
  action, 356–357
  awareness, 354–356
  desire, 356
  interest, 356
Aided recall, 354
Airplane industry consolidation, 397
Alpha testing, 253
Alternatives evaluation, 108–111
  attribute sets, 109
  consumer decision rules, 110–111
  in ethical decision-making, 74, 75
American Horror Story, 57
American Idol, 352
American Marketing Association, 5, 13, 71
  Code of Ethics, 74
  marketing research guidelines, 213
America's Best Dance Crew, 43
Analysts, LinkedIn users, 139
and exchange rates, 152
Animal testing, 254
Anticipatory shipping system, 307–308
Antitrust laws, 304
Appeals, in advertising, 379–380
Apps; see Mobile apps
Architectural Digest, 183, 184
Asian Americans, 92
Associated services, 219
Association of Southeast Asian Nations, 152
Assurance, 270, 271, 272, 408
Attitude, 116
  components, 116
  incongruence among, 116–117
  influence of learning on, 118
  marketer influence on, 117
Attribute sets
  determinant attributes, 109
  evaluative criteria, 109
  evoked set, 109
  retrieval set, 109
  universal set, 109
Augmented product, 219
Autocratic buying center, 138
Automobile industry
  advertising by, 384–385
  in China, 151
  Ford Motor Company, 163
  General Motors, 181, 249
  innovations, 241
  Volkswagen, 38

Avengers, 117
Awareness, 354–356

B

Baby Boomers, 89
  clichéd image of, 88
  as TV audience, 182
Bait and switch, 304
BCG matrix; see Portfolio analysis
B2C marketing; see Business-to-consumer marketing
Behavioral component, 116
Behavioral segmentation, 177
  loyalty segmentation, 177–178
  occasion segmentation, 177
Believers, 176e
Benefit segmentation, 177
Beta testing, 254
  and Internet, 255
Better Business Bureau, Children's Advertising Review Unit, 387
Big Bang Theory, 352, 363, 392
Big box retailer, 336
Big data, 204, 308
  development of, 204
  General Motors use of, 249
  leading firms, 204
  software solutions, 204
  sources of growth, 205
Big Mac Index, 148–149
Biometric data, 214
Blogs, 56, 361
  corporate, 56
  FTC guidelines, 77
  function, 56
  to generate leads, 402
  personal, 57
  professional, 56–57
Blog trends, 47
Bloomberg Businessweek, 26
Body by Milk campaign, 12
Body copy, 384
Bon Appetit, 183
Bonus, 411
Bottled water labels, 234
Bottom of the pyramid market, 150
Bounce rate, 63
Boycott, 136
  in China, 137
Brainstorming
  for ethical decision-making, 74
  for product development, 250
Brand association, 228
Brand awareness, 226, 354
  building, 375
  creating, 227
  persuasive advertising, 375
Brand dilution, 231

Brand elements, 384
Brand equity, 226
   and brand dilution, 231
Brand extension, 230–231
   unsuccessful, 231
Brand image, 346
Branding
   customer loyalty and, 225
   facilitating purchases, 224–225
   introduction, 224
   protection from competition, 225
   value for customer, 225
Branding strategies
   brand and line extensions,
      230–231
   brand licensing, 231–232
   brand ownership, 229–230
   co-branding, 231
   naming brands
      family brands, 230
      individual brands, 230
   Red Bull, 217–218
   repositioning, 232
Brand licensing, 231
   risk of brand dilution, 232
   royalty payments, 232
Brand loyalty, 228
Brand names
   becoming generic, 227
   for new products, 230
Brand ownership
   manufacturer brands, 229
   private-label brands, 229–230
   retailer/store brands, 229–230
Brand repositioning, 232
Brands
   as assets, 225
   components, 224e
   customer loyalty to, 225
   easily recognizable, 224–225
   effect on market value,
      225–226
   evoked set, 109
   exclusive, 340
   failed products, 231
   global, 26
   perceived value, 227–228
   private-label/store, 340
   as protection from
      competition, 225
   Red Bull, 217–218
   world's ten most valuable, 226e
Brand value, loss of, 226
Brazil
   appeal of global marketing, 155
   versus China in social
      networking, 158
   size of economy, 155
Breadth, 220
   decrease or increase, 222
Break-even analysis, 295–297,
   295–297
Break-even point, 295
   determining, 296
Breakthroughs, 243
Bribery, 137

Bribery Index, 137
BRIC countries, 149–150, 258; see
   also Brazil; China; India;
   Russia
   appeal of, for global marketing,
      155–158
   literacy rates, 165
Browsing, 343
Budget
   for advertising, 378–379
   for IMC
      objective and task
         method, 364
      rule-of-thumb methods, 364
   for marketing campaign, 64
Bureau of Alcohol, Tobacco, and
   Firearms, 387
Bureau of Labor Statistics, 90
Business ethics, 70
   bribery and, 137
   at General Electric, 76
   and SWOT analysis, 76
Business relationships,
   improving, 242
Business-to-business buying
   process, 133e
   compared to B2C buying
      process, 132–133
   need recognition, 133
   order specification, 134
   proposal analysis, 134
   request for proposals, 133–134
   vendor negotiation and
      selection, 134
   vendor performance
      assessment, 134–135
   web portals, 133–134
Business-to-business marketing,
   10, 128
   advertising spending, 379
   buying centers
      building relationships, 138–140
      and organizational culture,
         136–138
      roles in, 135–136
      types of, 138
   buying situation
      changes over time, 142
      compared to B2C marketing,
         142–143
      modified rebuy, 142
      new buy, 130–132
      straight rebuy, 142
      strategies, 142
      types of, 140
   compared to B2C marketing,
      128–129, 132
   customer input for, 251
   and derived demand, 128
   by General Electric, 127–128
   generating leads, 402
   inbound marketing, 141
   order getters, 409
   personal selling, 359
   using LinkedIn, 139
   white papers, 139–140

Business-to-business markets
   government, 132
   institutions, 130
   iPad users, 132
   manufacturers, 129–130
   resellers, 130
   service providers, 129–130
Business-to-consumer
   marketing, 10
   advertising spending, 379
   compared to B2B marketing,
      128–129, 142–143
   customer input for, 251
   generating and qualifying
      leads, 404
Buyers, 135
   example, 136
Buying centers, 135
   roles in, 135–136
Buying decisions, 123
Buying situation
   changes over time, 142
   compared to B2C marketing,
      142–143
   marketing strategies for, 141
   modified rebuy, 141
   new buy, 140–142
   straight rebuy, 141
Buy one, get one free, 304

C

CAN-SPAM Act, 98
Cash cows, 41
Cash payment, 344
Category killer, 336
Celebrity endorsements, 21, 47, 388
Center for Democracy and
   Technology, 213
Central America Free Trade
   Agreement, 152
Cereal industry setbacks, 37
Channel conflict, 313
Channel members, 331
Checking, 322
Chief operating officer, 406, 407
Child Protection Act, 98
Children, in decision process, 119
Children's Television Act, 98, 387
China
   animal testing, 254
   boycott in, 137
   versus Brazil in social
      networking, 158
   car-buying, 151
   economic growth, 157
   gross domestic product, 157
   language differences, 166
   luxury goods, 166
   population size, 157
   recent history, 157
   social networking app, 58
   soup consumption, 163–164
   unequal economic distribution,
      157–158

Walmart in, 80
   working conditions, 318
Choice, 9
Churn, 204
Clayton Act, 304
Click farms, 77
Click path, 63
Click-through rate, 367
Closing the sale, 407
Cloud computing, 131, 405
Coalition for Consumer Information
   on Cosmetics, 254
Co-branding, 231
Coercive power, 315
Cognitive component, 116
Cognitive dissonance
   in attitudes, 116–117
   postpurchase, 112
Cold calls, 403
   to generate leads, 402
   loss of popularity, 403–404
College athletics tickets, 403
Commission, 411
Common goals, 317
Communication
   consumer perception of,
      353–354
   global strategies, 165–167
   in marketing, 349–350
   in marketing channels, 317
   in personal selling, 389–399
   verbal, 154
Communication channel, 352
Communication gap, 269, 276–278
   and customer expectations,
      277–278
   reducing, 277
Communication process, 351e
   channel, 352
   decoding, 353
   encoding, 352
   feedback loop, 353
   noise, 353
   receiver, 352–353
   sender, 352
Communication strategy, 351
Company capabilities, 85
Company sales force, 408
Compatibility, 247
Compensation of sales force
   financial, 411–412
   nonfinancial, 412
Compensatory decision rule, 110
Competition
   brands as protection from, 225
   for convenience stores, 335
   for drugstores, 336
   effect on consumers, 85
   forms of
      monopolistic, 298
      monopoly, 297
      oligopolistic, 297–298
      pure competition, 298
   global pricing, 165
   in maturity stage, 258
   from organic foods, 110

Competitive advantage; *see also* Sustainable competitive advantage
  based on location, 26
  function, 23
Competitive markets, 283
Competitive parity, 287
Competitive parity method, 364
Competitor orientation, 287
Competitors
  identifying position of, 190
  in immediate environment, 85–86
  for Starbucks, 3
  value proposition, 187
Competitors' products, for new ideas, 250–251
Complementary products, 294
Complexity, 247–248
Computer hacking, 95
Concentrated targeting strategy, 183–184, 185
Concept, 252
Concept testing, 252
  example, 253
Consensus buying center, 138
Consultative buying center, 138
Consumer behavior
  and AIDA model, 354–357
  cultural differences, 154–155
  decision process
    decision rules, 110–111
    evaluation of alternatives, 108–111
    information search, 105–108
    need recognition, 103–105
    postpurchase, 111–113
    purchase and consumption, 111
  decision process influences, 113–123
    marketing mix, 113
    psychological factors, 114–118
    situational factors, 120–123
    social factors, 118–120
    variety of, 114e
  health-related apps, 107
  involvement levels, 123–125
  laggard effect, 356
  natural and organic foods, 110
  reasons for buying goods, 102–103
  social and mobile marketing, 123
  and tax season, 105
  undesirable, 113
  and unethical practices, 117
  with untested technology, 101–102
Consumer decision process, 103e
Consumer decision rules, 110
  compensatory rule, 110–111
  noncompensatory rule, 111
Consumer Electronics Show, 97, 402–403
Consumer Privacy Bill of Rights, 360
Consumer Product Safety Act, 98

Consumer Product Safety Commission, 98
Consumer protection legislation, 98e
Consumer Reports, 106, 118
Consumers
  benefits of stores, 343–344
  biometric data, 214
  brand association, 228
  characteristics, 102
  communicating with, 351–357
  determining perceptions of, 190
  determining preferences of, 190–191
  device exhaustion, 259
  in economic downturn, 283
  effect of competition on, 85
  ethical, 72
  ethnic differences, 90–92
  influences on, 84
  levels of involvement, 123–125
  low-income, 90
  negative word of mouth, 113
  and neuromarketing, 214–215
  number of millennials, 88
  passive, 113
  perception of communication, 353–354
  perception of value, 283–285
  screening out ads, 373
  social trends among
    green marketing, 93–94
    health and wellness, 92–93
    privacy concerns, 95
  types of buying decisions, 123
Consumer spending
  by children, 119
  by millennials, 350
Consumer-to-consumer marketing, 10
Consumption, inseparable, 266
Contest, 392
Continuous advertising schedule, 382
Contractual vertical marketing system, 315
  franchising, 315–316
Contribution per unit, 296
Controlling the Assault of Non-Solicited Pornography and Marketing Act, 98
Control phase, 77–78
Control phase, 27
Convenience products/services, 220
Convenience store, 335
Conventional supermarket, 333
Conversational appliances, 97
Conversion rate, 63, 111
Cookie-blocking technology, 68
Cookies, 67, 68, 95, 185
Cooperative advertising, 341
Core competencies, 85
Core customer value, 218
Corporate blog, 56

Corporate Diversity Council, FedEx, 78
Corporate partners, 86
Corporate policy, and sales force, 413–414
Corporate social responsibility, 71
  and ethics, 71–72
  at FedEx, 78
  and investors, 72
  key stakeholders, 78–79e
    customers, 79
    employees, 79
    marketplace, 80
    society, 80–81
  versus profit motive, 78
  programs of major companies, 78e
  and sustainability, 81
  TOMS Shoes, 73
  at Walmart, 80
Corporate vertical marketing system, 316, 330
Cost-benefit analysis, 15
  in search process, 106
Costs, 294–297
  break-even analysis, 295–297
  fixed, 295
  markup and target return pricing, 297
  total, 295
  variable, 295
Council of Fashion Designers of America, 358
Countries, propensity to bribe, 137
Country culture, 87
Country market assessment, 148e
Coupon, 390
Credible commitments, 319
Credit card data, stolen, 77–78
Credit payment, 344
Cross-docking distribution center, 323
Cross-price elasticity, 294
Cross-promoting, 394
Cross-related marketing, 389
Crowding, 122
Crowd-sourced online opinions, 278
Cultural, demographic, social, technological, economic, and political forces, 28–29
Cultural differences; *see* Sociocultural factors
Culture, 86, 120
  classifying, 154
  country, 87
  demographic, social, technological, economic, and political forces, 86, 87e
  effect on consumer behavior, 154–155
  factor in decision process, 120
  regional, 87–88
  transmission of, 86–87
Currency fluctuations, 152

Customer complaints
  behaviors, 274
  and procedural fairness, 280–281
Customer dissatisfaction, 204
Customer excellence, 24
  outstanding customer service, 25
  retaining loyal customers, 24–25
Customer expectations, 330–331
  and communications gap, 277–278
  and follow-up, 408
  marketing research on, 271–272
  understanding, 270–274
Customer information, 405
Customer loyalty
  achieving, 24–25
  and Amazon Prime, 263
  and blogs, 56
  brand loyalty, 225, 228
  ethical considerations, 180
  in postpurchase behavior, 112–113
  segmentation, 177–178
  and service quality, 279
  Starbucks, 178
Customer needs, 187–188
  changing, 239–240
Customer orientation, 287
Customer product, 220
Customer relationship management, 15–16
  for customer loyalty, 24
  integrated, 345
  programs, 113
Customer relationship management systems, 405
Customers
  databases, 359
  demand curve and prices, 289–291
  demographic data on, 214
  early adopters, 245
  early majority, 245–246
  ethics of using information on, 213–215
  for ideas for new products, 250
  innovators, 245
  input from, for new products, 251–252
  laggards, 246
  late majority, 246
  lead users, 252
  LinkedIn users, 139
  listening to, 60–61, 280
  located by smartphone use, 68
  market segments, 31–32
  micromarketing by, 185–186
  online tracking, 67–68
  options for, 8
  potential, 6
  price elasticity of demand, 291–294
  and salesperson, 414
  and showrooming, 58

Customers—*Cont.*
  social and mobile marketing
    engagement, 60–64
  in social media 4E framework,
    48–52
  as stakeholders, 79
  use of corporate blogs, 56
Customer satisfaction, 6
  and customer expectations, 112
  loyalty programs, 177–178
  and service quality, 279
  steps to assure, 112
Customer service, 264, 342
  American Express, 277
  compared to services, 264
  personalized, 344–345
  provision of, 25
  rewarding employees for, 275–276
  Walt Disney Company, 193–195

D

Data, 198
  biometric, 214
  demographic, 214
  in marketing research, 198
Data analysis
  from customers, 60–61
  by eHarmony, 62
  in marketing research, 198–199
  measures for social media, 61–63
Data analytics platform, 105
Data collection
  in marketing research, 198
  misuse, 72–73
  by Nielsen Company, 202
  on people's locations, 77
Data disruption, 267
Data mining, 203
  by Lowe's, 204
  statistical models from, 204
  by Tesco, 203
  watchdogs over, 214
Data warehouses, 203
  electronic data interchange, 320
  vendor-managed inventory,
    320–321
Deal, 392
Death of a Salesman (Miller), 399
Deceptive advertising, 70
Deciders, 135
  example, 136
Decline stage, 256, 259–260; *see
    also* Product life cycle
Decoding, 353
Delivery gap, 269
  empowering service
    providers, 275
  incentives for employees,
    275–276
  technology to overcome, 276, 277
Demand curve, 289
  benefit for firms, 289e
  downward-sloping, 289e
  and prestige products, 289–291

Democratic buying center, 138
Demographics, 88
  China, 157–158
  education, 90
  ethnicity, 90–92
  gender, 90, 91
  generational cohorts, 88–89
  income distribution, 89–90
  India, 156
  information sources, 88
  TV audiences, 182
Demographic segmentation, 172
  and gender, 172
  inadequacy for firms, 172
  variables, 172
Department of Agriculture, 94
  National Organic Program, 110
Department store, 335
Depth, 220
  decrease or increase, 222
Derived demand, 128
Designed to Sell, 414
Desire, 356
Determinant attributes, 109
Device exhaustion, 259
**Differentiated targeting
    strategy, 183**
Diffusion of innovation, 243
  curve, 244e–245
  early adopters, 245
  early majority, 245–246
  first movers, 243
  innovators, 245
  and laggards, 246
  and late majority, 246
  pioneers/breakthroughs, 243
  product failures, 244e
  using theory of, 246–248
    benefit for firms, 246–247
    compatibility, 247
    complexity and trialability,
      247–248
    observability, 247
    relative advantage, 247
Digitalized spending worldwide,
    365e
Digital Learning Center, Nikon, 52
Digital Natives, 89
Direct and indirect channel
    strategies, 312e
Direct investment, 161
Direct mail advertising, 382e
Direct marketing, 359
  in IMC, 359–360
Direct marketing channel, 312
Direct store delivery, 321–322
Dispatcher, 322
Distance learning programs, 411
Distribution
  gray market, 299
  quick delivery, 309
Distribution and information
    systems, 25
Distribution center, 311
  activities
    dispatchers, 322

  floor ready merchandise, 323
  inbound transportation, 322
  planners, 322
  prepare shipments, 324
  receiving and checking,
    322–323
  shipping, 324
  storing and cross-docking, 323
  ticketing and marking, 323
  versus direct store delivery,
    321–322
  omnichannel retailing, 346–347
Distribution channels in global
    marketing, 165
Distribution intensity, 331
  exclusive distribution, 332
  intensive distribution, 331–332
  selective distribution, 332
Distributive fairness, 280
Distributor, 130
Diversification
  related, 44
  unrelated, 45
Diversification strategy, 48
Diversity, risk management
    through, 242
Dogs, 41–42
Doing, in social media strategy,
    63–64
Dollar, 95
Domo (data analytics), 105
Do Not Spam Law, 98
Doris Day Animal League, 254
Dr. Oz Show, 387
Driverless cars, 97
Drugstore, 336
Duty, 151
Dynamic pricing, 292

E

Early adopters, 245
  and price skimming, 302
Early majority, 245
Easy Rider, 175
Economic downturns, 161
Economic environment
  gross domestic product, 148–149
  purchasing power parity, 148–149
  trade deficit, 148
  trade surplus, 148
Economic situation, 95
  effect on marketing, 96–97
  foreign currency fluctuations, 95
  for global marketing
    general environment, 148–149
    market size, 149–150
    population growth rate, 149–150
    real income, 150
  inflation, 95
  interest rates, 95–96
  in Russia, 156
Economies of scale, 258
Economist, 148–149
Educating customers, 57

Education
  of customers, 50–51
  and income prospects, 90
Elastic, 291
Electronic data interchange, 320
  in just-in-time systems, 325
Electronic Privacy Information
    Center, 214
Emotional appeal, 380
Emotional support, 275
Empathy, 270, 271, 272, 408, 410
Employees
  empowering, 275
  LinkedIn users, 139
  as stakeholders, 79
  support and incentives for,
    275–276
Empowerment, 275
Encoding, 352
Engaging customers, 52, 56, 60–64
Entertainment, 344
Entrepreneur, 316
Environmental awareness
  FedEx, 78
  green marketing, 93–94
  at Nike, 22
  Walmart, 80
Environmentally friendly
    products, 80
Environmental Protection Agency,
    81, 94, 234
Environment analysis
  factors affecting, 85e
  framework for, 84–85
  hotel pet accommodations,
    83–84
  immediate environment
    company capabilities, 85
    competitors, 85–86
    corporate partners, 86
  macroenvironmental factors
    company response to, 99
    culture, 86–88
    demographics, 88–92
    economic situation, 95–97
    political/regulatory
      environment, 97–98
    social trends, 92–95
    technological advances, 95
Esteem needs, 115
Ethical and societal dilemma
  animal testing, 254
  bribery, 137
  car-buying in China, 151
  cosmetics and makeup, 385
  customer loyalty programs, 180
  fake reviews, 278
  gen ethically modified
    organisms, 69
  green cereal, 93
  iBeacon software, 18
  Integrated marketing
    communications, 358
  label information, 234
  marketing sugary drinks, 227
  natural and organic foods, 110

pharmaceutical companies, 117
pricing strategies, 301
privacy rights, 360
real estate TV, 414
shareholder interests *vs.*
society's interests, 68
shoppers' demographic data, 214
smoking and advertising, 378
Volkswagen in China, 38
working conditions in China, 318
Ethical consumers, 72
Ethical decision-making
framework, 72–75
brainstorming, 74
choosing course of action, 74–75
gather information, 73–74
identify issues, 72–73
identify stakeholders, 73–74
metric, 73e
Ethics; *see also* Business ethics;
Marketing ethics; Unethical
behavior
American Marketing Association
statement, 71
and corporate social
responsibility, 71–72
at General Electric, 76
in marketing research, 213–215
personal, 70–71
personal selling, 413–414
in planning process, 76
versus social responsibility, 72e
Ethnicity, 90–92
Euro, 95
European Commission, 304
European Union
advertising restrictions, 387
animal testing, 254
membership, 152
pricing regulations, 164
Evaluative criteria, 109
Event sponsorship, 389
of sports teams, 11
and universities, 140
Everyday low pricing, 299
Evoked set, 109
Exchange, 7, 7e
Exchange control, 152
Exchange rate, 152
Excitement of customers, 49–50, 53
Exclusive brand, 340
Exclusive distribution, 332
Experience curve effect, 300
Experience product or service,
52, 55
Experiencers, 176e
Experiment, 211
Experimental research, 211
and Facebook, 211–212
McDonald's, 211
Expertise power, 315
Exporting, 159
Extended problem solving, 124
External locus of control, 107
External search for information, 105
External secondary data, 201–203

Extreme-value food retailer, 333
Extreme-value retailer, 337
EyeSee mannequins, 214

F

Facial recognition software, 213
Fair Packaging and Labeling Act,
98, 235
Fake reviews, 278
Family brand, 230
Family Circle, 116
Family purchase decisions, 118–119
Farmed and Dangerous, 372–373
Fashion cycles, 242
Fast and Furious, 117
Fast-food surveys, 199e
Federal Cigarette Labeling and
Advertising Act, 98
Federal Communications
Commission, 99
on advertising, 387
on public service
announcements, 377
Federal Emergency Management
Agency, 267
Federal Reserve System, 152
Federal Trade Commission, 77,
98, 304
on advertising, 387, 388
National Do Not Call List, 404
Federal Trade Commission Act, 98,
235, 304
Feedback loop, 353
FIFA World Cup, 350
Financial performance metrics,
37–39
Financial rewards
bonuses, 411
commission, 411–412
salary, 411–412
sales contests, 411
Financial risk, 108
Financial Services Oversight
Council, 98
Firms
brand equity, 226
communication strategy, 351
consistency in communication,
349–350
corporate blogs, 56
corporate partners, 86
macroenvironment, 84
marketing analytics by, 15–18
marketing campaign steps, 64
online chats, 344
pricing objectives, 285–288
privacy practice disclosure, 214
profit *vs.* protecting customers, 68
propensity to bribe, 137
reasons for new products, 23–242
responding to negative word of
mouth, 113
response to environment, 99
social media to engage
customers, 60–64

social media uses, 48–49
spending on marketing
research, 195
value-driven, 15
value proposition, 187
First movers, 243
Fitness devices, 97
Five Cs of pricing
channel members, 299
company objectives, 285–288
competition, 297–298
costs, 294–297
customers, 289–294
Fixed costs, 181, 295
**Flighting (advertising
schedule), 382**
Floor-ready merchandise, 323
Focus group interviews, 209
Follow-up, 407–408
Food and Drug Administration, 69,
81, 98, 234, 387
Food and Drug Administration Act, 98
Food retailers, 332–333
number of stores, 338
Foreign currency fluctuation, 95
Fortune 500 companies, 139, 265
Four Ps of marketing, 7, 23; *see
also* Marketing mix
for retailing, 338–342
Franchisee, 160
Franchising, 160, 315
entrepreneurial advantage, 316
top ten firms, 316
Franchisor, 160
Freemium app, 59
Frequency, 365
Friending, 54
Frozen, 232
Fulfillment center, 311
Full-line discount stores, 336
food retailers, 332
Functional needs, 103

G

Gatekeepers, 135
example, 136
Gender, 90
and buying patterns, 91
and demographic
segmentation, 172
General merchandise retailers
category specialists, 336–337
department stores, 335–336
drugstores, 336
extreme-value, 337
full-line discount stores, 336
off-price, 337–338
specialty stores, 336
Generational cohorts, 88
Baby Boomers, 89
generation X, 89
generation Y, 89
generation Z, 89
shopping habits, 119
statistics on, 89e

Generation gap, 88
Generation X, 89
Generation Y, 89
Generation Z, 89
Genetically modified organisms, 69
**Geodemographic
segmentation, 179**
benefits for retailers, 179–180
Tapestry System, 179
Geographic segmentation, 171
types of, 171–172
Germany, privacy law, 214
Glee, 106
Glengarry Glen Ross (Mamet), 399
Global advertising expenditures, 373
Global brands, 26
Coke, 146
Global communication strategies,
165–167
Global distribution strategies, 165
Global entry strategies, 159e
Globalization, 146
Global marketing
Coca Cola Company, 145–146
driving forces, 155
market assessment
appeal of BRIC countries,
155–158
economic analysis, 147–150
governmental actions, 151–152
infrastructure, 150–151
sociocultural factors, 153–155
technological capabilities,
150–151
Global marketing strategies
communication, 165–167
distribution, 165
for market entry
control *vs.* risk in, 160
direct investment, 161–162
exporting, 159
franchising, 160
joint ventures, 160–161
strategic alliances, 160
pricing, 164–165
product or service, 163–164
segmentation and
positioning, 162
target market, 162
Global pricing strategies
and competitive forces, 165
difficulty in, 164
European restrictions, 164
Global products or services
glocalization, 164
same, 163–164
totally new, 164
Glocalization, 164
Goals
aligning short-term with
long-term, 71
identifying, 64
of integrated marketing
communications, 352, 363
in marketing channels, 313, 317
Going green, 86

Golf Digest, 183, 184
Good Morning America, 356
Goods, 8; *see also* Products
    differentiated from services, 266e
Government, business-to-business
    market, 131
Government Accounting Office, 234
Governmental actions; *see*
    Political/regulatory
    environment
Government spending, 131
GQ, 183
Green cereal, 93
Greener customers, 93–94
Green marketing, 54, 86, **93**
    demand for, 94
    versus greenwashing, 93
    U.S. and Europe, 94
Greenwashing, 94
Grey market, 299
Gross domestic product, 148
    services percent of, 265
Gross national income, 148
Gross rating points, 365
Growth stage, 256, 257–258; *see*
    also Product life cycle
Growth strategies
    components, 42e
    diversification, 44–45
    market development, 43–44
    market penetration, 43
    product development, 44

H

Habitual decision making, 125
Harry's Law, 182
Headline, 384
Health and wellness concerns,
    92–93
Health Insurance Portability and
    Accountability Act, 267
Heterogeneity, 266
Hierarchy of needs; *see* Maslow's
    hierarchy of needs
High-involvement consumers, 124
High/low pricing, 299
Hispanic consumers, 90–91
Hit, 61
Horizontal channel conflict, 313
Horizontal price fixing, 305
House Hunters, 414
House of Cards, 96, 169–170
Hunger Games, 246
Hunger Games: Catching Fire, 246
Hurricane Sandy, 52

I

Idea generation, 248–252
Ideal points, 189
Ideas, 9
Identifiable segments, 180
IMC; *see* Integrated marketing
    communications

Immediate environment, 85–86
Immediate gratification, 344
Immigrants, 91
Implementation phase, 27, 76–77;
    see also Marketing plan
Impressions, 367
Impulse buying, 124
In-app purchase, 59
Inbound marketing, 141, 402
Inbound transportation, 322
Income
    and education, 90
    real, 150
Income distribution, 89–90
Income effect, 293
Independent agents, 408
Independent (conventional)
    marketing channel, 314
In-depth interviews, 208
India
    Coca Cola Company in, 145–146
    coffee culture of, 161
    in global marketing, 156–157
    population size, 150, 156
    retailing environment, 157
    Unilever in, 165
Indirect marketing channel, 312
Individual brands, 230
Individualism, 153, 154, 155e
Individualized pricing, 292
Indulgence, 153
Inelastic, 292
Inflation, 95
Influencers, 135
    example, 136
Information, 198
    on customers from social media,
        60–64
    on demographics, 88
    for ethical decision-making, 73–74
    flow through marketing channels
        data warehouses, 320–321
        steps, 319–320
    from salespeople, 401
    from social media, 52
Information power, 315
Information search
    external, 105–106
    factors affecting
        actual or perceived risks, 108
        locus of control, 107
        perceived costs *vs.*
            benefits, 106
    internal, 105
Informative advertising, 375
Infrastructure, 150
    key elements of, 151
Initiator, 135
    example, 136
Innovation, 239; *see also* Diffusion
    of innovation; Reverse
    engineering; Technological
    advances
    broaden product line from, 242
    development over time,
        238–239

    at H&M, 327
    at Nike, 22
    percent of successes, 239
    reverse, 249
    at Starbucks, 3–4
    3D printing, 237–238
Innovators, 176e, 245
Inseparable, 266
Institutional advertisement, 376
Institutions, business-to-business
    market, 130
In-store demonstrations, 122
Instrumental support, 275
Intangible, 266
Integrated customer relationship
    management, 345
Integrated marketing
    communications, 36, 64, **351**
    and Coca Cola Company,
        349–350
    communicating
        AIDA model, 354–357
        perception of communication,
            353–354
        process, 351–353
    elements of, 351
    and harmful behavior, 358
    performance evaluation,
        366–368
    personal selling in, 398–402
    planning phase
        budget, 362–364
        goals, 362
        measurement metrics,
            364–366
    search engine marketing, 367
    social media components,
        48–49
    and social shopping, 367
    strategy elements, 357e
        advertising, 357–358
        direct marketing, 359–360
        online marketing, 360–362
        personal selling, 369
        public relations, 358–359
        sales promotions, 369
Intensive distribution, 331
Interdependence, 317
Interest, 356
Interest rates, 95
Internal locus of control, 107
Internal research and
    development, 248–249
Internal search for information, 105
International trade
    elimination of barriers, 146
    exporting, 159
    quotas, 152
    tariffs, 151, 152
Internet
    and beta testing, 255
    effect on direct marketing, 359
    expansion of communication, 349
    to generate leads, 402
    for information search, 106
    instant coupons, 390–391

    negative word of mouth on, 113
    omnichannel retailing, 344–347
    online training, 411
    privacy issues, 95
    search engine marketing, 367
    security breaches, 213
    social shopping, 367
Internet advertising, 382e
Introduction stage, 256, 257; *see*
    also Product life cycle
In-vehicle mobile apps, 97
Inventory management
    just-in-time systems
        increased availability, 325
        lower investment, 325
        versus order to deliver, 324
        reduced lead time, 324–325
    by manufacturers, 339
    vendor-managed, 320–321
Investors
    and corporate social
        responsibility, 72
    LinkedIn users, 139
Involvement, 122
    extended problem solving, 124
    habitual decision making, 125
    high *vs.* low, 124
    impulse buying, 124–125
    limited problem solving, 124–125
I Used to Be Fat, 44

J

Jersey Shore, 43
Joint ventures, 160
    restrictions on, 161
    Tata Starbucks, 161
Jungle, The (Sinclair), 78
Just-in-time inventory system, 324
    cost of, 325

K

Keyword analysis, 63
Kiosks, 267–268, 342
Knowledge gap, 269
    and customer expectations,
        270–274
    evaluating service quality,
        270–274

L

Labels
    information on, 234
    laws on, 235
Laggards, 246
    and decline stage, 260
Lagged effect, 356
Language
    advertising and differences in,
        165–166
    variations within countries, 166
Late majority, 246
    and maturity stage, 258

Late Night with Jimmy Fallon, 50
Leads, 402
    generating and qualifying,
        402–404
Lead time, 324
Lead users, 252
Learning, 118
Legitimate power, 315
Licensing for product
    development, 250
Lifestyles, 118, 174
    Harley way of life, 175
    limitations of analysis, 176
    VALS framework, 175–176
Lift, 386
**Limited-assortment
    supermarkets, 333**
Limited problem solving, 124
Line extension, 230
Listening, sentiment analysis, 60–61
Literacy in BRIC countries, 165
Litigation, pharmaceutical
    companies, 117
Local marketers, 150
Locational excellence, 26
    achieving, 26
Location-based software, 50
Location strategy, 10, 342
    Starbucks, 16
Locus of control, 107
Longmire, 182
Loss leader pricing, 303–304
Love needs, 115
Low-involvement consumers, 124
Loyalty; *see* Brand loyalty;
    Customer loyalty
Loyalty program, 393
Loyalty segmentation, 177
Luxury goods, 14, 104–105
    in China, 166

M

Macroenvironment, 87e
**Macroenvironmental
    factors, 86;** *see also*
    Environment analysis
    types of, 84
Magazine advertising, 382e
Makers, 176e
Management by walking
    around, 274
Manufacturer brands, 229
Manufacturers
    business-to-business market,
        129–130
    as channel members, 299
    corporate partners, 86
    flow of merchandise from,
        321–325
    lack of inventory storage, 339
    marketing by, 10e
    market power, 328–329
    omnichannel strategy, 329
    patterning with retailers, 330–332

    and retailers, 328–329
    sales to retailers, 12
    use of marketing channels,
        310–311
**Manufacturer's
    representatives, 408**
**Manufacturer's suggested retail
    price, 305**
    discount from, 337, 338
Manufacturing with 3D printing,
    127–128
Market(s)
    bottom of the pyramid, 150
    for business-to-business
        marketing, 129–131
    competitive, 283
    entry into new, 258–259
    ideal points of, 190
    millennial, 88
    price-sensitive, 283
    and service strategies, 24e
Market development strategy, 47
    MTV, 43–44
Market growth rate, 40
Marketing, 5; *see also* Business-
        to-business marketing
    aggressive tactics, 117
    to children, 119
    core aspects, 5e
    effect of economic situation on,
        96–97
    exchange in, 7
    of ideas, 9
    by local marketers, 150
    to low-income consumers, 90
    milestones in
        market-oriented era, 13
        production-oriented era, 12
        sales-oriented era, 12–13
        value-based marketing era,
            13–14
    performance of, 10e
        business-to-business, 10
        business-to-consumer, 10
        consumer-to-consumer, 10
        by individuals, 10–12
    satisfying needs and wants, 6
    of services, 265–268
    stakeholders, 12
    using age to identify customers,
        88–89
    value-based, 84–85
Marketing analytics
    airline ticket prices, 293
    cloud computing, 131
    cost-benefit analysis, 15
    customer relationship
        management, 15–16
    CVS, 391
    eHarmony, 62
    firms' reliance on, 15
    General Motors big data
        use, 249
    Google Analytics and Puma, 366
    Google Inc., 39
    IKEA, 343

    Kellogg's, 69
    location strategy, 16
    movie industry, 205
    Netflix predictive analytics, 96
    in performance evaluation, 37
    product lines, 221
    reducing wait time, 272
    relational orientation, 15
    Starbucks rewards program, 178
    tax season, 105
    using social and
        mobile media, 16–18
Marketing campaign
    budget for, 64
    Coca Cola Company, 349–350
    development, 64
    goals and strategy, 64
    monitoring and change, 64
    target audience, 64
**Marketing channel management,
    10, 308,** 311; *see also* Supply
    chain management
Marketing channels
    channel members, 299
    components, 312
    design of, 311–312
    for Nike, 23
    power in, 315
    specialized roles in, 312
    types of, 312
    value added by, 310–311
Marketing communication, 117
Marketing environment analysis;
    see also Environment
    analysis
Marketing ethics, 70
    compared to business
        ethics, 70
    and corporate social
        responsibility, 71–72, 78–81
    decision-making framework,
        70–74
    influence of personal ethics,
        70–71
    and marketing strategy, 75–78
    in online marketing, 67–68
    scope of, 70
    TOMS Shoes, 73
Marketing evolution, 13e
Marketing mix, 7
    components, 7–10
    in decision process, 113
    in marketing strategy, 23–26
    and market positioning, 32
    price in, 285
    products as key element in, 218
    role of place in, 308
    value capture, 34
    value communication, 35
    value creation products, 33–34
    value delivery, 34
Marketing plan, 5, 26
    Chipotle Mexican Grill, 372
    components, 5, 26–27
    control phase, 27
    function, 23

    implementation phase,
        27, 30–36
    marketing mix implementation,
        33–36
    market positioning, 32
    market segmentation, 31–32
    target marketing, 32
    performance evaluation, 36–42
    planning phase, 27
        mission statement, 27
        situation analysis, 28–30
        vision statement, 27
    stakeholders, 27
    steps, 27e
Marketing research, 195
    assessing value of, 196
    on consumer expectations,
        271–272
    on demographics, 88
    ethics in, 213–215
    factors to consider, 195
    guidelines for conducting, 213
    listening to customers, 60–61
    by nonprofits, 195
    online software for, 211
    by politicians, 195
    primary data
        advantages and
            disadvantages, 212–213
        blogs, 207–208
        definition, 198
        experimental research,
            211–212
        focus group interviews, 209
        in-depth interviews,
            208–209
        observation, 206–207
        panel-based, 211
        for qualitative research, 206
        for quantitative research, 206
        questionnaires, 209–211
        scanner-based, 211
        sentiment mining, 208
        social media, 207–208
        surveys, 209–211
    secondary data
        advantages and
            disadvantages, 212–213
        big data, 204–205
        data mining, 203–204
        data warehouses, 203
        definition, 198
        external, 201
        internal, 203–205
        panel data, 202–203
        in political setting, 200–201
        scanner data, 202–203
        sources, 200
        syndicated, 201–203
    spending on, 195
    technology for, 209
    value for marketers, 195
    voice-of-customer
        program, 272
    Walt Disney Company,
        193–195

Marketing research process
 action plan, 199–200
 data analysis, 198–199
 data collection, 198
 defining objectives, 196
 developing insights, 198–199
 research design, 196–198
 steps, 196e
Marketing strategy, 23
 based on product life cycle, 260
 and changing consumer
  demands, 83–84
 customer excellence, 23, 24–25
 digitally oriented, 22
 entry into global markets
  direct investment, 161–162
  exporting, 159
  franchising, 160
  joint venture, 160–161
  strategic alliance, 160
 for global marketing
  communication, 165–167
  distribution, 165
  pricing, 164–165
  product or services, 163–164
  target market, 162
 identifying, 64
 integrating ethics into
  control phase, 77–78
  implementation phase, 76–77
  planning phase, 76
 locational excellence, 23, 25
 macro strategies, 24e
 multiple sources of advantage, 26
 at Nike, 21–22
 operational excellence, 23, 25
 product excellence, 23, 25
 by Starbucks, 3–5
 for sustainable competitive
  advantage, 23
Market-orientation era, 13
**Market penetration strategy,
 47, 300**
Marketplace
 opportunities and uncertainties,
  28–29
 as stakeholder, 80
Market positioning, 32, 186
Market power, 328–329
Market presence, expanded, 345
Market saturation, 240–241
 in maturity stage, 258
Market segmentation, 6, 31; *see
 also* Segmentation;
 Segment *entries*
 at Hertz, 23e
Market segments, 31, 172e
 evaluation of attractiveness,
  180–182
 and maturity stage, 259
 profitability, 182e
Market share, 40
 of Boeing, 397
 and premium pricing, 286
Market size
 determining, 190

 evaluating, 149–150
 output metrics, 148
Market testing
 premarket tests, 255
 test marketing, 255
Market value, effect of brands on,
 225–226
Markup, and target return
 pricing, 297
Masculinity, 153
Maslow's hierarchy of needs, 114
 categories, 114
 love needs, 115
 physiological needs, 115
 safety needs, 115
 self-actualization, 115–116
Mass advertising, 358
Mass marketing, 183
Mass media, 382
Maturity stage, 256; *see also*
 Product life cycle
 development of new
  products, 259
 entry into new markets or
  segments, 258–259
 reminder advertising, 375–376
Maximizing profits, 286
M-commerce, 341
Media
 for advertising, 373
 evaluation and selection
  mass media, 382e
  media buy, 381
  niche media, 382
  planning, 381
  selection criteria, 382
 social *vs.* traditional, 49
 traditional, 364–365
 types available, 382e
 web-based, 365–366
Media buy, 381
Media mix, 381
Media planning, 381
Media-sharing sites
 Flickr, 56
 Instagram, 55–56
 photo sites, 56
 YouTube, 55
Men's Health, 116
Merchandise flow; *see* Supply
 chain management
Mercosur, 152
Message
 in advertising, 379
 in communication process,
  351–353
Metadata, 67
Metrics, 36
 to asses impact of
  advertising, 386
 for awareness
  aided recall, 354
  top-of-mind awareness,
   354–356
 for economic analysis, 147–150
 ethical decision-making, 74e

 to evaluate service quality,
  270–274
  customer feedback, 273–274
  voice-of-customer program, 272
  zone of tolerance, 272–273
 financial performance, 37–39
 for measuring IMC
  traditional media, 364–365
  web-based media, 365–366
 Nike *vs.* adidas, 39
 in performance evaluation, 37
 for sales force evaluation,
  412–413
 for vendor performance
  evaluation, 134–135
Microblog, 57
Micromarketing, 185
 by customers, 185–186
 examples, 184–185
 and Internet, 185
 retargeting technologies, 185
 of services, 267
Milk Life campaign, 12
Millennials, 89
 and social and mobile
  marketing, 88
 spending by, 350
Million Dollar Listing, 414
Mission Impossible, 393
Mission statement, 28
 adidas, 28
 Burt's Bees, 76
 Chipotle Mexican Grill, 372
 ethical, 76
 Nike, 28
 Pink Ribbon International, 28
Mobile advertising, 382e
Mobile apps
 An Affordable Wardrobe, 180
 Fabsugar, 180
 for health care, 107
 in-vehicle, 97
 notification of use of, 67–68
 number of downloads, 57
 pricing models
  ad-supported apps, 59
  at Apple App Store, 60e
  freemium apps, 59
  paid apps, 59
Mobile commerce, 341
Mobile marketing, 360
Mobile marketing campaigns, 361e
Mobile media; *see* Social and
 mobile marketing
Mode, 44
Modified rebuy, 142
Monitoring
 marketing campaign, 64
 social media, 61
Monopoly, 297
Motivation of salespeople, 411–413
Motive, 114
Movie industry
 benefit segmentation, 177
 Google Analytics, 205
 product placement, 392–393

 target audiences, 256
 3D films, 255
Multi-attribute model, 110
Multichannel strategy; *see*
 Omnichannel *entries*
Multiple segmentation methods,
 178–180
Mutual trust, 317

N

National Association for Sport and
 Physical Education, 390
National Association of
 Broadcasters, 387
National brands, 229
National Childhood Cancer
 Awareness Month, 389
National Do Not Call List/Registry,
 98, 404
National Eating Disorders
 Association, 358
National Employment Law
 Project, 72
National Highway Traffic Safety
 Administration, 97
National Institute for Fitness and
 Sport, 141
National Institutes of Health, 250
National Organic Program
 (Department of
 Agriculture), 110
National Transportation Safety
 Board, 398
Natural foods, 110
Nearfield communication
 technology, 95
Need recognition, 103
 in business-to-business
  marketing, 133
 functional needs, 103–104
 psychological needs, 104–105
Needs, 6; *see also* Maslow's
 hierarchy of needs
 functional, 103–104
 psychological, 104–105
 satisfied by mobile apps, 57–59
 versus wants, 103
Negative engagement, 52
Negative word of mouth, 113
Neuromarketing, 214–215
New buy, 140
New products; *see also* Product
 development
 brand names for, 230
 compatibility, 247
 complexity and trialability,
  247–248
 development over time,
  238–239
 and diffusion of innovation,
  244–245
 examples of failure, 244e
 introduction stage, 257
 lead users, 252
 observability, 247

pricing strategies
market penetration, 300–302
price skimming, 302
reasons for creating
changing customer needs, 29–240
fashion cycles, 242
improving supplier relationships, 242
managing risk through diversity, 242
market saturation, 240–241
relative advantage, 247
with 3D printing, 237–238
as unsought, 220
Newspaper advertising, 382e
New Yorker, 183
New York Times, 166
Niche media, 382
Noise, 353
Noncompensatory decision rule, 111
Nonfinancial rewards, 412
Nonprofit organizations
Newman's Own, 76
objectives, 28, 29
North American Free Trade Agreement, 152
Nutrition Labeling and Education Act, 98, 235

O

Objective-and-task method, 364
Objectives
of marketing research, 196
in STP process, 170–171
Observability, 247
Observation, 206
Occasion segmentation, 177
Occupational Safety and Health Act, 360
Off-price retailer, 337
Ohio State University, 142
Oligopolistic competition, 297
Omnichannel retailing
benefits
deeper and broader selection, 344
expanded market presence, 345
personalization, 344–345
effective
brand image, 346
integrated customer relationship management, 345
pricing, 346
supply chain, 346–347
Omnichannel strategy, 329
H&M, 327–328
One-to-one marketing, 185
Online advertising, 340–341
Online backups, 267
Online chat, 344

Online marketing, 35; *see also* Omnichannel retailing
blogs, 361
privacy issue, 67–68
social media, 361–362
websites, 360–361
Online reviews, 251–252, 278
Online training programs, 411
On-the-job training, 410–411
Open communication, 317
Operational excellence, 25
Opportunities; *see also* SWOT analysis
assessing, 28–29
identifying, 30–33
Optimism, 410
Order getter, 409
Order specification, 134
Order taker, 409
Organic foods, 110
Organizational culture, 136
bribery problem, 137
buying center types, 138
Outdoor advertising, 382e
Outsourcing by Boeing, 398

P

Packaging
changes for repositioning, 233
and consumer decision making, 122
key roles, 232–233
and labeling, 235
laws on, 235
primary and secondary, 232
recognizable, 234
to save costs, 234
sustainable, 234
Packaging conference, 234
Page view, 61
Paid app, 59
Paid app with in-app purchase, 59
Panel-based research, 211
Panel data, 202
Partnering relationships
Amazon and Procter & Gamble, 308
brand licensing, 231–232
joint ventures, 160–161
manufacturers and retailers, 330–332
in manufacturing, 86
in marketing channels, 317–319
Nike and Apple, 22
research and development consortia, 24–250
strategic alliances, 160
Passive consumers, 113
Pay-for-performance, 79
Penetration pricing, 300–302
Perceived value, 227
Percentage-of-sales method, 364
Perception, 118
influence of learning on, 118

Perceptual map, 189
ideal points, 189
steps in deriving, 190–191
Performance evaluation
accountability, 36–37
financial performance metrics, 37–39
IMC program, 366–367
marketing metrics for, 36–42
Nike *vs.* adidas, 39
objectives, analytics, and metrics, 37
portfolio analysis, 39–42
of product development, 256
salespeople, 412–413
uses of, 37
of vendors, 134–135
Performance objectives, 37
Performance risk, 108
Perishability, 268
Personal blog, 57
Personal ethics, 70–71
Personality, 410
Personality traits, 410
Personalization
of customer service, 344–345
of offerings, 345
Personal selling, 342, 359, 398
by Boeing, 398
as career, 399
ethical and legal issues
sales force and corporate policy, 413–414
sales manager and sales force, 413
salespeople and customers, 414
follow-up, 407–408
in IMC, 359
scope and nature of, 398–402
Personal selling process
closing the sale, 407
customer relationship management systems, 405
follow-up, 407–408
generating and qualifying leads, 402–404
handling reservations, 407
preapproach, 404–405
sales presentation, 406–407
value added by, 399–402
building relationships, 401–402
information and advice, 401
simplified buying, 401
time saved, 401
Personal service, 344
Persuasive advertising, 375
Pharmaceutical companies, unethical practices, 117
Philanthropy
Newman's Own, 76
versus questionable business practices, 72
by TOMS Shoes, 73
Walt Disney Company, 79
Photo sites, 56
Physiological needs, 115

Physiological risk, 108
Pick ticket, 324
Pioneers, 243
Place (strategy), 308
in marketing mix, 9–10
in retailing, 342
value delivery, 34
Planner, 322
Planning phase, 27, 76; *see also* Marketing plan
in Integrated marketing communications, 362–366
Point-of-purchase display, 393
Point-of-sale displays, 341
Political/regulatory environment, 97
advertising, 378–388
antitrust laws, 98
car-buying in China, 151
consumer protection laws, 98
for global marketing
exchange controls, 152
quotas, 151–152
tariffs, 151, 152
trade agreements, 152
packaging and labeling laws, 235
pricing in Europe, 164
pricing strategies, 303–305
privacy laws, 214
social media in China, 158
Pollution in China, 151
Population
of China, 157
of India, 156
Population distribution, 149
Population growth, 90
Population growth rate, 149–150
Portfolio analysis
BCG matrix, 41e
cash cows, 41
dogs, 41–42
question marks, 41
stars, 40, 41
market growth rate, 40
market share, 40
purpose, 39–40
at strategic business unit level, 40
Positioning, 32
Positioning methods
against competitors, 189
with perceptual maps, 189–191
product attributes, 188–189
symbols, 189
value method, 188
Positioning strategy
and firm's value proposition, 186–187
market positioning, 186
monitoring, 191
product/service location, 187–188
Postpurchase behavior
cognitive dissonance, 112
components, 112e
customer loyalty, 112–113
satisfaction, 112
undesirable, 113

Postpurchase cognitive dissonance, 112
Postpurchase evaluation, 279
Posttesting, 386
Power, 314
  types of, 315
Power distance, 153, 154, 155e
Preapproach, 404–405
Predatory lenders, 180
Predatory pricing, 298, 304
Predictive analytics
  Macy's, Inc., 221
  Netflix, 96
Premarket test, 255
Premium, 392
Premium pricing, 287
Prestige products or services, 289
  demand curve, 289–291
Pretesting, 386
Price(s), 285
  and demand curve, 289–291
  in marketing mix, 9
  in maturity stage, 258
  reference, 300
  regular, 303
  value capture, 34
Price competition, brands as
  protection from, 225
Price discrimination, 304
Price elasticity of demand, 291
  demand curve, 291
  and dynamic pricing, 292–293
  factors influencing
    cross-price elasticity, 294
    income effect, 293
    substitution effect, 293–294
  and price-sensitivity, 292
Price fixing, 304
  horizontal, 305
  vertical, 305
Price-insensitive products, 292
Price-sensitive markets, 283
Price skimming, 302
Price war, 297
Pricing
  and channel members, 299
  company objectives
    competitor orientation, 287
    customer orientation, 278–288
    profit orientation, 286
    sales orientation, 286–287
  and costs, 294–297
    break-even analysis, 295–297
    markup and target return
      pricing, 297
    types of cost, 295
  and customers
    demand curves, 289–291
    price elasticity of demand,
      291–294
  dynamic, 292–293
  and forms of competition
    monopolistic, 297–298
    monopolistic competition, 298
    monopoly, 297
    pure competition, 298

  legal & ethical aspects
    deceptive advertising,
      303–304
    predatory pricing, 304
    price discrimination, 304
    price fixing, 304–305
  loss leader, 303–304
  in omnichannel retailing, 346
  predatory, 289, 304
  premium, 286
  status quo, 287
  target profit, 286
  target return, 286
  in value proposition, 283
Pricing strategies
  as challenge for firms, 285
  and company objectives,
    285–288
  everyday low pricing, 299
  global, 164–165
  high/low pricing, 299–300
  for impoverished populations, 150
  mobile apps, 58–60
  for new products
    market penetration, 300–302
    price skimming, 302
  Procter & Gamble, 283–285
  in retailing, 340
Primary data, 198
  advantages and disadvantages,
    212–213
  experimental research, 211–212
  focus group interviews, 209
  in-depth interviews
    definition, 208
    disadvantages, 209
    uses of, 209
  from observation, 206–207
  panel-based, 211
  for qualitative research, 206
  for quantitative research, 206
  scanner-based, 211
  from social media
    blogs, 207–208
    sentiment mining, 208
    virtual communities, 208
  survey research, 209–211
Primary package, 232
Privacy issues, 95
  and capture of demographic
    data, 214
  and Internet, 67–68
Privacy laws
  lacking in U.S., 214
  strict in Germany, 214
Privacy protection, 68
Privacy rights, 360
Private-label branding, 229
Private-label brands, 340
Private sale online sites, 301
Procedural fairness, 280
  return policy, 281
Product(s), 218
  actual, 219
  Apple Inc., 41–42
  associated services, 219

  attribute sets, 109
  augmented, 219
  cash cows, 41
  of competitors for ideas,
    250–251
  complementary, 294
  complexity of, 218–219
  customer experience, 52
  determinant attributes, 109
  dogs, 41–42
  environmentally friendly, 80
  evaluative criteria, 109
  in global marketing strategy
    same, 163
    similar, 163–164
    totally new, 164
  glocalization strategy, 164
  in marketing mix, 7–9
  modified by lead users, 252
  multi-attribute model, 111–112e
  multiple, 242
  question marks, 41
  and safety needs, 115
  and service strategies, 24e
  showrooming, 58
  stars, 40, 41
  substitute, 294
  touching and feeling,
    343–344
  types of, 219–220
    consumer products, 229
    convenience, 220
    shopping, 220
    specialty, 220
    unsought, 220
  value-creating, 33–34
  variety of, 9
Product deletion, 222
Product design, 253
Product development, 253
  alpha testing, 253
  beta testing, 254–255
  concept testing, 252–253
  evaluation of results, 256
  high costs of, 248–249
  idea generation
    competitors' products,
      250–251
    customer input, 251–252
    internal research and
      development, 248–249
    research and development
      consortia, 249–250
  market testing, 255
  and maturity stage, 259
  process, 248e
  product launch, 255–256
  prototypes, 253
  reverse engineering, 251
  start of, 219
Product development strategy, 48
  MTV, 44
Product differentiation, 379
Product excellence, 26
  achieving, 26
Product-focused advertising, 376

Production
  globally integrated processes, 146
  inseparable, 266
  at Nike, 22
  with 3D printing, 237–238
  by TOMS Shoes, 73
Production-oriented era, 12
Product labels; see Labels
Product launch, 255–256
Product life cycle, 256, 257e
  characteristics of stages, 257e
  decline stage, 256, 259–260
  growth stage, 256, 257–258
  introduction stage, 256, 257
  as management tool, 256–257
  and marketplace trends, 256
  and market saturation, 240–241
  maturity stage, 256, 258–259
  and persuasive advertising, 375
  and reminder advertising, 376
  shape of curve, 260
  strategies based on, 260
  variations in, 256
Product line extension, 222, 223,
  230–231
Product lines, 40, 220
  added, 222
  BMW, 220–221
  deletion of, 222
  Macy's, Inc., 221
  TOMS Shoes, 73
Product mix, 220
  BMW, 220e
  breadth, 221
  changes to, 222
  depth, 221
  disadvantage of too much, 221
Product placement, 393
Product recalls, 70
Product specification, 133
Product strategy in retailing,
  338–340
Professional blog, 56
Profitable segments, 181–182
Profit margin percentage, 181
Profit orientation, 286
Promotion
  and brand association, 228
  cooperative advertising, 341
  and decision process, 122
  and marketing channels, 312
  in marketing mix, 10
  mobile commerce, 341
  personal selling, 342
  point-of-sale displays, 341
  in retailing, 340–342
  service representatives, 342
  in social and mobile
    marketing, 123
  by sponsorships, 11
  store ambiance, 341–342
  traditional advertising, 340
  value communication, 36
  on websites, 340–341
Property Virgins, 414
Proposal analysis, 134

Prototype, 253
Psychographics, 174
Psychographic segmentation, 172–176
  lifestyles analysis, 174–176
  limitations of analysis, 176
  self-concept, 174
  self-values, 174
  VALS framework, 175–176
Psychological factors in decision process
  attitudes, 116–117
  learning, 118
  lifestyle, 118
  motives, 114–118
  perception, 118
Psychological needs, 105
Psychological risk, 108
Public relations, 358, 388
  cause-related marketing, 389
  celebrities and, 388
  event sponsorship, 389–390
  growth in influence, 389
  in IMC, 358–359
Public relations toolkit, 390
Public service advertising, 377
Puffery, 387
Pull strategy, 374
Pulsing (advertising schedule), 383
Purchase behavior, 181
Purchase decision
  and conversion rate, 111
  risks in, 108
Purchase situation, 120
Purchasing power parity, 148
  Big Mac Index, 148–149
Pure competition, 298
Push strategy, 374

Q

Qualitative research, 206
Quantitative research, 206
Question marks, 41
Questionnaires, 209
  developing, 210
  McDonald's, 198, 199
  online *vs.* offline, 210
  response rates, 210–211
  software for, 211
  structured questions, 209–210
  unstructured questions, 209
  what to avoid in, 210e
QueVision, Kroger, 272
Quick delivery, 309
Quick-response inventory system, 324
Quota, 151

R

Radio advertising, 382e
Radio frequency identification tags, 95, 322–323

Reach, 365
  estimating, 367
  of marketing campaign, 65
Reachable segments, 180–181
Real estate industry, 414
Real Housewives of Orange County, 414
Real income, 150
Reality TV, 414
Rebate, 393
Rebranding, 232
Receiver, 352
  decoding by, 353
Receiving, 322
Recruitment and selection of sales force, 409–410
Red Bull Air Race, 389
Reference group, 119
Reference groups
  blogs, 120
  consumer identification with, 119–120
  information sources, 119
Reference price, 300
  deceptive, 303
Referent power, 315
Regional culture, 87
Regular price, 303
Related diversification, 48
Relational orientation, 15
Relationship marketing, and salespeople, 401–402
Relationship selling, 401
Relative advantage, 247
Relative market share, 40
  difficulty in maintaining, 42
Relevance, 367
Relevancy, 49
Reliability, 270, 271, 272, 408
Reminder advertising, 375–376
Repositioning
  at American Airlines, 233
  by packaging changes, 233
Request for proposals, 133
  in business-to-business marketing, 133–134
Research and development consortia, 24–250
  internal, 248–249
Resellers, 130
  business-to-business market, 130
Reservations or objections, 407
Resilience, 410
Resource allocation, 33–36
Responsiveness, 270, 271, 272, 408
Responsive segments, 181
Retailers
  as channel members, 299
  conversion rate, 111
  crowding, 122
  and distribution centers, 321–322
  in-store demonstrations, 122
  in-store promotions, 123

kiosks, 267–268
locational excellence, 26
and manufacturers, 328–329
manufacturer sales to, 12
marketing by, 10e
omnichannel strategy, 329
packaging, 122
promotions, 122
reasons for using, 310–311
return policy, 281
salespeople, 120–121
store atmosphere, 120
types of, 333e
  category specialists, 336–337
  convenience stores, 335
  department stores, 335–336
  drugstores, 336
  extreme-value, 337
  food retailers, 332–333
  full-line discount stores, 336
  general merchandise, 335–338
  off-price, 337–338
  service retailers, 338
  specialty stores, 336
  supercenters, 333
  supermarkets, 333–335
  warehouse clubs, 333–335
Retailer/store brands, 229
Retailing, 328
  benefits of stores
    browsing, 343
    cash or credit payment, 344
    entertainment, 344
    immediate gratification, 344
    personal service, 344
    risk reduction, 344
    social experience, 344
    touching and feeling products, 343–344
  bricks and mortar *vs.* online, 35
  current changes in, 328
  in India, 157
  partner choices
    channel member characteristics, 331
    channel structure, 330
    customer expectations, 330–331
    distribution intensity, 331–332
  place strategy, 342
  price strategy, 340
  product strategy, 338–340
  promotion, 340–342
  qualifying leads, 404
  in supply chain, 328
  traditional *vs.* omnichannel, 344–347
  virtual stores, 35
Retargeting technologies, 185
Retrieval set, 109
Return on investment, 367
  assessing, 63
Return on marketing investment, 367–368
Revenue generation, 285

Reverse engineering, 251
Reverse innovation, 163, 249
Reward power, 314
Reward systems
  financial, 411–412
  nonfinancial, 412
Risk management, 242
Risk reduction, 344
Risks
  in buying decisions, 124
  by early adopters, 245
  by innovators, 245
  in purchase decision
    financial, 108
    physiological, 108
    psychological, 108
    safety, 108
    social, 108
Robinson-Patman Act, 304
ROI; *see* Return on investment
Role playing, 405
Rule-of-thumb methods, 364
Russia
  economic situation, 156
  in global marketing, 156
  soup consumption, 163–164

S

Safety needs, 115
Safety risk, 108
Salary, 411
Sales contest, 411
Sales force
  and corporate policy, 413–414
  and customers, 414
  and sales manager, 413
  structure
    company sales force, 408–409
    manufacturer's representatives, 408–409
Sales forecasts, 321
Sales management, 408
  motivation and compensation, 411–412
  recruitment and selection, 409–410
  sales force structure, 408–409
  sales force training, 410–411
Sales manager, and sales force, 413
Sales orientation, 286
Sales-oriented era, 12–13
Salespeople, 344
  buying simplified by, 401
  closing the sale, 407
  and customer decision making, 120–121
  in drama, 399
  duties
    combination of, 409
    order getters, 409
    order takers, 409
    support personnel, 409

Salespeople—*Cont.*
  earnings of, 399
  follow-up, 407–408
  handling reservations, 407
  information and advice from, 401
  personality traits, 410
  in personal selling, 399
  recruitment and selection,
    409–410
  relationship-building, 401–402
  in retailing, 404
  role playing, 405
  sales presentation, 406–407
  selling teams, 409
  terms for, 398–399
  time saved by, 401
  training, 121, 410–411
  value to management, 399
Sales presentation, 406–407
Sales promotions, 359, 390
  careful use of, 394
  contests, 392
  coupons, 390–391
  cross-promoting, 394
  deals, 392
  goal of, 394l
  in IMC, 359
  loyalty programs, 393
  point-of-sale displays, 390, 393
  premiums, 392
  product placement, 393–394
  rebates, 393
  samples, 393
  sweepstakes, 392–393
Sales support personnel, 409
Same product or service, 163
Sample, 198
Sampling, 392
Scanner-based research, 211
Scanner data, 202
Search engine marketing, 367
Secondary data, 198
  advantages and disadvantages,
    212–213
  external, 201
  internal
    big data, 204–205
    churn problem, 204
    data mining, 203–204
    data warehouses, 203
  in political setting, 200–201
  sources, 200
  syndicated
    definition, 201
    from Nielsen Co., 202
    panel data, 202–203
    providers of, 201e
    scanner data, 202
Secondary package, 232
Security breaches, 213
Segment adoption percentage, 181
Segmentation, 31–32
**Segmentation, targeting, and
  positioning, 31**
  evaluation of segment
    attractiveness

  identifiable, 180
  profitable, 180–181
  reachable, 180–181
  responsive, 181
  substantial, 180
in global marketing, 162
introduction, 170
market positioning, 32
market segmentation, 31–32
Netflix, 169–170
positioning methods
  against competitors, 189
  with perceptual maps, 189–191
  product attributes, 188–189
  symbols, 189
  value method, 188
positioning process, 31
positioning strategy
  market positioning, 186
  value proposition, 186–188
process, 171e
segmentation methods
  behavioral, 177–178
  benefit, 177
  demographic, 172
  geodemographic, 179–180
  geographic, 171–172
  multiple, 178–180
  psychographic, 172–176
strategies and objectives,
  170–171
and SWOT analysis, 171
target marketing, 32
target market selection
  concentrated targeting,
    183–184
  differentiated strategy, 183
  factors affecting, 182
  mass marketing, 183
  micromarketing, 184–186
  undifferentiated strategy, 183
Segmentation methods; *see*
  Segmentation, targeting,
  and positioning
Segmentation process, 170–171
Segment attractiveness, 181e
Segment size, 181
Selective distribution, 332
Self-actualization, 115
Self-concept, 174
Self-motivation, 410
Self-regulation, in online
  marketing, 67–68
Self-values, 174
Selling Network, 414
Selling teams, 409
Sender, 352
  message adjustments, 353–354
Sentiment analysis, 61
Sentiment mining, 208
Service failures, 279–280
Service gap, 268
Service gaps
  overcoming, 279–281
  types of, 269
Service industry, variable costs, 295

Service-product continuum, 265e
Service providers, business-to-
  business market, 129–130
Service quality, 270, 408
  Broadmoor resort, 271
  and customer satisfaction, 279
  customers' evaluation, 273e
  dimensions of, 270–271
  metrics for evaluation, 270–274
Service recovery
  listening to customers, 280
  quick resolution of failures, 281
  and service failures, 279–280
  solutions
    distributive fairness, 280
    procedural fairness, 280–281
Service representatives, 342
Service retailer, 338
Services, 9, 264
  Amazon Prime, 263–264
  compared to customer
    service, 264
  customer experience, 52
  differentiated from goods, 266e
  economic dependence on, 265
  expanded scope of, 265
  Gaps Model
    communications gap, 269,
      276–278
    and customer satisfaction, 279
    delivery gap, 269, 275–276
    improving retail services, 269e
    knowledge gap, 269, 271–274
    purpose, 268
    standards gap, 269, 274–275
  in global marketing strategy,
    163–164
  heterogeneous, 266–268
  inseparable production and
    consumption, 266
  intangible, 266
  online reviews, 278
  percent of GDP, 265
  perishable, 268
  specialized, 265
  types of
    convenience, 220
    shopping, 220
    specialty, 220
    unsought, 220
Services marketing, 265–268
Shake It Up, 356
Share of wallet, 342
Sherman Antitrust Act, 304
Shipping merchandise, 324
Shopping products/services, 220
Shopping situation
  crowding, 122
  in-store demonstrations, 122
  packaging, 122
  promotions, 122
  salespeople, 120–121
  store atmosphere, 120
Showcasing, 341
Showrooming, 58
Similar product or service, 163–164

Situational factors in decision
  process, **120**
  purchase situation, 120
  shopping situation, 120–122
  temporal state, 122–123
Situation analysis, 28
  SWOT analysis, 28–30
Smart gadgets, 14
Smartphones, 95
  to locate customers, 68
  number of, in U.S., 58
Soccer team sponsorships, 11
Social and mobile marketing, 11
  advertising innovations, 50
  American Express hashtags, 277
  Brazil and China, 158
  campaigns, 51e
  campaign steps, 64e
  catchup by Microsoft, 251
  click farms, 77
  to connect with customers, 16–18
  data collection, 202
  engagement of customers
    click path analysis, 63
    data analysis, 61–63
    doing, 63–64
    keyword analysis, 63
    listening, 60–61
    sentiment analysis, 60–61
  fake clicks, 77
  Ford Motor Company, 77
  4E framework, 48–52
  Gatorade, 47–48
  generational cohorts, 88
  Google and Coke, 355
  health care apps, 107
  Hy-Line Cruises, 51
  in-store promotions, 123
  iPad users, 132
  Late Night with Jimmy Fallon, 50
  LinkedIn users, 139
  location-based software, 50
  mobile apps, 57–60
  personal selling in
    cyberspace, 400
  Pizza Hut, 33
  problems for Facebook, 173
  product line extensions, 223
  technological advances, 97
  tracking customers, 68
Social experience, 344
Social factors in decision process
  culture, 120
  family, 118–119
  reference groups, 119–120
Social marketing, 11, 377
Social marketing channels, 5
Social media, 48, 361
  analysis measures for strategies
    bounce rate, 63
    click paths, 63
    conversion rate, 63
    hits, 61
    keyword analysis, 63
    page views, 63
  benefits for companies, 47

Brazil *vs.* China, 158
categories
 media-sharing sites, 55–56
 social network sites, 53–55
 thought-sharing sites, 56–57
to connect with customers, 16–18
customer engagement using, 60–64
determining ROI, 63
4E framework, 48–52, 49e
 customer experience of product, 52
 educate customers, 50–51
 engage the customers, 52
 excite customers, 49–50
to generate leads, 402
information provided by, 52
in IMC, 48–49, 361–362
LinkedIn, 139
marketing campaign steps, 64e
monitoring, 61
Twitter, 139
uses by firms, 48–49
Social Media Mission Control Center, Gatorade, 47–48
Social network sites
 to create excitement, 53
 Facebook, 54
 Google+, 55
 LinkedIn, 54–55
Social responsibility; *see also* Corporate social responsibility
 versus ethics, 72e
Social risk, 108
Social shopping, 367
Social trends
 green marketing, 92–94
 health and wellness concerns, 92–93
 privacy concerns, 95
Society as stakeholder, 80–81
Sociocultural factors
 in communication, 165–167
 cultural dimensions concept, 153–155
 examples, 153
 and global marketing, 153
 verbal communication, 154
South Africa, 155
Specialty products/services, 220
Specialty store, 336
Sponsorship; *see* Event sponsorship
Sports teams sponsorship, 11
Stakeholders, 12
 for corporate social responsibility, 79–81
 in ethical decision-making, 73–74
 types of, 73
Standards gap, 269
 overcoming, 274–275
Stars, 40, 41
Star Wars, 232
State of mind, 122–123

Status quo pricing, 287
Stock-keeping units, 221
Store atmosphere, 120
Store brands, 229–230, 340
Stores; *see also* Retailers
 ambiance, 341–342
 benefits for consumers, 343–344
STP; *see* Segmentation, targeting, and positioning
Straight rebuy, 142
Strategic alliance, 160
Strategic business units, 40
Strategic (partnering) relationship, 317
Strategic planning, 42; *see also* Marketing strategies
Strategic relationships, 316–319
Strategy, in STP process, 170–171
Strivers, 176e
Structured questions, 209
Structured *vs.* unstructured response, 210e
Subhead, 384
Substantial segments, 180
Substitute products, 294
Substitution effect, 293
Sugar Bowl, 389
Super Bowl XLVII, 11
Supercenter, 333
Supermarkets
 convenience stores, 335
 conventional, 333
 extreme-value retailers, 333
 as health providers, 93
 limited-assortment, 333
 percent of sales, 332
 supercenters, 333
 warehouse clubs, 333–335
Suppliers
 LinkedIn users, 139
 relationship with, 242
Supply chain
 components, 312
 in less-developed nations, 150
 in omnichannel retailing, 346–347
 retailing in, 328
 simplified, 310e
Supply chain management, 10, 308
 activities, 311–312
 Amazon, 307–308
 anticipatory shipping system, 307–308
 channel conflict, 313
 distribution centers, 311
 electronic data interchange, 320
 fulfillment centers, 311
 goals, 313
 importance of, 309–311
 information flow
  data warehouses, 320–321
  steps, 319–320
 manufacturer-retailer relationship, 330–332

marketing channel design
 direct channels, 312
 indirect channels, 312
merchandise flow
 direct store delivery, 321–322
 distribution centers, 321–322
 floor-ready merchandise, 323
 fulfillment center, 322–324
 inbound transportation, 322
 inventory management, 324–325
 preparing shipments, 324
 radio frequency identification tags, 323
 receiving and checking, 322–323
 shipping, 324
 storage and cross-docking, 323
 ticketing and marking, 323
strategic relationships, 316–319
 common goals, 317
 credible commitments, 319
 interdependence, 317
 mutual trust, 317
 open communications, 317
 value added by, 310–311
 vendor-managed inventory, 320–321
 vertical marketing systems, 314–316
Supply chain partners, 12
Surveys, 209
 developing, 210
 fast-food, 199e
 questionnaires, 209–210
 response rates, 210–211
 software for, 211
Survivors, 176e
Sustainability
 and corporate social responsibility, 81
 at Walmart, 80
Sustainable competitive advantage, 23
 from customer service, 25
 from educating customers, 51
 from locational excellence, 26
 multiple sources of, 26
 from operational excellence, 25
 from product excellence, 26
 to retain loyal customers, 24–25
Sustainable packaging, 234
Sweepstakes, 392
SWOT analysis, 28, 85, 171
 and business ethics, 76
 conduct of, 28–30
 elements of, 30e
Syndicated data, 201

T

Tangibles, 270, 271, 272, 408
Tapestry Segmentation system, 179
Target audience, 65e
 for advertising, 373–374
 identifying, 64

Targeting, 32
Target market
 adjustments, 191
 and cross-promoting, 394
 and customer loyalty, 24
 in global marketing, 162
 for H&M, 328
 for Harley-Davidson, 175
 from ideas, 9
 for Lexus, 6
 for MTV, 43
 unethical behavior, 76–77
Target marketing, 32
Target market selection
 concentrated targeting, 183–184
 differentiated strategy, 183
 mass marketing, 183
 micromarketing, 184–186
 and SWOT analysis, 182
 television demographics, 183
 undifferentiated strategy, 183
Target profit pricing, 286
Target return pricing, 286
 and markup, 297
Tariff, 151
Tax season, 105
Technological advances, 95; *see also* Diffusion of innovation; Innovation
 to close delivery gap, 276
 at Consumer Electronics Show, 97
 and device exhaustion, 259
 to meet customer needs, 239–240
 for personal selling, 400
Technological capabilities, 150–151
Technology
 to capture demographic data, 214
 cookie-blockers, 68
 facial recognition software, 213
 Geographic Information System, 16
 mobile media, 16–18
 at Nike, 22
 to overcome delivery gap, 276, 277
 for promotion, 341
 security breaches, 213
 social media, 16–18
 untested, 101–102
 wearable, 102
Telemarketing, 403
 loss of popularity, 403–404
 Telemarketing Sales Rule, 98
Telepresence, 400
Television advertising, 382e
Television sets, 97
Television viewership, 182
Temporal state, 122–123
Test marketing, 255
Thinkers, 176e
Thought-sharing sites
 blogs, 56–57
 microblogs, 57
Threats; *see* SWOT analysis

3D printing, 127–128
  new products from, 237–238
  and trademark infringement, 238
Ticketing and marking, 323
Time, 72
Time orientation, 153
Tonight Show, 50
Top-of-mind awareness, 354
Total cost, 295
Total cost curve, 296
Totally new product or service, 164
Total revenue curve, 296
Touching and feeling products,
  343–344
Tracking, 386
Trade agreements, 152
Trade barriers
  elimination of, 146
  quotas, 151–152
  tariffs, 151, 152
Trade deficit, 148
Trademark infringement, 238
Trade shows, 402
Trade surplus, 148
Trading bloc, 152
Traditional media, 364–365
Training
  of sales force, 410–411
  of salespeople, 121
Transmitter, 352
Transparency International Bribe
  Payers Index, 137
Trialability, 247–248
Trouble with the Curve, 177
Turbo: F.A.S.T., 170

U

Uncertainties, assessing, 28–29
Uncertainty avoidance, 152
**Undifferentiated targeting
  strategy, 183**

Unethical behavior
  bribery, 137
  in choice of target market, 76–77
  deceptive advertising, 70
  pharmaceutical companies, 117
  reasons for, 70–71
  in social and mobile marketing, 77
  types of, 70
United States
  ethnicity, 90–92
  generational cohorts, 88–89
  and globalization, 146
  income distribution, 89–90
  number of smartphones, 58
  trade deficit, 148
United States Humane Society, 254
United States Supreme Court, on
  pricing, 305
Universal Product Code, 319,
  322–323
Universal set, 109
University of Alabama, 140
University of California, 140
Unrelated diversification, 49
Unsought products/services, 220
Unstructured questions, 209
U.S. Bureau of the Census, 201
U.S. Centers for Disease Control
  and Prevention, 92
U.S. Congress Commerce
  Committee, 180
U.S. Food Waste Challenge, 94
U.S. Travel Association, 17
Users, 135
  example, 136
Usual Suspects, The, 169

V

VALS framework, 175–176
Value, 13, 188; *see also* Adding
  value

benefits and costs in, 283
  in competitor-oriented
    strategy, 288
  consumer perception of,
    283–285
  and deals, 392
  defined by price, 340
Value-based marketing,
  13–14, 84–85
Value capture, by price, 9
Value chain, 10
Value cocreation, 13
Value communication, 36
Value creation
  by marketing, 12–14
  from products, 7–8
Value creation products, 33–34
Value delivery, 34
Value-driven firms, 15
Value proposition, 36, 186
  communicating, 10
  delivering, 9–10
  determining, 186–188
  main components, 188
  role of pricing in, 283
Variable costs, 295
Vendor-managed inventory, 320
Vendors
  attracting buyers, 141
  negotiation and selection, 134
  performance evaluation, 134–135
  relations with, 25
  to Walmart, 80
Verbal communication, 154
Vertical channel conflict, 313
Vertical marketing system, 314
  administered, 315
  contractual, 315–316
  corporate, 316
  versus independent
    channels, 314
Vertical price fixing, 305

Viral marketing program, 309
Virtual community, 208
Virtual stores, 35
Vision statement, 28
Voice-of-customer program, 273

W

Wait time reduction, 272
Wants, 6, 103
Warehouse clubs, 333,
  333–335
Weaknesses; *see* SWOT analysis
Wearable technology, 102
Web-based media, 365–366
Weblog, 361
Web portal, 133
Websites
  for community-building, 361
  in online marketing, 360–361
Web tracking software, 366
Wedding magazine, 116
White papers, 139
Wholesalers, 130, 309
  as channel members, 299
  reasons for using, 310–311
Winter Olympics of 2014, 30
Word of mouth, negative, 113
Workplace diversity, 78
World Trade Organization,
  156, 161
World Wide Web, 55

Y

Yoga studios, 93

Z

Zone of tolerance, 273